AMERICAN
SIGN LANGUAGE
DICTIONARY

AMERICAN SIGN LANGUAGE DICTIONARY

Revised Edition

Martin L. A. Sternberg, Ed.D.

ILLUSTRATIONS BY HERBERT ROGOFF, EDUSELF, AND NORTH MARKET STREET GRAPHICS

Abridged edition of *American Sign Language*

COLLINS REFERENCE
An Imprint of HarperCollins*Publishers*

To the memory of
Fannie and Irving Sternberg

HarperCollins books may be purchased for educational, business, or sales promotional
use. For information, please e-mail the Special Markets Department at
SPsales@harpercollins.com

Library of Congress Cataloging-in-Publication Data
Sternberg, Martin L. A.
    American Sign Language dictionary / Martin L. A. Sternberg ; a
illustrations by Herbert Rogoff and EduSelf. — Rev. ed.
        p.   cm.
    "Abridged edtion of American Sign Language."
    ISBN 0-06-273634-5
    1. American Sign Language—Dictionaries.   I. Sternberg, Martin L.
A. American Sign Language.   II. Title.
419—dc21   98-25273
                                                          CIP

21 SCP 30 29 28 27 26 25

Contents

Acknowledgments

The original work from which this revised and enlarged third edition is derived, *American Sign Language,* is the culmination of a period of endeavor that goes back to 1962. Two abridgments have since appeared: *American Sign Language Dictionary* (1987), and *American Sign Language Concise Dictionary* (1990). The current work is a revised and enlarged edition of the *American Sign Language Dictionary.*

In order to maintain continuity in the evolution of this project, members of the original General Editorial Committee are listed on pages ix and x.

My many friends who use sign language have been a constant source of information and inspiration in the identification and inclusion of new signs in this book. Many have also served as models for the signs herein illustrated. To them, my sustained appreciation and applause.

Bringing this project into the computer age from its index card and hand-illustrated status has been a major challenge, sometimes a source of trepidation and frustration, but ultimately a unique achievement. This could never have been accomplished without the sustained help and guidance of Kenneth S. Rothschild, my teacher, friend, and major supporter, who not only set up the format for the computer but came to my side countless times to help me out when I was in trouble.

Herbert Rogoff, the talented illustrator who did the original free-hand drawings appearing in editions past—many of which remain among these pages—is thanked yet again. Thanks also to the many others involved in the illustration process.

Robert Wilson, my editor, is the latest and very much the best of a long line of editors under whom I have worked. Thirty-two years is a long time to be affiliated with a single publisher, and Rob's commitment to me and this always-expanding project demonstrates the wisdom of my choice of HarperCollins as my publisher.

Finally, Theodora Zavin, my literary advisor, has been a reassuring presence throughout the development of the new edition.

Martin L. A. Sternberg, Ed.D.
New York, 1998

General Editorial Committee

Abbreviations

adj.	Adjective
adv.	Adverb, adverbial
adv. phrase	Adverbial phrase
alt. phrase	Alteration
arch.	Archaic
Brit.	British
colloq.	Colloquial, colloquialism. Informal or familiar term or expression in sign
condition. suffix	Conditional suffix
eccles.	Ecclesiastical. Of or pertaining to religious signs. These signs are among the earliest and best developed, inasmuch as the first teachers of deaf people were frequently religious workers and instruction was often of a religious nature.
e.g.	*Exempli gratia.* L., for example
esp. interrog.	Especially interrogative
i.e.	*Id est.* L., that is
interj.	Interjection
L.	Latin
loc.	Localism. A sign peculiar to a local or limited area. This may frequently be the case in a given school for deaf children, a college or postsecondary program catering to their needs, or a geographical area around such school or facility where deaf persons may live or work.
obs.	Obscure, obsolete
pl.	Plural
poss.	Possessive
prep.	Preposition
prep. phrase	Prepositional phrase
pron.	Pronoun
q.v.	*Quod vide.* L., which see
sl.	Slang
v.	Verb

v.i.   Verb intransitive

viz.   *Videlicet.* L., namely

voc.   Vocational. These signs usually pertain to special-
                ized vocabularies used in workshops, trade and
                vocational classes and schools.

v.t.   Verb transitive

vulg.   Vulgarism. A vulgar term or expression, usually
                used only in a colloquial sense.

Pronunciation Guide

The primary stress mark (′) is placed after the syllable bearing the heavier stress or accent; the secondary stress mark (′) follows a syllable having a somewhat lighter stress, as in **interrogate** (ĭn tĕr′ ə gāt′).

Symbol	Example	Symbol	Example
ă	add, map	ŏŏ	took, hook
ā	ace, rate	p	pit, stop
â(r)	care, air	r	run, poor
ä	palm, father	s	see, pass
b	bat, rub	sh	sure, rush
ch	check, catch	t	talk, sit
d	dog, rod	th	thin, both
ĕ	end, pet	th̸	this, bathe
ē	even, tree	ŭ	up, done
f	fit, half	ū	unite, vacuum
g	go, log	û(r)	urn, term
h	hope, hate	yōō	use, few
ĭ	it, give	v	vain, eve
ī	ice, write	w	win, away
j	joy, ledge	y	yet, yearn
k	cool, take	z	zest, muse
l	look, rule	zh	vision, pleasure
m	move, seem	ə	the schwa, an
n	nice, tin		unstressed vowel
ng	ring, song		representing the
ŏ	odd, hot		sound spelled
ō	open, so		*a* in *above*
ô	order, jaw		*e* in *sicken*
oi	oil, boy		*i* in *clarity*
ou	out, now		*o* in *melon*
ōō	pool, food		*u* in *focus*

Explanatory Notes

Sign Rationale

This term, admittedly imprecise semantically, refers to the explanatory material in parentheses which follows the part of speech. This material is an attempt to offer a mnemonic cue to the sign as described verbally. It is a device to aid the user of the dictionary to remember how a sign is formed.

Verbal Description

The sign and its formation are described verbally. Such terms as "S" hand, "D" position, "both 'B' hands," refer to the positions of the hand or hands as they are depicted in the American Manual Alphabet on page xvii.

Terms such as counterclockwise and clockwise refer to movement from the signer's orientation. Care should be taken not to become confused by illustrations that appear at first glance to contradict a verbal description. In all cases the verbal description should be the one of choice, with the illustration reinforcing it. The reader should place himself or herself mentally in the position of the signer i.e., the illustration, in order to assume the correct orientation for signing an English gloss word.

Sign Synonyms

Sign synonyms are other glosses for which the same sign is used. They are found at the end of the verbal description and are given in SMALL CAPITAL LETTERS.

It is important to remember that the cross-referenced words do not carry an equivalent sense in and of themselves. Because meaning for the signer springs from the sign, apparently unrelated glosses can be expressed by similar movements.

Illustrations

1. Illustrations appearing in sequence should not be regarded as separate depictions of parts of a sign. They are fluid and continu-

ous, and should be used in conjunction with the verbal description of a sign, for they illustrate the main features of the sign as one movement flows into the next.

2. Arrows, broken or solid, indicate direction of movement. Again, they are designed to reinforce the verbal description, and, where confusion may arise, the reader is cautioned to review the verbal description, always keeping himself or herself mentally in the position of the illustration (the signer).

3. As a general rule, a hand drawn with dotted or broken lines indicates the sign's initial movement or position of the hand. This is especially true if a similar drawing appears next to it using solid lines. This indicates terminal position in the continuum.

4. Groups of illustrations have been arranged as far as possible in visually logical order. They are read from left to right, or from top to bottom. Where confusion is possible, they have been captioned with letter A, B, C, etc.

5. Small lines outlining parts of the hand, especially when they are repeated, indicate small, repeated, or wavy or jerky motions, as described in the verbal section of an entry. ANTICIPATE is an example.

6. Arrows drawn side by side but pointing in opposite directions indicate repeated movement, as described in the verbal section of an entry. APPLAUD is an example.

7. Illustrations giving side or three-quarter views have been placed to afford maximum visibility and to avoid foreshortening problems. The user of the dictionary should not assume a similar orientation when making the sign. As a general rule, the signer faces the person he or she is signing to.

8. Inclusion of the head in the figures permits proper orientation in the formation of certain signs. The head is omitted where there is no question of ambiguity.

American
Manual
Alphabet

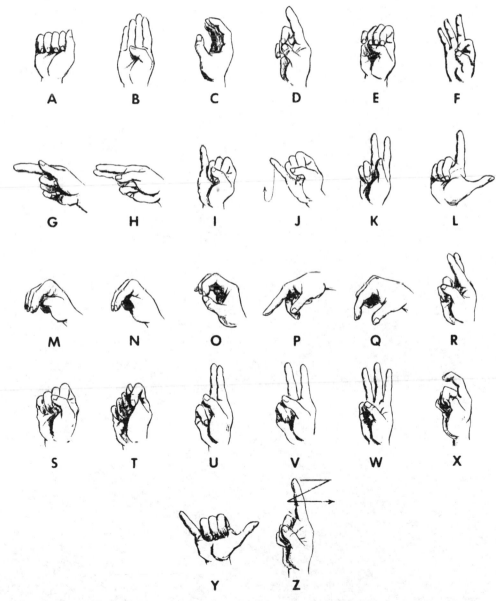

AMERICAN
SIGN LANGUAGE
DICTIONARY

A

ABANDON 1 (ə băn′ dən), *v.*, -DONED, -DONING. (To throw something aside.) Both "S" hands are held with palms facing at chest level and then thrown down and to the left, opening into the "5" position. Also CAST OFF, DEPOSIT 2, DISCARD 1, FORSAKE 3, LEAVE 2, LET ALONE, NEGLECT.

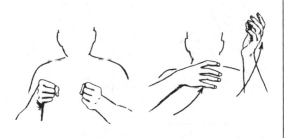

ABANDON 2, *v.* (To toss up and out.) Both "S" hands, held at chest level with palms facing, are swung down slightly and then up into the air toward the left, opening into the "5" position. Also CAST OUT, DISCARD 2, EVICT.

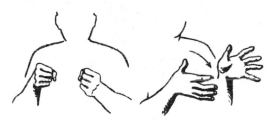

ABBREVIATE 1 (ə brē′ vĭ āt′), *v.*, -ATED, -ATING. (To squeeze or condense into a small space.) The "C" hands face each other, with the right hand nearer to the body than the left. Both hands draw together and close deliberately, squeezing an imaginary object. Also BRIEF 2, CONDENSE, MAKE BRIEF, SUMMARIZE 1, SUMMARY 1.

ABBREVIATE 2, *v.* (To make short; to measure off a short space.) The index and middle fingers of the right

"H" hand are placed across the top of the index and middle fingers of the left "H" hand, and move a short distance back and forth, along the length of the left index finger. Also BRIEF 1, SHORT 1, SHORTEN.

ABBREVIATION (-shən), *n.* See ABBREVIATE 1 or 2.

ABHOR (ăb hôr′), *v.*, -HORRED, -HORRING. (To push away and recoil from; avoid.) The two open hands, palms facing left, are pushed deliberately to the left, as if pushing something away. An expression of disdain or disgust is worn. Also AVOID 2, DESPISE 1, DETEST 1, HATE 1, LOATHE.

ABILITY (ə bĭl′ ə tĭ), *n.* (An affirmative movement of the hands, likened to a nodding of the head, to indicate ability or power to accomplish something.) Both "A" hands, held palms down, move down in unison a short distance before the chest. Also ABLE, CAN 1, CAPABLE, COMPETENT, COULD, FACULTY, MAY 2, POSSIBLE.

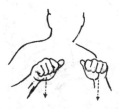

ABLE (ā′ bəl), *adj.* See ABILITY.

ABOLISH 1 (ə bŏl′ ĭsh), *v.,* -ISHED, -ISHING. (Wiping off.) The left "5" hand, palm up, is held slightly above the right "5" hand, held palm down. The right hand swings up, just brushing over the left palm. Both hands close into the "S" position, and the right is brought back with force to its initial position, striking a glancing blow against the left knuckles as it returns. Also ANNIHILATE, CORRUPT, DEFACE, DEMOLISH, DESTROY, HAVOC, PERISH 2, REMOVE 3, RUIN.

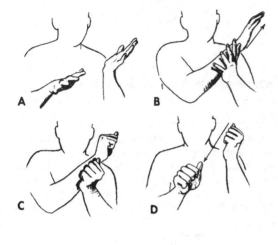

ABOLISH 2, *v.* (Removing.) The right "A" hand, resting in the palm of the left "5" hand, moves slightly up and away, describing a small arc. It is then cast downward, opening into the "5" position, palm down, as if removing something from the left hand and casting it down. Also ABSENCE 2, ABSENT 2, ABSTAIN, CHEAT 2, DEDUCT, DEFICIENCY, DELETE 1, LESS 2, MINUS 3, OUT 2, REMOVE 1, SUBTRACT, SUBTRACTION, TAKE AWAY FROM, WITHDRAW 2.

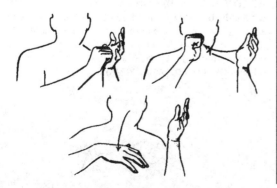

ABORTION 1 (ə bôr′ shən), *n.* (The baby is removed from its mother's womb.) The right hand grasps the stomach and then is thrown down and open.

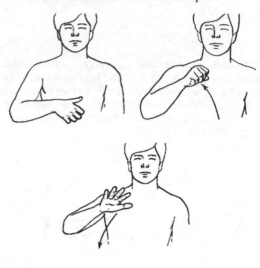

ABORTION 2, *n.* (A variation of ABORTION 1; taking from.) The right fingers scratch against the left palm as if removing something. The right hand is then thrown down and open.

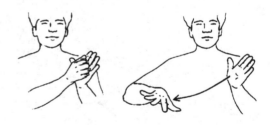

ABOUT 1 (ə bout′), *prep.* (Revolving about.) The left hand is held at chest height, all fingers extended and touching the thumb, and all pointing to the right. The right index finger circles about the left fingers several times. Also CONCERNING, ELECTRIC MOTOR, OF.

ABOUT 2, *adv.* The left hand is held at chest level in the right-angle position, with fingers pointing up and the back of the hand facing right. The right fingers are swept up along the back of the left hand. Also ALMOST, NEARLY.

ABOUT 3, *adv.* (In the general area.) The downturned open "5" hand moves in a counterclockwise direction in front of the body. Also THEREABOUTS.

ABOVE (ə bŭv′), *adv.* (One hand moves above the other.) Both hands, palms flat and facing down, are held before the chest. The right hand circles horizontally above the left in a counterclockwise direction. Also OVER 1.

ABSCESS (ab′ ses), *n.* (Swollen tissue.) The right fingertips are placed on the back of the left hand. They move up, opening into the claw position, defining the bulging abscess. This can be done at any appropriate spot on the body. Example: done on the cheek, it indicates a tooth abscess.

ABSENCE 1 (ăb′ səns), *n.* (A disappearance.) The right open hand, palm facing the body, is held by the

left hand and is drawn down and out, ending in a position with fingers drawn together. The left hand, meanwhile, may close into a position with fingers also drawn together. Also ABSENT 1, DEPLETE, DISAPPEAR, EMPTY 1, EXTINCT, FADE AWAY, GONE 1, MISSING 1, OMISSION 1, OUT 3, OUT OF, VANISH.

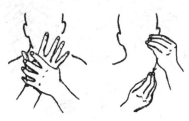

ABSENCE 2, *n.* (Removing.) The right "A" hand, resting in the palm of the left "5" hand, moves slightly up and away, describing a small arc. It is then cast downward, opening into the "5" position, palm down, as if removing something from the left hand and casting it down. Also ABOLISH 2, ABSENT 2, ABSTAIN, CHEAT 2, DEDUCT, DEFICIENCY, DELETE 1, LESS 2, MINUS 3, OUT 2, REMOVE 1, SUBTRACT, SUBTRACTION, TAKE AWAY FROM, WITHDRAW 2.

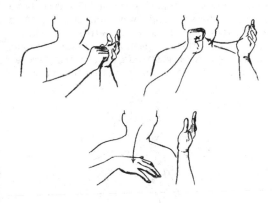

ABSENT 1 (-sənt), *adj.* See ABSENCE 1.

ABSENT 2, *adj.* See ABSENCE 2.

ABSENT-MINDED (mīn′ dĭd), *adj.* (The mind is gone.) The index finger of the right hand, palm back, touches the forehead (the modified sign for THINK, *q.v.*). The right open hand, palm facing the body, is held by the left hand and is drawn down and out, ending in a position with fingers drawn together. The left hand, meanwhile, has closed into a position with fingers also drawn together. Also ABSENCE 1.

DELETE 1, LESS 2, MINUS 3, OUT 2, REMOVE 1, SUBTRACT, SUBTRACTION, TAKE AWAY FROM, WITHDRAW 2.

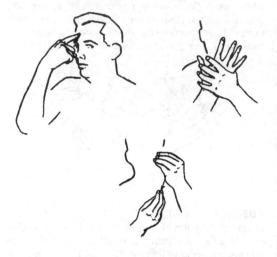

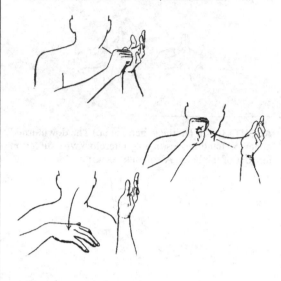

ABSOLUTE (ăb′ sə lo͞ot′), *adj.* (Coming forth directly from the lips; true.) The index finger of the right "D" hand, palm facing left, is placed against the lips. It moves up an inch or two and then describes a small arc forward and away from the lips. Also ABSOLUTELY, ACTUAL, ACTUALLY, AUTHENTIC, CERTAIN, CERTAINLY, FAITHFUL 3, FIDELITY, FRANKLY, GENUINE, INDEED, POSITIVE 1, POSITIVELY, REAL, REALLY, SINCERE 2, SURE, SURELY, TRUE, TRULY, TRUTH, VALID, VERILY.

ABSTAIN 2, *v.* (Withdrawing or getting off.) The curved right index and middle fingers, sitting in the hole formed by the left "C" or "O" hands, are pulled up and out.

ABSOLUTELY (ăb′ sə lo͞ot′ lĭ), *adv.* See ABSOLUTE.

ABUNDANCE (ə bŭn′ dəns), *n.* (A full cup.) The left hand, in the "S" position, is held palm facing right. The right "5" hand, palm down, is brushed outward several times over the top of the left, indicating a wiping off of the top of a cup. Also ABUNDANT, ADEQUATE, AMPLE, ENOUGH, PLENTY, SUBSTANTIAL, SUFFICIENT.

ABSTAIN 1 (ăb stān′), *v.,* -STAINED, -STAINING. (Removing.) The right "A" hand, resting in the palm of the left "5" hand, moves slightly up and away, describing a small arc. It is then cast downward, opening into the "5" position, palm down, as if removing something from the left hand and casting it down. Also ABOLISH 2, ABSENCE 2, ABSENT 2, CHEAT 2, DEDUCT, DEFICIENCY,

ABUNDANT (ə bŭn′ dənt), *adj.* See ABUNDANCE.

ABUSE (*v,* ə byo͞oz′; *n,* ə byo͞os′), ABUSED, ABUSING (Beating someone up.) The right fist strikes the upright left index finger back and forth several times.

ACCEPT (ăk sĕpt′), *v.,* -CEPTED, -CEPTING. (A taking of something unto oneself.) Both open hands, palms down, are held in front of the chest. They move in unison toward the chest, where they come to rest, all fingers closed. Also WILLING 1.

ACCESS (ak′ ses), *n., v.,* ACCESSED, ACCESSING. (Going into.) The downturned right fingers move under their left counterparts.

ACCOMPANY 1 (ə kŭm′ pə nǐ), *v.,* -NIED, -NYING. (To go along with.) Both "A" hands, knuckles together and thumbs up, are moved forward in unison, away from the chest. Also TOGETHER, WANDER AROUND WITH, WITH.

ACCOMPANY 2, *v.* (Going forward together.) Both "A" hands, knuckles and thumbs touching, move forward in unison. Also GO WITH.

ACCOMPLISH 1 (ə kŏm′ plĭsh), *v.,* -PLISHED, -PLISHING. (Penetrating the heights.) The "D" hands, palms back, are held at each side of the head near the temples. With a pivoting motion of the wrists, the hands swing up and around, simultaneously, to a position above the head, with palms facing out. Also ACHIEVE, PROSPER, SUCCEED, SUCCESS, SUCCESSFUL, TRIUMPH 2.

ACCOMPLISH 2, *v.* (Bring to an end.) The left hand, fingers together and pointing forward, is held palm facing right. The right, palm down, fingers also together, moves along the top of the left, goes over the tip of the left index finger, and drops straight down, indicating a cutting off or a finishing. This sign is also used to indicate the past tense of a verb, in the sense of accomplishing an action or state of being. Also ACHIEVE 2, COMPLETE 1, CONCLUDE, DONE 1, END 4, EXPIRE 1, FINISH 1, HAVE 2, TERMINATE.

ACCORDING (TO) (ə kôr′ dǐng), *adv.* (A likeness; a sameness.) Both index fingers, held together at one side of the body near waist level, point forward. As they travel to the other side of the body they separate an inch or two and come together again. Also ALSO 1, AS, DUPLICATE 2, SAME AS, TOO.

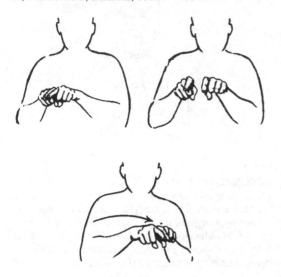

ACCUMULATE 1 (ə kū′ myə lāt′), *v.*, -LATED, -LATING. (Gathering in.) The right "5" hand, its little finger edge touching the upturned left palm, is drawn in an arc toward the body, closing into the "S" position as it sweeps over the base of the left hand. Also COLLECT, EARN, SALARY, WAGES.

ACCUMULATE 2, *v.* (A gathering together.) The right "5" hand, fingers curved and palm facing left, sweeps across and over the upturned left palm, several times, in a circular movement. Also GATHER 1, GATHERING TOGETHER.

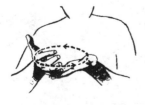

ACCUMULATE 3, *v.* (Assemble all together.) Both "5" hands, palms facing, are held with fingers point-

ing out from the body. With a sweeping motion they are brought in toward the chest, and all fingertips come together. This is repeated. Also ASSEMBLE, ASSEMBLY, CONFERENCE, CONVENE, CONVENTION, GATHER 2, GATHERING, MEETING 1.

ACCURATE 1 (ăk′ yə rĭt), *adj.* (The fingers come together precisely.) The thumb and index finger of each hand, palms facing, the right above the left, form circles. They are brought together with a deliberate movement, so that the fingers and thumbs now touch. Sometimes the right hand, before coming together with the left, executes a slow clockwise circle above the left. Also EXACT 1, EXACTLY, EXPLICIT 1, PRECISE, SPECIFIC.

ACCURATE 2, *adj.* The right index finger, held above the left index finger, comes down rather forcefully so that the bottom of the right hand comes to rest on top of the left thumb joint. Also CORRECT 1, DECENT, EXACT 2, JUST 2, PROPER, RIGHT 3, SUITABLE.

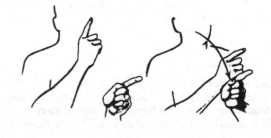

ACCUSE 1 (ə kuz′), *v.*, -CUSED, -CUSING. (The blame is firmly placed.) The right "A" hand, thumb pointing up, is brought down firmly against the back of the left hand, held palm down; the right thumb is then directed toward the person or object to blame. When personal blame is acknowledged, the thumb is brought in to the chest. Also BLAME, FAULT 1, GUILTY 1.

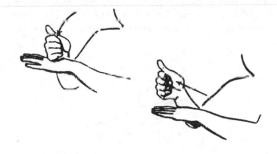

ACCUSE 2, *v.* (A fingering of someone.) The "D" hand, index finger pointing at an imaginary culprit, moves away from the body in short, stabbing steps.

ACCUSTOM (ə kŭs′ təm), *v.,* -TOMED, -TOMING. (Bound down to custom or habit.) Both "S" hands, palms down, are crossed and brought down in unison before the chest. Also BOUND, CUSTOM, HABIT, LOCKED, PRACTICE 3.

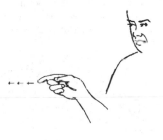

ACHE (āk), *n., v.,* ACHED, ACHING. (A stabbing pain.) The "D" hands, index fingers pointing to each other, are rotated in elliptical fashion before the chest—simultaneously but in opposite directions. Also HARM 1, HURT 1, INJURE 1, INJURY, MAR 1, OFFEND, OFFENSE, PAIN, SIN, WOUND,

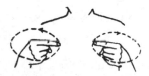

ACHIEVE 1 (ə chēv′), *v.,* -CHIEVED, -CHIEVING. (Penetrating the heights.) The "D" hands, palms back, are held at each side of the head, near the temples. With a pivoting motion of the wrists, the hands swing up and around, simultaneously, to a position above the head, with palms facing out. Also ACCOMPLISH 1, ATTAIN, PROSPER, SUCCEED, SUCCESS, SUCCESSFUL, TRIUMPH 2.

ACHIEVE 2, *v.* (Bring to an end.) The left hand, fingers together and pointing forward, is held palm facing right. The right, palm down, fingers also together, moves along the top of the left, goes over the tip of the left index finger, and drops straight down, indicating a cutting off or a finishing. This sign is also used to indicate the past tense of a verb, in the sense of achieving an action or state of being. Also ACCOMPLISH 2, COMPLETE 1, CONCLUDE, DONE 1, END 4, EXPIRE 1, FINISH 1, HAVE 2, TERMINATE.

ACID 1 (ăs′ ĭd), *n., adj.* (Something sour or bitter.) The right index finger is brought sharply up against the lips, while the mouth is puckered up as if tasting something sour. Also BITTER, DISAPPOINTED 1, LEMON 1, PICKLE, SOUR.

ACID 2, *n., adj.* (Eating away the skin.) With a repeated grasping motion, the right claw hand mimes eating away at the skin of the upturned left palm.

ACQUIRE (ə kwīr′), *v.,* -QUIRED, -QUIRING. (A grasping and bringing forward to oneself.) Both hands, in the "5" position, fingers curved, are crossed at the wrists, with the left palm facing right and the right palm facing left. They are brought in toward the chest, while closing into a grasping "S" position. Also GET, OBTAIN, PROCURE, RECEIVE.

ACROBAT (ak′ rə bat), *n.* (The body movement.) The right index and middle fingers rest in the upturned left palm. The right hand leaves the left, assuming a palm-up position. The index and middle fingers swing in the air in a clockwise circle, and then the two fingers "land" again in the left palm. Also GYMNASTICS.

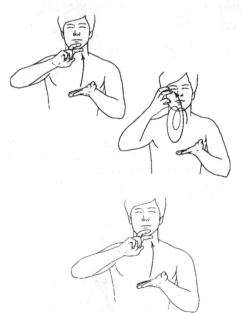

ACROSS (ə krôs′, ə krŏs′), *prep., adv.* (A crossing over.) The left hand is held before the chest, palm down and fingers together. The right hand, fingers together, glides over the left, with the right little finger touching the top of the left hand. Also CROSS 3, OVER 2.

ACT 1 (ăkt), *v.,* ACTED, ACTING, *n.* (Motion or movement, modified by the letter "A" for "act.") Both "A" hands, palms out, are held at shoulder height and rotate alternately toward the head. Also ACTOR, ACTRESS, DRAMA, PERFORM 2, PERFORMANCE 2, PLAY 2, SHOW 2.

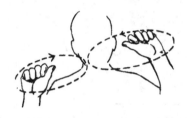

ACT 2, *v.* (An activity.) Both open hands, palms down, are swung right and left before the chest. Also ACTION, ACTIVE, ACTIVITY, BUSY 2, CONDUCT 1, DEED, DO, PERFORM 1, PERFORMANCE 1, RENDER 2.

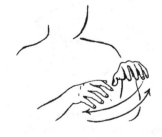

ACTION (ăk′ shən), *n.* (An activity.) See ACT 2.

ACTIVE (ăk′ tĭv), *adj.* (Activity.) See ACT 2.

ACTIVITY (ăk tĭv′ ə ti), *n.* See ACT 2.

ACTOR (ăk′ tər), *n.* (Male acting individual.) The right hand moves to the forehead and grasps an imaginary cap brim (MALE root sign). The sign for ACT 1 is then given. This is followed by the sign for INDIVIDUAL: both hands, fingers together, are placed at either side of the chest and are moved down to waist level. *Note:* The MALE root sign is optional.

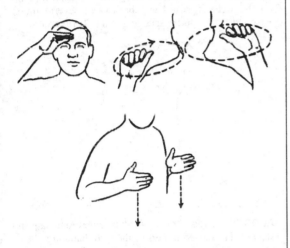

ACTRESS (ăk′ trĭs), *n.* (Female acting individual.) The thumb of the right "A" hand moves down along the line of the right jaw from ear to chin (FEMALE root sign). The sign for ACT 1 is then given. This is followed by the sign for INDIVIDUAL: both hands, fingers together, are placed at either side of the chest and are moved down to waist level. *Note:* The FEMALE root sign is optional.

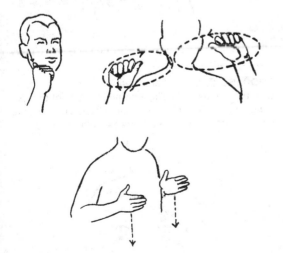

ACTUAL (ăk′ chŏŏ əl), *adj.* (Coming forth directly from the lips; true.) The index finger of the right "D" hand, palm facing left, is placed against the lips. It moves up an inch or two and then describes a small arc forward and away from the lips. Also ABSOLUTE, ABSOLUTELY, ACTUALLY, AUTHENTIC, CERTAIN, CERTAINLY, FAITHFUL 3, FIDELITY, FRANKLY, GENUINE, INDEED, POSITIVE 1, POSITIVELY, REAL, REALLY, SINCERE 2, SURE, SURELY, TRUE, TRULY, TRUTH, VALID, VERILY.

ACTUALLY (ăk′ chŏŏ ə lĭ), *adv.* (Truly.) See ACTUAL.

ADD 1 (ăd), *v.,* ADDED, ADDING. (To bring up all together.) The two open hands, palms and fingers facing each other, with the left hand above the right, are brought together, with all fingers closing simultaneously. This sign is used mainly in the sense of adding up figures or items. Also ADDITION, AMOUNT 1, SUM, SUMMARIZE 2, SUMMARY 2, SUM UP, TOTAL.

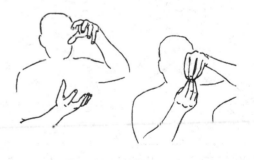

ADD 2, *v.* (A mathematical symbol.) The two index fingers are crossed in the sign for PLUS. Also ADDITION, PLUS, POSITIVE 2.

ADD 3, *v.* (Adding on.) The index and middle fingers of the right "H" hand, palm up, are swung up and over until they come to rest on the index and middle fingers of the left "H" hand, held palm down. Also ADDITION, EXTEND 1, EXTRA, GAIN 1, INCREASE, ON TO, RAISE 2.

ADD 4, *v.* (One hand is added to the other; an addition.) Both hands, palms facing, are held fingers together, the left a bit above the right. The right hand is brought up to the left until their fingertips touch. Also BESIDES, FURTHER 2, MORE, MOREOVER 2.

ADDICTED 1 (ə dĭkt′ əd), *adj.* (A weight is tied around the neck.) The signer mimes tying a rope around the neck.

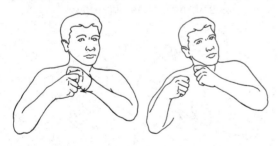

ADDICTED 2, *adj.* (Hooked.) The curved index finger, placed in the corner of the mouth, pulls back and slightly up. Also HOOKED.

ADDITION (ə dĭsh′ ən), *n.* See ADD 1, 2, or 3.

ADDRESS 1 (ə dres′), *n., v.,* -DRESSED, -DRESSING. (A gesture of an orator.) The right open hand, palm facing left, is held above and to the right of the head. It pivots on the wrist, forward and backward, several times. Also LECTURE, ORATE, SPEECH 2, TALK 2, TESTIMONY.

ADDRESS 2 (ăd′ rĕs), *n.* (A place where one eats and sleeps.) The closed fingers of the right hand are placed against the lips (the sign for EAT), and then, opening into a flat palm, against the right cheek (resting the head on a pillow, as in SLEEP). The head leans slightly to the right, as if going to sleep in the right palm, during this latter movement. Also HOME, RESIDENCE 1.

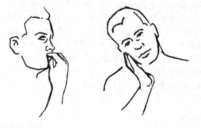

ADDRESS 3, *n., v.* (Same rationale as for LIFE 1, with the initials "L.") The upturned thumbs of the "A" hands move in unison up the chest. Also ALIVE, DWELL, EXIST, LIFE 1, LIVE 1, LIVING, MORTAL, RESIDE.

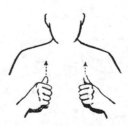

ADEPT (ə dĕpt′), *adj.* (A sharp-edged hand.) The right hand grasps the little finger edge of the left firmly. As it leaves this position, moving down and out, it assumes the "A" position, palm facing left. Also EXPERIENCE 1, EXPERT, SHARP 4, SHREWD, SKILL, SKILLFUL.

ADMINISTRATION 2, *n.* (A fingerspelled loan sign.) The letters "A-D-M" are spelled out.

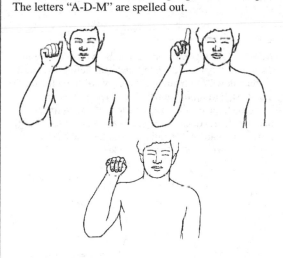

ADEQUATE (ăd′ a kwĭt), *adj.* (A full cup.) The left hand, in the "S" position, is held palm facing right. The right "5" hand, palm down, is brushed outward several times over the top of the left, indicating a wiping off of the top of a cup. Also ABUNDANCE, ABUNDANT, AMPLE, ENOUGH, PLENTY, SUBSTANTIAL, SUFFICIENT.

ADMISSION 1 (ăd mĭsh′ ən), *n.* (Getting something off the chest.) Both hands are held with fingers touching the chest and pointing down. They are then swung up and out, ending with both palms facing up before the body. Also ADMIT 1, CONCEDE, CONFESS, CONFESSION 1.

ADMINISTRATION 1 (ad min is trā′ shən), *n.* (Handling the reins.) The signer manipulates a pair of imaginary reins back and forth.

ADMISSION 2, *n.* (A nicking of or making a notch in the pocketbook, in the colloquial sense. This sign is used in the sense of ADMISSION to a theatre or public event.) The knuckle of the right "X" finger is nicked against the palm of the left hand, held in the "5" position, palm facing right. Also CHARGE 1, COST, DUTY 2, EXCISE, EXPENSE, FEE, FINE 2, IMPOST, PENALTY 3, PRICE 2, TAX 1, TAXATION 1, TOLL.

ADMIT 1 (ăd mĭt′), *v.*, -MITTED, -MITTING. See ADMISSION 1.

ADMIT 2, *v.* (Opening or leading the way toward something.) The open right hand, held up before the body, sweeps down in an arc and over toward the left side of the chest, ending in the palm-up position. Reversing the movement gives the passive form of the verb, except that the hand does not arc upward but rather simply moves outward in a small arc from the body. Also INVITATION, INVITE, INVITED, USHER, WELCOME.

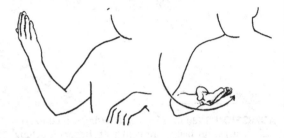

ADMONISH 1 (ăd mŏn′ ĭsh), *v.*, -ISHED, -ISHING. (Tapping one to draw attention to danger.) The right hand taps the back of the left several times. Also CAUTION, FOREWARN, WARN.

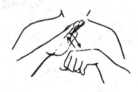

ADMONISH 2, *v.* (A scolding with the finger.) The right index finger shakes back and forth in a natural scolding movement. Also REPRIMAND, REPROVE, SCOLD 1.

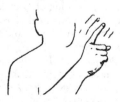

ADOPT 1 (ə dŏpt′), *v.*, -DOPTED, -DOPTING. (Taking unto oneself.) The right hand, palm out, is extended before the chest, index finger and thumb in an open position, the other fingers separated and pointing up. The hand is drawn in toward the chest, and the index and thumb

close at the same time, indicating something taken to oneself. Also APPOINT, CHOOSE 1, SELECT 2, TAKE.

ADOPT 2, *v.* (Take and keep.) The right hand grasps onto an imaginary object to the right, and then the two hands assume the "K" position, palms facing each other, with the right resting on the left.

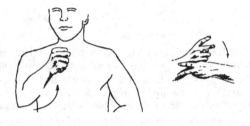

ADULT (ə dult′), *n., adj.* (The letter "A"; the FEMALE and MALE root signs.) The thumbtip of the right "A" hand is placed first on the right jawline and then moves up to touch the right temple.

ADULTERY 1 (ə dul′ tər ē), *n.* (Turning the corner, out of sight of the spouse.) The right cupped hand makes a U-turn around the left "D" hand. The movement is repeated.

ADULTERY 2, *n.* (Jumping from a spouse to another person.) The left hand is held in the "V" position, palm facing the signer. The right hand, in the "A" position, moves in a small arc from the left index to the left middle finger.

ADVANCE (ăd vănsʹ, -vänsʹ), *n., v.,* -VANCED, -VANCING. (Moving forward, step by step.) Both hands, in the right-angle position, palms facing, are held before the chest, a few inches apart, with the right hand slightly behind the left. The right hand is brought up, over and forward, so that it is now ahead of the left. The left hand then follows suit, so that it is now ahead of the right. Also PROGRESS 1.

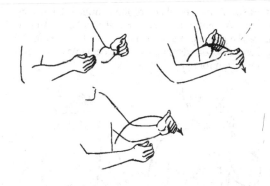

ADVANCED (ăd vănstʹ), *adj.* (Something high up.) Both hands, in the right-angle position, are held before the face, about a foot apart, palms facing. They are raised abruptly about a foot, in a slight outward curving movement. Also HIGH 1, PROMOTE, PROMOTION.

ADVANTAGE (ad vanʹ tij, -vänʹ-), *n.* (Gaining something and storing it in a pocket.) The downturned right index and thumb, holding an imaginary coin, place it in a vest pocket. Also PROFIT.

ADVENT (adʹ vent), *n.* (*eccles.*). (Coming from above.) Both index fingers, palms in, point upwards. They swing down in an arc to chest level.

ADVICE (ăd vīsʹ), *n.* (Take something, *advice,* and disseminate it.) The left hand, held limp in front of the body, has its fingers pointing down. The fingers of the right hand, held all together, are placed on the top of the left hand, and then move forward, off the left hand, assuming a "5" position, palm down. Also ADVISE, COUNSEL, COUNSELOR, INFLUENCE 4.

ADVISE (ăd vīzʹ), *v.,* -VISED, -VISING. See ADVICE.

ADVOCATE (adʹ və kātʹ), *v.,* -CATED, -CATING. (One hand upholds the other.) Both hands, in the "S" position, are held palms facing the body, the right under the left. The right hand pushes up the left in a gesture of support. Also ENDORSE 2, INDORSE 2, SUPPORT 2.

AFFILIATE 1 (ə fĭl′ ĭ āt′), v., -ATED, -ATING. (Joining together.) Both hands, held in the modified "5" position, palms out, move toward each other. The thumbs and index fingers of both hands then connect. Also ANNEX, ASSOCIATE 2, ATTACH, BELONG, COMMUNION OF SAINTS, CONCERN 2, CONNECT, ENLIST, ENROLL, JOIN 1, PARTICIPATE, RELATIVE 2, UNION, UNITE.

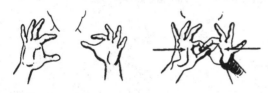

AFFILIATE 2, n. The sign for AFFILIATE 1 is made, followed by the sign for INDIVIDUAL: the open hands, placed at the sides of the chest, move down in unison, to waist level.

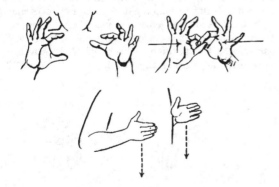

AFRAID (ə frād′), adj. (The heart is suddenly covered with fear.) Both hands, fingers together, are placed side by side, palms facing the chest. They quickly open and come together over the heart, one on top of

the other. Also COWARD, FEAR 1, FRIGHT, FRIGHTEN, SCARE(D), TERROR 1.

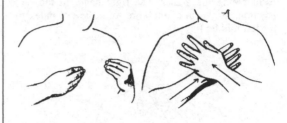

AFRICA 1 (af′ ri kə), n. The "A" hand, thumb pointing to the face, makes a counterclockwise circle around the face. This is considered a racist sign and should generally be avoided.

AFRICA 2, n. (The shape of the continent.) The hand, in the "A" position, opens, and the index and thumb trace the shape of the African continent in the air. This is generally considered the most acceptable and racially neutral sign for Africa.

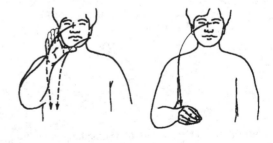

AFRICA 3, n. (A flattened nose.) The middle finger, after touching the tip of the nose, revolves in a counterclockwise direction around the face and comes to rest on the tip of the nose again. (This sign is considered somewhat improper and offensive.) Also NEGRO 2.

AFTER 1 (ăf′ tər, äf′-), *prep.* (Something occurring *after* a fixed place in time, represented by the hand nearest the body.) The right hand, held flat, palm facing the body, fingertips pointing left, represents the fixed place in time. The left hand is placed against the back of the right and moves straight out from the body. The relative positions of the two hands may be reversed, with the left remaining stationary near the body and the right moving out.

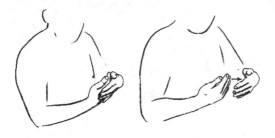

AFTER 2, *prep.* (One hand is after or behind the other.) Both hands, in the "A" position, are held knuckles to knuckles. The right hand moves back, describing a small arc, and comes to rest against the left wrist. Also BACK 1, BACKSLIDE, BEHIND.

AFTER A WHILE (hwīl), *adv. phrase.* (A moving on of the minute hand of the clock.) The right "L" hand, its thumb thrust into the palm of the left and acting as a pivot, moves forward a short distance. Also AFTERWARD, LATER 1, SUBSEQUENT, SUBSEQUENTLY.

AFTERNOON (ăf′ tər nōōn′, äf′ -), *n., adj.* (The sun is midway between zenith and sunset.) The right arm, fingers together and pointing forward, rests on the back of the left hand, its fingers also together and pointing

somewhat to the right. The right arm remains in a position about 45° from the vertical.

AFTERWARD (ăf′ tər wərd, äf′ -), *adv.* See AFTER A WHILE.

AGAIN (ə gĕn′), *adv.* The left hand, open in the "5" position, palm up, is held before the chest. The right hand, in the right-angle position, fingers pointing up, arches over and into the left palm. Also ENCORE, REPEAT.

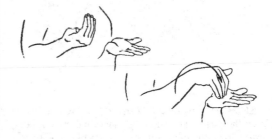

AGAINST (ə gĕnst′, -gānst′), *prep.* (Opposed to; restraint.) The tips of the right fingers, held together, are thrust purposefully into the open left palm, whose fingers are also together and pointing forward. Also OPPOSE.

AGE 1 (āj), *n.* (Age, in the sense of chronological age; the beard of an old man.) The right hand grasps an imaginary beard at the chin and pulls it downward. Also ANTIQUE, OLD.

AGE 2, *n.* (Time in the abstract, indicated by the rotating of the "T" hand on the face of a clock.) The right "T" hand is placed palm to palm in the open left hand. It describes a clockwise circle and comes to rest again in the left palm. Also EPOCH, ERA, PERIOD 2, SEASON, TIME 2.

AGENCY (ā′ jən sē), *n.* (The "A" letters; closing up a circle.) Both "A" hands, thumbs pointing to each other, describe an outward circle as they move around to form a circle, with the palms facing the signer. Also ASSOCIATION.

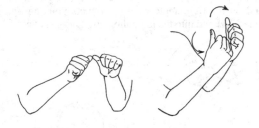

AGENDA (ə jen′ də), *n.* (The letter "A"; a listing down the page.) The right "A" hand, palm facing out, moves down the open left hand, describing an arc as it moves from fingertips to base.

AGGRAVATE 1 (ag′ rə vāt), *v.,* -VATED, -VATING. (The stomach turns.) The right claw hand makes a series of counterclockwise circles on the stomach. A look of distress or annoyance is assumed.

AGGRAVATE 2, *v.* (The emotions well up and explode.) Both downturned hands are placed at the stomach, right fingers pointing left and left fingers pointing right. Both hands move up slowly and then come apart explosively, with palms now facing each other. An expression of distress or annoyance is assumed.

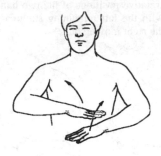

AGO (ə go′), *adj., adv.* (Something past, behind.) The upraised right hand, in the "5" position with palm facing the body, is held just above the right shoulder and is thrown back over it. Also FORMERLY, ONCE UPON A TIME, PAST, PREVIOUS, PREVIOUSLY, WAS, WERE.

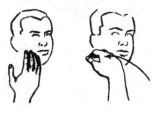

AGREE (ə grē′), *v.,* -GREED, -GREEING. (Of the same mind; thinking the same way.) The index finger of the right "D" hand, palm back, touches the forehead (the modified sign for THINK, *q.v.*), and then the two index fingers, both in the "D" position, palms down, are brought together so they are side by side, pointing away from the body (the sign for SAME). Also ACCORD, ACQUIESCE, ACQUIESCENCE, AGREEMENT, COINCIDE 2, COMPLY, CONCUR, CONSENT.

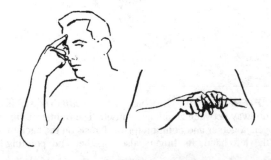

AGREEMENT (-mənt), *n.* See AGREE.

AHEAD (ə hĕd′), *adv.* (One hand moves *ahead* of the other.) The two "A" hands are placed side by side in front of the chest with thumbs and knuckles touching, and the thumbs pointing outward from the body. The right "A" hand moves ahead until its heel rests on the left knuckles.

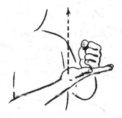

AID (ād), *n., v.,* AIDED, AIDING. (Helping up; supporting.) The left "S" hand, thumb side up, rests in the open right palm. In this position the left hand is pushed up a short distance by the right. Also ASSIST, ASSISTANCE, BENEFIT 1, BOOST, GIVE ASSISTANCE, HELP.

AIDS (ādz), *n.* (Branded with the letter "A.") The downturned open index and middle fingers of the left hand are crossed by the horizontal index finger of the right hand to form the written shape of "A." The word itself may also be fingerspelled.

AIM (ām), *v.,* AIMED, AIMING, *n.* (A thought directed upward, toward a goal.) The left "D" hand, palm facing the body, is held above the head, to represent the goal. The index finger of the right "D" hand, after touching the forehead (modified sign for THINK, *q.v.*), moves slowly and deliberately up to the tip of

the left index finger. Also AMBITION, ASPIRE, GOAL, OBJECTIVE, PERSEVERE 4, PURPOSE 2.

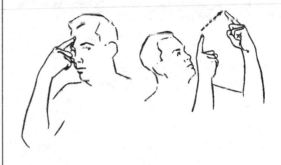

AIR (âr), *n.* (Creating a breeze with the hands.) Both hands, in the "5" position, palms facing, are held at face height. Pivoting at the wrists, they wave back and forth, fanning the face.

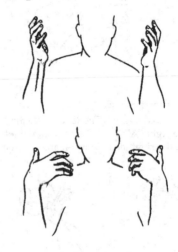

AIRPLANE 1 (âr′ plān′), *n.* (The wings of the airplane.) The "Y" hand, palm down and drawn up near the shoulder, moves forward, several times, up and away from the body. Either hand may be used. Also FLY 1, PLANE 1.

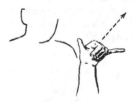

AIRPLANE 2, *n.* (The wings and fuselage of the airplane.) The hand assumes the same position as in

AIRPLANE 1, but the index finger is also extended, to represent the fuselage of the airplane. Either hand may be used, and the movement is the same as in AIR-PLANE 1. Also FLY 2, PLANE 2.

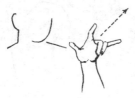

ALARM (ə lärm′), *n.* (The striker hits the bell.) The right index finger, pointing down or out, strikes the opposite palm repeatedly.

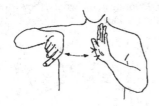

ALASKA (ə las′ kə), *n.* (The letter "A"; the fur-lined hood.) The right "A" hand moves from the left side of the face to the right, describing an arc over the head.

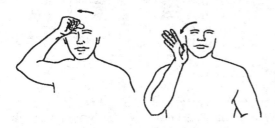

ALCOHOL (al′ kə hôl), *n.* (The size of the jigger.) The right hand, with index and little fingers extended and remaining fingers held against the palm by the thumb, strikes the back of the downturned "S" hand. Also LIQUOR 1, WHISKEY.

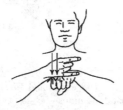

ALCOHOLICS ANONYMOUS, *n.* (The "A" letters.) The signer fingerspells "A-A," moving the "A" hand slightly to the right after the first letter.

ALIKE (ə līk′), *adv.* (Matching fingers are brought together.) The outstretched index fingers are brought together, either once or several times. Also IDENTICAL, LIKE 2, SAME 1, SIMILAR, SUCH.

ALIVE (ə līv′), *adj.* (The fountain [of LIFE] wells up from within the body.) The upturned thumbs of the "A" hands move in unison up the chest. Also ADDRESS 3, DWELL, EXIST, LIFE 1, LIVE 1, LIVING, MORTAL, RESIDE.

ALL 1 (ôl), *adj., n., pron.* (Encompassing; a gathering together.) Both hands are held in the right-angle position, palms facing the body, and the right hand in front of the left. The right hand makes a sweeping outward movement around the left and comes to rest with the back of the right hand resting in the left palm. Also ENTIRE, UNIVERSAL, WHOLE.

ALL 2, *adj., n., pron.* (An inclusion, in the sense of a total number.) The left hand is held in the "C" position, fingers pointing right. The right hand, in the "5" position, fingers facing out from the body, palm down, is held above the left. With a horizontal swing to the right, the right hand describes an arc, as the fingers close and are thrust into the left "C" hand, which closes over it. Also ALTOGETHER, INCLUDE, INCLUSIVE, WHOLE (THE).

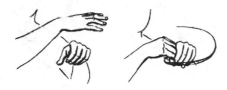

ALL AFTERNOON (ăf′ tər nōōn′, äf′-), *adv. phrase.* (The sun, at its zenith, travels across the sky to sunset position, at the horizon.) The left arm is held before the chest, with the hand extended, fingers together, and palm facing down. The right elbow rests on the left hand, with the right hand extended, palm facing out. The right arm, using its elbow as a pivot, moves slowly down until it reaches the horizontal. Also AFTERNOON.

ALL ALONG (ə lông′, ə lŏng′), *adv. phrase.* (From a point up and over.) In the "D" position, palms down, both index fingers touch the right shoulder and then are brought up and over, ending in a palm-up position, pointing straight ahead of the body. Also ALL THE TIME, EVER SINCE, SINCE, SO FAR, THUS FAR.

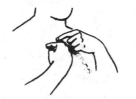 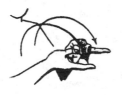

ALL DAY (dā), *phrase.* (From sunrise to sunset.) The left arm is held before the chest, palm down, fingers together. The right elbow rests on the back of the left

hand. The right hand, palm up, pivoted by its elbow, describes an arc, from as far to the right as it can be held to a point where it comes to rest on the left arm, indicating the course of the sun from sunrise to sunset.

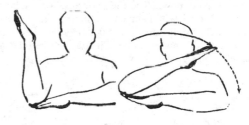

ALLEGIANCE (ə le′ jəns), *n.* (Support.) The knuckles of the right "S" hand push up the left "S" hand.

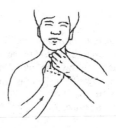

ALLIGATOR (al′ ə gā tər′), *n.* (The mouth.) Both "5" hands are held against each other, fingertips pointing forward. With the heels of the hands connected, the hands come apart in a wide arc, imitating the opening of a large mouth.

ALL MORNING (môr′ nĭng), *adv. phrase.* (The sun, at sunrise position, rises until it reaches its zenith.) The right arm is held horizontally before the body, palm up and fingers together. The left hand, palm facing the body, is placed in the crook of the right elbow, and the right arm rises slowly until it reaches the vertical.

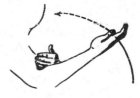

ALL NIGHT (nīt), *adv. phrase.* (The sun, having set over the horizon, continues around the other side of the earth until it reaches the opposite horizon.) The left arm is held before the chest, hand extended, fingers together, palm down. The right arm rests on the back of the left hand, with palm down, fingers extended and together. The right hand, pivoted at its wrist, describes a sweeping downward arc until it comes to a stop near the left elbow. Also LATE AT NIGHT.

ALL OF A SUDDEN, *phrase.* (The sign for WRONG 1, in the sense of an unexpected occurrence.) The right "Y" hand is placed on the chin, palm facing the signer. It swivels on the wrist over the chin, maintaining contact, as it moves from right to left. The signer assumes a look of sudden surprise. Also SUDDENLY.

ALLOW (ə lou′), *v.,* -LOWED, -LOWING. (A permissive upswinging of the hands, as if giving in.) Both hands, palms facing and fingers pointing away from the body, are held at chest level, almost a foot apart. With an upward movement, using their wrists as pivots, the hands sweep up until the fingers point almost straight up. Also GRANT 1, LET, LET'S, LET US, MAY 3, PERMISSION 1, PERMIT 1, TOLERATE 1.

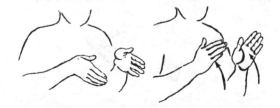

ALL RIGHT (rīt), *phrase.* (A straightening out.) The right hand, fingers together and palm facing left, is placed in the upturned left palm, whose fingers point away from the body. The right hand slides straight out along the left palm, over the left fingers, and stops with its heel resting on the left fingertips. Also O.K. 1, PRIVILEGE, RIGHT 1, RIGHTEOUS 1, YOU'RE WELCOME 2.

ALL THE TIME (tīm), *adv. phrase.* See ALL ALONG.

ALL YEAR; ALL YEAR ROUND (yĭr; round) (*colloq.*), *adv., v. phrase.* (Encircling the planet.) The left hand, in the "S" position, knuckles facing right, is encircled by the right index finger, which travels in a clockwise direction. It makes one revolution and comes to rest atop the left hand. Also AROUND THE WORLD, ORBIT 1.

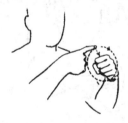

ALMOST (ôl′ mōst, ôl mōst′), *adv.* The left hand is held at chest level in the right angle position, with fingers pointing up and the back of the hand facing right. The right fingers are swept up along the back of the left hand. Also ABOUT 2, NEARLY.

ALONE (ə lōn′), *adj.* (One wandering around in a circle.) The index finger, pointing straight up, palm facing the body (the number *one*), is rotated before the face in a counterclockwise direction. Also LONE, ONE 2, ONLY, SOLE, UNITY.

ALPHABET 1 (ăl′ fə bĕt′), *n.* (The movement of the fingers in fingerspelling.) The right hand, palm out, is moved from left to right, with the fingers wriggling up and down. Also DACTYLOLOGY, FINGERSPELLING, MANUAL ALPHABET, SPELL, SPELLING.

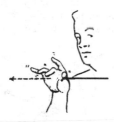

ALPHABET 2, *n.* (The A-B-C.) The signer fingerspells "A-B-C," and then the hand, with fingers wriggling, moves from left to right. See previous entry.

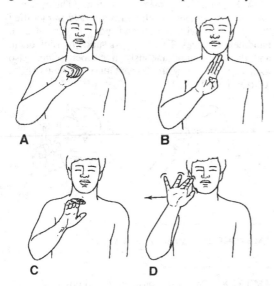

A   B

C   D

ALSO 1 (ôl′ sō), *adv.* (A likeness; a sameness.) Both index fingers, held together at one side of the body

near waist level, point forward. As they travel to the other side of the body they separate an inch or two and come together again. Also ACCORDING (TO), AS, DUPLICATE 2, SAME AS, TOO.

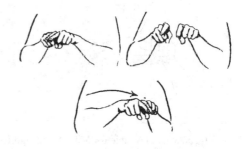

ALSO 2, *adv.* The right "5" hand, palm facing the body, fingers facing left, moves from left to right, meanwhile closing until all its fingers touch around its thumb. Also AND, MOREOVER 1.

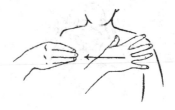

ALTAR 1 (ôl′ tər) (*eccles.*), *n.* (A table for kneeling.) The sign for TABLE is made: Both hands, held flat, palms down, touch at the thumbs. They are drawn apart about a foot (to represent the table top). The two index fingers, pointing down, move down simultaneously an inch or two, retract their course, move in toward the body, and again move down an inch or two (the table's four legs). The right index and middle fingers, bent at the knuckles, are then thrust into the upright palm of the left hand (to represent the act of kneeling).

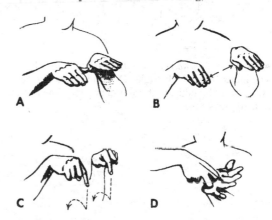

A   B

C   D

ALTAR 2, *n.* (The construction or shape of the altar.) Both "A" hands, palms down and thumbs touching, separate and move down.

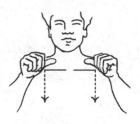

ALTAR 3 (*eccles.*), *n.* (A table for Mass.) The sign for ALTAR 1 is made; and then the two "F" hands, palms out, are drawn up and together so that the thumbs and index fingers of both hands touch before the face (bringing the Host to the lips in Roman Catholic practice). Also MASS.

ALTRUISM (al′ trōō iz əm), *n.* (The heart is open.) The right hand is held against the heart. It moves out and forward with a flourish, ending with the palm facing left.

ALWAYS (ôl′ wāz, -wĭz), *adv.* (Around the clock.) The index finger of the right "D" hand points outward, away from the body, with palm facing left. The arm is rotated clockwise.

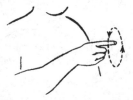

AM 1 (ăm; *unstressed* əm), *v.* (Part of the verb to BE.) The tip of the right index finger, held in the "D" position, palm facing left, is held at the lips, and the hand moves straight out and away from the lips. Also ARE 1, BE 1, IS 1.

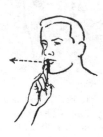

AM 2, *v.* (The "A" hand.) The tip of the right thumb, in the "A" position, palm facing left, is held at the lips. Then the hand moves straight out and away from the lips.

AMAZE (ə māz′), *v.,* -MAZED, -MAZING. (The eyes pop open in amazement.) Both hands are held in modified "O" positions with thumb and index fingers of each hand near the eyes. These fingers suddenly flick open, and the eyes simultaneously pop open wide. Also AMAZEMENT, ASTONISH, ASTONISHED, ASTONISHMENT, ASTOUND, SURPRISE 1.

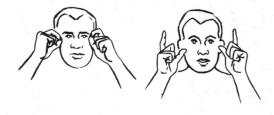

AMAZEMENT (-mənt), *n.* See AMAZE.

AMBITION (ăm bĭsh′ ən), *n.* (A thought directed upward, toward a goal.) The left "D" hand, palm facing the body, is held above the head, to represent the goal. The index finger of the right "D" hand, after touching the forehead (modified sign for THINK, *q.v.*), moves slowly and deliberately up to the tip of the left index finger. Also AIM, ASPIRE, GOAL, OBJECTIVE, PERSEVERE 4, PURPOSE 2.

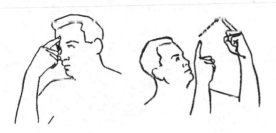

AMBITIOUS 1 (ăm bĭsh′ əs), *adj.* (Rubbing the hands together in zeal or ambition.) The open hands are rubbed vigorously back and forth against each other. Also ANXIOUS 1, ARDENT, DILIGENCE 1, DILIGENT, EAGER, EAGERNESS, EARNEST, ENTHUSIASM, ENTHUSIASTIC, INDUSTRIOUS, METHODIST, ZEAL, ZEALOUS.

AMBITIOUS 2, *adj.* (The self is carried uppermost.) The right "A" hand, thumb up, is brought up against the chest, from waist to breast. Also EGOTISM 1, SELF 2.

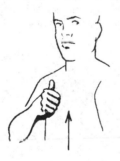

AMBULANCE (am′ byə ləns), *n.* (The flashing light.) The right hand, fingers extended, is positioned above the head. It rotates in imitation of a flashing emergency light.

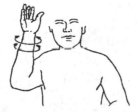

AMEND (ə mend′), *v.* -MENDED, -MENDING. (Add something on.) The open left hand is held either with palm facing the body or facing right. The right hand, palm down and a space maintained between the thumb and the other fingers, swivels up and grasps the little finger edge of the left hand, as if inserting a clip on a stack of papers.

AMERICA (ə mĕr′ ə kə), *n.* (The fences built by the early settlers as protection against the Indians.) The extended fingers of both hands are interlocked, and are swept in an arc from left to right as if encompassing an imaginary house or stockade. Also UNION, THE.

AMIABLE (ā′ mĭ ə bəl), *adj.* (A crinkling up of the face.) Both hands, in the "5" position, palms facing back, are placed on either side of the face. The fingers wiggle back and forth, while a pleasant, happy expression is worn. Also CHEERFUL, CORDIAL, FRIENDLY, JOLLY, PLEASANT.

AMID (ə′ mĭd′), *prep.* (Wandering in and out.) The right index finger weaves its way in and out between the outstretched fingers of the left hand. Also AMIDST, AMONG, MIDST.

AMIDST (ə' mǐdst'), *prep.* See AMID.

AMONG (ə mŭng'), *prep.* See AMID.

AMOUNT 1 (ə mount'), *n.* (To bring up all together.) The two open hands, palms and fingers facing each other, with the left hand above the right, are brought together, with all fingers closing simultaneously. This sign is used mainly in the sense of adding up figures or items. Also ADD 1, ADDITION, SUM, SUMMARIZE 2, SUMMARY 2, SUM UP, TOTAL.

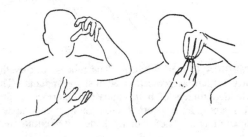

AMOUNT 2, *n.* (Throwing up a number of things before the eyes; a display of fingers to indicate a question of how many or how much.) The right hand, palm up, is held before the chest, all fingers touching the thumb. The hand is tossed straight up, while the fingers open to the "5" position. Also HOW MANY?, HOW MUCH?, NUMBER 2.

AMPLE (ăm' pəl), *adj.* (A full cup.) The left hand, in the "S" position, is held palm facing right. The right "5" hand, palm down, is brushed outward several times over the top of the left, indicating a wiping off of the top of a cup. Also ABUNDANCE, ABUNDANT, ADEQUATE, ENOUGH, PLENTY, SUBSTANTIAL, SUFFICIENT.

AMPUTATE (am' pyŏŏ tāt'), *v.,* -TATED, -TATING. (Sawing off a limb.) With the upturned open hand, the signer mimes sawing off an arm or a leg.

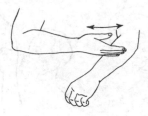

ANALYZE (an' ə līz), *v.,* -LYZED, -LYZING. (Pulling apart.) Both downturned curved index and middle fingers pull apart repeatedly.

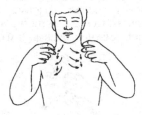

ANCESTORS 1 (ăn' sĕs tĕrz), *n. pl.* (A series of parents, in the past.) The upright open hands are held facing each other before the right shoulder, right palm facing left, left palm facing right. In this position the hands move back over the shoulder, alternately executing a series of up-down, circular motions.

ANCESTORS 2, *n. pl.* The upright, right open hand, palm facing left, moves back over the right shoulder in a series of up-down, circular motions. (This is similar to the sign for ANCESTORS 1, except that only the right hand is used.)

ANCHOR (ang′ kər), *n., v.,* ANCHORED, ANCHORING. (Dropping the hook.) The right "3" hand is held palm facing left. This represents the vessel floating on the surface of the water. The downturned curved left index finger is "thrown" overboard and goes down, and the signer leans back against an imaginary rope or line to set the anchor in place on the bottom.

AND (ănd; *unstressed* ənd; ən), *conj.* The right "5" hand, palm facing the body, fingers facing left, moves from left to right, meanwhile closing until all its fingers touch around its thumb. Also ALSO 2, MOREOVER 1.

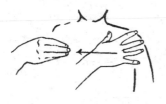

ANESTHESIA (an′ əs thē′ zhə), *n.* (Placing a mask over the mouth.) The cupped right hand is placed over the mouth. The eyes may close at the same time.

ANGEL (ān′ jəl), *n.* (A winged creature.) The fingertips of both hands rest on the shoulders, and then the hands go through the motions of flapping wings, pivoting up and down from the wrists, and held at shoul-

der level. The eyes are sometimes rolled upward, indicating something celestial.

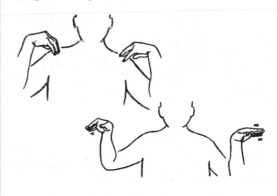

ANGER (ăn′ gər), *n.* (A violent welling up of the emotions.) The curved fingers of the right hand are placed in the center of the chest, and fly up suddenly and violently. An expression of anger is worn. Also ANGRY 2, ENRAGE, FURY, INDIGNANT, INDIGNATION, IRE, MAD 1, RAGE.

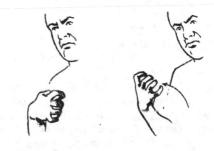

ANGLE 1 (ăn′ gəl), *n., v.,* -GLED, -GLING. (The natural sign.) Both hands, palms flat and fingers straight, are held in front of the body at right angles to each other with fingertips touching, the left fingertips pointing to the right and the right fingertips pointing forward. Also CORNER 1.

ANGLE 2, *n.* (Outlining an angle.) The left hand is held in the "L" position, palm facing forward. The right index finger moves down the left index and along the thumb, tracing a right angle as it does.

ANGRY 1 (ăn′ grĭ), *adj.* (Wrinkling the brow.) The "5" hand is held palm toward the face. The fingers partly open and close several times while an angry expression is worn on the face. Also CROSS 1, CROSSNESS, FIERCE, ILL TEMPER, IRRITABLE.

ANGRY 2, *adj.* See ANGER.

ANIMAL 1 (ăn′ ə məl), *n.* (Something with four legs that breathes.) With palms facing the body, both hands are placed on the chest, with one on top of the other, right fingers facing left and left fingers right. In this position both are moved alternately on and off the chest (signifying the rise and fall of the chest in breathing). The index and middle fingers of both hands are next brought into play, pointing downward, one in front of the other, and describing a walking motion outward from the body.

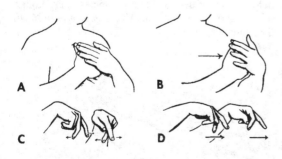

A B C D

ANIMAL 2, *n.* (A modification of the breathing movement described in ANIMAL 1.) With the curved fin-

gertips of both hands resting on either side of the chest, acting as anchors, the arms are moved alternately toward and away from each other.

ANKLE (ang′ kəl), *n.* (The anatomy is indicated.) The right index and thumb wrap around the left wrist, and then the signer points down to the foot.

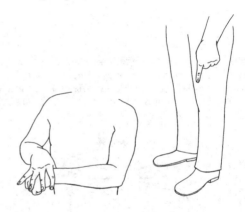

ANNEX (ə nĕks′), *v.,* -NEXED, -NEXING. (Joining together.) Both hands, held in the modified "5" position, palms out, move toward each other. The thumbs and index fingers of both hands then connect. Also AFFILIATE 1, ASSOCIATE 2, ATTACH, BELONG, COMMUNION OF SAINTS, CONCERN 2, CONNECT, ENLIST, ENROLL, JOIN 1, PARTICIPATE, RELATIVE 2, UNION, UNITE.

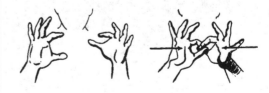

ANNOUNCE (ə nouns′), *v.,* -NOUNCED, -NOUNCING. (An issuance from the mouth.) Both index fingers are placed at the lips, with palms facing the body. They are rotated once and swung out in arcs until the left index finger points somewhat to the left and the right index somewhat to the right. Sometimes the rotation of the fingers is omitted in favor of a simple swinging out from the lips. Also ACCLAIM 1, ACCLAMATION,

ANNOUNCEMENT, DECLARE, MAKE KNOWN, PROCLAIM, PROCLAMATION.

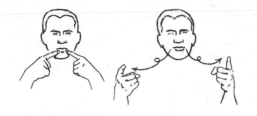

ANNOUNCEMENT (-mənt), *n.* See ANNOUNCE.

ANNOY 1 (ə noi′), *v.,* -NOYED, -NOYING. (Obstruct, block.) The left hand, fingers together and palm flat, is held before the body, facing somewhat down. The little finger side of the right hand, held with palm flat, makes one or several up-down chopping motions against the left hand, between its thumb and index finger. Also ANNOYANCE 1, BLOCK, BOTHER 1, CHECK 2, COME BETWEEN, DISRUPT, DISTURB, HINDER, HINDRANCE, IMPEDE, INTERCEPT, INTERFERE, INTERFERENCE, INTERFERE WITH, INTERRUPT, MEDDLE 1, OBSTACLE, OBSTRUCT, PREVENT, PREVENTION.

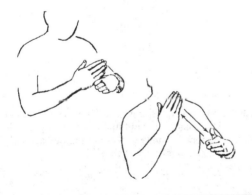

ANNOY 2 (*rare*), *v.* (A clouding over; a troubling.) Both "B" hands, palms facing each other, are rotated alternately before the forehead. Also ANNOYANCE 2, ANXIOUS 2, BOTHER 2, CONCERN 1, FRET, PROBLEM 1, TROUBLE, WORRIED, WORRY 1.

ANNOYANCE 1 (ə noi′ əns), *n.* See ANNOY 1.

ANNOYANCE 2 (*rare*), *n.* See ANNOY 2.

ANNUAL (ăn′ yŏŏ əl), *adj.* (Several years brought forward.) This sign is actually a modification of the sign for YEAR, *q.v.* The ball of the right "S" hand, moving straight out from the body, palm facing left, glances over the thumb side of the "S" hand, which is held palm facing right. As this contact is made, the right index finger is flung straight out, and the right hand, in this new position, continues forward. This is repeated several times, to indicate several years. Also EVERY YEAR, YEARLY.

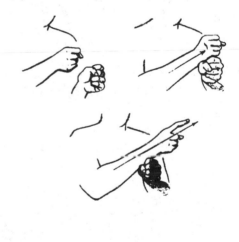

ANOINT 1 (ə noint′) (*eccles.*), *v.,* -NOINTED, -NOINTING. (A pouring of water over the head.) An imaginary cup of water is tilted and poured over the head.

ANOINT 2, *v.* (Pouring holy water on the head.) The "A" hand, holding an imaginary pitcher by the handle, tips it over above the head to pour water on the head.

ANOINT 3 (*eccles.*), *v.* (A crossing of the forehead.) In the "A" position, the right thumbnail is kissed, and then is used to describe a small cross on the forehead.

ANOINT 4 (*eccles.*), *v.* (Pouring the oil.) The downturned thumb of the right "A" hand makes a continuous counterclockwise circle over the back of the closed left hand.

ANOTHER (ə nŭth′ ər), *adj.* (Moving over to *another* position.) The right "A" hand, thumb up, is pivoted from the wrist and swung over to the right so that the thumb now points to the right. Also OTHER.

ANSWER 1 (ăn′ sər; än′-), *n., v.,* -SWERED, -SWERING. (Directing a reply from the mouth to someone.) The

tip of the right index finger, held in the "D" position, palm facing the body, is placed on the lips, while the left "D" hand, palm also facing the body, is held about a foot in front of the right hand. The right index finger, swinging around, moves toward and stops in a pointing position a few inches from the left index fingertip. Also MAKE RESPONSE, REPLY 1, RESPOND, RESPONSE 1.

ANSWER 2, *n.* (The letter "R"; coming out of the mouth.) Both "R" hands are held before the face, with the right "R" hand at the lips and behind the left "R" hand. Both hands move forward simultaneously, describing a small upward arc. Also REACTION, REPLY 2, REPORT, RESPONSE 2.

ANT (ant) *n.* (Squashing an ant between the thumbnails.) Both hands are held in the "A" position, and the right thumbnail comes down and presses against the left thumbnail a number of times.

ANTENNA 1 (an ten′ ə), *n.* (The shape of the aerial antenna placed to draw in signals.) The downturned right "3" hand pivots back and forth as it rests on top of the upturned left index finger.

ANTENNA 2, *n.* (The movement of the insect's antennae.) The downturned right "V" hand is placed on top of the head, the fingers pointing forward. The hand swivels from left to right, imitating the movement.

ANTICIPATE (ăn tĭs′ ə pāt′), *v.*, -PATED, -PATING. (A thought awaited.) The tip of the right index finger, held in the "D" position, palm facing the body, is placed on the forehead (modified THINK, *q.v.*). Both hands then assume right-angle positions, fingers facing, with the left hand held above left shoulder level and the right before the right breast. Both hands, held thus, wave to each other several times. Also ANTICIPA-TION, EXPECT, HOPE.

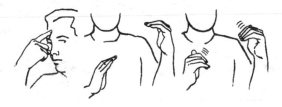

ANTICIPATION (-pā′ shən), *n.* See ANTICIPATE.

ANTLERS (ănt′ lərs), *n. pl.* (The branching of the antlers from the head.) Both hands, in the "5" position, palms up, are placed at the head, thumbs resting on the head above the temples. Also DEER, ELK, MOOSE.

ANXIOUS 1 (ăngk′ shəs, ăng′ shəs), *adj.* (Rubbing the hands together in zeal or ambition.) The open hands are rubbed vigorously back and forth against each other. Also AMBITIOUS 1, ARDENT, DILIGENCE 1, DILIGENT,

EAGER, EAGERNESS, EARNEST, ENTHUSIASM, ENTHUSIAS-TIC, INDUSTRIOUS, METHODIST, ZEAL, ZEALOUS.

ANXIOUS 2, *adj.* (A clouding over; a troubling.) Both "B" hands, palms facing each other, are rotated alternately before the forehead. Also ANNOY 2, ANNOYANCE 2, BOTHER 2, CONCERN 1, FRET, PROBLEM 1, TROUBLE, WORRIED, WORRY 1.

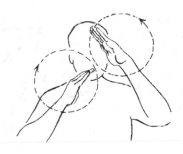

ANY 1 (ĕn′ ĭ), *adj., pron.* The "A" hand, palm out, moves down in an S-shaped curve to a point a bit above waist level.

ANY 2, *adj., pron.* The "A" hand, palm down and thumb pointing left, pivots around on the wrist, so the thumb now points down.

ANYHOW (ĕn′ ĭ hou′), *adv.* Both hands, in the "5" position, are held before the chest, fingertips facing each other. With an alternate back-forth movement, the fingertips are made to strike each other. Also ANY-WAY, DESPITE, DOESN'T MATTER, HOWEVER 2, INDIFFER-ENCE, INDIFFERENT, IN SPITE OF, MAKE NO DIFFERENCE, NEVERTHELESS, NO MATTER, WHEREVER.

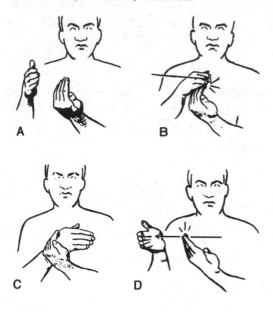

A   B

C   D

ANYONE (ĕn′ ĭ wŭn′), *pron.* (*Any* and *one*.) After forming either of the two signs for ANY, the "A" hand, moving up a bit, assumes the "1" position ("D"), palm out.

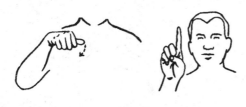

ANYWAY (ĕn′ ĭ wā′), *adv.* See ANYHOW.

APART (ə pärt′), *adv.* (The hands are moved *apart*.) Both hands, in the "A" position, thumbs up, are held together, with knuckles touching. With a deliberate movement they come apart. Also DIVORCE 1, PART 3, SEPARATE 1.

APOLOGIZE 1 (ə pŏl′ ə jīz′), *v.*, -GIZED, -GIZING. (The heart is circled to indicate feeling, modified by the let-ter "S" for SORROW.) The right "S" hand, palm facing the body, is rotated several times over the area of the heart. Also APOLOGY 1, CONTRITION, PENITENT, REGRET, REGRETFUL, REPENT, REPENTANT, RUE, SORROW, SOR-ROWFUL 2, SORRY.

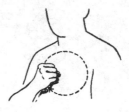

APOLOGIZE 2, *v.* (A wiped-off and cleaned slate.) The right hand wipes off the left palm several times. Also APOLOGY 2, EXCUSE, FORGIVE 2, PARDON, PAROLE.

APOLOGY 1 (ə pŏl′ ə jĭ), *n.* See APOLOGIZE 1.

APOLOGY 2, *n.* See APOLOGIZE 2.

APOSTLE (ə pos′ əl), *n.* (A follower.) Both "A" hands, one behind the other, move forward in unison. The sign for INDIVIDUAL is then made: both open hands, palms facing each other, move down the sides of the body, tracing its outline to the hips.

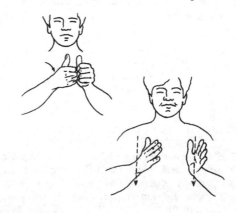

APPARENT (ə pắr′ ənt, ə pâr′-), *adj.* (Something presented before the eyes.) The open right hand, palm flat and facing out, with fingers together and pointing up, is positioned at shoulder level. Pivoting from the wrist, the hand is swung around so that the palm now faces the eyes. Sometimes the eyes glance at the newly presented palm. Also APPARENTLY, APPEAR 1, LOOK 2, SEEM.

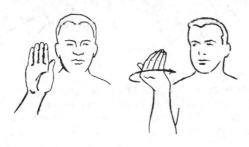

APPARENTLY (ə pắr′ ənt lē, ə pâr′-), *adv.* See APPARENT.

APPEAR 1 (ə pĭr′), *v.,* -PEARED, -PEARING. See APPARENT.

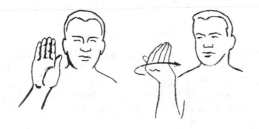

APPEAR 2, *v.* (Popping up before the eyes.) The right index finger, pointing up, pops up between the index and middle fingers of the left hand, whose palm faces down. Also POP UP, RISE 2.

APPEAR 3, *v.* (Face-to-face.) The left hand, fingers together, palm flat and facing the eyes, is held a bit above eye level. The right hand, fingers also together, is held in front of the mouth, with palm facing the left hand. With a sweeping upward movement the right hand moves toward the left, which moves straight up an inch or two at the same time. Also APPEARANCE, BEFORE 3, CONFRONT, FACE 2, FACE-TO-FACE, PRESENCE.

APPETITE (ăp′ ə tīt′), *n.* (The upper alimentary tract is outlined.) The right "C" hand, palm facing the body, is placed with fingertips touching midchest. In this position it moves down a bit. Also CRAVE, DESIRE 2, FAMINE, HUNGARIAN, HUNGARY, HUNGER, HUNGRY, STARVATION, STARVE, STARVED, WISH 2.

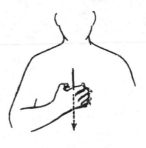

APPLAUD (ə plôd′), *v.,* -PLAUDED, -PLAUDING. (Good words coming from the mouth; clapping hands.) The fingertips of the right hand, palm flat and facing the body, are brought up to the lips so that they touch (part of the sign for GOOD, *q.v.*). The hands are then clapped together several times. Also ACCLAIM 2, APPLAUSE, APPROBATION, APPROVAL, APPROVE, CLAP, COMMEND, CONGRATULATE 1, CONGRATULATIONS 1, PRAISE.

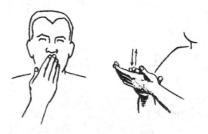

APPLAUSE (ə plôz′), *n.* See APPLAUD.

APPLE (ăp′ əl), *n.* (A chewing of the letter "A" for *apple*.) The right "A" hand is held at the right cheek, with the thumbtip touching the cheek and palm facing out. In this position the hand is swung over and back from the wrist several times, using the thumb as a pivot.

APPLESAUCE (ap′ əl sôs), *n.* (Eating an apple with a spoon.) The sign for APPLE is made. An imaginary spoon is then brought up to the mouth.

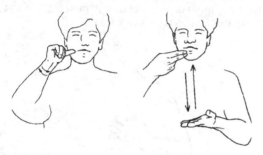

APPOINT (ə point′), *v.,* -POINTED, -POINTING. (Taking unto oneself.) The right hand, palm out, is extended before the chest, index finger and thumb in an open position, the other fingers separated and pointing up. The hand is drawn in toward the chest, and the index and thumb close at the same time, indicating something taken to oneself. Also ADOPT, CHOOSE 1, SELECT 2, TAKE.

APPOINTMENT (ə point′ mənt), *n.* (A binding of the hands together; a commitment.) The right "S" hand, palm down, is positioned above the left "S" hand, also palm down. The right hand circles above the left in a clockwise manner and is brought down on the back of

the left hand. At the same instant both hands move down in unison a short distance. Also ENGAGEMENT.

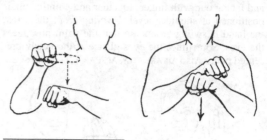

APPRECIATE (ə prē′ shĭ āt′), *v.,* -ATED, -ATING. (A pleasurable feeling on the heart.) The open right hand is circled on the chest over the heart. Also ENJOY, ENJOYMENT, GRATIFY 1, LIKE 3, PLEASE, PLEASURE, WILLING 2.

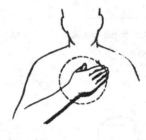

APPROACH (ə prōch′), *v.,* -PROACHED, -PROACHING. (Coming close to.) Both hands are held in the right-angle position, fingers facing each other, with the right hand held between the left hand and the chest. The right hand slowly moves toward the left. Also NEAR 2, TOWARD 2.

APPROVE (ə proov′), *v.,* -PROVED, -PROVING. (The letters "OK"; placing a stamp of approval.) The signer fingerspells "O" and "K." As the handshape for "K" appears, the hand is brought down into the palm of the other hand.

APRON 1 (ā′ prən), *n.* (Something worn at midriff.) The "L" hands, index fingers pointing down, palms facing the body, are placed in the center of the chest and are drawn apart, outlining the apron.

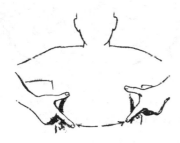

APRON 2, *n.* (Tying the apron.) The signer mimics tying apron strings behind the back.

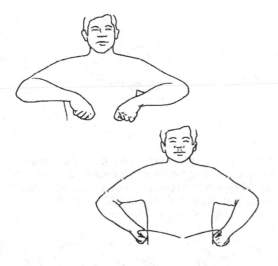

ARAB (ar′ əb) *n.* (The letter "A"; the Arab's headband.) The "A" hand makes a circle over the head.

ARCHDIOCESE (ärch′ dī′ə sēs′, -sis), *n.* (*eccles.*). (HIGH and DISTRICT.) Both right angle hands, palms down, move up a short distance from chest level. Both hands, then forming "D's," are held side by side, palms out. They swing apart in circles, coming together again with palms in.

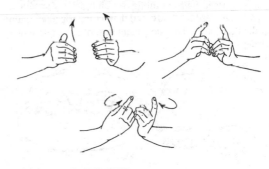

ARCHITECTURE (är′ kə tek chər), *n.* (The letter "A"; the roof and walls of a building.) Both "A" hands, palms facing forward and thumbtips touching, move apart and then straight down. Also ARCHITECT.

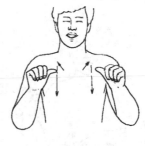

ARE 1 (är), *v.* (Part of the verb to BE.) The tip of the right index finger, held in the "D" position, palm facing left, is held at the lips, and the hand moves straight out and away from the lips. Also AM 1, BE 1, IS 1.

ARE 2, *v.* This is the same sign as for ARE 1, except that the "R" hand is used.

AREA (âr′ ĭ ə), *n.* (The letter "A"; the limitations or borders of the area.) The "A" hands, palms facing down, are positioned with thumbtips touching. They separate, move in toward the body, and then come together again at the thumbtips. The movement describes a square or a circle.

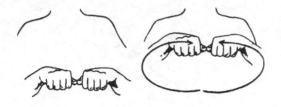

ARGENTINA 1 (är′ jen te′ na), *n.* (Playing a guitar.) The signer goes through the natural motions of playing a guitar.

ARGENTINA 2, *n.* The thumbtip of the "A" hand touches both sides of the forehead.

ARGUE (är′ gū), *v.,* -GUED, -GUING. (An expounding back and forth.) The index fingers here represent the two sides of the argument. First the left index finger is slapped into the open right palm, and then the right makes the same movement into the left palm. This is

repeated back and forth several times. Also ARGU-MENT, CONTROVERSY, DEBATE, DISPUTE.

ARGUMENT (-mənt), *n.* See ARGUE.

ARISE 1 (ə rīz′), *v.,* -ROSE, -RISEN, -RISING. (Rising up.) Both upturned hands, held at chest level, rise in unison to about shoulder height. Also RISE 3, STAND 3.

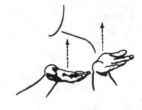

ARISE 2, *v.* (Getting onto one's feet.) The upturned index and middle fingers of the right hand, representing the legs, are swung up and over in an arc, coming to rest in the upturned left palm. Also ELEVATE, GET UP, RAISE 1, RISE 1, STAND 2, STAND UP.

ARITHMETIC (ə rĭth′ mə tĭk), *n.* (A multiplying.) The "V" hands, palms facing the body, alternately cross and separate several times. Also CALCULATE, ESTIMATE, FIGURE 1, MULTIPLY 1.

ARIZONA (ar′ ə zō′ nə), *n.* (The letter "A"; the dryness.) The thumbtip of the right "A" hand moves across the lips from left to right, as if drying the mouth.

ARMADILLO (är′ mə dil′ ō), *n.* (The shape and the tail.) Right hand rests on back of downturned left hand. The left index finger "wags" as both hands move together to the left.

ARMS (ärmz), *n. pl.* (Bearing arms.) Both "A" hands, palms facing the body, are placed at the left breast, with the right hand above the left, as if holding a rifle against the body. Also SOLDIER.

ARMY (är′ mǐ), *n.* (A group of arms bearers or soldiers.) The sign for ARMS is made. The "C" hands, palms facing each other, then pivot around on their wrists so that the palms now face the body (a class or category, all together as one unit). Also MILITARY.

AROUND 1 (ə round′), *adv.* (Circling *around*.) The left hand, all fingers pointed up and touching, is encir-

cled by the right index finger, pointing down and moving clockwise.

AROUND 2, *prep.* (Turning a corner.) The left open hand is held palm down. The right index finger moves around the left fingertips, from the index to the little finger.

AROUND 3, *adv, adj.* (Moving *around* an area.) The downturned "5" hand moves in a counterclockwise fashion.

AROUND THE WORLD (wûrld), *adv. phrase.* (Encircling the planet.) The left hand, in the "S" position, knuckles facing right, is encircled by the right index finger, which travels in a clockwise direction. It makes one revolution and comes to rest atop the left hand. Also ALL YEAR, ALL YEAR 'ROUND, ORBIT 1.

ARRANGE (ə rānj′), *v.*, -RANGED, -RANGING. (Placing things in order.) The hands, palms facing, fingers together and pointing away from the body, are positioned at the left side and held about a foot apart. With a slight up-down motion, as if describing waves, the hands travel in unison from left to right. Also ARRANGEMENT, CLASSED 2, DEVISE 1, ORDER 3, PLAN 1, POLICY 1, PREPARE 1, PROGRAM 1, PROVIDE 1, PUT IN ORDER, READY 1, SCHEME, SYSTEM.

ARRANGEMENT (ə rānj′ mənt), *n.* See ARRANGE.

ARREARS (ə rîrz′), *n. pl.* (Pointing to the palm, where the money should be placed.) The index finger of one hand is thrust into the upturned palm of the other several times. Also DEBIT, DEBT, DUE, OBLIGATION 3, OWE.

ARREST 1 (ə rĕst′), *v.*, -RESTED, -RESTING. (Seizing someone by the clothing.) The right hand quickly grasps the clothing at the left shoulder.

ARREST 2, *v.* (A stopping or cutting short.) The little finger edge of the right hand is thrust abruptly into the upturned left palm, indicating a cutting short. Also CEASE, HALT, STOP.

ARRIVAL (ə rī′ vəl), *n.* (Arrival at a designated place.) The right hand, palm facing the body and fingers pointing up, is brought forward from a position near the right shoulder and placed in the upturned palm of the left hand (the designated place). Also ARRIVE, REACH.

ARRIVE (ə rīv′), *v.*, -RIVED, -RIVING. See ARRIVAL.

ART (ärt), *n.* (Drawing on the hand.) The little finger of the right hand, representing a pencil, traces a curved line in the upturned left palm. Also DRAW 1, MAP.

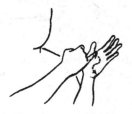

ARTERY (är′ tə rē), *n.* (The letter "A"; the path of an artery in the arm.) The "A" hand is run down along the bottom of the left arm, from elbow to wrist.

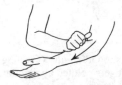

ARTICULATE (är tik′ yə lit), *adj.* (Speaking with skill.) The right index finger, pointing left, describes a continuous small circle in front of the mouth. This is a sign for SPEAK. It is followed by the sign for SKILL: the right hand grasps the little finger edge of the left firmly. As it leaves this position, moving down and out, it assumes the "A" position, palm facing left.

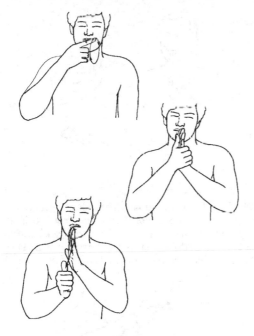

ARTIFICIAL (är tə fish′ əl), *adj.* (Words deflected from their path, straight out from the lips.) The index finger of the right "D" hand, pointing to the left, moves in front of the lips, from right to left.

ARTIST (är′ tĭst), *n.* (An individual who draws.) The sign for ART is made, followed by the sign for INDIVIDUAL: Both hands, fingers together, are placed at

either side of the chest and are moved down to waist level.

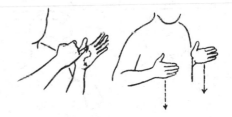

AS (ăz; *unstressed* əz), *adv.* (A likeness; a sameness.) Both index fingers, held together at one side of the body near waist level, point forward. As they travel to the other side of the body they separate an inch or two and come together again. Also ACCORDING (TO), ALSO 1, DUPLICATE 2, SAME AS, TOO.

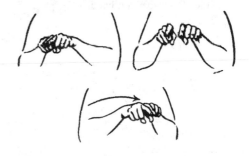

AS A MATTER OF FACT, *phrase.* (Straightforward, from the lips.) The right index finger is placed up against the lips. It moves up and forward, in a small arc.

ASHAMED 1 (ə shāmd′), *adj.* (The color rises in the cheek; an attempt is made to hide the head.) The backs of the fingers of the right hand, held in the right-angle position, are placed against the right cheek. The hand moves up along the cheek, pivoting at the wrist, so that the fingers finally point to the rear. Also BASHFUL 1, IMMODEST, IMMORAL, SHAME 1, SHAMEFUL, SHAME ON YOU, SHY 1.

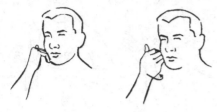

ASHAMED 2, *adj.* Similar to ASHAMED 1, but both hands are used at either cheek. Also BASHFUL 2, SHAME 2, SHY 2.

ASHTRAY (ash′ trā′), *n.* (The shape and function.) Holding an imaginary cigarette, the signer flicks the ashes into the "C"-shaped left hand.

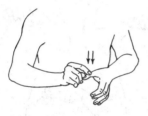

ASK 1 (ăsk, äsk), *v.*, ASKED, ASKING. (Pray tell.) Both hands, held upright about a foot in front of the chest, with palms facing and fingers pointing straight up, are positioned about a foot apart. Moving toward the chest, they come together until they touch, as if in prayer. Also CONSULT, INQUIRE 1, REQUEST 1.

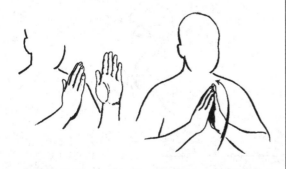

ASK 2 (*colloq.*), *v.*, (Fire a question.) The right hand, held in a modified "S" position with palm facing out, assumes a position with the thumb resting on the fin-

gernail of the index finger. The index finger is flicked out and forward, usually directed at the person being asked a question. Reversing the direction so that the index finger flicks out toward the speaker indicates the passive voice of the verb, *i.e.,* to be ASKED. Also EXAMINATION 2, INQUIRE 2, INTERROGATE 2, INTERROGATION 2, QUERY 2, QUESTION 2, QUIZ 2.

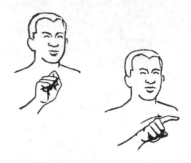

ASK 3, *v.* (Firing questions.) The index fingers of both "D" hands repeatedly curve and straighten out as the hands are alternately flung forward and back, as if firing questions. Also EXAMINATION 3, INQUIRE 3, INTERROGATE 1, INTERROGATION 1, QUERY 1, QUESTION 3, QUIZ 3.

ASL, *n.* (Abbreviation for AMERICAN SIGN LANGUAGE; an acronym and fingerspelled loan sign.) The signer fingerspells "A-S-L."

ASLEEP (ə slēp′), *adv.* (The eyes are closed.) The fingers of the right open hand, facing the forehead, are placed on the forehead. The hand moves down and away from the head, with the fingers closing so that they all touch. The eyes meanwhile close, and the head bows slightly, as in sleep. Also DOZE, NAP, SLEEP 1.

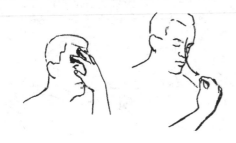

ASPARAGUS (ə spar′ ə gəs), *n.* (The "A"; the shape.) The left "A" hand is held thumb up. The right index and thumb briefly grasp the left thumbtip, and move up and away, indicating the length or shape of an asparagus stalk.

ASSEMBLE 1 (ə sĕm′ bəl), *v.,* -BLED, -BLING. (Assemble all together.) Both "5" hands, palms facing, are held with fingers pointing out from the body. With a sweeping motion they are brought in toward the chest, and all fingertips come together. This is repeated. Also ACCUMULATE 3, ASSEMBLY, CONFERENCE, CONVENE, CONVENTION, GATHER 2, GATHERING, MEETING 1.

ASSEMBLE 2, *v.* (Many people coming together in one place.) The downturned "5" hands, fingers wriggling, come toward each other until the fingertips almost touch.

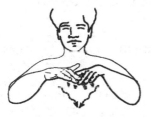

ASSEMBLY (ə sĕm′ blĭ), *n.* See ASSEMBLE.

ASSERTIVE (ə sŭr′ tĭv), *adj.* (Blows bounce off the chest.) Both "A" hands, palms facing each other, move in alternate clockwise circles, striking the chest each time.

ASSET (as′ ct), *n.* (Putting a plus into the pocket.) The index fingers form a plus (+) sign, and then the right "F" hand moves down an inch or two against the right side of the body as if placing a coin into a pocket.

ASSIST (ə sĭst′), *n., v.,* -SISTED, -SISTING. (Helping up; supporting.) The left "S" hand, thumb side up, rests in the open right palm. In this position the left hand is pushed up a short distance by the right. Also AID, ASSISTANCE, BENEFIT 1, BOOST, GIVE ASSISTANCE, HELP.

ASSISTANCE (ə sĭs′ təns), *n.* See ASSIST.

ASSOCIATE 1 (ə sō′ shĭ āt′), *v.,* -ATED, -ATING. (Mingling with.) Both hands are held in modified "A" positions, thumbs out. The left hand is positioned with its thumb pointing straight up, and the right hand, with its thumb pointing down, revolves above the left thumb in a counterclockwise direction. Also EACH OTHER, FEL-LOWSHIP, MINGLE 2, MUTUAL 1, ONE ANOTHER.

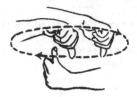

ASSOCIATE 2, *v.* (Joining together.) Both hands, held in the modified "5" position, palms out, move toward each other. The thumbs and index fingers of both hands then connect. Also AFFILIATE 1, ANNEX, ATTACH, BELONG, COMMUNION OF SAINTS, CONCERN 2, CONNECT, ENLIST, ENROLL, JOIN 1, PARTICIPATE, RELATIVE 2, UNION, UNITE.

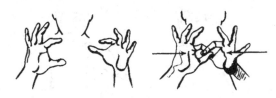

ASSOCIATION (ə sō′ sĭ ā′ shən), *n.* (A grouping together.) Both "C" hands, palms facing, are held a few inches apart at chest height. They are swung around in unison, so that the palms now face the body. Also AUDIENCE 1, CASTE, CIRCLE 2, CLASS, CLASSED 1, CLUB, COMPANY, FAMILY 2, GANG, GROUP 1, JOIN 2, ORGANIZATION 1.

ASSORTED (ə sôr′ tĭd), *adj.* (Separated many times; different.) The "D" hands, palms down, are crossed at the index fingers or are held side by side. They separate and return to their initial position a number of

times. Also DIFFERENCE, DIFFERENT, DIVERSE 1, DIVERSITY 1, UNLIKE, VARIED.

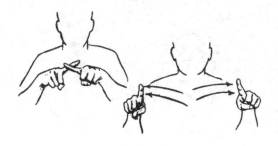

ASSUME (ə sōōm′), *v.,* -SUMED, -SUMING. (To take up.) Both hands, held palms down in the "5" position, are at chest level. With a grasping upward movement, both close into "S" positions before the face. Also PICK UP 1, TAKE UP.

ASTONISH (ə stŏn′ ĭsh), *v.,* -ISHED, -ISHING. (The eyes pop open in amazement.) Both hands are held in modified "O" positions with thumb and index fingers of each hand near the eyes. These fingers suddenly flick open, and the eyes simultaneously pop open wide. Also AMAZE, AMAZEMENT, ASTONISHED, ASTONISHMENT, ASTOUND, SURPRISE 1.

ASTONISHED, *adj.* See ASTONISH.

ASTONISHMENT (-mənt), *n.* See ASTONISH.

ASTOUND (ə stound′), *v.,* -TOUNDED, -TOUNDING. See ASTONISH.

ASTRONAUT (as′ trə nôt), *n.* (The "R" for "rocket"; the liftoff.) The base of the right "R" hand rests on the back of the downturned left hand. The "R" hand shoots up. The sign for INDIVIDUAL 1 then follows.

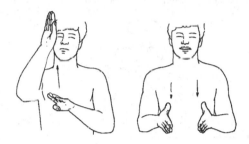

AT (ăt; *unstressed* ət; ĭt), *prep.* The left hand is held at eye level, palm facing out and fingers together. The right hand, palm down, fingers also together, moves over to the left so that the right fingertips come to touch the back of the left hand. This sign is seldom used; most signers prefer to spell out "AT" on the fingers.

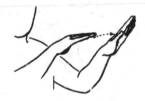

AT A LOSS (lôs, lŏs), *phrase.* (The mind is frozen; the thought is frozen.) The index finger of the right "D" hand, palm facing the body, touches the forehead (modified THINK sign, *q.v.*). Both hands, in the "5" position, palms down, are then suddenly and deliberately dropped down in front of the body. A look of surprise is assumed at this point, and the head jerks back slightly. Also DUMBFOUNDED 1, JOLT, SHOCKED 1, STUMPED.

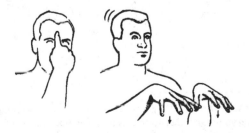

ATHENS (ăth′ ĭnz), *n.* (The letter "A"; a central location, i.e., the capital.) The downturned thumb of the right "A" hand is thrust into the upturned left palm.

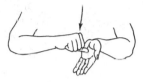

ATHLETE (ăth′ lēt), *n.* (One who does exercises.) Both "A" hands, palms facing the chest, move in alternate forward circles. The sign for INDIVIDUAL 1 then follows.

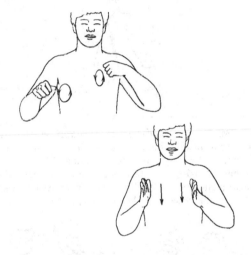

ATOM (ăt′ əm), *n.* (The letter "A"; around the world.) The right "A" hand makes a circle around the upright left fist.

ATTACH (ə tăch′), *v.,* -TACHED, -TACHING. (Joining together.) Both hands, held in the modified "5" position, palms out, move toward each other. The thumbs and index fingers of both hands then connect. Also AFFILIATE 1, ANNEX, ASSOCIATE 2, BELONG, COMMUNION

OF SAINTS, CONCERN 2, CONNECT, ENLIST, ENROLL, JOIN 1, PARTICIPATE, RELATIVE 2, UNION, UNITE.

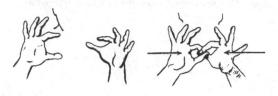

ATTACK (ə tăk′), *n., v.,* -TACKED, -TACKING. (Striking against.) The clenched right hand strikes against the open left palm.

ATTEMPT 1 (ə tĕmpt′), *n., v.,* -TEMPTED, -TEMPTING. (Trying to push through.) The "A" hands, palms facing before the body, are swung around and a bit down, so that the palms now face out. The movement indicates an attempt to push through a barrier. Also EFFORT 1, ENDEAVOR, PERSEVERE 1, PERSIST 1, TRY 1.

ATTEMPT 2, *n., v.* (Trying to push through, using the "T" hands, for "try.") This is the same sign as ATTEMPT 1, except that the "T" hands are employed. Also EFFORT 2, PERSEVERE 2, TRY 2.

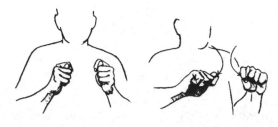

ATTEND (TO) (ə tĕnd′), *v.,* -TENDED, -TENDING. (Directing one's attention forward; applying oneself;

concentrating.) Both hands, fingers pointing up and together, are held at the sides of the face. They move straight out from the face. Also APPLY 2, ATTENTION, CONCENTRATE, CONCENTRATION, FOCUS, GIVE ATTENTION (TO), MIND 2, PAY ATTENTION (TO).

ATTENTION (ə tĕn′ shən), *n.* See ATTEND (TO).

ATTITUDE (ăt′ ə tūd′, -tōōd′), *n.* (The letter "A"; the inclination of the heart.) The right "A" hand describes a counterclockwise circle around the heart and comes to rest against the heart.

ATTORNEY (ə tûr′ nĭ), *n.* (A law individual.) The upright right "L" hand (for LAW), resting palm against palm on the upright left "5" hand, moves down in an arc, a short distance, coming to rest on the base of the left palm. The sign for INDIVIDUAL is then added: both hands, fingers together, are placed at either side of the chest and are moved down to waist level.

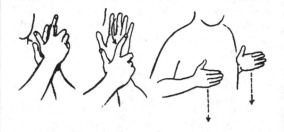

ATTRACT (ə trăkt′), *v.,* -TRACTED, -TRACTING. (Bringing everything together to one point.) The open "5" hands, palms down and held at chest level, draw together until all the fingertips touch. Also ATTRACTION, ATTRACTIVE 1.

ATTRACTION (ə trăk′ shən), *n*. See ATTRACT.

ATTRACTIVE 1 (ə trăk′ tĭv), *adj*. See ATTRACT.

ATTRACTIVE 2, *adj*. (Literally, a good face.) The right hand, fingers closed over the thumb, is placed at or just below the lips (indicating a tasting of something GOOD, *q.v.*). It then describes a counterclockwise circle around the face, opening into the "5" position, to indicate the whole face. At the completion of the circling movement the hand comes to rest in its initial position, at or just below the lips. Also BEAUTIFUL, BEAUTY, EXQUISITE, PRETTY, SPLENDID 3.

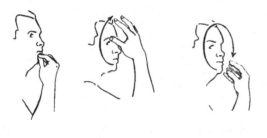

AUDIOLOGY (ô′ dē ol′ ə jē), *n*. (The "A"; at the ear.) The right "A" hand, held at the ear, pivots slightly back and forth. Both "A" hands may also be used, at both ears.

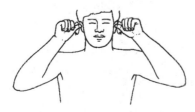

AUDITION (ô dish′ ən), *n*. (The "A's"; modification of the verb TRY. Both "A" hands are positioned with

thumbs pointing to the ears. The hands swing forward in a downward arc.

AUNT (ănt, änt), *n*. (A female, defined by the letter "A.") The "A" hand, thumb near the right jawline (see sign for FEMALE), quivers back and forth several times.

AUSTRALIA 1 (ô străl′ yə), *n*. (The turned back brim of an Australian hat.) The fingertips of the right "B" hand are placed against the forehead with palm toward the face. The hand is then drawn away from the face and turned so that the palm faces outward. The open hand then strikes back against the right side of the head.

AUSTRALIA 2, *n*. Both hands are held in the "8" position, palms down. The signer flicks out the middle fingers of both hands twice. This is a native Australian sign.

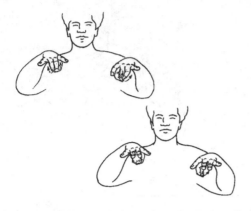

AUTHENTIC (ô thĕn′ tĭk), *adj.* (Coming forth directly from the lips; true.) The index finger of the right "D" hand, palm facing left, is placed against the lips. It moves up an inch or two and then describes a small arc forward and away from the lips. Also ABSOLUTE, ABSOLUTELY, ACTUAL, ACTUALLY, CERTAIN, CERTAINLY, FAITHFUL 3, FIDELITY, FRANKLY, GENUINE, INDEED, POSITIVE 1, POSITIVELY, REAL, REALLY, SINCERE 2, SURE, SURELY, TRUE, TRULY, TRUTH, VALID, VERILY.

AUTHORITY 1 (ə thôr′ ə tĭ, -thŏr′-), *n.* (Holding the reins over all.) The "A" hands, palms facing, move alternately back and forth, as if grasping and manipulating reins. The left "A" hand, still in position, swings over so that its palm now faces down. The right hand opens to the "5" position, palm down, and swings over the left which moves slightly to the right. Also CON-

TROL 1, DIRECT 1, GOVERN, MANAGE, MANAGEMENT, MANAGER, OPERATE, REGULATE, REIGN, RULE 1.

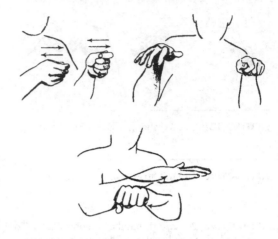

AUTHORITY 2, *n.* (The letter "A"; the muscle.) The right "A" hand describes an arc on the left arm muscle as it moves from shoulder to the crook of the elbow.

AUTISM (ô′ tiz əm), *n.* (Cut off from the world.) Both "C" hands, palms facing, are positioned at the temples. They move around so that they now cover the eyes.

AUTOMATIC (ô tə mat′ ik), *n., adj.* (The shift lever attached to the car's steering column.) The left index finger, slightly curved, is held up. The right index finger, also slightly curved, palm up, slides up and down the left index finger.

AUTOMOBILE (ô′ tə mə bēl′, ô′ tə mo′ bēl, -mə bēl′), *n.* (The steering wheel.) The hands grasp an imaginary steering wheel and manipulate it. Also CAR, DRIVE.

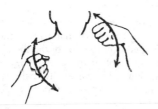

AUTONOMY (ô ton′ ə mē), *n.* (Alone by oneself.) The right "D" hand, index pointing up and palm facing the chest, twists slightly in a counterclockwise direction as it is brought into the chest.

AUTUMN 1 (ô′ təm), *n.* (The falling of leaves.) The left arm, held upright with palm facing back, represents a tree trunk. The right hand, fingers together and palm down, moves down along the left arm, from the back of the wrist to the elbow, either once or several times. This represents the falling of leaves from the tree branches, indicated by the left fingers. Also FALL 1.

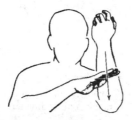

AUTUMN 2, *n.* (A chopping down during harvest time.) The right hand, fingers together and palm facing down, makes several chopping motions against the left elbow, to indicate the harvesting of growing things in autumn.

AVAILABLE (ə vā′ lə bəl), *adj.* (A spot or place is empty, therefore available.) The middle finger of the right downturned "5" hand makes a small counterclockwise circle against the back of the downturned left hand.

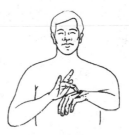

AVERAGE (ăv′ ər ĭj, ăv′ rĭj), *n. adj., v.,* -AGED, -AGING. (Halfway between top and bottom.) The right open hand, held upright, palm facing left, rests its little finger edge across the index finger edge of the downturned, open left hand. In this position the right hand moves back and forth several times, rubbing the base of the little finger along the edge of the left hand. Also MEAN 3.

AVIATOR (ā′ vĭ ā′ tər, ăv′ ĭ-), *n.* (An individual who flies a plane.) The sign for either AIRPLANE 1 or AIRPLANE 2 is made, and this is followed by the sign for INDIVIDUAL 1: both hands, fingers together, are placed at either side of the chest and are moved down to waist level. Also FLIER, PILOT.

AVOID 1 (ə void′), *v.*, -VOIDED, -VOIDING. (Ducking back and forth away from something.) Both "A" hands, thumbs pointing straight up, are held some distance before the chest, with the left hand in front of the right. The right hand, swinging back and forth, moves away from the left and toward the chest. Also EVADE, EVASION, SHIRK, SHUN.

AVOID 2, *v.* (To push away and recoil from; avoid.) The two open hands, palms facing left, are pushed deliberately to the left, as if pushing something away. An expression of disdain or disgust is worn. Also ABHOR, DESPISE 1, DETEST 1, HATE 1, LOATHE.

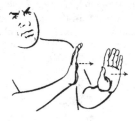

AWAKE (ə wāk′), *v.*, *adj.*, -WOKE or -WAKED, -WAKING. (Opening the eyes.) Both hands are closed, with thumb and index finger of each hand held together, extended, and placed at the corners of the closed eyes.

Slowly they separate, and the eyes open. Also AROUSE, AWAKEN, WAKE UP.

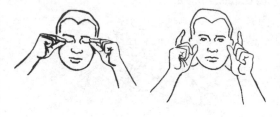

AWAKEN (ə wā′ kən), *v.*, -ENED, -ENING. See AWAKE.

AWARD (ə wôrd′), *n.*, *v.*, -WARDED, -WARDING. (A giving of something.) Both "A" hands, with index fingers somewhat draped over the tips of the thumbs, are held palms facing in front of the chest. They are pivoted forward and down, in unison, from the wrists. Also BEQUEATH, BESTOW, CONFER, CONSIGN, CONTRIBUTE, GIFT, PRESENT 2.

AWFUL (ô′ fəl), *adj.* (Throwing out the hands.) Both hands, their fingertips touching their respective thumbs, are held, palms facing each other, near the temples. They are thrown out before the face, assuming "5" positions, palms still facing. Also CALAMITOUS, CATASTROPHIC, DANGER 1, DANGEROUS 1, DREADFUL, FEARFUL, TERRIBLE, TRAGEDY, TRAGIC.

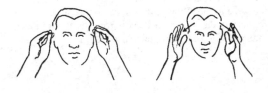

AWKWARD (ôk′ wərd), *adj.* (Clumsy in gait; all thumbs.) The "3" hands, palms down, move alternately up and down before the body. Also AWKWARDNESS, CLUMSINESS, CLUMSY 1, GREEN 2, GREENHORN 2, NAIVE.

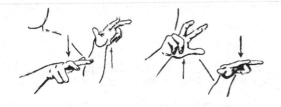

AWKWARDNESS, *n.* See AWKWARD.

AW SHIT! (*expletive, vulg.*). (The anus.) The thumb of the downturned right "5" hand is thrust into a cup formed by the left hand. The signer assumes an expression of great annoyance.

AX (aks), *n.* (The chopping.) The left arm is held straight up from the bent elbow. The little finger edge of the upturned right hand then makes a series of chopping movements against the left elbow. Also HATCHET.

B

BABY (bā′ bĭ), *n., adj., v.,* -BIED, -BYING. (The rocking of the baby.) The arms are held with one resting on the other, as if cradling a baby. They rock from side to side. Also DOLL 2, INFANT.

BABYSITTER (bā′ bĭ sit er), *n.* (The baby is kept or cared for.) The sign for BABY is made: the upturned right arm is placed atop the upturned left arm, and both arms rock back and forth. The right "K" hand is then placed on its left counterpart to keep the baby in place.

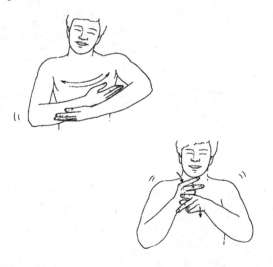

BACHELOR (băch′ ə lər, băch′ lər), *n.* (The letter "B.") The right "B" hand, held with palm facing left and fingers pointing up, touches the left side of the mouth and then moves back across the lips to touch the right side of the mouth.

BACK 1 (băk), *adv.* (One hand is after or behind the other.) Both hands, in the "A" position, are held knuckles to knuckles. The right hand moves back, describing a small arc, and comes to rest against the left wrist. Also AFTER 2, BACKSLIDE, BEHIND.

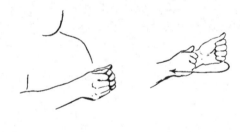

BACK 2, *n.* (The natural sign.) The right hand moves over the right shoulder to tap the back. Also REAR 1.

BACKGROUND 1 (băk′ ground′), *n.* (The area below.) Both hands, in the "5" position, palms down, are held before the chest, the right under the left. The right hand moves under the left in a counterclockwise fashion. Also BASIS 2, BELOW 1, BOTTOM, FOUNDATION.

BACKGROUND 2, *n.* (The letters "B" and "G"; underneath.) The right hand, in the "B" position, is held under the downturned left hand. The "B" changes to a "G."

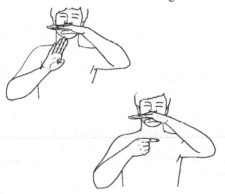

BACKPACKING (bak' pak ing), *n.* (Slapping the backpack.) Both hands reach over the shoulders to pat a backpack.

BACKUP (bak' up'), *n.* (Something behind.) The upturned right "A" hand sweeps behind its left counterpart. This sign is also used for a computer backup file.

BACON (bā' kən), *n.* (The curled up slice after frying.) Both hands, in the "H" position, are held with middle and index fingers touching. The hands move apart and the index and middle fingers execute wavy movements as they separate.

BAD 1 (băd), *adj.* (Tasting something, finding it unacceptable, and turning it down.) The tips of the right "B" hand are placed at the lips, and then the hand is thrown down. Also GRAVE 2, NAUGHTY, WICKED.

BAD 2 (*colloq.*), *adj.* The right "I" hand is held, palm facing forward, in front of the right shoulder. From this position, the right hand moves slightly to the right.

BADGE (baj), *n.* (The shape and position.) The thumbs and index fingers of both hands, palms out, form the shape of a badge, which is hung on the left chest.

BAGGAGE (băg' ĭj), *n.* (The natural sign.) The downturned right "S" hand grasps an imaginary piece of luggage and shakes it up and down slightly, as if testing its weight. Also LUGGAGE, SUITCASE, VALISE.

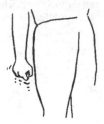

BAH! (bä), *interj.* The outstretched right hand, palm facing forward, is thrown forward and down in a forceful manner. The signer assumes an expression of annoyance or disapproval. An even more effective nonmanual accompaniment to this sign would be an explosive release of breath. Also PHOOEY!

BAKE (bāk), *v.*, BAKED, BAKING, *n.* (Placing the bread in the oven.) The downturned right "B" hand, representing the bread, is thrust slowly forward under the downturned left hand, representing the oven. Also OVEN.

BALANCE 1 (băl′ əns), *n.*, *v.*, -ANCED, -ANCING. (The natural sign.) The extended right index and middle fingers are placed across the extended index and middle fingers of the left hand, which is held with thumb edge up and fingers pointing forward. In this

position the right hand rocks back and forth, as if balancing.

BALANCE 2, *n.*, *v.* (The scales.) Both open hands, held palms down in front of the body, move alternately up and down, imitating a pair of scales. Also SCALE 3.

BALD 1 (bôld), *adj.* (A bald patch.) The middle finger of the open right hand makes several circles on the back of the left "S" hand, which is held with palm facing down. Also BARE 1.

BALD 2, *adj.* (Devoid of hair.) The right middle finger makes a continuous clockwise circle on top of the head.

BALL 1 (bôl), *n.* (The rhythmic swaying of the feet.) The downturned index and middle fingers of the right

"V" hand swing rhythmically back and forth over the upturned left palm. Also DANCE, PARTY 2.

BALL 2, *n.* (The shape.) The curved open hands are held with fingertips touching, as if holding a ball. Also ORB, ROUND 1, SPHERE.

BALLET (bal′ ā), *n.* (The toes held *en pointe.*) Both hands, fingers together, point straight down. They move up and down in successive order.

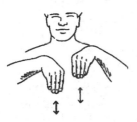

BALLOON (bə lōōn′), *n.* (Blowing up.) The signer mimes blowing up a balloon. The cupped "C" hands expand and the cheeks are puffed out.

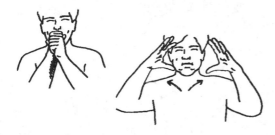

BALONEY (bə lō′ nĭ), (*sl.*), *n.* The right "S" hand is held with its thumb edge over the tip of the nose, palm

facing left; in this position the right hand is then twisted forcefully to the left until the palm faces down.

BALTIMORE (bôl′ tə môr′, -mōr′), *n.* (The "B"; the movement of a boat.) The right "B" hand, palm facing left, moves up and down a bit. Baltimore is known as a seaport.

BAN (băn), *v.*, BANNED, BANNING, *n.* (A modification of LAW, *q.v.;* "against the law.") The downturned right "D" or "L" hand is thrust forcefully into the left palm. Also FORBID 1, FORBIDDEN 1, PROHIBIT.

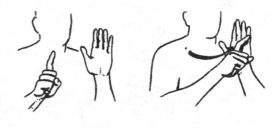

BANANA 1 (bə nan′ ə), *n.* (The natural sign.) Go through the motions of peeling a banana, the left index representing the banana and the right fingertips pulling off the skin.

BANANA 2, *n.* (Peeling a banana.) The left "AND" hand is held with fingers pointing up, representing a banana, while the left hand moves as if peeling the skin downward.

BANDAGE 1 (băn′ dĭj), *n., v.,* -AGED, -AGING. (Applying a Band-Aid.) The index and middle fingers of the right hand are drawn across the back of the downturned, left "S" hand, as if smoothing a Band-Aid. Also BAND-AID.

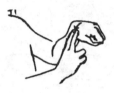

BANDAGE 2, *v., n.* (Bandaging the hand.) The right "H" hand makes a series of clockwise circles around the left fist.

BAND-AID (bănd′ ād), *n.* See BANDAGE.

BANDIT (băn′ dĭt), *n.* (A mustachioed thief.) The fingertips of both "H" hands, palms facing the body, are placed above the lips and are drawn slowly apart, describing a mustache. Sometimes one hand only is used. This is followed by the sign for INDIVIDUAL: both open hands, palms facing each other, move down

the sides of the body, tracing its outline to the hips. Also BURGLAR, BURGLARY, CROOK, ROB 3, ROBBER 1, STEAL 3, THEFT 3, THIEF 2.

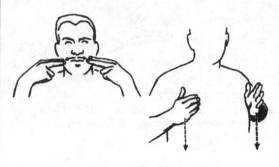

BANGS (bangz), *n.* (The shape on the forehead.) The right downturned claw hand is positioned with fingertips touching the left temple. The hand swings over to the right temple.

BANK 1 (bangk), *n.* (The "B" letters; a house or building.) Both downturned "B" hands describe the shape of a building's roof and walls.

BANK 2, *n.* (Stuffing money into a piggy bank.) The signer mimes stuffing money into a small toy bank.

BANKRUPT (băngk′ rŭpt, -rəpt), *n., adj.* (The head is chopped off.) The tips of the right fingers are thrust forcefully into the right side of the neck. Also BROKE.

BANQUET (băng′ kwĭt), *n., v.,* -QUETED, -QUETING. (Placing food in the mouth.) Both closed hands alternately come to the mouth, as if placing food in it. Also DINNER, FEAST.

BAPTISM (băp′ tĭz əm) (*eccles.*), *n.* (The sprinkling of water on the head.) The right hand sprinkles imaginary water on the head. Also SHOWER.

BAPTIST (băp′ tĭst) (*eccles.*), *n.* (The immersion.) Both "A" hands, palms facing and thumbs pointing up, swing over simultaneously to the left, with the thumbs describing a downward arc. Also BAPTIZE.

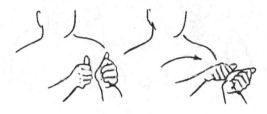

BAPTIZE (băp tīz′, băp′ tīz), *v.,* -TIZED, -TIZING. See BAPTIST.

BAR (bär), *n.* (Raising the beer stein or mug.) The thumb of the right "A" or "Y" hand is brought up to the mouth. Also SALOON.

BARBECUE 1 (bär′ bə kyōō), *n., v.,* -CUED, -CUING. (Turning the spit.) Both horizontal index fingers, pointing toward each other, execute simultaneous clockwise turns.

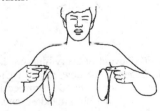

BARBECUE 2 (A fingerspelled loan sign.) The letters "B-B-Q" are fingerspelled.

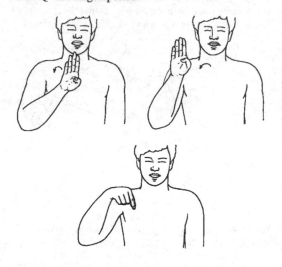

BARBER (bär′ bər), *n*. (The scissors at both sides of the head.) The two "V" hands, palms facing the sides of the head, open and close repeatedly as the hands move alternately back and forth. Also HAIRCUT.

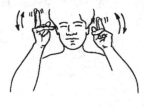

BARE 1 (băr), *adj*. (A bald patch.) The middle finger of the open right hand makes several circles on the back of the left "S" hand, which is held with palm facing down. Also BALD.

BARE 2, *adj*. (Devoid of everything on the surface.) The middle finger of the downturned right "5" hand sweeps over the back of the downturned left "A" or "S" hand, from wrist to knuckles, and continues beyond a bit. Also EMPTY 2, NAKED, NUDE, OMISSION 2, VACANCY, VACANT, VOID.

BARK (bärk), *v*., BARKED, BARKING (The opening and closing of the dog's mouth.) The hands are positioned palm against palm before the body, with the fingertips pointing forward. With the bases of the hands always touching and serving as a hinge, the hands open and close repeatedly, with the stress on the opening movement, which is sudden and abrupt. Also SCOLD 3.

BAROMETER (bə rom′ ə tər), *n*. (The letter "B"; rising and falling.) The downturned right "B" hand moves up and down along the upright left index finger.

BASE 1 (bās), *n., adj*. (Motion downward.) The "A" hand is held in front of the body, thumb pointing upward. The hand then moves straight downward several inches. Both hands may be used. Also LOW 1.

BASE 2, *n., adj.* (Motion downward.) The right-angle hands are held up before the head, fingertips pointing toward each other. From this position, the hands move down in an arc. Also DEMOTE, LOW 2, LOWER.

BASE 3, *adj.* (Striking down against.) Both "A" or "X" hands are held before the chest, the right above the left. The right hand strikes down and out, hitting the left thumb and knuckles with force. Also BACK-BITE, CRUEL 1, HARM 2, HURT 2, MAR 2, MEAN 1, SPOIL.

BASEBALL (băs′ bôl′), *n.* (Swinging a bat.) Both "S" hands, the right behind the left, grip an imaginary bat and move back and forth over the right shoulder, as if preparing to hit a baseball. Also BAT, BATTER.

BASHFUL 1 (băsh′ fəl), *adj.* (The color rises in the cheek; an attempt is made to hide the head.) The backs of the fingers of the right hand, held in the right-angle position, are placed against the right cheek. The hand moves up along the cheek, pivoting at the wrist, so that the fingers finally point to the rear. Also ASHAMED

1, IMMODEST, IMMORAL, SHAME 1, SHAMEFUL, SHAME ON YOU, SHY 1.

BASHFUL 2, *adj.* Similar to BASHFUL 1, but both hands are used, at either cheek. Also ASHAMED 2, SHAME 2, SHY 2.

BASIS 1 (bā′ sĭs), *n.* (Rays of influence emanating from a given source.) All the right fingertips, including the thumb, are positioned on the tip of the upturned thumb of the left "A" hand. The right hand, opening into the downturned "5" position, moves forward from its initial position. Instead of its initial position on the left thumb, the right hand is frequently placed on the back of the downturned left "S" hand, moving forward as described above. Also CAUSE, EFFECT 1, INFLUENCE 2, INTENT 2, LOGIC, PRODUCE 4, REASON 2.

BASIS 2, *n.* (The area below.) Both hands, in the "5" position, palms down, are held before the chest, the right under the left. The right hand moves under the left in a counterclockwise fashion. Also BACKGROUND, BELOW 1, BOTTOM, FOUNDATION.

BASKETBALL (băs′ kĭt bôl′), *n.* (Shooting a basket.) Both open hands are held with fingers pointing down and somewhat curved, as if grasping a basketball.

From this position the hands move around and upward, as if to shoot a basket.

BASTARD (băs′ tərd), *n., adj.* (The letter "B.") The right "B" hand, held with palm facing left, fingers pointing up, strikes the middle of the forehead.

BAT 1 (băt), *n., v.,* BATTED, BATTING. (Swinging a bat.) Both "S" hands, the right behind the left, grip an imaginary bat and move back and forth over the right shoulder, as if preparing to hit a baseball. Also BASE-BALL, BATTER.

BAT 2, *n.* (The hooked wings of the creature.) The index fingertips of the "X" hands, palms facing the body, are crossed and hooked on the shoulders, depicting a bat with folded wings.

BATH (băth, bäth), *n.* (The natural sign.) The closed hands move up and down against the chest as if scrubbing it. Also BATHE, WASH 3.

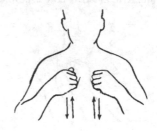

BATHE (bāth), *v.,* BATHED, BATHING. See BATH.

BATHROBE (băth′ rōb), *n.* (Bathing and slipping on a robe.) The signer rubs the body with the closed hands, and then mimes slipping on a bathrobe.

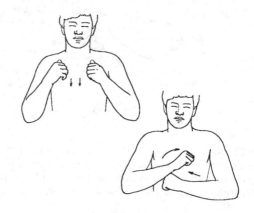

BATHROOM (băth′ rōōm′, -rŏŏm′, bäth′-), *n.* (The natural signs.) The sign for BATH is made, and then the sign for ROOM: the open hands, palms facing and fingers pointing out, are dropped an inch or two simultaneously. They then shift their relative positions so that both palms face the body, with one hand in front of the other. In this new position they again drop an inch or two simultaneously.

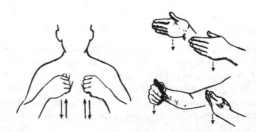

BATHTUB (băth′ tub), *n.* (Bathing and the shape of the tub.) The signer rubs the body with the closed hands and then mimes shaping the bottom and sides of a bathtub.

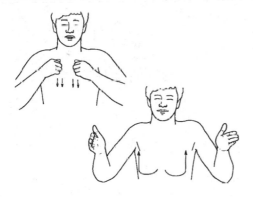

BATTER 1 (băt′ ər), *n.* (Swinging a bat.) Both "S" hands, the right behind the left, grip an imaginary bat and move back and forth over the right shoulder, as if preparing to hit a baseball. This is followed by the sign for INDIVIDUAL: both open hands, palms facing each other, move down the sides of the body, tracing its outline to the hips. Also BASEBALL, BAT.

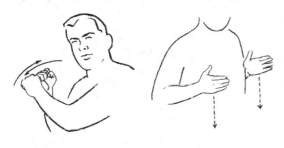

BATTER 2, *n.* (The mixing motion.) The downturned right finger, placed in a cup formed by the left "C" hand, makes a series of rapid clockwise movements, as if mixing up a batter.

BATTERY (bat′ ə rē), *n.* (The "B"; making contact.) The left "B" hand is held palm out. The knuckle of the

right index finger touches the left index finger repeatedly.

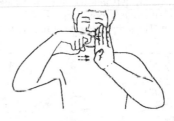

BAWL 1 (bôl), *v.,* BAWLED, BAWLING. (Tears streaming down the cheeks.) Both index fingers, in the "D" position, move down the cheeks, either once or several times. Sometimes one finger only is used. Also CRY 1, TEAR 2, TEARDROP, WEEP 1.

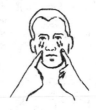

BAWL 2, *v.* (Tears gushing from the eyes.) Both "B" hands are held before the face, palms facing forward, with the backs of the index fingertips touching the face just below the eyes. From this position both hands move forward and over in an arc to indicate a flow of tears. Also CRY 2, WEEP 2.

BAWL 3, *v. sl.* (A flood from the eyes.) Both downturned claw hands move forward and down from the eyes.

BAWL OUT, *v. phrase.* (Words coming out force-fully.) The "S" hands are held one atop the other, the right palm facing left and the left palm facing right. Both hands suddenly shoot straight out, opening to the "5" position. The sign is repeated once or twice.

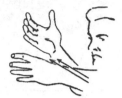

BE 1 (bē; *unstressed* bǐ), *v.,* BEEN, BEING. (Part of the verb to BE.) The tip of the right index finger, held in the "D" position, palm facing left, is held at the lips, and the hand moves straight out and away from the lips. Also AM 1, ARE 1, IS 1.

BE 2, *v.* (The "B" hand.) This is the same sign as for BE 1 except that the "B" hand is used.

BE 3 (*arch.*), *v.* The crooked index finger of the right "G" hand moves from right to left in front of the body.

BEADS (bēdz), *n. pl.* (The shape.) With the "F" hand, the signer traces a series of round objects around the throat.

BEAN(S) (bēn), *n.* (The beans in a pod.) The tips of the four right fingers move up and down simultaneously as they move along the left index finger from knuckle to tip. This sign is used generally for different grains. Also GRAIN, OATMEAL, RICE.

BEANPOLE (bēn′ pōl′) (*sl.*), *n.* (A thin, tapering object is described with the little fingers, the thinnest of all.) The tips of the little fingers, touching, one above the other, are drawn apart. The cheeks may also be drawn in for emphasis. Also SKINNY, THIN 2.

BEAR 1 (bâr). *n.* (Scratching; the bear hug.) Cross the arms, placing the right hand on the left upper arm and the left hand on the right upper arm; pull the hands across the arms toward the center, with a clawing movement.

BEAR 2, *v.,* BORE, BORN(E), BEARING. (Coming from the uterus.) The open hands are held with both palms toward the body, the back of one hand resting against the palm of the other. From a position near the abdomen, the hands turn slightly upward or downward and push out away from the body.

BEAR 3, *v.* (A clenching of the fists; the rise and fall of pain.) Both "S" hands, tightly clenched, revolve about each other, slowly and deliberately, while a pained expression is worn. Also AGONY, DIFFICULT 3, ENDURE 1, PASSION 2, SUFFER 1, TOLERATE 2.

BEAR 4, *v.* (Something that weighs down or burdens one with responsibility.) The fingertips of both hands, placed on the right shoulder, bear down. Also ATTRIBUTE 1, BURDEN, OBLIGATION 1, RELY 1, RESPONSIBILITY 1, RESPONSIBLE 1.

BEARD 1 (bĭrd), *n.* (The natural sign.) The thumb and fingers of the right hand move down either side of the lower face, tracing the outline of a beard and coming together just below the chin.

BEARD 2, *n.* (In need of a shave.) The fingers of both open hands move up and down along either cheek.

BEAT 1 (bēt), *v.,* BEAT, BEATEN, BEATING. (The natural sign.) The left hand is held in a fist before the face, as if grasping something or someone. The right hand, at the same time, is held as if grasping a stick or whip; it strikes repeatedly at the imaginary object or person dangling from the left hand. Also PUNISH 2, WHIP.

BEAT 2, *v.* (Forcing the head into a bowed position.) The right "S" hand, placed across the left "S" hand, moves over and down a bit. Also CONQUER, DEFEAT, OVERCOME, SUBDUE.

BEAT 3, *n.* (A blow is struck.) The right fist strikes the left palm. Also BLOW 2.

BEAT 4, *v.* (Throwing someone over.) The right hand is held in a loose fist with the thumb touching the middle and index fingers. The hand is thrust forward suddenly, with the index and middle fingers suddenly shooting out.

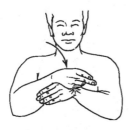

BEATEN (bē′ tən), *adj.* (The head is forced into a bowed position.) The right "S" hand, palm up, is placed under and across the left "S" hand, whose palm faces down. The right "S" hand moves up and over, toward the body. This sign is used as the passive voice of the verb BEAT. Also CONQUERED.

BEAU (bō) (*colloq.*), *n.* (Heads nodding toward each other.) The "A" hands are placed together before the body with thumbs up. The thumbs wiggle up and down. Also COURTING, COURTSHIP, LOVER, MAKE LOVE 1, SWEETHEART 1.

BEAUTIFUL (bū′ tə fəl), *adj.* (Literally, a good face.) The right hand, fingers closed over the thumb, is placed at or just below the lips (indicating a tasting of something GOOD, *q.v.*). It then describes a counterclockwise circle around the face, opening into the "5" position, to indicate the whole face. At the completion of the circling movement the hand comes to rest in its initial position, at or just below the lips. Also ATTRACTIVE 2, BEAUTY, EXQUISITE, PRETTY, SPLENDID 3.

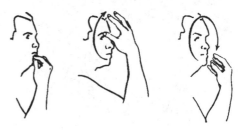

BEAUTY (bū′ tĭ), *n.* See BEAUTIFUL.

BEAVER (bē′ vər), *n.* (The action of the tail.) Both downturned hands are held at chest level, the right under the left. The right hand moves up sharply, its back slapping against the left palm. The action is repeated.

BE CAREFUL (kâr′ fəl), *v. phrase.* (The "K" for *keep* in the sense of *keeping carefully*.) Both "K" hands are crossed, the right atop the left. The right hand moves up and down a very short distance, several times, each time coming to rest on top of the left. Also CAREFUL 3, TAKE CARE OF 1.

BECAUSE (bǐ kôz′, -kŏz′), *conj.* (A thought or knowledge uppermost in the mind.) The fingers of the right hand or the index finger are placed on the center of the forehead, and then the hand is brought strongly up above the head, assuming the "A" position, with thumb pointing up. Also FOR 2.

BECKON (běk′ ən), *v.,* BECKONED, BECKONING. The right index finger makes a natural beckoning movement. Also COME 2.

BECOME (bǐ kŭm′), *v.,* -CAME, -COME, -COMING. (To change from one position to another.) The palms of both hands, fingers closed and slightly curved, face each other a few inches apart, with the right above the left. They are pivoted around simultaneously, in a clockwise manner, so that their relative positions are reversed.

BECOME SUCCESSFUL, *phrase.* (Soaring up into the stars.) The downturned right "B" hand is placed against the palm of the left hand. The "B" hand shoots upward smartly.

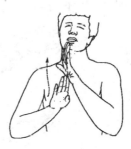

BECOMING (bǐ kŭm′ ǐng), *adj.* (Something that agrees with.) Both hands, in the "D" position, index fingers pointing straight out, are held before the body, palms facing and several inches apart. They are swung down in unison until the palms face down—bringing the two index fingers almost together and side by side, in "agreement" with each other.

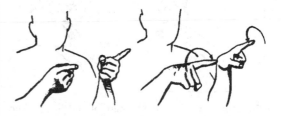

BED (běd), *n.* (A sleeping place with four legs.) The head is tilted to one side, with the cheek resting in the palm, to represent the head on a pillow. Both index fingers, pointing down, move straight down a short distance, in unison (the two front legs of the bed), and then are brought up slightly, and move down again a bit closer to the body (the rear legs).

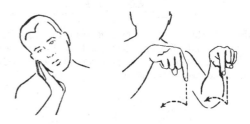

BEDROOM (-rōōm; -rŏŏm), *n.* The sign for BED is made, followed by the sign for ROOM. The open palms facing and fingers pointing out are dropped an inch or two simultaneously. They then shift their relative positions so that both palms face the body, with one hand in front of the other. In this new position they again drop an inch or two simultaneously. This indicates the four sides of a room. The "R" hands are often substituted for the open palms.

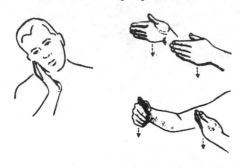

BEE (bē), *n.* (The bee's stinger is brushed away.) The index finger is placed on the cheek, and then the same hand makes a quick brushing motion off the cheek.

BEEF (bēf), *n.* (The fleshy part of the hand.) The right index finger and thumb squeeze the fleshy part of the open left hand, between thumb and index finger. Also FLESH, MEAT.

BEEPER (bē′ pər), *n.* (Hanging from the waist and going on and off.) The right hand, all fingers positioned against the belt on the right side of the body, opens and closes repeatedly.

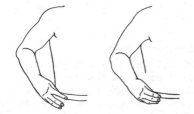

BEER 1 (bĭr), *n.* (Raising a beer stein to the lips.) The right "Y" hand is raised to the lips as the head tilts back a bit.

BEER 2, *n.* (The letter "B.") The right "B" hand moves down the right cheek a short distance.

BEFORE 1 (bĭ fōr′), *adv.* (One hand precedes the other.) The left hand is held before the body, fingers together and pointing to the right. The right hand, fingers also together and pointing to the left, is placed so that its back rests in the left palm. The right hand moves rather quickly toward the body. The sign is used as an indication of time or of precedence: *He arrived before me.*

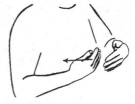

BEFORE 2 (*alt.*), *adv.* (One hand precedes the other.) The left hand, palm out and fingers together, is held before the body. The right, fingers also together, is placed back to back against the left and moves rather quickly toward the body. The sign is used alternatively, but less commonly, than BEFORE 1.

BEFORE 3, *adv.* (Face-to-face.) The left hand, fingers together, palm flat and facing the eyes, is held a bit above eye level. The right hand, fingers also together, is held in front of the mouth, with palm facing the left hand. With a sweeping upward movement the right hand moves toward the left, which moves straight up an inch or two at the same time. Also APPEAR 3, APPEARANCE, CONFRONT, FACE 2, FACE-TO-FACE, PRESENCE.

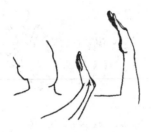

BEG 1 (bĕg), *v.*, BEGGED, BEGGING. (Holding out the hand and begging.) The right open hand, palm up and fingers slightly cupped, is moved up and down by the left hand, positioned under it. Also ASK ALMS, BEGGAR, PANHANDLER.

BEG 2, *v.* (An act of supplication.) With the right hand clasped over the left, both hands are shaken gently before the body. The eyes often are directed upward. Also BESEECH, ENTREAT, IMPLORE, PLEA, PLEAD, SUPPLICATION.

BEGIN (bĭ gĭn′), *v.*, -GAN, -GUN, -GINNING. (Turning a key to open up a new venture.) The right index finger, resting between the left index and middle fingers, executes a half turn once or twice. Also COMMENCE, INITIATE, INSTITUTE 2, ORIGIN 1, ORIGINATE 1, START.

BEHAVE (bi hāv′), *v.*, HAVED, -HAVING. (The "B" letters; doing or acting.) Both downturned "B" hands move from side to side in unison. Also BEHAVIOR.

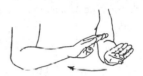

BEHIND (bĭ hīnd′), *prep.* (One hand is after or behind the other.) Both hands, in the "A" position, are held knuckles to knuckles. The right hand moves back, describing a small arc, and comes to rest against the left wrist. Also AFTER 2, BACK, BACKSLIDE.

BE IGNORED, *v.* (A form of thumbing the nose.) The index fingertip of the right "4" hand is placed on the nose, and then the hand sweeps down in a flourish so that the little finger edge strikes the midchest, with palm facing up.

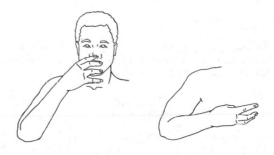

BELCH (bĕlch), *n., v.,* BELCHED, BELCHING. (The natural sign.) The downturned "S" hand is positioned against the lower chest. It moves up suddenly for a short distance as the upper part of the body contracts slightly, as it does in emitting a belch.

BELIEF (bĭ lēf'), *n.* (A thought clasped onto.) The index finger touches the middle of the forehead (where the thought lies), and then both hands are clasped together. Also BELIEVE, CONVICTION 2, DOCTRINE 2.

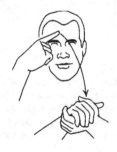

BELIEVE (bĭ lēv'), *v.,* -LIEVED, -LIEVING. See BELIEF.

BELL 1 (bĕl), *n.* (The bell's reverberations.) The right fist strikes the front of the left hand and then opens and moves away from the left in an undulating manner to indicate the sound waves. Also RING 2.

BELL 2, *n.* (Ringing a small bell to summon someone.) An imaginary small bell is held in the hand and daintily shaken back and forth.

BELL 3, *n.* (Pressing the button of the bell.) The right thumb is thrust into the open left palm several times, indicating the pressing of a bell button.

BELONG (bĭ lông', -lŏng'), *v.,* -LONGED, -LONGING. (Joining together.) Both hands, held in the modified "5" position, palms out, move toward each other. The thumbs and index fingers of both hands then connect. Also AFFILIATE 1, ANNEX, ASSOCIATE 2, ATTACH, COMMUNION OF SAINTS, CONCERN 2, CONNECT, ENLIST, ENROLL, JOIN 1, PARTICIPATE, RELATIVE 2, UNION, UNITE.

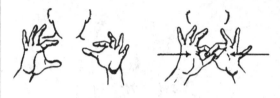

BELOVED (bĭ lŭv' ĭd), *adj.* (Clasping the heart.) The "5" hands are held one atop the other over the heart. Sometimes the "S" hands are used, in which case they are crossed at the wrists. Also CHARITY, DEVOTION, LOVE, REVERE 2.

BELOW 1 (bĭ lō'), *adv.* (The area below.) Both hands, in the "5" position, palms down, are held before the chest, the right under the left. The right hand moves under the left in a counterclockwise fashion. Also BACKGROUND, BASIS 2, BOTTOM, FOUNDATION.

BELOW 2, *adv.* (Underneath something.) The right hand, in the "A" position, thumb pointing straight up, moves down under the left hand, held outstretched, fingers together, palm down. Also BENEATH 1, UNDER 1, UNDERNEATH.

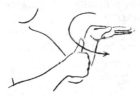

BELOW 3, *adv.* (The area below.) The right "A" hand, thumb pointing up, moves in a counterclockwise fashion under the downturned left hand. Also BENEATH 2, UNDER 2.

BENCH 1 (hĕnch) (*arch.*), *n.* (The expanse of bench with its supports.) With both hands in the "S" position, the left hand is held before the chest, palm facing the body. The right hand is placed under the left wrist and then, describing an arc, moves over to the left elbow, indicating supports. Both hands are then placed together, palm to palm, fingers pointing away from the body. They separate to describe the expanse of bench.

BENCH 2, *n.* (The stretched-out seat.) Both hands are held with curved index and middle fingers pointing down, depicting the sitting position. The palms may

face either inward or outward. The hands separate, moving in opposite directions.

BE QUIET 1 (kwi' ət), *v. phrase.* (The natural sign.) The index finger is brought up against the pursed lips. Also CALM 2, HUSH, NOISELESS, QUIET 1, SILENCE 1, SILENT, STILL 2.

BE QUIET 2 (Quiet and peace.) The open hands are crossed before the mouth, the right palm facing left, left facing right. Then both hands, held palms down, move down from the mouth, curving outward to either side of the body. Also BE STILL, CALM 1, QUIET 2, SILENCE 2.

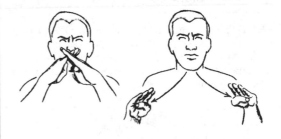

BERRY (ber' ē), *n.* (A small item being picked off a branch.) The right fingertips grasp the tip of the left little finger and twist, as if plucking a berry. This sign is used for any berry, often with classifiers. Also CHERRY, VIRGIN 3.

BE SEATED, *v. phrase.* (The act of sitting.) The extended right index and middle fingers are draped across the back of the same two fingers of the down-turned left hand. The hands then move straight downward a short distance. Also CHAIR 1, SEAT, SIT 1.

BEST (běst), *adj.* (The most good.) The fingertips of one hand are placed at the lips, as if tasting something (also GOOD), and then the hand is brought high above the head into the "A" position, thumb up, indicating the superlative degree.

BE STILL, *v. phrase.* See BE QUIET 2.

BET (bět) *n., v.,* BET, BETTED, BETTING. (The placing or slamming down of bets by two parties.) Both open hands, palms up, are suddenly swung over in unison to the palms-down position. Sometimes they are swung over one at a time. Also WAGER.

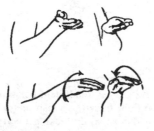

BETTER (bět′ ər), *adj.* (More good.) The fingertips of one hand are placed at the lips, as if tasting something (*see* GOOD). Then the hand is moved up to a position just above the head, where it assumes the "A" position, thumb up. This latter position, less high up than the one indicated in BEST, denotes the comparative degree. Also PREFER.

 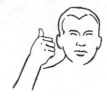

BETWEEN (bǐ twēn′), *prep.* (Between the fingers.) The left hand, in the "C" position, is placed before the chest, all fingers facing up. The right hand, in the "B" position, is placed between the left fingers and moves back and forth several times. This sign may also be made by pointing the left fingers to the right, with the left thumb pointing up and the right hand making the same back and forth motion as before, with the right little finger resting on the left index finger.

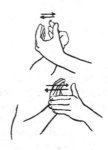

BEYOND (bǐ yŏnd′), *prep.* (One hand moves on to a place *beyond* the other.) Both hands, fingers together and slightly cupped, are held before the chest, with the left hand in front of the right. The right hand moves up and over the left and then straight out.

BIB (bib), *n.* (The bib is indicated.) The signer mimes placing a bib on the chest and fastening its strings behind the neck.

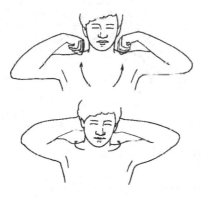

BIBLE 1 (bī′ bəl), *n.* (Literally, Jesus book.) The sign for JESUS is made: the left middle finger touches the right palm, and then the right middle finger touches the left palm (the crucifixion marks). The sign for BOOK is then made: the open hands are held together, fingers pointing away from the body; they open with little fingers remaining in contact, as in the opening of a book. This BIBLE sign signifies the Christian Bible. Also TESTAMENT 1.

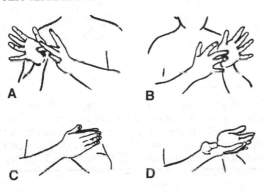

BIBLE 2, *n.* (Literally, holy book.) The right "H" hand makes a clockwise circular movement and is then opened and wiped across the open left palm (something nice or clean with an "H," *i.e.,* HOLY). The sign for BOOK, as in BIBLE 1, is then made. This sign may be used by all religious faiths. Also TESTAMENT 2.

BIBLE 3, *n.* (Literally, Jewish book; the Old Testament.) The sign for JEW is formed: the fingers and thumb of each hand are placed at the chin, and stroke an imaginary beard, as worn by the old Jewish patriarchs or Orthodox rabbis. The sign for BOOK, as in BIBLE 1, is then made. Also HEBREW BIBLE, HOLY SCRIPTURE, JEWISH BIBLE, TESTAMENT 3.

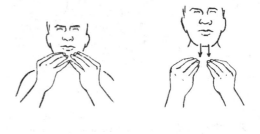

BIBLE 4, *n.* (The book from above.) The sign for BOOK is made: the hands, held together palm to palm, open and part, as if opening a book. They then close again as both hands, palms touching, are raised to a level above the head.

BIBLIOGRAPHY (bib′ lē og′ rə fē), *n.* (A book with lists.) The sign for BOOK is made: the hands, held together palm to palm, open and part, as if opening a book. The little finger edge of the right hand then moves down along the upturned left palm in a series of small jumps, from fingertips to the heel of the left hand, as if listing items one after the other.

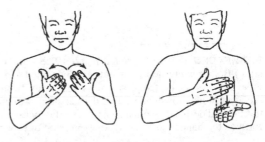

BICYCLE, (bī′ sə kəl), *n., v.,* -CLED, -CLING. (The motion of the feet on the pedals.) Both hands, in the "S" position, rotate alternately before the chest. Also PEDAL, TRICYCLE.

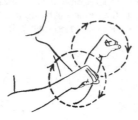

BIG 1 (bĭg), *adj.* (A delineation of something big, modified by the letter "L," which stands for LARGE.) Both "L" hands, palms facing out, are placed before the face and separated rather widely. Also ENORMOUS, GREAT 1, HUGE, IMMENSE, LARGE.

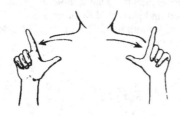

BIG 2, *adj.* (The height is indicated.) The right right-angle hand, palm facing the left, is held at the height the signer wishes to indicate. Also HEIGHT 2, HIGH 3, TALL 2.

BIG-HEADED (hĕd′ ĭd) (*colloq.*), *adj.* (The natural sign.) Both downturned "L" hands are positioned with index fingers at the temples. They move away from the head rather slowly, indicating the size or growth of the head. The head is often moved slightly back and forth as the hands move away. An expression of supe-

riority is assumed. Also BIG SHOT, CONCEITED, SWELL-HEADED.

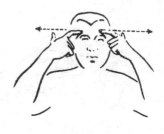

BIG SHOT (shŏt), (*sl.*). See BIG-HEADED.

BIG WORDS (wûrdz) (*sl.*). (Large expanses of written material as they appear on the page.) The right "Y" hand, palm down, is placed on the left "G" hand above the wrist. The right hand, in this position, arcs up and over, coming to rest on the left index finger. In this sign the two fingers of the right hand represent the widest possible space that can be indicated, and the left "G" hand represents a single line on the page.

BILLFOLD 1 (bil′ fōld), *n.* (Placing the bills inside.) The little finger edge of the open right hand, palm facing the body, is slipped into the space created by the thumb and other fingers of the left hand. The signer then mimes placing the billfold into a back pocket. Also WALLET 2.

BILLFOLD 2, *n.* (Placing the bills in and folding the billfold.) Same as BILLFOLD 1, but after placing the bills in the billfold, the two hands, fingertips touching, are brought together palm to palm.

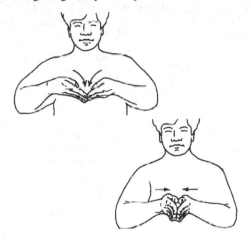

BILLIARDS (bil′ yərdz), *n*. (The game of billiards.) The signer, hunched over an imaginary cue stick, mimes striking the ball. Also POOL.

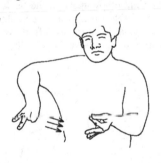

BILLION (bĭl′ yən), *adj., n.* (A thousand thousand thousands.) The sign for THOUSAND is made three times: the tips of the right "M" hand are thrust into the upturned left palm three times, each time a little closer to the left fingertips.

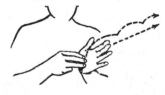

BIND (bīnd), *v.*, BOUND, BINDING. (The act of tying.) Both hands, in the "A" position, go through the natural hand-over-hand motions of tying and drawing out a knot. Also FASTEN, KNOT, TIE 1.

BINOCULARS (bə nŏk′ yə lərz, bī-), *n. pl.* (The natural sign.) The "C" hands are held in front of the eyes. Also GOGGLES, OPERA GLASSES.

BIOLOGY (bī ŏl′ ə jē), *n*. (The "B"s; pouring from a test tube.) Both "B" hands, palms out, execute continuous alternating circles: the right moving counter-clockwise and the left clockwise.

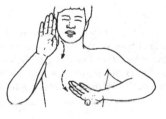

BIRD (bûrd), *n*. (The shape and movement of a beak.) The right thumb and index finger are placed against the mouth, pointing straight out. They open and close. Also BEAK.

BIRTH 1 (bûrth), *n*. (Presenting the baby from womb to hand; a coming out from the womb to the waiting hand.) The upturned right hand is brought forward from the stomach to the upturned left palm. Also BORN 1, NÉE.

BIRTH 2, *n*. (The baby is presented.) Both open hands are held against the breast, one on top of the other, as if holding something to oneself. From this position the hands move out from the body and to either side, ending palms up. Also BORN 2.

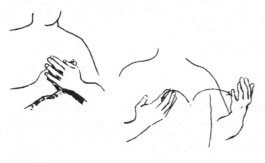

BIRTH 3, *n*. (The baby is brought forth from the womb.) Both cupped hands, palms facing the body, are placed at the stomach or lower chest, one on top of the other. Both hands are moved out and away from the body in unison, describing a small arc. Also BORN 3.

BIRTH CONTROL, *n. phrase*. (Preventing a baby from being conceived.) The sign for BABY is made: the upturned right arm rests on its upturned left counterpart, and both arms rock back and forth. Next the

sign for PREVENT is made: the left hand, fingers together and palm flat, is held facing somewhat down. The little finger edge of the right hand, striking the thumb side of the left, pushes the left hand slightly forward.

BIRTHDAY 1 (bûrth′ dā′), *n*. The sign for BIRTH 1 or BIRTH 2 is made, followed by the sign for DAY: the left arm, held horizontally, palm down, represents the horizon. The right elbow rests on the back of the left hand, with the right arm in a perpendicular position. The right "D" hand, palm facing left, moves in an arc to the left until it is just above the left elbow.

BIRTHDAY 2 (*colloq*.). (Something sweet, *e.g.,* ice cream or cake.) The right middle finger touches the lips, then moves down to touch the chest.

BIRTHDAY 3 (*colloq.*). The knuckles of the right fist strike the heart twice.

BIRTHDAY 4 (*colloq.*). (Showing relative height of a person.) The downturned "B" hand is placed against the stomach and moves off and up, coming to rest at chest level. This sign indicates the growth marks some parents make on the wall to chronicle the growth of children, especially on their birthdays. Also YEARS OLD.

BIRTHDAY 5, *n.* (*colloq.*) (Music is made.) The right "B" hand, palm down over the downturned left arm, makes a series of elongated figure eights.

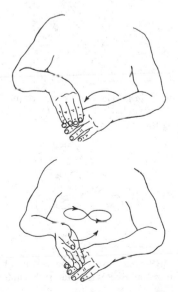

BIRTHDAY 6, *n.* (*colloq.*) Pull the earlobe.

BIRTHDAY 7, *n.* (*colloq.*) (An old sign for "cake.") The middle finger of the right "K" hand is thrust twice into the right cheek.

BIRTHDAY 8, *n.* (*colloq.*) (An old sign for "party.") The elongated fingers of the right closed hand are placed against the right chin. The hand is thrust out and thrown down. Also PARTY 3.

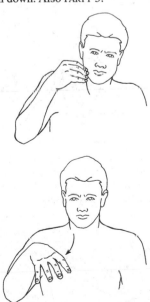

BISEXUAL (bī sek′ shōō əl), *n., adj.* (Swinging from one sexual orientation to another.) The right curved downturned index and middle fingers, swiveling at the wrist, move to the left and right.

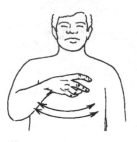

BISHOP 1 (bĭsh′ əp) (*eccles.*), *n.* (Kissing the ring.) The extended index and middle fingers make the sign of the cross before the face. Then the ring finger of the right "S" hand is kissed. This is the sign for a Catholic bishop.

BISHOP 2, *n.* (The shape.) The downturned open hands, fingers together, move up from either side of the head, and the fingertips come together, forming an arch over the head, to describe the bishop's mitre. Also MITRE.

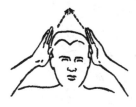

BIT (bit), *n. Computer term.* (The "B.") The right "B" hand is placed against the outfacing left palm. It moves down to the base of the left hand. Refers to a binary digit, a unit of binary language.

BITCH (bĭch) (*sl.*), *n.* (The letter "B"; the "female" portion of the head.) The right "B" hand is brought up to the chin.

BITE (bīt), *n., v.,* BIT, BITTEN, BITING. (The natural sign.) The index finger of the downturned hand is bitten.

BITTER (bĭt′ ər), *adj.* (Something sour or bitter.) The right index finger is brought sharply up against the lips, while the mouth is puckered up as if tasting something sour. Also ACID, DISAPPOINTED 1, LEMON 1, PICKLE, SOUR.

BLACK (blăk), *adj.* (The darkest part of the face, *i.e.,* the brow, is indicated.) The tip of the index finger moves along the eyebrow.

BLACKBERRY (blak′ bər′ ē, -bə rē), *n.* (The color and the sign for BERRY.) The right index finger moves along the right eyebrow from left to right (the sign for BLACK). The right thumb plus index and middle fingers then grasp the tip of the left little finger and twist it clockwise.

BLACKBOARD 1 (blăk' bōrd'), *n.* (Black, hard, write.) The sign for BLACK is made. This is followed by the sign for HARD: the bent right index and middle fingers strike the back of the left fist. Then the sign for WRITE is made: the right index finger and thumb, grasping an imaginary piece of chalk, write across the open left palm. Also SLATE.

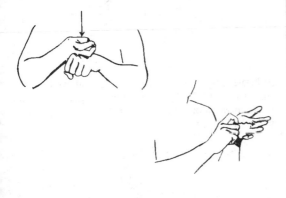

BLACKBOARD 2, *n.* (The signs for black and write.) The right index finger moves over the right eyebrow from left to right. This is the sign for BLACK. The right hand then mimes writing something on the upturned left palm.

BLACK EYE, *n.* (Swollen eye.) The right claw hand, palm facing the body, is placed over the right eye.

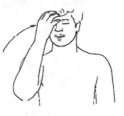

BLAME (blām), *v.,* BLAME, BLAMING, *n.* (The blame is firmly placed.) The right "A" hand, thumb pointing up, is brought down firmly against the back of the left hand, held palm down; the right thumb is then directed toward the person or object to blame. When personal blame is acknowledged, the thumb is brought in to the chest. Also ACCUSE 1, FAULT 1, GUILTY 1.

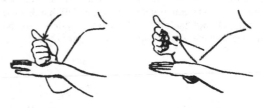

BLANKET (blang' kit), *n.* (Pulling up the cover.) The downturned hands grasp an imaginary blanket edge and pull it up over the chest.

BLANK MIND, *n. phrase.* (Wiping off the mind.) The right middle finger moves across the forehead from left to right, indicating an emptiness within. This sign is derived from BARE or EMPTY.

BLEED (blēd), v., BLED, BLEEDING, adj. (Blood trickles down from the hand.) The left "5" hand is held palm facing the body and fingertips pointing right. The right "5" hand touches the back of the left and moves down, with the right fingers wiggling. Also BLOOD.

BLESS 1 (blĕs), v., BLESSED or BLEST, BLESSING. (Blessed; forgiveness.) The "A" hands are held near the lips, thumbs up and almost touching. Both hands move down and out simultaneously, ending in the "5" position, palms down. The right hand, palm flat, facing down, is then brushed over the left hand, held palm flat and facing up. This latter action may be repeated twice. Also ABSOLUTION 1, FORGIVE 1.

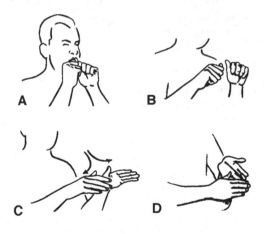

BLESS 2, v. (Pronouncing a blessing over a kneeling figure.) The index finger of the right "D" hand is placed at the lips to indicate the source of the blessing. Both hands then assume the "A" position, thumbs up and knuckles touching. They sweep down and out, opening to the "5" position, palms down, as if placing the hands on bowed heads. Also BENEDICTION 2.

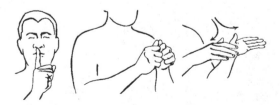

BLIND (blīnd), adj. (The eyes are blocked.) The tips of the "V" fingers are thrust toward the closed eyes. Also BLINDNESS.

BLINDFOLD (blīnd' fōld), n., v., -FOLDED, -FOLDING. (The natural sign.) The signer mimes tying a blindfold over the eyes and fastening it behind the head.

BLINDNESS, n. See BLIND. This is followed by the sign for -NESS: The downturned right "N" hand moves down along the left palm, which is facing away from the body.

BLINK (blingk), n., v., BLINKED, BLINKING. (The closing eyes.) Both index fingers and thumbs close at either side of the head. The eyes may also close simultaneously.

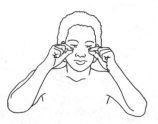

BLOCKHEAD (blok′ hed′), *n., sl.* (The head is like a block of stone.) The right index finger touches the forehead, and then both fists are banged together.

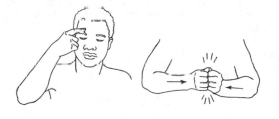

BLOND (blond), *adj., n.* (Yellow hair.) As it moves up over the right side of the head, the right "Y" hand makes the sign for YELLOW: it twists back and forth repeatedly, swiveling at the right wrist.

BLOOD (blŭd), *n.* See BLEED.

BLOOD PRESSURE, *n.* (The armband.) The right hand repeatedly squeezes the left upper arm.

BLOOM (bloŏm), *n.* (Flowers or plants emerge from the ground.) The right fingers, pointing up, emerge from the closed left hand, and they spread open as they do. Also DEVELOP 1, GROW, GROWN, MATURE, PLANT 1, RAISE 3, REAR 2, SPRING 1.

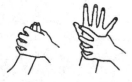

BLOOMINGDALE'S, *n. loc.* The right index finger, held pointing into the throat, twists back and forth repeatedly, swiveling at the wrist. Refers to dabbing perfume on the neck; the perfume counter at the main store, in New York City, which is near the site of the old Lexington School for the Deaf.

BLOW 1 (blō), *v.,* BLEW, BLOWN, BLOWING, *n.* (The blowing back and forth of the wind.) The "5" hands, palms facing and held up before the body, sway gracefully back and forth, in unison. The cheeks meanwhile are puffed up and the breath is being expelled. The nature of the swaying movement—graceful and slow, fast and violent, etc.—determines the type of wind. The strength of exhalation is also a qualifying device. Also BREEZE, GALE, STORM, WIND.

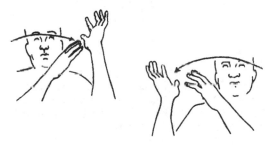

BLOW 2, *n.* (A blow is struck.) The right fist strikes the left palm. Also BEAT 3.

BLOW YOUR STACK, *sl. phrase.* (The lid blows off the pot.) The downturned right hand rests on the left hand in the "C" or "O" position. The right hand suddenly goes up, its wrist swiveling back and forth as it does.

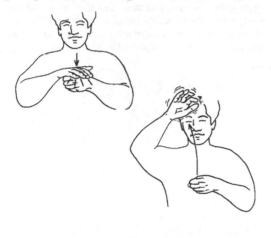

BLUE (blōo), *n., adj.* (The letter "B.") The right "B" hand shakes slightly, pivoting at the wrist.

BLUFF (blŭf), *n.* (A double face, *i.e.,* a mask covers the face.) The right hand is placed over the back of the left hand and pushes it down and a bit in toward the body. Also FAKE, HUMBUG, HYPOCRITE 1, IMPOSTOR.

BLUNT (blunt), *adj.* (The letter "B"; straightforward.) The right "B" hand is placed on the forehead, palm facing left. It moves straight out forcefully.

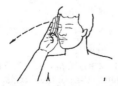

BLURRY (blûr' ĭ), *adj.* (One hand obscures the other.) The "5" hands are held up, palm against palm, in front of the body. The right hand moves in a slow, continuous clockwise circle over the left palm as the signer tries to see between the fingers. Also UNCLEAR, VAGUE.

BLUSH (blŭsh), *v.,* BLUSHED, BLUSHING. (The red rises in the cheeks.) The sign for RED is made: the tip of the right index finger of the "D" hand moves down over the lips, which are red. Both hands are then placed palms facing the cheeks and move up along the face, to indicate the rise of color. Also EMBARRASS, EMBARRASSED, FLUSH, MORTIFICATION.

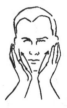

BOARD OF DIRECTORS, *n.* (The letters "B-D"; the Roman toga.) The right "B" hand, starting at either shoulder, sweeps across the chest, ending in a "D" at the opposite shoulder.

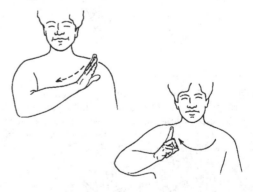

BOARD OF TRUSTEES, *n.* (The letters "B-T"; the Roman toga.) The right "B" hand, starting at either shoulder, sweeps across the chest, ending in a "T" at the opposite shoulder.

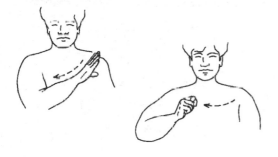

BOAT (bōt), *n.* (The shape; the bobbing on the waves.) Both hands are cupped together to form the hull of a boat. They move forward in a bobbing motion.

BODY (bŏd′ ĭ), *n.* (The body is indicated.) One or both hands are placed against the chest and then are removed and replaced at a point a bit below the first. Also PHYSICAL.

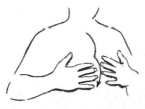

BOMB (bom), *n., v.,* BOMBED, BOMBING. (Releasing the bomb.) The right index finger, palm down, is placed under the downturned open left hand. It drops straight down.

BONE 1 (bōn), *n.* (The finger touches a brittle substance.) The index finger is brought up to touch the

exposed front teeth. Also CHINA 2, DISH, GLASS 1, PLATE, PORCELAIN.

BONE 2, *n.* (The skeleton's crossed bones.) Both hands, crossed and palms facing the signer, are held with index and middle fingers curved inward.

BONE 3, *n.* (The shape.) The open right hand, index and thumb forming a circle, is drawn back and forth along the back of the left arm, outlining the bone inside.

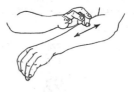

BONNET (bon′ it), *n.* (Tying the strings.) Both hands, starting at the top of the head, mime slipping on a bonnet and tying the strings under the chin.

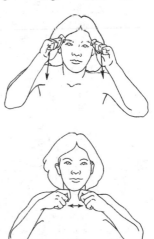

BOOK (bŏŏk), *n.* (Opening a book.) The open hands are held together, fingers pointing away from the body. They open with little fingers remaining in contact, as in the opening of a book. Also TEXTBOOK, VOLUME.

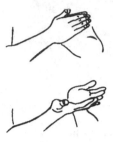

BOOKLET (bŏŏk′ lĭt), *n.* (A book with a narrow spine.) The left hand, fingers together, is held upright, palm facing right. The right hand wraps around the lower edge of the left and travels up to the little finger. This denotes a narrow object. The sign for BOOK is then made. Sometimes this latter sign is omitted. Also CATALOG, MAGAZINE, MANUAL, PAMPHLET.

BOOKSHELF (bŏŏk′ shelf), *n.* (Books side by side along the shelf.) The sign for BOOKS is made: the hands open repeatedly. The right hand, palm facing left, then moves to the right, slowly and deliberately.

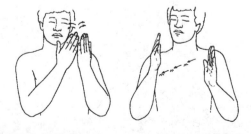

BOOT (bŏŏt), *n.* (The height of the boot.) The little finger edge of the right hand is drawn across the wrist of the downturned left hand.

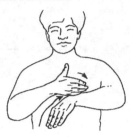

BORDER/BORDERLINE (bôr′ dər), *n., v.,* BORDERED, BORDERING. (The line.) The fingertips of the downturned right hand are drawn along the index finger edge of the left hand, held palm facing the body. The tip of the right little finger alone may be substituted for the right fingertips.

BORE 1 (bōr), *v.,* BORED, BORING, *n.* (A dryness, indicated by a wiping of the lips.) The "X" finger is drawn across the lips, from left to right, as if wiping them. Also ARID, DROUGHT, DRY, DULL 2.

BORE 2, *v.* (Act of boring a hole with a brace.) The left "S" hand, palm down, grasps an imaginary brace top. The right hand, also in the "S" position, palm facing left, rotates the brace, as if drilling something. Also DRILL 1.

BORING 1 (bōr′ ĭng), *adj.* (The nose is pressed as if to a grindstone wheel.) The right index finger touches the tip of the nose as a bored expression is assumed. The right hand is sometimes pivoted back and forth slightly as the fingertip remains against the nose. Also MONOTONOUS 1, TEDIOUS.

BORING 2, *adj.* (The movement of the grindstone.) The left hand is held with palm facing right. The thumb edge of the right "S" hand is placed on the left palm and does a series of clockwise circles. This sign may be preceded by the index finger briefly touching the nose.

BORN 1 (bôrn), *adj.* (Presenting the baby from womb to hand; a coming out from the womb to the waiting hand.) The upturned right hand is brought forward from the stomach to the upturned left palm. Also BIRTH 1, NÉE.

BORN 2, *adj.* (The baby is presented.) Both open hands are held against the breast, one on top of the other, as if holding something to oneself. From this position the hands move out from the body and to either side, ending palms up. Also BIRTH 2.

BORN 3, *adj.* (The baby is brought forth from the womb.) Both cupped hands, palms facing the body, are placed at the stomach or lower chest, one on top of the other. Both hands are moved out and away from the body in unison, describing a small arc. Also BIRTH 3.

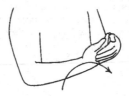

BORROW (bŏr′ ō, bôr′ ō), *v.,* -ROWED, -ROWING, (Bring to oneself.) The "K" hands are crossed and moved in toward the body.

BOSTON (bôs′ tən, bos′ tən), *n.* (The "B.") The right "B" hand, palm facing out, moves to the right and down with a sharp movement.

BOTH (bōth), *adj., pron.* (Two fingers are drawn together.) The right "2" hand, palm facing the body, is drawn down through the left "C" hand. As it does, the right index and middle fingers come together. Also MUTUAL 2, PAIR.

BOTHER 1 (bŏth′ ər), *v.*, -ERED, -ERING. (Obstruct, block.) The left hand, fingers together and palm flat, is held before the body, facing somewhat down. The little finger side of the right hand, held with palm flat, makes one or several up-down chopping motions against the left hand between its thumb and index finger. Also ANNOY 1, ANNOYANCE 1, BLOCK, CHECK 2, COME BETWEEN, DISRUPT, DISTURB, HINDER, HINDRANCE, IMPEDE, INTERCEPT, INTERFERE, INTERFERENCE, INTERFERE WITH, INTERRUPT, MEDDLE 1, OBSTACLE, OBSTRUCT, PREVENT, PREVENTION.

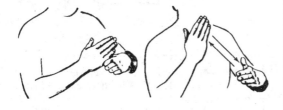

BOTHER 2, *v.* (A clouding over; a troubling.) Both "B" hands, palms facing each other, are rotated alternately before the forehead. Also ANNOY 2, ANNOYANCE 2, ANXIOUS 2, CONCERN 1, FRET, PROBLEM 1, TROUBLE, WORRIED, WORRY 1.

BOTH OF US, *phrase.* (Two people interacting.) The right "V" hand, palm up and fingers pointing left, is

swung in and out to and from the chest. Also US TWO, WE TWO.

BOTTOM (bŏt′ əm), *n.* (The area below.) Both hands, in the "5" position, palms down, are held before the chest, the right under the left. The right hand moves under the left in a counterclockwise fashion. Also BACKGROUND, BASIS 2, BELOW 1, FOUNDATION.

BOUND (bound), *adj.* (Bound down to custom or habit.) Both "S" hands, palms down, are crossed and brought down in unison before the chest. Also ACCUSTOM, CUSTOM, HABIT, LOCKED, PRACTICE 3.

BOX 1 (bŏks), *n.* (The dimensions are indicated.) The open hands, palms facing and fingers pointing out, are dropped an inch or two simultaneously. They then shift their relative positions so that both palms face the body, with one hand in front of the other. In this new position they again drop an inch or two simultaneously. Also PACKAGE, ROOM 1, SQUARE 1, TRUNK.

Box 81 Braille

BOX 2, *v.*, BOXED, BOXING. (The natural sign.) Both clenched fists go through the motions of boxing. Also FIGHT 2.

BOY 1 (boi), *n.* (A small male.) The MALE root sign is made: the thumb and extended fingers of the right hand are brought up to grasp an imaginary cap brim, representing the tipping of caps by men in olden days. The downturned right hand then indicates the short height of a small boy.

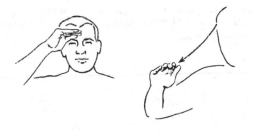

BOY 2, *n.* (A modification of the MALE root sign; the familiar sign for BOY 1.) The right hand, palm down, is held at the forehead. The fingers open and close once or twice. Also LAD.

BOY SCOUT (skout), *n.* (The salute.) The Boy Scout salute is given.

BRA (brä), *n.* (The shape.) The thumbs and index fingers of each hand outline the shape of a brassiere across the chest, with the left hand moving left and the right moving right. Also BRASSIERE.

BRACELET (brās′ lit), *n.* (The natural sign.) The curved thumb and index finger of the open right hand are wrapped around the left wrist.

BRAG (brăg), *v.*, BRAGGED, BRAGGING. (Indicating the self, repeatedly.) The thumbs of both "A" hands are alternately thrust into the chest a number of times. Also BOAST, SHOW OFF 1.

BRAILLE (brāl), *n.* (Feeling the raised dots.) The curved index and middle fingers are thrust in toward the eyes to indicate BLIND, and then the fingertips run back and forth against the upturned palm of the other hand.

BRAINSTORMING (brān′ stôr′ ming), *n., v. (colloq.)* (Culling the brain and throwing the pieces together.) With both hands moving alternately, the signer picks off pieces from the brain and throws them into an imaginary pot or other receptacle.

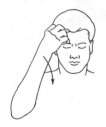

BRAKE (brāk), *n., v.,* BRAKED, BRAKING. (Pressing the brake pedal.) The signer uses the right hand to mime pressing the brake pedal of a car.

BRANCH 1 (brănch, bränch), *n.* (The shape.) The elbow of the upright right arm rests on the palm of the upturned left hand. This is the trunk. The right "5" fingers wiggle to imitate the movement of the branches and leaves. Also TREE.

BRANCH 2, *n.* (The offshoot of the tree.) Both open hands, facing out, are held with index finger edges

touching. The right hand moves up along the edge of the left, curving right as it reaches the left fingertips.

BRAVE (brāv), *adj., n., v.,* BRAVED, BRAVING. (Strength emanating from the body.) Both "5" hands are placed palms against the chest. They move out and away forcefully, closing and assuming the "S" position. Also BRAVERY, COURAGE, COURAGEOUS, FORTITUDE, HALE, HEALTH, HEALTHY, MIGHTY 2, STRENGTH, STRONG 2, WELL 2.

BRAVERY (brā′ və rĭ), *n.* See BRAVE.

BRAZIL (brə zil′), *n.* (Possibly having to do with the feathered headdress of a native.) The fingers are placed on the forehead and the hand moves in a slight counterclockwise direction. A native sign.

BREAD (brĕd), *n.* (Act of cutting a loaf of bread.) The left arm is held against the chest, representing a loaf of bread. The little finger edge of the right hand is drawn down over the back of the left hand several times to indicate the cutting of slices. Also COMMUNION (HOLY) 2, HOLY COMMUNION 2, WINE 2.

upright angle. The signs may also be reversed, as MORNING, FOOD.

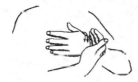

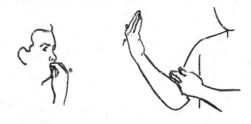

BREAK (brāk), n., v., BROKE, BROKEN, BREAKING. (The natural sign.) The hands grasp an imaginary object and break it in two. Also FRACTURE.

BREASTS 1 (brestz), n. (The location.) The right fingertips touch the left breast and then the right.

BREAKDOWN (-doun), n. (A collapsing.) Both "5" hands, fingertips joined before the chest, swing down so that the fingertips face down. Also CAVE IN, COLLAPSE.

BREASTS 2, n. (The shape.) Both cupped hands are held over the breasts, to indicate the shape.

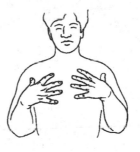

BREASTS 3, n. (The breasts hang.) Both upturned cupped hands are positioned under the breasts and move up and down an inch or so.

BREAKFAST (brĕk′ fəst), n. (Morning food.) The sign for FOOD is given: the closed right hand goes through the natural motion of placing food in the mouth. This movement is repeated, followed by the sign for MORNING: the little finger edge of the left hand rests in the crook of the right elbow; the left arm, held horizontally, represents the horizon; the open right hand, fingers together and pointing up, with palm facing the body, rises slowly to an almost

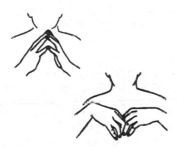

BREATH (brĕth), *n.* (The rise and fall of the chest in respiration.) The hands, folded over the chest, move forward and back to the chest to indicate the breathing. Also BREATHE, RESPIRATION.

BREATHE (brĕth), *v.,* BREATHED, BREATHING. See BREATH.

BREEZE (brēz), *n.* (The blowing back and forth of the wind.) The "5" hands, palms facing and held up before the body, sway gracefully back and forth in unison. The cheeks meanwhile are puffed up and the breath is being expelled. The nature of the swaying movement—graceful and slow, fast and violent, etc.—determines the type of wind. The strength of exhalation is also a qualifying device. Also BLOW 1, GALE, STORM, WIND.

BRIBE (brīb), *n., v.,* BRIBED, BRIBING. (Underhanded payment of money.) The right hand, grasping an imaginary dollar bill, moves under the downturned left hand.

BRICK (brik), *n.* (The color red and the shape.) The sign for RED is made: the index finger moves down across the lips. The thumbs and index fingers then out-

line the shape of a brick, moving apart to indicate the length and then closing to show the height.

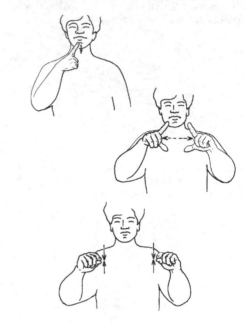

BRIDE (brīd), *n.* (The veil.) The downturned "5" hands, starting on top of the head, move down and apart, tracing a veil over the face.

BRIEF 1 (brēf), *adj.* (To make short; to measure off a short space.) The index and middle fingers of the right "H" hand are placed across the top of the index and middle fingers of the left "H" hand and move a short distance back and forth along the length of the left index finger. Also ABBREVIATE 2, SHORT 1, SHORTEN.

BRIEF 2, *adj.* (To squeeze or condense into a small space.) Both "C" hands face each other, with the right hand nearer to the body than the left. Both hands draw together and close deliberately, squeezing an imaginary object. Also ABBREVIATE 1, CONDENSE, MAKE BRIEF, SUMMARIZE 1, SUMMARY 1.

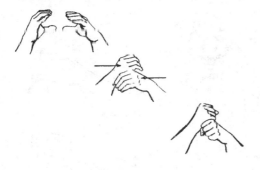

BRIGHT 1 (brīt), *adj.* (Rays of light clearing the way.) Both hands are held at chest height, palms out, all fingertips together. They open into the "5" position in unison, the right hand moving toward the right and the left toward the left. The palms of both hands remain facing out. Also BRILLIANCE 1, BRILLIANT 2, CLEAR, EXPLICIT 2, OBVIOUS, PLAIN 1.

BRIGHT 2 *adj.* (Reflected glistening of light rays.) The left hand, held supinely before the chest, palm down, represents the object from which the rays glisten. The right hand, in the "5" position, touches the back of the left lightly and moves up toward the right, pivoting slightly at the wrist, with fingers wiggling. Also GLISTEN, SHINE, SHINING.

BRIGHT 3, *adj.* (The mind is bright.) The middle finger is placed at the forehead, and then the hand, with an outward flick, turns around so that the palm faces outward. This indicates a brightness flowing from the mind. Also BRILLIANT 1, CLEVER 1, INTELLIGENT, SMART.

BRIGHT 4, *adj.* (Light rays glistening upward.) Both "5" hands, palms facing out, are held before the chest. They move up and out, all fingers wiggling to convey the glistening of light rays upward. This sign is an alternate for BRIGHT 2 and GLISTEN. Also BRILLIANCE 2.

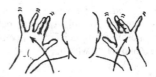

BRILLIANCE 1 (brĭl′ yəns), *n.* See BRIGHT 1.

BRILLIANCE 2, *n.* See BRIGHT 4.

BRILLIANT 1 (brĭl′ yənt), *adj.* See BRIGHT 3.

BRILLIANT 2, *adj.* See BRIGHT 1.

BRING (brĭng), *v.,* BROUGHT, BRINGING. (Carrying something over.) Both open hands, palms up, move in an arc from left to right, as if carrying something from one point to another. Also CARRY 2, DELIVER 2, FETCH, PRODUCE 1, TRANSPORT.

BRITAIN (brĭt' ən), *n.* (The English are supposed to be handshakers.) The right hand grasps and shakes the left. Also BRITISH, ENGLAND, ENGLISH, GREAT BRITAIN.

BRITISH (brĭt' ĭsh), *adj.* See BRITAIN.

BROAD (brôd), *adj.* (The width is indicated.) The open hands, fingers pointing out and palms facing each other, separate from their initial position an inch or two apart. Also WIDE, WIDTH.

BROADCAST (brôd' kast', -käst'), *n., v.,* -CAST, or -CASTED, -CASTING. (Tooting a horn.) Holding an imaginary trombone, the signer works the sliding part back and forth. Also ADVERTISE, PROPAGANDA.

BROAD-MINDED (brôd' mīn' dĭd), *adj.* (The mind is open, or wide.) The index finger touches the forehead to indicate the MIND. Then the sign for BROAD is made: the open hands, fingers pointing out and palms

facing each other, separate from their initial position an inch or two apart.

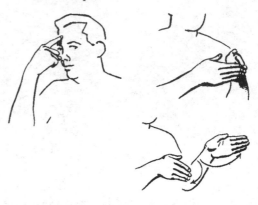

BROADWAY 1 (brôd' wā'), *n.* (The letter "B.") The right "B" hand, held upright and palm facing left, swivels at the wrist forward and back again several times.

BROADWAY 2, *n.* (The letter "B"; acting.) Both "B" hands, held at chest level, palms facing each other, move in alternate circles.

BROKE (brōk) (*sl.*), *adj.* (The head is chopped off.) The tips of the right fingers are thrust forcefully into the right side of the neck. Also BANKRUPT.

BROOKLYN (brŏok′ lin), *n.* (The "B.") The right "B" hand, facing out, moves up and down. The movement is a bit more pronounced than for BOSTON.

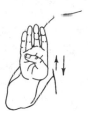

BROOM (brōom, brŏom), *n.* (The natural sign.) The hands grasp and manipulate an imaginary broom. Also SWEEP.

BROTHER 1 (brŭth′ ər), *n.* (A male who is the same, *i.e.,* from the same family.) The root sign for MALE is made: the thumb and extended fingers of the right hand are brought up to grasp an imaginary cap brim, representing the tipping of caps by men in olden days. Then the sign for SAME 1 is made: the outstretched index fingers are brought together, either once or several times.

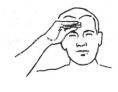

BROTHER 2 (*eccles.*), *n.* (The white collar-piece worn by religious brothers.) The thumb and index finger of one hand are placed just below the throat and

move down, describing the white hanging collar-piece. Also CHRISTIAN BROTHERS.

BROTHER-IN-LAW (brŭth′ ər ĭn lô′), *n.* (The sign for BROTHER 1 is made, followed by the sign for IN: the fingers of the right hand are thrust into the left. The sign for LAW is then made: the upright right "L" hand, resting palm against palm on the upright left "5" hand, moves down in an arc a short distance, coming to rest on the base of the left palm.

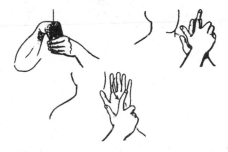

BROWN (broun), *adj.* The "B" hand is placed against the face, with the index finger touching the upper cheek. The hand is then drawn straight down the cheek.

BRUISE (brōoz) *n., v.,* BRUISED, BRUISING. (Indicating where a blow was struck.) The right fist strikes the left upper arm, and then the signer, with index and thumb forming a circle, places the circle on the spot just struck.

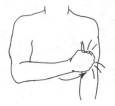 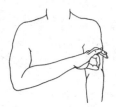

BUCKET (buk′ it), *n.* (Hanging from the arm.) The arm is held outstretched, palm down. The index finger of the other hand makes a downward arch from wrist to elbow. Also PAIL.

BUCKLE (buk′ əl), *n., v.,* -LED, -LING. (Locking the buckle's catch.) Both hands are held palms facing the waist, with curved thumbs, index and middle fingers. These fingers slide together, knuckles interlocking, as if fastening the catch of a buckle.

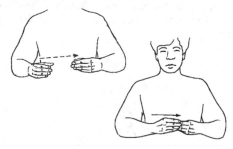

BUFFALO 1 (bŭf′ ə lō′), *n.* (The horns.) The "Y" hand, pivoted at the wrist, is shaken slightly beside the

head. This sign is used for both the animal and the city of Buffalo, in New York State.

BUFFALO 2, *n.* (The horns.) Both outstretched "S" hands are positioned palms out at the temples. They move away and twist so that the palms now face the signer. The "C" hands may be used initially at the temples, changing to "S" as they move away.

BUILD (bĭld), *v.,* BUILT, BUILDING. (Piling bricks one on top of another.) The downturned hands are placed repeatedly atop each other. Each time this is done the arms rise a bit, to indicate the raising of a building. Also CONSTRUCT 1, CONSTRUCTION, ERECT.

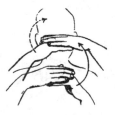

BULB (bulb), *n.* (Twisting the bulb into its socket.) The sign for ELECTRIC may be made: the knuckles of the bent index fingers touch each other twice. The signer then mimes twisting a light bulb into its socket.

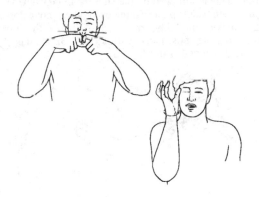

BULL 1 (bŏŏl), *n.* (The flattened brow of the bull.) The "A" hand, palm facing the body, is placed at the forehead and rotated counterclockwise. This sign is sometimes used to indicate any male animal.

BULL 2, *n.* (The ring in the bull's nose.) The thumb and index fingers indicate a ring in the nose.

BULLDOZER (bŏŏl′ dō′ zər), *n.* (The shape and action.) The right index finger, placed in the left open palm, pushes forward.

BULLSHIT 1 (bŏŏl′ shit), *n., expletive.* (A finger-spelled loan sign.) The signer makes the letters "B" and "S." The hand is flung out while making the "S."

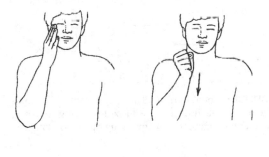

BULLSHIT 2, *n., expletive.* (The horns of a bull; the animal defecating.) The left downturned "Y" hand is held near the right shoulder. The closed left hand, positioned under the left elbow, opens suddenly into the "5" position. The movement may be repeated.

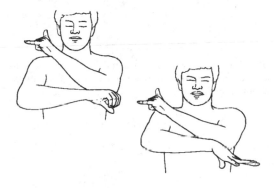

BULLY (bŏŏl′ ē), *n., v.,* -LIED, -LYING. (Coming up sharply against someone.) The downturned "Y" hand swings up repeatedly against the upturned left index finger.

BUMPER-TO-BUMPER, *adj.* (Bumpers touching.) The two flattened hands, palms down, are placed one in front of the other. They move forward together, in successive small movements, never separating.

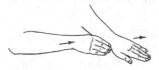

BUNDLE (bun′ dəl), *n.* (The shape.) Both "C" hands, held about a foot apart with palms facing, move up and come together as if squeezing the top of a bag.

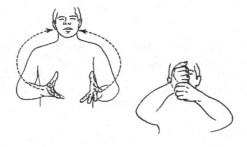

BUNK (bungk), *n.* (A two-tiered bed.) Both down-turned "U" hands are positioned one atop the other, about an inch apart.

BUNK BEDS, *n.* (One atop the other.) Both down-turned "U" hands are positioned one above the other. The sign for SLEEP, head resting on the back of the hand, may precede the sign.

BURGLAR (bûr′ glər), *n.* (A mustachioed thief.) The fingertips of both "H" hands, palms facing the body, are placed above the lips and are drawn slowly apart, describing a mustache. Sometimes one hand only is used. This is followed by the sign for INDIVIDUAL: both open hands, palms facing each other, move down the sides of the body, tracing its outline to the hips. Also BANDIT, BURGLARY, CROOK, ROB 3, ROBBER 1, STEAL 3, THEFT 3, THIEF 2.

BURGLARY (bûr′ glə rĭ), *n.* See BURGLAR.

BURN (bûrn), *n., v.,* BURNED or BURNT, BURNING. (The leaping of flames.) The "5" hands are held with palms facing the body. They move up and down alternately while the fingers wiggle. Also FIRE 1, FLAME, HELL 2.

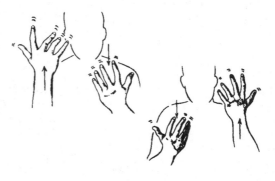

BURY 1 (bĕr′ ĭ), *v.,* BURIED, BURYING. (The mound of a grave.) The downturned open hands, slightly cupped, are held side by side. They describe on arc as they are drawn in toward the body. Also CEMETERY, GRAVE 1.

BURY 2, *v.* (The coffin is lowered.) The downturned right "U" hand slides down the outstretched left palm, whose fingertips face forward.

BUSY 1 (bĭz′ ĭ), *adj.* (An activity of the hands.) The right "S" hand, palm out, glances back and forth against the left "S" hand, whose palm faces down. Also the alternate sign for BUSINESS.

BUSY 2, *adj.* (An activity.) Both open hands, palms down, are swung right and left before the chest. Also ACT 2, ACTION, ACTIVE, ACTIVITY, CONDUCT 1, DEED, DO, PERFORM 1, PERFORMANCE 1, RENDER 2.

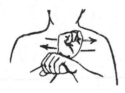

BUSYBODY (biz′ ē bod ē), *n.* (One whose nose is into others' business.) The nose is touched with the index finger, which is then curved and thrust into a hole formed by the other hand.

BUT (bŭt; *unstressed* bət), *conj.* (A divergence or a difference; the opposite of SAME.) The index fingers of both "D" hands, palms facing down, are crossed near their tips. The hands are drawn apart. Also ALTHOUGH, HOWEVER 1, ON THE CONTRARY.

BUTCHER (bŏŏch′ ər), *n., v.,* -ERED, -ERING. (Stabbing a creature in the neck.) The right thumb stabs the right side of the neck. For the noun, the sign for INDIVID-UAL 1 then follows.

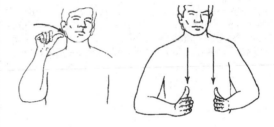

BUTTER (bŭt′ ər), *n., v.,* -TERED, -TERING. (The spreading of butter.) The tips of the fingers of the downturned right "U" hand are brushed repeatedly over the upturned left palm.

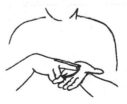

BUTTERFLY (bŭt′ ər flī′), *n.* (The natural sign.) The "5" hands, palms facing the body, are crossed and intertwined at the thumbs. The hands, hooked in this manner, move to and fro in vague figure eights, while the individual hands flap back and forth.

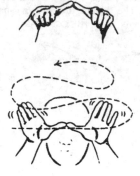

BUY (bī), *n., v.,* BOUGHT, BUYING. (Giving out money.) The sign for MONEY is made: the upturned right hand, grasping some imaginary bills, is brought down into the upturned left palm, and then the right hand

moves forward and up in a small arc, opening up as it does. Also PURCHASE.

BY A HAIR, *phrase.* The signer, grasping an imaginary hair at the forehead, pulls it straight out. Also CLOSE CALL.

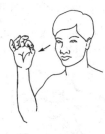

CABINET 1 (kăb′ ə nĭt), *n.* (Opening the doors.) The outstretched "B" hands are held side by side near the left shoulder at eye level, facing out. They turn in repeatedly, as if doors are swinging in. At each successive opening, the hands move slightly to the right.

CABINET 2, *n.* (Grasping the handles.) The signer mimes opening a pair of cabinet doors by grasping the handles. Also CUPBOARD.

CABLE (kā′ bəl), *n.* (The "C's" and the length.) Both "C" hands are side by side, both facing out. The right

hand moves right, away from the left, in a series of undulating, wavy motions.

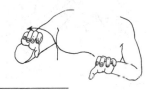

CACTUS (kak′ təs), *n.* (The sharp needles.) The outstretched fingers of the right "4" hand, palm facing in, move up the back of the left "C" hand, whose palm also faces in. The right fingers continue up until they are resting on top of the left.

CAFETERIA 1 (kaf′ ə tir′ ē ə), *n.* (The letter "C"; a restaurant.) The right "C" hand is placed at the left corner of the mouth and moves over to the right corner.

CAFETERIA 2, *n.* (Eating and pushing the tray.) The signer lifts food to the mouth twice and guides a tray from left to right.

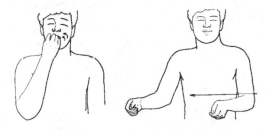

CAGE (kāj), *n.*, *v.*, CAGED, CAGING. (The bars.) Both "4" hands are held up, right facing left and left facing right. They switch positions and may move down slightly.

CAKE 1 (kāk), *n.* (The rising of the cake.) The fingertips of the right "5" hand are placed in the upturned left palm. The right rises slowly an inch or two above the left.

CAKE 2 (*loc.*), *n.* (The letter "K," the last initial of an instructor of baking at a school for the deaf.) The middle finger of the right "K" hand touches the right cheek twice. Also PIE 2.

CAKE 3, *n.* The same position is assumed as in CAKE 1 except that the right hand moves up and down several times.

CAKE 4, *n.* (The letter "C"; cutting a slice.) The little finger edge of the right "C" hand, resting on the upturned left hand, cuts an imaginary slice of cake.

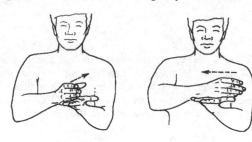

CALCULATOR (kal′ kyə lā′ tər), *n.* (The function and shape.) The left open hand, palm up, represents the keyboard. The index or middle finger of the right hand taps in numbers at random. The right thumb and index are then drawn down the left palm, outlining the shape of the calculator.

CALENDAR 1 (kal′ ən dər), *n.* (Turning the pages.) The right "C" hand, palm facing left, moves up the left palm, over the fingertips, and down the back of the hand.

CALENDAR 2, *n.* (A monthly schedule.) The sign for MONTH is made: the right index finger moves down along the inside edge of the left finger, which is pointing up. This is followed by SCHEDULE: the right "4" hand, palm against the left palm and fingers pointing up, moves down from the index finger edge to the little finger edge. The right palm next flips over so that it faces the body and moves from the base of the left palm to the left fingertips.

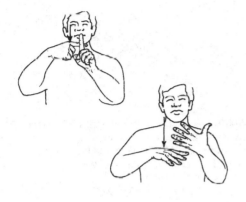

CALF 1 (kaf), *n.* (A small cow.) The sign for COW: one or both "Y" hands, palms facing forward, are positioned with thumbs touching the temples. The cupped hands, palms facing, are then brought together to indicate something small.

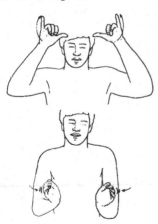

CALF 2, *n.* (Small horns.) The index fingers are wiggled slightly at the temples.

CALIFORNIA (kăl′ ə fôr′ nyə, -fôr′ nĭ ə), *n.* (Yellow earrings, *i.e.*, gold, which was discovered in California.) The earlobe is pinched, and then the sign for YELLOW is made: the "Y" hand, pivoted at the wrist, is shaken back and forth repeatedly. Also GOLD.

CALL 1 (kôl), *v.*, CALLED, CALLING. (To tap someone for attention.) The right hand is placed on the back of the left, held palm down. The right hand then moves up and in toward the body, assuming the "A" position. As an optional addition, the right hand may then assume a beckoning movement. Also SUMMON 2.

CALL 2 *n.*, *v.* (The natural sign.) The cupped right hand is held against the right cheek. The mouth is slightly open.

CALLED, *adj.* (NAME, indicating who is named.) The sign for NAME is made: the right "H" hand, palm facing left, is brought down on the left "H" hand, palm facing right. The hands, in this position, move forward a few inches. Also NAMED.

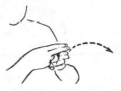

CALM 1 (käm), *adj., v.,* CALMED, CALMING. (Quiet and peace.) The open hands are crossed before the mouth, the right palm facing left, left facing right. Then both hands, held palms down, move down from the mouth, curving outward to either side of the body. Also BE QUIET 2, BE STILL, QUIET 2, SILENCE 2.

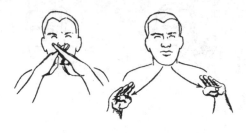

CALM 2, *adj.* (The natural sign.) The index finger is brought up against the pursed lips. Also BE QUIET 1, HUSH, NOISELESS, QUIET 1, SILENCE 1, SILENT, STILL 2.

CAMEL 1 (käm' əl), *n.* (The shape of the neck.) The two "C" hands are placed at the neck. The right hand, palm facing up, moves up and forward in a long undulating curve, as if tracing the camel's long neck.

CAMEL 2, *n.* (The two humps.) The downturned right hand describes the two humps on the camel's back.

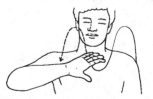

CAMERA 1 (käm' ər ə, käm' rə), *n.* (The natural sign.) The eye peers through the viewfinder of an imaginary camera, and the index finger clicks the shutter. This sign is used for a camera of the 35mm type.

CAMERA 2, *n.* (The natural sign.) The signer peers down into the viewfinder of an imaginary camera held at the waist, and the thumb clicks the shutter. This sign is used for a camera of the box type.

CAMPFIRE (kamp' fïr), *n.* (CAMP and FIRE.) Both "V" hands, fingertips touching, move down and out, describing a pyramid. This is the shape of a tent, associated with camp. The upturned wriggling fingers then move up and down alternately, describing the leaping of flames.

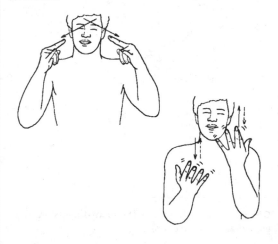

CAN 1 (kän, kən), *v.,* CANNED, CANNING. (An affirmative movement of the hands, likened to a nodding of the head, to indicate ability or power to accomplish something.) Both "A" hands, held palms down, move down in unison a short distance before the chest. Also

ABILITY, ABLE, CAPABLE, COMPETENT, COULD, FACULTY, MAY 2, POSSIBLE.

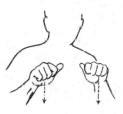

CAN 2, *n.* (Turning the cover of jar.) The right hand is laid palm down over the upturned thumb edge of the left "S" hand. In this position the right hand twists in a clockwise circle, as if turning the cover of a jar. Also CONTAINER, CANNING.

CANADA (kăn′ ə də), *n.* (Shaking the snow from the lapel of an overcoat.) The hand grasps and shakes the right lapel. Also CANADIAN.

CANCEL (kăn′ səl), *n., v.,* -CELED, -CELING. (A canceling out.) The right index finger makes a cross on the open left palm. Also ANNUL, CHECK 1, CORRECT 2, CRITICISM, CRITICIZE, FIND FAULT 1, REVOKE.

CANCER (kan′ sər), *n.* (Eating away the tissues of the body.) The right claw hand is placed on the thumb edge of the left hand and "eats" against the hand repeatedly.

CANDIDATE (kăn′ də dāt′, -dĭt), *n.* (Bringing oneself forward.) The right index finger and thumb grasp the clothing near the right shoulder (often the lapel of a suit or the collar of a dress) and tug it up and down gently several times. Sometimes one tug only is used. Also APPLY 1, OFFER 2, RUN FOR OFFICE, VOLUNTEER.

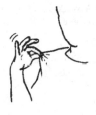

CANDLE (kăn′ dəl), *n., v.,* -DLED, -DLING. (Blowing the flame of the candle; the flickering flames.) The tip of the index finger of the right hand is placed at the lips, and then it is placed at the base of the outstretched left hand, whose palm is facing out and whose fingers are wiggling to denote the flickering of flames.

CANDY 1 (kăn′ dĭ), *n.* (Titillating to the taste.) The fingertips of the right "U" hand, palm facing the body, brush against the chin a number of times beginning at the lips. Also CUTE 1, SUGAR, SWEET.

CANDY 2, *n.* (Wiping the lips; licking the finger.) The right index finger, pointing left, is drawn across the lips from left to right.

CANE (kān), *n.* (A walking stick.) The signer mimes swinging a cane in the act of walking.

CANNING (kan′ ing), *v.* (Tightening the cover.) The signer mimes tightening the cover of a jar or can.

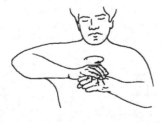

CANNON 1 (kăn′ ən), *n.* (The recoil.) The right index finger points out and slightly upward. The right arm is

jerked quickly forward and back, like the recoil of a cannon.

CANNON 2, *n.* (Describing the physical length.) The back of the right hand travels along the length of the outstretched left arm from shoulder to wrist.

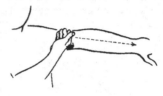

CANNOT 1 (kăn′ ŏt), *v.* (One finger encounters an unyielding quality in striking another.) The right index finger strikes the left and continues moving down. The left index finger remains in place. Also CAN'T, IMPOSSIBLE 1, UNABLE.

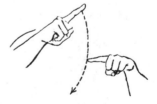

CANNOT 2, *v.* (Not able.) The sign for CAN is formed, followed by the sign for NOT: both hands, fingers together and palms facing down, are held before the body, with the right slightly above the left. They separate with a deliberate movement, the right hand moving to the right and the left moving to the left.

CANOEING (kə nōō′ ĭng), *n*. (The natural sign.) The hands, grasping an imaginary paddle, go through the motions of paddling a canoe. Also PADDLE.

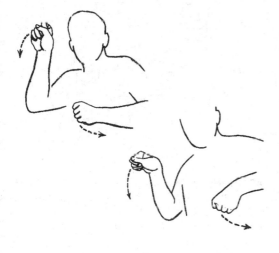

CANONIZE (kan′ ə nīz′), *v.*, -IZED, -IZING. (*eccles.*). (NAME, SAINT.) The sign for NAME: the right "H" hand, palm facing left, is brought down on the left "H" hand, palm facing right. The downturned right fist then slides forward on the upturned left palm, from base to fingertips (SAINT).

CAN'T (kănt, känt), *v*. See CANNOT 1, 2.

CANTOR (kan′ tər, -tôr), *n*. (*eccles.*). (The "C" and rhythm of music.) The right "C" hand, palm facing out, describes a continuous figure-eight movement back and forth over the upturned left arm.

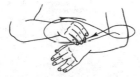

CAP (kăp), *n., v.,* CAPPED, CAPPING. (The natural sign.) The hand grasps the brim of an imaginary cap and pulls it down slightly.

CAPABLE (kā′ pə bəl), *adj*. (An affirmative movement of the hands, likened to a nodding of the head, to indicate ability or power to accomplish something.) Both "A" hands, held palm down, move down in unison a short distance before the chest. Also ABILITY, ABLE, CAN 1, COMPETENT, COULD, FACULTY, MAY 2, POSSIBLE.

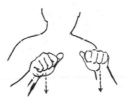

CAPACITY (kə păs′ ə tĭ), *n*. (The upper and lower limits are defined.) The right-angle hands, palms facing, are held before the body, the right above the left. They swing out 45° simultaneously, pivoted from their wrists. Also LIMIT, QUANTITY 1, RESTRICT.

CAPITAL 1 (kăp′ ə təl), *n*. (The head indicates the head or seat of government.) The right index finger, pointing toward the right temple, describes a small clockwise circle and comes to rest on the right temple. Also GOVERNMENT, ST. PAUL (MINN.)

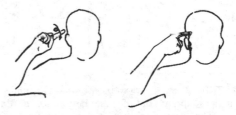

CAPITAL 2, *n*. (Slapping of paper money in the palm.) The upturned right hand, grasping some imaginary bills, is brought down into the upturned left palm a number of times. Also CURRENCY, FINANCES, FUNDS, MONEY 1.

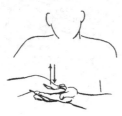

CAPITAL LETTER (lĕt′ ər), *n*. (The size.) The right index and thumb, forming a "C," are held far apart. This sign is usually made only in context; here we are discussing printing.

CAPTAIN (kăp′ tən, -tĭn), *n*. (The epaulets.) The fingertips of the downturned right "5" hand strike the right shoulder twice. Also OFFICER.

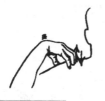

CAPTION 1 (kăp′ shən), *n*. (The quotation marks are indicated.) The curved index and middle fingers of both hands, held palms out, move slightly to either side of the body, as if drawing quotation marks in the air. Also CITE, QUOTATION, QUOTE, SO-CALLED, SUBJECT, THEME, TITLE, TOPIC.

CAPTION 2, *n*., *v*., -TIONED, -TIONING. (Language or sentences spread out on the bottom of a filmed

image.) Both "F" hands, palms out, are held together. As they separate they wriggle, pivoted by the wrists.

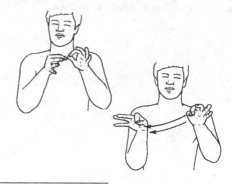

CAPTURE (kăp′ chər), *n*., *v*., -TURED, -TURING. (Grasping something and holding it down.) Both hands, palms down, quickly close into the "S" position, the right on top of the left. Also CATCH 2, GRAB, GRASP, SEIZE.

CAR (kär), *n*. (The steering wheel.) The hands grasp an imaginary steering wheel and manipulate it. Also AUTOMOBILE, DRIVE.

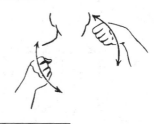

CARBURETOR (kär′ bə rā′ tər, -byə-), *n*. (Actually, the choke, a device designed to feed a fuel/oxygen mixture into an internal combustion engine, a device largely supplanted by fuel injection today.) The right or left claw hand is placed on the throat. Also CHOKE 1.

CARD (kärd), *n.* (The natural sign.) The sides of the card are outlined with the thumb and index finger of each hand. Also TICKET 1.

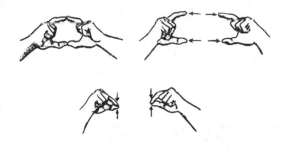

CARDINAL (kär′ də nəl) (*eccles.*), *n.* (A red bishop.) The sign for RED is made: the tip of the right index finger moves down across the lips; the "R" hand may also be used. This is followed by the sign for BISHOP 1: the ring finger of the right "S" hand is kissed. This is the sign for a Catholic bishop. The red refers to the cardinal's red hat or biretta.

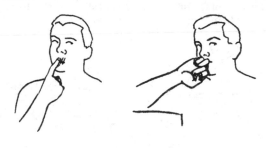

CARD PLAYING (plā′ ĭng). (The action of dealing out cards.) The signer goes through the motions of dealing out imaginary playing cards. Also CARDS, DISTRIBUTE 2, PLAYING CARDS.

CARDS (kärdz), *n. pl.* See CARD PLAYING.

CARE 1 (kâr), *n., v.,* CARED, CARING. (Slow, careful movement.) The "K" hands are crossed, the right above the left, little finger edges down. In this position they describe a small counterclockwise circle in front of the chest. Also CARE FOR, CAREFUL 1, TAKE CARE OF 3.

CARE 2, *n., v.* With the hands in the same position as in CARE 1, they are moved up and down a short distance. Also CAREFUL 2, KEEP, MAINTAIN 1, MIND 3, PRESERVE, RESERVE 2, TAKE CARE OF 2.

CAREER (kə rēr′) *n.* (Line of work.) The fingers of the right "B" hand, pointing down and held together, move forward along the index finger edge of the left "B" hand, whose palm faces right. This is followed by the sign for WORK: the right downturned fist comes down twice on the top of its left counterpart.

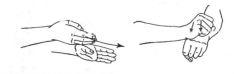

CARE FOR (fôr), *v. phrase.* See CARE 1.

CAREFUL 1 (kâr′ fəl), *adj.* See CARE 1.

CAREFUL 2, *adj.* See CARE 2.

CAREFUL 3, *adj.* (The "K" for *keep* in the sense of *keeping carefully.*) Both "K" hands are crossed, the right atop the left. The right hand moves up and down a very short distance several times, each time coming to rest on top of the left. Also BE CAREFUL, TAKE CARE OF 1.

CARELESS (kâr′ lĭs), *adj.* (The vision is sidetracked, causing one to lose sight of the object in view.) The right "V" hand, representing the vision, is held in front of the face, palm facing left. The hand, pivoted at the wrist, moves back and forth a number of times. Also HEEDLESS, RECKLESS, THOUGHTLESS.

CARPENTER (kär′ pən tər), *n.* (Manipulating a carpenter's plane.) The hands grasp and manipulate an imaginary carpenter's plane. This is followed by the sign for INDIVIDUAL: both open hands, palms facing each other, move down the sides of the body, tracing its outline to the hips. Also CABINETMAKER.

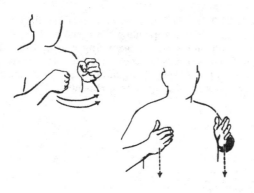

CARPET (kär′ pit), *n.* (The letter "C"; spread out over a surface.) The right "C" hand, facing left, slides over the downturned left arm from forearm to wrist.

CARRIAGE 1 (kăr′ ĭj), *n.* (Holding the carriage.) The downturned hands grasp the handlebar of an imaginary carriage and move it forward and back once or twice.

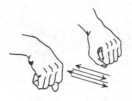

CARRIAGE 2, *n.* (The rolling wheels and the ears of the horse, defined by FINE or ELEGANT.) The index fingers of the "D" hands, pointing to each other, describe small circles in the air. They are then moved forward in unison and describe another series of circles to define the wheels of the carriage. The "H" hands, palms facing out, are then placed at the sides of the head and the index and middle fingers of both hands move back and forth to describe the movement of a horse's ears. The thumb of the right "5" hand is then thrust into the chest—an act that indicates the fineness of the ruffled bosoms of ladies and shirtfronts of gentlemen of old. Also CART, CHARIOT.

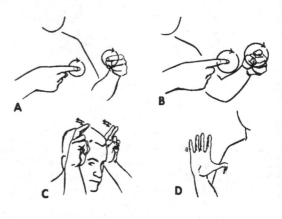

A   B

C   D

CARROT 1 (kar′ ət), *n.* (Shredding.) The right thumb vigorously shaves the outstretched index of the left "D" hand.

CARROT 2, *n.* (Biting a carrot.) The signer bites off a piece of imaginary carrot.

CARRY 1 (kăr′ ĭ), *v.,* -RIED, -RYING. (Act of conveying an object from one point to another.) The open hands are held palms up before the chest on the right side of the body. Describing an arc, they move up and forward in unison. Also CONVEY.

CARRY 2, *v.* (Carrying something over.) Both open hands, palms up, move in an arc from left to right, as if carrying something from one point to another. Also BRING, DELIVER 2, FETCH, PRODUCE 1, TRANSPORT.

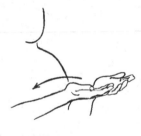

CARTOON(S) (kär tōōn′), *n.* (Funny drawings.) The sign for FUNNY is made: the index and middle fingertips brush repeatedly over the tip of the nose. The sign for DRAW then follows: the tip of the right little finger is repeatedly drawn down over the upturned left palm.

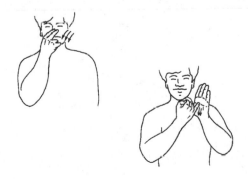

CARVE (kärv), *v.,* CARVED, CARVING. (Chipping or cutting out.) The right thumbtip repeatedly gouges out imaginary pieces of material from the palm of the left hand, held facing right. Also ENGRAVE, ETCH.

CASTLE 1 (kăs′ ol), *n.* (The buttresses and bulwarks.) Both hands, held in fists, are placed one on top of the other, arms held horizontally. The right arm then rises into the vertical position and its elbow is brought smartly down about an inch. The left arm then follows suit.

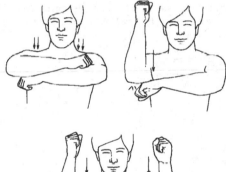

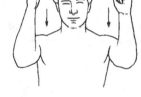

CASTLE 2, *n.* (The ramparts and towers.) Both "C" hands, held aloft and palms facing, are brought down and apart in a series of successive movements.

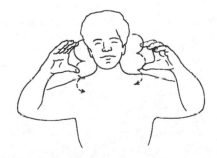

CAST OFF (kăst ôf′), *v. phrase*, CAST, CASTING. (To throw something aside.) Both "S" hands are held with palms facing at chest level and then thrown down and to the left, opening into the "5" position. Also ABANDON 1, DEPOSIT 2, DISCARD 1, FORSAKE 3, LEAVE 2, LET ALONE, NEGLECT.

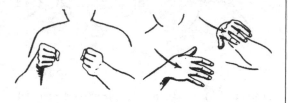

CAT (kăt), *n.* (The whiskers.) The thumbs and index fingers of both hands stroke an imaginary pair of whiskers at either side of the face. The right hand then strokes the back of the left, as if stroking the fur. This latter sign is seldom used today, however. Also, one hand may be used in place of two for the stroking of the whiskers.

CATCH 1 (kăch), *n., v.,* CAUGHT, CATCHING. (The act of catching.) Both hands quickly come together, as if catching a ball.

CATCH 2, *v.* (Grasping something and holding it down.) Both hands, palms down, quickly close into the "S" position, the right on top of the left. Also CAPTURE, GRAB, GRASP, SEIZE.

CATCH 3, *v.* (Catching a ball.) Both hands go through the motions of catching a ball.

CATCHER (kăch′ ər), *n.* (One who catches a ball.) The sign for CATCH 3 is made, followed by the sign for INDIVIDUAL: both open hands, palms facing each other, move down the sides of the body, tracing its outline to the hips.

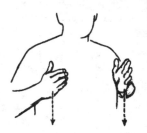

CATERPILLAR (kat′ ər pil ər), *n.* (The insect's crawling motion.) The right index finger makes a series of undulating forward motions as it crawls up the downturned left arm.

CATHOLIC (kăth′ ə lĭk, kăth′ lĭk), *adj.* (The cross.) The extended index and middle fingers make the sign of the cross before the face, moving down from the forehead and then across the face from left to right.

CAUGHT IN THE ACT 1 (kôt ĭn thĭ ăkt), *v. phrase*. (A pinning down.) The left "D" finger represents the one who is caught. The curved index and middle fingers of the right hand, palm facing down, are thrust against the left "D" finger, impaling it. Also CONTACT 2, CORNER 2.

CAUGHT IN THE ACT 2, *v. phrase*. (Impaled on a stick, as a snake's head.) The "V" fingers are thrust into the throat. Also CHOKE 2, STRANDED, STUCK 2, TRAP.

CAUSE (kôz), *n., v.*, CAUSED, CAUSING. (Rays of influence emanating from a given source.) All the right fingertips, including the thumb, are positioned on the tip of the upturned thumb of the left "A" hand. The right hand, opening into the downturned "5" position, moves forward from its initial position. Instead of its initial position on the left thumb, the right hand is frequently placed on the back of the downturned left "S" hand, moving forward as described above. Also BASIS 1, EFFECT 1, INFLUENCE 2, INTENT 2, LOGIC, PRODUCE 4, REASON 2.

CAUTION (kô′ shən), *n*. (Tapping one to draw attention to danger.) The right hand taps the back of the left several times. Also ADMONISH 1, FOREWARN, WARN.

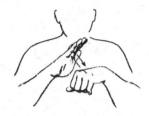

CAVE 1 (kāv), *n*. (Walking in and under a low ceiling.) With the left "C" hand downturned, the right index and middle fingers, bent over, creep under the left hand.

CAVE 2, *n*. (Entering a cave through its opening.) The left "C" hand is held palm facing forward. The right index finger makes a clockwise circle at the left "C" and enters the space between the left thumb and other fingers.

CAVE IN (kāv ĭn′), *v. phrase*, CAVED, CAVING. (A collapsing.) Both "5" hands, fingertips joined before the chest, swing down so that the fingertips face down. Also BREAKDOWN, COLLAPSE.

CAVITY (kăv′ ə tĭ), *n.* (The hole in a tooth.) The right index finger drills into a tooth. The mouth is of course held wide open. Also CARIES.

CEILING (sē′ ling), *n.* (An overhead covering.) Both hands are held palms down above the head, index fingers side by side. The arms are separated while the signer looks up.

CELEBRATE (sĕl′ ə brāt′), *v.,* -BRATED, -BRATING. (Waving of flags.) Both upright hands, grasping imaginary flags, wave them in small circles. Also CELEBRATION, CHEER, REJOICE, VICTORY 1, WIN 1.

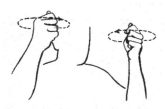

CELEBRATION (sĕl′ ə brā′ shən), *n.* See CELEBRATE.

CELERY (sel′ ər ē), *n.* (The "C"; the stalk.) The thumbtip of the right "C" hand is placed on the tip of the left upturned index finger.

CELLAR (sel′ ər), *n.* (The "C" underneath.) The right "C" hand, palm facing left, makes a series of counterclockwise circles under the open downturned left hand.

CELSIUS (sel′ sē əs), *n.* (The letter "C"; temperature.) The thumb of the right "C" hand moves up and down the upturned left index finger.

CEMETERY (sĕm′ ə tĕr′ ĭ), *n.* (The mound of a grave.) The downturned open hands, slightly cupped, are held side by side. They describe an arc as they are drawn in toward the body. Also BURY, GRAVE 1.

CENSUS (sen′ səs), *n.* (Counting people.) The fingertips of the right "F" hand move straight up the palm of the left, from heel to tips of fingers, as if adding up a column of figures. The sign for PEOPLE is then made: both "P" hands, palms down, swing in toward the body in alternate and repeated counterclockwise circles.

CENT (sĕnt), *n.* (The Lincoln head.) The right index finger touches the right temple and moves up and away quickly. This is one cent. For two cents, the "2" hand is used, etc. Also CENTS, PENNY.

CENTER (sĕnt′ ər), *n., v.,* -TERED, -TERING. (The natural sign.) The downturned right fingers describe a small clockwise circle and come to rest in the center of the upturned left palm. Also CENTRAL, MIDDLE.

CENTIMETER (sen′ tə mē tər), *n.* (The "C" hands; the distance between.) Both "C" hands, palms out, are held with thumbtips touching. The hands move straight apart.

CENTRAL (sĕn′ trəl), *adj.* See CENTER.

CENTS, *n. pl.* See CENT.

CEREAL (sēr′ ē əl), *n.* (Emphasizing the chewing.) The right index finger, wriggling, moves across the mouth from right to left.

CERTAIN (sûr′ tən), *adj.* (Coming forth directly from the lips; true.) The index finger of the right "D" hand, palm facing left, is placed against the lips. It moves up an inch or two and then describes a small arc forward and away from the lips. Also ABSOLUTE, ABSOLUTELY, ACTUAL, ACTUALLY, AUTHENTIC, CERTAINLY, FAITHFUL 3, FIDELITY, FRANKLY, GENUINE, INDEED, POSITIVE 1, POSITIVELY, REAL, REALLY, SINCERE 2, SURE, SURELY, TRUE, TRULY, TRUTH, VALID, VERILY.

CERTAINLY (sûr′ tən lĭ), *adv.* See CERTAIN.

CERTIFICATE (sər tif′ i kit), *n.* (The "C.") Both "C" hands face each other. The thumbtips touch each other twice.) Also CREDENTIAL.

CESAREAN SECTION (si zâr′ ē ən sek′ shən), *n.* (Cutting out the baby.) The sign for PREGNANT 1 is made: one or both open hands are placed on the stomach and move forward an inch or two to indicate the swollen belly. The right thumb is then drawn across the stomach as if making an incision.

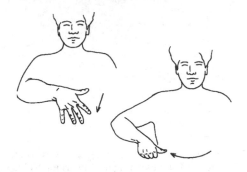

CHAIN (chān), *n.* (The links.) The thumbs and index fingers of both hands interlock, separate, reverse their relative positions, and interlock again.

CHAIR 1 (châr), *n.* (The act of sitting.) The extended right index and middle fingers are draped across the back of the same two fingers of the downturned left hand. The hands then move straight downward a short distance. Also BE SEATED, SEAT, SIT 1.

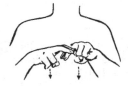

CHAIR 2, *n.* (Act of sitting down; the legs of the chair.) Both hands, palms down, are held before the chest, and they move down a short distance in unison.

The downturned index fingers are then thrust downward a few inches, moved in toward the body, and thrust downward once again to represent the four legs of the chair. Also SIT 2.

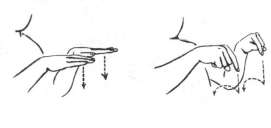

CHAIR 3, *n.* (A rocking chair.) The "L" hands, palms facing each other and about two feet apart, are held before the chest. They arc up and down toward the shoulders a number of times. The body is sometimes rocked back and forth in time with the movement of the hands. Also ROCKING CHAIR 1.

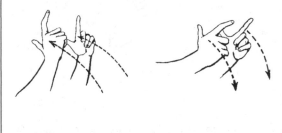

CHALLENGE (chăl′ ĭnj), *n., v.,* -LENGED, -LENGING. (Two individuals pitted against each other.) The hands are held in the "A" position, thumbs pointing straight up, palms facing the body. They come together forcefully, moving down a bit as they do, and the knuckles of one hand strike those of the other. Also GAME 1, OPPORTUNITY 2, VERSUS.

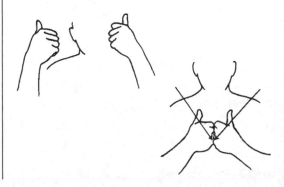

CHAMPAGNE (sham pān′), *n.* (Popping the cork.) The thumb flicks up from its position hidden in the closed hand.

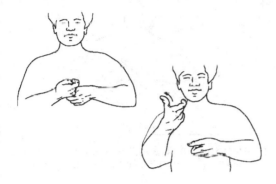

CHAMPION (chăm′ pĭ ən) (*sports*), *n.* (The head is crowned.) The upturned left index finger represents the victorious individual. The downturned "5" hand, fingers curved, is brought down on the left index finger as if draping it with a crown. Also CROWNED.

CHANCE 1 (chăns, chäns), *n., v.,* CHANCED, CHANCING, *adj.* (A befalling.) Both "D" hands, index fingers pointing away from the body, are simultaneously pivoted over so that the palms face down. Also ACCIDENT, BEFALL, COINCIDE 1, COINCIDENCE, EVENT, HAPPEN 1, INCIDENT, OCCUR, OPPORTUNITY 4.

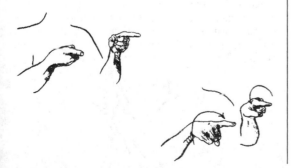

CHANCE 2, *n.* (Grabbing an opportunity.) The right cupped hand grabs an imaginary object from the upturned open left hand.

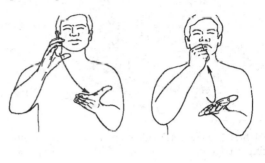

CHANCE 3, *n.* (Trying to push through to an opportunity.) Both "C" hands, palms facing each other, move forward simultaneously, palms coming around to face forward.

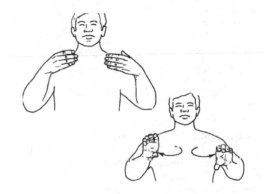

CHANGE 1 (chānj), *v.,* CHANGED, CHANGING, *n.* (The position of the hands is altered.) Both "A" hands, thumbs up, are held before the chest, several inches apart. The left hand is pivoted over so that its thumb points to the right. Simultaneously, the right hand is moved up and over the left, describing a small arc, with its thumb pointing to the left. Also ADJUST, ALTER, ALTERATION, CONVERT, MODIFY, REVERSE 2, TRANSFER 1.

CHANGE 2, *n., v.* The "A" hands are held before the chest, right behind the left. The right hand swings under the left.

CHANGE 3, *n., v.* (Dividing up or sharing.) The little finger edge of the open right "5" hand, held perpendicular to the index finger edge of the left, sweeps back and forth. This sign is used to mean changing money. Some signers use the right index finger over the left index finger, with the same orientation and motion as described before.

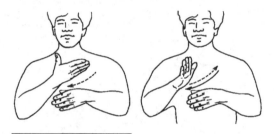

CHANGEABLE (chăn′ jə bəl), *adj.* (Changing again and again.) The "5" hands, fingers curved and palms facing, swing in unison in alternate clockwise and counterclockwise directions, with the left and right hands alternating in front of each other. Also WISHY-WASHY.

CHAPTER (chăp′ tər), *n.* (A section of a page.) The palm of the left "C" hand faces right, representing a page. The fingertips of the right "C" hand, representing a section of the page, move straight down against the left palm.

CHARACTER 1 (kăr′ ĭk tər), *n.* (The heart is defined by the letter "C.") The right "C" hand, palm facing left, describes a circle against the heart.

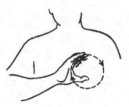

CHARACTER 2, *n.* The "C" is again placed on the heart, and then the index fingers outline the heart itself.

CHARACTER 3, *n.* (The letter "C"; the face or appearance of something.) The right "C" hand, held palm facing left, executes a single counterclockwise circle, coming to rest against the left palm, which is facing forward.

CHARGE 1 (chärj), *v.,* CHARGED, CHARGING, *n.* (Nicking into one.) The knuckle of the right "X" finger is nicked against the palm of the left hand, held in the "5" position, palm facing right. Also ADMISSION 2, COST, DUTY 2, EXCISE, EXPENSE, FEE, FINE 2, IMPOST, PENALTY 3, PRICE 2, TAX 1, TAXATION 1, TOLL.

CHARGE 2, *v., n.* (A bank or charge account—act of signing the name on paper.) The index finger and thumb of the right hand go through the natural motion of scribbling across the left palm. Then the fingers of the right "H" hand, palm facing down, are thrust against the left palm, as if placing the name on a piece of paper. As an alternate, the closed fingers of the right hand may be thrust into the left palm. Also ACCOUNT.

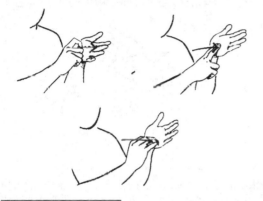

CHASE 1 (chās), *v.,* CHASED, CHASING. (The natural sign.) The "A" hands are held in front of the body, with the thumbs facing forward, the right palm facing left, and the left palm facing right. The left hand is held slightly ahead of the right; it then moves forward in a straight line while the right hand follows after, executing a circular motion or swerving back and forth, as if in pursuit. Also PURSUE.

CHASE 2 (*voc.*), *n.* (The printer's chase outlined.) The downturned index finger and thumb of each hand outline the square shape of a frame. Also FRAME.

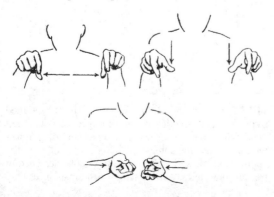

CHAT 1 (chăt), *n., v.,* CHATTED, CHATTING. (Words tossed back and forth.) The open hands are held side by side with palms up, fingers pointing forward and slightly curved. In this position the hands swing back and forth from side to side before the chest. Also CONVERSATION 2.

CHAT 2, *n., v.* (Moving the hands as in using sign language.) Both "C" hands, palms facing out, move alternately up and down.

CHAT 3, *n., v.* (A modified version of CHAT 2.) Both hands are held in the "C" position, palms facing out, but only the right hand moves up and down.

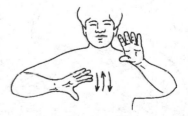

CHAUFFEUR (shō′ fər, shō fûr′), *n., v.,* -FEURED, -FEURING. (A driver with epaulets, to signify a uniform.) One or both claw hands, palm down, touches the shoulder twice. Both hands then grasp an imaginary steering wheel and maneuver it right and left.

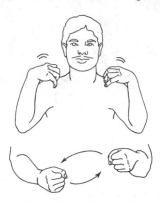

CHEAP 1 (chēp), *adj.* (A small amount of money.) The sign for MONEY is made: the upturned right hand, grasping some imaginary bills, is brought down into the upturned left palm a number of times. The downturned cupped right hand is then positioned over the upturned cupped left hand. The right hand descends a short distance but does not touch the left. Also INEXPENSIVE.

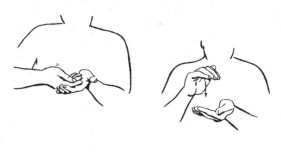

CHEAP 2 (*colloq.*), *adj.* (Something easily moved, therefore of no consequence.) The right fingertips slap the little finger edge of the upturned left hand.

CHEAT 1 (chēt), *v.,* CHEATED, CHEATING. (Underhandedness.) The right hand, palm down, is held with index and little fingers pointing out. The left hand, in a similar position, is held above the right. The right hand moves forward repeatedly, each time emerging briefly from under the left hand. The positions may be reversed, with the left hand doing the movement, or both hands can move simultaneously. Also DECEIT, DECEIVE, DECEPTION, DEFRAUD, FRAUD, FRAUDULENT 1.

CHEAT 2, *v.* (Removing.) The right "A" hand, resting in the palm of the left "5" hand, moves slightly up and away, describing a small arc. It is then cast downward, opening into the "5" position, palm down, as if removing something from the left hand and casting it down. Also ABOLISH 2, ABSENCE 2, ABSENT 2, ABSTAIN, DEDUCT, DEFICIENCY, DELETE 1, LESS 2, MINUS 3, OUT 2, REMOVE 1, SUBTRACT, SUBTRACTION, TAKE AWAY FROM, WITHDRAW 2.

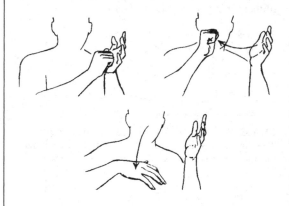

CHEAT 3, *v., n. sl.* (Riding a pony.) The downturned right "V" hand straddles the index finger edge of the left hand, whose palm faces right. An up-down riding movement is used. This somewhat archaic sign refers to the "pony"—small, old, softcover study books designed to prepare one quickly for a school examination, usually high school or college undergraduate. These books seldom helped and often confused or hurt.

CHECK 1 (chĕk), v., CHECKED, CHECKING. (A canceling out.) The right index finger makes a cross on the open left palm. Also ANNUL, CANCEL, CORRECT 2, CRITICISM, CRITICIZE, FIND FAULT 1, REVOKE.

CHECK 2, v. (Obstruct, block.) The left hand, fingers together and palm flat, is held before the body, facing somewhat down. The little finger side of the right hand, held with palm flat, makes one or several up-down chopping motions against the left hand, between its thumb and index finger. Also ANNOY 1, ANNOYANCE 1, BLOCK, BOTHER 1, COME BETWEEN, DISRUPT, DISTURB, HINDER, HINDRANCE, IMPEDE, INTERCEPT, INTERFERE, INTERFERENCE, INTERFERE WITH, INTERRUPT, MEDDLE 1, OBSTACLE, OBSTRUCT, PREVENT, PREVENTION.

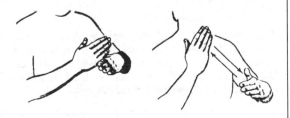

CHECK 3, n. (A bank check.) The sign for CARD is made: the sides of the card are outlined with the thumb and index finger of each hand. This is followed by the sign for MONEY: the back of the right hand,

palm up and fingers touching the thumb, is placed in the upturned left hand.

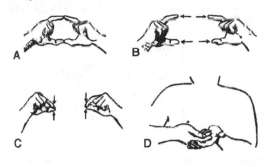

CHECK 4, n. (A baggage check or ticket.) The sign for CARD is made: the sides of the card are outlined with the thumb and index finger of each hand. This is followed by the sign for TICKET: the middle knuckles of the second and third fingers of the right hand squeeze the outer edge of the left palm, as a conductor's ticket punch. Also TICKET 2.

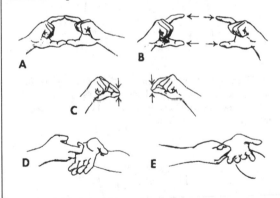

CHECKERS (chek' ərz), n. (The movement of the pieces.) The curved thumb plus index and middle fingers of the downturned right hand grasp an imaginary checker piece and move it in a series of jumps from one place to another.

CHEER (chĭr), *n.* (Waving of flags.) Both upright hands, grasping imaginary flags, wave them in small circles. Also CELEBRATE, CELEBRATION, REJOICE, VICTORY 1, WIN 1.

CHEERFUL (chĭr′ fəl), *adj.* (A crinkling up of the face.) Both hands, in the "5" position, palms facing back, are placed on either side of the face. The fingers wiggle back and forth, while a pleasant, happy expression is worn. Also AMIABLE, CORDIAL, FRIENDLY, JOLLY, PLEASANT.

CHEESE (chēz), *n.* (The pressing of cheese.) The base of the downturned right hand is pressed against the base of the upturned left hand, and the two rotate back and forth against each other.

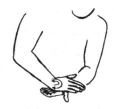

CHEMISTRY 1 (kĕm′ ĭs trĭ), *n.* (Pouring alternately from test tubes.) The upright thumbs of both "A" hands swing over alternately, as if pouring out the contents of a pair of test tubes. Also SCIENCE 2.

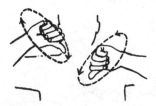

CHEMISTRY 2, *n.* (The letter "C"; pouring from test tubes.) Both "C" hands mime alternately pouring out the contents of laboratory test tubes.

CHERRY 1 (cher′ ē), *n.* (Loosening a cherry from a branch.) The fingertips of the right hand grasp the end of the left little finger and twist back and forth as if loosening a cherry from a branch. Also BERRY, VIRGIN 3.

CHERRY 2, *n.* (Flinging a pit from the mouth.) The signer, using the index and thumb, mimes taking a cherry pit from the mouth and flinging it down.

CHEWING GUM (chōō′ ing gum), *n.* (The chewing motion.) The thumb of the right "A" hand, held against the right cheek, swivels forward and back several times. Alternatively, the tips of the right "V" hand are placed at the right cheek and bend in and out. Also GUM.

CHICAGO (shĭ kô′ gō, -kä′ -), *n.* (The letter "C.") The right "C" hand, palm facing out, describes an inverted "S" curve, moving down as it does.

CHICK (chĭk), *n.* (A small chicken.) The sign for CHICKEN is made: the right index and thumb, pointing forward, open and close at the lips. The cupped hands are then brought together as if holding a small object.

CHICKEN (chĭk′ ən, -ĭn), *n.* (The bill and the scratching.) The right index finger and thumb open and close as they are held pointing out from the mouth. (This is the root sign for any kind of bird.) The right "X" finger then scratches against the upturned left palm, as it scratching for food. The scratching is sometimes omitted. Also FOWL, HEN.

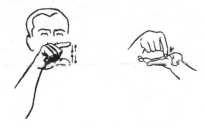

CHILD (chīld), *n.* (The child's height.) The downturned right palm is extended before the body as if resting on a child's head.

CHILDREN (chĭl′ drən), *n.* (Indicating different heights of children; patting the children on their heads.) The downturned right palm, held before the body, executes a series of movements from left to right, as if patting a number of children on their heads.

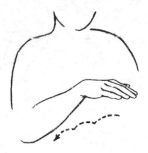

CHILE (chil′ ē), *n.* The right middle finger flicks an imaginary speck of dust from the left shoulder. A native sign.

CHILL (chĭl), *n.* (Chattering teeth.) Both "V" hands, fingers curved and the right hand held above the left, move very rapidly back and forth, in opposite directions each time, imitating the chattering of teeth. Also SHIVER 2.

CHILLY (chĭl′ ĭ), *adj.* (The trembling from cold.) Both "S" hands, palms facing, are placed at the sides of the body. In this position the arms and hands shiver. Also COLD 1, FRIGID, SHIVER 1, WINTER 1.

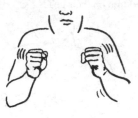

CHIMNEY (chim′ nē), *n.* (The shape.) The open hands, palms facing each other, are held a few inches apart. They move up together a short distance, come together an inch or two, and then continue their upward movement. Also SMOKESTACK.

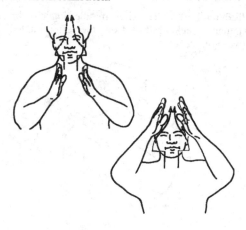

CHIN (chĭn), *n.* The chin is touched with the extended index finger.

CHINA 1 (chī′ nə), *n.* (Slanting eyes.) The index fingers draw back the corners of the eyes, causing them to slant. One hand is often used. In either case, this sign, formerly very popular and widely used, is today considered offensive and derogatory. Also CHINESE.

CHINA 2, *n.* (Same as above, but initialed with "C.") The thumb of the "C" hand is placed at the corner of the eye. Also derogatory and offensive.

CHINA 3, *n.* (Tracing the buttons on the Mao uniform.) The right "G" hand, palm facing the upper chest, moves across from left to right, then down to the right side of the chest. This sign is used by native Chinese. It is slowly replacing other signs for CHINA.

CHINA 4, *n.* (The finger touches a brittle substance.) The index finger is brought up to touch the exposed front teeth. Also BONE, DISH, GLASS 1, PLATE, PORCELAIN.

CHINESE (chī nēz′, -nēs′), *n., adj.* See CHINA 1.

CHIP (chip), *n. Computer term.* (A very small item.) Both index fingers and thumbs outline a tiny square.

CHOCOLATE (chôk′ ə lĭt, chŏk′-, chôk′ lĭt, chŏk′-), *n., adj.* The thumb of the right "C" hand, resting against the back of the downturned left "S" hand, makes a series of small counterclockwise circles.

CHOICE (chois), *n.* (Making a choice.) The left "V" hand faces the body. The right thumb and index finger close first over the left index fingertip and then over the left middle fingertip. Also EITHER 2.

CHOKE 1 (chōk), *v.* CHOKED, CHOKING. (Catching one by the throat.) The right hand makes a natural movement of grabbing the throat. Also STUCK 1.

CHOKE 2, *v., n.* (Impaled on a stick, as a snake's head.) The "V" fingers are thrust into the throat. Also CAUGHT IN THE ACT 2, STRANDED, STUCK 2, TRAP.

CHOOSE 1 (chōōz), *v.,* CHOSE, CHOSEN, CHOOSING. (Taking unto oneself.) The right hand, palm out, is extended before the chest, index finger and thumb in an open position, the other fingers separated and pointing up. The hand is drawn in toward the chest, and the index and thumb close at the same time, indicating something taken to oneself. Also ADOPT, APPOINT, SELECT 2, TAKE.

CHOOSE 2, *v.* (The natural motion of selecting something from the hand.) The thumb and index fingers of the outstretched right hand grasp an imaginary object on the upturned left palm. The right hand then moves straight up. Also DISCOVER, FIND, PICK 1, SELECT 1.

CHOREOGRAPHER (kôr ē og′ rə fer), *n.* (DANCE and TEACHER.) The sign for DANCE: the index and middle fingers of the right hand execute a rhythmic back-and-forth movement against the upturned left hand. Next, the sign for TEACH: the fingertips of each hand are placed at the temples; they then swing out and open into the "5" position. The sign for INDIVIDUAL 1 then follows.

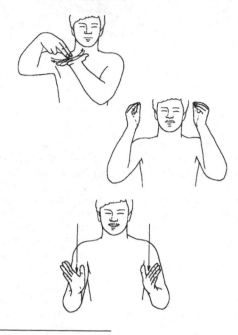

CHRIST (krīst) (*eccles.*), *n.* The right "C" hand is placed against the left shoulder and slides down across the chest to the right hip. The movement from shoulder to hip outlines the band worn across the chest by royalty.

CHRISTIAN (krĭs′ chən), *n., adj.* (An individual who follows Jesus.) The sign for JESUS is made: both "5" hands are used; the left middle finger touches the right palm, and then the right middle finger touches the left palm. This is followed by the sign for INDIVIDUAL: both open hands, palms facing each other, move down the sides of the body, tracing its outline to the hips. Other ways to make this sign involve the signs for JESUS, BELIEVER, FOLLOWER, or FRIEND. Another way is to make the signs for CHRIST and INDIVIDUAL.

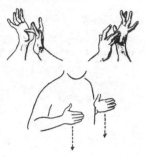

CHRISTMAS 1 (krĭs′ məs), *n.* (The shape of the wreath.) The right "C" hand, palm facing out, describes an arc from left to right. Also WREATH.

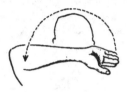

CHRISTMAS 2, *n.* (Jesus's birthday.) The sign for JESUS is made. This is followed by the sign for BIRTHDAY: the sign for BIRTH, 1, 2, or 3 is made, followed by the sign for DAY, in which the right "D" hand, pointing straight up, elbow resting on the down-turned left hand, moves down to a horizontal position, describing the path of the sun across the sky, and comes to a rest atop the left arm.

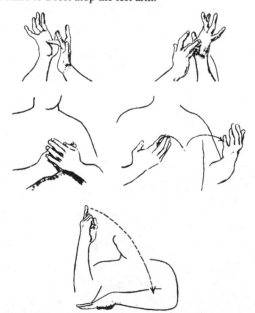

CHURCH 1 (chûrch), *n.* (The letter "C," set up on a firm foundation, as a building.) The base of the thumb of the right "C" hand is brought down to rest on the back of the downturned open left hand. The action may be repeated twice. Also CHAPEL.

CHURCH 2, *n.* ("Sunday house.") The fingertips of both hands are placed together to indicate the sloping roof of a house. The sign for SUNDAY is then made: the "5" hands, held side by side, palms out before the body, move straight down a short distance. They may also move slightly out as they move down.

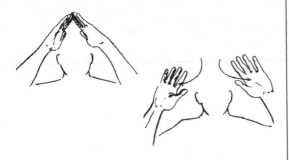

CIGAR 1 (sĭ gär′), *n.* (The shape.) The right hand, in the "1" position, is placed with the base of the thumb against the lips. The extended index finger indicates the cigar.

CIGAR 2, *n.* (The shape.) The right hand, in a grasping position and palm facing left, moves forward from the slightly open mouth, closing into the "S" position.

CIGARETTE (sĭg′ ə rĕt′, sĭg′ ə rĕt′), *n.* (The dimensions of the cigarette.) The index and little fingers of the right hand, palm facing down, are placed on the left index finger so that the right index finger rests on the knuckle of the left index finger and the right little finger rests on the tip of the left index finger.

CIRCLE 1 (sûr′ kəl), *n., v.,* -CLED, -CLING. (The circle is described.) The index finger, pointing down or out, describes a circle. Also ROUND 2.

CIRCLE 2, *n., v.* (A grouping together.) Both "C" hands, palms facing, are held a few inches apart at chest height. They are swung around in unison so that the palms now face the body. Also ASSOCIATION, AUDIENCE 1, CASTE, CLASS, CLASSED 1, CLUB, COMPANY, FAMILY 2, GANG, GROUP 1, JOIN 2, ORGANIZATION 1.

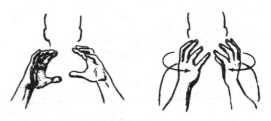

CIRCUMCISION 1 (sûr′ kəm sizh en), *n.* (Cutting the foreskin.) The tip of the right thumb makes a clockwise circular movement around the tip of the left thumb.

CIRCUMCISION 2, *n.* (A variant of CIRCUMCISION 1.) The fingertips of the right hand grasp the tip of the left index and pivot in a clockwise manner.

CIRCUS 1 (sûr′ kəs), *n.* (The shape of the tent.) The "V" hands, fingers touching, move apart and down in a series of arcs.

CIRCUS 2, *n.* (The circus ring.) The right downturned curved "V" hand makes a counterclockwise circle over the back of the downturned left open hand.

CITY (sĭt′ ĭ), *n.* (A collection of rooftops.) The fingertips of both hands are joined, the hands and arms forming a pyramid. The fingertips separate and rejoin a number of times. Both arms may move a bit from left to right each time the fingertips separate and rejoin. Also COMMUNITY 2, TOWN.

CIVILIZATION (siv ə lə zā′ shən), *n.* (Around the world with the letter "C.") The right "C" hand makes a circle around the left fist.

CLAP 1 (klăp), *v.,* CLAPPED, CLAPPING, *n.* (Good words coming from the mouth; clapping hands.) The fingertips of the right hand, palm flat and facing the body, are brought up to the lips so that they touch (part of the sign for GOOD, *q.v.*). The hands are then clapped together several times. Also ACCLAIM 2, APPLAUD, APPLAUSE, APPROBATION, APPROVAL, APPROVE, COMMEND, CONGRATULATE 1, CONGRATULATIONS 1, PRAISE.

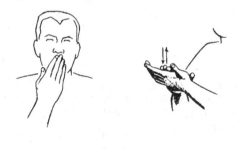

CLAP 2, *n., sl.* (A slang term for GONORRHEA: the penis is infected, *i.e.,* covered with the disease.) The right claw hand is brought down on the tip of the left index. Although gender-specific here, this sign may also be used for female gonorrhea. Also GONORRHEA.

CLASH (klash) *n., v.,* CLASHED, CLASHING. (A confrontation.) Both elongated "O" or "A" hands, palms facing, are brought smartly together, opening into "5"s, palms touching.

CLASS (klăs, kläs), *n.* (A grouping together.) Both "C" hands, palms facing, are held a few inches apart at chest height. They are swung around in unison so that the palms now face the body. Also ASSOCIATION, AUDIENCE 1, CASTE, CIRCLE 2, CLASSED 1, CLUB, COMPANY, FAMILY 2, GANG, GROUP 1, JOIN 2, ORGANIZATION 1.

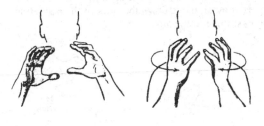

CLASSED 1, *v.* See CLASS.

CLASSED 2, *v.* (Placing things in order.) The hands, palms facing, fingers together and pointing away from the body, are positioned at the left side and held about a foot apart. With a slight up-down motion, as if describing waves, the hands travel in unison from left to right. Also ARRANGE, ARRANGEMENT, DEVISE 1, ORDER 3, PLAN 1, POLICY 1, PREPARE 1, PROGRAM 1, PROVIDE 1, PUT IN ORDER, READY 1, SCHEME, SYSTEM.

CLAWS (klôz), *n.* (Indicating the claws.) The open left hand is held palm down. The index finger and thumb of the right hand grasp each fingertip in turn, starting with the left index, and move off a short distance, indicating the extended fingertips or claws.

CLEAN 1 (klēn), *adj.* (Everything is wiped off the hand, to emphasize an uncluttered or clean condition.) The right hand slowly wipes the upturned left palm, from wrist to fingertips. Also IMMACULATE, NEAT, NICE, PLAIN 2, PURE 1, PURITY, SIMPLE 2.

CLEAN 2, *v.,* CLEANED, CLEANING. (Rubbing the clothes.) The knuckles of the "A" hands rub against one another in circles. Also WASH 1.

CLEANSER (klenz′ ər), *n.* (The powder and the rubbing.) The signer mimes sprinkling powder into the left palm. The right hand then rubs vigorously back and forth against the left palm.

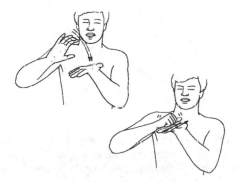

CLEAR (klĭr), *adj*. (Rays of light clearing the way.) Both hands are held at chest height, palms out, all fingertips together. They open into the "5" position in unison, the right hand moving toward the right and the left toward the left. The palms of both hands remain facing out. Also BRIGHT 1, BRILLIANCE 1, BRILLIANT 2, EXPLICIT 2, OBVIOUS, PLAIN 1.

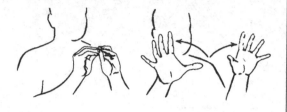

CLERC, LAURENT, *n*. An early educator of French Deaf people, who became America's first Deaf teacher of Deaf pupils. The extended right index and middle fingers sweep back once or twice against the lower right cheek. Clerc, as a very young child, suffered a fall that left a scar on his face.

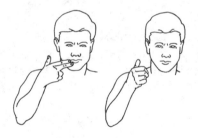

CLEVER 1 (klĕv′ ər), *adj*. (The mind is bright.) The middle finger is placed at the forehead, and then the hand, with an outward flick, turns around so that the palm faces outward. This indicates a brightness flowing from the mind. Also BRIGHT 3, BRILLIANT 1, INTELLIGENT, SMART.

CLEVER 2, *adj*. (Modification of CLEVER 1.) The right "5" hand, palm facing the signer, is placed with the tip of the middle finger touching the forehead. The hand swings quickly out and around, moving up an inch or two as it does so. Also SHARP 3.

CLIENT 1 (klī′ ənt), *n*. (One who is advised.) The sign for ADVICE is reversed: the closed fingertips of the right hand rest on top of the downturned left hand; the right hand is brought in toward the chest, opening into the downturned "5" position. This is followed by the sign for INDIVIDUAL: both open hands, palms facing each other, move down the sides of the body, tracing its outline to the hips.

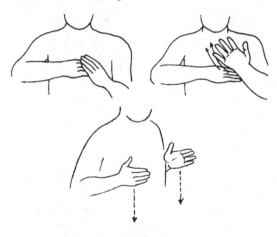

CLIENT 2, *n*. (The letter "C.") The "C" hands move down the sides of the body, as in INDIVIDUAL 1, *q.v.*

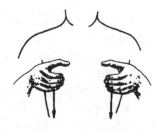

CLIMB 1 (klīm), *v.*, CLIMBED, CLIMBING, *n.* (One hand over the other.) One hand is lifted above the other, as if climbing a pole or tree.

CLIMB 2, *v.*, *n.* (Rising.) The right open hand, palm up, moves slowly up. Also ASCEND, LADDER.

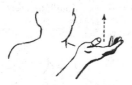

CLIMB 3, *v.* (Climbing up a ladder.) The left "V" hand, palm facing out, serves as the ladder. The right index and middle fingers walk up along the back of the left hand, starting at the wrist.

CLINIC (klin′ ik), *n.* (The "C"; describing a red cross on the sleeve.) The right "C" hand describes a cross on the upper left sleeve.

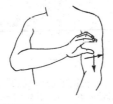

CLOCK 1 (klŏk), *n.* (Time by the clock, indicated by the ticking of the clock or watch.) The curved right index finger taps the back of the left wrist several times. Also TIME 1, WATCH 3.

CLOCK 2, *n.* (A timepiece on the wall.) The signer taps the top of the wrist, indicating a wristwatch. The index fingers and thumbs are then used to form a pair of "C"s, and an imaginary clock is held up, as if hanging it on a wall or placing it on a shelf.

CLOSE 1 (*adj.*, *adv.* klōs; *v.* klōz), CLOSED, CLOSING. (The act of closing.) Both "B" hands, held palms out before the body, come together with some force. Also SHUT.

CLOSE (TO) 2, *adj.* (One hand is near the other.) The left hand, cupped, fingers together, is held before the chest, palm facing the body. The right hand, also cupped, fingers together, moves a very short distance back and forth as it is held in front of the left. Also ADJACENT, BESIDE, BY 1, NEAR 1, NEIGHBOR, NEIGHBORHOOD, VICINITY.

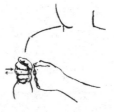

CLOSE EYES (klōs' īz), *v.* (The action.) One hand, held at the eyes in the modified "C" position, with thumb and index finger forming the letter "C," closes so that the index fingers and thumbs come together. The eyes close simultaneously.

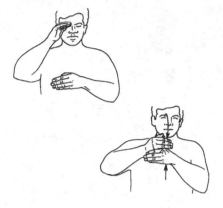

CLOSET 1 (klŏz' ĭt), *n., v.,* -ETED, -ETING. The extended index and middle fingers of the right hand strike across the back and then the front of the same two fingers of the left hand, which is held with palm facing the chest.

CLOSET 2, *n.* (The hangers.) The right curved index finger is repeatedly hung over the extended left index finger, starting at the lower knuckle and moving successively to the fingertip. Also HANGER 1.

CLOTH (klôth), *n.* (Plucking the fabric.) The right index and middle fingers and thumb pluck the fabric covering the chest.

CLOTHES (klōz, klōthz), *n. pl.* (Draping the clothes on the body.) With fingertips resting on the chest, both hands move down simultaneously. The action is repeated. Also CLOTHING, DRESS, FROCK, GARMENT, GOWN, SHIRT, SUIT, WEAR 1.

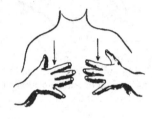

CLOTHESPIN 1 (klōz' pĭn', klōthz'-), *n.* The index and thumb of the right hand squeeze the left index finger, first at the knuckle and then at the tip, indicating the position of the clothespin on a line.

CLOTHESPIN 2, *n.* (The clipping.) The thumb, index, and middle fingers of the downturned right hand clamp down twice on the index finger edge of the left hand. Instead of the clamping, they may slide down.

CLOTHING (klō′ thĭng), *n.* See CLOTHES.

CLOUD(S) (kloud), *n.* (Black objects gathering over the head.) The sign for BLACK is made: the right index finger is drawn over the right eyebrow from left to right. Both open hands are then rotated alternately before the forehead, outlining the shape of the clouds.

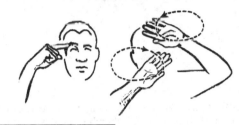

CLOWN (kloun), *n.* (The big nose.) The fingertips of the right claw hand are placed over the nose.

CLUB (klŭb), *n.* (A grouping together.) Both "C" hands, palms facing, are held a few inches apart at chest height. They are swung around in unison so that the palms now face the body. Also ASSOCIATION, AUDIENCE 1, CASTE, CIRCLE 2, CLASS, CLASSED 1, COMPANY, FAMILY 2, GANG, GROUP 1, JOIN 2, ORGANIZATION 1.

CLUMSINESS (klŭm′ zĭ nĭs), *n.* (Clumsy in gait; all thumbs.) The "3" hands, palms down, move alternately up and down before the body. Also AWKWARD, AWKWARDNESS, CLUMSY 1, GREEN 2, GREENHORN 2, NAIVE.

CLUMSY 1 (klŭm′ zĭ), *adj.* See CLUMSINESS.

CLUMSY 2 (*colloq.*), *adj.* (The thickness of the skull is indicated to stress intellectual density.) With the thumb of the right "C" hand grasped by the closed left hand, the right hand is swung in toward the body, describing a small arc as it moves. The space between the curved right fingers and the closed left hand indicates the thickness of the skull. Also DUMB 2, MORON, STUPID 2, THICK-SKULLED, UNSKILLED.

COAT (kōt), *n.* (The lapels are outlined.) The tips of the "A" thumbs outline the lapels of the coat. Also CLOAK, OVERCOAT.

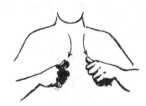

COAX (kōks), *v.,* COAXED, COAXING. (Shaking someone to implant one's will into another.) Both "A" hands, palms facing, are held before the chest, the left slightly in front of the right. In this position the hands move back and forth a short distance. Also CONVINCE, INDUCE, PERSUADE, PERSUASION, PROD, URGE 2.

COCA-COLA (kō′ kə kō′ lə) (*colloq.*) (A shot in the arm.) The right index finger is thrust into the left upper arm and the thumb wiggles back and forth a number of times, as if implanting a shot in the arm. Also COKE, DOPE, INOCULATE, MORPHINE, NARCOTICS.

COCAINE 1 (kō kān′), *n*. (The powder is pushed into the nostrils.) The right thumbtip is pressed up against each nostril.

COCAINE 2, *n*. (Inhaling the powder.) The powder is sniffed up through an imaginary straw from the upturned left palm.

COCHLEAR IMPLANT (kok′ le ər im plant), *n*. (The implant's position behind the ear.) The curved right thumb, index, and middle fingers touch the head at a position behind the right ear.

COCONUT (kō′ kə nut′, -nət), *n*. (Shaking to make sure it is full.) The signer mimes shaking a coconut near the ear.

COCOON (kə kōōn′), *n*. (Covering the contents of the cocoon.) The tip of the left thumb protrudes from the tightly cupped right hand.

COERCE 1 (kō ûrs′), *v.,* -ERCED, -ERCING. (Forcing the head to bow.) The right "C" hand pushes down on an imaginary neck. Also COERCION 1, COMPEL 1, FORCE 1, IMPEL 1.

COERCE 2, *v.* (Pushing something forward.) The open right hand is held palm down at chin level, fingers pointing left. From this position the hand turns to point forward and moves forcefully forward and away from the body, as if pushing something ahead of it. Also COERCION 2, COMPEL 2, FORCE 2, IMPEL 2.

COERCION 1 (kō ûr′ shən), *n.* See COERCE 1.

COERCION 2, *n.* See COERCE 2.

COFFEE (kôf′ ĭ, kŏf′ ĭ), *n.* (Grinding the coffee beans.) The right "S" hand, palm facing left, rotates in a counterclockwise manner atop the left "S" hand, palm facing right.

COFFIN (kô′ fin, kof′ in), *n.* (A box that is buried.) The sign for BURY: both downturned cupped hands move simultaneously in an arc from the front of the body toward the chest. This is the mound of earth on the burial site. The sign for BOX is next made: the open hands, palms facing and fingers pointing out, are dropped an inch or two simultaneously. They then shift their relative positions so that both palms face the body, with one hand in front of the other. In this new position they again drop an inch or two simultaneously. Also CASKET.

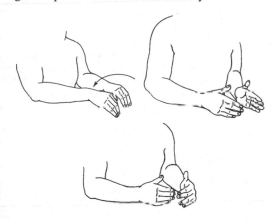

COINCIDE 1 (kō′ in sid′), *v.,* -CIDED, -CIDING. (A befalling.) Both "D" hands, index fingers pointing away from the body, are simultaneously pivoted over so that the palms face down. Also ACCIDENT, BEFALL, CHANCE, COINCIDENCE, EVENT, HAPPEN 1, INCIDENT, OCCUR, OPPORTUNITY 4.

COINCIDE 2, *v.* (Agreement; of the same mind; thinking the same way.) The index finger of the right "D" hand, palm back, touches the forehead (the modified sign for THINK), and then the two index fingers, both in the "D" position, palm down, are brought together so they are side by side, pointing away from the body (the sign for SAME). Also ACCORD, ACQUIESCE, ACQUIESCENCE, AGREE, AGREEMENT, COMPLY, CONCUR, CONSENT.

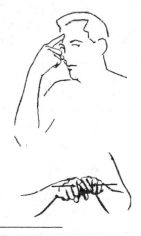

COINCIDENCE (kō ĭn′ sə dəns), *n.* See COINCIDE 1.

COKE (kōk) (*colloq.*), *n.* See COCA-COLA.

COLD 1 (kōld), *adj.* (The trembling from cold.) Both "S" hands, palms facing, are placed at the sides of the body. In this position the arms and hands shiver. Also CHILLY, FRIGID, SHIVER 1, WINTER 1.

COLD 2, *n.* (Wiping the nose.) The signer makes the motions of wiping the nose several times with an imaginary handkerchief. This is the common cold. Also HANDKERCHIEF.

COLLAPSE (kə lăps′), *v.*, -LAPSED, -LAPSING, *n.* (A collapsing.) Both "5" hands, fingertips joined before the chest, swing down so that the fingertips face down. Also BREAKDOWN, CAVE IN.

COLLAR (kŏl′ ər), *n.* (Outlining the collar.) The fingertips of both "Q" hands are placed at either side of the neck. They encircle the neck, coming together under the chin.

COLLATE (kō′ lāt, kol′ āt), *v.*, -LATED, -LATING. *Computer term.* Both hands, palms facing, are held fingers pointing straight forward. The right hand executes several up-down movements as it moves toward the right, away from the left.

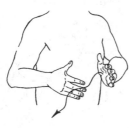

COLLECT (kə lĕkt′), *v.*, -LECTED, -LECTING. (Gathering in.) The right "5" hand, its little finger edge touching the upturned left palm, is drawn in an arc toward the body, closing into the "S" position as it sweeps over the base of the left hand. Also ACCUMULATE 1, EARN, SALARY, WAGES.

COLLEGE (kŏl′ ĭj), *n.* (Above ordinary school.) The sign for SCHOOL, *q.v.,* is made, but without the clapping of hands. The upper hand swings up in an arc above the lower. The upper hand may form a "C" instead of assuming a clapping position.

COLLIDE 1 (kə līd′), *v.*, -LIDED, -LIDING. The fists come together with force. Also COLLISION 1, CRASH, RUN UP AGAINST, WRECK.

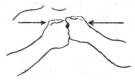

COLLIDE 2, *v.* (A coming together.) Both "5" hands, palms facing, are held about a foot apart in front of the chest. They both sweep upward in unison until their palms come together with force. Also COLLISION 2.

COLLISION 1 (kə lĭzh′ en), *n.* See COLLIDE 1.

COLLISION 2, *n.* See COLLIDE 2.

COLOMBIA (kə lum′ bē a), *n.* (The letter "C.") The right "C" hand, palm facing forward, makes a counterclockwise circle as it rests on the back of the left hand. A native sign.

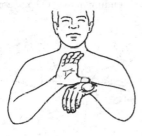

COLOR 1 (kŭl′ ər), *n*. The fingertips of the right "5" hand, palm facing the body, are placed against the chin and wiggle back and forth.

COLOR 2 (*rare*), *n*. (Mixing the colors on the palette.) The fingertips of the downturned right "B" hand rub against the upturned left palm in a clockwise-counterclockwise fashion.

COLOR 3 (*rare*), *n*. (Bringing an object into view to observe its color.) The fingertips of the right "V" hand are thrust into the upturned left palm. They are then brought up quickly before the eyes.

COLOR 4, *v.*, -ORED, -ORING. The downturned right "5" hand is held above the upturned left palm. The right fingers, wriggling, are passed back and forth over the left palm, from the base of the hand to the fingertips.

COLORADO (kol′ ə rad′ ō, rä′ dō), *n*. (The "C"; mountaintops.) The right "C" hand, palm facing left, moves in a wavy line over the downturned left arm, from elbow to wrist.

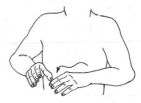

COLUMBUS (kə lum′ bəs), *n*. (The letter "C"; a name sign.) The thumb of the right "C" hand is placed against the right temple.

COMB (kōm) *n.*, *v.*, COMBED, COMBING. (Act of combing the hair.) The downturned curved fingertips of the right hand, representing the teeth of the comb, are drawn through the hair.

COME 1 (kŭm), *v.*, CAME, COME, COMING. (Movement toward the body.) The index fingers, pointing to each other, are rolled in toward the body.

COME 2, *v.* (A beckoning.) The right index finger makes a natural beckoning movement. Also BECKON.

COME 3, *v.* (The natural sign.) The upright hand beckons.

COME ON, *v. phrase.* (The natural beckoning motion.) One right-angle hand, held at shoulder level, palm facing the body, is moved toward the body in a beckoning motion while the signer assumes an appropriately encouraging or anxious expression.

COMET (kom′ it), *n.* (The comet's tail.) The right "C" hand, palm out, describes a broad sweeping arc in the sky as it moves, ending in the "O" position.

COMFORT (kŭm′ fərt), *n., v.,* -FORTED, -FORTING. (A stroking motion.) Each downturned open hand alternately strokes the back of the other, moving forward from wrist to fingers. Also COMFORTABLE, CONSOLE, COZY.

COMFORTABLE (kŭmf′ tə bəl, kŭm′ fər tə bəl), *adj.* See COMFORT.

COMIC (kŏm′ ĭk), *n.* (The nose wrinkles in laughter.) The tips of the right index and middle fingers brush repeatedly off the tip of the nose. Also COMICAL, FUNNY, HUMOR, HUMOROUS.

COMICAL (kŏm′ ə kəl), *adj.* See COMIC.

COMMA (kŏm' ə), *n.* (The natural sign.) The right thumb and index finger are held together. In this position they draw a comma in the air before the face.

COMMAND (kə mănd'), *n., v.,* -MANDED, -MANDING. (An issuance from the mouth.) The tip of the index finger of the "D" hand, palm facing the body, is placed at the closed lips. It moves around and out rather forcefully. Also BID 1, DIRECT 2, ORDER 1.

COMMANDMENTS (kə mănd' mənts), *n. pl.* Hold up the left open hand, palm facing right; place the side of the right "C" hand against the left palm twice, the second time slightly lower than the first.

COMMENCE (kə mĕns'), *v.,* -MENCED, -MENCING. (Turning a key to open up a new venture.) The right index finger, resting between the left index and middle fingers, executes a half turn once or twice. Also BEGIN, INITIATE, INSTITUTE 2, ORIGIN 1, ORIGINATE 1, START.

COMMEND (kə mĕnd'), *v.,* -MENDED, -MENDING. (Good words coming from the mouth; clapping hands.) The fingertips of the right hand, palm flat and facing the body, are brought up to the lips so that they touch (part of the sign for GOOD, *q.v.*). The hands are then clapped together several times. Also ACCLAIM 2, APPLAUD, APPLAUSE, APPROBATION, APPROVAL, APPROVE, CLAP, CONGRATULATE 1, CONGRATULATIONS 1, PRAISE.

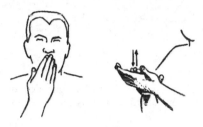

COMMON (kom' ən), *adj.* (The same all around.) Both downturned "Y" hands execute counterclockwise circles. Also STANDARD.

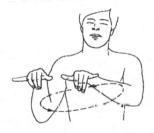

COMMON LAW (kom' ən law), *n.* (Everyday law.) The sign for DAILY is made: the right "A" hand moves forward several times from its initial resting place on the right cheek. This is followed by the sign for LAW: the upright "L" hand, resting palm against palm on the upright left "5" hand, moves down in an arc a short distance, coming to rest on the base of the left palm.

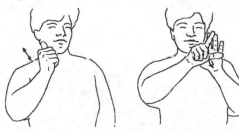

COMMUNIST (kŏm′ yə nĭst), *n.* (The salute.) The right fist is raised above the signer's line of vision.

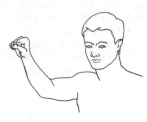

COMMUNITY 1 (kə mū′ nə tĭ). *n.* (A collection of roofs; nearness to one another.) The sign for CITY or TOWN is made: the fingertips of the "B" hands come together once or twice to describe the slanting roofs. With the left open hand facing the body and fingers pointing right, the right hand, fingers pointing left, is then placed over the back of the left. This movement is then repeated, with the hands in reversed position, and the left hand placed over the back of the right.

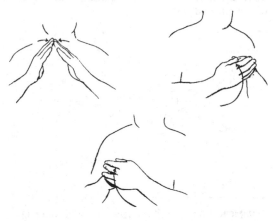

COMMUNITY 2, *n.* (A collection of rooftops.) The fingertips of both hands are joined, the hands and arms forming a pyramid. The fingertips separate and rejoin a number of times. Both arms may move a bit from left to right each time the fingertips separate and rejoin. Also CITY, TOWN.

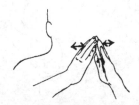

COMPANY 1 (kŭm′ pə nĭ), *n.* (A grouping together.) Both "C" hands, palms facing, are held a few inches apart at chest height. They are swung around in unison so that the palms now face the body. Also ASSOCIATION, AUDIENCE 1, CASTE, CIRCLE 2, CLASS, CLASSED 1, CLUB, FAMILY 2, GANG, GROUP 1, JOIN 2, ORGANIZATION 1.

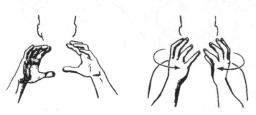

COMPANY 2, *n.* (The abbreviation; a fingerspelled loan sign.) The letters "C-O" are fingerspelled. To avoid misunderstanding, as in "coworker," the hand may move in a small arc between the "C" and "O."

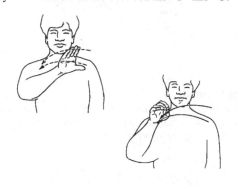

COMPARE (kəm pâr′), *v.,* -PARED, -PARING. (Comparing both palms.) Both open hands are held before the body, with palms facing each other and fingers pointing upward. The hands then turn toward the face while the signer looks from one to the other, as if comparing them. Also CONTRAST 1.

COMPASS (kum′ pəs), *n.* (The needle's movement.) The right index finger, held above the left "C" hand, moves back and forth, from left to right.

COMPASSION (kəm păsh′ ən), *n.* (Feelings from the heart, conferred on others.) The middle finger of the open right hand moves up the chest over the heart. The same open hand then moves in a small, clockwise circle in front of the right shoulder, with palm facing forward and fingers pointing up. The signer assumes a kindly expression.

COMPETE 1 (kəm pēt′), *v.,* -PETED, -PETING. (Two opponents come together.) Both hands are closed, with thumbs pointing straight up and palms facing the body. From their initial position about a foot apart, the hands are brought together sharply so that the knuckles strike. The hands, as they are drawn together, also move down a bit so that they describe a "V." Also COMPETITION 1, CONTEND 1, CONTEST 1, RACE 1, RIVAL 2, RIVALRY 1, VIE 1.

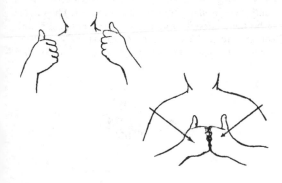

COMPETE 2, *v.* (Opposing objects.) The "A" hands are held side by side before the chest, palms facing each other and thumbs pointing forward. In this posi-

tion the hands move alternately back and forth, toward and away from the body. Also COMPETITION 2, CONTEND 2, CONTEST 2, RACE 2, RIVAL 3, RIVALRY 2, VIE 2.

COMPETE 3, *v.* (The changing fortunes of competitors.) The "A" hands are held facing each other, thumbs pointing up in front of the body. Both hands are moved alternately backward and forward past each other several times. Also COMPETITION 3, CONTEND 3, CONTEST 3, RACE 3, RIVAL 4, RIVALRY 3, VIE 3.

COMPETENT (kŏm′ pə tənt), *adj.* (An affirmative movement of the hands, likened to a nodding of the head, to indicate ability or power to accomplish something.) Both "A" hands, held palms down, move down in unison a short distance before the chest. Also ABILITY, ABLE, CAN 1, CAPABLE, COULD, FACULTY, MAY 2, POSSIBLE.

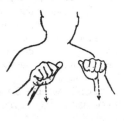

COMPETITION 1 (kŏm′ pə tĭsh′ ən), *n.* See COMPETE 1.

COMPETITION 2, *n.* See COMPETE 2.

COMPETITION 3, *n*. See COMPETE 3.

COMPLAIN 1 (kəm plān′), *v.*, -PLAINED, -PLAINING. (The hand is thrust into the chest to force a complaint out.) The curved fingers of the right hand are thrust forcefully into the chest. Also COMPLAINT, OBJECT 2, OBJECTION, PROTEST.

COMPLAIN 2 (*sl.*), *v.* (Kicking.) Both "S" hands are held before the chest. Then the hands move sharply to the side, opening into a modified "V" position, palms down, as if kicking. Also KICK 2, OBJECT 3.

COMPLAINT (kəm plānt′), *n.* See COMPLAIN 1.

COMPLETE 1 (kəm plēt′), *adj., v.,* -PLETED, -PLETING. (Bring to an end.) The left hand, fingers together and pointing forward, is held palm facing right. The right, palm down, fingers also together, moves along the top of the left, goes over the tip of the left index finger, and drops straight down, indicating a cutting off or a finishing. This sign is also used to indicate the past tense of a verb, in the sense of completing an action or state of being. Also ACCOMPLISH 2, ACHIEVE 2, CONCLUDE, DONE 1, END 4, EXPIRE 1, FINISH 1, HAVE 2, TERMINATE.

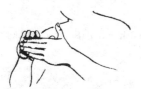

COMPLETE 2, *v.* (Wiping off the top of a container to indicate its condition of fullness.) The downturned open right hand wipes across the index finger edge of the left "S" hand, whose palm faces right. The movement of the right hand is toward the body. Also FILL, FULL 1.

COMPLEX (kəm pleks′), *adj.* The wriggling fingers indicate the involved nature.) Both downturned "W" hands, fingers facing each other, are moved toward each other while the fingers wriggle and open and close a bit.

COMPLICATE (kŏm′ plə kāt′), *v.,* -CATED, -CATING. (Scrambling or mixing up.) The downturned right hand is positioned above the upturned left. The fingers of both are curved. Both hands move in opposite horizontal circles. Also CLUTTER, CONFUSE, CONFUSED, CONFUSION, DISORDER, MINGLE 1, MIX, MIXED, MIX UP, SCRAMBLE.

COMPOSITION (kom pə zish′ ən), *n.* (Writing down.) Grasping an imaginary pencil, the right hand scribbles across the open left palm. The right thumb and index finger, held apart, then move down the left palm from the index finger edge to the little finger edge. This second part of the sign is optional.

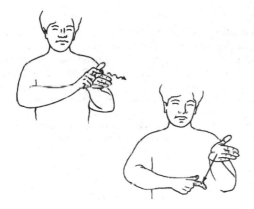

COMPUTER 1 (kəm pyo͞o′ tər), *n.* The thumb of the right "C" hand is placed on the back of the left hand and moves up the left arm in an arc.

COMPUTER 2, *n.* (Reference to the mind.) The thumb of the right "C" hand touches the forehead or the temple, and the hand twists slightly up and down.

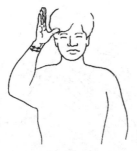

COMPUTER 3, *n.* (The tape in a mainframe drive.) Both index fingers describe clockwise circles.

COMPUTER 4, *n.* Same as COMPUTER 3, using "C" hands.

CONCEITED (kən sē′ tĭd) (*colloq.*), *adj.* (The natural sign.) Both downturned "L" hands are positioned with index fingers at the temples. They move away from the head rather slowly, indicating the size or growth of the head. The head is often moved slightly back and forth as the hands move away. An expression of superiority is assumed. Also BIG-HEADED, BIG SHOT, SWELL-HEADED.

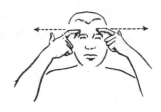

CONCEIVE 1 (kən sēv′), *v.,* -CEIVED, -CEIVING. (Thought reflected in a mirror.) The extended right index finger touches the forehead briefly. The right palm is then turned back and forth like a mirror before the face, as if reflecting a thought.

CONCEIVE 2, *v.* (A thought coming forward from the mind, modified by the letter "I" for "idea.") With the "I" position on the right hand, palm facing the body, touch the little finger to the forehead, and then move the hand up and away in a circular, clockwise motion. The hand may also be moved up and away without this circular motion. Also CONCEPT 1, CONCEPTION, FANCY 2, IDEA, IMAGINATION, IMAGINE 1, JUST THINK OF IT!, NOTION, POLICY 2, THEORY, THOUGHT 2.

CONCEIVE 3 (*eccles.*), *v.* The right "AND" hand is held above the head, fingers pointing down, while the left "AND" hand is held before the body, fingers pointing up toward the right hand. The two hands then move toward each other, opening as they come together.

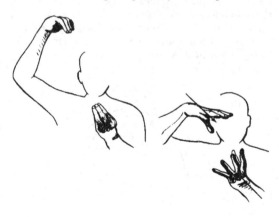

CONCENTRATE (kŏn' sən trāt'), *v.,* -TRATED, -TRATING, *n.* (Directing one's attention forward; applying oneself; concentrating.) Both hands, fingers pointing up and together, are held at the sides of the face. They move straight out from the face. Also APPLY 2, ATTEND (TO), ATTENTION, CONCENTRATION, FOCUS, GIVE ATTENTION (TO), MIND 2, PAY ATTENTION (TO).

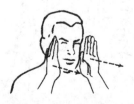

CONCENTRATION (kŏn' sən tra' shən), *n.* See CONCENTRATE.

CONCEPT 1 (kŏn' sĕpt), *n.* (A thought coming forward from the mind, modified by the letter "I" for "idea.") With the "I" position on the right hand, palm facing the body, touch the little finger to the forehead, and then move the hand up and away in a circular, clockwise motion. The hand may also be moved up and away without this circular motion. Also CONCEIVE 2, CONCEPTION, FANCY 2, IDEA, IMAGINATION, IMAGINE 1, JUST THINK OF IT!, NOTION, POLICY 2, THEORY, THOUGHT 2.

CONCEPT 2, *n.* (The letter "C"; an idea popping out of the head.) The right "C" hand is held near the right side of the forehead. It moves up and out a bit.

CONCERN 1 (kən sûrn'), *n., v.,* -CERNED, -CERNING. (A clouding over; a troubling.) Both "B" hands, palms facing each other, are rotated alternately before the forehead. Also ANNOY 2, ANNOYANCE 2, ANXIOUS 2, BOTHER 2, FRET, PROBLEM 1, TROUBLE, WORRIED, WORRY 1.

CONCERN 2, *n., v.* (Joining together.) Both hands, held in the modified "5" position, palms out, move toward each other. The thumbs and index fingers of both hands then connect. Also AFFILIATE 1, ANNEX, ASSOCIATE 2, ATTACH, BELONG, COMMUNION OF SAINTS, CONNECT, ENLIST, ENROLL, JOIN 1, PARTICIPATE, RELATIVE 2, UNION, UNITE.

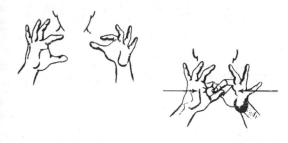

CONDENSE (kən děns'), *v.,* -DENSED, -DENSING. (To squeeze or condense into a small space.) The "C" hands face each other, with the right hand nearer to the body than the left. Both hands draw together and close deliberately, squeezing an imaginary object. Also ABBREVIATE 1, BRIEF 2, MAKE BRIEF, SUMMARIZE 1, SUMMARY 1.

CONDESCEND (kon di send'), *v.,* -SCENDED, -SCENDING. (Looking down upon.) Both downturned "V" hands point somewhat down, indicating the gaze is directed down at someone. To indicate the signer is the subject of condescension, the "V" hands are held at eye level, pointing down toward the signer.

CONDOM 1 (kon' dəm), *n.* (Slipping on a condom.) The inner edge of the curved right index finger is

slipped around the left index finger and moves down.

CONDOM 2, *n.* The same sign as CONDOM 1, but the index and thumb, in the "G" position, slip on the condom.

CONDUCT 1 (*n.* kŏn' dŭkt; *v.* kən dŭkt') -DUCTED, -DUCTING. (An activity.) Both open hands, palms down, are swung right and left before the chest. Also ACT 2, ACTION, ACTIVE, ACTIVITY, BUSY 2, DEED, DO, PERFORM 1, PERFORMANCE 1, RENDER 2.

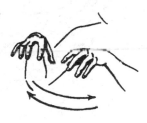

CONDUCT 2, *n.* (One hand leads the other.) The right hand grasps the tips of the left fingers and pulls the left hand forward. Also GUIDE, LEAD 1.

CONFERENCE (kŏn′ fər əns), *n.* (Assemble all together.) Both "5" hands, palms facing, are held with fingers pointing out from the body. With a sweeping motion they are brought in toward the chest, and all fingertips come together. This is repeated. Also ACCUMULATE 3, ASSEMBLE, ASSEMBLY, CONVENE, CONVENTION, GATHER 2, GATHERING, MEETING 1.

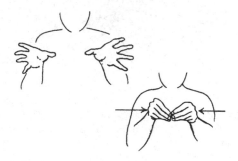

CONFESS (kən fĕs′), *v.*, -FESSED, -FESSING. (Getting something off the chest.) Both hands are held with fingers touching the chest and pointing down. They are then swung up and out, ending with both palms facing up before the body. Also ADMISSION 1, ADMIT 1, CONCEDE, CONFESSION 1.

CONFESSION 1 (kən fĕsh′ ən), *n.* See CONFESS.

CONFESSION 2 (*eccles.*), n. (The grating through which confession is heard.) The fingers of the right open hand are spread slightly and placed with their backs resting diagonally across the front of the spread fingers of the left open hand so as to form a grid held

just to the side of the face, palms toward the face. Also CONFESSIONAL, PENANCE 2.

CONFESSIONAL (kən fĕsh′ ən əl), *adj., n.* See CONFESSION 2.

CONFIDENCE (kŏn′ fə dəns), *n.* (Planting a flagpole, *i.e.,* planting one's trust.) The "S" hands grasp and plant an imaginary flagpole in the ground. This sign may be preceded by BELIEVE, *q.v.* Also FAITH, TRUST.

CONFIGURATION (kən fig′ yə rā′ shən), *n. Computer term.* (The shape.) Both outfacing "C" hands, side by side, move apart and straight down.

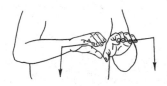

CONFRONT (kən frŭnt′), *v.*, -FRONTED, -FRONTING. (Face-to-face.) The left hand, fingers together, palm flat and facing the eyes, is held a bit above eye level. The right hand, fingers also together, is held in front of the mouth, with palm facing the left hand. With a sweeping upward movement the right hand moves toward the left, which moves straight up an inch or two at the same time. Also APPEAR 3, APPEARANCE, BEFORE 3, FACE 2, FACE-TO-FACE, PRESENCE.

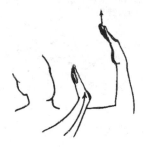

CONFUSE (kən fūz′), v., -FUSED, -FUSING. (Scrambling or mixing up.) The downturned right hand is positioned above the upturned left. The fingers of both are curved. Both hands move in opposite horizontal circles. Also CLUTTER, COMPLICATE, CONFUSED, CONFUSION, DISORDER, MINGLE 1, MIX, MIXED, MIX UP, SCRAMBLE.

CONFUSED (kən fūzd′), adj. See CONFUSE.

CONFUSION (kən fū′ zhən), n. See CONFUSE.

CONGRATULATE 1 (kən grăch′ ə lāt′), v., -LATED, -LATING. (Good words coming from the mouth; clapping hands.) The fingertips of the right hand, palm flat and facing the body, are brought up to the lips so that they touch (part of the sign for GOOD, q.v.). The hands are then clapped together several times. Also ACCLAIM 2, APPLAUD, APPLAUSE, APPROBATION, APPROVAL, APPROVE, CLAP, COMMEND, CONGRATULATIONS 1, PRAISE.

CONGRATULATE 2, v. (Shaking the clasped hands in triumph.) The hands are clasped together in front of the face and are shaken vigorously back and forth. The signer smiles. Also CONGRATULATIONS 2.

CONGRATULATIONS 1 (kən grăch′ ə lā′ shənz), n. pl. See CONGRATULATE 1.

CONGRATULATIONS 2, n. pl. See CONGRATULATE 2.

CONGRESS (kong′ gris), n. (The letter "C"; the fastening of the Roman toga.) The right "C" hand is brought from the left shoulder to the right shoulder. The movement may also be done from right to left.

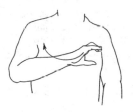

CONNECT (kə nĕkt′), v., -NECTED, -NECTING. (Joining together.) Both hands, held in the modified "5" position, palms out, move toward each other. The thumbs and index fingers of both hands then connect. Also AFFILIATE 1, ANNEX, ASSOCIATE 2, ATTACH, BELONG, COMMUNION OF SAINTS, CONCERN 2, ENLIST, ENROLL, JOIN 1, PARTICIPATE, RELATIVE 2, UNION, UNITE.

CONNECTION (kə nĕk′ shən), *n.* (The fingers are connected.) The index fingers and thumbs of both hands interlock, and the hands move back and forth from right to left. Also RELATIONSHIP 1.

CONQUER (kŏng′ kər), *v.,* -QUERED, -QUERING. (Forcing the head into a bowed position.) The right "S" hand, placed across the left "S" hand, moves over and down a bit. Also BEAT 2, DEFEAT, OVERCOME, SUBDUE.

CONQUERED, *adj.* (The head is forced into a bowed position.) The right "S" hand, palm up, is placed under and across the left "S" hand, whose palm faces down. The right "S" hand moves up and over, toward the body. This sign is used as the passive voice of the verb CONQUER. Also BEATEN.

CONSCIENCE 1 (kŏn′ shəns), *n.* The index finger is shaken scoldingly at the heart. Also CONVICTION 1.

CONSCIENCE 2, *n.* (Shaking a warning finger at yourself.) The right "G" hand is held just above the right side of the head, with the index fingertip pointing toward the right temple. Then the hand drops toward the head but does not touch it. This movement is repeated several times.

CONSCIENCE 3, *n.* (A guilty heart.) The side of the right "G" hand strikes against the heart several times.

CONSCIOUS (kŏn′ shəs), *adj.* (Indicating the mind.) The fingertips of the open right hand are placed against the forehead. Also CONSCIOUSNESS, KNOWING.

CONSENSUS (kən sen′ səs), *n.* (Of the same mind all around.) The sign for AGREE is made: the index finger of the right hand touches the forehead, and then both index fingers come together side by side, palms down. Both "Y" hands, palms down, then simultaneously describe a counterclockwise circle.

CONSENT (kən sĕnt'), *n., v.,* -SENTED, -SENTING. (Agreement; of the same mind; thinking the same way.) The index finger of the right "D" hand, palm back, touches the forehead (the modified sign for THINK), and then the two index fingers, both in the "D" position, palm down, are brought together so they are side by side, pointing away from the body (the sign for SAME). Also ACCORD, ACQUIESCE, ACQUIESCENCE, AGREE, AGREEMENT, COINCIDE 2, COMPLY, CONCUR.

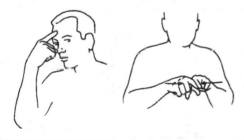

CONSIDER 1 (kən sĭd' ər), *v.,* -ERED, -ERING. (A thought is turned over in the mind.) The index finger makes a small circle on the forehead. Also MOTIVE 1, RECKON, SPECULATE 1, SPECULATION 1, THINK, THOUGHT 1, THOUGHTFUL.

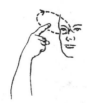

CONSIDER 2, *v.* (Turning thoughts over in the mind.) Both index fingers, pointing to the forehead, describe

continuous alternating circles. Also CONTEMPLATE, PONDER, SPECULATE 2, SPECULATION 2, WEIGH 2, WONDER 1.

CONSIDER 3, *v.* (The scales move up and down.) The two "F" hands, palms facing each other, move alternately up and down. Also COURT, EVALUATE 1, IF, JUDGE 1, JUDGMENT, JUSTICE 1.

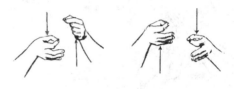

CONSISTENT (kən sĭs' tənt), *adj.* (Coming together with regular frequency.) Both "D" hands are held with index fingers pointing forward, the right hand above the left. The right "D" hand is brought down on the left several times in rhythmic succession. Also FAITHFUL 1, REGULAR.

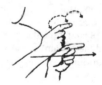

CONSTELLATION (kon stə lā' shən), *n.* (Stars in the sky.) The sign for STARS is made: both index fingers, held together and pointing up, move up alternately. The open right hand, palm facing out, then sweeps up and across the sky.

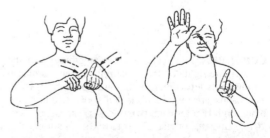

CONSTIPATION (kon' stə pā' shən), *n.* (The bowels are backed up.) The right thumb is thrust twice up and into the little finger side of the closed left hand.

CONSTITUTION (kŏn' stə tū' shən, -tōo'-), *n.* (The letter "C.") The right "C" hand moves downward along the left palm, in two stages, from fingertips to wrist.

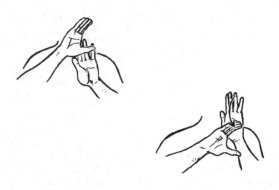

CONSTRUCT 1 (kən strŭkt'), *v.*, -STRUCTED, -STRUCT- ING. (Piling bricks one on top of another.) The down-turned hands are placed repeatedly atop each other. Each time this is done the arms rise a bit, to indicate the raising of a building. Also BUILD, CONSTRUCTION, ERECT.

CONSTRUCT 2, *v.* (Fashioning something with the hands.) The right "S" hand, palm facing left, is placed on top of its left counterpart, whose palm faces right. The hands are twisted back and forth, striking each other slightly after each twist. Also COMPOSE, CONSTI- TUTE, CREATE, DEVISE 2, FABRICATE, FASHION, FIX,

MAKE, MANUFACTURE, MEND 1, PRODUCE 3, RENDER 1, REPAIR.

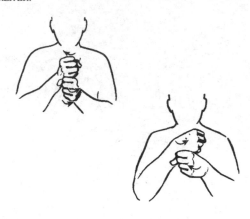

CONSTRUCTION (kən strŭk' shən), *n.* See CON- STRUCT 1.

CONSUME 1 (kən sōōm'), *v.*, -SUMED, -SUMING. (The natural sign.) The closed right hand goes through the natural motion of placing food in the mouth. This movement is repeated. Also CONSUMPTION, DEVOUR, DINE, EAT, FEED 1, FOOD 1, MEAL.

CONSUME 2, *v.* (To use; the letter "U.") The right "U" hand describes a small clockwise circle. Also USE, USED, USEFUL, UTILIZE, WEAR 2.

CONSUMER 1 (kən sōō' mər), *n.* (One who buys.) The sign for BUY is made: the upturned right hand, grasping imaginary dollar bills, is positioned in the upturned left palm. The hand moves forward in a

small arc, opening up as it does. The sign for INDI-VIDUAL 1 then follows.

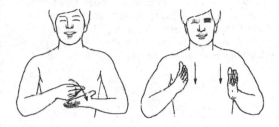

CONSUMER 2, *n.* (One who uses.) The sign for USE is made: the letter "U" describes a small clockwise circle. The sign for INDIVIDUAL 1 then follows.

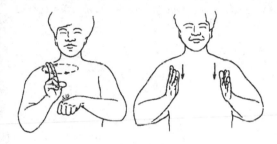

CONSUMPTION (kən sŭmp' shən), *n.* See CONSUME 1.

CONTACT 1 (kŏn' tăkt), *n., v.,* -TACTED, -TACTING. (The natural movement of touching.) The tip of the middle finger of the downturned right "5" hand touches the back of the left hand a number of times. Also FEEL 1, TOUCH, TOUCHDOWN.

CONTACT 2, *v.* (A pinning down.) The left "D" finger represents the one who is caught. The curved index and middle fingers of the right hand, palm facing down, are thrust against the left "D" finger, impaling it. Also CAUGHT IN THE ACT 1, CORNER 2.

CONTACT LENSES (kon' takt lenz' ez), *n.* (Inserting the lens.) Leaning over the upturned index or middle finger, the signer mimes placing a contact lens in the eye.

CONTEMPLATE (kŏn' təm plāt', kən těm' plāt), *v.,* -PLATED, -PLATING. (Turning thoughts over in the mind.) Both index fingers, pointing to the forehead, describe continuous alternating circles. Also CONSIDER 2, PONDER, SPECULATE 2, SPECULATION 2, WEIGH 2, WONDER 1.

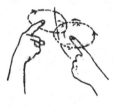

CONTEMPT 1 (kən těmpt'), *n.* (The gaze is cast downward.) Both "V" hands, side by side and palms facing out, are swept downward so that the fingertips now point down. A haughty expression or one of mild contempt is sometimes assumed. Also LOOK DOWN, SCORN 1.

CONTEMPT 2 (*rare*), *n*. (The finger is flicked to indicate something petty, small; *i.e.,* to be scorned as inconsequential.) The right index finger and thumb are used to press the lips down into an expression of contempt. The right thumb is then flicked out from the closed hand. Also DESPISE 2, DETEST 2, DISLIKE, HATE 2, SCORN 2.

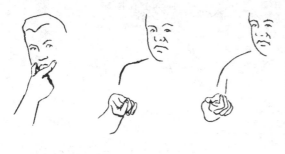

CONTENT (kən těnt′), *adj*. (The inner feelings settle down.) Both "B" hands (or "5" hands, fingers together) are placed palms down against the chest, the right above the left. Both move down simultaneously a few inches. Also CONTENTED, GRATIFY 2, SATISFACTION, SATISFIED, SATISFY 1.

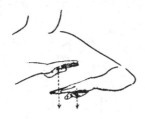

CONTENTED (kən těn′ tĭd), *adj*. See CONTENT.

CONTINENT (kon′ tn ənt), *n*. (The "C"; a spread of land.) The right "C" hand, palm out, makes a counterclockwise circle over the downturned left arm.

CONTINUE 1 (kən tĭn′ ū), *v.*, -TINUED, -TINUING. (Steady, uninterrupted movement.) The "A" hands are held with palms out, thumbs extended and touching, the right behind the left. In this position the hands move forward in a straight, steady line. Also ENDURE 2, EVER 1, LAST 3, LASTING, PERMANENT, PERPETUAL, PERSEVERE 3, PERSIST 2, REMAIN, STAY 1, STAY STILL.

CONTINUE 2, *v*. (Duration of movement from past to present.) The right "Y" hand is held palm down in front of the right shoulder and is then moved slowly down and forward in a smooth curve. Also STAY 2, STILL 1, YET 1.

CONTRACT 1 (kon′ trakt), *n*. (Signing the papers.) Both downturned "U" hands, side by side, fingers pointing forward, move down suddenly, an inch or two, as if two people are signing something simultaneously.

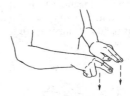

CONTRACT 2, *n., v.*, -TRACTED, -TRACTING. (kən trakt′). (Putting the signature on paper.) The fingers of the downturned right "H" hand are slapped into the upturned left palm.

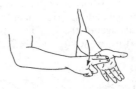

CONTRAST 1 (*n*. kŏn′ trăst; *v*. kən trăst′), -TRASTED, -TRASTING. (Comparing both palms.) Both open hands are held before the body, with palms facing each other and fingers pointing upward. The hands then turn toward the face while the signer looks from one to the other, as if comparing them. Also COMPARE.

CONTRAST 2, *n., v.* (Separateness.) The tips of the extended index fingers touch before the chest, the right finger pointing left and the left finger pointing right. The fingers then draw apart sharply to either side. Also OPPOSITE, REVERSE 1.

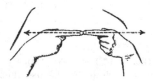

CONTRIBUTE (kən trĭb′ ūt), *v.,* -UTED, -UTING. (A giving of something.) Both "A" hands, with index fingers somewhat draped over the tips of the thumbs, are held palms facing in front of the chest. They are pivoted forward and down, in unison, from the wrists. Also AWARD, BEQUEATH, BESTOW, CONFER, CONSIGN, GIFT, PRESENT 2.

CONTRITION (kən trĭsh′ ən), *n.* (The heart is circled to indicate feeling, modified by the letter "S" for SORRY.) The right "S" hand, palm facing the body, is rotated several times over the area of the heart. Also APOLOGIZE 1, APOLOGY 1, PENTITENT, REGRET, REGRETFUL, REPENT, REPENTANT, RUE, SORROW, SORROWFUL 2, SORRY.

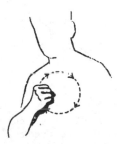

CONTROL 1 (kən trōl′), *v.,* -TROLLED, -TROLLING. (Holding the reins over all.) The "A" hands, palms facing, move alternately back and forth as if grasping and manipulating reins. The left "A" hand, still in position, swings over so that its palm now faces down. The right hand opens to the "5" position, palm down, and swings over the left, which moves slightly to the right. Also AUTHORITY, DIRECT 1, GOVERN, MANAGE, MANAGEMENT, MANAGER, OPERATE, REGULATE, REIGN, RULE 1.

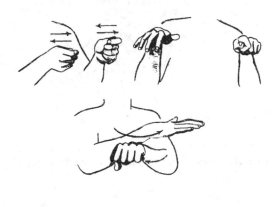

CONTROL 2, *n., v.* (Keeping the feelings down.) The curved fingertips of both hands are placed against the chest. The hands slowly move down as the fingers close into the "S" position. One hand only may also be used. Also SUPPRESS FEELINGS.

CONTROVERSY (kŏn′ trə vûr′ sĭ), *n.* (An expounding back and forth.) The index fingers here represent the two sides of the argument. First the left index finger is slapped into the open right palm, and then the right makes the same movement into the left palm. This is repeated back and forth several times. Also ARGUE, ARGUMENT, DEBATE, DISPUTE.

CONVENE (kən vēn′), *v.,* -VENED, -VENING. (Assemble all together.) Both "5" hands, palms facing, are held with fingers pointing out from the body. With a sweeping motion they are brought in toward the chest, and all fingertips come together. This is repeated. Also ACCUMULATE 3, ASSEMBLE, ASSEMBLY, CONFERENCE, CONVENTION, GATHER 2, GATHERING, MEETING 1.

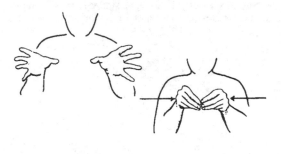

CONVENTION (kən vĕn′ shən), *n.* See CONVENE.

CONVENTIONAL (kən ven′ shən əl), *adj.* (Bound down by custom or habit.) Both "Y" hands are held side by side. They move in a continuous counterclockwise direction.

CONVERSATION 1 (kŏn′ vər sā′ shən), *n.* (Movement forward from, and back to, the mouth.) The tips of both index fingers, held pointing up, move alternately forward from, and back to, the lips. Also COMMUNICATE WITH, CONVERSE, TALK 3.

CONVERSATION 2, *n.* (Words tossed back and forth.) The open hands are held side by side with palms up, fingers pointing forward and slightly curved. In this position the hands swing back and forth from side to side before the chest. Also CHAT.

CONVERSE (kən vûrs′), *v.,* -VERSED, -VERSING. See CONVERSATION 1.

CONVERT (kən vûrt′), *v.,* -VERTED, -VERTING. (To change positions.) Both "A" hands, thumbs up, are held before the chest, several inches apart. The left hand is pivoted over so that its thumb points to the right. Simultaneously, the right hand is moved up and over the left, describing a small arc, with its thumb pointing to the left. Also ADJUST, ALTER, ALTERATION, CHANGE 1, MODIFY, REVERSE 2, TRANSFER 1.

CONVICTION 1 (kən vĭk′ shən), *n.* The index finger is shaken scoldingly at the heart. Also CONSCIENCE 1.

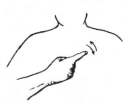

CONVICTION 2, *n.* (A thought clasped onto.) The index finger touches the middle of the forehead (where the thought lies), and then both hands are clasped together. Also BELIEF, BELIEVE, DOCTRINE 2.

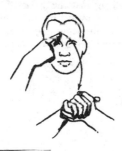

CONVICTION 3, *n.* (Feel strongly.) The sign for FEEL 2 is made: The right middle finger, touching the heart, moves up an inch or two a number of times. This is followed by the sign for STRONG: both "5" hands are placed palms against the chest; they move out and away, forcefully, closing and assuming the "S" position.

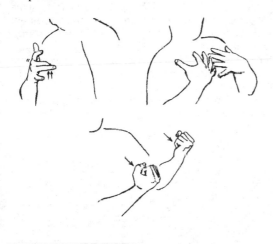

CONVINCE 1 (kən vĭns'), *v.,* -VINCED, -VINCING. (Shaking someone to implant one's will into another.) Both "A" hands, palms facing, are held before the chest, the left slightly in front of the right. In this position the hands move back and forth a short distance. Also COAX, INDUCE, PERSUADE, PERSUASION, PROD, URGE 2.

CONVINCE 2, *v.* (The karate chop to the neck wins the prize, *i.e.,* convinces the victim.) One or both upturned open hands mimes a karate chop.

COOK (kŏŏk), *n., v.,* COOKED, COOKING. (Turning over a pancake.) The open right hand rests on the upturned left palm. The right hand flips over and comes to rest with its back on the left palm. This is the action of turning over a pancake. The sign for INDIVIDUAL, for a noun, then follows: both open hands, palms facing each other, move down the sides of the body, tracing its outline to the hips. Also CHEF, KITCHEN 1, PANCAKE.

COOKIE (kŏŏk' ĭ), *n.* (Act of cutting cookies with a cookie mold.) The right hand, in the "C" position, palm down, is placed into the open left palm. It then rises a bit, swings or twists around a little, and in this new position is placed again in the open left palm. Also BISCUIT, MUFFIN.

COOL (kŏŏl), *adj., v.,* COOLED, COOLING. (Fanning the face.) Both open hands are held with palms down and fingers spread and pointing toward the face. The hands move up and down as if fanning the face.

COOPERATE (kō ŏp′ ə rāt′), *v.*, -ATED, -ATING. (Joining in movement.) Both "D" hands, thumbs and index fingers interlocked, rotate in a counterclockwise circle in front of the body.

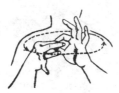

COP (kŏp) (*colloq.*), *n.* (The letter "C" for "cop"; the shape and position of the badge.) The right "C" hand, palm facing left, is placed against the heart. Also POLICE, POLICEMAN, SHERIFF.

COPULATE (kŏp′ yə lāt′), *v.*, -LATED, -LATING. (The motions of the legs during the sexual act.) The upturned left "V" hand remains motionless while the downturned right "V" hand comes down repeatedly on the left. Also FORNICATE, SEXUAL INTERCOURSE.

COPY 1 (kŏp′ ĭ), *n., v.,* COPIED, COPYING. (The natural sign.) The right fingers and thumb close together and move onto the upturned, open left hand, as if taking something from one place to another. Also DUPLICATE 1, IMITATE, MIMIC, MODEL.

COPY 2, *v.* (The motion of removing something and transferring it.) The fingertips and thumb of the right hand are placed against the back of the left hand, which is held palm toward the face, fingers pointing up. The fingers of the right hand then close into the "AND" position and move forward, away from the left hand, as they do.

COPYRIGHT (kop′ ē rīt′), *n., v.,* -RIGHTED, -RIGHTING. (COPY and RIGHT.) The right fingers and thumb close together and move onto the upturned open left hand as if taking something from one place to another. Next, the sign for RIGHT: the right hand, fingers together and palm facing left, is placed in the upturned left palm, whose fingers point away from the body. The right hand slides straight out along the left palm, over the left fingers, and stops with its heel resting on the left fingertips.

CORDIAL (kôr′ jəl), *adj.* (A crinkling up of the face.) Both hands, in the "5" position, palms facing back, are placed on either side of the face. The fingers wiggle back and forth while a pleasant, happy expression is worn. Also AMIABLE, CHEERFUL, FRIENDLY, JOLLY, PLEASANT.

CORN (kôrn), *n.* (Scraping kernels from the corncob.) The extended left index finger points forward, representing the corncob, while the right thumb and index finger rub back and forth along the finger, as if scraping off kernels.

CORNER 1 (kôr′ nər), *n.* (The natural sign.) Both hands, palms flat and fingers straight, are held in front of the body at right angles to each other with fingertips touching, the left fingertips pointing to the right and the right fingertips pointing forward. Also ANGLE.

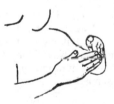

CORNER 2, *v.*, -NERED, -NERING. (A pinning down.) The left "D" finger represents the one who is caught. The curved index and middle fingers of the right hand, palm facing down, are thrust against the left "D" finger, impaling it. Also CAUGHT IN THE ACT 1, CONTACT 2.

CORN ON THE COB (kôrn, kŏb), *n.* (Act of eating an ear of corn.) The index fingers, touching each other, are brought up against the teeth. Both hands are pivoted around and back several times. One index finger may be used instead of two.

CORRECT 1, *adj.* The right index finger, held above the left index finger, comes down rather forcefully so that the bottom of the right hand comes to rest on top of the left thumb joint. Also ACCURATE 2, DECENT, EXACT 2, JUST 2, PROPER, RIGHT 3, SUITABLE.

 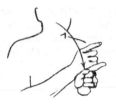

CORRECT 2 (kə rĕkt′), *v.*, -RECTED, -RECTING. (A canceling out.) The right index finger makes a cross on the open left palm. Also ANNUL, CANCEL, CHECK 1, CRITICISM, CRITICIZE, FIND FAULT 1, REVOKE.

CORRELATION (kôr ə lā′ shən), *n.* (Connection.) The indexes and thumbs of both hands form a link together. Both hands move repeatedly left to right and back.

CORRESPOND (kôr′ ə spŏnd′), *v.*, -PONDED, -PONDING. The "AND" hands face each other, one slightly higher than the other. The two hands then move toward and past each other, opening as they do.

CORRIDOR (kôr′ ə dər, kŏr′ -), *n.* (The movement.) Both hands, palms facing and fingers together and extended straight out, move in unison away from the body in a straight or winding manner. Also HALL, HALLWAY, MANNER 2, METHOD, OPPORTUNITY 3, PATH, ROAD, STREET, TRAIL, WAY 1.

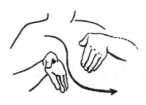

COSMETICS (kŏz mĕt′ ĭks), *n. pl.* (Applying something to the face.) The thumbtip and fingertips of each hand are held together and rotated in small counterclockwise circles on both cheeks simultaneously. Also MAKEUP.

COST (kôst, kŏst), *n., v.,* COST, COSTING. (Nicking into one.) The knuckle of the right "X" finge'r is nicked against the palm of the left hand, held in the "5" position, palm facing right. Also ADMISSION 2, CHARGE 1,

DUTY 2, EXCISE, EXPENSE, FEE, FINE 2, IMPOST, PENALTY 3, PRICE 2, TAX 1, TAXATION 1, TOLL.

COSTA RICA (kos′ tə rē kə) *n.* (The shape of the North American and South American continents with Costa Rica in between.) The tips of the right "C" hand, palm facing left, rest on the thumb of the left "C" hand, palm facing right. Alternatively, the modified "C" hands may be used, with only thumbs and index fingers forming the "C." In this case, the right index rests on the left thumb. A native sign.

COSTLY (kôst′ lĭ), *adj.* (Throwing away money.) The right "AND" hand lies in the palm of the upturned, open left hand (as if holding money). The right hand then moves up and away from the left, opening abruptly as it does (as if dropping the money it holds). Also DEAR 2, EXPENSIVE.

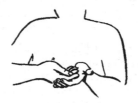 

COSTUME (kos′ tōōm), *n.* (The letter "C"; slipping clothes on.) Both "C" hands, palms facing, move down the chest simultaneously. The movement is repeated.

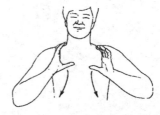

COTTON 1 (kŏt′ ɔn), *n.* (White, pick.) The sign for WHITE is formed: the fingertips of the "5" hand are placed against the chest. The hand moves straight out from the chest, while the fingers and thumb all come together. Then the fingertips and thumbtip of the down-turned, open right hand come together, and the hand moves up a short distance, as if picking something.

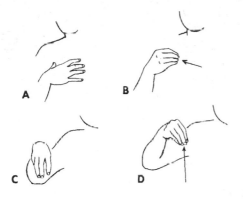

COTTON 2, *n.* (Picking cotton.) The left hand is held with extended thumb touching fingertips. The right hand closes over the left and pulls away, as if plucking cotton from the plant.

COUGH 1 (kôf), *n., v.,* COUGHED, COUGHING. (An irritation in the throat.) The fingertips of the right "V" hand are jabbed into the right side of the neck. The signer imitates coughing.

COUGH 2, *n., v.* The right claw hand is held with fingertips on the chest. The fingertips alternately open and bend as the signer mimes coughing.

COULD (kŏŏd), *v.* (An affirmative movement of the hands, likened to a nodding of the head, to indicate ability or power to accomplish something.) Both "A" hands, held palms down, move down in unison a short distance before the chest. Also ABILITY, ABLE, CAN 1, CAPABLE, COMPETENT, FACULTY, MAY 2, POSSIBLE.

COUNSEL (koun′ sǝl), *n., v.,* -SELED, -SELING. (Take something, *counsel,* and disseminate it.) The left hand, held limp in front of the body, has its fingers pointing down. The fingers of the right hand, held all together, are placed on top of the left hand and then move forward, off the left hand, assuming a "5" position, palm down. This may be repeated. Also ADVICE, ADVISE, COUNSELOR, INFLUENCE 4.

COUNSELOR (koun′ sə lər), *n.* The sign for COUN-SEL is made. This is followed by the sign for INDI-VIDUAL: both open hands, palms facing each other, move down the sides of the body, tracing its outline to the hips.

COUNT (kount), *v.,* COUNTED, COUNTING. The thumb-tip and index fingertip of the right "F" hand move up along the palm of the open left hand, which is held facing right with fingers pointing up.

COUNTRY 1 (kun′ trĭ), *n.* (The elbow reinforcement on the jacket of a "country squire" type; also, a place where one commonly "roughs it," *i.e.,* gets rough elbows.) The open right hand describes a continuous counterclockwise circle on the left elbow. Also FARM 3.

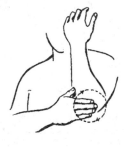

COUNTRY 2, *n.* (An established area.) The right "N" hand, palm down, executes a clockwise circle above the downturned prone left hand. The tips of the "N" fingers then move straight down and come to rest on the back of the left hand. Also LAND 2, NATION.

COURAGE (kûr′ ĭj, kŭr′-), *n.* (Strength emanating from the body.) Both "5" hands are placed palms against the chest. They move out and away forcefully, closing and assuming the "S" position. Also BRAVE, BRAVERY, COURAGEOUS, FORTITUDE, HALE, HEALTH, HEALTHY, MIGHTY 2, STRENGTH, STRONG 2, WELL 2.

COURAGEOUS (kə rā′ jəs), *adj.* See COURAGE.

COURT (kōrt), *n.* (The scales move up and down.) The two "F" hands, palms facing each other, move alternately up and down. Also CONSIDER 3, EVALUATE 1, IF, JUDGE 1, JUDGMENT, JUSTICE 1.

COURTEOUS (kûr′ tĭ əs), *adj.* (The ruffled shirtfront of a gentleman of old.) The thumb of the right "5" hand is thrust into the chest. The hand then pivots down, with thumb remaining in place. This latter part of the sign, however, is optional. Also COURTESY, FINE 4, POLITE.

COURTESY (kûr′ tə sĭ), *n.* See COURTEOUS.

COUSIN (kŭz′ ən) (*f.*), *n.* (The letter "C" in female position.) The right "C" hand is shaken back and forth next to the right cheek.

COUSIN (*m.*), *n.* (The letter "C" in male position.) The right "C" hand is shaken back and forth next to the right temple.

COVENANT (kuv ′ə nənt), *n.* (*eccles.*). (Agree and connect with.) The sign for AGREE: the right index touches the forehead, then is brought down to touch the left index, both pointing forward. The sign for CONNECT follows: both right and left thumbs and index fingers interconnect. This refers to an agreement made with God.

COVER 1 (kŭv′ ər), *n., v.,* -ERED, -ERING. (The natural sign.) This sign is used to mean "to cover up something." The right hand, held curved and palm down, slides from fingertips to wrist over the back of the left hand, which is also held curved and palm down.

COVER 2, *n.* (The natural sign.) The open right hand lies over the upturned thumb edge of the left "S" hand. In this position the right hand turns in a clockwise direction several times, as if screwing on a cover. Also LID.

COVER 3, *n.* (The natural sign.) This sign is used to mean "to place a cover on." The open right hand, held palm down before the chest, moves downward, coming to rest atop the upturned thumb edge of the left "S" hand, as if to cover it.

COVER 4, *v.* (One hand is hidden under the other.) This sign is used to mean "to hide." The thumb of the right "A" hand, whose palm faces left, is placed against the lips. The hand then swings down and under the downturned left hand. The initial contact with the lips is sometimes omitted. Also HIDE.

COVER 5, *n. v.* (The natural motion.) The signer lifts an imaginary cover and pulls it up over his body.

COVER-UP (kuv′ ər up′), *n.* (Obscuring the view.) The right "5" hand sweeps repeatedly in a counterclockwise direction over the facing left palm.

COW (kou), *n.* (The cow's horns.) The "Y" hands, palms facing away from the body, are placed at the temples, with thumbs touching the head. Both hands are brought out and away simultaneously, in a gentle curve.

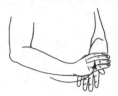

COWBOY 1 (kou′ boi), *n.* (The pistols.) Using both "L" hands, the signer waves them forward and back repeatedly.

COWBOY 2, *n.* (Twirling a lariat.) The signer twirls an imaginary lariat and pulls back. For added effect, the body may bounce up and down slightly, as if on horseback. Also LARIAT, LASSO.

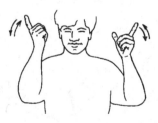

CRAB 1 (krab), *n.* (The claws.) The indexes and thumbs open and close repeatedly.

CRAB 2, *n.* A variant of CRAB 1. The upturned "V" fingers open and close repeatedly.

CRACKER 1 (krăk′ ər), *n.* The thumb edge of the right fist strikes several times against the left elbow, while the left arm is bent so that the left fist is held against the right shoulder. Also MATZOTH, PASSOVER.

CRACKER 2, *n.* (Modification of CRACKER 1.) The elbow is brought down into the upturned palm as if to break a cracker in it.

CRADLE (krād'l) *n.* (The shape; rocking the baby.) The signer rocks an imaginary baby; then the up-turned cupped hands trace the outline of a cradle by separating and moving up in a curve.

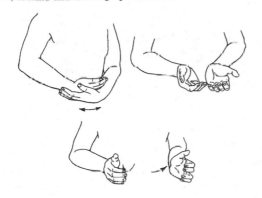

CRANKY (krang'kē) *adj.* (The facial features are screwed up.) The palm of the right claw hand is held in front of the face and the fingers open and close several times. The facial features are contorted to portray anger or annoyance.

CRASH (krăsh), *n., v.,* CRASHED, CRASHING. The fists come together with force. Also COLLIDE 1, COLLISION 1, RUN UP AGAINST, WRECK.

CRAVE (krāv), *v.,* CRAVED, CRAVING. (The upper alimentary tract is outlined.) The right "C" hand, palm facing the body, is placed with fingertips touching mid-chest. In this position it moves down a bit. Also

APPETITE, DESIRE 2, FAMINE, HUNGARIAN, HUNGARY, HUNGER, HUNGRY, STARVATION, STARVE, STARVED, WISH 2.

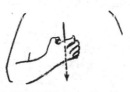

CRAYON (krā' ən), *n.* (Color and writing.) The sign for COLOR is made: the fingertips of the right "5" hand, palm facing the body, are placed on or just in front of the chin and wiggle back and forth. This is followed by the sign for WRITE: the right hand, holding an imaginary writing implement, writes on the palm of the upturned left hand.

CRAZY 1 (krā' zǐ), *adj.* (Turning of wheels in the head.) The open right hand is held palm down before the face, fingers spread, bent, and pointing toward the forehead. The fingers move in circles before the forehead. Also INSANE, INSANITY, MAD 2, NUTS 1.

CRAZY 2, *adj.* (Wheels in the head.) The sign for THINK is made. Then both index fingers, positioned one on top of the other and pointing to each other, spin around. Also NUTS 2.

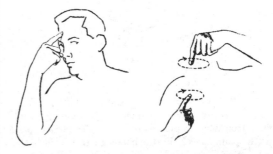

CRAZY 3, *adj.* (Turning of wheels in the head.) The right index finger revolves in a clockwise circle at the right temple. Also NUTS 3.

CRAZY FOR, *phrase.* (Kissing something to indicate a liking for it.) The back of the fist is kissed.

CRAZY FOR/ABOUT, *phrase.* (Something that makes you dizzy.) The right claw hand, facing the signer, shakes from right to left repeatedly. The mouth is usually held open.

CREAM (krēm), *n.* (The motion of skimming cream.) The right hand is held slightly cupped and is moved repeatedly across the upturned, open left palm, as if skimming cream from the top of a container of milk.

CREATE 1 (krē āt′), *v.,* CREATED, CREATING. (Fashioning something with the hands.) The right "S" hand, palm facing left, is placed on top of its left counterpart, whose palm faces right. The hands are twisted back and

forth, striking each other slightly after each twist. Also COMPOSE, CONSTITUTE, CONSTRUCT 2, DEVISE 2, FABRICATE, FASHION, FIX, MAKE, MANUFACTURE, MEND 1, PRODUCE 3, RENDER 1, REPAIR.

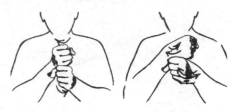

CREATE 2, *v.* (Something springs from the mind, and then the hands go to work to make it.) The right "4" hand, palm facing left, moves up the forehead. The right hand changes to the "S" position, palm facing left, and is placed on top of its left counterpart, whose palm faces right. The hands are twisted back and forth, striking each other slightly after each twist.

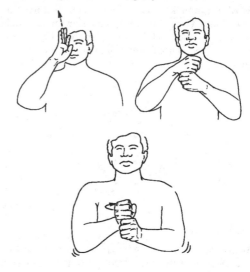

CREDENTIAL (kri dən′ shəl), *n.* (The "C." Both "C" hands face each other. The thumbtips touch each other twice. Also CERTIFICATE.

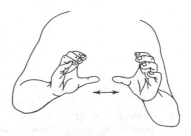

CREDIBLE (krĕd′ ə bəl), *adj.* (Fall for something, *i.e.,* swallowing the bait.) The right-angle hand is brought up toward the open mouth. Also GULLIBLE.

CREDIT CARD (kred′ it kard), *n.* (The credit card machine is used to make an impression on the sales slip.) The left hand is held palm up. The right hand, closed in a fist, is placed with the edge of the little finger on the left palm. The right hand moves back and forth.

CREW CUT, (krōō′ kŭt′), *n.* (Tracing the hair over the head.) The thumb side of the "G" hand is drawn over the head. Squinting and blowing out slightly will indicate a very short crew cut.

CRIB (krib), *n.* (An interlaced support.) The upturned hands are held with fingers interlocked. They separate and move up, forming a cradle or crib.

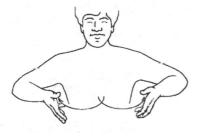

CRICKET (krik′ it), *n.* (The natural sign.) The signer mimes swinging a cricket bat.

CRIPPLE (krĭp′ əl), *n., v.,* -PLED, -PLING. (The uneven movement of the legs.) The downturned index fingers move alternately up and down. The body sways to and fro a little, keeping time with the movement of the fingers. Also LAME.

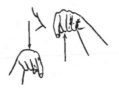

CRITERIA (krī tēr′ ē ə), *n.* (The "C"; moving across fingers, indicating options.) The thumb edge of the right "C" hand runs over the upright left fingers, beginning at the left thumb.

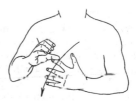

CRITICISM (krĭt′ ə sĭz′ əm), *n.* (A canceling out.) The right index finger makes a cross on the open left palm. Also ANNUL, CANCEL, CHECK 1, CORRECT 2, CRITICIZE, FIND FAULT 1, REVOKE.

CRITICIZE (krĭt′ ə sīz′), *v.*, -CIZED, -CIZING. See CRITI-CISM.

CROOK (krŏŏk), *n.* (A mustachioed thief.) The fingertips of both "H" hands, palms facing the body, are placed above the lips and are drawn slowly apart, describing a mustache. Sometimes one hand only is used. This is followed by the sign for INDIVIDUAL: both open hands, palms facing each other, move down the sides of the body, tracing its outline to the hips. Also BANDIT, BURGLAR, BURGLARY, ROB 3, ROBBER 1, STEAL 3, THEFT 3, THIEF 2.

CROSS 1 (krôs), *adj.* (Wrinkling the brow.) The "5" hand is held palm toward the face. The fingers open and close partly, several times, while an angry expression is worn on the face. Also ANGRY 1, CROSSNESS, FIERCE, ILL TEMPER, IRRITABLE.

CROSS 2 (*eccles.*), *n.* (The cross on the mountain.) The back of the right "S" hand is struck several times against the back of the left "S" hand to denote something hard, like a ROCK or a MOUNTAIN, *q.v.* The sign for CROSS 2 is then made: the right "C" hand, palm facing out, makes the sign of the cross. Also CALVARY 1, CRUCIFIX.

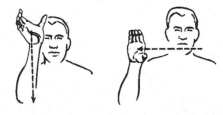

CROSS 3, *v.*, CROSSED, CROSSING. (A crossing over.) The left hand is held before the chest, palm down and

fingers together. The right hand, fingers together, glides over the left, with the right little finger touching the top of the left hand. Also ACROSS, OVER 2.

CROSS 4, *v.* (Intersecting lines.) The extended index fingers move toward each other at right angles and cross. Also CROSSING, INTERSECT, INTERSECTION.

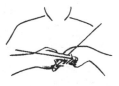

CROSS-COUNTRY SKIING, *n.* (The natural movement.) Using a swinging rhythm, the signer takes long sliding strides as the ski poles maneuver back and forth.

CROSSING (krôs′ ĭng), *n.* See CROSS 4.

CROSSNESS, *n.* See CROSS 1.

CROWD (kroud), *n.*, *v.*, CROWDED, CROWDING. (The movement of many people.) Both open hands are held side by side, palms down. The hands are then moved forward while the fingers wiggle.

CROWDED, *adj.* (Squeezed in.) The "5" hands are held about a foot apart in front of the body, fingers pointing forward. The hands are slowly pushed toward each other without touching, as if compressing something into a smaller space. The signer assumes a strained expression.

CROWN 1 (kroun), *n.* (The natural sign.) Both "C" hands, held in a modified position, with middle, ring, and little fingers extended and little finger edges down, are held over the head and slowly lowered, as if placing a crown on the head. Also CORONET.

CROWN 2, *n., v.,* CROWNED, CROWNING. (Placing a crown on the head.) The right hand, its thumb and fingers spread and curved, is placed with thumbtip and fingertips touching the top of the head to represent a crown.

CRUCIFIX (krōō sə fĭks'), *n.* See CROSS 2.

CRUEL 1 (krōō' əl), *adj.* (Striking down against.) Both "A" or "X" hands are held before the chest, the right above the left. The right hand strikes down and

out, hitting the left thumb and knuckles with force. Also BACKBITE, BASE 3, HARM 2, HURT 2, MAR 2, MEAN 1, SPOIL.

CRUEL 2, *adj.* (A heart that is rough.) The sign for HEART 1 is made: the index fingers outline either half of a small heart on the left side of the chest. Then the sign for ROUGH is made: the right thumbtip and fingertips are placed at the base of the upturned, open left palm. From this position they move forward forcefully, off and away from the left hand.

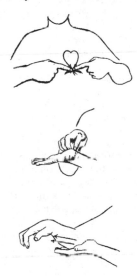

CRUEL 3, *adj.* The movements in TEASE 1, *q.v.,* are duplicated, except that the "G" hands are used. Also TEASE 3.

CRUSH (krush), *v.*, CRUSHED, CRUSHING. (Pressing together.) The heels of both open hands are pressed forcefully together, and the right hand pivots to the right.

CRY 1 (krī), *v.*, CRIED, CRYING. (Tears streaming down the cheeks.) Both index fingers, in the "D" position, move down the cheeks, either once or several times. Sometimes one finger only is used. Also BAWL 1, TEAR 2, TEARDROP, WEEP 1.

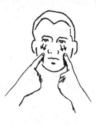

CRY 2, *v.* (Tears gushing from the eyes.) Both "B" hands are held before the face, palms facing forward, with the backs of the index fingertips touching the face just below the eyes. From this position both hands move forward and over in an arc to indicate a flow of tears. Also BAWL 2, WEEP 2.

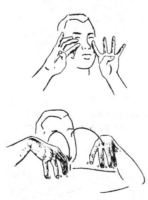

CRY 3, *v.* (Harsh words thrown out.) The right hand, as in BLASPHEME 1, appears to claw words out of the mouth. This time, however, it turns and throws

them out, ending in the "5" position. Also BLASPHEME 2, CALL OUT, CRY OUT, CURSE 2, SCREAM, SHOUT, SUMMON 1, SWEAR 3.

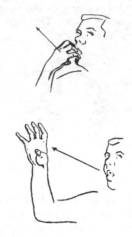

CUBA (kyo͞o′ bə), *n.* (The cap worn by the militia.) The back of the right open hand is placed against the forehead. A native sign.

CULTURE (kul′ chər), *n.* (The "C"; surrounding one.) The right "C" hand makes a counterclockwise circle around the upright left index finger.

CUP (kŭp), *n.* (The natural sign.) The little finger edge of the right "C" hand rests on the palm of the upturned, open left hand. Also CUP AND SAUCER.

CUP AND SAUCER (kŭp, sô′ sər), *n. phrase.* See CUP.

CUPBOARD (kub′ ərd), *n.* (Grasping the handles.) The signer mimes opening a pair of cabinet doors by grasping the handles. Also CABINET 2.

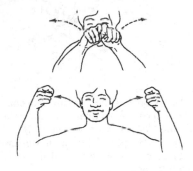

CURAÇAO (kyōō′ ə sō′), *n.* The right "C" hand, palm facing out and held at chest level, moves to the right and then down a few inches. A native sign.

CURIOSITY (kyōōr′ ĭ ŏs′ ə tĭ), *n.* See CURIOUS 3.

CURIOUS 1 (kyōō′ ĭ əs), *adj.* (Directing the vision from place to place.) The right "C" hand, palm facing left, moves from right to left across the line of vision in a series of counterclockwise circles. The signer's gaze remains concentrated and his head turns slowly from right to left. Also EXAMINE, INVESTIGATE 1, LOOK FOR, PROBE 1, QUEST, SEARCH, SEEK.

CURIOUS 2, *adj.* (Something that distorts the vision.) The "C" hand describes a small arc in front of the face. Also GROTESQUE, ODD, PECULIAR, QUEER 1, STRANGE 1, WEIRD.

CURIOUS 3 (*colloq.*), *adj.* (The Adam's apple.) The right thumb and index finger pinch the skin over the Adam's apple while the hand wiggles up and down. Also CURIOSITY.

CURRICULUM (kə rik′ yə ləm), *n.* (The "C" and "M"; outlining a sheet of paper.) The right "C" hand is placed near the fingertips of the forward-facing left palm. As it moves down toward the heel of the hand, the left hand changes to an "M."

CURSE 1 (kûrs), *n., v.,* CURSED, CURSING. (Harsh words and a threatening hand.) The right hand appears to claw words out of the mouth. It ends in the "S" position, above the head, shaking back and forth in a threatening manner. Also BLASPHEME 1, SWEAR 2.

CURSE 2, *n., v.* (Harsh words thrown out.) The right hand, as in CURSE 1, appears to claw words out of the mouth. This time, however, it turns and throws them out, ending in the "5" position. Also BLASPHEME 2, CALL OUT, CRY 3, CRY OUT, SCREAM, SHOUT, SUMMON 1, SWEAR 3.

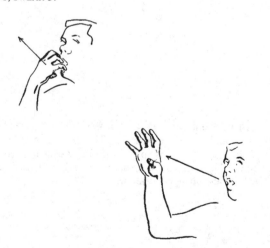

CURSE 3 (*sl.*), *n., v.* (Curlicues, as one finds in cartoon-type swearwords.) The right "Y" hand, palm down, pivots at the wrist along the left "G" hand, from the wrist to the tip of the finger. Also BLASPHEME 3, SWEAR 4.

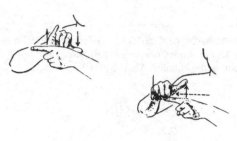

CURSOR (kûr′ sər), *n.* (The blinking movement on the computer screen.) With right index touching the right thumb, the hand moves from left to right, while the thumb and index open and close in a methodical fashion. They may also move up and down as they move from left to right.

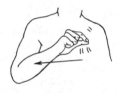

CUSTOM (kŭs′ təm), *n.* (Bound down to custom or habit.) Both "S" hands, palms down, are crossed and brought down in unison before the chest. Also ACCUSTOM, BOUND, HABIT, LOCKED, PRACTICE 3.

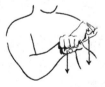

CUT (kŭt), *v.,* CUT, CUTTING. (Cutting the finger with a knife.) The extended right index finger makes a cutting motion across the extended left index finger. Both hands are held palms down.

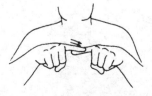

CUTE 1 (kūt), *adj.* (Titillating to the taste.) The fingertips of the right "U" hand, palm facing the body, brush against the chin a number of times, beginning at the lips. Also CANDY 1, SUGAR, SWEET.

CUTE 2, *adj.* (Tickling.) The open right hand is held with fingers spread and pointing up, palm facing the chest. In this position the fingertips wiggle up and down, tickling the chin several times.

CYCLE (sī′ kəl), *n. Computer term.* (Around the clock to the beginning.) The right index finger touches its left counterpart. It then makes a small clockwise circle around the left, coming back to its original position.

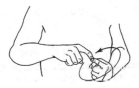

CYLINDER (sil′ in dər), *n. automotive.* (The shape and movement.) Both clenched fists, held upright, one behind the other, move alternately up and down, tracing the movement of automobile or marine engine cylinders.

CYNIC (sĭn′ ĭk), *n.* (The nose is wrinkled in disbelief.) The right "V" hand faces the nose. The index and middle fingers bend as a cynical expression is assumed. This is followed by the sign for INDIVIDUAL: both open hands, palms facing each other, move down the sides of the body, tracing its outline to the hips. Also CYNICAL, DISBELIEF 1, DON'T BELIEVE, DOUBT 1, INCREDULITY, SKEPTIC 1, SKEPTICAL 1.

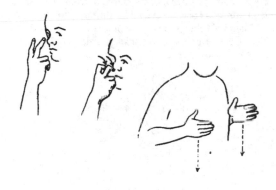

CYNICAL (sĭn′ ə kəl), *adj.* See CYNIC. The sign for INDIVIDUAL is omitted.

D

DACTYLOLOGY (dăk′ tə lŏl′ ə jĭ), *n.* (The movement of the fingers in fingerspelling.) The right hand, palm out, is moved from left to right, with the fingers wriggling up and down. Also ALPHABET, FINGERSPELLING, MANUAL ALPHABET, SPELL, SPELLING.

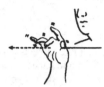

DAD (dăd) (*informal*), *n.* (Derived from the formal sign for FATHER 1, *q.v.*) The thumbtip of the right "5" hand touches the right temple a number of times. The other fingers may also wiggle. Also DADDY, FATHER 2, PAPA, POP 2.

DADDY (dăd′ ĭ), *n.* See DAD.

DAILY (dā′ lĭ), *adj.* (Tomorrow after tomorrow.) The sign for TOMORROW, *q.v.*, is made several times: the right "A" hand moves forward several times from its initial resting place on the right cheek. Also EVERYDAY.

DAISY (dā′ zē), *n.* (Plucking the petals.) The right index and thumb pluck imaginary petals from the upright left index finger.

DALLAS (dal′ əs), *n.* (The letter "D.") The thumbtip and the tip of the middle finger of the right "D" hand are placed on the right temple.

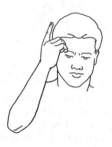

DAM (dam), *n., v.,* DAMMED, DAMMING. (Closing off the water.) The sign for WATER is made: the index finger of the right "W" sign is placed against the lips. The signer then forms both hands into right angles, one above the other. The little finger edge of the upper hand comes down against the index finger edge of the other, as if closing something.

DAMN! (dam), *interj.* The right "D" hand, palm facing down, is moved forcefully to the right. An expression of annoyance or disapproval is assumed. Also DARN!

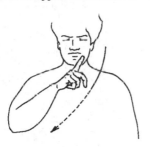

DAMP (dămp), *adj.* (The wetness.) The right fingertips touch the lips, and then the fingers of both hands open and close against the thumbs a number of times. Also CERAMICS, CLAY, MOIST, WET.

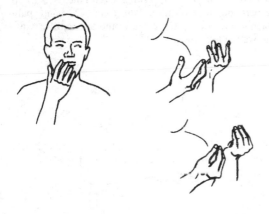

DANCE (dăns, däns), *n., v.,* DANCED, DANCING. (The rhythmic swaying of the feet.) The downturned index and middle fingers of the right "V" hand swing rhythmically back and forth over the upturned left palm. Also BALL 1, PARTY 2.

DANGER 1 (dān′ jər), *n.* (Throwing out the hands.) Both hands, their fingertips touching their respective thumbs, are held, palms facing each other, near the temples. They are thrown out before the face, assuming "5" positions, palms still facing. Also AWFUL, CALAMITOUS, CATASTROPHIC, DANGEROUS 1, DREADFUL, FEARFUL, TERRIBLE, TRAGEDY, TRAGIC.

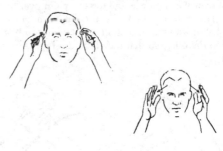

DANGER 2, *n.* (An encroachment; parrying a knife thrust.) The left "A" hand is held palm toward the body, knuckles facing right. The extended thumb of the right "A" hand is brought sharply over the back of the left. Also DANGEROUS 2, INJURE 2, PERIL, TRESPASS, VIOLATE.

DANGEROUS 1 (dān′ jər əs), *adj.* See DANGER 1.

DANGEROUS 2, *adj.* See DANGER 2.

DARE (dâr), *n., v.,* DARED, DARING. (The letter "D"; challenge or confront.) Both hands are held in the "D" position, facing each other. The right "D" hand is brought up sharply against the left, and both hands continue away from the body an inch or so.

DARK(NESS) (därk), *adj., n.* (Shutting out the light.) Both open hands are held in front of the face, the right palm over the right eye and the left palm over the left eye. The hands then move toward each other and slightly downward in a short arc, coming to rest one behind the other so that they hide the face. Also TWI-LIGHT.

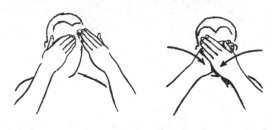

DARN (därn), *v.,* DARNED, DARNING. (The threads are interwoven.) Both "5" hands, palms down, are brought slowly together, with the right sliding over the left. As they move together, the fingers wiggle. Also INFIL-TRATE, WEAVE.

DAUGHTER (dô′ tər), *n.* (Female baby.) The FEMALE prefix sign is made: the thumb of the right "A" hand traces a line on the right jaw from just below the ear to the chin. The sign for BABY is then made: the right arm is folded on the left arm. Both palms face up.

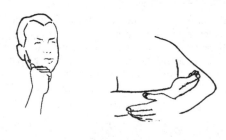

DAVEN (dä′ vən), *v.,* DAVENED, DAVENING. (*eccles.*). (The traditional way to recite Jewish prayers, bowing repeatedly.) With the hands clasped palm to palm or one hand resting in the other, the signer bows the head and upper torso repeatedly.

DAY (dā), *n., adj.* (The letter "D"; the course of the sun across the sky.) The left arm, held horizontally, palm down, represents the horizon. The right elbow rests on the back of the left hand, with the right arm in a perpendicular position. The right "D" hand, palm facing left, moves in an arc to the left until it is just above the left elbow.

DEAD 1 (děd), *adj.* (Turning over on one's side.) The open hands, fingers pointing ahead, are held side by side, with the right palm down and the left palm up. The two hands reverse their relative positions as they move from the left to the right. Also DEATH, DIE 1, DYING, EXPIRE 2, PERISH 1.

DEAD 2 (*sl.*), *adj.* (An animal's legs sticking up in the air, in death.) Both hands are held with palms facing each other and curved index and middle fingers prescnted. The hands pivot up a bit, simultaneously, assuming the "V" position as they do. Also DIE 2, PASS OUT.

DEAF 1 (dĕf), *adj.* (Deaf and mute.) The tip of the extended right index finger touches first the right ear and then the closed lips.

DEAF 2 (dĕf), *adj.* (The ear is shut.) The right index finger touches the right ear. Both "B" hands, palms out, then draw together until their index finger edges touch.

DEATH (dĕth), *n.* Scc DEAD 1.

DEBATE (dĭ bat'), *n., v.,* -BATED, -BATING. (An expounding back and forth.) The index fingers here represent the two sides of the argument. First the left index finger is slapped into the open right palm, and then the right makes the same movement into the left palm. This is repeated back and forth several times. Also ARGUE, ARGUMENT, CONTROVERSY, DISPUTE.

DEBIT (dĕb' ĭt), *n.* (Pointing to the palm where the money should be placed.) The index finger of one hand is thrust into the upturned palm of the other several times. Also ARREARS, DEBT, DUE, OBLIGATION 3, OWE.

DEBT (dĕt), *n.* Scc DEBIT.

DECAY (dĭ kā'), *v.,* -CAYED, -CAYING. (Fingering the small pieces resulting from the breaking up of something.) The thumbs rub slowly across the fingertips of the upturned hands, from the little fingers to the index fingers, and then continue to the "A" position, palms up. Also DIE OUT, DISSOLVE, FADE, MELT, ROT.

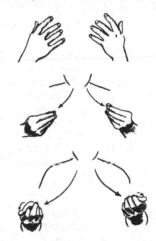

DECEIT (dĭ set'), *n.* (Underhandedness.) The right hand, palm down, is held with index and little fingers pointing out. The left hand, in a similar position, is held above the right. The right hand moves forward repeatedly, each time emerging briefly from under the left hand. The positions may be reversed, with the left hand doing the movement, or both hands can move simultaneously. Also CHEAT 1, DECEIVE, DECEPTION, DEFRAUD, FRAUD, FRAUDULENT 1.

DECEIVE (dǐ sēv'), *v.,* -CEIVED, -CEIVING. See DECEIT.

DECENT (dē' sənt), *adj.* The right index finger, held above the left index finger, comes down rather forcefully so that the bottom of the right hand comes to rest on top of the left thumb joint. Also ACCURATE 2, CORRECT 1, EXACT 2, JUST 2, PROPER, RIGHT 3, SUITABLE.

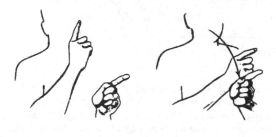

DECEPTION (dǐ sĕp' shən), *n.* See DECEIT.

DECIDE (dǐ sīd'), *v.,* -CIDED, -CIDING. (The mind stops wavering, and the pros and cons are resolved.) The right index finger touches the forehead, the sign for THINK, *q.v.* Both "F" hands, palms facing each other and fingers pointing straight out, then drop down simultaneously. The sign for JUDGE, *q.v.,* explains the rationale behind the movement of the two hands here. Also DECISION, DECREE 1, DETERMINE, MAKE UP ONE'S MIND, MIND 5, RENDER JUDGMENT, RESOLVE, VERDICT.

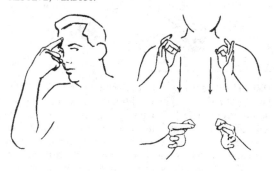

DECISION (dǐ sǐzh' ən), *n.* See DECIDE.

DECLARE (dǐ klâr'), *v.,* -CLARED, -CLARING. (An issuance from the mouth.) Both index fingers are placed at the lips, with palms facing the body. They are rotated once and swung out in arcs until the left

index finger points somewhat to the left and the right index somewhat to the right. Sometimes the rotation of the fingers is omitted in favor of a simple swinging out from the lips. Also ACCLAIM 1, ACCLAMATION, ANNOUNCE, ANNOUNCEMENT, MAKE KNOWN, PROCLAIM, PROCLAMATION.

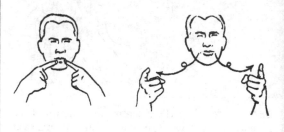

DECLINE 1 (dǐ klīn'), *n., v.,* -CLINED, -CLINING. (A downward movement.) The right "A" hand, held with thumb pointing up, moves straight downward in front of the body. Both "A" hands may also be used. Also DEGENERATION.

DECLINE 2, *v.* (Going down step by step.) The little finger edge of the open right hand is placed on the upper side of the extended left arm, which is held with the open left hand palm down. The right hand moves down along the left arm in a series of short movements. This is the opposite of IMPROVE, *q.v.* Also DETERIORATE, DETERIORATION, NOT IMPROVE.

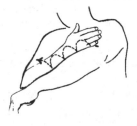

DECLINE 3, *v.* (The hands are shaken, indicating a wish to rid them of something.) The "5" hands, palms facing the body, suddenly swing around to the palms-down position. Also DON'T WANT.

DECLINE IN HEALTH, *phrase.* Both upturned thumbs move down in stages.

DECODE (dē kōd′), *v. Computer term.* (Changing; the letter "D.") Both "D" hands are held together, index fingers pointing up. They swing around so that the right "D" is now underneath the left "D."

DECORATE 1 (dĕk′ ə rāt′), *v.,* -RATED, -RATING. (The hands describe the flounces of draperies.) Both "C" hands, palms out, are held somewhat above the head. They move out and down in a series of successive arcs. Also ADORN, ORNAMENT 1, TRIM 1.

DECORATE 2, *v.* (Embellishing; adding to.) Both "O" hands, palms facing each other, move alternately back and forth in a curving up and down direction.

The fingertips come in contact each time the hands pass each other. Also ORNAMENT 2, TRIM 2.

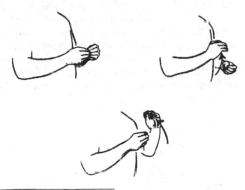

DECREASE 1 (*n.* de′ krēs; *v.* dĭ krēs′), -CREASED, -CREASING. (The diminishing size or amount.) With palms facing, the right hand is held above the left. The right hand moves slowly down toward the left, but does not touch it. Also LESS 1, REDUCE.

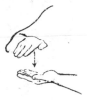

DECREASE 2, *v., n.* (Dropping off what has been added.) Both "H" hands, palms down, are positioned with the right resting on the left. The right "H" swings off the left in an arc to the right, ending in the palm-up position.

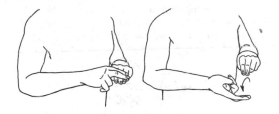

DEDICATE (ded′ i kāt′), *v.,* -CATED, -CATING. *Computer term.* (The letter "D"; established.) The base of the right "D" hand rests on the back of the downturned left fist. Also DEDICATED.

DEDUCT (dǐ dŭkt′), *v.*, -DUCTED, -DUCTING. (Removing.) The right "A" hand, resting in the palm of the left "5" hand, moves slightly up and away, describing a small arc. It is then cast downward, opening into the "5" position, palm down, as if removing something from the left hand and casting it down. Also ABOLISH 2, ABSENCE 2, ABSENT 2, ABSTAIN, CHEAT 2, DEFICIENCY, DELETE 1, LESS 2, MINUS 3, OUT 2, REMOVE 1, SUBTRACT, SUBTRACTION, TAKE AWAY FROM, WITHDRAW 2.

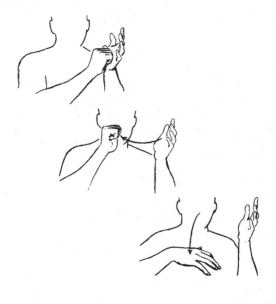

DEED (dēd), *n.* (An activity.) Both open hands, palms down, are swung right and left before the chest. Also ACT 2, ACTION, ACTIVE, ACTIVITY, BUSY 2, CONDUCT 1, DO, PERFORM 1, PERFORMANCE 1, RENDER 2.

DEEP (dēp), *adj.* (The "D" hand, movement downward.) The right "D" hand is held with index finger pointing down. In this position it moves down along the left palm, which is held facing right with fingertips pointing forward. Also DEPTH.

DEER (dǐr), *n.* (The branching of the antlers from the head.) Both hands, in the "5" position, palms up, are placed at the head, thumbs resting on the head above the temples. Also ANTLERS, ELK, MOOSE.

DEFEAT (dǐ fēt′), *v.*, -FEATED, -FEATING. (Forcing the head into a bowed position.) The right "S" hand, placed across the left "S" hand, moves over and down a bit. Also BEAT 2, CONQUER, OVERCOME, SUBDUE.

DEFEATED, *adj.* (Overpowered by great strength.) The right "S" hand (a fist) is held with palm facing the right shoulder. In this position it moves back toward the shoulder, pivoting from the elbow. The left "S" hand at the same time is held palm down with knuckles facing right and is positioned below the right hand and over the right biceps.

DEFECATE (dĕf′ ə kāt′) (*sl., vulg.*), *v.,* -CATED, -CAT-ING. (The passing of fecal material.) The left hand grasps the upturned right thumb. The right hand drops down and the right thumb is exposed. Also FECES.

DEFEND (dĭ fĕnd′), *v.,* -FENDED, -FENDING. (Hold down firmly; cover and strengthen.) The "S" hands, downturned, are held side by side in front of the body, the arms almost horizontal and the left hand in front of the right. Both arms move a short distance forward and slightly downward. Also DEFENSE, FORTIFY, GUARD, PROTECT, PROTECTION, SHIELD 1.

DEFENDANT (di fen′ dənt), *n.* (One who wards off or shields against.) Both downturned "S" hands, the right above the left, move out sharply a short distance. The sign for INDIVIDUAL 1 then follows.

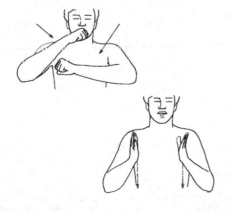

DEFENSE (dĭ fĕns′), *n.* See DEFEND.

DEFER (dĭ fûr′), *v.,* -FERRED, -FERRING. (Putting off; moving things forward repeatedly.) The "F" hands, palms facing and fingers pointing out from the body, are moved forward simultaneously in a series of short movements. Also DELAY, POSTPONE, PROCRASTINATE, PUT OFF.

DEFICIT (def′ ə sit), *n.* (Something is lacking or missing.) The downturned left open hand is held with middle finger hanging down from the rest. The right index finger strikes the left middle finger several times, pushing it back each time toward the left palm, *i.e.,* causing it to be missing.

DEFINE 1 (dĭ fīn′), *v.,* -FINED, -FINING. (Unraveling something to get at its parts.) The "F" hands, palms facing and fingers pointing straight out, are held about an inch apart. They move alternately back and forth a few inches. Also DESCRIBE 1, DESCRIPTION, EXPLAIN 1.

DEFINE 2, *v.* This is the same sign as for DEFINE 1, except that the "D" hands are used.

DEFLATE (dĭ flāt′), v., -FLATED, -FLATING. (A flattening.) The thumb of the right "C" hand rests on the back of the downturned left "B" hand. The fingers suddenly come down on the right thumb. Also DEFLATION.

DEFLATION (dĭ flā′ shən), n. See DEFLATE.

DEFRAUD (dĭ frôd′), v., -FRAUDED, -FRAUDING. (Underhandedness.) The right hand, palm down, is held with index and little fingers pointing out. The left hand, in a similar position, is held above the right. The right hand moves forward repeatedly, each time emerging briefly from under the left hand. The positions may be reversed, with the left hand doing the movement, or both hands can move simultaneously. Also CHEAT 1, DECEIT, DECEIVE, DECEPTION, FRAUD, FRAUDULENT 1.

DEFY (di fī′), v., -FIED, -FYING. (Swing away from.) The right fist is held up, palm facing the signer. It swings around abruptly to the palm-out position while the signer assumes a stubborn or determined look.

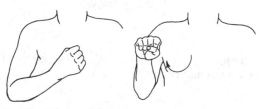

DEGREE 1 (di grē′), n. (A unit of temperature.) The tip of the index finger of the right "D" hand travels up

and down the upturned left index finger. Also TEMPERATURE 2.

DEGREE 2, n. (Drawing a percent symbol in the air.) The right "O" hand traces a percent symbol (%) in the air. Also PERCENT, RATE.

DEGREE 3, n. (The rolled up diploma.) With thumbs and index fingers forming circles, both hands, held together initially, separate, describing the shape of a rolled up diploma. Also DIPLOMA.

DEJECTED (dĭ jĕk′ tĭd), adj. (The facial features drop.) Both "5" hands, palms facing the eyes and fingers slightly curved, drop simultaneously to a level with the mouth. The head drops slightly as the hands move down, and an expression of sadness is assumed.

Also DEPRESSED, GLOOM, GLOOMY, GRAVE 3, GRIEF 1, MELANCHOLY, MOURNFUL, SAD, SORROWFUL 1.

DELAWARE (del′ ə wâr′), *n.* (The letter "D"; the first state.) The right "D" hand, palm out, with a flourish, twists straight up.

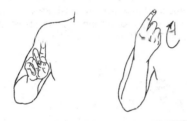

DELAY (dĭ lā′), *n., v.,* -LAYED, -LAYING. (Putting off; moving things forward repeatedly.) The "F" hands, palms facing and fingers pointing out from the body, are moved forward simultaneously in a series of short movements. Also DEFER, POSTPONE, PROCRASTINATE, PUT OFF.

DELEGATE (del′ i git), *n.* (The shape of the ribbon hanging down from a delegate's badge.) The right thumb and index finger trace a ribbon hanging down over the chest. The movement is usually repeated.

DELETE 1 (dĭ lēt′), *v.,* -LETED, -LETING. (Removing.) The right "A" hand, resting in the palm of the left "5" hand, moves slightly up and away, describing a small arc. It is then cast downward, opening into the "5" position, palm down, as if removing something from the left hand and casting it down. Also ABOLISH 2, ABSENCE 2, ABSENT 2, ABSTAIN, CHEAT 2, DEDUCT, DEFICIENCY, LESS 2, MINUS 3, OUT 2, REMOVE 1, SUBTRACT, SUBTRACTION, TAKE AWAY FROM, WITHDRAW 2.

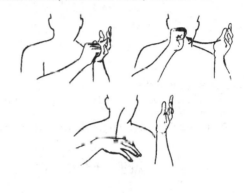

DELETE 2, *v.* (Scratching something out and throwing it away.) The fingertips of the open right hand scratch downward across the palm of the upright left hand. In one continuous motion, the right hand then closes as if holding something and finally opens again forcefully and motions as if throwing something away. Also DISCARD 3, ELIMINATE.

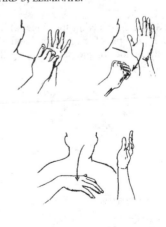

DELETE 3, *v.* (The printer flicks a piece of type out of the composing stick.) The thumb, positioned initially inside the closed hand, flicks out. The hand moves up a bit as the thumb makes its appearance. Also EXPUNGE.

the heart after each strike. Also GAIETY 1, GAY, GLAD, HAPPINESS, HAPPY, JOY, MERRY.

DELICIOUS 1 (dǐ lǐsh′ əs), *adj.* (Smooth to the taste.) The right middle finger is placed on the lips, and then the hand moves down and out a bit. As it does, the thumb rubs over the middle finger. Both hands may be used.

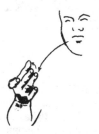

DELIVER 1 (dǐ lǐv′ ər), *v.,* -ERED, -ERING. (Breaking the bonds.) The "S" hands, crossed in front of the body, swing apart and face out. Also EMANCIPATE, FREE 1, INDEPENDENCE, INDEPENDENT, LIBERATION, REDEEM 1, RELIEF, RESCUE, SAFE, SALVATION, SAVE 1.

DELICIOUS 2, *adj.* (Licking the fingers.) The signer draws the fingertips of one open hand downward across the tip of the tongue, as if licking the fingers one at a time.

DELIVER 2, *v.* (Carrying something over.) Both open hands, palms up, move in an arc from left to right, as if carrying something from one point to another. Also BRING, CARRY 2, FETCH, PRODUCE 1, TRANSPORT.

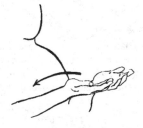

DELIGHT (dǐ līt′), *n.* (The heart is stirred; the spirits bubble up.) The open right hand, palm facing the body, strikes the heart repeatedly, moving up and off

DEMAND (dǐ mănd′, -mänd′), *v.,* -MANDED, -MANDING. (Something specific is moved in toward oneself.) The palm of the left "5" hand faces right. The right index finger is thrust into the left palm, and both hands are drawn sharply in toward the chest. Also INSIST, REQUEST 2, REQUIRE.

DEMOCRAT (dĕm′ ə krăt), *n.* (The "D" hand.) The right "D" hand is shaken back and forth several times before the right shoulder.

DEMON (dē′ mən), *n.* (The horns.) With the thumbs resting on the temples, the index and middle fingers of both hands open and close repeatedly. Also DEVIL, DEVILMENT, HELL 1, SATAN.

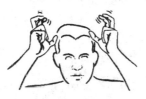

DEMONSTRATE (dĕm′ ən strāt′), *v.,* -STRATED, -STRATING. (Directing the attention to something, and bringing it forward.) The right index finger points into the left palm, held facing out before the body. The left palm moves straight out. For the passive form of this verb, *i.e.,* BE SHOWN or DEMONSTRATED, the movement is reversed: the left hand, palm facing in, is moved in toward the body, while the right index finger remains pointing into the left palm. Also DISPLAY, EVIDENCE, EXAMPLE, EXHIBIT, EXHIBITION, ILLUSTRATE, INDICATE, INFLUENCE 3, PRODUCE 2, REPRESENT, SHOW 1, SIGNIFY 1.

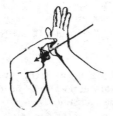

DEMOTE (dĭ′ mōt), *v.,* -MOTED, -MOTING. (Motion downward.) The right-angle hands are held up before the head, fingertips pointing toward each other. From this position, the hands move down in an arc. Also BASE 2, LOW 2, LOWER.

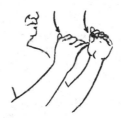

DENMARK 1 (dĕn′ märk), *n.* (The letter "D"; the top or northern part of the body.) The right "D" hand, palm facing left, makes a small counterclockwise circle on the forehead. Also DANE.

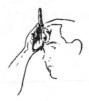

DENMARK 2, *n.* (The markings on the flag; waving in the breeze.) The right "3" hand, palm facing the chest, moves in a wavy fashion from left to right.

DENTIST (dĕn′ tĭst), *n.* (The teeth.) The index finger touches the lower teeth, and then the sign for INDIVIDUAL 1, *q.v.,* is made. Instead of the latter sign, the sign for DOCTOR, *q.v.,* may be made. Also, instead of the index finger alone, the middle finger and the index may both be used to touch the lower teeth.

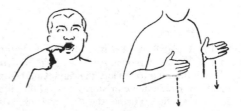

DENY 1 (dǐ nī′), *v.*, -NIED, -NYING. (An emphatic NOT 2, *q.v.*) The thumbs of both "A" hands, positioned under the chin, move out simultaneously, each toward their respective sides of the body. The head may be shaken slightly as the hands move out.

DENY 2, *v.* (Turning down.) The right "A" hand swings down sharply, its thumb pointing down. Both hands are sometimes used here.

DEODORANT (dē ō′ dər ənt), *n.* (The activity of applying deodorant to the underarm.) The signer either sprays or applies a liquid to the underarm.

DEPART (dǐ pärt′), *v.*, -PARTED, -PARTING. (Pulling away.) The downturned open hands are held in a line, with fingers pointing to the left, the right hand behind the left. Both hands move in unison toward the right. As they do so, they assume the "A" position. Also

EVACUATE, FORSAKE 1, GRADUATE 2, LEAVE 1, RETIRE 1, WITHDRAW 1.

DEPEND 1 (dǐ pěnd′), *v.*, -PENDED, -PENDING. (Hanging onto.) With the right index finger resting across its left counterpart, both hands drop down a bit. Also DEPENDABLE, DEPENDENT, HINGE 2, RELY 2.

DEPEND 2, *v.* (One hand depending on the other.) The extended index and middle fingers of the downturned right hand rest across the back of their left counterparts. In this position the right fingers push down slightly on the left fingers.

DEPEND 3, *v.* (The letter "D"; DEPEND 1.) The base of the right "D" hand rests on the back of the downturned left "S" hand. Both hands move down simultaneously.

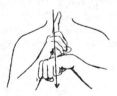

DEPENDABLE (dǐ pěn′ də bəl), *adj.* See DEPEND 1.

DEPOSIT 1 (dǐ pŏz′ ǐt), *v.*, -ITED, -ITING. (The natural motion.) The downturned "O" hands are brought down and to the left simultaneously from an initial side-by-side position near the right shoulder. Also PUT DOWN.

DEPOSIT 2, *v.* (To throw something aside.) Both "S" hands are held with palms facing at chest level and then thrown down and to the left, opening into the "5" position. Also ABANDON 1, CAST OFF, DISCARD 1, FORSAKE 3, LEAVE 2, LET ALONE, NEGLECT.

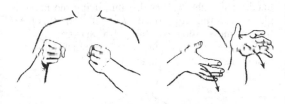

DEPRESSED 1 (dǐ prěst′), *adj.* (The facial features drop.) Both "5" hands, palms facing the eyes and fingers slightly curved, drop simultaneously to a level with the mouth. The head drops slightly as the hands move down, and an expression of sadness is assumed. Also DEJECTED, GLOOM, GLOOMY, GRAVE 3, GRIEF 1, MELANCHOLY, MOURNFUL, SAD, SORROWFUL 1.

DEPRESSED 2, *adj.* (The inner feelings are "down.") Both open hands, palms down, fingers pointing down, slide down the chest to waist level.

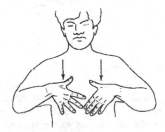

DEPTH (děpth), *n.* (The "D" hand, movement downward.) The right "D" hand is held with index finger pointing down. In this position it moves down along the left palm, which is held facing right with fingertips pointing forward. Also DEEP.

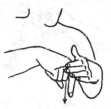

DESCRIBE 1 (dǐ skrīb′), *v.*, -SCRIBED, -SCRIBING. (Unraveling something to get at its parts.) The "F" hands, palms facing and fingers pointing straight out, are held about an inch apart. They move alternately back and forth a few inches. Also DEFINE 1, DESCRIPTION, EXPLAIN 1.

DESCRIBE 2, *v.* (The unraveling or stretching out of words or sentences.) Both open hands are held close to each other, with fingers open and palms facing and almost touching. As the hands are drawn apart, the thumb and index finger of each hand come together to form circles. This is repeated several times. Also EXPLAIN 2, FABLE, FICTION, GOSPEL 1, NARRATE, NARRATIVE, STORY 1, TALE, TELL ABOUT.

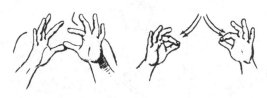

DESCRIBE 3, *v.* (The letter "D"; unraveling something.) The "D" hands, palms facing and index fingers pointing straight forward, are held an inch or two apart. They move alternately forward and back.

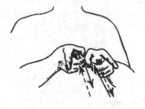

DESCRIPTION (dǐ skrǐp′ shən), *n*. See DESCRIBE 1.

DESERT (dez′ ərt), *n*. (A dry area.) The downturned curved right index finger draws across the lips, from left to right. The open hands, palms down, then spread forward and apart, indicating an expanse of land.

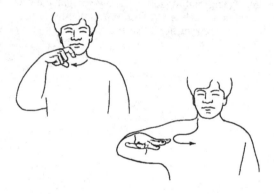

DESIGN (di zīn′), *n., v,* -SIGNED, -SIGNING. (Drawing and inventing.) The right "I" hand moves across the upturned left palm, from index finger edge to little finger edge, describing a series of curves. Optionally, the signer then places the index finger of the right "4" hand against the forehead and moves straight up.

DESIRE 1 (dǐ zīr′), *v.,* -SIRED, -SIRING, *n*. (Grasping something and pulling it in.) The upturned "5" hands,

held side by side before the chest, close slightly into a grasping position as they move in toward the body. Also COVET 1, LONG 2, NEED 2, WANT, WILL 2, WISH 1.

DESIRE 2, *v., n*. (The upper alimentary tract is outlined.) The right "C" hand, palm facing the body, is placed with fingertips touching midchest. In this position it moves down a bit. Also APPETITE, CRAVE, FAMINE, HUNGARIAN, HUNGARY, HUNGER, HUNGRY, STARVATION, STARVE, STARVED, WISH 2.

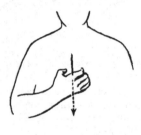

DESPISE 1 (dǐ spīz′), *v.,* -SPISED, -SPISING. (To push away and recoil from; avoid.) The two open hands, palms facing left, are pushed deliberately to the left, as if pushing something away. An expression of disdain or disgust is worn. Also ABHOR, AVOID 2, DETEST 1, HATE 1, LOATHE.

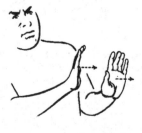

DESPISE 2, *v*. (The finger is flicked to indicate something petty, small; *i.e.,* to be scorned as inconsequential.) The right index finger and thumb are used to press the lips down into an expression of contempt.

The right thumb is then flicked out from the closed hand. Also CONTEMPT 2, DETEST 2, DISLIKE, HATE 2, SCORN 2.

DESPITE (dĭ spīt'), *prep., n.* Both hands, in the "5" position, are held before the chest, fingertips facing each other. With an alternate back-forth movement, the fingertips are made to strike each other. Also ANYHOW, ANYWAY, DOESN'T MATTER, HOWEVER 2, INDIFFERENCE, INDIFFERENT, IN SPITE OF, MAKE NO DIFFERENCE, NEVERTHELESS, NO MATTER, WHEREVER.

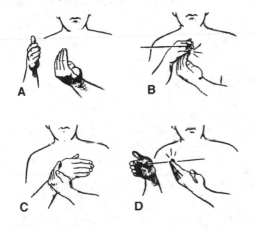

DESSERT (di zûrt'), *n.* Both hands, held in the "D" position, palms facing, come together once or twice.

DESTROY (dĭ stroi'), *v.,* -STROYED, -STROYING. (Wiping off.) The left "5" hand, palm up, is held slightly

above the right "5" hand, held palm down. The right hand swings up, just brushing over the left palm. Both hands close into the "S" position, and the right is brought back with force to its initial position, striking a glancing blow against the left knuckles as it returns. Also ABOLISH 1, ANNIHILATE, CORRUPT, DEFACE, DEMOLISH, HAVOC, PERISH 2, REMOVE 3, RUIN.

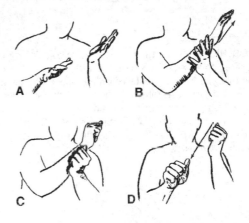

DETACH (dĭ tăch'), *v.,* -TACHED, -TACHING. (An unlocking.) With thumbs and index fingers interlocked initially (the links of a chain), the hands draw apart, showing the break in the chain. Also DISCONNECT, PART FROM.

DETECTIVE 1 (dĭ tĕk' tĭv), *n.* (The badge.) The right "D" hand circles over the heart.

DETECTIVE 2, *n.* (The badge hung over the heart.) The right "T" hand moves down slightly from its position on the heart. This movement is repeated a number of times.

DETERIORATE (dǐ tǐr′ ǐ ə rāt′), *v.*, -RATED, -RATING. (Going down step by step.) The little finger edge of the open right hand is placed on the upper side of the extended left arm, which is held with the open left-hand palm down. The right hand moves down along the left arm in a series of short movements. This is the opposite of IMPROVE, *q.v.* Also DECLINE 2, DETERIORATION, NOT IMPROVE.

DETERIORATION (dǐ tǐr′ ǐ ə rā′ shən), *n.* See DETERIORATE.

DETERMINE (dǐ tûr′ mǐn), *v.*, -MINED, -MINING. (The mind stops wavering, and the pros and cons are resolved.) The right index finger touches the forehead, the sign for THINK, *q.v.* Both "F" hands, palms facing each other and fingers pointing straight out, then drop down simultaneously. The sign for JUDGE, *q.v.*, explains the rationale behind the movement of the two hands here. Also DECIDE, DECISION, DECREE 1, MAKE UP ONE'S MIND, MIND 5, RENDER JUDGMENT, RESOLVE, VERDICT.

DETEST 1 (dǐ tĕst′), *v.*, -TESTED, -TESTING. (To push away and recoil from; avoid.) The two open hands, palms facing left, are pushed deliberately to the left, as if pushing something away. An expression of dis-

dain or disgust is worn. Also ABHOR, AVOID 2, DESPISE 1, HATE 1, LOATHE.

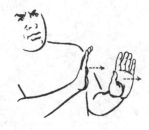

DETEST 2, *v.* (The finger is flicked to indicate something petty, small; *i.e.,* to be scorned as inconsequential.) The right index finger and thumb are used to press the lips down into an expression of contempt. The right thumb is then flicked out from the closed hand. Also CONTEMPT 2, DESPISE 2, DISLIKE, HATE 2, SCORN 2.

DEVELOP 1 (dǐ vĕl′ əp), *v.*, -OPED, -OPING. (Flowers or plants emerge from the ground.) The right fingers, pointing up, emerge from the closed left hand, and they spread open as they do. Also BLOOM, GROW, GROWN, MATURE, PLANT 1, RAISE 3, REAR 2, SPRING 1.

DEVELOP 2, *v.* (The letter "D"; moving upward, as if in growth.) The right "D" hand is placed against the left palm, which is facing right with fingers pointing up. The "D" hand moves straight up to the left fingertips.

DEVIATE 1 (dē′ vĭ āt′), *v.*, -ATED, -ATING. (Going astray.) The open right hand, palm facing left, is placed with its little finger edge resting on the upturned left palm. The right hand curves rather sharply to the left as it moves across the palm. Also WRONG 2.

DEVIATE 2, *v.* (The natural motion.) The "G" hands are held side by side and touching, palms down, index fingers pointing forward. Then the right hand moves forward, curving toward the right side as it does. Also DEFLECT, GO OFF THE TRACK, STRAY, WANDER 1.

DEVIATION (dē′ vĭ ā′ shən), *n.* See DEVIATE 1.

DEVIL (dĕv′ əl), *n.* (The horns.) With the thumbs resting on the temples, the index and middle fingers of both hands open and close repeatedly. Also DEMON, DEVILMENT, HELL 1, SATAN.

DEVISE 1 (dĭ vīz′), *v.*, -VISED, -VISING, *n.* (Placing things in order.) The hands, palms facing, fingers together and pointing away from the body, are positioned at the left side and held about a foot apart. With a slight up-down motion, as if describing waves, the hands travel in unison from left to right. Also ARRANGE, ARRANGEMENT, CLASSED 2, ORDER 3, PLAN 1,

POLICY 1, PREPARE 1, PROGRAM 1, PROVIDE 1, PUT IN ORDER, READY 1, SCHEME, SYSTEM.

DEVISE 2, *v.* (Fashioning something with the hands.) The right "S" hand, palm facing left, is placed on top of its left counterpart, whose palm faces right. The hands are twisted back and forth, striking each other slightly after each twist. Also COMPOSE, CONSTITUTE, CONSTRUCT 2, CREATE, FABRICATE, FASHION, FIX, MAKE, MANUFACTURE, MEND 1, PRODUCE 3, RENDER 1, REPAIR.

DEVOTION (dĭ vō′ shən), *n.* (Clasping the heart.) The "5" hands are held one atop the other over the heart. Sometimes the "S" hands are used, in which case they are crossed at the wrists. Also BELOVED, CHARITY, LOVE, REVERE 2.

DIABETES (dī′ ə bē′ tis, tēz), *n.* (Pertaining to sugar or sweet.) The fingertips of the right "U" hand, palm facing the body, brush down against the chin a number of times, beginning with the lips. Also CANDY 1, SUGAR.

DIAGNOSIS (dī əg nō′ sis), *n.* (Pulling apart to get to the source of the trouble.) The index and middle fingers of both hands are held curved and pointing down. The hands come apart simultaneously a number of times.

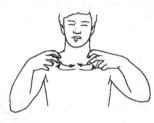

DIALOGUE (dī′ ə lôg, -log), *n.* (Back-and-forth conversation.) Both upturned index fingers move alternately back and forth in front of the mouth.

DIAMOND 1 (dī′ mənd, dī′ ə-), *n.* (The letter "D"; sparkling with scintillating rays of light.) The right "D" hand is shaken slightly as it is held slightly above the ring finger of the downturned left hand.

DIAMOND 2, *n.* (Fingering the gem.) The right thumb and index finger hold an imaginary diamond. The right hand moves around slightly, as if causing the gem to catch the light and flash. An expression of pleasure is assumed, and the eyes follow the flashing of the stone.

DIAMOND 3, *n.* (A sparkling ring.) The downturned right "S" hand is shaken slightly over the ring finger of the downturned open left hand.

DIAPER (dī′ ə pər), *n., v.,* -PERED, -PERING. (The natural sign.) The thumbs and index and middle fingers of each hand point down and rest on each hip as the signer mimes the closing of clips to fasten the diaper.

DIARRHEA 1 (dī ə rē′ ə), *n.* (Defecating repeatedly.) The right thumb is drawn repeatedly down and out from the left closed hand.

DIARRHEA 2 (Going back and forth to the bathroom.) The upturned thumb goes back and forth from left to right.

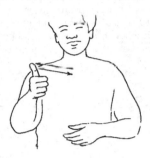

DIARRHEA 3 (The bowels in a state of constant movement.) Both hands, with fingertips close to the stomach, palms up, move down repeatedly.

DICTIONARY 1 (dĭk′ shə nĕr′ ĭ), n. (The letter "D.") The right "D" hand is shaken slightly back and forth. This may be preceded by the sign for BOOK, q.v.: the open hands are held together, fingers pointing away from the body; they open with little fingers remaining in contact, as in the opening of a book.

DICTIONARY 2, n. (Thumbing the pages.) The right "D" hand moves across the left palm quickly, from the fingers to the base, several times, as if thumbing through the pages.

DIE 1 (dī), v., DIED, DYING. (Turning over on one's side.) The open hands, fingers pointing ahead, are held side by side, with the right palm down and the left palm up. The two hands reverse their relative positions as they move from the left to the right. Also DEAD 1, DEATH, DYING, EXPIRE 2, PERISH 1.

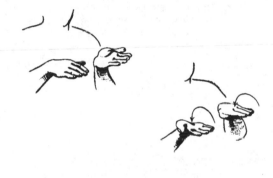

DIE 2 (sl.), v. (An animal's legs sticking up in the air in death.) Both hands are held with palms facing each other and curved index and middle fingers presented. The hands pivot up a bit, simultaneously, assuming the "V" position as they do. Also DEAD 2, PASS OUT.

DIE OUT, v. phrase. (Fingering the small pieces resulting from the breaking up of something.) The thumbs rub slowly across the fingertips of the upturned hands, from the little fingers to the index fingers, and then continue to the "A" position, palms up. Also DECAY, DISSOLVE, FADE, MELT, ROT.

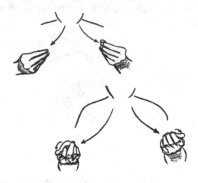

DIFFER (dĭf′ ər), v., -FERED, -FERING. (To think in opposite terms.) The sign for THINK is made: the right index finger touches the forehead. The sign for OPPOSITE is then made: the "D" hands, palms facing the body and index fingers touching, draw apart sharply. Also CONTRADICT, CONTRARY TO, DISAGREE.

DIFFERENCE (dĭf′ ər əns, dĭf′ rəns), n. (Separated many times; different.) The "D" hands, palms down, are crossed at the index fingers or are held side by side. They separate and return to their initial position a number of times. Also ASSORTED, DIFFERENT, DIVERSE 1, DIVERSITY 1, UNLIKE, VARIED.

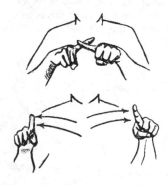

DIFFERENT (dĭf′ ər ənt, dĭf′ rənt), adj. See DIFFERENCE.

DIFFICULT 1 (dĭf′ ə kŭlt′), adj. (The knuckles are rubbed to indicate a condition of being worn down.) The knuckles of the curved index and middle fingers of both hands are rubbed up and down against each other. Instead of the up-down rubbing, they may rub against each other in an alternate clockwise/counterclockwise manner. Also DIFFICULTY, HARD 1, HARDSHIP, POVERTY 2, PROBLEM 2.

DIFFICULT 2, adj. (Striking a hard object.) The curved index and middle fingers of the right hand, whose palm faces the body or the left, are brought down sharply against the back of the downturned left "S" hand. Also HARD 2, SOLID.

DIFFICULT 3, adj. (A clenching of the fists; the rise and fall of pain.) Both "S" hands, tightly clenched, revolve about each other slowly and deliberately while a pained expression is worn. Also AGONY, BEAR 3, ENDURE 1, PASSION 2, SUFFER 1, TOLERATE 2.

DIFFICULTY (dĭf′ ə kŭl′ tĭ, -kəl tĭ), n. See DIFFICULT 1.

DIG 1 (dĭg), v., DUG or DIGGED, DIGGING. (The natural sign.) The slightly cupped right hand, palm up, goes through the motions of digging into a mound of earth and turning it over.

DIG 2, *v.* (The natural motion.) Both hands, in the "A" position, right hand facing up and left hand facing down, grasp an imaginary shovel. They go through the natural movements of shoveling earth—first digging in and then tossing the earth aside. Also SHOVEL, SPADE.

DIGRESS (di gres′), *v.*, -GRESSED, -GRESSING. (Moving off the track.) Both "S" hands are held at chest height, palms facing each other. The right index finger shoots out as the right hand crosses over the left.

DILIGENCE 1 (dĭl′ ə jəns), *n.* (Rubbing the hands together in zeal or ambition.) The open hands are rubbed vigorously back and forth against each other. Also AMBITIOUS 1, ANXIOUS 1, ARDENT, DILIGENT, EAGER, EAGERNESS, EARNEST, ENTHUSIASM, ENTHUSIASTIC, INDUSTRIOUS, METHODIST, ZEAL, ZEALOUS.

DILIGENCE 2 (*colloq.*), *n.* (Rationale obscure; possibly an emphasis on sharpness.) The upturned open right hand is poised with thumb resting on the chin and the middle finger bent back under the thumb. The middle finger suddenly flicks out sharply. An intense expression is assumed, with brows furrowed.

DILIGENT (dĭl′ ə jənt), *adj.* See DILIGENCE 1.

DIMPLE (dim′ pəl), *n.* (The facial indentation.) The signer indicates a dimple by twisting the index finger around in a clockwise fashion as it rests on the cheek. Both fingers are used to indicate bilateral dimples.

DINOSAUR (dī′ nə sôr), *n.* (The swinging neck.) The right arm is held upright, with the hand facing forward, all fingers touching the thumb. The hand swivels from right to left in a slow, deliberate movement. The cupped left hand may be used to support the right elbow.

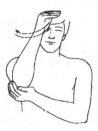

DIPLOMA (di plō′ mə), *n.* (The rolled-up diploma.) With thumbs and index fingers forming circles, both hands, held together initially, separate, describing the shape of a rolled-up diploma. Also DEGREE 3.

DIRECT 1 (dĭ rĕkt′, dī-), v., -RECTED, -RECTING. (Holding the reins over all.) The "A" hands, palms facing, move alternately back and forth, as if grasping and manipulating reins. The left "A" hand, still in position, swings over so that its palm now faces down. The right hand opens to the "5" position, palm down, and swings over the left, which moves slightly to the right. Also AUTHORITY, CONTROL 1, GOVERN, MANAGE, MANAGEMENT, MANAGER, OPERATE, REGULATE, REIGN, RULE 1.

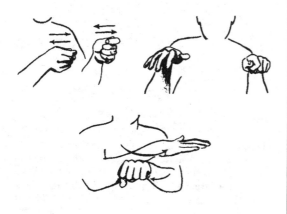

DIRECT 2, v. (An issuance from the mouth.) The tip of the index finger of the "D" hand, palm facing the body, is placed at the closed lips. It moves around and out rather forcefully. Also BID 1, COMMAND, ORDER 1.

DIRECTION 1 (dĭ rĕk′ shən), n. (Alternate directions are indicated.) The right "D" hand, with palm out and index finger straight or slightly curved, moves a short distance back and forth, from left to right. Also WHERE 1.

DIRECTION 2, n. The open "5" hands, palms up and fingers slightly curved, move back and forth in front of the body, the right hand to the right and the left hand to the left. Also HERE, WHERE 2.

DIRECTION 3, n. (The "D" letters; one hand follows the other.) The right "D" hand is positioned behind its left counterpart, and both hands move forward together.

DIRECTION 4, n. (The letter "D"; moving forward.) The little finger edge of the right "D" hand, index pointing forward, slides forward, either straight or in a weaving back-forth fashion over the extended left index finger.

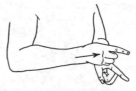

DIRT (dûrt), *n.* (Fingering the soil.) Both hands, held upright before the body, finger imaginary pinches of soil. Also EARTH 2, GROUND, SOIL 1.

DIRTY (dûr' tĭ), *adj.* (A modification of the pig's snout groveling in a trough.) The downturned right hand is placed under the chin. Its fingers, pointing left, wiggle repeatedly. Also FILTHY, FOUL, IMPURE, NASTY, SOIL 2, STAIN.

DISAGREE (dĭs' ə grē'), *v.,* -GREED, -GREEING. (To think in opposite terms.) The sign for THINK is made: the right index finger touches the forehead. The sign for OPPOSITE is then made: the "D" hands, palms facing the body and index fingers touching, draw apart sharply. Also CONTRADICT, CONTRARY TO, DIFFER.

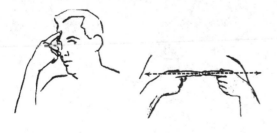

DISAPPEAR (dĭs' ə pir'), *v.,* -PEARED, -PEARING. (A disappearance.) The right open hand, palm facing the body, is held by the left hand and is drawn down and out, ending in a position with fingers drawn together. The left hand, meanwhile, may close into a position with fingers also drawn together. Also ABSENCE 1,

ABSENT 1, DEPLETE, EMPTY 1, EXTINCT, FADE AWAY, GONE 1, MISSING 1, OMISSION 1, OUT 3, OUT OF, VANISH.

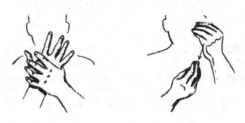

DISAPPOINT (dĭs' ə point'), *v.,* -POINTED, -POINTING. (The feelings sink.) The middle fingers of both "5" hands, one above the other, rest on the heart. They both move down a few inches.

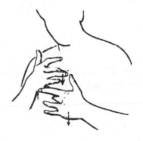

DISAPPOINTED 1, *adj.* (Something sour or bitter.) The right index finger is brought sharply up against the lips while the mouth is puckered up as if tasting something sour. Also ACID, BITTER, LEMON 1, PICKLE, SOUR.

DISAPPOINTED 2, *adj.* (Coming up against a wall; a door is slammed in the face.) The open right hand is brought up sharply, and its back strikes the mouth and nose. The head moves back a bit at the same time. Also FRUSTRATED.

DISAPPOINTMENT (dĭs′ ə point′ mənt), *n.* Use any sign for DISAPPOINT, DISAPPOINTED 1, or DISAPPOINTED 2.

DISBELIEF 1 (dĭs bĭ lēf′), *n.* (The nose is wrinkled in disbelief.) The right "V" hand faces the nose. The index and middle fingers bend as a cynical expression is assumed. Also CYNIC, CYNICAL, DON'T BELIEVE, DOUBT 1, INCREDULITY, SKEPTIC 1, SKEPTICAL 1.

DISBELIEF 2, *n.* (The wavering.) The downturned "S" hands swing alternately up and down. Also DOUBT 2, DOUBTFUL, WAVER 2.

DISC (disk), *n.* (The shape and movement.) The palm of the downturned "D" hand makes a clockwise circle on the upturned left palm. This refers to a computer or compact disc. Also DISK, VIDEODISC.

DISCARD 1 (*v.* dĭs kärd′; *n.* dĭs′ kärd), -CARDED, -CARDING. (To throw something aside.) Both "S" hands are held with palms facing at chest level and then thrown down and to the left, opening into the "5"

position. Also ABANDON 1, CAST OFF, DEPOSIT 2, FORSAKE 3, LEAVE 2, LET ALONE, NEGLECT.

DISCARD 2, *v.* (To toss up and out.) Both "S" hands, held at chest level with palms facing, are swung down slightly and then up into the air toward the left, opening into the "5" position. Also ABANDON 2, CAST OUT, EVICT.

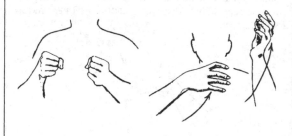

DISCARD 3, *v.* (Scratching something out and throwing it away.) The fingertips of the open right hand scratch downward across the palm of the upright left hand. In one continuous motion, the right hand then closes, as if holding something, and finally opens again forcefully and motions as if throwing something away. Also DELETE 2, ELIMINATE.

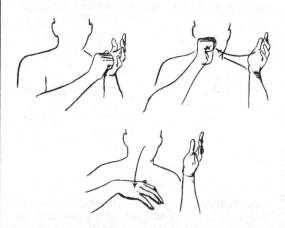

DISCHARGE 1 (dĭs chärj′), *v.,* -CHARGED, -CHARGING. ("Getting the axe"; the head is chopped off.) The upturned open right hand is swung sharply over the index finger edge of the left "S" hand, whose palm faces right. Also EXPEL 1, FIRE 2.

DISCHARGE 2, v. (To cut one down.) The right index finger strikes the tip of the upturned left index finger, in a right to left direction, causing the left index finger to bend slightly. Also EXPEL 2.

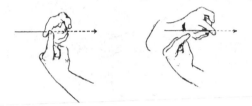

DISCO (dis′ kō), n. (The natural sign.) The signer mimes dancing to a disco beat.

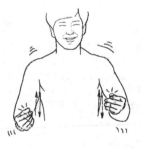

DISCONNECT (dĭs′ kə nĕkt′), v., -NECTED, -NECTING. (An unlocking.) With thumbs and index fingers interlocked initially (the links of a chain), the hands draw apart, showing the break in the chain. Also DETACH, PART FROM.

DISCONTENTED (dĭs′ kən tĕn′ tĭd), adj. (NOT, SATISFIED.) The sign for NOT 1 is made: the crossed downturned open hands draw apart. The sign for SATISFIED then follows: the downturned "B" hands, the right above the left, are positioned on the chest. They move straight down simultaneously. Also DISSATISFACTION, DISSATISFIED.

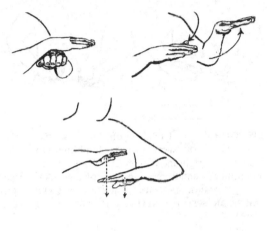

DISCOUNT (dis′ kount, dis kount′), n., v., -COUNTED, -COUNTING. (The letter "D"; making smaller.) Both "D" hands are positioned palm to palm, fingers pointing forward. The upper "D" hand moves down toward the lower "D" hand.

DISCOURAGE 1 (dĭs kûr′ ĭjd), adj., v., -AGED, -AGING. (Throwing up the hands in a gesture of surrender.) Both "A" hands are held palms down before the chest and then thrown up in unison, ending in the "5" position. Also ABDICATE, CEDE, FORFEIT, GIVE UP, LOSE HOPE, RELINQUISH, RENOUNCE, RENUNCIATION, SURRENDER 1, YIELD.

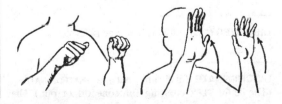

DISCOURAGE 2, *adj., v.* (The hands collapse in exhaustion.) Both "C" hands are placed either on the lower chest or at the waist. The palms face the body. They fall away into a palms-up position. At the same time, the shoulders suddenly sag in a very pronounced fashion. An expression of weariness may be used for emphasis. Also EXHAUST, FATIGUE, TIRE, TIRED, WEARY.

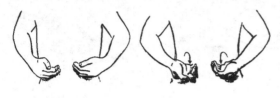

DISCOURSE (*n.* dĭs′ kôrs, dĭs kôrs′; *v.* dĭs kôrs′), -COURSED, -COURSING. (Words tumbling from the mouth.) The right index finger, pointing left, describes a continuous small circle in front of the mouth. Also BID 3, HEARING, MAINTAIN 2, MENTION, REMARK, SAID, SAY, SPEAK, SPEECH 1, STATE, STATEMENT, TALK 1, TELL, VERBAL 1.

DISCOVER (dĭs kŭv′ ər), *v.*, -ERED, -ERING. (The natural motion of selecting something from the hand.) The thumb and index fingers of the outstretched right hand grasp an imaginary object on the upturned left palm. The right hand then moves straight up. Also CHOOSE 2, FIND, PICK 1, SELECT 1.

DISCOVERY (dĭs kŭv′ ə rĭ), *n.* See DISCOVER.

DISCRIMINATE (di skrim′ ə nāt′), *v.*, -NATED, -NATING. (The letter "D"; crossing someone off or out.) The

downturned right "D" hand traces a large "X" over the upturned left palm.

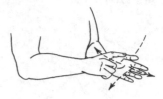

DISCUSS (dĭs kŭs′), *v.*, -CUSSED, -CUSSING. (Expounding one's points.) The right "D" hand is held with the palm facing the body. It moves down repeatedly so that the side of the index finger strikes the upturned left palm. Also DISCUSSION 1.

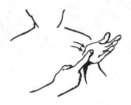

DISCUSSION 1 (dĭs kŭsh′ ən), *n.* See DISCUSS.

DISCUSSION 2, *n.* (Back-and-forth talk.) The "5" hands, palms facing and somewhat cupped, swing alternately toward and away from the face. Each time they move away they also swing down a bit. The movement is graceful and continuous.

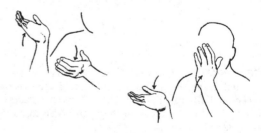

DISEASE 1 (dĭ zēz′), *n., v.*, -EASED, -EASING. (The sick parts of the anatomy are indicated.) The right middle finger rests on the forehead, and its left counterpart is placed against the stomach. The signer assumes an expression of sadness or physical distress. Also ILL, ILLNESS, SICK, SICKNESS.

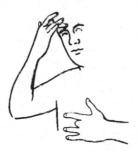

DISEASE 2, *n.* (Something inside is emphasized.) The "5" hands, palms facing the body, are positioned with middle fingers resting on the chest. The hands move alternately up and down.

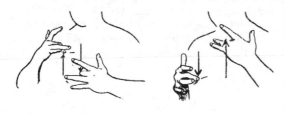

DISGUST (dĭs gŭst'), *n.*, *v.*, -GUSTED, -GUSTING. (Turning the stomach.) The fingertips of the curved right hand describe a continuous circle on the stomach. The signer assumes an exaggerated expression of disgust. Also DISGUSTED, DISGUSTING, DISPLEASED, MAKE ME DISGUSTED, MAKE ME SICK, NAUSEA, NAUSE-ATE, NAUSEOUS, OBNOXIOUS, REVOLTING.

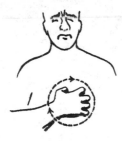

DISGUSTED (dĭs gŭs' tĭd), *adj.* See DISGUST.

DISGUSTING (dĭs gŭs' tĭng), *adj.* See DISGUST.

DISH (dĭsh), *n.* (The finger touches a brittle substance.) The index finger is brought up to touch the exposed front teeth. Also BONE, CHINA 2, GLASS 1, PLATE, PORCELAIN,

DISHWASHER (dĭsh' wŏsh ər), *n.* (The action of the water inside the machine.) Both hands, in the claw position, palms facing and one above the other, move back and forth in opposite clockwise/counterclockwise motions.

DISHWASHING (dĭsh' wŏsh ĭng -wŏsh-), *n.* (The natural sign.) The downturned right "5" hand describes a clockwise circle as it moves over the upturned left "5" hand. Also WASH DISHES.

DISK (dĭsk), *n.* See DISC.

DISMOUNT (dis mount'), *v.*, -MOUNTED, -MOUNTING. (Getting off the saddle.) The downturned right "V"

hand straddles the index finger edge of the left "B" hand. The right hand moves up and off of this position.

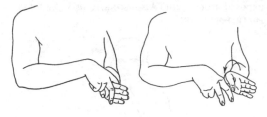

DISOBEDIENCE (dĭs′ ə bē′ dĭ əns), *n.* See DISOBEY.

DISOBEY (dĭs′ ə bā′), *v.,* -BEYED, -BEYING. (Turning the head.) The right "S" hand, held up with its palm facing the body, swings sharply around to the palm-out position. The head meanwhile moves slightly toward the left. Also DISOBEDIENCE, REBEL.

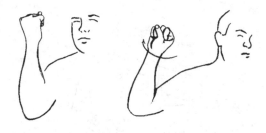

DISPLAY (dĭs plā′), *v.,* -PLAYED, -PLAYING. (Directing the attention to something and bringing it forward.) The right index finger points into the left palm, held facing out before the body. The left palm moves straight out. For the passive form of this verb, *i.e.,* BE SHOWN or DISPLAYED, the movement is reversed: the left hand, palm facing in, is moved in toward the body, while the right index finger remains pointing into the left palm. Also DEMONSTRATE, EVIDENCE, EXAMPLE, EXHIBIT, EXHIBITION, ILLUSTRATE, INDICATE, INFLUENCE 3, PRODUCE 2, REPRESENT, SHOW 1, SIGNIFY 1.

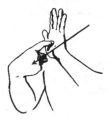

DISPOSE (dĭs pōz′), *v.,* -POSED, -POSING, *n.* (The feelings of the heart move toward a specific object.) The

tip of the right middle finger touches the heart. The open right hand, palm facing the body, then moves away from the heart toward the palm of the open left hand. Also DISPOSED TO, DISPOSITION, INCLINATION, INCLINE, INCLINED, TEND, TENDENCY.

DISPOSED TO (dĭs pōzd′), *adj. phrase.* See DISPOSE.

DISPUTE (dĭs pūt′), *n., v.,* -PUTED, -PUTING. (An expounding back and forth.) The index fingers here represent the two sides of the argument. First the left index finger is slapped into the open right palm, and then the right makes the same movement into the left palm. This is repeated back and forth several times. Also ARGUE, ARGUMENT, CONTROVERSY, DEBATE.

DISREGARD (dĭs′ rĭ gärd′), *v.,* -GARDED, -GARDING. (Thumbing the nose.) The index finger of the right "B" hand is placed under the tip of the nose. From this position the right hand moves straight forward, away from the face. Also IGNORE.

DISRUPT (dĭs rŭpt′), *v.,* -RUPTED, -RUPTING. (Obstruct, bother.) The left hand, fingers together and palm flat, is held before the body, facing somewhat down. The little finger side of the right hand, held with palm flat, makes one or several up-down chopping motions against the left hand, between its thumb and index finger. Also ANNOY 1, ANNOYANCE 1, BLOCK, BOTHER 1, CHECK 2, COME BETWEEN, DISTURB, HINDER, HINDRANCE, IMPEDE, INTERCEPT, INTERFERE, INTERFERENCE, INTERFERE WITH, INTERRUPT, MEDDLE 1, OBSTACLE, OBSTRUCT, PREVENT, PREVENTION.

DISSATISFACTION (dĭs′ săt ĭs fāk′ shən), *n.* (NOT, SATISFIED.) The sign for NOT 1 is made: the crossed downturned open hands draw apart. The sign for SATISFIED then follows: the downturned "B" hands, the right above the left, are positioned on the chest. They move straight down simultaneously. Also DISCONTENTED, DISSATISFIED.

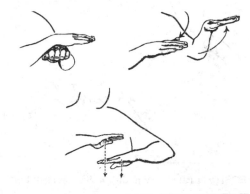

DISSATISFIED (dĭs săt′ ĭs fīd′), *adj.* See DISSATISFACTION.

DISSERTATION (dis′ ər tā′ shən), *n.* (The letter "D"; writing.) The right "D" hand, palm down, makes writing motions as it moves across the upturned left palm.

DISSOLVE (dĭ zŏlv′), *v.,* -SOLVED, -SOLVING. (Fingering the small pieces resulting from the breaking up of something.) The thumbs rub slowly across the finger tips of the upturned hands from the little fingers to the index fingers and then continue to the "A" position, palms up. Also DECAY, DIE OUT, FADE, MELT, ROT.

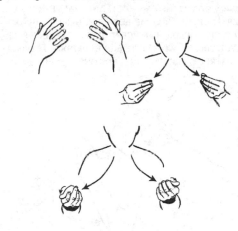

DISTRIBUTE 1 (dĭs trĭb′ ūt), *v.,* -UTED, -UTING. (Giving out widely.) The "AND" hands are held with palms up and fingertips touching each other, the right fingertips pointing left and the left fingertips pointing right. From this position, the hands sweep forward and curve to either side, opening, palms up, as they do.

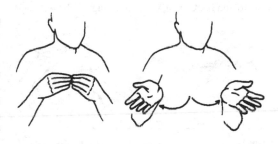

DISTRIBUTE 2, *v.* (The action of dealing out cards.) The signer goes through the motions of dealing out imaginary playing cards. Also CARD PLAYING, CARDS, PLAYING CARDS.

DISTURB (dĭs tûrb′), *v.*, -TURBED, -TURBING. (Obstruct, bother.) The left hand, fingers together and palm flat, is held before the body, facing somewhat down. The little finger side of the right hand, held with palm flat, makes one or several up-down chopping motions against the left hand, between its thumb and index finger. Also ANNOY 1, ANNOYANCE 1, BLOCK, BOTHER 1, CHECK 2, COME BETWEEN, DISRUPT, HINDER, HINDRANCE, IMPEDE, INTERCEPT, INTERFERE, INTERFERENCE, INTERFERE WITH, INTERRUPT, MEDDLE 1, OBSTACLE, OBSTRUCT, PREVENT, PREVENTION.

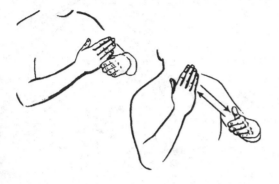

DIVE 1 (dīv), *v.*, DIVED or DOVE, DIVED, DIVING. (The natural motion.) The extended right index and middle fingertips are placed on the back of the same two fingers of the left hand, which is held palm down in front of the body. From this position the right hand moves upward and back in an arc, as if diving off the left hand.

DIVE 2, *n., v.* (The natural sign.) The hands are held together in praying fashion. Always in contact, they swing down in an arc, as if diving into the water.

DIVERSE 1 (dĭ vûrs′, dī-, dī′ vûrs), *adj.* (Separated many times; different.) The "D" hands, palms down, are crossed at the index fingers or are held side by side. They separate and return to their initial position a number of times. Also ASSORTED, DIFFERENCE, DIFFERENT, DIVERSITY 1, UNLIKE, VARIED.

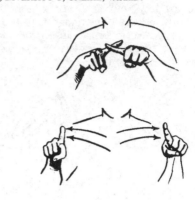

DIVERSE 2, *adj.* (The fingertips indicate many things.) Both hands, in the "D" position, palms out and index fingertips touching, are drawn apart. As they move apart, the index fingers wiggle up and down. Also DIFFERENT OBJECTS, DIVERSITY 2, VARIOUS, VARY.

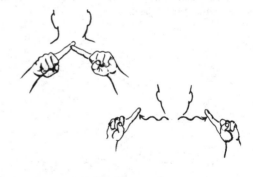

DIVERSITY 1 (dĭ vûr′ sə tĭ, dī-), *n.* See DIVERSE 1.

DIVERSITY 2, *n.* See DIVERSE 2.

DIVIDE 1 (dĭ vīd′), *v.*, -VIDED, -VIDING. (A splitting apart or dividing.) The two hands are crossed, with the right little finger resting on the left index finger. Both hands are dropped down and separated simultaneously, so that the palms face down. Also APPORTION, SHARE 2.

DIVIDE 2, *v.* (Separating or splitting apart.) The "D" hands, palms facing and index fingers pointing straight out, swing down sharply, moving toward their respective sides of the body. Also DIVISION.

DIVIDEND 1 (dĭv' ə dĕnd'), *n.* (A regular taking in.) The outstretched open left hand, held palm facing right, moves in toward the body, assuming the "A" position, palm still facing right. This is repeated several times. Also INCOME, INTEREST 4, SUBSCRIBE, SUBSCRIPTION.

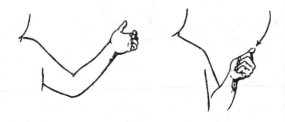

DIVIDEND 2, *n.* The right fingers trace a continuous circle in the upturned left palm.

DIVISION (dĭ vĭzh' ən), *n.* See DIVIDE 2.

DIVORCE 1 (dĭ vōrs'), *n., v.,* -VORCED, -VORCING. (The hands are moved apart.) Both hands, in the "A" position, thumbs up, are held together, with knuckles touching. With a deliberate movement they come apart. Also APART, PART 3, SEPARATE 1.

DIVORCE 2, *n., v.* (The hands, locked in marriage, come apart.) The clasped hands draw apart, into the "A" position, palms facing each other.

DIVORCE 3, *n., v.* (The letter "D"; a separating.) The "D" hands, palms facing and fingertips touching, draw apart.

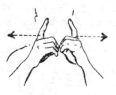

DIZZY (dĭz' ĭ), *adj.* (Images swinging around before the eyes.) The right "5" hand, palm facing the body and fingers somewhat curved, swings around in a continuous counterclockwise circle before the eyes.

DO (dōō), *v.,* DOES, DID, DONE, DOING. (An activity.) Both open hands, palms down, are swung right and left before the chest. Also ACT 2, ACTION, ACTIVE, ACTIVITY, BUSY 2, CONDUCT 1, DEED, PERFORM 1, PERFORMANCE 1, RENDER 2.

DO AS ONE WISHES, *phrase.* (Think for yourself.) The sign for THINK is made: the right index finger touches the center of the forehead. The SELF sign follows: the upturned right thumb moves straight forward from the signer toward the person addressed. Also UP TO YOU.

DOCTOR (dŏk′ tər), *n.* (The letter "M," from "M.D.";feeling the pulse.) The fingertips of the right "M" hand lightly tap the left pulse a number of times. The right "D" hand may also be used, in which case the thumb and fingertips tap the left pulse. Also SURGEON.

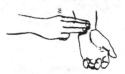

DOESN'T MATTER, *v. phrase.* Both hands, in the "5" position, are held before the chest, fingertips facing each other. With an alternate back-forth movement, the fingertips are made to strike each other. Also ANYHOW, ANYWAY, DESPITE, HOWEVER 2, INDIFFERENCE, INDIFFERENT, IN SPITE OF, MAKE NO DIFFERENCE, NEVERTHELESS, NO MATTER, WHEREVER.

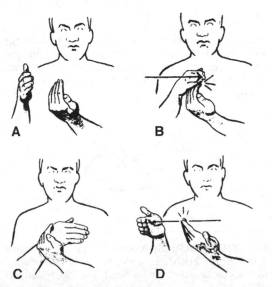

A B

C D

DOG 1 (dôg), *n.* (Patting the knee and snapping the fingers to beckon the dog.) The right hand pats the right knee, and then the fingers are snapped.

DOG 2 (*colloq.*), *n.* (The dog's habit of scratching behind the ear.) The right "B" hand, imitating a paw, brushes the right ear repeatedly.

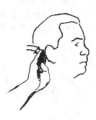

DOG 3, *n.* (*loc.*). (The cold nose.) The middle finger rubs back and forth against the tip of the nose. This sign, identified in Pennsylvania, can easily be mistaken for the disparaging and racist sign for NEGRO.

DOLL 1 (dŏl), *n.* (Pulling the nose.) The right "X" finger, resting on the nose, pulls the head with it as it moves down slightly. It does not leave its position on the nose. Also FOOL 2, HOAX, JOKE.

DOLL 2, *n.* (The rocking of the baby.) The arms are held with one resting on the other, as if cradling a baby. They rock from side to side. Also BABY, INFANT.

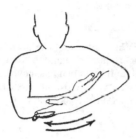

DOLL 3, *n.* (*rare*). (Shaking the doll.) The signer hits the right temple twice with the heel of the right hand.

DOLLAR(S) 1 (dŏl′ ər), *n.* (The natural sign; drawing a bill from a billfold.) The right thumb and index finger trace the outlines of a bill on the upturned left palm. Or the right thumb and fingers may grasp the base of the open left hand, which is held palm facing right and fingers pointing forward; the right hand, in this position, then slides forward along and off the left hand, as if drawing bills from a billfold. Also BILL(S) 1, COIN(S) 1.

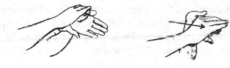

DOLLAR(S) 2, *n.* (The shape of a coin.) The right index finger traces a small circle on the upturned left palm. Also BILL(S) 2, COIN(S) 2.

DOLPHIN (dol′ fin), *n.* (The diving.) The right "B" hand makes a series of undulating dive movements in front of the downturned left arm, which represents the surface of the water.

DOMINICAN REPUBLIC, *n.* (də min′ i ken re pub′ lik) (The initials.) The right "D" is placed at the right temple, and then it moves down to chin level, changing to the letter "R."

DONE 1 (dŭn), *v.* (Bring to an end.) The left hand, fingers together and pointing forward, is held palm facing right. The right, palm down, fingers also together, moves along the top of the left, goes over the tip of the left index finger, and drops straight down, indicating a cutting off or a finishing. This sign is also used to indicate the past tense of a verb, in the sense of accomplishing an action or state of being. Also ACCOMPLISH 2, ACHIEVE 2, COMPLETE 1, CONCLUDE, END 4, EXPIRE 1, FINISH 1, HAVE 2, TERMINATE.

DONE 2, *v.* (Shaking the hands to rid them of some-thing.) The upright "5" hands, palms facing each other, are suddenly and quickly swung around to a palm-out position. Also END 3, FINISH 2.

DONKEY (dǒng′ kǐ), *n.* (The donkey's broad ear; the animal is traditionally a stubborn one.) The open hand, or the "B" hand, is placed at the side of the head, with palm out and fingers pointing straight up. The hand moves forward and back, pivoting at the wrist, as in the case of a donkey's ears flapping. Both hands may also be used, at either side of the head. Also MULE, MULISH, OBSTINATE, STUBBORN.

DO NOT 1, *v. phrase.* (The natural sign.) The crossed "5" hands, palms facing out (or down), separate and recross quickly and repeatedly. The head is usually shaken simultaneously. This sign is from NOT 1, *q.v.* Also DON'T 1.

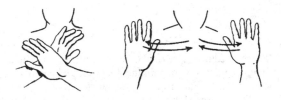

DO NOT 2, *v. phrase.* The thumb of the right "A" hand is placed under the chin. From this position it is flicked outward in an arc. Also DON'T 2.

DON'T 1 (dōnt) *v.* See DO NOT 1.

DON'T 2, *v.* See DO NOT 2.

DON'T BELIEVE, *v. phrase.* (The nose is wrinkled in disbelief.) The right "V" hand faces the nose. The index and middle fingers bend as a cynical expression is assumed. Also CYNIC, CYNICAL, DISBELIEF 1, DOUBT 1, INCREDULITY, SKEPTIC 1, SKEPTICAL 1.

DON'T CARE 1 (*colloq.*), *v. phrase.* (Wiping the nose, *i.e.,* "keeping the nose clean" or not becoming involved.) The downturned right "D" hand, index finger touching the nose, is suddenly flung down and to the right.

DON'T CARE 2 (*colloq.*), *v. phrase.* (The thoughts, *i.e.,* the concern for, is thrown away.) The fingertips of the closed right hand rest on the forehead. The right hand is suddenly flung down and to the right, opening into the downturned "5" position.

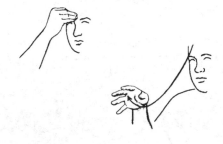

DON'T CARE 3 (*colloq.*), *v. phrase.* (A variation of DON'T CARE 2.) The thumb of the right "Y" hand touches the right ear. The right "Y" hand is then flung down and to the right. Also DON'T CARE FOR 2, DON'T LIKE 1.

DON'T CARE FOR 1, *v. phrase*. (An indication of disdain.) The right "5" hand is placed over the heart, and the head moves back slightly to the right. An expression of disdain is assumed. Also DON'T LIKE 2.

DON'T CARE FOR 2 (*colloq.*), *v. phrase*. See DON'T CARE 3.

DON'T KNOW, *v. phrase*. (Knowledge is lacking.) The sign for KNOW is made: the right fingertips tap the forehead several times. The right hand is then flung over to the right, ending in the "5" position, palm out.

 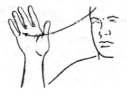

DON'T LIKE 1 (*colloq.*), *v. phrase*. See DON'T CARE 3.

DON'T LIKE 2, *v. phrase*. See DON'T CARE FOR 1.

DON'T WANT, *v. phrase*. (The hands are shaken, indicating a wish to rid them of something.) The "5"

hands, palms facing the body, suddenly swing around to the palms-down position. Also DECLINE 3.

DOOR (dōr), *n*. (The opening and closing of the door.) The "B" hands, palms out and edges touching, are drawn apart and then come together again. Also DOORWAY, OPEN THE DOOR.

DOORKNOB (dōr′ nob), *n*. (The natural sign.) The signer mimes twisting a doorknob.

DOORWAY (dōr′ wā′), *n*. See DOOR.

DOPE (dōp) (*colloq.*), *n*. (A shot in the arm.) The right index finger is thrust into the left upper arm and the thumb wiggles back and forth a number of times, as if implanting a shot in the arm. Also COCA-COLA, COKE, INOCULATE, MORPHINE, NARCOTICS.

DORMITORY (dôr′mi tôr′ē, tōr′ē), *n*. (The letter "D"; where one eats and sleeps.) The right "D" hand moves from chin to cheek.

DOS (dôs, dos), *n*. (Computer acronym for Disk Operating System.) The signer fingerspells D-O-S.

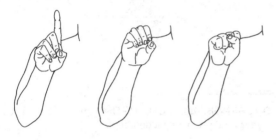

DOUBT 1 (dout), *n., v.,* DOUBTED, DOUBTING. (The nose is wrinkled in disbelief.) The right "V" hand faces the nose. The index and middle fingers bend as a cynical expression is assumed. Also CYNIC, CYNICAL, DISBELIEF 1, DON'T BELIEVE, INCREDULITY, SKEPTIC 1, SKEPTICAL 1.

DOUBT 2, *n., v.* (The wavering.) The downturned "S" hands swing alternately up and down. Also DISBELIEF 2, DOUBTFUL, WAVER 2.

DOUBT 3, *n., v.* (On the fence.) One extended index finger makes a seesaw motion across the other.

DOUBTFUL (dout′ fəl), *adj.* See DOUBT 2.

DOWN (doun), *prep.* (The natural sign.) The right hand, pointing down, moves down an inch or two.

DRAMA (dra′ mə, drăm′ ə), *n*. (Motion or movement, modified by the letter "A" for "act.") Both "A" hands, palms out, are held at shoulder height and rotate alternately toward the head. Also ACT 1, ACTOR, ACTRESS, PERFORM 2, PERFORMANCE 2, PLAY 2, SHOW 2.

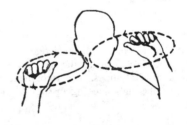

DRAW 1 (drô), *v.,* DREW, DRAWN, DRAWING. (Drawing on the hand.) The little finger of the right hand, representing a pencil, traces a curved line in the upturned left palm. Also ART, MAP.

DRAW 2, *v.* See DRAG.

DRAWBRIDGE (drô' brij), *n.* (The opening of the bridge.) Both hands are held palms down, fingertips touching. They sweep up in individual arcs, miming the opening of a drawbridge.

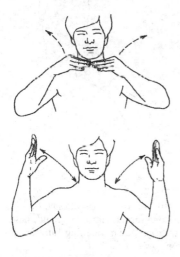

DRAWER (drôr), *n.* (The natural sign.) The upturned hands grasp imaginary drawer pulls and pull the drawer toward the body.

DREAD (drĕd), *v.,* DREADED, DREADING. (The hands attempt to ward off something that causes fear.) The "5" hands, right behind left, move downward before the body in a wavy motion. Also FEAR 2, TERROR 2, TIMID.

DREADFUL (drĕd' fəl), *adj.* (Throwing out the hands.) Both hands, their fingertips touching their respective thumbs, are held, palms facing each other, near the temples. They are thrown out before the face, assuming "5" positions, palms still facing. Also AWFUL, CALAMITOUS, CATASTROPHIC, DANGER 1, DANGEROUS 1, FEARFUL, TERRIBLE, TRAGEDY, TRAGIC.

DREAM (drem), *n., v.,* DREAMED, DREAMT, DREAMING. (A thought wanders off into space.) The right curved index finger opens and closes quickly as it leaves its initial position on the forehead and moves up into the air. Also DAYDREAM, DISTRACTION.

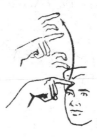

DRESS (drĕs), *n., v.,* DRESSED, DRESSING. (Draping the clothes on the body.) With fingertips resting on the chest, both hands move down simultaneously. The action is repeated. Also CLOTHES, CLOTHING, FROCK, GARMENT, GOWN, SHIRT, SUIT, WEAR 1.

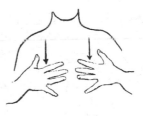

DRINK 1 (drĭngk), *n., v.,* DRANK, DRUNK, DRINKING. (The natural sign.) An imaginary glass is tipped at the open lips.

DRINK 2, *n., v.* (The act of drinking.) The thumbtip of the right "Y" hand is tilted toward the mouth as if it were a drinking glass or bottle. The signer tilts his head back slightly as if drinking. Also DRUNK, DRUNKARD, DRUNKENNESS, INTOXICATE, INTOXICATION, LIQUOR 2.

DRIVE (drīv), *v.,* DROVE, DRIVEN, DRIVING, *n.* (The steering wheel.) The hands grasp an imaginary steering wheel and manipulate it. Also AUTOMOBILE, CAR.

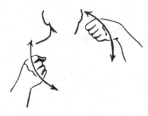

DRIVE TO (drīv to), *v.* (The steering wheel moves forward.) Holding an imaginary steering wheel, the hands move straight forward. Also GO BY CAR.

DROOL (drōōl), *v.,* DROOLED, DROOLING. (The saliva drips from a corner of the mouth.) The index finger of the right "4" hand moves down from its position against the right mouth's corner. The mouth is held slightly open, and the tip of the tongue may protrude

from the mouth. This sign usually indicates strong desire or lust.

DROP (drŏp), *v.,* DROPPED, DROPPING. (The natural sign.) The downturned right "S" hand, held at shoulder height, drops down, opening into the downturned "5" position.

DROWN 1 (droun), *v.,* DROWNED, DROWNING. (The legs go under.) The index and middle fingers of the right "V" hand, palm facing the body, are drawn down between the index and middle fingers of the downturned left "4" hand. The right index finger alone may be substituted for the "V" fingers.

DROWN 2, *v.* (The downward movement.) The downturned right hand, fingers touching thumb, is thrust down into the cup formed by the open left hand. The right hand continues straight down through this cup.

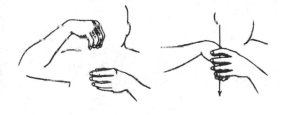

DRUG (drŭg), *n.*, *v.*, DRUGGED, DRUGGING. (Mixing of medicine; rolling a pill.) The ball of the middle fingertip of the right "5" hand describes a small counterclockwise circle in the upturned left palm. Also MEDICINE, POISON 1, PRESCRIPTION.

DRUM (drŭm), *n.*, *v.*, DRUMMED, DRUMMING. (The natural sign.) The hands play an imaginary drum.

DRUNK 1 (drŭngk), *adj.* (The glass misses the lips.) The thumbtip of the right "A" hand moves quickly across the lips, from right to left.

DRUNK 2, *adj.* (Wavy motion indicates unsteadiness.) The downturned right hand, flat and open, undulating up and down, moves across the forehead from right to left.

DRUNK 3, *adj.* (The act of drinking.) The thumbtip of the right "Y" hand is tilted toward the mouth, as if it were a drinking glass or bottle. The signer tilts his head back slightly as if drinking. Also DRINK 2, DRUNKARD, DRUNKENNESS, INTOXICATE, INTOXICATION, LIQUOR 2.

DRUNKARD (drŭngk' ərd), *n.* See DRUNK.

DRUNKENNESS (drŭngk' ən nĭs), *n.* See DRUNK.

DRY (drī), *adj.*, *v.*, DRIED, DRYING. (A dryness, indicated by a wiping of the lips.) The "X" finger is drawn across the lips, from left to right, as if wiping them. Also ARID, BORE 1, DROUGHT, DULL 2.

DRYER (drī' ər), *n.* (The circular movement.) The sign for DRY is made: the downturned curved index finger is wiped across the lips. The right index finger then twirls around in a cup formed by the left "C" hand.

DUCK (dŭk), *n.* (The broad bill.) The right hand is held with its back resting against the mouth. The thumb plus index and middle fingers come together repeatedly, indicating the opening and closing of a broad bill. Also GOOSE.

DUCKLING (dŭk′ ling), *n.* (A small duck.) The sign for DUCK is made: the right hand is held with the back of the hand resting against the mouth. The thumb and index and middle fingers open and close together, depicting the broad bill of the duck. The cupped hands then come together, indicating a small item within.

DUE (dū, dōō), *adj.* (Pointing to the palm where the money should be placed.) The index finger of one hand

is thrust into the upturned palm of the other several times. Also ARREARS, DEBIT, DEBT, OBLIGATION 3, OWE.

DULL 1 (dŭl), *adj.* (Knocking the head to indicate its empty state.) The "S" hand, palm facing the body, knocks against the forehead. Also DUMB 1, DUNCE, STUPID 1.

DULL 2, *adj.* See DRY.

DUMB 1 (dŭm), *adj.* See DULL 1.

DUMB 2 (*colloq.*), *adj.* (The thickness of the skull is indicated to stress intellectual density.) With the thumb of the right "C" hand grasped by the closed left hand, the right hand is swung in toward the body, describing a small arc as it moves. The space between the curved right fingers and the closed left hand indicates the thickness of the skull. Also CLUMSY 2, MORON, STUPID 2, THICK-SKULLED, UNSKILLED.

DUMBFOUNDED 1 (dŭm found′), *adj.* (The mind is frozen; the thought is frozen.) The index finger of the right "D" hand, palm facing the body, touches the forehead (modified THINK sign, *q.v.*). Both hands, in the "5" position, palms down, are then suddenly and deliberately dropped down in front of the body. A look of surprise is assumed at this point, and the head jerks back slightly. Also AT A LOSS, JOLT, SHOCKED 1, STUMPED.

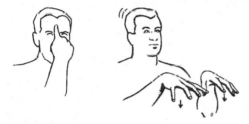

DUMBFOUNDED 2 (*colloq.*), *adj.* (The mouth drops open.) The fingertips of both "V" hands are held curved and touching before the body, one hand above the other. Then the hands are suddenly drawn apart and, at the same instant, the mouth drops open and the eyes open wide. Also FLABBERGASTED. OPENMOUTHED, SPEECHLESS, SURPRISE 2.

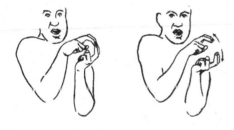

DUMMY (dum′ ē), *n.* The thumb of the right "C" hand is placed inside the closed left hand. Pivoting on the thumb, the right hand moves up and over the back of the left.

DUNCE (dŭns), *n.* See DULL 1.

DUPLICATE 1 (*adj., n.,* dū′ plə kĭt, dōō′-; *v.,* dū′ plə kāt′, dōō′-), -CATED, -CATING. (The natural sign.) The

right fingers and thumb close together and move onto the upturned, open left hand, as if taking something from one place to another. Also COPY 1, IMITATE, MIMIC, MODEL.

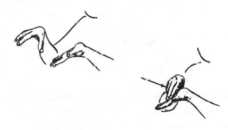

DUPLICATE 2, *n.* (A likeness; a sameness.) Both index fingers, held together at one side of the body near waist level, point forward. As they travel to the other side of the body they separate an inch or two and come together again. Also ACCORDING (TO), ALSO 1, AS, SAME AS, TOO.

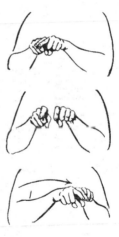

DURING (dyŏŏr′ ĭng, dŏŏr′-), *prep.* (Parallel time.) Both "D" hands, palms down, move forward in unison, away from the body. They may move straight forward or may follow a slight upward arc. Also IN THE MEANTIME, IN THE PROCESS OF, MEANTIME, WHILE.

DUST (dust), *v.*, DUSTED, DUSTING. (Manipulating a dusting cloth.) The signer mimes moving a cloth over a surface at random.

DUSTPAN (dust' pan), *n.* (The sweeping.) The upturned left hand is the dustpan. The little finger edge of the right hand repeatedly "sweeps" dust into the left.

DWELL ON, (dwel on), *v.* (The mind is fixed on one thing.) The right index finger touches the forehead and is then brought down to touch the back of the down-turned left "S" hand, which moves up and down slightly. Also FIXATED, OBSESSED.

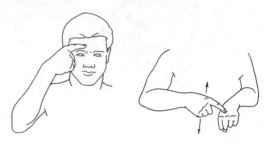

E

EACH (ēch), *adj.* (Peeling off, one by one.) The left "A" hand is held palm facing the right. The knuckles of the right "A" hand are drawn repeatedly down the left thumb from its tip to its base. Also EVERY.

EACH ONE, *pron. phrase.* (EVERY; ONE.) The sign for EVERY is made, followed by the sign for ONE. Also EVERYBODY, EVERYONE.

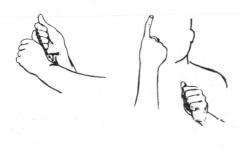

EACH OTHER, *pron. phrase.* (Mingling with.) Both hands are held in modified "A" positions, thumbs out. The left hand is positioned with its thumb pointing straight up, and the right hand, with its thumb pointing down, revolves above the left thumb in a counterclockwise direction. Also ASSOCIATE 1, FELLOWSHIP, MINGLE 2, MUTUAL 1, ONE ANOTHER.

EAGER (ē′ gər), *adj.* (Rubbing the hands together in zeal or ambition.) The open hands are rubbed vigor-

ously back and forth against each other. Also AMBITIOUS 1, ANXIOUS 1, ARDENT, DILIGENCE 1, DILIGENT, EAGERNESS, EARNEST, ENTHUSIASM, ENTHUSIASTIC, INDUSTRIOUS, METHODIST, ZEAL, ZEALOUS.

EAGERNESS, *n.* See EAGER.

EAGLE (ē′ gəl), *n.* (The hooked beak and the wings.) The index finger of the right "X" hand is placed on the nose, either facing out or across it. The hands and arms then flap slowly, in imitation of the bird's majestic flight.

EAR (ĭr), *n.* (The natural sign.) The right index finger touches the right ear.

EARACHE (ĭr′ āk′), *n.* (A stabbing pain in the ear.) The sign for EAR is made, followed by the sign for ACHE: the "D" hands, index fingers pointing to each other and palms facing the body, are rotated in elliptical fashion before the chest—simultaneously but in opposite directions.

EARLY 1 (ûr′ lē), *adj.* (The sun is coming up.) The little finger edge of the open right hand rests in the crook of the left elbow. (The right arm here represents the horizon and should therefore be held in a horizontal position.) The left "5" hand is held palm up, and the left arm is held at a 45° angle from the horizontal. This represents the sun coming up over the horizon, and is a modified sign for MORNING, *q.v.,* but with no motion.

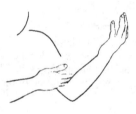

EARLY 2, *adj.* The middle finger of the downturned right hand rests on the back of the downturned left hand. The top hand moves forward, while the middle finger is drawn back against the palm.

EARN (ûrn), *v.*, EARNED, EARNING. (Gathering in.) The right "5" hand, its little finger edge touching the upturned left palm, is drawn in an arc toward the body, closing into the "S" position as it sweeps over the base of the left hand. Also ACCUMULATE 1, COLLECT, SALARY, WAGES.

EARRING (ĭr′ rĭng′), *n.* (The natural sign.) The signer squeezes the earlobe, which may also be shaken slightly.

EARTH 1 (ûrth), *n.* (The earth and its axes are indicated.) The downturned left "S" hand indicates the earth. The thumb and index finger of the downturned right "5" hand are placed at each edge of the left. In this position the right hand swings back and forth while maintaining contact with the left. Also GEOGRAPHY, GLOBE 1, PLANET.

EARTH 2, *n.* (Fingering the soil.) Both hands, held upright before the body, finger imaginary pinches of soil. Also DIRT, GROUND, SOIL 1.

EARTHQUAKE (ûrth′ kwāk′), *n.* (Earth, noise.) The sign for EARTH 1 is made. This is followed by the sign for NOISE. After placing the index finger on the ear, both hands assume the "S" position, palms down. They move alternately back and forth forcefully.

EASTER 1 (ēs′ tər), *n.* (The letter "E.") The right "E" hand, pivoted at the wrist, is shaken slightly.

EASTER 2, *n.* (A rising.) The right index and middle fingers, representing the legs, are positioned in the upturned left palm. The right hand moves slowly up and off the left. *Note:* This sign is considered vulgar by some; it is at best used in a colloquial sense. Also ASCENSION, RESURRECTION.

EASTER 3, *n.* (A modification of EASTER 1.) The right "E" hand swings in an arc from left to right.

EASY 1 (ē′ zĭ), *adj.* (The fingertips are easily moved.) The right fingertips brush repeatedly over their upturned left counterparts, causing them to move. Also FACILITATE, SIMPLE 1.

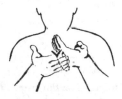

EASY 2 (*loc., colloq.*), *adj.* (Rationale obscure.) The thumb and index finger of the right "F" hand are placed on the chin.

EAT (ēt), *v.,* ATE, EATEN, EATING. (The natural sign.) The closed right hand goes through the natural motion of placing food in the mouth. This movement is repeated. Also CONSUME 1, CONSUMPTION, DEVOUR, DINE, FEED 1, FOOD 1, MEAL.

EAVESDROP 1 (ēvz′ drop), *v.,* DROPPED, DROPPING. (Information is pulled into the eye.) The hand is held with thumb below the eye, index and middle fingers pointing forward. The index and middle fingers repeatedly move in and out, as if bringing something into the eye. This is a culturally related sign, taking into account that deaf people gather information with their eyes rather than their ears.

EAVESDROP 2, *v.* (Information is pulled into the ear.) The same hand position as in EAVESDROP 1, above. The thumbtip is placed on the ear, and the index and middle fingers move in and out, as if bringing something into the ear.

ECONOMIC (ek ə nom′ ik), *adj.* (The "E" hand; money.) The back of the upturned right "E" hand is brought down twice on the upturned left open hand.

ECCENTRIC (ĭk sĕn′ trĭk), *adj.* -TRICALLY, *adv.* (Something that distorts the vision.) The "C" hand describes a small arc in front of the face.

ECUADOR (ek′ wə dôr), *n.* The right "E" hand makes a clockwise circle at the right temple. A native sign.

ECHO (ek ′ō), *n., v.,* ECHOED, ECHOING. (The knocking sound bounces back.) The ear is touched with the index finger, and then the knuckles of the right fist strike against the left open hand, palm facing right. The right hand then opens and moves up and back, with fingers wriggling.

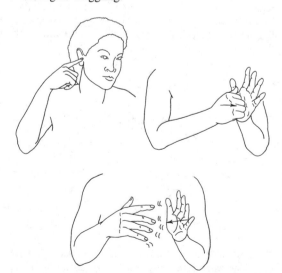

EDITING (video or film). (The snipping in the cutting room.) The signer mimes snipping film with both hands working simultaneously.

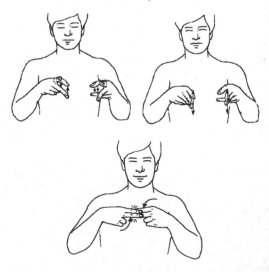

EDUCATE (ĕj′ ŏŏ kāt′), *v.,* -CATED, -CATING. (Giving forth from the mind.) The fingertips of each hand are placed on the temples. They then swing out and open into the "5" position. Also INDOCTRINATE, INDOCTRINATION, INSTRUCT, INSTRUCTION, TEACH.

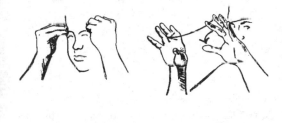

EDUCATION 1 (ej′ ōō kā ′shən), *n.* (The letters "E" and "D"; teaching or imparting knowledge.) Both "E" hands are positioned at the temples, palms facing the head. They are thrown out and forward, changing to the "D" position.

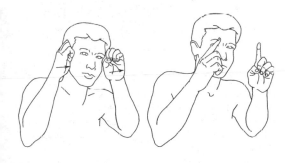

EDUCATION 2, *n.* (Taking knowledge from a book and placing it in the head.) The downturned fingers of the right hand are placed on the upturned left palm. They close, and then the hand rises and the right fingertips are placed on the forehead. Also LEARN.

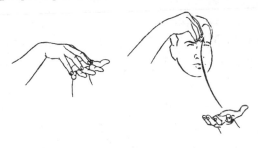

EFFEMINATE (i fem′ ə nit), *adj.* (The mincing gestures.) Both "F" hands, palms out, are held at shoulder height. The signer moves them alternately forward and

back, while the shoulders keep pace with the forward-and-back movements. Also GAY 4, HOMOSEXUAL 4.

EFFORT 1 (ĕf′ ərt), *n.* (Trying to push through.) The "A" hands, palms facing before the body, are swung around and a bit down so that the palms now face out. The movement indicates an attempt to push through a barrier. Also ATTEMPT 1, ENDEAVOR, PERSEVERE 1, PERSIST 1, TRY 1.

EFFORT 2, *n.* (Trying to push through, using the "T" hands, for "try.") This is the same sign as EFFORT 1 except that the "T" hands are employed. Also ATTEMPT 2, PERSEVERE 2, TRY 2.

EFFORT 3, *n.* (The letter "E"; attempting to break through.) Both "E" hands move forward simultaneously, describing a small, downturned arc.

EGG (ĕg), *n.* (Act of breaking an egg into a bowl.) The right "H" hand is brought down on the left "H"

hand, and then both hands are pivoted down and slightly apart.

EGOTISM 1 (ē′ gə tĭz′ əm, ĕg′ ə-), *n.* (The self is carried uppermost.) The right "A" hand, thumb up, is brought up against the chest, from waist to breast. Also AMBITIOUS 2, SELF 2.

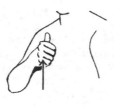

EGOTISM 2 *n.* (Repeated "I"s.) The "I" hands are alternately swung in toward and away from the chest. The movement is repeated a number of times.

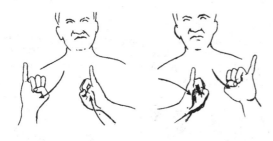

EGOTISM 3 (*colloq.*), *n.* (A big "I.") The right "I" hand, palm facing left, rests on the chest. The left hand, wrapped loosely around the right little finger, is drawn straight up as if to extend the right little finger.

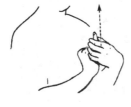

EGYPT 1 (ē′ jĭpt), *n.* (The dark face.) The right fingertips rest initially on the nose. The right hand sweeps

around the face, describing a counterclockwise circle and returning to its original position. Also EGYPTIAN.

EGYPT 2, *n.* (The asp in the headdress of the pharaohs.) The right "X," palm facing forward, is positioned against the forehead.

EGYPT 3, *n.* (The "E"; the shape of the headdress or hairstyle. Also the pyramids.) Both "E" hands, positioned at the top of the head, move down the sides of the head, widening as they move down to chin level, where they move in toward the jaws, describing a triangle.

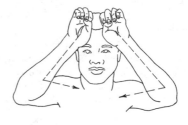

EIFFEL TOWER, *n.* (The shape.) Both "V" hands, palms facing, move up above the head, fingertips coming in contact. Also PARIS, TOWER.

EITHER 1 (ē′ thər *or, esp. Brit.,* ī′ thər), *conj.* (Selection between two or among multiple choices.) The left "L" hand is held palm facing the body and thumb pointing straight up. The right index finger touches the left thumbtip and then the left index fingertip. Also OR 1.

EITHER 2, *adj* (Making a choice.) The left "V" hand faces the body. The right thumb and index finger close first over the left index fingertip and then over the left middle fingertip. Also CHOICE.

EITHER 3, *conj.* (Considering one thing against another.) The "A" hands, palms facing and thumbs pointing straight up, move alternately up and down before the chest. Also OR 2, WHETHER, WHICH 1.

EJACULATE 1 (ĭ jak′ yə lăt), *n. v.,* -LATED, -LATING. (The pulsing of the penis during release.) The left index finger, representing the penis, is positioned at the base of the right "E" or "S" hand, whose palm faces left. The fingers of the right hand open and close twice, as the two hands, connected, move forward an inch or so. This sign is used for male ejaculation. Also EJACULATION 1, SEMEN, SPERM.

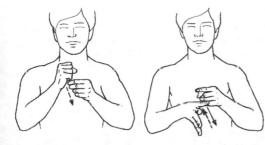

EJACULATE 2, *v., n.* (Pulsation within the vagina.) The left hand grasps the right wrist as the right fingers are thrown open repeatedly. Also EJACULATION 2.

EJACULATION 1 (ĭ jak yə lă′ shən), *n.* See EJACU-LATE 1.

EJACULATION 2, *n.* See EJACULATE 2.

ELBOW (el′ bō), *n.* (The elbow is pointed to.) The signer touches his elbow.

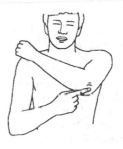

ELDER (ĕl′ dər), *adj., comparative degree.* The sign for OLD is made, followed by the comparative degree sign: the upturned right thumb moves up to a position in line with the right temple. Also OLDER.

ELECT (ĭ lĕkt′), *n., v.,* -LECTED, -LECTING (Placing a ballot in a box.) The right hand, holding an imaginary ballot between the thumb and index finger, places it into an imaginary box formed by the left "O" hand, palm facing right. Also ELECTION, VOTE.

ELECTION (ĭ lĕk′ shən), *n.* See ELECT.

ELECTRIC (ĭ lĕk′ trĭk), *adj.* (The points of the electrodes.) The "X" hands are held palms facing the body, thumb edges up. The knuckles of the index fingers touch each other repeatedly. Also ELECTRICITY, PHYSICS.

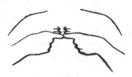

ELECTRICITY (ĭ lĕk′ trĭs′ ə tĭ), *n.* See ELECTRIC.

ELECTRIC OUTLET (out′ lət). (Plugging in.) Both "V" hands, palms facing each other, are held before the body. The right "V" hand, representing the prongs of a plug, is brought into an interlocking position with the left. Also ELECTRIC PLUG, SOCKET.

ELECTRIC PLUG (plŭg). See ELECTRIC OUTLET.

ELECTRON (i lek′ tron), *n.* (The letter "E"; circling.) The right "E" makes a circle around the left fist.

ELEGANT (el′ ə gənt), *adj.* (The feelings are titillated.) With the thumb resting on the upper part of the chest, the fingers are wiggled back and forth. Also FINE 1, GRAND 2, GREAT 4, SPLENDID 2, SWELL 2, WONDERFUL 2.

ELEMENTARY (el ə men′ tər ē), *adj.* (The letter "E"; something basic, *i.e.,* necessary to support one's knowledge.) The upturned right thumb is placed underneath the downturned left palm. The thumb makes a continuous counterclockwise circle.

ELEPHANT (ĕl′ ə fənt), *n.* (The movement of the trunk.) The cupped downturned right hand is placed with its back resting on the nose. The hand moves down, out, and around, imitating the motion of the trunk in bringing food up to the mouth. The hand may also be moved in random undulations.

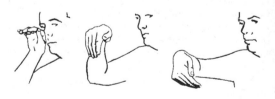

ELEVATOR 1 (ĕl′ ə vā′ tər), *n.* (A rising platform.) With the downturned right "V" fingers standing on the upturned left palm, the left hand rises straight up.

ELEVATOR 2, *n.* (The letter "E"; the rising.) The right "E" hand, palm facing left and thumb edge up, rises straight up.

ELIMINATE (ĭ ·lĭm′ ə nāt), *v.*, -NATED, -NATING. (Scratching something out and throwing it away.) The fingertips of the open right hand scratch downward across the palm of the upright left hand. In one continuous motion, the right hand then closes as if holding something and finally opens again forcefully and motions as if throwing something away. Also DELETE 2, DISCARD 3.

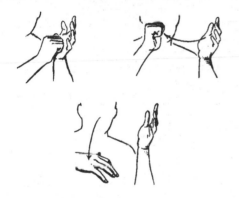

ELK (elk), *n.* (The antlers.) Both upturned "5" hands are placed with thumbtips against either side of the head. They move slightly.

ELOPE (i lōp′), *v.*, ELOPED, ELOPING. (Escaping and joining hands in marriage.) The right index finger, positioned between the left index and middle fingers,

suddenly shoots forward. Both hands are then clasped together.

ELSE (els), *adj.* (Moving over to *another* position.) The right "A" hand, thumb up, is pivoted from the wrist and swung over to the right so that the thumb now points to the right. Also ANOTHER, OTHER.

EMANCIPATE (ĭ măn′ sə pāt′), *v.*, -PATED, -PATING. (Breaking the bonds.) The "S" hands, crossed in front of the body, swing apart and face out. Also DELIVER 1, FREE 1, INDEPENDENCE, INDEPENDENT, LIBERATION, REDEEM 1, RELIEF, RESCUE, SAFE, SALVATION, SAVE 1.

EMBARRASS (ĕm băr′ əs), *v.*, -RASSED, -RASSING. (The red rises in the cheeks.) The sign for RED is made: the tip of the right index finger of the "D" hand moves down over the lips, which are red. Both hands are then placed palms facing the cheeks and move up along the face, to indicate the rise of color. Also BLUSH, EMBARRASSED, FLUSH, MORTIFICATION.

EMBARRASSED, *adj.* See EMBARRASS.

EMBRACE (ĕm brās′), *v.,* -BRACED, -BRACING, *n.* (The natural sign.) The arms clasp the body in a natural hugging position. Also HUG.

EMERGENCY (ĭ mûr′ jən sē), *n., adj.* (The flashing light.) The right "E" hand is positioned above the head. It rotates in imitation of a flashing emergency light.

EMOTION 1 (ĭ mō′ shən), *n.* (The welling up of feelings or emotions in the heart.) The right middle finger, touching the heart, moves up an inch or two a number of times. Also FEEL 2, FEELING, MOTIVE 2, SENSATION, SENSE 2.

EMOTION 2, *n.* (The letter "E"; that which moves about in the chest, *i.e.* the heart.) The "E" hands, palms facing in, are positioned close to the chest. Both hands describe alternate circles, the left hand clockwise and the right hand counterclockwise. The right hand alone may be used.

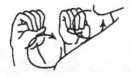

EMPEROR (ĕm′ pər ər), *n.* (The letter "E"; the sash worn by royalty.) The right "E" hand, palm facing left, moves down in an arc from the left shoulder to the right hip.

EMPHASIS (ĕm′ fə sĭs), *n.* (Pressing down to emphasize.) The right thumb is pressed down deliberately against the upturned left palm. Both hands move forward a bit. Also EMPHASIZE, EMPHATIC, STRESS.

EMPHASIZE (ĕm′ fə sīz′), *v.,* -SIZED, -SIZING. See EMPHASIS.

EMPHATIC (ĕm făt′ ĭk), *adj.* See EMPHASIS.

EMPTY 1 (ĕmp′ tĭ), *adj.* (A disappearance.) The right open hand, palm facing the body, is held by the left hand and is drawn down and out, ending in a position with fingers drawn together. The left hand, meanwhile, may close into a position with fingers also drawn together. Also ABSENCE 1, ABSENT 1, DEPLETE, DISAPPEAR, EXTINCT, FADE AWAY, GONE 1, MISSING 1, OMISSION 1, OUT 3, OUT OF, VANISH.

EMPTY 2, *adj.* (Devoid of everything on the surface.) The middle finger of the downturned right "5" hand sweeps over the back of the downturned left "A" or "S" hand, from wrist to knuckles, and continues beyond a bit. Also BARE 2, NAKED, NUDE, OMISSION 2, VACANCY, VACANT, VOID.

ENCODE (en kōd′), *v.*, ENCODED, ENCODING. (The "E"; changing to something else. Computer term indicating conversion of data into a program code for a computer.) Both "E" hands, knuckle to knuckle, twist around each other.

ENCOUNTER (ĕn koun′ tər), *v.*, -TERED, -TERING. (A coming together of two persons.) Both "D" hands, palms facing each other, are brought together. Also MEET.

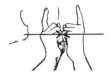

ENCOURAGE (ĕn kûr′ ĭj), *v.*, -AGED, -AGING. (Pushing forward.) Both "5" hands are held, palms out, the right fingers facing right and the left fingers left. The hands move straight forward in a series of short movements. Also MOTIVATE, MOTIVATION, URGE 1.

ENCYCLOPEDIA (en sī klə pē′ dē ə), *n.* (The letter "E"; turning the pages.) The upturned left hand indicates the open page. The right "E" hand, palm down,

repeatedly brushes against the left palm, from fingertips to heel.

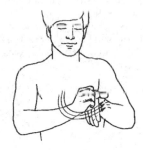

END 1 (ĕnd), *n., v.*, ENDED, ENDING. (The little, *i.e.*, LAST, fingers are indicated.) With the hands in the "I" position, the tip of the right little finger strikes the tip of its left counterpart. The right index finger may be used instead of the right little finger. Also EVENTUALLY, FINAL 1, FINALLY 1, LAST 1, ULTIMATE, ULTIMATELY.

END 2, *n., v.* (A single little, *i.e.*, LAST, finger is indicated.) The tip of the index finger of the right "D" hand strikes the tip of the little finger of the left "I" hand. Also FINAL 2, FINALLY 2, LAST 2.

END 3, *n., v.* (Shaking the hands to rid them of something.) The upright "5" hands, palms facing each other, are suddenly and quickly swung around to a palm-out position. Also DONE 2, FINISH 2.

END 4, *n., v.* (Bring to an end.) The left hand, fingers together and pointing forward, is held palm facing right. The right, palm down, fingers also together, moves along the top of the left, goes over the tip of the left index finger, and drops straight down, indicating a cutting off or a finishing. This sign is also used to indicate the past tense of a verb, in the sense of ending an action or state of being. Also ACCOMPLISH 2, ACHIEVE 2, COMPLETE 1, CONCLUDE, DONE 1, EXPIRE 1, FINISH 1, HAVE 2, TERMINATE.

ENDEAVOR (ĕn dĕv′ ər), n. (Trying to push through.) The "A" hands, palms facing before the body, are swung around and a bit down, so that the palms now face out. The movement indicates an attempt to push through a barrier. Also ATTEMPT 1, EFFORT 1, PERSEVERE 1, PERSIST 1, TRY 1.

ENDORSE 1 (ĕn dôrs′), v., -DORSED, -DORSING. (Holding up.) The right "S" hand pushes up the left "S" hand. Also FAVOR, INDORSE 1, MAINTENANCE, SUPPORT 1, SUSTAIN, SUSTENANCE, UPHOLD, UPLIFT.

ENDORSE 2, v. (One hand upholds the other.) Both hands, in the "S" position, are held palms facing the body, the right under the left. The right hand pushes up the left in a gesture of support. Also ADVOCATE, INDORSE 2, SUPPORT 2.

ENDORSE 3, v. ("Second"—two fingers.) The right "L" hand, held somewhat above the head, index finger pointing straight up, pivots forward a bit so that the index finger now points forward. Used in parliamentary procedure. Also INDORSE 3, SECOND 2, SUPPORT 3.

ENDURE 1 (ĕn dyŏŏr′, -dŏŏr′), v., -DURED, -DURING. (A clenching of the fists; the rise and fall of pain.) Both "S" hands, tightly clenched, revolve about each other, slowly and deliberately, while a pained expression is worn. Also AGONY, BEAR 3, DIFFICULT 3, PASSION 2, SUFFER 1, TOLERATE 2.

ENDURE 2, v. (Steady, uninterrupted movement.) The "A" hands are held with palms out, thumbs extended and touching, the right behind the left. In this position the hands move forward in a straight, steady line. Also CONTINUE 1, EVER 1, LAST 3, LASTING, PERMANENT, PERPETUAL, PERSEVERE 3, PERSIST 2, REMAIN, STAY 1, STAY STILL.

ENEMY (ĕn′ ə mǐ), n. (At sword's point.) The two index fingers, after pointing to each other, are drawn sharply apart. This is followed by the sign for INDIVIDUAL: both open hands, palms facing each other, move down the sides of the body, tracing its outline to the hips. Also FOE, OPPONENT, RIVAL 1.

ENERGY (en′ ər jē), *n.* (The letter "E"; power or muscle.) The left arm, fist closed, is extended, palm up. The right "E" hand, palm down, describes an arc over the upper muscle area.

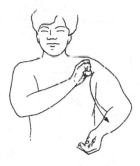

ENGAGED 1 (ĕn gājd′), *adj.* (The letter "E"; the ring finger.) The right "E" hand moves in a clockwise circle over the downturned left hand and then comes to rest on the left ring finger.

ENGAGED 2, *adj.* (The natural sign.) The right hand goes through the natural motion of placing a ring on the left ring finger.

ENGINE (ĕn′ jən), *n.* (The meshing gears.) With the knuckles of both hands interlocked, the hands pivot up and down, imitating the meshing of gear teeth. Also FACTORY, MACHINE, MACHINERY, MECHANIC 1, MECHANISM, MOTOR.

ENGINEER (en′ jə nēr′), *n.* (Measuring something.) Both "Y" hands, palms out and thumbs touching, rotate alternately back and forth. Alternatively, the hands, in this same position, separate and come together repeatedly. Also MEASURE.

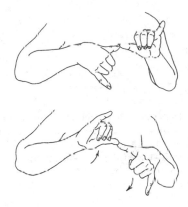

ENGLAND (ĭng′ glənd), *n.* (The English are supposed to be handshakers.) The right hand grasps and shakes the left. Also BRITAIN, BRITISH, ENGLISH, GREAT BRITAIN.

ENGLISH (ing′ glĭsh), *adj.* See ENGLAND.

ENJOY (ĕn joi′), *v.,* -JOYED, -JOYING. (A pleasurable feeling on the heart.) The open right hand is circled on the chest, over the heart. Also APPRECIATE, ENJOYMENT, GRATIFY 1, LIKE 3, PLEASE, PLEASURE, WILLING 2.

ENJOYMENT (ĕn joi′ mənt), *n.* See ENJOY.

ENLIST (ĕn lĭst′), *v.,* -LISTED, -LISTING. (Joining together.) Both hands, held in the modified "5" position, palms out, move toward each other. The thumbs and index fingers of both hands then connect. Also AFFILIATE 1, ANNEX, ASSOCIATE 2, ATTACH, BELONG, COMMUNION OF SAINTS, CONCERN 2, CONNECT, ENROLL, JOIN 1, PARTICIPATE, RELATIVE 2, UNION, UNITE.

ENOUGH (ĭ nŭf′), *adj.* (A full cup.) The left hand, in the "S" position, is held palm facing right. The right "5" hand, palm down, is brushed outward several times over the top of the left, indicating a wiping off of the top of a cup. Also ABUNDANCE, ABUNDANT, ADEQUATE, AMPLE, PLENTY, SUBSTANTIAL, SUFFICIENT.

ENRAGE (ĕn rāj′), *v.,* -RAGED, -RAGING. (A violent welling up of the emotions.) The curved fingers of the right hand are placed in the center of the chest and fly up suddenly and violently. An expression of anger is worn. Also ANGER, ANGRY 2, FURY, INDIGNANT, INDIGNATION, IRE, MAD 1, RAGE.

ENROLL (ĕn rōl′), *v.,* -ROLLED, -ROLLING. See ENLIST.

ENTER (ĕn′ tər), *v.,* -TERED, -TERING. (Going in.) The downturned open right hand sweeps under its downturned left counterpart. Also ENTRANCE 1.

ENTHUSIASM (ĕn thōō′ zĭ ăz′ əm), *n.* (Rubbing the hands together in zeal or ambition.) The open hands are rubbed vigorously back and forth against each other. Also AMBITIOUS 1, ANXIOUS 1, ARDENT, DILIGENCE 1, DILIGENT, EAGER, EAGERNESS, EARNEST, ENTHUSIASTIC, INDUSTRIOUS, METHODIST, ZEAL, ZEALOUS.

ENTHUSIASTIC (ĕn thōō′ zĭ ăs′ tĭk), *adj.* See ENTHUSIASM.

ENTIRE (ĕn tīr′), *adj.* (Encompassing; a gathering together.) Both hands are held in the right-angle position, palms facing the body, and the right hand in front of the left. The right hand makes a sweeping outward movement around the left and comes to rest with the back of the right hand resting in the left palm. Also ALL, UNIVERSAL, WHOLE.

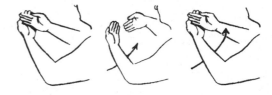

ENTRANCE 1 (ĕn′ trəns), *n.* See ENTER.

ENTRANCE 2 (*sl.*), *v.,* -TRANCED, -TRANCING. (The tongue drops out of the mouth; gawking.) The right thumb and curved index finger are placed in front of the open mouth. The right hand moves straight forward as the tongue comes out of the mouth a bit.

ENTREAT (ĕn trēt′), *v.,* -TREATED, -TREATING. (An act of supplication.) With the right hand clasped over the left, both hands are shaken gently before the body.

The eyes often are directed upward. Also BEG 2, BESEECH, IMPLORE, PLEA, PLEAD, SUPPLICATION.

ENVELOPE (en′ və lōp), *n.* (Licking the flap.) The shape of the envelope is indicated with the curved thumbs and index fingers, which move apart to show the length. The tongue then emerges and licks back and forth against the flap.

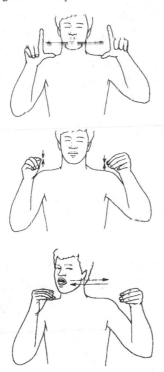

ENVIOUS (ĕn′ vĭ əs), *adj.* (Biting the finger to suppress the feelings.) The tip of the index finger is bitten. The tip of the little finger is sometimes used. Also COVET 2, ENVY, JEALOUS, JEALOUSY.

ENVIRONMENT 1 (ĕn vī′ rən mənt), *n.* (The surrounding area.) The downturned right hand circles around the upturned left in a counterclockwise direc-

ENVIRONMENT 2, *n.* (The letter "E"; encircling the individual, represented by the index finger.) The right "E" hand travels around the upright left index finger.

ENVY (en′ vĭ), *n.* See ENVIOUS.

EPIDEMIC (ep ə dem′ ik), *n.* (Sickness spreads.) The sign for SICK is made: the right middle finger rests on the forehead and its left counterpart on the stomach. Both hands are then held palms down, in the modified "O" position. The hands move out and spread apart, with fingers opening wide.

EPILEPSY (ep′ ə lep sē), *n.* (The body shakes in a fit.) The right hand, palm up, index and middle fingers curved, is placed in the upturned left palm. The right hand's index and middle fingers open and close slightly as the two fingers tremble. Also FIT, SEIZURE.

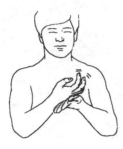

EPILOGUE (ep′ ə lôg), *n.* (The letter "E"; coming to the end.) The right "E" hand moves along the index finger edge of the left and drops down over the left fingertips.

EPISCOPAL (ĭ pĭs′ kə pəl), *adj.* (The surplice sleeve.) The left arm is held horizontally, and the right index finger describes an arc under it, from wrist to elbow. Also BASKET, EPISCOPALIAN, STORE 3.

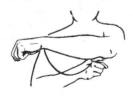

EQUAL (ē′ kwəl), *adj., n., v.,* -QUALED, -QUALING. (Sameness is stressed.) The downturned "B" hands, held at chest height, are brought together repeatedly so that the index finger edges or fingertips come into contact. Also EQUIVALENT, EVEN, FAIR 1, IMPARTIAL, JUST 1, LEVEL.

EQUATOR (i kwā′ tər), *n.* (The letter "E"; circling the globe.) The right "E" hand describes a circle around the left fist, which represents the planet.

EQUIPMENT (i kwip′ mənt), *n.* (The letter "E"; things.) The upturned right "E" hand moves to the right in a series of small, arched movements.

EQUIVALENT (ĭ kwĭv′ ə lənt), *adj.* See EQUAL.

ERECTION (i rek′ shən), *n.* (The arm portrays the erection of the penis.) The left hand grasps the right arm or the crook of the right elbow as the right "S" hand moves up in an arc from a horizontal position.

ERROR (ĕr′ ər), *n.* (Rationale obscure; the thumb and little finger are said to represent, respectively, right and wrong, with the head poised between the two.) The right "Y" hand, palm facing the body, is brought up to the chin. Also FAULT 2, MISTAKE, SACRILEGIOUS, WRONG 1.

ESCALATOR (es′ kə lā tər), *n.* (Standing on moving stairs.) The right index and middle fingers stand on the left hand, which is held either up or down. The left hand moves up at an angle, carrying the right hand with it.

ESCAPE (ĕs kāp′), *v.,* -CAPED, -CAPING. (Emerging from a hiding place.) The downturned right "D" hand is positioned under the downturned open left hand. The right "D" hand suddenly emerges and moves off quickly to the right. Also FLEE.

ESKIMO 1 (es′ kə mō), *n.* (The letter "E"; the fur hood.) The "E" hand, palm facing out, describes a circle over the head, from left to right.

ESKIMO 2, *n.* (The "E"; rubbing the nose, an Eskimo custom in greeting.) The right "E" hand, palm facing the body, rubs the nose back and forth.

ESTABLISH (ĕs tăb′ lĭsh), *v.,* -LISHED, -LISHING. (To set up.) The right "A" hand, thumb up and palm facing left, comes down to rest on the back of the down-turned left "S" hand. Before doing so, the right "A" hand may describe a clockwise circle above the left hand, but this is optional. Also FOUND, FOUNDED.

ETERNITY 1 (ĭ tûr′ nə tĭ), *n.* (Around the clock and ahead into the future.) The right index finger, pointing forward, traces a clockwise circle in the air. The downturned right "Y" hand then moves forward, either in a straight line or in a slight downward curve. Also EVER 2, EVERLASTING, FOREVER.

ETERNITY 2 (*rare*), *n.* (The letter "E"; continuous motion.) The right "E" hand, palm out, moves in a continuous clockwise circle. Also EUROPE.

ETHICS (eth′ iks), *n.* (The letter "E"; having to do with the heart or character.) The right "E" hand, palm facing the signer, describes a counterclockwise circle over the heart.

EVADE (ĭ vād′), *v.,* -VADED, -VADING. (Ducking back and forth, away from something.) Both "A" hands, thumbs pointing straight up, are held some distance before the chest, with the left hand in front of the right. The right hand, swinging back and forth, moves away from the left and toward the chest. Also AVOID 1, EVASION, SHIRK, SHUN.

EVALUATE 1 (ĭ văl′ yŏŏ āt′), *v.,* -ATED, -ATING. (The scales move up and down.) The two "F" hands, palms facing each other, move alternately up and down. Also CONSIDER 3, COURT, IF, JUDGE 1, JUDGMENT, JUSTICE 1.

EVALUATE 2, *v.* (The letter "E"; weighing up and down.) The "E" hands, palms facing out from the body, move alternately up and down.

EVASION (ĭ vā′ zhən), *n.* See EVADE.

EVEN (ē′ vən), *adj.* (Sameness is stressed.) The downturned "B" hands, held at chest height, are brought together repeatedly so that the index finger edges or fingertips come into contact. Also EQUAL, EQUIVALENT, FAIR 1, IMPARTIAL, JUST 1, LEVEL.

EVENT (ĭ vĕnt′), *n.* (A befalling.) Both "D" hands, index fingers pointing away from the body, are simultaneously pivoted over so that the palms face down. Also ACCIDENT, BEFALL, CHANCE, COINCIDE 1, COINCIDENCE, HAPPEN 1, INCIDENT, OCCUR, OPPORTUNITY 4.

EVENTUALLY (ĭ vĕn′ chŏŏ ə lĭ), *adv.* (The little, *i.e.,* LAST, fingers are indicated.) With the hands in the "I" position, the tip of the right little finger strikes the tip of its left counterpart. The right index finger may be used instead of the right little finger. Also END 1, FINAL 1, FINALLY 1, LAST 1, ULTIMATE, ULTIMATELY.

EVER 1 (ĕv′ ər), *adv.* (Steady, uninterrupted movement.) The "A" hands are held with palms out, thumbs extended and touching, the right behind the left. In this position the hands move forward in a straight, steady line. Also CONTINUE 1, ENDURE 2, LAST 3, LASTING, PERMANENT, PERPETUAL, PERSERVERE 3, PERSIST 2, REMAIN, STAY 1, STAY STILL.

EVER 2, *adv.* (Around the clock and ahead into the future.) The right index finger, pointing forward, traces a clockwise circle in the air. The downturned right "Y" hand then moves forward, either in a straight line or in a slight downward curve. ETERNITY 1, EVERLASTING, FOREVER.

EVER 3, *adv.* (Around the clock again and again.) The index finger of the right "D" hand points outward, away from the body, with palm facing left. The arm is rotated clockwise.

EVERLASTING (ĕv′ ər lăs′ tĭng, -läs′-), *adj.* See EVER 2.

EVER SINCE (ĕv′ ər sĭns), *phrase.* (From a point up and over.) In the "D" position, palms down, both index fingers touch the right shoulder and then are brought up and over, ending in a palm-up position, pointing straight ahead of the body. Also ALL ALONG, ALL THE TIME, SINCE, SO FAR, THUS FAR.

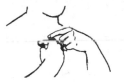

EVERY (ĕv′ rĭ), *adj.* (Peeling off, one by one.) The left "A" hand is held palm facing the right. The knuckles of the right "A" hand are drawn repeatedly down the left thumb, from its tip to its base. Also EACH.

EVERY AFTERNOON, *phrase.* (Afternoons one after the other.) The sign for AFTERNOON is made while both hands move from left to right.

EVERYDAY (ĕv′ rĭ dā′), *adj.* (Tomorrow after tomorrow.) The sign for TOMORROW, *q.v.,* is made several times: the right "A" hand moves forward several times from its initial resting place on the right cheek. Also DAILY.

EVERY FRIDAY, *phrase.* (The letter "F"; down the calendar.) The letter "F," palm in or out, moves straight down a short distance.

EVERY MONDAY, *phrase.* (The letter "M"; down the calendar.) The letter "M," palm in or out, moves straight down a short distance.

EVERY MORNING, *phrase.* (Mornings, one after the other.) The sign for MORNING is made while both hands move from left to right.

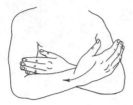

***

EVERY NIGHT, *phrase.* (Nights one after the other.) The sign for NIGHT is made while both hands move from left to right.

***

EVERY TWO WEEKS, *phrase.* (Two individual weeks.) The "2" hand, palm down, is placed on the upturned left palm. It moves from the heel of the hand to the fingertips, repeating the movement. Also BIWEEKLY.

***

EVERY YEAR (yĭr), *phrase.* (Several years brought forward.) This sign is actually a modification of the sign for YEAR, *q.v.* The ball of the right "S" hand, moving straight out from the body, palm facing left, glances over the thumb side of the left "S" hand, which is held palm facing right. As this contact is made, the right index finger is flung straight out, and the right hand, in this new position, continues for-

ward. This is repeated several times to indicate several years. Also ANNUAL, YEARLY.

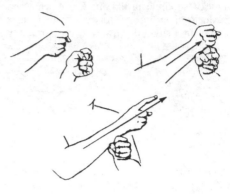

***

EVIDENCE (ĕv′ ə dəns), *n., v.,* -DENCED, -DENCING. (Directing the attention to something and bringing it forward.) The right index finger points into the left palm, held facing out before the body. The left palm moves straight out. For the passive form of this verb, *i.e.,* BE SHOWN, the movement is reversed: the left hand, palm facing in, is moved in toward the body, while the right index finger remains pointing into the left palm. Also DEMONSTRATE, DISPLAY, EXAMPLE, EXHIBIT, EXHIBITION, ILLUSTRATE, INDICATE, INFLUENCE 3, PRODUCE 2, REPRESENT, SHOW 1, SIGNIFY 1.

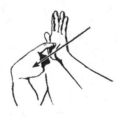

***

EVIDENT (ev′ ə dənt), *adj.* (Rays of light clearing the way.) Both hands are held at chest height, palms out, all fingertips together. They open into the "5" position in unison, the right hand moving toward the right and the left toward the left. The palms of both hands remain facing out. Also CLEAR, OBVIOUS, PLAIN 1.

EXACT 1 (ĭg zăkt′), *adj.* (The fingers come together precisely.) The thumb and index finger of each hand, palms facing, the right above the left, form circles. They are brought together with a deliberate movement so that the fingers and thumbs now touch. Sometimes the right hand, before coming together with the left, executes a slow clockwise circle above the left. Also ACCURATE 1, EXACTLY, EXPLICIT 1, PRECISE, SPECIFIC.

EXACT 2, *adj.* The right index finger, held above the left index finger, comes down rather forcefully so that the bottom of the right hand comes to rest on top of the left thumb joint. Also ACCURATE 2, CORRECT 1, DECENT, JUST 2, PROPER, RIGHT 3, SUITABLE.

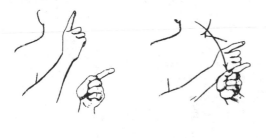

EXACTLY (ĭg zăkt′ lĭ), *adv.* See EXACT 1.

EXAGGERATE 1 (ĭg zăj′ ə rāt′), *v.*, -ATED, -ATING. (Thoughts pop up and are added on to something.) The right index finger moves straight up on the forehead. The sign for MORE is then made: the left hand, fingers touching the thumb, and palm down, moves down in an arc to come in contact with the right hand, held in the same position but with palm up. The sign is repeated with both hands reversing their roles.

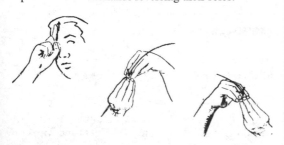

EXAGGERATE 2 (*sl.*), *v.*, -ATED, -ATING. (Stretching out one's words.) The left "S" hand, palm facing right, is held before the mouth. Its right counterpart, palm facing left, is moved forward in a series of short up-and-down arcs.

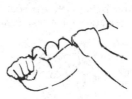

EXAMINATION 1 (ĭg zăm′ ə nā′ shən), *n.* (A series of questions spread out on a page.) Both "D" hands, palms down, simultaneously execute a single circle, the right hand moving in a clockwise direction and the left in a counterclockwise direction. Upon completion of the circle, both hands open into the "5" position and move straight down a short distance. (The hands actually draw question marks in the air.) Also QUIZ 1, TEST.

EXAMINATION 2 (*colloq.*), *n.* (Fire a question.) The right hand, held in a modified "S" position with palm facing out, assumes a position with the thumb resting on the fingernail of the index finger. The index finger is flicked out and forward, usually directed at the person being asked a question. Also ASK 2, INQUIRE 2, INTERROGATE 2, INTERROGATION 2, QUERY 2, QUESTION 2, QUIZ 2.

EXAMINATION 3, *n.* (Firing questions.) The index fingers of both "D" hands repeatedly curve and straighten out as the hands are alternately flung forward and back, as if firing questions. Also ASK 3, INQUIRE 3, INTERROGATE 1, INTERROGATION 1, QUERY 1, QUESTION 3, QUIZ 3.

EXAMINE (ĭg zăm′ ĭn), *v.*, -INED, -INING. (Directing the vision from place to place.) The right "C" hand, palm facing left, moves from right to left across the line of vision in a series of counterclockwise circles. The signer's gaze remains concentrated and his head turns slowly from right to left. Also CURIOUS 1, INVESTIGATE 1, LOOK FOR, PROBE 1, QUEST, SEARCH, SEEK.

EXAMPLE (ĭg zăm′ pəl, -zăm′ -), *n., v.*, -PLED, -PLING. (Directing the attention to something and bringing it forward.) The right index finger points into the left palm, held facing out before the body. The left palm moves straight out. For the passive form of this verb, *i.e.,* BE SHOWN, the movement is reversed: the left hand, palm facing in, is moved in toward the body, while the right index finger remains pointing into the left palm. Also DEMONSTRATE, DISPLAY, EVIDENCE, EXHIBIT, EXHIBITION, ILLUSTRATE, INDICATE, INFLUENCE 3, PRODUCE 2, REPRESENT, SHOW 1, SIGNIFY 1.

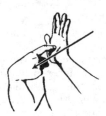

EXCELLENT (ĕk′ sə lənt), *adj.* (The hands gesture toward the heavens.) The "5" hands, palms out and arms raised rather high, are positioned somewhat above the line of vision. The arms move abruptly forward and up once or twice. An expression of pleasure or surprise is usually assumed. Also GRAND 1, GREAT 3, MARVEL, MARVELOUS, MIRACLE, O!, SPLENDID 1, SWELL 1, WONDER 2, WONDERFUL 1.

EXCEPT (ĭk sĕpt′), *prep., conj.* (Selecting a particular item from among several.) The index finger and thumb of the right hand grasp and pull up the left index finger. Also ESPECIAL, EXCEPTION, SPECIAL.

EXCEPTION (ĭk sĕp′ shən), *n.* See EXCEPT.

EXCHANGE (ĭks chānj′), *v.*, -CHANGED, -CHANGING. (Exchanging places.) The right "A" hand, positioned above the left "A" hand, swings down and under the left, coming up a bit in front of it. Also INSTEAD OF 1, REPLACE, SUBSTITUTE, TRADE.

EXCITE (ĭk sīt′), *v.*, -CITED, -CITING. (The heart beats violently.) Both middle fingers move up alternately to strike the heart sharply. Also EXCITEMENT, EXCITING, THRILL 1.

EXCITEMENT (ĭk sīt′ mənt), *n.* See EXCITE.

EXCITING (ĭk sī′ tĭng), *adj.* See EXCITE.

EXCUSE (*n.* ĭk skūs′; *v.* ĭk skūz′), -CUSED, -CUSING. (A wiped-off and cleaned slate.) The right hand wipes off

Exhibit   229   Expel

the left palm several times. Also APOLOGIZE 2, APOL-OGY 2, FORGIVE 2, PARDON, PAROLE.

EXHIBIT (ĭg zĭb′ ĭt), v., -ITED, -ITING. (Directing the attention to something and bringing it forward.) The right index finger points into the left palm, held facing out before the body. The left palm moves straight out. For the passive form of this verb, *i.e.,* BE SHOWN, the movement is reversed: the left hand, palm facing in, is moved in toward the body, while the right index finger remains pointing into the left palm. Also DEMONSTRATE, DISPLAY, EVIDENCE, EXAMPLE, EXHIBITION, ILLUSTRATE, INDICATE, INFLUENCE 3, PRODUCE 2, REPRESENT, SHOW 1, SIGNIFY 1.

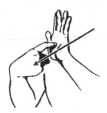

EXHIBITION (ĕk′ sə bĭsh′ ən), n. See EXHIBIT.

EXODUS (ek′ sə dəs), n. (*eccles.*). (Mass movement forward.) Both downturned "S" hands open and wiggle as they move forward.

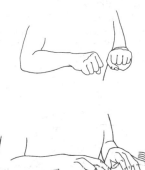

EXPAND (ĭk spănd′), v., -PANDED, -PANDING. (A large amount.) The "5" hands face each other, fingers curved and touching. They move apart rather quickly. Also GREAT 2, INFINITE, LOT, MUCH.

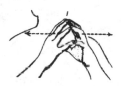

EXPECT (ĭk spĕkt′), v., -PECTED, -PECTING. (A thought awaited.) The tip of the right index finger, held in the "D" position, palm facing the body, is placed on the forehead (modified THINK, *q.v.*). Both hands then assume right-angle positions, fingers facing, with the left hand held above left shoulder level and the right before the right breast. Both hands, held thus, wave to each other several times. Also ANTICIPATE, ANTICIPATION, HOPE.

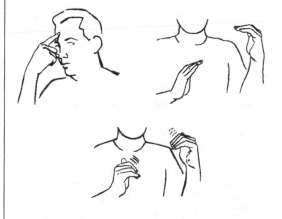

EXPEL 1 (ĭk spĕl′), v., -PELLED, -PELLING. ("Getting the axe"; the head is chopped off.) The upturned open right hand is swung sharply over the index finger edge of the left "S" hand, whose palm faces right. Also DISCHARGE 1, FIRE 2.

EXPEL 2, v. (To cut one down.) The right index finger strikes the tip of the upturned left index finger in a right to left direction, causing the left index finger to bend slightly. Also DISCHARGE 2.

EXPENSE (ĭk spĕns′), *n.* (Nicking into one.) The knuckle of the right "X" finger is nicked against the palm of the left hand, held in the "5" position, palm facing right. Also ADMISSION 2, CHARGE 1, COST, DUTY 2, EXCISE, FEE, FINE 2, IMPOST, PENALTY 3, PRICE 2, TAX 1, TAXATION 1, TOLL.

EXPENSIVE (ĭk spĕn′ sĭv), *adj.* (Throwing away money.) The right "AND" hand lies in the palm of the upturned, open left hand (as if holding money). The right hand then moves up and away from the left, opening abruptly as it does (as if dropping the money it holds). Also COSTLY, DEAR 2.

EXPERIENCE 1 (ĭk spĭr′ ĭ əns), *n.* (A sharp-edged hand.) The right hand grasps the little finger edge of the left firmly. As it leaves this position, moving down and out, it assumes the "A" position, palm facing left. Also ADEPT, EXPERT, SHARP 4, SHREWD, SKILL, SKILL-FUL.

 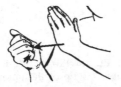

EXPERIENCE 2, *n.* (White hair.) The right fingertips gently pull the hair of the right temple. The movement is repeated.

EXPERIENCE SOMETHING, *phrase.* (Coming in contact; finish, meaning "to have done so.") The sign for TOUCH is made: the tip of the middle finger of the downturned right "5" hand touches the back of the downturned left hand. This is followed by the sign for FINISH: the upright "5" hands, palms facing each other, are suddenly and quickly swung around to a palm-out position. One hand only may also be used.

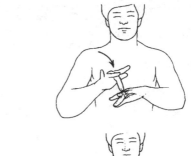

EXPERIMENT (ĭk sper′ ə mənt), *n., v.* (The "E" letters; manipulating the test tubes.) Both "E" hands, palms out, make a series of alternating circles, the right in a counterclockwise manner and the left in a clockwise fashion. The movement looks like pouring out the contents of test tubes.

EXPERT (*n.* ĕks′ pûrt; *adj.* ĭk spûrt′). See EXPERI-ENCE 1.

EXPLAIN 1 (ĭk splān′), *v.*, -PLAINED, -PLAINING. (Unraveling something to get at its parts.) The "F" hands, palms facing and fingers pointing straight out, are held about an inch apart. They move alternately back and forth a few inches. Also DEFINE 1, DESCRIBE 1, DESCRIPTION.

EXPLAIN 2, *v.* (The unraveling or stretching out of words or sentences.) Both open hands are held close to each other, with fingers open and palms facing and almost touching. As the hands are drawn apart, the thumb and index finger of each hand come together to form circles. This is repeated several times. Also DESCRIBE 2, FABLE, FICTION, GOSPEL 1, NARRATE, NARRATIVE, STORY 1, TALE, TELL ABOUT.

EXPLICIT 1 (ĭk splĭs′ ĭt), *adj.* (The fingers come together precisely.) The thumb and index finger of each hand, palms facing, the right above the left, form circles. They are brought together with a deliberate movement so that the fingers and thumbs now touch. Sometimes the right hand, before coming together with the left, executes a slow clockwise circle above the left. Also ACCURATE 1, EXACT 1, EXACTLY, PRECISE, SPECIFIC.

EXPLICIT 2, *adj.* (Rays of light clearing the way.) Both hands are held at chest height, palms out, all fingertips together. They open into the "5" position in unison, the right hand moving toward the right and the

left toward the left. The palms of both hands remain facing out. Also BRIGHT 1, BRILLIANCE 1, BRILLIANT 2, CLEAR, OBVIOUS, PLAIN 1.

EXPOSURE (ik spō′ zhər), *n.* (Rays emanating.) The right fingertips are placed on the top of the left index finger. The right hand opens into the "5" position, its base resting against the left fingertip.

EXPRESS (ĭk spres′), *v.*, -ED, -ING. (Getting something out of the system.) Both "S" (or "E") hands, palms facing up, are positioned on the chest. They move forward simultaneously in an arc, opening into the "5" position.

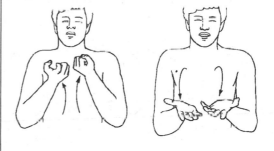

EXTRAVAGANT (ĭk străv′ ə gənt), *adj.* (Repeated giving forth.) The back of the upturned right hand, thumb touching fingertips, is placed in the upturned left palm. The right hand moves off and away from the left once or several times, each time opening into the "5" position, palm up. Also SPEND, SQUANDER, WASTE 1.

EXULTATION (ĕg′ zŭl tā′ shən), *n.* (Waving a flag.) The right "A" hand goes through the natural movement of waving a flag in circular fashion. Preceding this, the right hand may go through the motion of grabbing the flagstaff out of the left hand. Also TRIUMPH 1, VICTORY 2, WIN 2.

EYE (ī), *n., v.,* EYED, EYING or EYEING. (The natural sign.) The right index finger touches the lower lid of the right eye.

EYEBROW (ī′ brou), *n.* (Tracing the eyebrow.) The right index finger runs along the eyebrow from left to right.

EYEGLASSES (ī′ glăs′ əs), *n. pl.* (The shape.) The thumb and index finger of the right hand, placed flat against the right temple, move back toward the right ear, tracing the line formed by the eyeglass frame. Also GALLAUDET, THOMAS HOPKINS; GLASSES; SPECTACLES.

EYELASHES (ī′ lash ez), *n.* (The shape.) Both downturned "4" hands are held at the eyes, fingers pointing forward. The hands move slightly forward in an upturned arc.

EYES ROLLING AROUND (*colloq.*), *n. phrase.* (The natural sign.) Both "F" hands, palms facing, are held at eye level. They execute a series of small circular movements before the eyes.

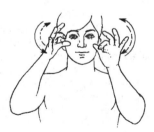

F

FACE 1 (fās), *n*. (The natural sign.) The index finger outlines the face without touching it.

FACE 2, *v.*, FACED, FACING. (Face-to-face.) The left hand, fingers together palm flat and facing the eyes, is held a bit above eye level. The right hand, fingers also together, is held in front of the mouth, with palm facing the left hand. With a sweeping upward movement the right hand moves toward the left, which moves straight up an inch or two at the same time. Also APPEAR 3, APPEARANCE, BEFORE 3, CONFRONT, FACE-TO-FACE, PRESENCE.

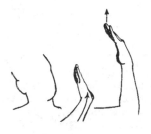

FACE-TO-FACE, *adj.*, *adv.* See FACE 2.

FACTORY (făk′ tə rĭ), *n*. (The meshing gears.) With the knuckles of both hands interlocked, the hands pivot up and down, imitating the meshing of gear teeth. Also ENGINE, MACHINE, MACHINERY, MECHANIC 1, MECHANISM, MOTOR.

FACULTY 1 (făk′ əl tĭ), *n*. (An affirmative movement of the hands, likened to a nodding of the head, to indicate ability or power to accomplish something.) Both "A" hands, held palms down, move down in unison a short distance before the chest. Also ABILITY, ABLE, CAN 1, CAPABLE, COMPETENT, COULD, MAY 2, POSSIBLE.

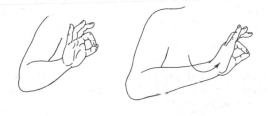

FACULTY 2, *n*. (The letter "F"; the Roman toga, a mark of power.) The right "F" hand moves from one shoulder to the other.

FADE (fād), *v.*, FADED, FADING. (Fingering the small pieces resulting from the breaking up of something.) The thumbs rub slowly across the fingertips of the upturned hands, from the little fingers to the index fingers, and then continue to the "A" position, palms up. Also DECAY, DIE OUT, DISSOLVE, MELT, ROT.

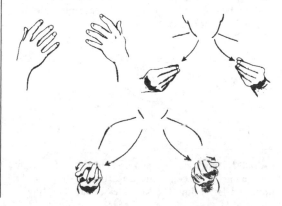

233

FAHRENHEIT (far' ən hīt), *n.* (The letter "F"; rise and fall of temperature.) The thumb and index finger of the right "F" hand move up and down the upturned left index finger.

FAIL 1 (fāl), *v.,* FAILED, FAILING. (Tumbling down.) The open hands, palms facing the body, rotate around each other as they move downward and a bit outward from the body. Also FAILURE.

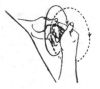

FAIL 2, *v.* (A sliding.) The right "V" hand, palm up, slides along the upturned left palm from its base to its fingertips. Also FAILURE.

FAIL 3, *v.* The right "F" hand strikes forcefully against the open left palm, which faces right with fingers pointing forward. Also FLUNK.

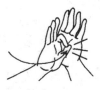

FAINT 1 (fānt), *adj.* (The knees buckle.) The right "V" hand is placed with fingertips resting in the upturned left palm. The knuckles of the "V" fingers buckle a bit. This motion may be repeated. Also FEEBLE, FRAIL, WEAK, WEAKNESS.

FAINT 2, *v.,* FAINTED, FAINTING. (Attempting to grasp something as one falls.) The downturned open hands, fingers somewhat curved, suddenly separate and close into the "S" position. The head, meanwhile, falls back a bit, and the eyes close.

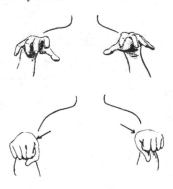

FAIR 1 (fâr), *adj.* (Sameness is stressed.) The downturned "B" hands, held at chest height, are brought together repeatedly so that the index finger edges or fingertips come into contact. Also EQUAL, EQUIVALENT, EVEN, IMPARTIAL, JUST 1, LEVEL.

FAIR 2, *adj.* (The letter "F" at the midpoint of the mouth, *i.e.,* neither good nor bad.) The tip of the middle finger of the right "F" hand, whose palm faces left, touches the middle of the lips repeatedly.

FAIRY TALE (fair′ y tale′), *n.* (Something popping from the mind and narrated.) The right "4" hand, index finger edge on the forehead, moves straight up. Both open hands are then held side by side, palms down. As the hands are drawn apart, the thumb and index finger of each hand come together to form circles. This is repeated several times.

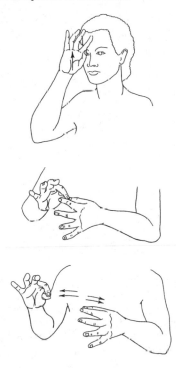

FAITHFUL 1 (fāth′ fəl), *adj.* (Coming together with regular frequency.) Both "D" hands are held with index fingers pointing forward, the right hand above the left. The right "D" hand is brought down on the left several times in rhythmic succession. Also CONSISTENT, REGULAR.

FAITHFUL 2, *adj.* (A modification of FAITHFUL 1, above, with the "F" hands.) The "F" hands execute the same movements as in FAITHFUL 1.

FAITHFUL 3, *adj.* (Coming forth directly from the lips; true.) The index finger of the right "D" hand, palm facing left, is placed against the lips. It moves up an inch or two and then describes a small arc forward and away from the lips. Also ABSOLUTE, ABSOLUTELY, ACTUAL, ACTUALLY, AUTHENTIC, CERTAIN, CERTAINLY, FIDELITY, FRANKLY, GENUINE, INDEED, POSITIVE 1, POSITIVELY, REAL, REALLY, SINCERE 2, SURE, SURELY, TRUE, TRULY, TRUTH, VALID, VERILY.

FAKE (fāk), *v.*, FAKED, FAKING. (A double face, *i.e.*, a mask covers the face.) The right hand is placed over the back of the left hand and pushes it down and a bit in toward the body. Also BLUFF, HUMBUG, HYPOCRITE 1, IMPOSTOR.

FALL 1 (fôl), *n.* (The falling of leaves.) The left arm, held upright with palm facing back, represents a tree trunk. The right hand, fingers together and palm down, moves down along the left arm, from the back of the wrist to the elbow, either once or several times.

This represents the falling of leaves from the tree branches, indicated by the left fingers. Also AUTUMN 1.

FALL 2, *n.* (A chopping down during harvesttime.) The left arm is held in the same manner as in FALL 1. The right hand, fingers together and palm facing down, makes several chopping motions against the left elbow to indicate the felling of growing things in autumn.

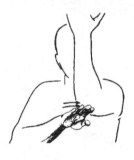

FALL 3, *n., v.,* FELL, FALLEN, FALLING. (Falling on one's side.) The downturned index and middle fingers of the right "V" hand are placed in a standing position on the upturned left palm. The right "V" hand flips over, coming to rest palm up on the upturned left palm.

FALL 4, *v.* (Falling on one's side.) The "V" hand, held palm down, flips over toward the right, to the palm-up position.

FALL ASLEEP, *v. phrase,* FELL, FALLEN, FALLING. (The eyes close hard.) The right "5" hand is placed palm facing the eyes. The hand closes into a fist, moving downward and coming to rest against the upturned left fist.

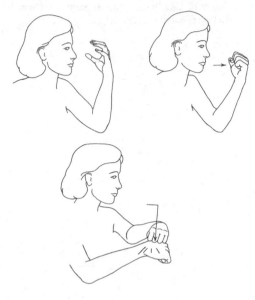

FALL FOR 1 (*colloq.*), *v. phrase.* (Falling flat on one's face.) The right "D" hand, palm out, falls down into the upturned left palm. This sign is used in the sense of "falling for" someone, *i.e.,* becoming enamored of someone.

FALL FOR 2, *v.* (Swallowing the bait.) The mouth is held wide open. The right hand, fingers pointing to the rear of the signer, moves as if to enter the mouth, but brushes the right cheek as it passes to the rear. This sign is used in the context of someone who has been duped or has proved gullible.

FALSE 1 (fôls), *adj.* (Words diverted instead of coming straight, or truthfully, out.) The index finger of the right "D" hand, pointing to the left, moves along the lips from right to left. Also FALSEHOOD, FRAUDULENT 2, LIAR, LIE 1, PREVARICATE, UNTRUTH.

FALSE 2, *adj.* (The words are deflected from their normal straight path from the lips.) The right "D" hand, palm facing left, moves quickly in front of the lips, from right to left. Also FIB.

FALSEHOOD (fôls' hŏŏd), *n.* See FALSE 1.

FAME (fām), *n.* (One's fame radiates far and wide.) The extended index fingers rest on the lips (or on the temples). Moving in small, continuous spirals, they move up and to either side of the head. Also CELEBRATED, FAMOUS, PROMINENT 1, RENOWNED.

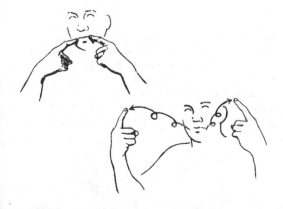

FAMILIAR (fə mil' yər), *adj.* (Patting the head to indicate something of value inside.) The right fingers pat the forehead several times. Also KNOW.

FAMILY 1 (făm' ə lĭ), *n.* (The letter "F"; a circle or group.) The thumb and index fingers of both "F" hands are in contact, palms facing. The hands swing open and around, coming together again at their little finger edges, palms now facing the body.

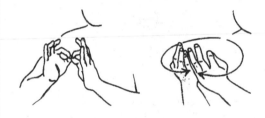

FAMILY 2, *n.* (A grouping together.) Both "C" hands, palms facing, are held a few inches apart at chest height. They are swung around in unison so that the palms now face the body. Also ASSOCIATION, AUDIENCE 1, CASTE, CIRCLE 2, CLASS, CLASSED 1, CLUB, COMPANY, GANG, GROUP 1, JOIN 2, ORGANIZATION 1.

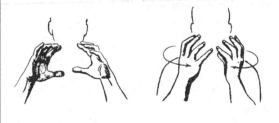

FAMOUS (fā' məs), *adj.* See FAME.

FAN 1 (fan), *n.* (Electric; blowing on the face.) The sign for ELECTRIC is made. The knuckles of both bent index fingers come together several times, indicating the electrodes coming in contact. The right index finger, pointing at the face, makes a clockwise circle and then the right hand moves toward the face, fingers spread open. The sign for ELECTRIC may be omitted.

FAN 2, *n., v.,* FANNED, FANNING. (Fanning oneself.) The signer, grasping an imaginary fan, mimes fanning the face.

FANTASY 1 (fan′ tə sē, -zē), *n.* (Thoughts whirling around.) The index finger of the right "4" hand touches the forehead. The hand moves up and off the forehead in a continuous clockwise circle.

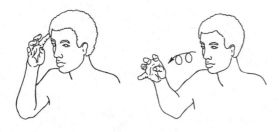

FANTASY 2, *n.* (A revelation forms in the head and becomes clear.) Both "S" hands are placed against the

forehead, with one behind the other. Both hands simultaneously open up, palms now facing.

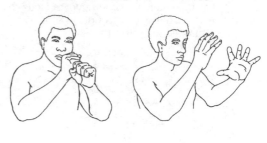

FAR (fär), *adj.* (Moving beyond, *i.e.,* the concept of distance or "farness.") The "A" hands are held together, thumbs pointing away from the body. The right hand moves straight ahead in a slight arc. The left hand does not move. Also DISTANCE, DISTANT, OFF 2, REMOTE.

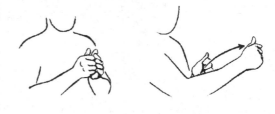

FAR-FETCHED (fär′ fĕcht′), *adj.* (The mind wanders off into space or fantasy.) The index finger of the right "5" hand is placed at the right temple. The hand then moves toward the right in a series of clockwise spirals up and away from the head.

FARM 1 (färm), *n.* (The action of the plow's blade in making a furrow.) The open right hand is placed upright in a perpendicular position on the upturned left palm, with the little finger edge resting in the palm. The right hand moves forward along the left palm. As it does so, it swings over to a palm-down position and moves off a bit to the right. Also PLOW.

FARM 2, *n., sl.* (The stubbled beard commonly associated with an uncouth backwoods type.) The open right "5" hand is placed with thumb resting on the left side of the chin. The hand moves over to the right side of the chin, with the thumb always in contact with it.

FARM 3 (*colloq.*), *n.* (The elbow reinforcement on the jacket of a "country squire" type; also, a place where one commonly "roughs it," *i.e.,* gets rough elbows.) The open right hand describes a continuous counterclockwise circle on the left elbow. Also COUNTRY 1.

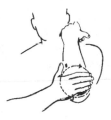

FART 1 (färt), *v., n., sl.,* -ED, -ING. (The escaping gas.) The right index finger, pointing up, moves suddenly forward from a position between two fingers of the downturned open left hand.

FART 2, *v., n., sl.* (Gas escaping.) The right hand, fingers and thumbs touching, is held under the left elbow. The right hand opens and closes quickly.

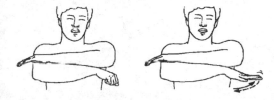

FASCINATE 1 (făs′ ə nāt′), *v.,* -NATED, -NATING. (Drawing one out.) The index and middle fingers of both hands, one above the other, are placed on the middle part of the chest. Both hands move forward simultaneously. As they do, the index and middle fingers of each hand come together. Also INTEREST 1, INTERESTED 1, INTERESTING 1.

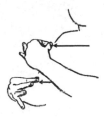

FASCINATE 2, *v.* (A modification of FASCINATE 1.) The same movements are employed, except that one of the hands is positioned in front of the mouth. Also ENGROSS, INTEREST 2.

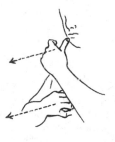

FAST 1 (făst), *adj.* (A quick movement.) The thumbtip of the upright right hand is flicked quickly off the tip of the curved right index finger, as if shooting marbles. Also IMMEDIATELY, QUICK, QUICKNESS, RAPID, RATE 1, SPEED, SPEEDY, SWIFT.

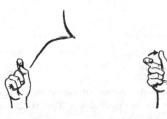

FAST 2, *v.,* FASTED, FASTING. (The "F" hand, zipping closed.) The thumb of the right "F" hand is drawn along the lips from left to right.

FAT 1 (făt), *adj.* (The swollen cheeks.) The cheeks are puffed out, and the open "C" hands, positioned at either cheek, move away to their respective sides. Also STOUT.

FAT 2 (*colloq.*), *adj.* (The legs are spread wide to accommodate a wide torso.) The downturned right "Y" hand is placed in the upturned left palm, so that the right little finger supports the right hand. The right hand pivots forward on the little finger until the right thumb comes to rest on the left palm. The right hand then pivots forward again until the little finger comes to rest again on the left palm. The action is similar to the manipulation of a pair of dividers. Also OBESE.

FAT 3, *n.* (The drippings from a fleshy, *i.e.,* animal, substance. Used, however, to indicate both organic and inorganic types of oil.) The right thumb and middle finger grasp the fleshy part of the open left hand. The right hand moves straight down. This is repeated

once or twice. Also FATTY, GRAVY, GREASE, GREASY, OIL 2, OILY.

FATHER 1 (fä′ thər), *n.* (Male who holds the baby.) The sign for MALE, *q.v.,* is made: the thumb and extended fingers of the right hand are brought up to grasp an imaginary cap brim, representing the tipping of caps by men in olden days. Both hands are then held open with palms facing up, as if holding a baby. This is the formal sign.

FATHER 2 (*informal*), *n.* (Derived from the formal sign for FATHER 1, *q.v.*) The thumbtip of the right "5" hand touches the right temple a number of times. The other fingers may also wiggle. Also DAD, DADDY, PAPA, POP 2.

FATHER 3, *n.* (The ecclesiastical collar.) The thumbs and index fingers of both hands indicate the shape of the collar as they move around the neck, coming together in front of the throat. Sometimes only one hand is used. Also PRIEST 1.

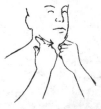

FATTY (făt′ ĭ), *adj.* (The drippings from a fleshy, *i.e.*, animal, substance. Used, however, to indicate both organic and inorganic types of oil.) The right thumb and middle finger grasp the fleshy part of the open left hand. The right hand moves straight down. This is repeated once or twice. Also FAT 3, GRAVY, GREASE, GREASY, OIL 2, OILY.

FAULT 1 (fôlt), *n.* (The blame is firmly placed.) The right "A" hand, thumb pointing up, is brought down firmly against the back of the left hand, held palm down; the right thumb is then directed toward the person or object to blame. When personal blame is acknowledged, the thumb is brought in to the chest. Also ACCUSE 1, BLAME, GUILTY 1.

FAULT 2, *n.* (Rationale obscure; the thumb and little finger are said to represent, respectively, right and wrong, with the head poised between the two.) The right "Y" hand, palm facing the body, is brought up to the chin. Also ERROR, MISTAKE, SACRILEGIOUS, WRONG 1.

FAVORITE 1 (fā′ vər ĭt), *adj.* (The thoughts are directed to a single thing.) The right index finger, placed initially at the forehead, palm facing the body, swings away, the palm coming around to face out and the index finger coming to rest on the tip of the left upturned index finger.

FAVORITE 2 (*colloq.*), *adj.* (Something or someone that turns the head.) The open right "5" hand is placed with its index finger resting near the right temple, palm facing the left. The hand suddenly pivots sharply around and out toward the right, moving away from the head and ending in a position with the palm facing the head and held about a foot from it.

FAVORITE 3, *adj.* (Hooked on to; a good friend.) Both index fingers interlock and move down forcefully an inch or two. The lips are held together tightly and an expression of pleasure is shown. Also GOOD FRIEND.

FAVORITE 4, *adj.* (To the taste.) The middle finger is placed against the lips and the signer assumes an expression indicating pleasure.

FAVORITE 5, *adj.* (Kissing, to indicate a high approval rating.) The back of either fist is kissed, and an expression of pleasure is shown. *Cultural note:* this sign is considered overused by many deaf people. To them it indicates a lack of discrimination (everything is a "favorite").

FAX 1 (faks), *n., v.,* -ED, -ING. (The paper coming out.) The downturned left hand undulates a little as it moves under and out of the downturned right hand.

FAX 2, *n., v.* (A fingerspelled loan sign.) The signer fingerspells "F-A-X."

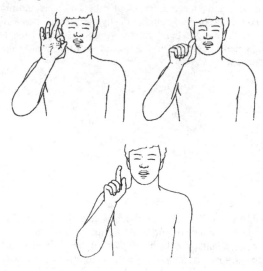

FAY, EDWARD ALLEN, *n.* (The letter "F"; a name sign.) An early educator of young Deaf Americans. The thumb and index fingers of the right "F" hand move forward and slightly up from their position on the right temple.

FEAR 1 (fĭr), *n., v.,* FEARED, FEARING. (The heart is suddenly covered with fear.) Both hands, fingers together, are placed side by side, palms facing the chest. They quickly open and come together over the heart, one on top of the other. Also AFRAID, COWARD, FRIGHT, FRIGHTEN, SCARE(D), TERROR 1.

FEAR 2, *n., v.* (The hands attempt to ward off something that causes fear.) The "5" hands, right behind left, move downward before the body in a wavy motion. Also DREAD, TERROR 2, TIMID.

FEAST (fēst), *n.* (Placing food in the mouth.) Both closed hands alternately come to the mouth, as if placing food in it. Also BANQUET, DINNER.

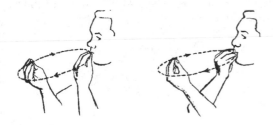

FEASTDAY (fēst' dā), *n.* (CARE, DAY.) The sign for CARE 1 is made: the "K" hands are crossed, the right above the left, little finger edges down. In this position they describe a small counterclockwise circle in front of the chest. This is followed by the sign for DAY: the left arm, held horizontally, palm down, represents the horizon. The right elbow rests on the back of the left hand, with the right arm in a perpendicular position. The right "D" hand, palm facing left, moves in an arc to the left until it is just above the left elbow.

FEATHER 1 (feth' ər), *n.* (The "F"; covering the skin.) The right "F" hand moves up the back of the left, plucking a succession of imaginary feathers.

FEATHER 2, *n.* (The shape.) With the thumb and index finger of the right hand, the signer mimes a feather standing up from the head.

FECES (fē' sēz) (*sl., vulg.*), *n.* (The passing of fecal material.) The left hand grasps the upturned right thumb. The right hand drops down and the right thumb is exposed. Also DEFECATE.

FEDERAL (fed' ər əl), *adj.* (The "F"; at the head of government.) The right "F" hand, palm facing left, makes a clockwise circle near the right temple and comes to rest on the temple.

FEE (fē), *n.* (Nicking into one.) The knuckle of the right "X" finger is nicked against the palm of the left hand, held in the "5" position, palm facing right. Also ADMISSION 2, CHARGE 1, COST, DUTY 2, EXCISE, EXPENSE, FINE 2, IMPOST, PENALTY 3, PRICE 2, TAX 1, TAXATION 1, TOLL.

FEEBLE (fē′ bəl), *adj.* (The knees buckle.) The right "V" hand is placed with fingertips resting in the upturned left palm. The knuckles of the "V" fingers buckle a bit. This motion may be repeated. Also FAINT 1, FRAIL, WEAK, WEAKNESS.

FEED 1 (fēd), *v.,* FED, FEEDING. (The natural sign.) The closed right hand goes through the natural motion of placing food in the mouth. This movement is repeated. Also CONSUME 1, CONSUMPTION, DEVOUR, DINE, EAT, FOOD 1, MEAL.

FEED 2, *v.* (Placing food before someone; the action of placing food in someone's mouth.) The upturned hands, holding imaginary pieces of food, the right behind the left, move forward simultaneously, in a gesture of placing food in someone's mouth.

FEEDBACK (fēd′ bak), *n.* (The letters "F" and "B"; back and forth.) Both "F" hands are positioned in front of the face, the left facing in and the right facing out. They move in and out alternately, changing from "F" to "B" each time.

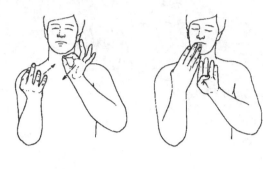

FEEL 1 (fēl), *v.,* FELT, FEELING. (The natural movement of touching.) The tip of the middle finger of the downturned right "5" hand touches the back of the left hand a number of times. Also CONTACT 1, TOUCH, TOUCHDOWN.

FEEL 2, *v.* (The welling up of feelings or emotions in the heart.) The right middle finger, touching the heart, moves up an inch or two a number of times. Also EMOTION 1, FEELING, MOTIVE 2, SENSATION, SENSE 2.

FEEL HURT (hŭrt), *v. phrase.* (The feelings are those that give pain and cause the hand to be removed quickly from the source of this pain.) The sign for FEEL 2 is made, and then the right hand is thrown down and out, opening into the downturned "5" position. Also HURT 4.

FEELING (fē' lǐng), *n*. See FEEL 2.

FEEL TOUCHED (tŭcht), *v. phrase*. (A piercing of the heart.) The tip of the middle finger of the right "5" hand is thrust against the heart. The head, at the same time, moves abruptly back a very slight distance. Also TOUCHED, TOUCHING.

FELLOWSHIP (fĕl' ō shǐp'), *n*. (Mingling with.) Both hands are held in modified "A" positions, thumbs out. The left hand is positioned with its thumb pointing straight up, and the right hand, with its thumb pointing down, revolves above the left thumb in a counter-clockwise direction. Also ASSOCIATE 1, EACH OTHER, MINGLE 2, MUTUAL 1, ONE ANOTHER.

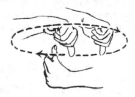

FEMALE (fē' māl), *n., adj*. (The bonnet string used by women of old.) The right "A" hand's thumb moves down along the line of the right jaw, from ear almost to chin. This outlines the string used to tie ladies' bonnets in olden days. This is a root sign to modify many

others. *Viz:* FEMALE plus BABY; DAUGHTER, FEMALE plus SAME; SISTER, etc.

FERRIS WHEEL (fer' is), *n* (The circling seat.) The downturned right index and middle fingers are draped over the downturned left thumb, which is held rigid. Both hands, thus held, execute a series of large, clockwise, forward circles, imitating the action of a ferris wheel.

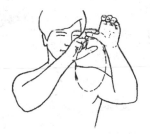

FETTER (fĕt' ər), *n., v.*, -TERED, -TERING. (The course of the chain or shackle around the ankles.) The right "X" finger describes a half circle around the left wrist, and then the hands are switched and the movement repeated with the left "X" finger and the right wrist.

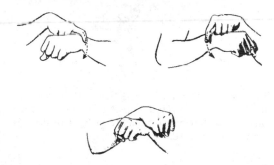

FEVER (fē' vər), *n*. (The rise and fall of the mercury in the thermometer.) The index finger of the right "D" hand, pointing left, moves slowly up and down the index finger of the left "D" hand, which is held pointing up. Also TEMPERATURE, THERMOMETER.

FEW (fū), *adj.* (The fingers are presented in order to convey the concept of "several.") The right "A" hand is held palm facing up. One by one the fingers open, beginning with the index finger and ending with the little finger. Some use only the index and middle fingers. Also RARE, SCARCE, SEVERAL, SUNDRY.

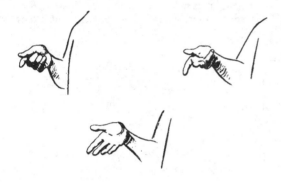

FEW SECONDS AGO, A, *adv. phrase.* (Time moved backward a bit.) The right "D" hand, palm facing the body, is placed in the palm of the left hand, which is facing right. The right hand swings back a bit toward the body, with the index finger describing an arc. Also JUST A MOMENT AGO, WHILE AGO 3.

FIB (fĭb), *n.* (The words are deflected from their normal straight path from the lips.) The right "D" hand, palm facing left, moves quickly in front of the lips, from right to left. Also FALSE 2.

FIDELITY (fĭ dĕl′ ə tĭ, fə-), *n.* (Coming forth directly from the lips; true.) The index finger of the right "D" hand, palm facing left, is placed against the lips. It moves up an inch or two and then describes a small arc forward and away from the lips. Also ABSOLUTE, ABSOLUTELY, ACTUAL, ACTUALLY, AUTHENTIC, CERTAIN, CERTAINLY, FAITHFUL 3, FRANKLY, GENUINE, INDEED, POSITIVE 1, POSITIVELY, REAL, REALLY, SINCERE 2, SURE, SURELY, TRUE, TRULY, TRUTH, VALID, VERILY.

FIELD 1 (fēld), *n.* (An expanse of ground.) The sign for SOIL 1 is made: both hands, held upright before the body, finger imaginary pinches of soil. The down-turned open right "5" hand then sweeps in an arc from right to left. Also LAND 1.

FIELD 2, *n.* (A fenced-in enclosure.) The "5" hands are held with palms facing the body and fingers interlocked but not curved. The hands separate, swinging first to either side of the body and then moving in toward the body, tracing a circle and coming together palms out and bases touching. Also GARDEN, YARD 2.

FIELD 3, *n.* (A straight, *i.e.,* special, path.) The hands are held in the "B" position, one above the other, with left palm facing right and right palm facing left. The little finger edge of the right hand moves straight forward along the index finger edge of the left. Also IN THE FIELD OF, SPECIALIZE, SPECIALTY.

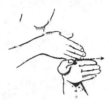

FIELD 4, *n.* (The letter "F"; straight line denotes a specific "line" or area of pursuit.) The thumb edge of the right "F" hand moves forward along the outstretched left index finger. Also PROFESSION 1.

FIELD 5, *n.* (The letter "F"; outlining the space.) Both downturned "F" hands, thumbs and index fingers touching, are held several inches in front of the chest. They describe a circle as they separate and move in toward the chest.

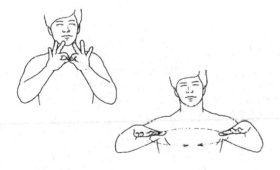

FIERCE (fîrs), *adj.* (Wrinkling the brow.) The "5" hand is held palm toward the face. The fingers open and close partly, several times, while an angry expression is worn on the face. Also ANGRY 1, CROSS 1, CROSSNESS, ILL TEMPER, IRRITABLE.

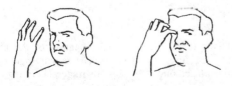

FIGHT 1 (fît), *n., v.,* FOUGHT, FIGHTING. (The fists in combat.) The "S" hands, palms facing, swing down simultaneously toward each other. They do not touch, however. Also COMBAT.

FIGHT 2, *n., v.* (The natural sign.) Both clenched fists go through the motions of boxing. Also BOX 2.

FIGURE 1 (fîg' yər), *n., v.,* -URED, -URING. (A multiplying.) The "V" hands, palms facing the body, alternately cross and separate several times. Also ARITHMETIC, CALCULATE, ESTIMATE, MULTIPLY 1.

FIGURE 2, *n., v.* (Contours are indicated or outlined.) Both "A" hands, held about a foot apart before the face, with palms facing each other, move down simultaneously in a wavy, undulating motion. Also FORM, IMAGE, SCULPT, SCULPTURE, SHAPE 1, STATUE.

FILE 1 (fîl) (*voc.*), *n., v.,* FILED, FILING. (The natural sign.) The index and middle fingers of the right "H"

hand rub back and forth over the edge of the index finger of the left "H" hand, whose palm faces right.

FILE 2, *v.* (Impaling a piece of paper on a spike.) The right "V" hand is brought down over the upturned left index finger.

FILE 3, *n., v.* (Standing up files in proper order.) The left "5" hand, fingers spread, faces right. The open or "B" right hand, palm facing the signer, moves down repeatedly between the different fingers of the left hand.

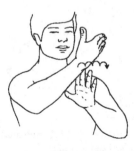

FILL 1 (fĭl), *v.,* FILLED, FILLING. (Wiping off the top of a container to indicate its condition of fullness.) The downturned open right hand wipes across the index finger edge of the left "S" hand, whose palm faces right. The movement of the right hand is toward the body. Also COMPLETE 2, FULL 1.

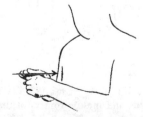

FILL 2, *v.* (Fill to the brim.) The left hand is held palm facing the body. The little finger edge of the downturned right hand moves up the left, from little finger edge to index.

FILM (fĭlm), *n.* (The frames of the film speeding through the projector.) The left "5" hand, palm facing right and thumb pointing up, is the projector. The right "5" hand is placed against the left and moves back and forth quickly. Also CINEMA, MOTION PICTURE, MOVIE(S), MOVING PICTURE.

FILMSTRIP (fĭlm′ strĭp), *n.* (A strip of movie film.) The sign for MOVIE is made: the left "5" hand is held palm facing right. The right "5" or "F" hand is placed on the left palm and moves back and forth quickly. The right thumb and index then move straight down the left palm.

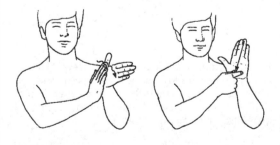

FILTHY (fĭl′ thĭ), *adj.* (A modification of the pig's snout groveling in a trough.) The downturned right hand is placed under the chin. Its fingers, pointing left, wiggle repeatedly. Also DIRTY, FOUL, IMPURE, NASTY, SOIL 2, STAIN.

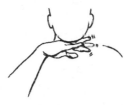

FINAL 1 (fī′ nǝl), *adj.* (The little, *i.e.*, LAST, fingers are indicated.) With the hands in the "I" position, the tip of the right little finger strikes the tip of its left counterpart. The right index finger may be used instead of the right little finger. Also END 1, EVENTU-ALLY, FINALLY 1, LAST 1, ULTIMATE, ULTIMATELY.

FINAL 2, *adj.* (A single little, *i.e.*, LAST, finger is indicated.) The tip of the index finger of the right "D" hand strikes the tip of the little finger of the left "I" hand. Also END 2, FINALLY 2, LAST 2.

FINALLY 1 (fī′ nǝ lǐ), *adv.* See FINAL 1.

FINALLY 2, *adv.* See FINAL 2.

FINANCE (fi nans′), *v.*, FINANCED, FINANCING. (PAY and SUPPORT.) The sign for PAY: the right index finger, resting in the upturned left palm, flicks forward.

This is followed by the sign for SUPPORT: the right "S" hand pushes up its left counterpart.

FINANCES (fĭ năn′ sǝs, fī′ năn sǝs), *n. pl.* (Slapping of paper money in the palm.) The upturned right hand, grasping some imaginary bills, is brought down into the upturned left palm a number of times. Also CAPITAL 2, CURRENCY, FUNDS, MONEY 1.

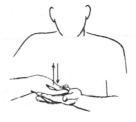

FIND (fīnd), *n., v.,* FOUND, FINDING. (The natural motion of selecting something from the hand.) The thumb and index fingers of the outstretched right hand grasp an imaginary object on the upturned left palm. The right hand then moves straight up. Also CHOOSE 2, DISCOVER, PICK 1, SELECT 1.

FIND FAULT 1 (fôlt), *v. phrase.* (A canceling out.) The right index finger makes a cross on the open left palm. Also ANNUL, CANCEL, CHECK 1, CORRECT 2, CRITICISM, CRITICIZE, REVOKE.

FIND FAULT 2 (*arch.*), *v. phrase.* (Selecting something by pulling it out of a receptacle or container.) The cupped left "C" hand is the container. The right index finger and thumb are placed in this imaginary container and pull something out.

FINE 1 (fīn), *adj., interj.* (The feelings are titillated.) With the thumb resting on the upper part of the chest, the fingers are wiggled back and forth. Also ELEGANT, GRAND 2, GREAT 4, SPLENDID 2, SWELL 2, WONDERFUL 2.

FINE 2, *n., v.,* FINED, FINING. (Nicking into one.) The knuckle of the right "X" finger is nicked against the palm of the left hand, held in the "5" position, palm facing right. Also ADMISSION 2, CHARGE 1, COST, DUTY 2, EXCISE, EXPENSE, FEE, IMPOST, PENALTY 3, PRICE 2, TAX 1, TAXATION 1, TOLL.

FINE 3, *adj.* (The fineness of sand or dust.) The index finger and thumb of the right "F" hand rub each other, as if fingering sand or dust.

FINE 4, *adj.* (The ruffled shirtfront of a gentleman of old.) The thumb of the right "5" hand is thrust into the chest. The hand then pivots down, with thumb remaining in place. This latter part of the sign, however, is optional. Also COURTEOUS, COURTESY, POLITE.

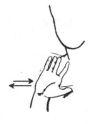

FINGER (fing′ gər), *n.* (Indicating a finger.) The right index finger and thumb grasp the left index finger and shake it very slightly.

FINGERSPELLING (fĭng′ ger, spĕl ĭng), *n.* (The movement of the fingers in fingerspelling.) The right hand, palm out, is moved from left to right, with the fingers wriggling up and down. Also ALPHABET, DACTYLOLOGY, MANUAL ALPHABET, SPELL, SPELLING.

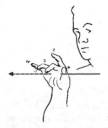

FINISH 1 (fĭn′ ĭsh), v., -ISHED, -ISHING. (Bring to an end.) The left hand, fingers together and pointing forward, is held palm facing right. The right, palm down, fingers also together, moves along the top of the left goes over the tip of the left index finger, and drops straight down, indicating a cutting off or a finishing. This sign is also used to indicate the past tense of a verb, in the sense of finishing an action or state of being. Also ACCOMPLISH 2, ACHIEVE 2, COMPLETE 1, CONCLUDE, DONE 1, END 4, EXPIRE 1, HAVE 2, TERMINATE.

FINISH 2 (colloq.), n., v. (Shaking the hands to rid them of something.) The upright "5" hands, palms facing each other, are suddenly and quickly swung around to a palm-out position. Also DONE 2, END 3.

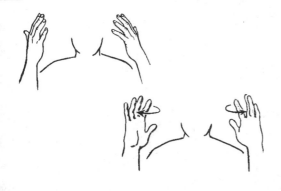

FINLAND 1 (fĭn′ lənd), n. (The letter "F"; the uppermost part of the body, to indicate the northern or Scandinavian sector of Europe.) The right "F" hand moves in a small counterclockwise circle on the forehead. Also FINN.

FINLAND 2, n. The curved index finger taps the chin twice. This is a native Finnish sign.

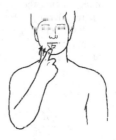

FIRE 1 (fīr), n., v., FIRED, FIRING. (The leaping of flames.) The "5" hands are held with palms facing the body. They move up and down alternately while the fingers wiggle. Also BURN, FLAME, HELL 2.

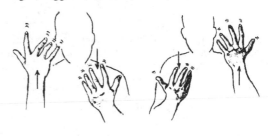

FIRE 2, v. ("Getting the axe"; the head is chopped off.) The upturned open right hand is swung sharply over the index finger edge of the left "S" hand, whose palm faces right. Also DISCHARGE 1, EXPEL 1.

FIREFIGHTER (fīr′ fī tər), n. (The shield on the hat.) The right "B" hand, palm out, is placed above the forehead.

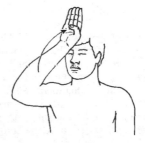

FIREPLACE (fīr′ plās), *n.* (FIRE; the shape of the mantel.) The sign for FIRE is made: the upturned wriggling fingers, hands facing the signer, move alternately up and down in imitation of the flames. The downturned open hands, held together, move apart and then down, palms now facing each other, to describe the sides of the mantel.

FIRST 1 (fûrst), *adj.* (The first finger is indicated.) The right index finger touches the upturned left thumb. Also INITIAL, ORIGIN 2, PRIMARY.

FIRST 2, *adj.* (The natural sign.) The right "1" hand, palm facing left, is swung around so that the palm now faces the signer.

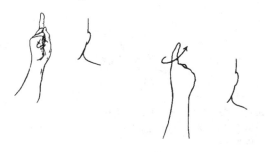

FISH 1 (fĭsh), *n.* (The natural motion.) The open right hand, palm facing left and fingers pointing forward, represents the fish. The open left hand, palm facing right and fingers also pointing forward, is positioned behind the right hand so that its fingertips rest against the base of the right hand. The right hand flaps back and forth, from right to left, moving very slightly forward meanwhile. The left hand remains in contact

with the right, but its only movement is forward. The left hand may also be dispensed with.

FISH 2, *v.,* FISHED, FISHING. (The natural motion of fishing.) The hands grasp and shake an imaginary fishing rod. The right hand may also go through the motions of operating the fishing reel.

FIT (fit), *n.* (The body shakes in a fit.) The right hand, palm up, index and middle fingers curved, is placed in the upturned left palm. The right hand's index and middle fingers open and close slightly as the two fingers tremble. Also EPILEPSY, SEIZURE.

FIVE OF US, *n. phrase.* ("Five," all in a circle.) The right "5" hand swings in an arc from right shoulder to left shoulder.

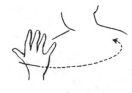

FLAME (flām), *n., v.,* FLAMED, FLAMING. (The leaping of flames.) The "5" hands are held with palms facing the body. They move up and down alternately while the fingers wiggle. Also BURN, FIRE 1, HELL 2.

side. The initial dropping down of the hands is often omitted.

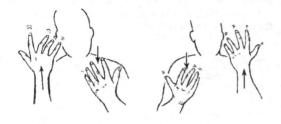

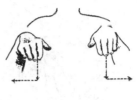

FLASH (flash), *n., v.,* FLASHED, FLASHING. (A sudden opening and closing of light.) The right modified "O" hand, palm forward, suddenly and quickly opens and closes. This sign may be made with the palm facing down, indicating an overhead flashing.

FLATBED PRESS (flăt bĕd prĕs) (*voc.*). (The natural motion of feeding sheets of paper into the flatbed press.) The downturned open hands, held side by side, move over to the right, grasp an imaginary sheet of paper, and, moving to the left, feed it into the press. The movement is usually repeated.

FLAT 1 (flat), *adj.* (The flatness is indicated.) Both open hands are positioned with palms down, right on top of left. The right hand moves off straight to the right.

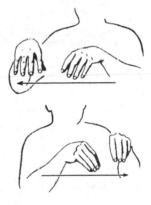

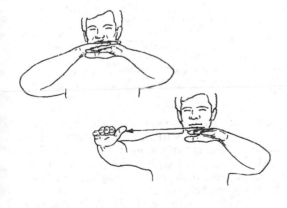

FLATTER 1 (flăt′ ər), *v.,* -TERED, -TERING. (Blinding one with sparkling words.) The downturned open hands are joined at the thumbtips. The fingers wiggle at random. Sometimes the hands sway up and down alternately, but in any case the thumbtips remain in contact at all times. Also FLATTERY 1.

FLAT 2, *adj.* (The concept of flatness is emphasized.) The downturned hands, fingers together and pointing straight out from the body, are held side by side, about a foot apart. They drop down simultaneously an inch or two, and then move to the respective sides of the body—the right to the right side and the left to the left

FLATTER 2, *v.* (All eyes are directed to the signer, the one being flattered.) The "V" hands, palms facing the body, wave back and forth before the face. Also FLAT-TERY 2.

FLATTER 3, *v.* (Massaging the ego.) The fingertips of the right hand, pointing forward or left, brush back and forth against the upright left index finger. This sign is used to indicate flattery of someone.

FLATTERY 1 (flăt′ ə rĭ), *n.* See FLATTER 1.

FLATTERY 2, *n.* See FLATTER 2.

FLAT TIRE, *n.* (The natural sign.) The right hand, palm down and fingers pointing forward, is placed with thumb on top of left hand. The right hand closes down suddenly on the right thumb, imitating a flat tire.

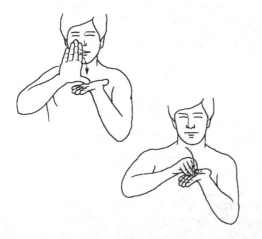

FLEE (flē), *v.*, FLED, FLEEING. (Emerging from a hiding place.) The downturned right "D" hand is positioned under the downturned open left hand. The right "D" hand suddenly emerges and moves off quickly to the right. Also ESCAPE.

FLESH (flĕsh), *n.* (The fleshy part of the hand.) The right index finger and thumb squeeze the fleshy part of the open left hand between thumb and index finger. Also BEEF, MEAT.

FLEXIBLE (flek′ sə bəl), *adj.* (Bendable back and forth.) The right fingers grasp the tips of the left fingers and bend them back and forth.

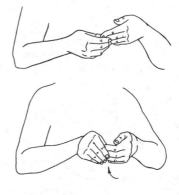

FLIER (flī′ ər), *n.* (An individual who flies a plane.) The sign for either AIRPLANE 1 or AIRPLANE 2 is made, and this is followed by the sign for INDIVIDUAL: both open hands, palms facing each other, move down the sides of the body, tracing its outline to the hips. Also AVIATOR, PILOT.

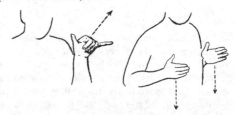

FLIGHT ATTENDANT (flīt ə ten′ dənt) *n.* (A person who flies and serves food.) The downturned open right hand, with thumb, little finger, and (optionally) index fingers extended, moves forward above the head, as an airplane in flight. Both upturned hands then mime serving a succession of dishes to someone. The sign for INDIVIDUAL 1 then follows.

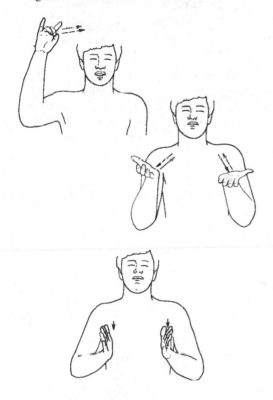

FLIP THE LID (flĭp thə lĭd) (*sl.*), *v. phrase*, FLIPPED, FLIPPING. (The lid or cover of a pot pops off into the air.) This sign is used to indicate a loss of temper. The left "O" hand, thumb side up and palm facing right, is the pot. The downturned right hand, resting on the left, suddenly pops up and, pivoted at the wrist, moves up in a wavy manner. Also FLY OFF THE HANDLE.

FLIRT 1, *v.*, FLIRTED, FLIRTING. (Dazzling someone with the wiggling fingers.) Both downturned "5" hands are held thumb to thumb, and the fingers wiggle while the signer assumes a flirtatious look.

FLIRT 2, *v.* (Fanning someone.) The hands are held as in FLIRT 1, but the signer moves them alternately up and down while maintaining contact between the two thumbs. As before, a flirtatious look is assumed.

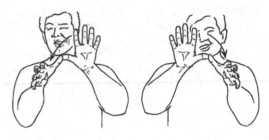

FLOAT 1 (flōt), *n., v.*, FLOATED, FLOATING. (Resting on an object that bobs up and down on the water.) Both hands are held in the palms-down position. The right index and middle fingers rest on their left counterparts. The left hand moves forward in a series of bobbing movements, carrying the right hand along with it.

FLOAT 2, *n., v.* (Prone on a floating object.) The downturned right open hand rests on the downturned left hand. Both hands move forward in a series of bobbing actions.

FLOOR (flōr), *n.* (Boards arranged side by side.) The downturned open hands, fingers together, are held side by side at the left side of the body. They separate and come together repeatedly as they move toward the right.

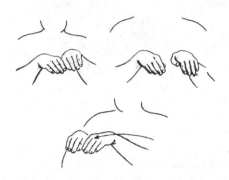

FLOPPY (flop′ ē), *adj., n. Computer term.* (Easily bent.) Both hands, grasping an imaginary disk, bend it forward and back.

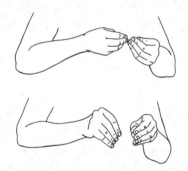

FLOUR 1 (flour), *n.* (The sign for WHITE; the grinding process.) The sign for WHITE is made: the right "5" hand is placed at midchest, palm facing the body. It moves off the chest, closing into the "O" position, palm still facing the body. The fingertips of the right hand, held palm down, move in a continuous counterclockwise circle on the upturned left palm.

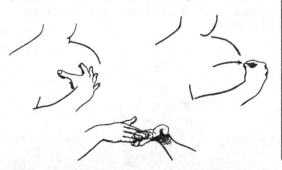

FLOUR 2, *n.* (The sign for WHITE; feeling the flour.) The sign for WHITE is made, as in FLOUR 1. The right hand then fingers an imaginary pinch of flour.

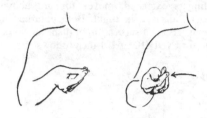

FLOWER (flou′ ər), *n.* (The natural motion of smelling a flower.) The right hand, grasping an imaginary flower, holds it first against the right nostril and then against the left. Also BLOSSOM.

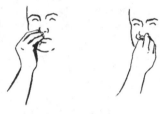

FLUNK (flŭngk), *v.,* FLUNKED, FLUNKING. The right "F" hand strikes forcefully against the open left palm, which faces right with fingers pointing forward. Also FAIL 3.

FLUSH (flŭsh), *v.,* FLUSHED, FLUSHING. (The red rises in the cheeks.) The sign for RED is made: the tip of the right index finger of the "D" hand moves down over the lips, which are red. Both hands are then places palms facing the cheeks and move up along the face to indicate the rise of color. Also BLUSH, EMBARRASS, EMBARRASSED, MORTIFICATION.

FLUTE (flōōt), *n.* (Playing the instrument.) The signer mimes playing a flute.

FLY 1 (flī), *v.,* FLEW, FLOWN, FLYING. (The wings of the airplane.) The "Y" hand, palm down and drawn up near the shoulder, moves forward, up and away from the body. Either hand may be used. Also AIRPLANE 1, PLANE 1.

FLY 2, *v., n.* (The wings and fuselage of the airplane.) The hand assumes the same position as in FLY 1, but the index finger is also extended to represent the fuselage of the airplane. Either hand may be used, and the movement is the same as in FLY 1. Also AIRPLANE 2, PLANE 2.

FLY 3, *n.* (Act of catching a fly.) The open right hand, poised over the raised left arm, quickly swoops down and grasps an imaginary fly resting on the left arm.

FLY A KITE, *phrase.* (Holding the kite string.) Looking up, the signer pulls on an imaginary string several times. Both hands may be used. Also KITE.

FLY TO HERE, *v. phrase.* (The aircraft comes to the signer.) With the right thumb and index and little fingers extended and pointing to the signer, the hand moves up in an arc toward the chest. It stops short of touching.

FOCUS (fō′ kəs), *n., v.,* -CUSED, -CUSING. (Directing one's attention forward; applying oneself; concentrating.) Both hands, fingers pointing up and together, are held at the sides of the face. They move straight out from the face. Also APPLY 2, ATTEND (TO), ATTENTION, CONCENTRATE, CONCENTRATION, GIVE ATTENTION (TO), MIND 2, PAY ATTENTION (TO).

FOE (fō), *n.* (At sword's point.) The two index fingers, after pointing to each other, are drawn sharply apart. This is followed by the sign for INDIVIDUAL: both open hands, palms facing each other, move down the sides of the body, tracing its outline to the hips. Also ENEMY, OPPONENT, RIVAL 1.

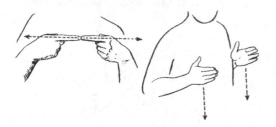

FOLLOW (fŏl′ ō), v., -LOWED, -LOWING. (One hand follows the other.) The "A" hands are used, thumbs pointing up. The right is positioned a few inches behind the left. The left hand moves straight forward, while the right follows behind in a series of wavy movements. Also CONSECUTIVE, FOLLOWING, SEQUEL.

FOLLOWING (fŏl′ ō ĭng), adj. See FOLLOW.

FOLLY (fŏl′ ĭ), n. (Thoughts flickering back and forth.) The right "Y" hand, thumb almost touching the forehead, is shaken back and forth across the forehead several times. Also ABSURD, DAFT, FOOLISH, NONSENSE, RIDICULOUS, SILLY, TRIFLING.

FOOD 1 (fōōd), n. (The natural sign.) The closed right hand goes through the natural motion of placing food in the mouth. This movement is repeated. Also CONSUME 1, CONSUMPTION, DEVOUR, DINE, EAT, FEED 1, MEAL.

FOOD 2, n. (Various things to eat.) The sign for FOOD 1 is made, followed by the sign for VARIOUS: the index fingers, pointing at each other, are drawn apart. As they do so, they wiggle slightly.

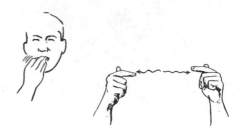

FOOL AROUND (fōōl ə rownd′) v. (Frivolous activity.) Both "Y" hands, swiveling at the wrists, move alternately back and forth. This sign is derived from the verb PLAY.

FOOLISH (fōō′ lĭsh), adj. (Thoughts flickering back and forth.) The right "Y" hand, thumb almost touching the forehead, is shaken back and forth across the forehead several times. Also ABSURD, DAFT, FOLLY, NONSENSE, RIDICULOUS, SILLY, TRIFLING.

FOOT 1 (fŏŏt), *n.* (The natural sign.) The signer points to his foot.

FOOT 2, *n.* (The length is indicated.) The "A" hands, palms down and thumbtips touching, are held before the chest. They separate until they are about a foot apart.

FOOT 3, *n.* (The measurement.) The left hand is held palm down. The heel of the right "F" hand is placed on the left wrist, and then moves in an arc to the left fingertips.

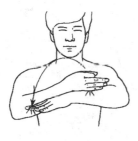

FOOTBALL 1 (fŏŏt′ bôl′), *n.* (The teams lock in combat.) The "5" hands, facing each other, are interlocked suddenly. They are drawn apart and the action is repeated.

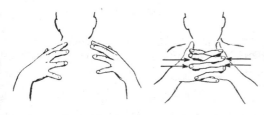

FOOTBALL 2, *n.* (The shape of the ball.) The "5" hands face each other, the right fingers in contact with

their left counterparts. The hands are drawn apart into the "O" position, palms facing each other.

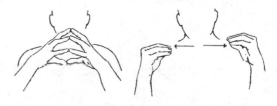

FOR 1 (fôr), *prep.* (The thoughts are directed outward toward a specific goal or purpose.) The right index finger, resting on the right temple, leaves its position and moves straight out in front of the face. Also TO 2, TOWARD 3

FOR 2, *prep.* (A thought or knowledge uppermost in the mind.) The fingers of the right hand or the index finger are placed on the center of the forehead, and then the hand is brought strongly up above the head, assuming the "Λ" position, with thumb pointing up. Also BECAUSE.

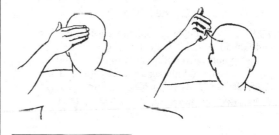

FORBID 1 (fər bĭd′), *v.,* -BADE *or* -BAD, -BIDDEN *or* -BID, -BIDDING. (A modification of LAW, *q.v.;* "against the law.") The downturned right "D" or "L" hand is thrust forcefully into the left palm. Also BAN, FORBIDDEN 1, PROHIBIT.

FORBID 2, *v.* (The letter "F"; the same sign as above.) The right "F" hand makes the same sign as in FORBID 1. Also FORBIDDEN 2.

FORBIDDEN 1 (fər bĭd′ ən), *v.* See FORBID 1.

FORBIDDEN 2, *adj.* See FORBID 2.

FORCE 1 (fōrs), *v.*, FORCED, FORCING. (Forcing the head to bow.) The right "C" hand pushes down on an imaginary neck. Also COERCE 1, COERCION 1, COMPEL 1, IMPEL 1.

FORCE 2, *v.* (Pushing something forward.) The open right hand is held palm down at chin level, fingers pointing left. From this position the hand turns to point forward and moves forcefully forward and away from the body, as if pushing something ahead of it. Also COERCE 2, COERCION 2, COMPEL 2, IMPEL 2.

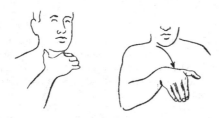

FORECAST (fōr′ kăst′, -käst′), *v.*, -CAST or -CASTED, -CASTING. (The vision is directed forward, into the distance.) The right "V" fingertips are placed under the eyes, with palm facing the body. The hand is then swung around and forward, moving under the down-turned prone left hand and continuing forward and

upward. Also FORESEE, FORETELL, PERCEIVE 2, PREDICT, PROPHECY, PROPHESY, PROPHET, VISION 2.

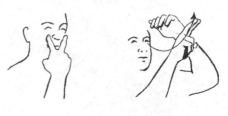

FORESEE (fōr sē′), *v.*, -SAW, -SEEN, -SEEING. See FORECAST.

FOREST (fôr′ ĭst), *n.* (A series of trees.) The open right "5" hand is raised, with elbow resting on the back of the left hand, as in TREE, *q.v.* As the right hand swings around and back a number of times, pivoting at the wrist, the left arm carries the right arm from left to right. Also WOODS.

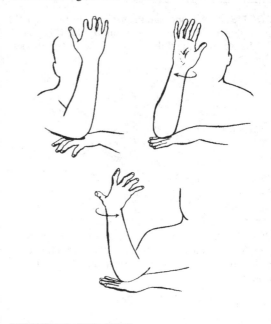

FORETELL (fōr tĕl′), *v.*, -TOLD, -TELLING. See FORE-CAST.

FOREVER (fôr ĕv′ ər), *adv.* (Around the clock and ahead into the future.) The right index finger, pointing forward, traces a clockwise circle in the air. The downturned right "Y" hand then moves forward, either in a straight line or in a slight downward curve. Also ETERNITY 1, EVER 2, EVERLASTING.

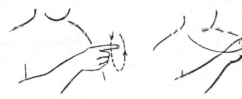

FOREWARN (fōr wôrn'), v., -WARNED, -WARNING. (Tapping one to draw attention to danger.) The right hand taps the back of the left hand several times. Also ADMONISH 1, CAUTION, WARN.

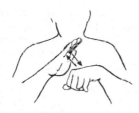

FORFEIT (fôr' fĭt), n. (Throwing up the hands in a gesture of surrender.) Both "A" hands are held palms down before the chest and then thrown up in unison, ending in the "5" position. Also ABDICATE, CEDE, DIS-COURAGE 1, GIVE UP, LOSE HOPE, RELINQUISH, RENOUNCE, RENUNCIATION, SURRENDER 1, YIELD.

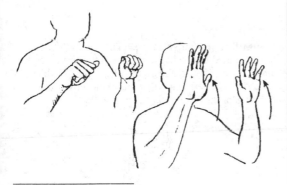

FORGET 1 (fər gĕt'), v., -GOT, -GOTTEN, -GETTING. (Wiping knowledge from the mind.) The right hand, fingers pointing left, rests on the forehead. It moves off to the right, assuming the "A" position, thumb up and palm facing the signer's rear. Also FORSAKE 2.

FORGET 2, v. (The thought is gone.) The sign for THINK is made: the index finger makes a small circle on the forehead. This is followed by the sign for GONE 1: the right open hand, palm facing the body, is held by the left hand and is drawn down and out, ending in a position with fingers drawn together. The left hand, meanwhile, has closed into a position with fingers also drawn together.

FORGIVE 1 (fər gĭv') (eccles.), v., -GAVE, -GIVEN, -GIVING. (Blessed; forgiveness.) The "A" hands are held near the lips, thumbs up and almost touching. Both hands move down and out simultaneously, ending in the "5" position, palms down. The right hand, palm flat, facing down, is then brushed over the left hand, held palm flat and facing up. This latter action may be repeated twice. Also ABSOLUTION 1, BLESS 1.

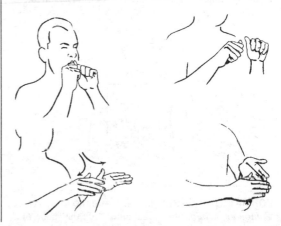

FORGIVE 2, *v.* (A wiped-off and cleaned slate.) The right hand wipes off the left palm several times. Also APOLOGIZE 2, APOLOGY 2, EXCUSE, PARDON, PAROLE.

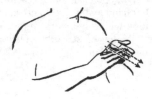

FORK (fôrk), *n., v.,* FORKED, FORKING. (The natural sign.) The downturned fingertips of the right "V" hand are thrust repeatedly into the upturned left palm.

FORM 1 (fôrm), *n.* (Contours are indicated or outlined.) Both "A" hands, held about a foot apart before the face, with palms facing each other, move down simultaneously in a wavy, undulating motion. Also FIGURE 2, IMAGE, SCULPT, SCULPTURE, SHAPE 1, STATUE.

FORM 2, *n.* (The letters "F"; outlining the shape.) Both "F" hands, palms facing out, outline the shape of a piece of paper.

FORMAT (fôr′ mat), *n., v.,* -MATTED, -MATTING. *Computer terminology.* (The letter "F"; the shape of a computer disk.) The right "F" hand makes a clockwise circle around the outstretched left palm and comes to rest on the palm.

FORMERLY (fôr′ mər lĭ), *adv.* (Something past, behind.) The upraised right hand, in the "5" position with palm facing the body, is held just above the right shoulder and is thrown back over it. Also AGO, ONCE UPON A TIME, PAST, PREVIOUS, PREVIOUSLY, WAS, WERE.

FORMULA (fôr′ myə lə), *n.* (The letter "F"; something spelled out to be seen.) The left palm faces forward or slightly to the right. The right "F" hand is placed at the left fingertips and then moves down to the base of the left hand.

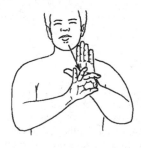

FORNICATE (fôr′ nə kāt′), *v.,* -CATED, -CATING. (The motions of the legs during the sexual act.) The upturned left "V" hand remains motionless while the downturned right "V" hand comes down repeatedly on the left. Also COPULATE, SEXUAL INTERCOURSE.

FORSAKE 1 (fôr sāk′), *v.,* -SOOK, -SAKEN, -SAKING. (Pulling away.) The downturned open hands are held in a line, with fingers pointing to the left, the right hand behind the left. Both hands move in unison toward the right. As they do so, they assume the "A" position. Also DEPART, EVACUATE, GRADUATE 2, LEAVE 1, RETIRE 1, WITHDRAW 1.

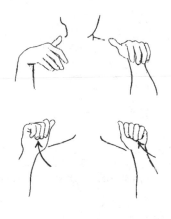

FORSAKE 2, *v.* (Wiping knowledge from the mind.) The right hand, fingers pointing left, rests on the forehead. It moves off to the right, assuming the "A" position, thumb up and palm facing the signer's rear. Also FORGET 1.

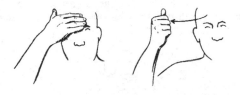

FORSAKE 3, *v.* (To throw something aside.) Both "S" hands are held with palms facing at chest level and then thrown down and to the left, opening into the "5"

position. Also ABANDON 1, CAST OFF, DEPOSIT 2, DISCARD 1, LEAVE 2, LET ALONE, NEGLECT.

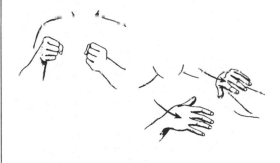

FORT (fôrt, fōrt), *n.* (The fence spread around a fort.) The upturned right "4" hand, palm out, is placed in front of the downturned left arm. It moves along the edge of the left arm from left to right.

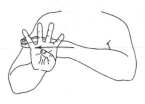

FORTIFY (fôr′ tə fī′), *v.,* -FIED, -FYING. (Hold down firmly; cover and strengthen.) The "S" hands, downturned, are held side by side in front of the body, the arms almost horizontal and the left hand in front of the right. Both arms move a short distance forward and slightly downward. Also DEFEND, DEFENSE, GUARD, PROTECT, PROTECTION, SHIELD 1.

FORTITUDE (fôr′ tə tūd′, -tōōd′), *n.* (Strength emanating from the body.) Both "5" hands are placed palms against the chest. They move out and away forcefully, closing and assuming the "S" position. Also BRAVE, BRAVERY, COURAGE, COURAGEOUS, HALE,

HEALTH, HEALTHY, MIGHTY 2, STRENGTH, STRONG 2, WELL 2.

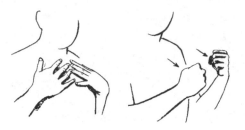

FOUL 1 (foul), *adj.* (A modification of the pig's snout groveling in a trough.) The downturned right hand is placed under the chin. Its fingers, pointing left, wiggle repeatedly. Also DIRTY, FILTHY, IMPURE, NASTY, SOIL 2, STAIN.

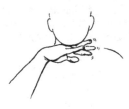

FOUL 2 (foul), *n.* (*sports*). The index finger brushes forward quickly against the ear located on the same side as the hand.

FOUND (found), *v.,* FOUNDED, FOUNDING. (To set up.) The right "A" hand, thumb up and palm facing left, comes down to rest on the back of the downturned left "S" hand. Before doing so, the right "A" hand may describe a clockwise circle above the left hand, but this is optional. Also ESTABLISH, FOUNDED.

FOUNDATION (foun dā' shən), *n.* (The area below.) Both hands, in the "5" position, palms down, are held before the chest, the right under the left. The right hand moves under the left in a counterclockwise fashion. Also BACKGROUND, BASIS 2, BELOW 1, BOTTOM.

FOUNDED, *v.* See FOUND.

FOUR (fōr), *adj.* (The natural sign.) Four fingers are displayed.

FOUR OF US, *n. phrase.* ("Four"; an encompassing movement.) The right "4" hand, palm facing the body, moves from the right shoulder to the left shoulder.

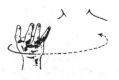

FOX (fŏks), *n.* (The letter "F"; the pointed snout.) The tip of the nose is placed in the circle formed by the right "F" hand, which swings back and forth a short distance. Also FOXY, SLY 1.

FOXY (fŏk' sĭ), *adj.* See FOX.

FRACTURE (frăk′ chər), *n., v.,* -TURED, -TURING. (The natural sign.) The hands grasp an imaginary object and break it in two. Also BREAK.

FRAGRANT (frā′ grənt), *adj.* (Bringing something up to the nose.) The upturned right hand moves slowly up to and past the nose, and the signer breathes in as the hand sweeps by. Also ODOR, SCENT, SMELL.

FRAIL (frāl), *adj.* (The knees buckle.) The right "V" hand is placed with fingertips resting in the upturned left palm. The knuckles of the "V" fingers buckle a bit. This motion may be repeated. Also FAINT 1, FEEBLE, WEAK, WEAKNESS.

FRAME (frām), *n., v.,* FRAMED, FRAMING. (The frame is outlined.) The downturned index finger and thumb of each hand outline the square shape of a frame. Also CHASE 2.

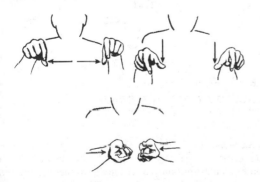

FRANK (frăngk), *adj.* (The letter "H," for HONEST; a straight and true path.) The index and middle fingers of the right "H" hand, whose palm faces left, move straight forward along the upturned left palm. Also HONEST, HONESTY, SINCERE 1.

FRANKFURTER 1 (frăngk′ fər tər), *n.* (The shape.) The "C" hands are held side by side, palms out, thumbs and index fingers touching. They change to the "S" position as they are drawn apart. Also HOT DOG.

FRANKFURTER 2, *n.* (The shape in a roll or bun.) The left hand is held with the fingers pointing up. The right index finger is placed between the thumb and the other fingers. Also HOT DOG 2.

FRANKLY (frăngk′ lĭ), *adv.* (Coming forth directly from the lips; true.) The index finger of the right "D" hand, palm facing left, is placed against the lips. It moves up an inch or two and then describes a small arc forward and away from the lips. Also ABSOLUTE, ABSOLUTELY, ACTUAL, ACTUALLY, AUTHENTIC, CERTAIN, CERTAINLY, FAITHFUL 3, FIDELITY, GENUINE, INDEED,

POSITIVE 1, POSITIVELY, REAL, REALLY, SINCERE 2, SURE, SURELY, TRUE, TRULY, TRUTH, VALID, VERILY.

FRAUD (frôd), *n.* (Underhandedness.) The right hand, palm down, is held with index and little fingers pointing out. The left hand, in a similar position, is held above the right. The right hand moves forward repeatedly, each time emerging briefly from under the left hand. The positions may be reversed, with the left hand doing the movement, or both hands can move simultaneously. Also CHEAT 1, DECEIT, DECEIVE, DECEPTION, DEFRAUD, FRAUDULENT 1.

FRAUDULENT 1 (frô′ jə lənt), *adj.* See FRAUD.

FRAUDULENT 2, *adj.* (Words diverted instead of coming straight, or truthfully, out.) The index finger of the right "D" hand, pointing to the left, moves along the lips from right to left. Also FALSE 1, FALSEHOOD, LIAR, LIE 1, PREVARICATE, UNTRUTH.

FRECKLES (frek′ əlz), *n.* (Little spots on the face.) Both claw hands, palms facing the signer, touch the face at various places.

FREE 1 (frē), *adj., v.,* FREED, FREEING. (Breaking the bonds.) The "S" hands, crossed in front of the body, swing apart and face out. Also DELIVER 1, EMANCIPATE, INDEPENDENCE, INDEPENDENT, LIBERATION, REDEEM 1, RELIEF, RESCUE, SAFE, SALVATION, SAVE 1.

FREE 2, *adj., v.* (The letter "F.") The "F" hands make the same sign as in FREE 1.

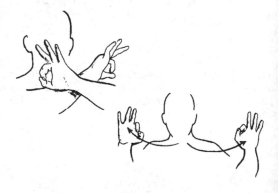

FREEDOM (frē′ dəm), *n.* See FREE 1.

FREEWAY (frē′ wā), *n.* (Traffic flowing in opposite directions.) The downturned "4" hands pass each other as the right moves repeatedly to the left and the left repeatedly to the right. The downturned "V" hands are often used instead of the "4"s. Also HIGHWAY.

FREEZE (frēz), *v.*, FROZE, FROZEN, FREEZING. (The stiff fingers.) The fingers of the "5" hands, held palms down, stiffen and contract. Also FROZEN, ICE, RIGID.

FREQUENT (*adj.* frē′ kwənt; *v.* frĭ kwĕnt′), -QUENTED, -QUENTING. The left hand, open in the "5" position, palm up, is held before the chest. The right hand, in the right-angle position, fingers pointing up, arches over and into the left palm. This is repeated several times. Also OFTEN.

FRESHMAN (fresh′ mən), *n., adj.* (The first year after the preparatory year at Gallaudet University.) The right index finger touches the ring finger of the other hand.

FRET (frĕt), *v.*, FRETTED, FRETTING, *n.* (A clouding over; a troubling.) Both "B" hands, palms facing each other, are rotated alternately before the forehead. Also ANNOY 2, ANNOYANCE 2, ANXIOUS 2, BOTHER 2, CONCERN 1, PROBLEM 1, TROUBLE, WORRIED, WORRY 1.

FREUD (froid), *n.* (The letter "F"; PSYCHOLOGY.) The right hand forms the letter "F." The little finger edge is thrust twice into the open left hand, its palm facing out, between thumb and index finger. This is the sign for PSYCHOLOGY, shaping the Greek letter "psi." Strictly speaking, Freud was not a psychologist but a psychoanalytic psychiatrist. This so-called name sign applies nevertheless.

FRIEND (frĕnd), *n.* (Locked together in friendship.) The right and left hands are interlocked at the index fingers. The hands separate, change their relative positions, and come together again as before. Also FRIENDSHIP.

FRIENDLY (frĕnd′ lĭ), *adj.* (A crinkling up of the face.) Both hands, in the "5" position, palms facing back, are placed on either side of the face. The fingers wiggle back and forth while a pleasant, happy expression is worn. Also AMIABLE, CHEERFUL, CORDIAL, JOLLY, PLEASANT.

FRIENDSHIP (frĕnd′ shĭp), *n.* See FRIEND.

FRIGHT (frīt), *n.* (The heart is suddenly covered with fear.) Both hands, fingers together, are placed side by side, palms facing the chest. They quickly open and come together over the heart, one on top of the other. Also AFRAID, COWARD, FEAR 1, FRIGHTEN, SCARE(D), TERROR 1.

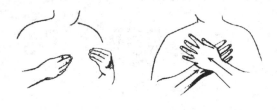

FRIGHTEN (frī′ tən), *v.*, -TENED, -TENING. See FRIGHT.

FRINGE (frinj), *n.* (The shape.) The downturned right "4" hand, covered by the left, moves from left to right as the four hanging fingers wriggle.

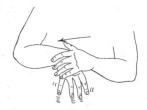

FROCK (frŏk), *n.* (Draping the clothes on the body.) With fingertips resting on the chest, both hands move down simultaneously. The action is repeated. Also

CLOTHES, CLOTHING, DRESS, GARMENT, GOWN, SHIRT, SUIT, WEAR 1.

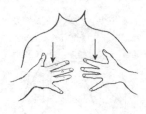

FROM (frŏm), *prep.* (The "away from" action is indicated.) The knuckle of the right "X" finger is placed against the base of the left "D" or "X" finger and then moved away in a slight curve toward the body.

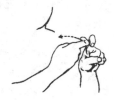

FROM TIME TO TIME, *adv. phrase.* (Forward in slow, deliberate movements.) The right hand, palm facing the signer, fingers pointing left, makes a series of small forward movements, describing a small arc each time. Also NOW AND THEN, ONCE IN A WHILE 2.

FRONT 1 (frunt), *n., adv.* (In front of the face.) The right "B" hand, palm facing the body and fingertips pointing left, is drawn up and down close to the front of the face. Also IN FRONT OF.

FRONT 2, *n.* (The front of the hand is indicated.) The right "5" hand is held palm facing out, and the left index finger is placed in it. The hand positions may be reversed.

FROZEN (frō′ zən), *adj.* (The stiff fingers.) The fingers of the "5" hands, held palms down, stiffen and contract. Also FREEZE, ICE, RIGID.

FRUIT 1 (frōōt), *n.* (The growth and the shape.) The sign for GROW is made: the right hand, palm facing the body and fingers touching the thumb, is thrust up through the closed left hand, opening into the "5" position as it emerges. The right hand is then placed over the left "O" hand, whose fingers point to the right. The right hand is drawn toward the right, closing into the "O" position.

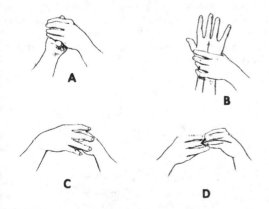

FRUIT 2, *n.* (Peeling the fruit.) The right index and thumb grasp an imaginary piece of skin on the back of the downturned left hand and peel it downward.

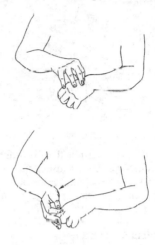

FRUSTRATED (frŭs′ trāt ĭd), *adj.* (Coming up against a wall; a door is slammed in the face.) The open right hand is brought up sharply, and its back strikes the mouth and nose. The head moves back a bit at the same time. Also DISAPPOINTED 2.

FULL 1 (fŏŏl), *adj.* (Wiping off the top of a container to indicate its condition of fullness.) The downturned open right hand wipes across the index finger edge of the left "S" hand, whose palm faces right. The movement of the right hand is toward the body. Also COMPLETE 2, FILL.

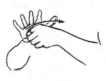

FULL 2, *adj., adv.* (Full—up to the chin.) The downturned open right hand moves up until its back comes into contact with the underside of the chin. The signer assumes an expression of annoyance. Also FED UP.

FUN (fŭn), *n.* (The wrinkled nose—indicative of laughter or fun.) The index and middle fingers of the right "U" hand, whose palm faces the body, are placed on the nose. The right hand swings down in an arc and, palm down, the "U" fingers strike their left counterparts on the downturned left "U" hand and either stop at that point or continue on.

FUND (fund), *v.,* FUNDED, FUNDING. (Support from money.) The sign for MONEY 1 is made: the upturned right hand, grasping some imaginary bills, is brought down into the upturned left palm. The right "S" hand then pushes up the left "S" hand.

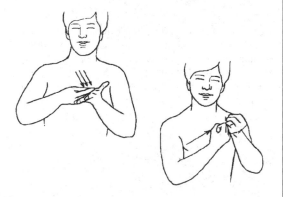

FUNDAMENTAL (fun′ də men′ təl), *adj.* (The letter "F"; basic or underlying.) The right "F" moves in a

continuous clockwise circle under the downturned left hand.

FUNDRAISING, *v. phrase.* (Money is raised.) The sign for MONEY 1 is made: the upturned right hand, grasping some imaginary bills, is brought down into the upturned left palm a number of times. Both upturned open hands then move up together.

FUNDS (fŭndz), *n. pl.* (Slapping of paper money in the palm.) The upturned right hand, grasping some imaginary bills, is brought down into the upturned left palm a number of times. Also CAPITAL 2, CURRENCY, FINANCES, MONEY 1.

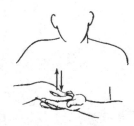

FUNNY (fŭn′ ĭ), *adj.* (The nose wrinkles in laughter.) The tips of the right index and middle fingers brush repeatedly off the tip of the nose. Also COMIC, COMICAL, HUMOR, HUMOROUS.

FUR (fûr), *n.* (Fingering the fur.) The downturned right hand repeatedly fingers imaginary fur covering the back of the downturned left hand.

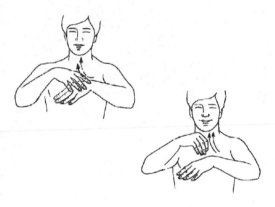

FURNITURE (fûr′ nı chər), *n.* (The letter "F"; things in front of you.) The right "F" hand, palm facing up or out, moves in a series of small back-and-forth movements in front of the body.

FURY (fyŏor′ ĭ), *n.* (A violent welling up of the emotions.) The curved fingers of the right hand are placed in the center of the chest and fly up suddenly and violently. An expression of anger is worn. Also ANGER, ANGRY 2, ENRAGE, INDIGNANT, INDIGNATION, IRE, MAD 1, RAGE.

FUTURE (tu′ chər), *n.* (Something ahead or in the future.) The upright, open right hand, palm facing left, moves straight out and slightly up from a position beside the right temple. Also BY AND BY, IN THE FUTURE, LATER 2, LATER ON, SHALL, WILL 1, WOULD.

G

GAIETY 1 (gā′ ə tǐ), *n.* (The heart is stirred; the spirits bubble up.) The open right hand, palm facing the body, strikes the heart repeatedly, moving up and off the heart after each strike. Also DELIGHT, GAY, GLAD, HAPPINESS HAPPY, JOY, MERRY.

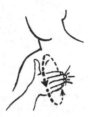

GAIETY 2, *n.* (The swinging of tambourines.) Both open hands, held somewhat above the head, are pivoted back and forth repeatedly, as if swinging a pair of tambourines. Also PARTY 1.

GAIN 1 (gān), *v.*, GAINED, GAINING. (Adding on.) The index and middle fingers of the right "H" hand, palm up, are swung up and over until they come to rest on the index and middle fingers of the left "H" hand, held palm down. Also ADD 3, ADDITION, EXTEND 1, EXTRA, INCREASE, ON TO, RAISE 2.

GAIN 2, *n., v.* (To get a profit; a coin popped into the vest pocket.) The sign for GET is made: both outstretched hands, held in a grasping "5" position, close into "S" positions, with the right on top of the left. At the same time, both hands are drawn in to the body. The thumb and index finger of the right hand, holding an imaginary coin, are then popped into an imaginary vest or breast pocket. Note: the sign for GET is sometimes omitted. Also BENEFIT 2, PROFIT.

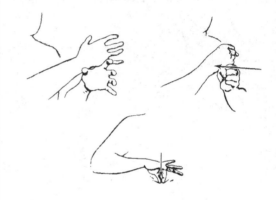

GALLEY (găl′ ĭ) (*voc.*), *n.* (The shape of the galley or of the galley proof.) Both downturned open hands rest on the edges of an imaginary galley frame. The left hand moves forward, tracing the elongated shape of the frame.

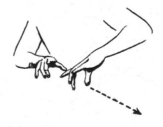

GALLOP (gal′ əp), *v., n.*, GALLOPED, GALLOPING. (The horse's legs.) Both "V" hands, palms down, are held one before the other, fingers curved down. Both hands move forward in unison in a series of circles. Each time they rise, the curved fingers close up, opening again as they fall.

GAME (gām), *n.*, *v.*, GAMED, GAMING. (Two individuals pitted against each other.) The hands are held in the "A" position, thumbs pointing straight up, palms facing the body. They come together forcefully, moving down a bit as they do, and the knuckles of one hand strike those of the other. Also CHALLENGE, OPPORTUNITY 2, VERSUS.

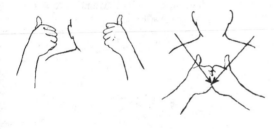

GANG 1 (găng), *n.* (A grouping together.) Both "C" hands, palms facing, are held a few inches apart at chest height. They are swung around in unison so that the palms now face the body. Also ASSOCIATION, AUDIENCE 1, CASTE, CIRCLE 2, CLASS, CLASSED 1, CLUB, COMPANY, FAMILY 2, GROUP 1, JOIN 2, ORGANIZATION 1.

GANG 2, *n.* (*loc.*). (Someone surrounded by a retinue or a following.) The right claw hand surrounds the left upright index finger. The right hand moves straight back toward the signer's chest and away from the left index.

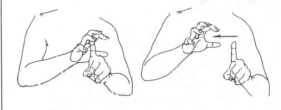

GARAGE (gə räzh′, -räj′), *n.* (A vehicle is placed under cover.) The right "3" hand, thumb up, palm facing left or the signer's chest, moves under a shield formed by the downturned open left hand. The so-called "3" hand is a generic sign for many vehicles.

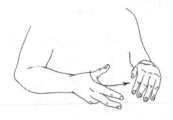

GARDEN 1 (gär′ dən), *n.* (A fenced-in enclosure.) The "5" hands are held with palms facing the body and fingers interlocked but not curved. The hands separate, swinging first to either side of the body and then moving in toward the body, tracing a circle and coming together palms out and bases touching. Also FIELD 2, YARD 2.

GARDEN 2, *n.* (The letter "G"; an area.) The right "G" hand circles counterclockwise around the downturned open left hand.

GARLIC (gär′ lik), *n.* (Garlic breath.) The right hand, in the claw position, fingers placed at the open mouth, spins forward.

GARMENT (gär′ mənt), *n.* (Draping the clothes on the body.) With fingertips resting on the chest, both hands move down simultaneously. The action is repeated. Also CLOTHES, CLOTHING, DRESS, FROCK, GOWN, SHIRT, SUIT, WEAR 1.

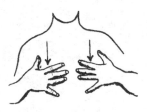

GAS 1 (găs), *n.* (The emission and the foul smell.) The upturned right index finger and thumb, in contact with each other, move up through the hole formed by the left "F" hand. The right hand then grasps the tip of the nose. The signer assumes an appropriate expression to indicate the foulness of the odor. Another sign involves the left hand resting on top of the right, whose fingers open and close.

GAS 2, *n.* (The act of pouring gasoline into an automobile tank.) The thumb of the right "A" hand is placed into the hole formed by the left "O" hand. Also GASOLINE, POUR.

GASOLINE (găs′ ə lēn′, găs ə lēn′), *n.* See GAS 2.

GATE (gāt), *n.* (The natural sign.) The fingertips of both open hands touch each other before the body, palms toward the chest, thumbs pointing upward. Then the right fingers swing forward and back to their original position several times, imitating the movement of a gate opening and closing.

GATHER 1 (găth′ ər), *v.,* -ERED, -ERING. (A gathering together.) The right "5" hand, fingers curved and palm facing left, sweeps across and over the upturned left palm several times in a circular movement. Also ACCUMULATE 2, GATHERING TOGETHER.

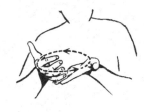

GATHER 2, *v.* (Assemble all together.) Both "5" hands, palms facing, are held with fingers pointing out from the body. With a sweeping motion they are brought in toward the chest, and all fingertips come together. This is repeated. Also ACCUMULATE 3, ASSEMBLE, ASSEMBLY, CONFERENCE, CONVENE, CONVENTION, GATHERING, MEETING 1.

GATHERING (găth′ ər ĭng), *n.* See GATHER 2.

GATHERING TOGETHER, *phrase.* See GATHER 1.

GAY 1 (gā), *n., adj.* (Homosexual.) The tips of the "G" fingers are placed on the chin. Also HOMOSEXUAL 1.

GAY 2, *n., adj.* (Supposedly a code originally.) The signer pulls the earlobe. Also HOMOSEXUAL 2.

GAY 3, *n., adj.* (Mutual masturbation.) Both fists, palms facing down, come together repeatedly. Also HOMOSEXUAL 3.

GAY 4, *n., adj.* (An effeminate gesture.) Both "F" hands, palms out, are held at shoulder height. The signer moves them alternately forward and back, while the shoulders keep pace with the forward-and-back movements. Also EFFEMINATE, HOMOSEXUAL 4.

GAY 5, *adj.* (The heart is stirred; the spirits bubble up.) The open right hand, palm facing the body, strikes the heart repeatedly, moving up and off the heart after each strike. Also DELIGHT, GAIETY 1, GLAD, HAPPINESS, HAPPY, JOY, MERRY.

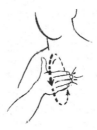

GAZE (gāz), *v.,* GAZED, GAZING, *n.* (The vision is directed forward.) The tips of the right "V" fingers point to the eyes. The right hand is then swung around and forward a bit. Also LOOK AT, OBSERVE 1, WITNESS.

GENERAL (jen′ ər əl), *n.* (The insignia of rank.) The right "G" hand is placed on the right shoulder and moves down an inch or two.

GENERATION (jěn′ ə rā′ shən), *n.* (Persons descending, one after another, from an original or early person.) The downturned cupped hands are positioned one above the other at the right shoulder. They roll over each other as they move alternately downward and a bit away from the body. This sign is used only when talking about people.

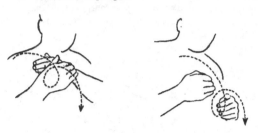

GENEROUS 1 (jĕn′ ər əs), *adj.* (The heart rolls out.) Both right-angle hands roll over each other as they move down and away from their initial position at the heart. Also BENEVOLENT, GENTLE 1, GENTLENESS, GRACIOUS, HUMANE, KIND 1, KINDNESS, MERCY 1, TENDER 3.

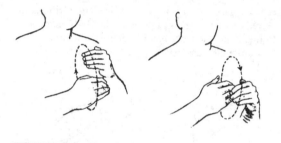

GENEROUS 2, *adj.* (The heart is encircled and its largeness indicated.) The right index finger traces a circle around the heart. The two "L" hands, held palms out and thumbs pointing at each other, then move apart from their initial position in front of the chest.

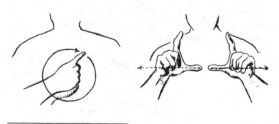

GENETIC (jə net′ ik), *adj.* (The "G" letters; coming from behind into the present.) Both "G" hands are placed above the right shoulder. They roll alternately forward over each other.

GENIUS (jēn′ yəs), *n.* (Doubly smart.) Both "C" hands are placed on the forehead, with the right thumb resting on the forehead and the left thumb on the fingertips of the right.

GENTLEMAN (jĕn′ təl mən), *n.* (A fine or polite man.) The MALE prefix sign is made: the right hand grasps the edge of an imaginary cap. The sign for POLITE is then made: the thumb of the right "5" hand is placed slowly and deliberately on the right side of the chest.

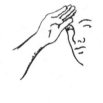

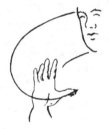

GENUINE (jĕn′ yŏŏ ĭn), *adj.* (Coming forth directly from the lips; true.) The index finger of the right "D" hand, palm facing left, is placed against the lips. It moves up an inch or two and then describes a small arc forward and away from the lips. Also ABSOLUTE, ABSOLUTELY, ACTUAL, ACTUALLY, AUTHENTIC, CERTAIN, CERTAINLY, FAITHFUL 3, FIDELITY, FRANKLY, INDEED, POSITIVE 1, POSITIVELY, REAL, REALLY, SINCERE 2, SURE, SURELY, TRUE, TRULY, TRUTH, VALID, VERILY.

GEOGRAPHY (jĭ ŏg′ rə fĭ), *n.* (The earth and its axis are indicated.) The downturned left "S" hand indicates the earth. The thumb and index finger of the downturned right "5" hand are placed at each edge of the left. In this position the right hand swings back and forth while maintaining contact with the left. Also EARTH 1, GLOBE 1, PLANET.

GERBIL (jûr′ bil), *n.* (The letter "G"; MOUSE.) The back of the right "G" hand brushes the nose several times.

GERMANY 1 (jûr′ mə nĭ), *n.* See GERMAN.

GERMANY 2, *adj., n.* (The spike worn on the World War 1 soldier's helmet.) The index finger, pointing straight up, is placed on top of the head.

GET (gĕt), *v.,* GOT, GOTTEN, GETTING. (A grasping and bringing forward to oneself.) Both hands, in the "5" position, fingers curved, are crossed at the wrists, with the left palm facing right and the right palm facing left. They are brought in toward the chest while closing into a

grasping "S" position. Also ACQUIRE, OBTAIN, PROCURE, RECEIVE.

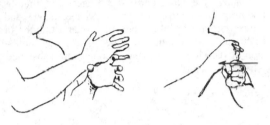

GET AWAY, *phrase, interj.* (Shooing someone away with a wave of the hand.) The downturned right hand is flung away to the right. The signer usually assumes an expression of annoyance.

GET IN FRONT OF, *phrase.* (The movement.) Both "A" hands are placed with the right behind the left. The right hand moves ahead, passing the left, and positions itself in front of the left.

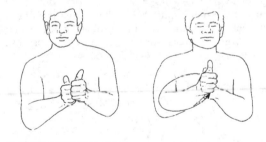

GET UP (ŭp), *v. phrase.* (Getting onto one's feet.) The upturned index and middle fingers of the right hand, representing the legs, are swung up and over in an arc, coming to rest in the upturned left palm. Also ARISE 2, ELEVATE, RAISE 1, RISE 1, STAND 2, STAND UP.

GHOST (gōst), *n.* (Something thin and filmy, *i.e.*, ephemeral.) The hands are held palms facing, with one above the other and index fingers and thumbs touching and almost connected. As the upper hand moves straight up, the index fingers and thumbs of both hands slowly come together, giving the impression of drawing out a thread or other thin substance. Also SOUL, SPIRIT.

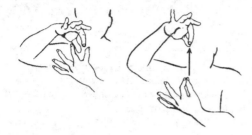

GIANT (jī′ ənt), *n., adj.* (The wide shoulders.) The thumbs and curved index fingers of both hands, forming "C" shapes, are placed on the shoulders and move off in opposite directions in a large arc.

GIFT (gĭft), *n.* (A giving of something.) Both "A" hands, with index fingers somewhat draped over the tips of the thumbs, are held palms facing in front of the chest. They are pivoted forward and down, in unison, from the wrists. Also AWARD, BEQUEATH, BESTOW, CONFER, CONSIGN, CONTRIBUTE, PRESENT 2.

GIGABYTE (gig′ ə bīt′, jig′-), *n. Computer term.* (The initials.) The signer fingerspells "G-B."

GIGGLE (gig′ əl), *n., v.,* -GLED, -GLING. (The mouth contorts repeatedly in laughter.) Both index fingers, at each corner of the mouth, move back quickly and repeatedly, as if forcing the mouth to open in laughter.

GILLS (gilz), *n.* (The fluttering movement.) Both hands are placed at either side of the throat, fingertips touching the throat. They flip open and shut repeatedly, imitating the fluttering movement of gills.

GIRDLE (gûr′ dl), *n.* (Stretching a girdle around the abdomen to slim up the figure.) Both "S" hands grasp the edges of an imaginary elasticized garment, pull the edges forward and around the abdomen, and finish with one "S" on top of the other. During the pulling, the signer shows effort expended, and the breath is sucked in.

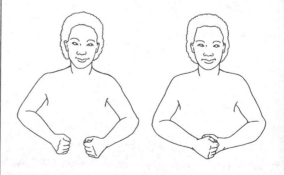

GIRL (gûrl), *n.* (A female who is small.) The FE-MALE root sign is given: the thumb of the right "A"

hand moves down along the line of the right jaw, from ear almost to chin. This outlines the string used to tie ladies' bonnets in olden days. The downturned open right hand is then held at waist level, indicating the short height of the female. Also MAIDEN.

GIVE 1 (gĭv), *v.*, GAVE, GIVEN, GIVING. (The hands move forward and open.) Both hands are held, palms up or down, about a foot apart, thumbs resting on fingertips. The hands are extended forward in a slight arc, opening to the "5" position as they do. Also EXTEND 2.

GIVE 2, *v.* (Holding something and extending it toward someone.) The right "O" hand is held before the right shoulder and then moved outward in an arc, away from the body.

GIVE ASSISTANCE (ə sĭs′ təns), *v. phrase.* (Helping up; supporting.) The left "S" hand, thumb side up, rests in the open right palm. In this position the left hand is pushed up a short distance by the right. Also AID, ASSIST, ASSISTANCE, BENEFIT 1, BOOST, HELP.

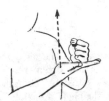

GIVE ATTENTION (TO) (ə tĕn′ shən), *v. phrase.* (Directing one's attention forward; applying oneself; concentrating.) Both hands, fingers pointing up and together, are held at the sides of the face. They move straight out from the face. Also APPLY 2, ATTEND (TO), ATTENTION, CONCENTRATE, CONCENTRATION, FOCUS, MIND 2, PAY ATTENTION (TO).

GIVE ME (mē), *v. phrase.* (Extending the hand toward oneself.) This sign is a reversal of GIVE 2.

GIVE UP (gĭv ŭp′), *v. phrase.* (Throwing up the hands in a gesture of surrender.) Both "A" hands are held palms down before the chest and then thrown up in unison, ending in the "5" position. Also ABDICATE, CEDE, DISCOURAGE 1, FORFEIT, LOSE HOPE, RELINQUISH, RENOUNCE, RENUNCIATION, SURRENDER 1, YIELD.

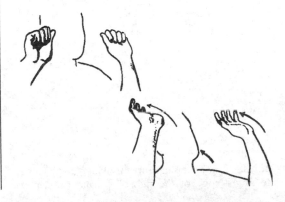

GLACIER (glā' shər), *n.* (The movement forward.) The downturned claw hands move very slowly forward.

GLAD (glăd), *adj.* (The heart is stirred; the spirits bubble up.) The open right hand, palm facing the body, strikes the heart repeatedly, moving up and off the heart after each strike. Also DELIGHT, GAIETY 1, GAY, HAPPINESS, HAPPY, JOY, MERRY.

GLASS 1 (glăs, gläs), *n.* (The finger touches a brittle substance.) The index finger is brought up to touch the exposed front teeth. Also BONE, CHINA 2, DISH, PLATE, PORCELAIN.

GLASS 2, *n.* (The shape of a drinking glass.) The little finger edge of the right "C" hand rests in the

upturned left palm. The right hand moves straight up a few inches, tracing the shape of a drinking glass.

GLASSES (glăs' əs), *n. pl.* (The shape.) The thumb and index finger of the right hand, placed flat against the right temple, move back toward the right ear, tracing the line formed by the eyeglass frame. Also EYE-GLASSES; GALLAUDET, THOMAS HOPKINS; SPECTACLES.

GLIMPSE (glimps), *n., v.,* GLIMPSED, GLIMPSING. (The quick and sudden movement of the eyeballs.) Both "F" hands, palms out and side by side below the chin, suddenly jerk toward the left and back again.

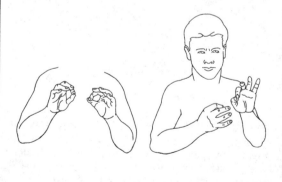

GLISTEN (glis' ən), *v.,* -TENED, -TENING. (Reflected glistening of light rays.) The left hand, held supinely before the chest, palm down, represents the object from which the rays glisten. The right hand, in the "5" position, touches the back of the left lightly and moves up toward the right, pivoting slightly at the wrist, with fingers wiggling. Also BRIGHT 2, SHINE, SHINING.

GLOBE 1 (glōb), *n.* (The earth and its axes are indicated.) The downturned left "S" hand indicates the earth. The thumb and index finger of the downturned right "5" hand are placed at each edge of the left. In this position the right hand swings back and forth while maintaining contact with the left. Also EARTH 1, GEOGRAPHY, PLANET.

GLOBE 2, *n.* (The letter "W," for WORLD in orbit.) The right "W" hand makes a complete circle around the left "W" hand and comes to rest on the thumb edge of the left "W" hand. The left hand frequently assumes the "S" position, instead of the "W," to represent the stationary sun. Also WORLD.

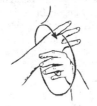

GLOOM (glōōm), *n.* (The facial features drop.) Both "5" hands, palms facing the eyes and fingers slightly curved, drop simultaneously to a level with the mouth. The head drops slightly as the hands move down, and an expression of sadness is assumed. Also DEJECTED,

DEPRESSION, GLOOMY, GRAVE 3, GRIEF 1, MELANCHOLY, MOURNFUL, SAD, SORROWFUL 1.

GLOOMY (glōō' mĭ), *adj.* See GLOOM.

GLORIOUS 1 (glōr' ĭ əs), *adj.* See GLORY 1.

GLORIOUS 2, *adj.* (With glory.) The sign for WITH is made: both "A" hands, knuckles together and thumbs up, are moved forward in unison, away from the chest. This is followed by the sign for GLORY 1.

GLORY 1 (glōr' ĭ), *n.* (The letter "G"; scintillating or shining.) The right "G" hand moves in a clockwise circle or is simply held stationary above the downturned left "S" or "A" hand. The right hand then opens into the "5" position, palm facing the left hand, and moves up in a deliberate wavy motion. Also GLORIOUS 1.

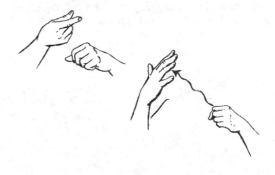

GLORY 2 (*rare*), *n.* (A modification of GLORY 1.) The hands are clasped, and then both separate into the

"5" position, palms facing, with the right hand moving up in a deliberate wavy motion, pivoted at the wrist.

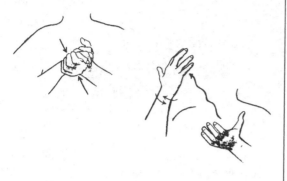

GLUE 1 (glo͞o), *n., v.,* GLUED, GLUING. (Squeezing a tube of glue; indicating the stickiness.) The right hand squeezes an imaginary tube, pressing its contents onto the upturned left palm. The right hand, using the thumb and middle finger, then demonstrates the stickiness by touching the left palm and then indicating the difficulty in separating the finger from the thumb.

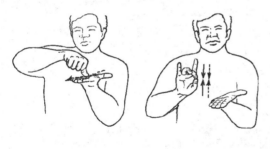

GLUE 2, *n.* (The spreading and pressing together of the glued parts.) The index and middle fingers of the right hand spread imaginary glue on the upturned left palm. Both hands, in the "5" position, are then pressed firmly together.

GO 1 (gō), *v.,* WENT, GONE, GOING. (Continuous motion forward.) With palms facing each other, the index fin-

gers of the "D" hands revolve around each other as both hands move forward.

GO 2, *v., interj.* (The natural sign.) The right index finger is flung out as a command to go. A stern expression is usually assumed.

GO AHEAD (ə hĕd'), *v. phrase.* (Moving forward.) Both right-angle hands, palms facing each other and knuckles facing forward, move forward simultaneously. Also FORWARD, MOTION FORWARD, ONWARD, PROCEED, PROGRESS 2, RESUME.

GOAL (gōl), *n.* (A thought directed upward toward a goal.) The left "D" hand, palm facing the body, is held above the head to represent the goal. The index finger of the right "D" hand, after touching the forehead (modified sign for THINK, *q.v.*), moves slowly and deliberately up to the tip of the left index finger. Also AIM, AMBITION, ASPIRE, OBJECTIVE, PERSEVERE 4, PURPOSE 2.

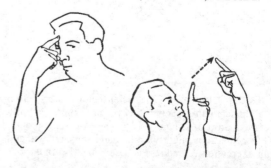

GO AS A GROUP, *phrase.* (Many people, forming a circle, move forward.) Both "C" hands, palms facing each other and fingers facing forward, form a circle or a ball and move forward in unison.

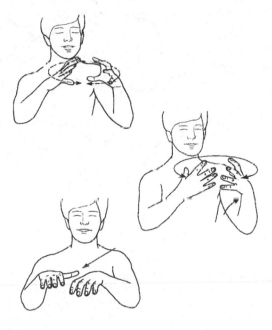

GO BACK, *v. phrase.* (Walking backwards.) The downturned index fingers move alternately in toward the chest.

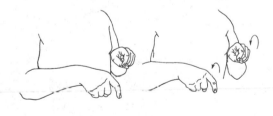

GO BY BOAT, *phrase.* (The boat moves forward.) With upright cupped hands held side by side, both hands move straight forward.

GO BY CAR, *phrase.* (The steering wheel moves forward.) Holding an imaginary steering wheel, the hands move straight forward. Also DRIVE TO.

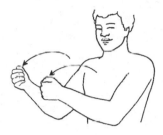

GO BY TRAIN, *phrase.* (The train moves forward.) The downturned right index and middle fingers, placed on top of their left counterparts, move suddenly forward.

GOD (gŏd), *n.* (A motion indicating the One above.) The right open hand, palm facing left, swings up above the head and is then moved down about an inch. The signer looks up while making the sign. Also LORD 2.

GODFATHER 1 (gŏd′ fä′ thər), *n.* (FATHER, RESPONSIBLE 1.) The sign for FATHER 1 is made: the thumb and extended fingers of the right hand are brought up to grasp an imaginary cap brim, representing the tipping of caps by men in olden days. Both hands are then held open and palms facing up, as if holding a baby. This is followed by the sign for

RESPONSIBLE 1: the fingertips of both hands, placed on the right shoulder, bear down.

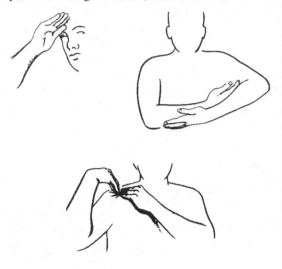

RESPONSIBLE 1: the fingertips of both hands, placed on the right shoulder, bear down.

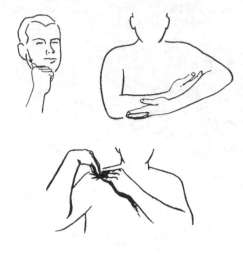

GODFATHER 2, *n.* (Second father.) The right "2" hand is twisted around (SECOND), and then the signer makes the sign for FATHER 2: the tip of the thumb of the right "5" hand is placed against the right forehead or temple. The signer may make the two signs in reverse order.

GODMOTHER 2, *n.* (Second mother.) The right "2" hand is twisted around (SECOND), and then the signer makes the sign for MOTHER 2: the tip of the thumb of the right "5" hand is placed against the right cheek. The signer may make the two signs in reverse order.

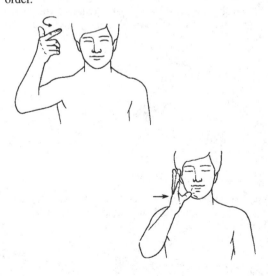

GODMOTHER 1 (gŏd′ mŭth′ ər), *n.* (MOTHER, RESPONSIBLE 1.) The sign for MOTHER 1 is made: the thumb of the right "A" hand moves down along the line of the right jaw, from ear almost to chin. Both hands are then held open and palms facing up, as if holding a baby. This is followed by the sign for

GOLD (gōld), *n.* (Yellow earrings, *i.e.,* gold, which was discovered in California.) The earlobe is pinched, and then the sign for YELLOW is made: the "Y"

hand, pivoted at the wrist, is shaken back and forth repeatedly. Also CALIFORNIA.

GONE 1 (gôn, gŏn), *adj.* (A disappearance.) The right open hand, palm facing the body, is held by the left hand and is drawn down and out, ending in a position with fingers drawn together. The left hand, meanwhile, may close into a position with fingers also drawn together. Also ABSENCE 1, ABSENT 1, DEPLETE, DISAPPEAR, EMPTY 1, EXTINCT, FADE AWAY, MISSING 1, OMISSION 1, OUT 3, OUT OF, VANISH.

 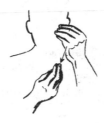

GONE 2, *adj.* (A wiping-off motion to indicate a condition of no longer being present.) The little finger edge of the "5" hand, held palm facing the body, rests on the back of the downturned left hand. The right hand moves straight forward suddenly, closing into the "S" position, palm still facing the body. Also EXHAUSTED.

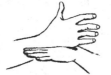 

GONE 3 (*sl.*), *adj.* (A modification of GONE 2, indicating a disappearance into the distance. The narrowing perspective is the main feature here.) The right "L" hand, resting on the back of the downturned left

hand, moves straight forward suddenly. As it does, the index finger and thumb come together.

GONORRHEA (gon ə rē′ ə), *n.* (The penis is infected, *i.e.,* covered with the disease.) The right claw hand is brought down on the tip of the left index. Also CLAP. Although this is essentially a male sign, it may also be used in a non-gender-specific context.

GOOD 1 (gŏod), *adj.* (Tasting something, approving it, and offering it forward.) The fingertips of the right "5" hand are placed at the lips. The right hand then moves out and into a palm-up position on the upturned left palm. Also WELL 1.

GOOD 2 (*colloq.*), *adj., interj.* (Thumbs up!) The right "A" hand is held with thumb pointing straight up. The right hand moves forward and out about an inch. This motion may be repeated.

GOODBYE 1 (good′ bī′), *n., interj.* (Words extended politely from the mouth.) The fingertips of the right "5" hand are placed at the mouth. The hand moves away from the mouth to a palm-up position before the body. The signer, meanwhile, usually nods smilingly. Also FAREWELL 1, HELLO 1, THANKS, THANK YOU, YOU'RE WELCOME 1.

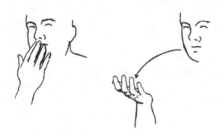

GOODBYE 2, *interj.* (A wave of the hand.) The right open hand waves back and forth several times. Also FAREWELL 2, HELLO 2, SO LONG.

GOOD FRIEND (good frĕnd), *n.* (Hooked on to.) Both index fingers interlock and move down forcefully an inch or two. The lips are held together tightly and an expression of pleasure is shown. Also FAVORITE 2.

GOOD LUCK, *phrase.* (Thumbs up!) The right "A" hand is held with thumb pointing straight up. The

hand moves forward and out about an inch. This may be repeated. Also GOOD 2.

GO OFF THE TRACK, *v. phrase.* (The natural motion.) The "G" hands are held side by side and touching, palms down, index fingers pointing forward. Then the right hand moves forward, curving toward the right side as it does. Also DEFLECT, DEVIATE 2, STRAY, WANDER 1.

GOOSE (goos), *n.* (The broad bill.) The right hand is held with its back resting against the mouth. The thumb, index and middle fingers come together repeatedly, indicating the opening and closing of a broad bill. Also DUCK.

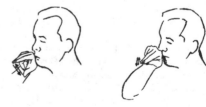

GOOSE BUMPS (*colloq.*), *n.* (Fingertips indicate where the bumps appear.) The downturned right claw hand moves up the back of the left arm.

GORILLA (gə ril′ ə), *n.* (Thumping the chest.) Both fists alternately beat against the chest.

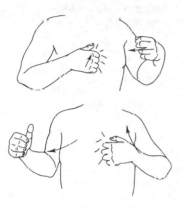

GO TO BED 1, *v. phrase.* (Laying the head on the pillow.) The head is placed on its side in the open palm, and the eyes are closed.

GO TO BED 2 (*colloq.*), *v. phrase.* (Tucking the legs beneath the covers.) The index and middle fingers of the right "U" hand, held either palm down or palm up, are thrust into the downturned left "O" hand. Also RETIRE 2.

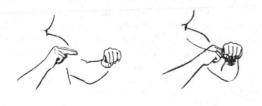

GOVERN (gŭv′ ərn), *v.*, -ERNED, -ERNING. (Holding the reins over all.) The "A" hands, palms facing, move alternately back and forth as if grasping and manipulating reins. The left "A" hand, still in position, swings over so that its palm now faces down. The right hand opens to the "5" position, palm down, and swings over the left, which moves slightly to the right. Also AU-

THORITY, CONTROL 1, DIRECT 1, MANAGE, MANAGEMENT, MANAGER, OPERATE, REGULATE, REIGN, RULE 1.

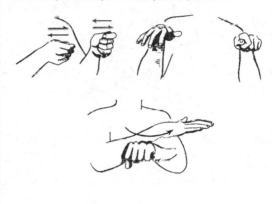

GOVERNMENT (gŭv′ ərn mənt, -ər-), *n.* (The head indicates the head or seat of government.) The right index finger, pointing toward the right temple, describes a small clockwise circle and comes to rest on the right temple. Also CAPITAL 1, ST. PAUL (Minn.).

GO WITH, *phrase.* (Going forward together.) Both "A" hands, knuckles and thumbs touching, move forward in unison. Also ACCOMPANY 2.

GOWN (goun), *n.* (Draping the clothes on the body.) With fingertips resting on the chest, both hands move down simultaneously. The action is repeated. Also

CLOTHES, CLOTHING, DRESS, FROCK, GARMENT, SHIRT, SUIT, WEAR 1.

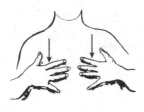

GRAB (grăb), *v.*, GRABBED, GRABBING, *n.* (Grasping something and holding it down.) Both hands, palms down, quickly close into the "S" position, the right on top of the left. Also CAPTURE, CATCH 2, GRASP, SEIZE.

GRAB OPPORTUNITY, *v. phrase.* (Grasping what is at hand.) The right hand grabs an imaginary object on the upturned left palm and sweeps it in toward the chest.

GRADE (grād), *n.* (The letter "G"; the level.) Both "G" hands, palms facing out, move apart, indicating a level or stage.

GRADUATE 1 (*n.* grăj′ ŏŏ ĭt; *v.* grăj′ ŏŏ āt′), -ATED, -ATING. (The letter "G"; the ribbon around the diploma.) The right "G" hand makes a single clockwise circle and drops down into the upturned left palm.

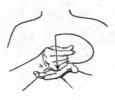

GRADUATE 2 (*loc.*), *adj., n., v.* (Pulling away.) The downturned open hands are held in a line, with fingers pointing to the left, the right hand behind the left. Both hands move in unison toward the right. As they do so, they assume the "A" position. Also DEPART, EVACUATE, FORSAKE 1, LEAVE 1, RETIRE 1, WITHDRAW 1.

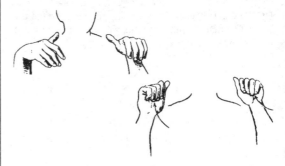

GRADUATE 3, *adj.* (Fingers represent a total of seven years of college.) The left "5" hand is held palm facing the chest. The right "2" hand, palm also facing the chest, is placed across the left so that the index and middle fingers are next to the left thumb, making a total of seven fingers presented. This sign is traditionally used at Gallaudet University, where the first five fingers represent years at school, with the little finger corresponding to the preparatory year and the remaining four signifying freshman through senior years. Thus the two extra fingers added on will be the two extra years beyond the senior year required in most cases for a master's degree. This sign is today applicable to any graduate school or program.

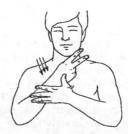

GRAM (gram), *n.* (The letter "G"; weighing.) The right "G" fingers rock back and forth on the extended left index.

GRAND 1 (grănd), *adj.* (The hands gesture toward the heavens.) The "5" hands, palms out and arms raised rather high, are positioned somewhat above the line of vision. The arms move abruptly forward and up once or twice. An expression of pleasure or surprise is usually assumed. Also EXCELLENT, GREAT 3, MARVEL, MARVELOUS, MIRACLE, O!, SPLENDID 1, SWELL 1, WONDER 2, WONDERFUL 1.

GRAND 2, *adj., interj.* (The feelings are titillated.) With the thumb resting on the upper part of the chest, the fingers are wiggled back and forth. Also ELEGANT, FINE 1, GREAT 4, SPLENDID 2, SWELL 2, WONDERFUL 2.

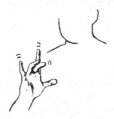

GRANDDAUGHTER (grăn' dô tər), *n.* (The letter "G"; DAUGHTER.) The "G" is formed with the right hand. The sign for DAUGHTER is then made: the FEMALE prefix sign is formed, with the thumb of the right hand tracing a line on the right jaw from just below the ear

to the chin. The right upturned arm then rests on its left counterpart, as if holding a baby.

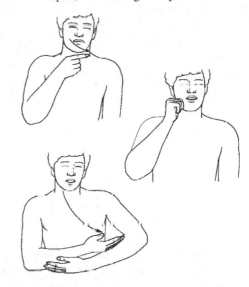

GRANDFATHER 1 (grănd' fä' thər), *n.* (A holder of a male baby; a predecessor.) The sign for FATHER 2 is made: the thumbtip of the right "5" hand touches the right temple a number of times. Then both open hands, palms up, are extended in front of the chest, as if supporting a baby. From this position they sweep over the left shoulder. The whole sign is smooth and continuous.

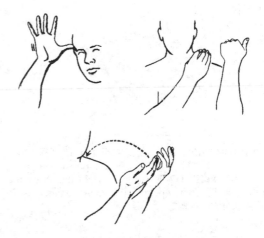

GRANDFATHER 2, *n.* (A variation of GRANDFATHER 1.) The "A" hands are held with the left in front of the right and the right thumb positioned against the forehead. Both hands open into the "5"

position so that the right little finger touches or almost touches the left thumb. Both hands may, as they open, move forward an inch or two.

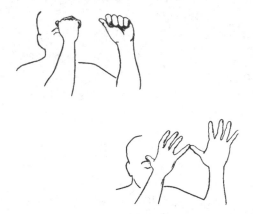

GRANDMOTHER 1 (grănd′ mŭth′ ər), *n.* (Same rationale as for GRANDFATHER 1.) The sign for MOTHER 2 is made: the thumb of the right "5" hand rests on the right cheek or on the right chin bone. The rest of the sign follows that for GRANDFATHER 1.

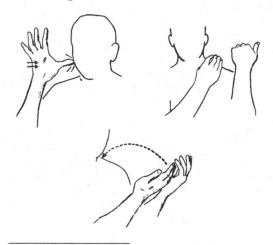

GRANDMOTHER 2, *n.* (A variation of GRAND-MOTHER 1.) The "A" hands are positioned as in GRANDFATHER 2 but with the right thumb on the right cheek. They open in the same manner as in GRANDFATHER 2.

GRANDSON (grănd′ sun), *n.* (The letter "G"; SON.) The "G" is formed with the right hand. The sign for SON is then made: the MALE prefix sign is formed, with the thumb and extended fingers of the right hand brought up to grasp an imaginary cap brim. The right upturned arm then rests on its left counterpart, as if holding a baby.

GRANT 1 (grănt, gränt), *v.*, GRANTED, GRANTING. (A permissive upswinging of the hands, as if giving in.) Both hands, palms facing and fingers pointing away from the body, are held almost a foot apart at chest level. With an upward movement, using their wrists as pivots, the hands sweep up until the fingers point almost straight up. Also ALLOW, LET, LET'S, LET US, MAY 3, PERMISSION 1, PERMIT 1, TOLERATE 1.

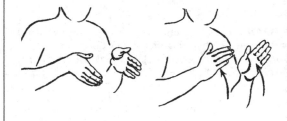

GRANT 2, *v.* The modified "O" hand, little finger edge down, moves forward and down in an arc before the body, as if giving something to someone.

GRAPEFRUIT (grāp′ frōōt), *n.* (The two "G"s.) Both "G" hands, palms facing, make clockwise circles around each other.

GRAPES 1 (grāps), *n. pl.* (A clump of the fruit is outlined.) The curved right fingertips move along the back of the downturned open left hand, from wrist to knuckles, in a series of short, up-down, curved movements, outlining a clump of grapes.

GRAPES 2, *n. pl.* (A variation of GRAPES 1.) The thumb and index fingers of the right "Q" hand execute the same movement as in GRAPES 1.

GRAPH (graf), *n.* (Drawing the lines of a graph.) The right "G" hand traces the imaginary up-down lines of a graph in the air.

GRASP (grăsp, gräsp), *v.,* GRASPED, GRASPING. See GRAB.

GRASS 1 (grăs), *n.* (GREEN; an expanse.) The right "G" hand makes the sign for GREEN: it pivots at the wrist a number of times. As it does so, it swings from left to right.

GRASS 2, *n.* (The letter "G"; growing.) The index and thumb of the right "G" hand is pushed up through the left hand, which forms a cup.

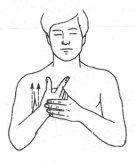

GRASS 3, *n.* (Blades of grass obscuring the view; the smell of new-mown grass.) The open right hand, palm facing the signer, moves up in front of the lips and nose. The movement is usually repeated.

GRASSHOPPER (gras′ hop′ ər), *n.* (The jumping.) The right index and middle fingers execute a series of jumping motions as they move up the downturned left arm.

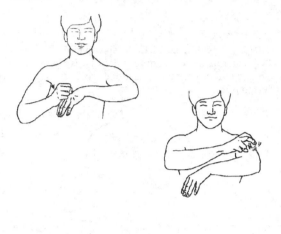

GRATEFUL (grāt′ fəl), *adj.* (Expressions from the heart and mouth.) The open right hand is placed against the mouth, the open left hand against the heart. Both move forward, away from the body, simultaneously.

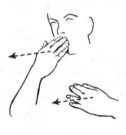

GRATIFY 1 (grăt′ ə fī′), *v.,* -FIED, -FYING. (A pleasurable feeling on the heart.) The open right hand is circled on the chest over the heart. Also APPRECIATE, ENJOY, ENJOYMENT, LIKE 3, PLEASE, PLEASURE, WILLING 2.

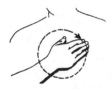

GRATIFY 2, *v.* (The inner feelings settle down.) Both "B" hands (or "5" hands, fingers together) are placed palms down against the chest, the right above the left. Both move down simultaneously a few inches.

Also CONTENT, CONTENTED, SATISFACTION, SATISFIED, SATISFY 1.

GRAVE 1 (grāv), *n.* (The mound of a grave.) The downturned open hands, slightly cupped, are held side by side. They describe an arc as they are drawn in toward the body. Also BURY, CEMETERY.

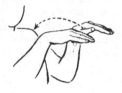

GRAVE 2, *adj.* (Tasting something, finding it unacceptable, and turning it down.) The tips of the right "B" hand are placed at the lips, and then the hand is thrown down. Also BAD 1, NAUGHTY, WICKED.

GRAVE 3, *adj.* (The facial features drop.) Both "5" hands, palms facing the eyes and fingers slightly curved, drop simultaneously to a level with the mouth. The head drops slightly as the hands move down, and an expression of sadness is assumed. Also DEJECTED, DEPRESSED, GLOOM, GLOOMY, GRIEF 1, MELANCHOLY, MOURNFUL, SAD, SORROWFUL 1.

GRAVITY (grav′ ə te), *n.* (The letter "G"; dropping down.) The right "G" hand, positioned under the downturned left palm, drops straight down.

GRAVY (grā′ vĭ), *n.* (The drippings from a fleshy, *i.e.*, animal, substance. Used, however, to indicate both organic and inorganic types of oil.) The right thumb and middle finger grasp the fleshy part of the open left hand. The right hand moves straight down. This is repeated once or twice. Also FAT 3, FATTY, GREASE, GREASY, OIL 2, OILY.

GRAY 1 (grā) (*rare*), *adj.* (Mixing of colors, in this case black and white, to produce the necessary shade.) The fingertips of the open right hand describe a continuous clockwise circle in the upturned left palm.

GRAY 2 (*rare*), *adj.* (Rationale unknown.) The right "R" hand, held with palm toward the face, swings around to the palm-out position.

GRAY 3 (*loc.*), *adj.* (Rationale unknown.) The right "O" hand traces an S curve in the air as it moves down before the body.

GRAY 4, *adj.* (Intermingling of colors, in this case black and white.) The open "5" hands, fingers pointing to one another and palms facing the body, alternately swing in toward and out from the body. Each time they do so, the fingers of one hand pass through the spaces between the fingers of the other.

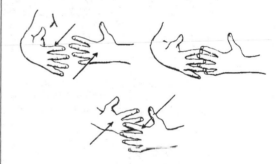

GRAY 5, *adj.* (The letter "G"; modified sign for BLACK.) The right "G" hand, fingers pointing left, moves across the brow from left to right.

GREASE (*n.* grēs; *v.* grēs, grēz), *n., v.,* GREASED, GREASING. (The drippings from a fleshy, *i.e.*, animal, substance. Used, however, to indicate both organic and inorganic types of oil.) The right thumb and middle finger grasp the fleshy part of the open left hand. The right hand moves straight down. This is repeated once or twice. Also FAT 3, FATTY, GRAVY, GREASY, OIL 2, OILY.

GREASY (grē′ sĭ, -zĭ), *adj.* See GREASE.

GREAT 1 (grāt), *adj.* (A delineation of something big, modified by the letter "L," which stands for LARGE.) Both "L" hands, palms facing out, are placed before the face and separate rather widely. Also BIG 1, ENORMOUS, HUGE, IMMENSE, LARGE.

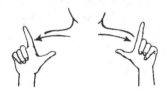

GREAT 2, *adj.* (A large amount.) The "5" hands face each other, fingers curved and touching. They move apart rather quickly. Also EXPAND, INFINITE, LOT, MUCH.

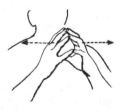

GREAT 3, *adj.* (The hands gesture toward the heavens.) The "5" hands, palms out and arms raised rather high, are positioned somewhat above the line of vision. The arms move abruptly forward and up once or twice. An expression of pleasure or surprise is usually assumed. Also EXCELLENT, GRAND 1, MARVEL, MARVELOUS, MIRACLE, O!, SPLENDID 1, SWELL 1, WONDER 2, WONDERFUL 1.

GREAT 4, *adj., interj.* (The feelings are titillated.) With the thumb resting on the upper part of the chest, the fingers are wiggled back and forth. Also ELEGANT, FINE 1, GRAND 2, SPLENDID 2, SWELL 2, WONDERFUL 2.

GREAT BRITAIN (brĭt ən), *n.* (The English are supposed to be handshakers.) The right hand grasps and shakes the left. Also BRITAIN, BRITISH, ENGLAND, ENGLISH.

GREAT GRANDFATHER (grāt′ grănd′ fä′ thər), *n.* (A male holder of a baby, two predecessors removed.) The sign for GRANDFATHER 1, *q.v.,* is made, except that the hands swing over the left shoulder in two distinct steps.

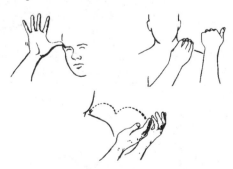

GREAT GRANDMOTHER (grāt′ grănd′ mŭth′ ər), *n.* (Same rationale as for GREAT GRANDFATHER.) The sign for GRANDMOTHER 1, *q.v.,* is made, followed by the same end sign as employed for GREAT GRANDFATHER.

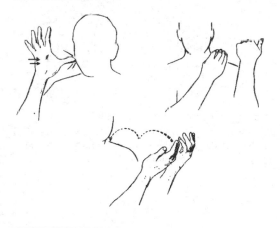

GREAT GRANDPARENTS, *n.* See GREAT GRAND-FATHER.

GREEDY 1 (grē′ dĭ), *adj.* (Pulling things toward one-self.) Both prone open or "V" hands are held in front of the body with fingers bent. The hands are then drawn quickly and forcefully inward, as if raking things toward oneself. Also SELFISH 1, STINGY 1, TIGHTWAD 1.

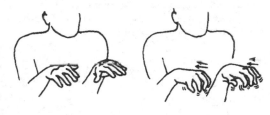

GREEDY 2, *adj.* (Scratching the palm in greed.) The right fingers scratch the upturned left palm several times. A frowning expression is often used. Also AVARICIOUS, SELFISH 2, STINGY 2, TIGHTWAD 2.

GREEDY 3, *adj.* (Scratching in greed.) The down-turned "3" hands, held side by side, make a scratching

motion as they move in toward the body. Also SELFISH 3, STINGY 3.

GREY (grā), *adj.* See GRAY.

GRIEF 1 (grēf), *n.* (The facial features drop.) Both "5" hands, palms facing the eyes and fingers slightly curved, drop simultaneously to a level with the mouth. The head drops slightly as the hands move down, and an expression of sadness is assumed. Also DEJECTED, DEPRESSED, GLOOM, GLOOMY, GRAVE 3, MELANCHOLY, MOURNFUL, SAD, SORROWFUL 1.

GRIEF 2, *n.* (Wringing the heart.) Both clenched hands, held at the heart with knuckles touching, go through back-and-forth wringing motions. A sad expression is usually assumed. Also GRIEVE, MOURN.

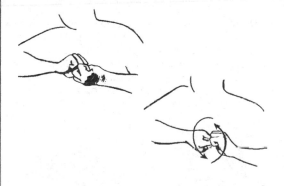

GRIEVE (grēv), *v.,* GRIEVED, GRIEVING. See GRIEF 2.

GRIMACE (grĭ mās′, grĭ′ məs), *n., v.,* -MACED, -MACING. (The facial features are distorted.) The "X" hands are moved alternately up and down in front of the face, whose features are distorted with a pronounced frown. Also HOMELY 1, MAKE A FACE, UGLINESS 1, UGLY 1.

GROTESQUE (grō tĕsk′), *adj.* (Something that distorts the vision.) The "C" hand describes a small arc in front of the face. Also CURIOUS 2, ODD, PECULIAR, QUEER 1, STRANGE 1, WEIRD.

GROUND (ground), *n.* (Fingering the soil.) Both hands, held upright before the body, finger imaginary pinches of soil. Also DIRT, EARTH 2, SOIL 1.

GROUP 1 (gro͞op), *n.* (A grouping together.) Both "C" hands, palms facing, are held a few inches apart at chest height. They are swung around in unison so that the palms now face the body. Also ASSOCIATION, AUDIENCE 1, CASTE, CIRCLE 2, CLASS, CLASSED 1, CLUB, COMPANY, FAMILY 2, GANG, JOIN 2, ORGANIZATION 1.

GROUP 2, *n.* (The letter "G.") The sign for GROUP 1 is made, using the "G" hands.

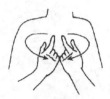

GROVEL (gruv′ əl), *v.,* GROVELED, GROVELING. (Walk on knees.) The knuckles of the right index and middle fingers walk on the upturned left palm.

GROW (grō), *v.,* GREW, GROWN, GROWING. (Flowers or plants emerge from the ground.) The right fingers, pointing up, emerge from the closed left hand, and they spread open as they do. Also BLOOM, DEVELOP 1, GROWN, MATURE, PLANT 1, RAISE 3, REAR 2, SPRING 1.

GROWL 1 (groul), *n., v.,* -ED, -ING. (Sound coming out of the throat.) The right claw hand, palm facing the signer, is positioned at the throat. The fingers wriggle as the hand moves forward from the throat. The signer assumes a threatening countenance, baring the teeth.

GROWL 2, *n., v.* (The threatening face and bared teeth.) With both claw hands facing forward, the signer assumes a threatening countenance and bares the teeth.

GROWN (grōn), *adj.* See GROW.

GROW UP TOGETHER (*phrase*) (Rising together.) Both downturned hands rise together.

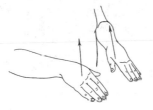

GUARANTEE 1 (găr′ ən tē′), *n., v.,* -TEED, -TEEING. (The arm is raised.) The right index finger is placed at the lips. The right arm is then raised, palm out and elbow resting on the back of the left hand. Also LOYAL, OATH, PLEDGE, PROMISE 1, SWEAR 1, SWORN, TAKE OATH, VOW.

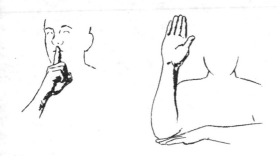

GUARANTEE 2 (*colloq.*), *n., v.* (The natural sign.) The right hand grasps an imaginary rubber stamp and

presses it against the upturned left palm. Also SEAL 1, STAMP 2.

GUARD (gärd), *v.,* GUARDED, GUARDING. (Hold down firmly; cover and strengthen.) The "S" hands, down-turned, are held side by side in front of the body, the arms almost horizontal and the left hand in front of the right. Both arms move a short distance forward and slightly downward. Also DEFEND, DEFENSE, FORTIFY, PROTECT, PROTECTION, SHIELD 1.

GUATEMALA (gwä′ tə mä′ lä), *n.* The open right hand rubs the stomach in a counterclockwise direction. A native sign.

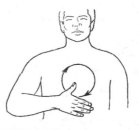

GUESS 1 (gĕs), *n., v.,* GUESSED, GUESSING. (A thought comes into view.) The index finger of the right "D" hand is placed at midforehead, pointing straight up. The slightly cupped right hand, palm facing left, then swings around so that the palm is toward the face.

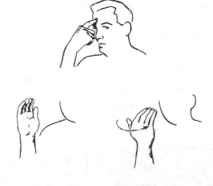

GUESS 2, *n., v.* (A thought is grasped.) The right fingertip touches the forehead; then the right hand makes a quick grasping movement in front of the head, ending in the "S" position.

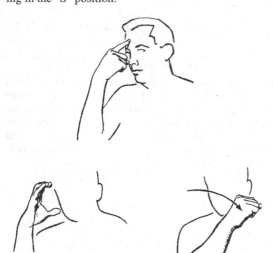

GUESS 3 (*rare*), *n., v.* (A typical gesture of hesitation or uncertainty.) The index fingertip of the right "V" hand is placed against the edge of the upper teeth. A look of slight puzzlement is sometimes assumed.

GUESS 4, *v.* (Weighing one thing against another.) The upturned open hands move alternately up and down. Also MAY 1, MAYBE, MIGHT 2, PERHAPS, POSSIBILITY, POSSIBLY, PROBABLE, PROBABLY, SUPPOSE.

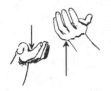

GUIDE (gīd), *n., v.,* GUIDED, GUIDING. (One hand leads the other.) The right hand grasps the tips of the left

fingers and pulls the left hand forward. Also CONDUCT 2, LEAD 1.

GUILTY 1 (gĭl′ tĭ), *adj.* (The blame is firmly placed.) The right "A" hand, thumb pointing up, is brought down firmly against the back of the left hand, held palm down; the right thumb is then directed toward the person or object to blame. When personal blame is acknowledged, the thumb is brought in to the chest. Also ACCUSE 1, BLAME, FAULT 1.

GUILTY 2, *adj.* (The "G" hand; a guilty heart.) The index finger edge of the right "G" hand taps the chest over the heart.

GUINEA PIG, *n.* (The letter "G"; PIG.) The right "G" hand brushes the tip of the nose twice, then the sign for PIG is made: the downturned right prone hand is placed under the chin, fingers pointing forward. The hand swings alternately up and down.

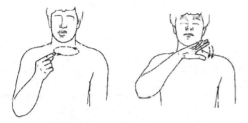

GUM (gŭm), *n.* (The chewing.) The side of the right "X" finger moves up and down on the right cheek. The mouth is held open, and may engage in a chewing motion, keeping time with the right "X" finger. Also RUBBER 1.

GYM 1 (jǐm), *n.* (Typical calisthenic exercises.) The downturned "S" hands move back and forth simultaneously and then up and down simultaneously. Also EXERCISE 1.

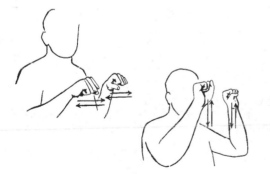

GYM 2, *n.* (Jumping rope.) The signer mimes jumping rope, with the hands held closely to the respective shoulders.

GYMNASTICS (jim nas' tiks), *n.* (The body movement.) The right index and middle fingers rest in the upturned left palm. The right hand leaves the left, assuming a palm-up position. The index and middle fingers swing in the air in a clockwise circle, and then the two fingers land again in the left palm. Also ACROBAT.

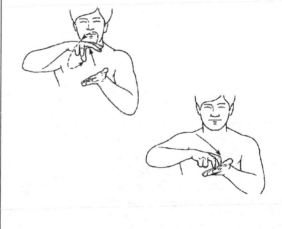

H

HABIT (hăb′ ĭt), *n.* (Bound down to custom or habit.) Both "S" hands, palms down, are crossed and brought down in unison before the chest. Also ACCUSTOM, BOUND, CUSTOM, LOCKED, PRACTICE 3.

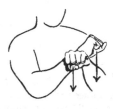

HAIFA (hī′ fə), *n.* (Apparently something to do with an army camp or base located there.) The signer executes a salute. A native sign.

HAIR (hâr), *n.* (The natural sign.) A lock of hair is grasped by the right index finger and thumb.

HAIRCUT (hâr′ kut), *n.* (The scissors at both sides of the head.) The two "V" hands, palms facing the sides of the head, open and close repeatedly as the hands move alternately back and forth. Also BARBER.

HAIRDRESSER (hâr′ drĕs′ ər), *n.* (Working on the hair.) The "S" hands, palms out, are positioned above the head. They move alternately toward and away from the head, as if pulling locks of hair. This sign is followed by the sign for INDIVIDUAL: both open hands, palms facing each other, move down the sides of the body, tracing its outline to the hips. Also BEAUTY PARLOR.

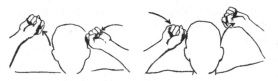

HAIR DRYER (hâr′ drī′ ər), *n.* (Holding the machine above the head.) The right "L" hand, thumb pointing up, aims the index finger at the hair as the hand moves at random over the head.

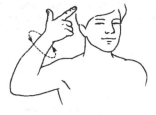

HAITI (hā′ tē), *n.* The right "H" hand moves repeatedly across the line of vision of the right eye. A native sign.

HALE (hāl), *adj.* (Strength emanating from the body.) Both "5" hands are placed palms against the chest. They move out and away forcefully, closing and assuming the "S" position, Also BRAVE, BRAVERY, COURAGE,

300

COURAGEOUS, FORTITUDE, HEALTH, HEALTHY, MIGHTY 2, STRENGTH, STRONG 2, WELL 2.

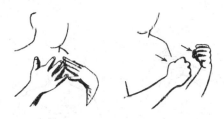

HALF 1 (hăf), *n., adj.* (The fraction ½.) Using the same hand for each sign, first make the "1" sign, then drop the hand straight down a bit and make the "2" sign.

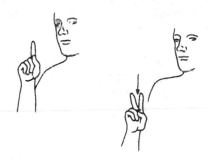

HALF 2, *adj.* (Half of the finger is indicated.) The right index finger is drawn across the midpoint of the left index finger, moving toward the body.

HALL 1 (hôl), *n.* (The movement.) Both hands, palms facing and fingers together and extended straight out, move in unison away from the body, in a straight or winding manner. Also CORRIDOR, HALLWAY, MANNER 2, METHOD, OPPORTUNITY 3, PATH, ROAD, STREET, TRAIL, WAY 1.

HALL 2, *n.* (The "H" and the shape.) Both upright "H" hands, actually the "U," palms facing each other, move forward in unison, tracing the outline of the walls.

HALLOWED 1 (hăl′ ōd, hăl′ ō ĭd), *adj.* (Made holy.) The sign for MAKE is made: the right "S" hand, palm facing left, is placed on top of its left counterpart, whose palm faces right. The hands are twisted back and forth, striking each other slightly after each twist. This is followed by the sign for HOLY: the right "H" hand makes a clockwise circular movement and is then opened and wiped across the open left palm.

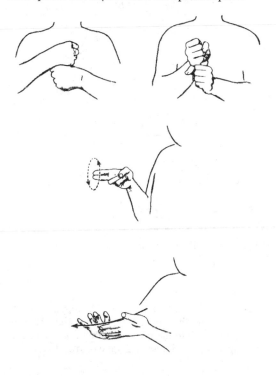

HALLOWED 2, *adj.* (The letter "H"; a gesture of respect.) The right "H" hand, palm facing left, swings down in an arc from its initial position in front of the forehead. The head bows slightly during this movement of the hand. Also HONOR 1, HONORARY.

HALLOWEEN (hal′ ə wēn′, -ō ēn′, hol′), *n.* (The mask.) Both "C" hands are placed at the eyes, palms facing each other. The hands open slightly and move back from the eyes, outlining a mask.

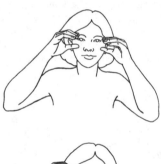

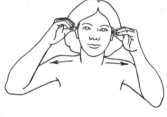

HALLWAY (hôl′ wā′), *n.* See HALL.

HALT (hôlt), *v.,* HALTED, HALTING. (A stopping or cutting short.) The little finger edge of the right hand is thrust abruptly into the upturned left palm, indicating a cutting short. Also ARREST 2, CEASE, STOP.

HAMBURGER 1 (hăm′ bûr′ gər), *n.* (Making patties.) Both open hands go through the motions of forming patties.

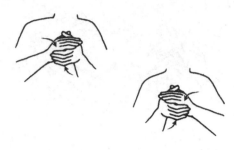

HAMBURGER 2, *n.* (Chopping meat.) The open hands face each other, little finger edges down. In this position both hands move up and down alternately, imitating chopping blades.

HAMMER (hăm′ ər), *n., v.,* -MERED, -MERING. (The natural sign.) The right hand, grasping an imaginary hammer, swings down toward the left fist, which represents the object being hammered. The right hand does not touch the left, however. The action is usually repeated.

HAMSTER (ham′ stər), *n.* (The letter "H"; a rodent or rat.) The right "H" fingers brush repeatedly across the tip of the nose.

HAND 1 (hănd), *n*. (The natural sign.) The right index finger touches the back of the prone left hand.

HAND 2, *n*. (The natural sign.) The prone right hand is drawn over the back of the prone left hand. For the plural, the action is repeated with the hands switched. The little finger edge of the right hand may instead be drawn across the back of the left wrist, as if cutting off the left hand; for the plural the action is repeated with the hands switched.

HANDCUFF (hand' kuf), *n.*, *v.*, -CUFFED, -CUFFING. (Placing handcuffs on the wrists.) The right index and thumb, forming a "C," close over the left wrist. The left hand then does the same to the right.

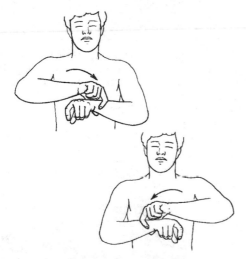

HANDICAP (han' dē kap'), *n.*, *v.*, -CAPPED, -CAPPING. (The letters.) The signer fingerspells "H-C".

HANDKERCHIEF (hăng' kər chĭf, -chēf'), *n*. (Wiping the nose.) The signer makes the motions of wiping the nose several times with an imaginary handkerchief. This is the common cold. Also COLD 2.

HANG 1 (hăng), *v.*, HUNG, HANGED, HANGING. (The natural sign.) The curved right index finger hangs on the extended left index finger. Also SUSPEND 1.

HANG 2, *v*. (Hanging by the throat.) The thumb of the "Y" hand is placed at the right side of the neck, and the head hangs toward the left, as if it were caught in a noose. Also SCAFFOLD.

HANG 3, *v*. (The hanger attached to the closet pole.) The right curved index finger is draped over the horizontal left index finger. The sign may be repeated a number of times, or the right index finger may slide along the left toward the tip.

HANGAR (hang′ ər), *n.* (A shelter for airplanes.) The downturned right hand, with thumb plus index and little fingers extended, moves under a curved shelter formed by the downturned left cupped hand.

HANGER 1 (hang′ ər), *n.* (The hangers.) The right curved index finger is repeatedly hung over the extended left index finger, starting at the lower knuckle and moving successively to the fingertip. Also CLOSET 2.

HANGER 2, *n, loc.* (Clothing hanging from the hanger.) The right "Y" hand, palm facing the body, is positioned under the chin.

HANGER 3, *n., loc.* (The curved hook.) The knuckle of the curved right index finger is placed beneath the chin.

HAPPEN 1 (hăp′ ən), *v.,* -ENED, -ENING. (A befalling.) Both "D" hands, index fingers pointing away from the body, are simultaneously pivoted over so that the palms face down. Also ACCIDENT, BEFALL, CHANCE, COINCIDE 1, COINCIDENCE, EVENT, INCIDENT, OCCUR, OPPORTUNITY 4.

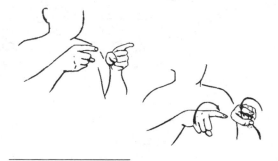

HAPPEN 2, *v.* The same sign as for HAPPEN 1, but the "H" hands are used.

HAPPY (hăp′ ĭ), *adj.* (The heart is stirred; the spirits bubble up.) The open right hand, palm facing the body, strikes the heart repeatedly, moving up and off the heart after each strike. Also DELIGHT, GAIETY 1, GAY, GLAD, HAPPINESS, JOY, MERRY.

HARD 1 (härd), *adj.* (The knuckles are rubbed to indicate a condition of being worn down.) The knuckles of the curved index and middle fingers of both hands are rubbed up and down against each other. Instead of the up-down rubbing, they may rub against each other in an alternate clockwise/counterclockwise manner. Also DIFFICULT 1, DIFFICULTY, HARDSHIP, POVERTY 2, PROBLEM 2.

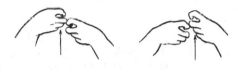

HARD 2, *adj.* (Striking a hard object.) The curved index and middle fingers of the right hand, whose palm faces the body or the left, are brought down sharply against the back of the downturned left "S" hand. Also DIFFICULT 2, SOLID.

HARD OF HEARING, *adj. phrase.* (The "H" is indicated twice.) The right "H" hand drops down an inch or so, rises, moves in a short arc to the right, and drops down an inch or so again.

HARDSHIP (härd′ shĭp), *n.* See HARD 1.

HARM 1 (härm), *n.* (A stabbing pain.) The "D" hands, index fingers pointing to each other, are rotated in elliptical fashion before the chest—simultaneously but in opposite directions. Also ACHE, HURT 1, INJURE 1, INJURY, MAR 1, OFFEND, OFFENSE, PAIN, SIN, WOUND.

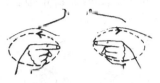

HARM 2 (härm), *v.*, HARMED, HARMING. (Striking down against.) Both "A" or "X" hands are held before the chest, the right above the left. The right hand strikes down and out, hitting the left thumb and knuckles with force. Also BACKBITE, BASE 3, CRUEL 1, HURT 2, MAR 2, MEAN 1, SPOIL.

HARMONICA (här mon′ i kə), *n.* (The act of playing a harmonica.) The signer, one hand clasped over the other and both hands held with thumb edges against the mouth, mimes playing a harmonica, with the clasped hands opening and closing rhythmically and the head bobbing slightly to keep tune.

HARVEST 1 (här′ vĭst), *n., v.*, -VESTED, -VESTING. (Cutting the stalks.) The left hand holds an imaginary bunch of stalks, and the right hand, holding an imaginary sickle, sweeps under the left as if cutting the stalks. Also REAP 1.

HARVEST 2, *v.* (Gathering in the harvest.) The right open hand sweeps across the upturned left palm and closes into the "A" position, as if gathering up some stalks. Also REAP 2.

HARVEST 3, *v.* (The cutting.) The left hand grasps the heads of imaginary wheat stalks. The upturned right hand, imitating a sickle blade, then swings in to cut the stalks. Also REAP 3.

HASIDIC (has' i dik), *adj.* (The *pais,* or earlocks, worn by ultra-Orthodox Jewish males.) The signer twirls an imaginary curl hanging down on the side of the head. Also ORTHODOX 2.

HASTE (hāst), *n.* (Letter "H"; quick movements.) The "H" hands, palms facing each other and held about six inches apart, shake alternately up and down. One hand alone may be used. Also HURRY, HUSTLE.

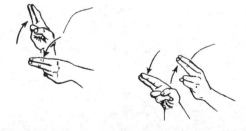

HAT (hăt), *n.* (The natural sign.) The right hand pats the head.

HATCH (hach), *v.,* HATCHED, HATCHING. (Cracking the shell.) The right "H" hand is brought down on the left "H" hand, and then both hands are pivoted down and slightly apart. Also EGG.

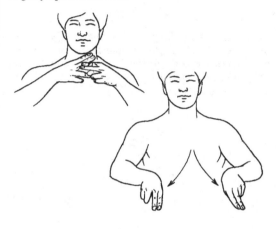

HATCHET (hach' it), *n.* (The chopping.) The left arm is held straight up from the bent elbow. The little finger edge of the upturned right hand (or "H" hand) then makes a series of chopping movements against the left elbow. Also AX.

HATE 1 (hāt), *n., v.,* HATED, HATING. (To push away and recoil from; avoid.) The two open hands, palms facing left, are pushed deliberately to the left, as if pushing something away. An expression of disdain or disgust is worn. Also ABHOR, AVOID 2, DESPISE 1, DETEST 1, LOATHE.

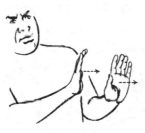

HATE 2, *v., n.* (The finger is flicked to indicate something petty, small, i.e., to be scorned as inconsequential.) The right index finger and thumb are used to press the lips down into an expression of contempt. The right thumb is then flicked out from the closed hand. The modern version of this sign omits pressing down of the lips and includes only the flicking out of the middle finger of one or both hands. Also CONTEMPT 2, DESPISE 2, DETEST 2, DISLIKE, SCORN 2.

HAVE 1 (hăv), *v.,* HAS, HAD, HAVING. (The act of bringing something over to oneself.) The right-angle hands, palms facing and thumbs pointing up, are swept toward the body until the fingertips come to rest against the middle of the chest. Also POSSESS 2.

HAVE 2, *v.* (Bring to an end.) The left hand, fingers together and pointing forward, is held palm facing right. The right, palm down, fingers also together, moves along the top of the left, goes over the tip of the left index finger, and drops straight down, indicating a cutting off or a finishing. This sign is also used to indicate the past tense of a verb, in the sense of accomplishing an action or state of being. Also ACCOMPLISH 2, ACHIEVE 2, COMPLETE 1, CONCLUDE, DONE 1, END 4, EXPIRE 1, FINISH 1, TERMINATE

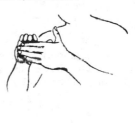

HAVE 3, *v.* (A modification of HAVE 1.) The hands are crossed over each other as they rest on the chest. Also POSSESS 1.

HAVE TO, *v. phrase.* (Being pinned down.) The right hand, in the "X" position, palm down, moves forcefully up and down once or twice. An expression of determination is frequently assumed. Also IMPERATIVE, MUST, NECESSARY 1, NECESSITY, NEED 1, OUGHT TO, SHOULD, VITAL 2.

HAWAII 1 (hə wī′ ē, -wä′ yə), *n.* (The dancing.) The hands and arms wave in the traditional undulating manner of the Hawaiian dance. Also HAWAIIAN.

HAWAII 2, *n.* ("H"; beautiful.) The right "H" hand makes a counterclockwise circle around the face. This movement is from the sign for BEAUTIFUL.

HAY 1 (hā) (*rare*), *n.* (The stalks rise before the face.) The index finger of the right "4" hand, whose palm faces left, rests on the nose. The hand moves straight up.

HAY 2, *n.* (Blades of grass obscuring the view; the smell of newly mown hay.) The open right hand, palm facing the signer, moves up in front of the lips and nose. The movement is usually repeated. Also GRASS.

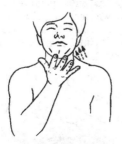

HAYLOFT (ha′ lôft), *n.* (Stuffing the hay.) The sign for HAY, above, is made, followed by the right hand stuffing imaginary hay into a cup formed by the left hand.

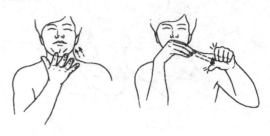

HAYSTACK (hā′ stak), *n.* (A pile of hay or grass.) The sign for HAY, above, is made. The downturned cupped hands, held together, then move down and apart, describing a mound or pile.

HE (hē), *pron.* (Pointing at a male.) The MALE prefix sign is made: the right hand grasps an imaginary cap brim. The right index finger then points at an imaginary male. If in context the gender is clear, the prefix sign is usually omitted. Also HIM.

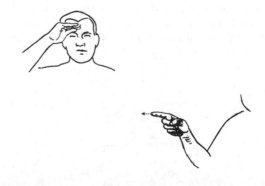

HEAD (hĕd), *n.* (The head is indicated.) The tips of the fingers of the right right-angle hand are placed at the right temple and then move down in an arc to the right jaw.

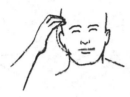

HEADACHE (hĕd' āk'), *n.* (A stabbing pain in the head.) The index fingers, pointing to each other, move back and forth on the forehead.

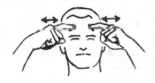

HEADLIGHTS (hed' līts'), *n.* (The rays shining forward.) Both hands, palms out and fingers touching respective thumbs, jump forward, opening into the "5" position.

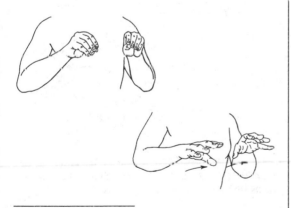

HEADLINE (hed' līn), *n.* (A banner across a newspaper.) The right curved index and thumb sweep across an imaginary newspaper page, from left to right.

HEALTH (hĕlth), *n.* (Strength emanating from the body.) Both "5" hands are placed palms against the chest. They move out and away forcefully, closing and assuming the "S" position. Also BRAVE, BRAVERY, COURAGE, COURAGEOUS, FORTITUDE, HALE, HEALTHY, MIGHTY 2, STRENGTH, STRONG 2, WELL 2.

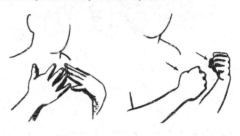

HEALTHY (hĕl' thǐ), *adj.* See HEALTH.

HEAR (hǐr), *v.,* HEARD (hûrd), HEARING. (Cupping the hand at the ear.) The right hand is placed, usually slightly cupped, behind the right ear. Also HARK, HEARKEN, LISTEN.

HEARING (hǐr' ǐng), *n., adj.* (Words tumbling from the mouth, indicating the old association of being able to hear with being able to speak.) The right index finger, pointing left, describes a continuous small circle in front of the mouth. Also BID 3, DISCOURSE, MAINTAIN 2, MENTION, REMARK, SAID, SAY, SPEAK, SPEECH 1, STATE, STATEMENT, TALK 1, TELL, VERBAL 1.

HEARING AID 1, *n.* (Behind the ear.) The right curved index finger is hooked onto the right ear, fingertip facing either forward or backward.

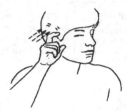

HEARING AID 2, *n.* (The wire leading down from the hearing aid.) The thumb and index finger trace an imaginary wire leading down from the ear to the chest.

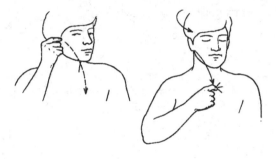

HEART 1 (härt), *n.* (The natural sign.) The index fingers trace a heart at the appropriate spot on the chest.

HEART 2, *n.* (The natural sign.) The middle fingers are used to trace a heart as in HEART 1.

HEART ATTACK (ə tăk′), *n. phrase.* (The heart is struck.) The sign for HEART 1 is made. Then the closed right fist strikes the open left palm, which faces right.

HEARTBEAT 1 (härt′ bēt′), *n.* (The opening and closing of a heart valve.) The middle finger of the right "5" hand touches the heart. The open right hand, fingers together, then moves rhythmically up and down on the thumb edge of the left "O" hand, in imitation of a valve alternately releasing and blocking the passage of blood in the heart.

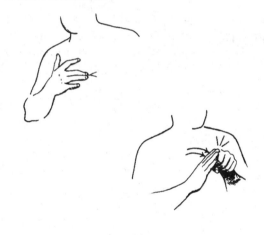

HEARTBEAT 2, *n.* (The natural sign.) The right fist beats rhythmically against the heart.

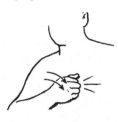

HEARTBURN (härt′ bûrn′), *n.* (Fire in the chest.) Both open hands rest facing the chest. The fingers wriggle as the hands move slowly up. The signer looks distressed.

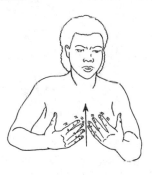

HEAT 1 (hēt), *n., v.,* HEATED, HEATING. (The warmth of the breath is indicated.) The upturned cupped right hand is placed at the slightly open mouth. It moves up and away from the mouth, opening into the upturned "5" position, with fingers somewhat curved. Also WARM 1.

HEAT 2, *v.* (The action of flames under a pot or pan.) The upturned left hand is the pot. The fingers of the upturned right hand, held underneath the left hand, wiggle in imitation of the action of flames.

HEAVEN (hĕv' ən), *n.* (Entering heaven through a break in the clouds.) Both open hands, fingers straight and pointing up, move upward in an arc on either side of the head. Just before they touch above the head, the right hand, palm down, sweeps under the left and moves up, its palm now facing out. Also SKY 1.

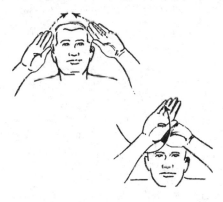

HEAVY (hĕv' ĭ), *adj.* (The hands drop under a weight.) The upturned "5" hands, held before the chest, suddenly drop a short distance. Also CRUSHING, WEIGHTY.

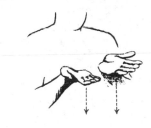

HEBREW (hē' brōō), *n., adj.* (The beard of the old Jewish patriarchs.) The fingers and thumb of each hand are placed at the chin and stroke an imaginary beard. Also ISRAELITE, JEW, JEWISH.

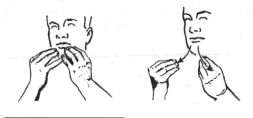

HEIGHT 1 (hīt), *n.* (The height is indicated.) The index finger of the right "D" hand moves straight up against the palm of the left "5" hand. Also TALL 1.

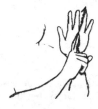

HEIGHT 2, *n.* (The height is indicated.) The right right-angle hand, palm facing the left, is held at the height the signer wishes to indicate. Also BIG 2, HIGH 3, TALL 2.

HELICOPTER (hel′ ə kop′ tər), *n.* (The rotor.) The downturned left "5" hand is placed on the upturned right index and trembles or quivers as the right index pushes it up.

HELL 1 (hĕl), *n.* (The devil; pointing down.) The sign for DEVIL is made: with the thumbs resting on the temples, the index and middle fingers of both hands open and close repeatedly. The right index finger, pointing down, then moves straight down a few inches. The pointing may be omitted. Also DEMON, DEVIL, DEVILMENT, SATAN.

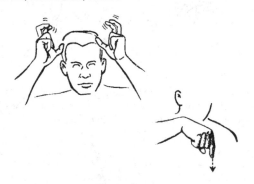

HELL 2, *n.* (The leaping of flames.) The "5" hands are held with palms facing the body. They move up

and down alternately while the fingers wiggle. Also BURN, FIRE 1, FLAME.

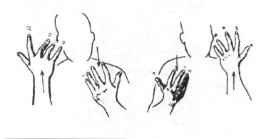

HELL 3, *n.* (The letter "H.") The right "H" hand, palm facing the body, moves sharply in an arc to the right.

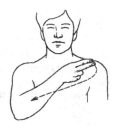

HELLO 1 (hĕ lō′), *interj., n.* (Words extended politely from the mouth.) The fingertips of the right "5" hand are placed at the mouth. The hand moves away from the mouth to a palm-up position before the body. The signer meanwhile usually nods smilingly. Also FAREWELL 1, GOODBYE 1, THANKS, THANK YOU, YOU'RE WELCOME 1.

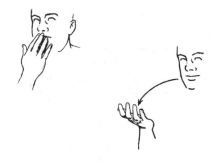

HELLO 2, *interj.* (A wave of the hand.) The right open hand waves back and forth several times. Also FAREWELL 2, GOODBYE 2, SO LONG.

HELP (hĕlp), *n., v.,* HELPED, HELPING. (Helping up; supporting.) The left "S" hand, thumb side up, rests in the open right palm. In this position the left hand is pushed up a short distance by the right. Also AID, ASSIST, ASSISTANCE, BENEFIT 1, BOOST, GIVE ASSISTANCE.

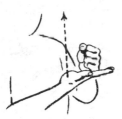

HEN 1 (hĕn), *n.* (The bill and the scratching.) The right index finger and thumb open and close as they are held pointing out from the mouth. (This is the root sign for any kind of bird.) The right "X" finger then scratches against the upturned left palm, as if scratching for food. The scratching is sometimes omitted. Also CHICKEN, FOWL.

HEN 2, *n.* (The flapping wings.) Both downturned "S" hands are placed with the elbows against the sides of the body. They flap up and down, imitating the wings.

HENPECK (hĕn′ pĕk′), *v.,* -PECKED, -PECKING (The hen's beak pecks.) The index finger and thumb of the right hand, held together, are brought against the index finger of the left "D" hand a number of times. Also NAG, PECK, PICK ON.

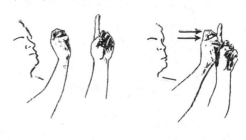

HER 1 (hûr), *pron.* (Pointing at a female.) The FEMALE prefix sign is made: the right "A" hand's thumb moves down along the line of the right jaw, from ear almost to chin. The right index finger then points at an imaginary female. If in context the gender is clear, the prefix sign is usually omitted. Also SHE. For the possessive sense of this pronoun, see HERS.

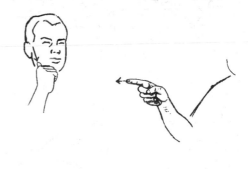

HER 2, *pron.* (honorific) (The shape or presence of the person in question.) The upturned open hand, fingers pointing toward the female person in question, moves down a few inches. Roughly equivalent to the English gloss "that's her, in person."

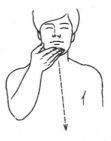

HERE (hĭr), *adv.* The open "5" hands, palms up and fingers slightly curved, move back and forth in front of the body, the right hand to the right and the left hand to the left. Also DIRECTION 2, WHERE 2.

HERESY (hĕr′ ə sĭ), *n.* (False faith.) The sign for FALSE 2 is made: the index finger of the right "D" hand, pointing to the left, moves along the lips from right to left. This is followed by the sign for FAITH: the "S" hands grasp and plant an imaginary flagpole in the ground.

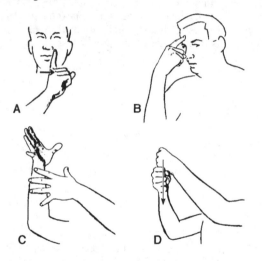

A

B

C

D

HERETIC (hĕr′ ə tĭk), *n.* (False believer.) The sign for FALSE 2, as in HERESY, is made. This is followed by the sign for BELIEVE: the index finger touches the middle of the forehead, and then both hands are clasped together. This is followed by the sign for INDIVIDUAL: both open hands, palms facing each other, move down the sides of the body, tracing its outline to the hips.

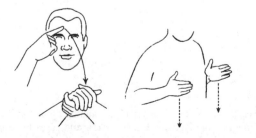

HERITAGE (hĕr′ ə tĭj), *n.* (The "H" hands; rolling down from the past into the present.) The "H" hands, palms down, are positioned over the shoulder, one atop the other but not touching. They roll down over each other as they move down and forward. See also GENERATION.

HERMIT (hûr′ mĭt) (*colloq.*), *n.* (A lone person with himself.) The "I" hands, palms facing the body, touch repeatedly along their little finger edges.

HERMIT CRAB, *n.* (The shape and function.) The downturned bent left "V" fingers creep forward as they pull the right hand (the shell) along.

HEROIN (her′ ō in), *n.* (Jabbing in the needle.) The right fist grasps an imaginary needle and jabs it into the crook of the left elbow.

HERS (hûrz), *pron.* (Belonging to a female.) The FEMALE prefix sign is made. The open right hand, palm facing out, then moves straight forward a few inches. If in context the gender is clear, the prefix sign is usually omitted.

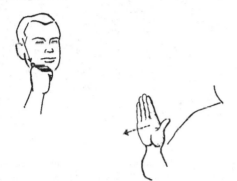

HERSELF (hər sĕlf'), *pron.* (The thumb indicates an individual who is stressed above others.) The FEMALE prefix sign is made. The right "A" hand, thumb upturned, then moves forward an inch or two, either once or twice. If in context the gender is clear, the prefix sign is usually omitted.

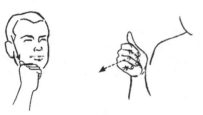

HESITATE (hĕz' ə tāt'), *v.,* -TATED, -TATING. (A faltering gesture.) The right "D" hand, palm facing left, moves forward in steps, an inch or so at a time. Each time it moves forward the head nods slightly.

HETEROSEXUAL (het ər ə sek' shōō əl), *adj.* (Straight) The upright right arm, palm facing left, moves straight forward in an arc. Also STRAIGHT 2.

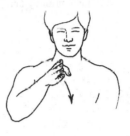

HEY! (hā), *interj.* (Waving for attention.) The open hand waves vigorously, with fingers pointing either up or at the person being addressed. This of course takes into account that deaf people communicate visually.

HIDE (hīd), *v.,* HID, HIDDEN, HIDING. (One hand is hidden under the other.) The thumb of the right "A" hand, whose palm facefs left, is placed against the lips. The hand then swings down and under the downturned left hand. The initial contact with the lips is sometimes omitted. Also COVER 4.

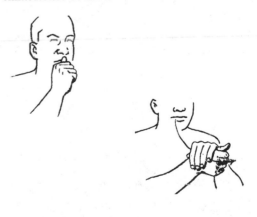

HIERARCHY (hī' ə rär' kē, hī' rär-), *n.* (Successive steps beginning at the top and opening up into further steps on a lower plane.) Both downturned "H" or open hands, fingers pointing to each other, are held in front of the upper chest. They separate, move down a bit, and continue in this fashion until they are lower and wider apart.

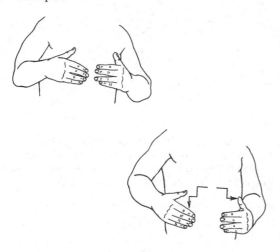

HIGH 1 (hī), *adj.* (Something high up.) Both hands, in the right-angle position, are held before the face, about a foot apart, palms facing. They are raised abruptly about a foot, in a slight outward-curving movement. Also ADVANCED, PROMOTE, PROMOTION.

HIGH 2, *adj.* (Indicating height.) The right "A" hand, held with thumb pointing upward, moves straight up above the right shoulder. Also PROMINENT 3, SUPERIOR.

HIGH 3, *adj.* (The height is indicated.) The right right-angle hand, palm facing the left, is held at the height the signer wishes to indicate. Also BIG 2, HEIGHT 2, TALL 2.

HIGH 4, *adj.* (The letter "H"; the natural movement.) The right "H" hand, palm facing the body, is moved up about a foot, to a position somewhat above the head.

HIGHBROW (hī′ brou′) (*colloq.*), *n., adj.* (The natural sign.) The wide-open right "C" hand is placed with thumb against the forehead and palm facing left. The position of the hand thus indicates the height of the brow.

HIGH SCHOOL, *n. phrase.* (The letters "H" and "S.") The letters "H" and "S" are fingerspelled.

HIGHWAY (hī′ wā), *n.* (Traffic flowing in opposite directions.) The downturned "4" hands pass each other as the right moves repeatedly to the left and the left repeatedly to the right. The downturned "V" hands are often used instead of the "4"s. Also FREEWAY.

HILL 1 (hĭl), *n.* (A rocky mound.) The sign for ROCK is made: the back of the right "S" hand is struck several times against the back of the left "S" hand. Both "5" hands, palms down, then move in a wavy, undulating manner either from left to right or from right to left. The sign for ROCK is frequently omitted.

HILL 2, *n.* (The shape.) With the right downturned hand positioned above its left counterpart, a hill is described by moving the right hand up and forward in a hump or arc.

HIM 1 (hĭm), *pron.* (Pointing at a male.) The MALE prefix sign is made: the right hand grasps an imaginary cap brim. The right index finger then points at an imaginary male. If in context the gender is clear, the prefix sign is usually omitted. Also HE.

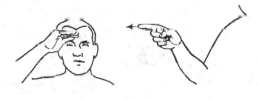

HIM 2, *pron.* (honorific) (The shape or presence of the person in question.) The upturned open hand, fingers pointing toward the male person in question, moves down a few inches. Roughly equivalent to the English gloss "that's him, in person."

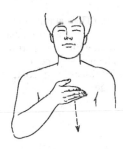

HIMSELF (hĭm sĕlf′), *pron.* (The thumb indicates an individual who is stressed above others.) The MALE prefix sign is made. The right "A" hand, thumb upturned, then moves forward an inch or two, either once or twice. If in context the gender is clear, the prefix sign is usually omitted.

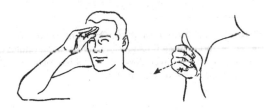

HINDER (hĭn′ dər), *v.,* -DERED, -DERING. (Obstruct, block.) The left hand, fingers together and palm flat, is held before the body, facing somewhat down. The little finger side of the right hand, held with palm flat, makes one or several up-down chopping motions against the left hand, between its thumb and index finger. Also ANNOY 1, ANNOYANCE 1, BLOCK, BOTHER 1, CHECK 2, COME BETWEEN, DISRUPT, DISTURB, HINDRANCE, IMPEDE, INTERCEPT, INTERFERE, INTERFERENCE,

INTERFERE WITH, INTERRUPT, MEDDLE 1, OBSTACLE, OBSTRUCT, PREVENT, PREVENTION.

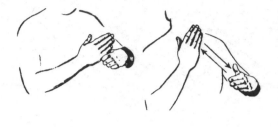

HINDRANCE (hĭn′ drəns), *n.* See HINDER.

HINGE 1 (hĭnj), *n.* (The natural sign.) The hands are joined at the fingertips and are positioned at right angles to each other, with the fingertips pointing away from the body. The hands come together and separate again, always with fingertips in contact. This imitates the action of a hinge.

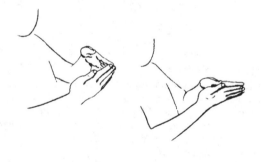

HINGE 2, *v.,* HINGED, HINGING. (Hanging onto.) With the right index finger resting across its left counterpart, both hands drop down a bit. Also DEPEND 1, DEPENDABLE, DEPENDENT, RELY 2.

HIPPOPOTAMUS (hip′ ə pot′ ə məs), *n.* (The large mouth opens.) Both "C" hands are placed on top of each other, fingertips pointing forward. The hands pivot wide open and close again. Another way to make this sign is with the extended index and little fingers

of each hand, with the same open-and-close movement as before. The fingers here represent the teeth.

HIS (hĭz), *poss. pron.* (Belonging to a male.) The MALE prefix sign is made. The open right hand, palm facing out, then moves straight forward a few inches. If in context the gender is clear, the prefix sign is usually omitted.

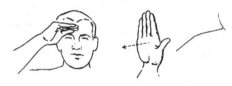

HISTORY 1 (hĭs′ tə rĭ), *n.* (The letter "H"; moving down toward the present from the past.) The right "H" hand, palm facing left, swings down in an arc from its initial position a bit above shoulder height.

HISTORY 2, *n.* (Occurrences or happenings coming down from the past and into the present.) The "D" hands, index fingers pointing ahead and palms facing each other, are initially poised near the right shoulder. They execute a series of downward movements, pivoted at the wrists. Each of these downward movements represents an event in history.

HIT 1 (hĭt), *n., v.,* HIT, HITTING. (The natural sign.) The right "S" hand strikes its knuckles forcefully against the open left palm, which is held facing right. Also POUND 3, PUNCH 1, STRIKE 1.

HIT 2, *v.* (The natural sign.) The left "5" hand, palm facing the right, is the object hit. The right "S" hand swings down in an arc, its knuckles just missing the left palm.

HIT 3, *n., v.* (Hitting the ball with a baseball bat.) The signer mimes hitting a ball with a baseball bat. Also BASEBALL.

HIT 4, *n., v.* (Hit with a bullet.) The left "5" hand, palm facing right, is the object hit. The right hand, imitating a gun, fires an imaginary bullet at the left hand, and the projectile's path is traced until the right index finger strikes the left palm.

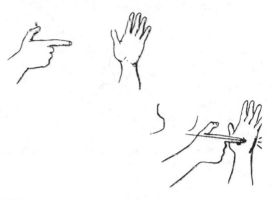

HITCH (hĭch), *n., v.,* HITCHED, HITCHING. (Hooking onto something and pulling.) With index fingers interlocked, the right hand pulls the left hand from left to right. Also HOOK, PULL 2, TOW.

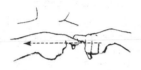

HIT THE NAIL ON THE HEAD, *colloq. phrase.* (Hitting the mark.) The right fist hits the left index finger on the side.

HOCKEY (hok′ē), *n.* (The hockey stick.) The knuckle of the curved right index finger strikes against the upturned left palm, from fingertips to base, as if hitting a hockey puck.

HOE, *n., v.,* HOED, HOEING. (Cutting a chunk of earth from a mound.) The right "C" hand digs repeatedly into the left palm, which is held either up or facing right.

HOLD (hōld), *n., v.,* HELD, HOLDING. (The gripping is emphasized.) Both "S" hands, one resting on the other, tremble slightly as they grip an imaginary object.

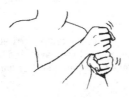

HOLDUP (hōld′ ŭp′) (*colloq.*), *n.* (The guns.) Both "L" hands, palms facing each other, thumbs pointing straight up, are thrown forward slightly, as if presenting a pair of revolvers. Also ROBBERY 2.

HOLE 1 (hōl), *n.* (A hole is traced.) Both index fingers, pointing down, are positioned side by side. They move in half circles toward the body until they come in contact with each other again. The right index finger then moves down a few inches in the center of the imaginary circle just traced.

HOLE 2, *n.* (The natural sign.) The left index finger and thumb form a circle. The right index finger is placed on this circle and traces its outline.

HOLIDAY (hŏl′ ə dā′), *n.* (A position of idleness.) With thumbs tucked in the armpits, the remaining fingers of both hands wiggle. Also IDLE, LEISURE, RETIRE 3, VACATION.

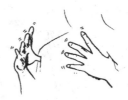

HOLLYWOOD (hol′ ē wŏŏd′), *n.* (Acting.) Both "5" hands are held up, the middle fingers extending somewhat forward. The hands and shoulders move alternately back and forth.

HOLY (hō′ lĭ), *adj.* (The letter "H"; cleanliness or purity.) The right "H" hand makes a clockwise circular movement and is then opened and wiped across the open left palm

HOME (hōm), *n.* (A place where one eats and sleeps.) The closed fingers of the right hand are placed against the lips (the sign for EAT) and then, opening into a flat palm, against the right cheek (resting the head on a pillow, as in SLEEP). The head leans slightly to the right, as if going to sleep in the right palm, during this latter movement. Also ADDRESS 2, RESIDENCE 1.

HOMELY 1 (hōm′ lĭ), *adj.* (The facial features are distorted.) The "X" hands are moved alternately up and down in front of the face, whose features are distorted with a pronounced frown. Also GRIMACE, MAKE A FACE, UGLINESS 1, UGLY 1.

HOMELY 2, *adj.* The "X" hands, palms down, move back and forth in a horizontal direction in front of the face, whose features are distorted with a pronounced frown. Also UGLINESS 2, UGLY 2.

HOMOSEXUAL 1 (hō′ mə sek′ shōō əl), *n., adj.* The tips of the "G" fingers are placed on the chin. Also GAY 1.

HOMOSEXUAL 2, *n., adj.* (Supposedly a code originally.) The signer pulls the earlobe. Also GAY 2.

HOMOSEXUAL 3, *n., adj.* (Mutual masturbation.) Both fists, palms facing down, come together repeatedly. Also GAY 3.

HOMOSEXUAL 4, *n., adj.* (An effeminate gesture.) Both "F" hands, palms out, are held at shoulder height. The signer moves them alternately forward and back, while the shoulders keep pace with the forward-and-back movements. Also EFFEMINATE, GAY 4.

HONDURAS (hon dŏŏr′ əs), *n.* The downturned right "V" hand moves down an inch or two on the right side of the body, as if putting something into a side pocket. A native sign.

HONEST (ŏn′ ĭst), *adj.* (The letter "H," for HONEST; a straight and true path.) The index and middle fingers of the right "H" hand, whose palm faces left, move straight forward along the upturned left palm. Also FRANK, HONESTY, SINCERE 1.

HONESTY (ŏn′ ĭs tǐ), *n.* See HONEST.

HONEY 1 (hun′ ē), *n.* (Wiping the lips.) The upturned right index finger is swept across the mouth, from left to right.

HONEY 2, *n.* (Wiping the lips.) With right index and little fingers extended, the signer wipes the lips from left to right and then throws the hand down.

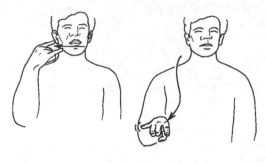

HONEYMOON (hun′ ē mōōn′), *n.* (Wiping the honey from the lips.) The right middle fingertip wipes across the lips, from left to right.

HONG KONG (hong′ kong′, hông′ kông′), *n.* The closed hand is held in front of the mouth, palm facing out. The hand is thrown forward twice, each time with the fingers opening.

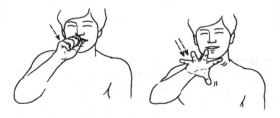

HONOR 1 (ŏn′ ər), *n., v.,* -ORED, -ORING. (The letter "H"; a gesture of respect.) The right "H" hand, palm facing left, swings down in an arc from its initial position in front of the forehead. The head bows slightly during this movement of the hand. Also HALLOWED 2, HONORARY.

HONOR 2, *n.* The right open hand faces the chest, with the thumb and index finger touching the midchest. The hand is drawn straight out and away, while the thumb and index finger come together and touch. The "H" position is next assumed, and, with a sweeping motion, the index and middle fingers describe an arc directed inward to the forehead. Also ADMIRE 2.

HONORARY (ŏn′ ə rĕr′ ĭ), *adj.* See HONOR 1.

HOOK (hŏŏk), *n.* (Hooking onto something and pulling.) With index fingers interlocked, the right hand pulls the left hand from left to right. Also HITCH, PULL 2, TOW.

HOPE (hōp), *n., v.,* HOPED, HOPING. (A thought awaited.) The tip of the right index finger, held in the "D" position, palm facing the body, is placed on the forehead (modified THINK, *q.v.*). Both hands then assume right-angle positions, fingers facing, with the left hand held above left shoulder level and the right before the right breast. Both hands, held thus, wave

to each other several times. Also ANTICIPATE, ANTICIPATION, EXPECT.

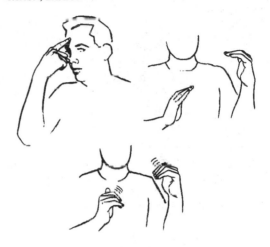

HOPSCOTCH (hop′ skoch), *n.* (The movement of the feet or legs.) The index and middle fingers, placed on the heel of the left hand, run forward about half the distance between the heel and the fingertips. The running fingers then execute a series of short jumps forward until they reach the fingertips.

HORDES (hôrdz), *n.* (Many people coming together in one place.) The downturned "5" hands, fingers wriggling, come toward each other until the fingertips almost touch.

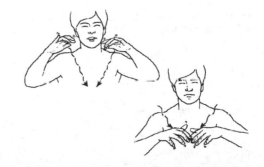

HORNY 1 (hôr′ nē), *adj., sl.* (The horns.) One or both index fingers are placed at the top of the forehead, pointing out.

HORNY 2, *adj., sl.* (The pulse in the throat.) The right hand, index and little fingers extended and palm facing out, is held at the right side of the throat. The index finger repeatedly strikes the side of the throat.

HORROR (hôr′ ər), *n.* (A threatening gesture, much used in childhood.) Both claw hands, palms out, are positioned in front of the face. The signer's teeth are bared, or the mouth is held open.

HORSE (hôrs), *n.* (The ears.) The "U" hands are placed palms out at either side of the head. The index and middle fingers move forward and back repeatedly, imitating the movement of a horse's ears.

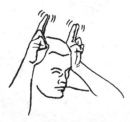

HORSEBACK (hôrs′ băk′), *n.* (Mounted on horseback.) The right index and middle fingers straddle the left hand, which is held palm facing right. The left hand moves in a rhythmic up-down motion, carrying the right hand with it. Also RIDE.

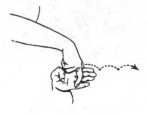

HOSPITAL 1 (hŏs′ pĭ təl), *n.* (The letter "H"; the red cross on the sleeve.) The index and middle fingers of the right "H" hand trace a cross on the upper part of the left arm. Also INFIRMARY 1.

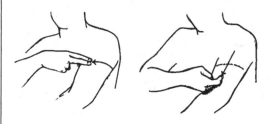

HOSPITAL 2, *n.* (The wide, birdlike hood worn by the French nursing sisters.) The right "B" hand, palm facing left, swings over from the left side of the forehead to the right side.

HOT (hŏt), *adj.* (Removing hot food from the mouth.) The cupped hand, palm facing the body, moves up in front of the slightly open mouth. It is then flung down to the palm-down position.

HOTCHKISS, JOHN BURTON, *n.* (The two parts of the surname.) Hotchkiss was an early educator of Deaf Americans. The sign for HOT: the cupped "5" hand, palm facing the body, moves up in front of the slightly open mouth. It is then flung down to the palm-down position. The sign for KISS then follows: with fingers touching their thumbs, both hands are brought together. Alternatively, the right hand, fingers touching thumb, is placed against the lips and then moves over to the right cheek. While not disparaging, this sign is probably a part of classroom humor and should be used with that in mind.

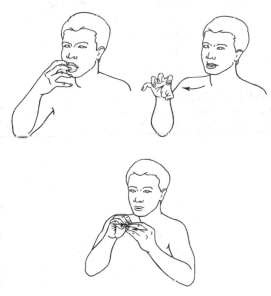

HOT DOG 1 (*colloq.*), *n.* (The shape.) The "C" hands are held side by side, palms out, thumbs and index fin-

gers touching. They change to the "S" position as they are drawn apart. Also FRANKFURTER.

HOT DOG 2, *n.* (The shape in a roll or bun.) The left hand is held with the fingers pointing up. The right index finger is placed between the thumb and the other fingers. Also FRANKFURTER 2.

HOT ROD (hŏt′ rŏd), *n.* (The stick shift.) The signer mimes shifting automobile gears violently while holding the top of the steering wheel in the other hand. The body may show bouncing as the car takes off.

HOUR (our), *n.* (The minute hand completes a circle around the clock's face.) The left "5" hand, palm facing right and fingers pointing forward or upward, is the clock's face. The right "D" hand is placed against it so that the right index finger points straight up. The right hand, always in contact with the left palm, executes a full clockwise circle, tracing the movement of the minute hand.

HOUSE (hous), *n.* (The shape of the house.) The open hands are held with fingertips touching so that they form a pyramid a bit above eye level. From this position, the hands separate and move diagonally downward for a short distance; then they continue straight down a few inches. This movement traces the outline of a roof and walls. Also BARN, DOMICILE, RESIDENCE 2.

HOW (hou), *adv.* (The hands come into view to reveal something.) The right-angle hands, palms down and knuckles touching, swing up and open to the palms-up position. Also MANNER 1.

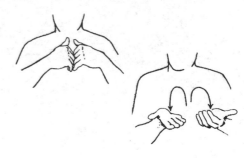

HOW ARE YOU? 1, *interrogative sent.* (The strength of the body; the inquisitive expression.) The "5" hands are placed on the chest rather forcefully. They then close into the "S" position, palms facing the body, as they leave the chest and move up a bit. In this terminal position they shake or tremble a bit. An inquisitive expression is all-important here.

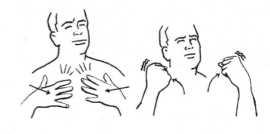

HOW ARE YOU? 2, *phrase.* (What are your feelings?) Both middle fingers quickly sweep up and out from the chest. The eyebrows are raised in inquiry. Also WHAT'S NEW? 2

HOWEVER 1 (hou ĕv′ ər), *conj.* (A divergence or a difference; the opposite of SAME.) The index fingers of both "D" hands, palms facing down, are crossed near their tips. The hands are drawn apart. Also ALTHOUGH, BUT, ON THE CONTRARY.

HOWEVER 2, *conj.* Both hands, in the "5" position, are held before the chest, fingertips facing each other. With an alternate back-forth movement, the fingertips are made to strike each other. Also ANYHOW, ANYWAY, DESPITE, DOESN'T MATTER, INDIFFERENCE, INDIFFERENT, IN SPITE OF, MAKE NO DIFFERENCE, NEVERTHELESS, NO MATTER, WHEREVER.

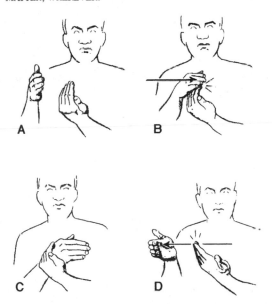

A   B

C   D

HOW MANY? *interrogative phrase.* (Throwing up a number of things before the eyes; a display of fingers to indicate a question of how many or how much.) The right hand, palm up, is held before the chest, all fingers touching the thumb. The hand is tossed straight up while the fingers open to the "5" position. Also AMOUNT 2, HOW MUCH?, NUMBER 2.

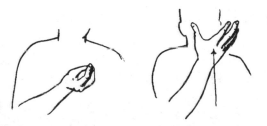

HOW MUCH? *interrogative phrase.* See HOW MANY?

HOW MUCH MONEY? *interrogative sent.* (Amount of money is indicated.) The sign for MONEY, is made: the upturned right hand, grasping some imaginary bills, is brought down into the upturned left palm a number of times. The right hand then moves straight up, opening into the "5" position, palm up. Also PRICE 1, WHAT IS THE PRICE?

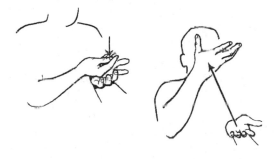

HUG (hŭg), *v.*, HUGGED, HUGGING, *n.* (The natural sign.) The arms clasp the body in a natural hugging position. Also EMBRACE.

HUH? (hu), *interj.* (Throwing out a question.) The downturned curved right index finger is thrown out and forward very slightly, while the signer follows the finger with a very slight forward movement of the body. An expression of inquiry or perplexity is assumed.

HUM (hum), *n., v.,* HUMMED, HUMMING. (The letter "M"; coming from the mouth or being heard by the ear.) The downturned right "M" hand, moving forward from the closed mouth, indicates a hum being sounded. Moving away from the ear indicates the humming is being heard.

HUMAN 1 (hū′ mən), *adj.* (The man's cap.) The thumb and extended fingers of the right hand are brought up to grasp an imaginary cap brim, representing the tipping of caps by men in olden days. This is a root sign used to modify many others. As an alternative, the "H" hands are drawn up the sides of the chest. Also MALE, MAN, MANKIND.

HUMAN 2, *adj., n.* (The "H"; life emanating from the body.) Both "H" hands, fingers up, move upward simultaneously from the chest.

HUMANITY (hū măn′ ə tĭ), *n.* (People, indicated by the rotating "P" hands.) The "P" hands, side by side, are moved alternately in continuous counterclockwise circles. Also AUDIENCE 2, PEOPLE, PUBLIC.

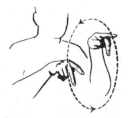

HUMBLE 1 (hŭm′ bəl, ŭm′-), *adj.* (The head bows; a turtle's head retreats into its shell; an act of humility.) The index finger edge of the right "B" hand, palm facing left, is placed at the lips. The right "B" hand is then brought down and under the downturned open left hand. The head, at the same time, bows. Also MEEK, MODEST.

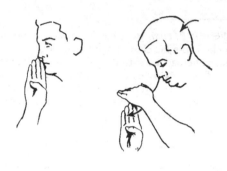

HUMBLE 2, *adj.* Same as HUMBLE 1, but only the right hand is used.

HUMBLE 3, *adj.* (Dropping the hands and bowing the head; an act indicating humility.) The open hands, held with palms out or slightly facing each other, are dropped from their initial position before the head. As they drop the head bows.

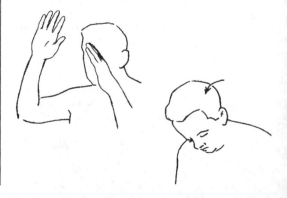

HUMBUG (hŭm′ bŭg), *n.* (A double face, *i.e.,* a mask covers the face.) The right hand is placed over the back of the left hand and pushes it down and a bit in toward the body. Also BLUFF, FAKE, HYPOCRITE 1, IMPOSTOR

HUMOR (hū′ mər, ū′-), *n.* (The nose wrinkles in laughter.) The tips of the right index and middle fingers brush repeatedly off the tip of the nose. Also COMIC, COMICAL, FUNNY, HUMOROUS.

HUMOROUS (hū′ mər əs, ū′-), *adj.* See HUMOR.

HUNDRED (hŭn′ drəd), *n., adj.* (The Roman "C," *centum,* for "hundred.") The letter "C" is formed. This is preceded by a "1" for a simple hundred or by whatever number of hundreds one wishes to indicate.

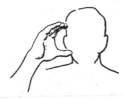

HUNGARY (hung′ gə rē), *n.* The curved right index finger is draped over the right thumb. The hand moves out and forward from a position under the chin. A native sign.

HUNGER (hŭng′ gər), *n.* See HUNGARIAN.

HUNGRY (hŭng′ grĭ), *adj.* See HUNGARIAN.

HUNT (hŭnt), *n., v.,* HUNTED, HUNTING. (Firing a rifle.) The left hand grasps the barrel of an imaginary rifle, while the right hand grasps the base, its thumb extended upward to represent the sight, and index finger wiggling back and forth, as if pulling the trigger. At the same time, both hands make short back-and-forth movements, as if the rifle is firing.

HURRICANE (hûr′ i kān′, hur′-), *n.* (The "H"s; the circular motion.) The right "H" hand is positioned palm out, thumb pointing down. The left "H" hand is placed thumb pointing up and palm facing in. The two thumbs touch each other and the two "H" hands flick back and forth in imitation of a whirling wind.

HURRY (hûr′ ĭ), *v.,* -RIED, -RYING. (Letter "H"; quick movements.) The "H" hands, palms facing each other and held about six inches apart, shake alternately up and down. One hand alone may be used. Also HASTE, HUSTLE.

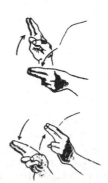

HURT 1 (hûrt), *v.,* HURT, HURTING, *n.* (A stabbing pain.) The "D" hands, index fingers pointing to each other, are rotated in elliptical fashion before the chest—simultaneously but in opposite directions. Also ACHE, HARM 1, INJURE 1, INJURY, MAR 1, OFFEND, OFFENSE, PAIN, SIN, WOUND.

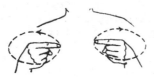

HURT 2, *v., n.* (Striking down against.) Both "A" or "X" hands are held before the chest, the right above the left. The right hand strikes down and out, hitting the left thumb and knuckles with force. Also BACKBITE, BASE 3, CRUEL 1, HARM 2, MAR 2, MEAN 1, SPOIL.

HURT 3, *v.* (Silence; an avoidance of an outcry or impatience.) The index finger of the right "D" hand, palm facing left, is placed at the sealed lips. The head is held slightly bowed. Also PATIENCE 2, PATIENT 2.

HURT 4, *v., n.* (The feelings are those that give pain and cause the hand to be removed quickly from the source of the pain.) The sign for FEEL 2 is made: the right middle finger, touching the heart, moves up an inch or two a number of times. The right hand is then thrown down and out, opening into the downturned "5" position. Also FEEL HURT.

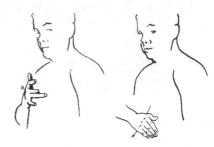

HUSBAND (hŭz′ bənd), *n.* (A male joined in marriage.) The MALE prefix sign is formed: the right hand grasps the brim of an imaginary cap. The hands are then clasped together.

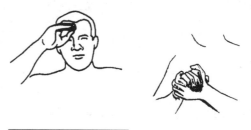

HYMN 1 (hĭm), *n.* (A rhythmic, wavy movement of the hand to indicate a melody; the movement of a conductor's hand in directing a musical performance.) The right "5" hand, palm facing left, is waved back and forth over the downturned left hand in a series of elongated figure eights. Also CHANT, MELODY, MUSIC, SING, SONG.

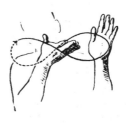

HYMN 2, *n.* (The letter "H.") The sign for HYMN 1 is made, but with the right "H" hand.

HYPNOSIS (hip nō′ sis), *n.* (The movement of the fingers.) The outstretched hands, palms down and positioned facing out from the eyes, make small continuous wriggles. This indicates performing hypnosis. With the fingers facing in toward the signer's eyes, this indicates being hypnotized.

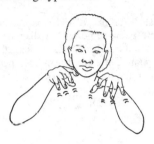

HYPOCRITE 1 (hĭp′ ə krĭt), *n.* (A double face, *i.e.,* a mask covers the face.) The right hand is placed over the back of the left hand and pushes it down and a bit in toward the body. Also BLUFF, FAKE, HUMBUG, IMPOSTOR.

HYPOCRITE 2, *n.* (Covering the real face.) Both hands are held open, with palms down. The right hand, from a position above the left, swings out and under the left and then moves straight out. Also FALSE-FACED, TWO-FACED, UNDERHAND.

HYSTERECTOMY (his tə rek′ tə mē), *n.* (WOMAN, CUT, REMOVE.) The sign for WOMAN is made: the thumb of the open "5" hand leaves the chin and moves down to the chest. Next is the sign for CUT, as in operation: the right thumb slashes across the belly. This is followed by REMOVE: the right hand makes a grasping movement from the palm of the left hand and is thrown down.

I 1 (ī), *pron.* (The "I," held to the chest.) The right "I" hand is held with its thumb edge to the chest and little finger pointing up.

I 2, *pron.* (The natural sign.) The signer points to himself. Also ME.

ICE (īs), *n., v.,* ICED, ICING. (The stiff fingers.) The fingers of the "5" hands, held palms down, stiffen and contract. Also FREEZE, FROZEN, RIGID.

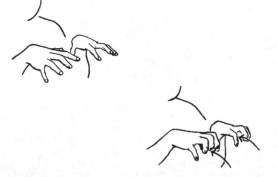

ICE CREAM 1 (krēm), *n.* (The eating action.) The upturned left palm represents a dish or plate. The curved index and middle fingers of the right hand represent the spoon. They are drawn up repeatedly from the left palm to the lips. Also SPOON.

ICE CREAM 2, *n.* (The natural sign.) The signer goes through the act of licking an imaginary ice cream pop. Also LOLLIPOP.

IDENTICAL (ī děn′ tə kəl), *adj.* (Matching fingers are brought together.) The outstretched index fingers are brought together, either once or several times. Also ALIKE, LIKE 2, SAME 1, SIMILAR, SUCH.

IDIOM (ĭd′ ē əm), *n.* (The "I" letters; quotation marks.) Both "I" hands, palms out, move apart. The signer then curves the index and middle fingers of each hand, describing a pair of quotation marks in the air.

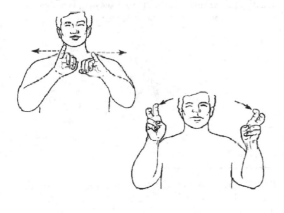

IDLE (ī′ dəl), *adj.* (A position of idleness.) With thumbs tucked in the armpits, the remaining fingers of both hands wiggle. Also HOLIDAY, LEISURE, RETIRE 3, VACATION.

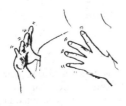

IF 1 (ĭf), *conj.* (The scales move up and down.) The two "I" hands, palms facing each other, move alternately up and down. Also CONSIDER 3, COURT, EVALUATE 1, JUDGE 1, JUDGMENT, JUSTICE 1.

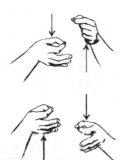

IF 2 (ĭf), *conj.* The tip of the right little finger touches the forehead or the area under the right eye. Also SUPPOSE 2.

IGNITE (ĭg nīt′) *v.,* IGNITED, IGNITING. (Striking a match to cause flames.) The signer strikes an imaginary match on the palm, and then both hands, palms facing the body, are held upright with fingers wriggling.

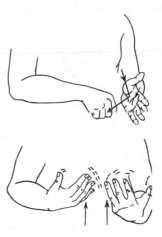

IGNORANT (ĭg′ nə rənt), *adj.* (The head is struck to emphasize its emptiness or lack of knowledge.) The back of the right "V" hand strikes the forehead once or twice. Two fingers represent prison bars across the mind—the mind is imprisoned.

IGNORE (ĭg nôr'), *v.*, -NORED, -NORING. (Thumbing the nose.) The index finger of the right "B" hand is placed under the tip of the nose. From this position the right hand moves straight forward, away from the face. Also DISREGARD.

ILL (ĭl), *adj., n., adv.* (The sick parts of the anatomy are indicated.) The right middle finger rests on the forehead, and its left counterpart is placed against the stomach. The signer assumes an expression of sadness or physical distress. Also DISEASE 1, ILLNESS, SICK, SICKNESS.

ILLNESS (ĭl' nĭs), *n.* See ILL. This is followed by the sign -NESS: the downturned right "N" hand moves down along the left palm, which is facing away from the body.

ILLUSTRATE (ĭl' ə strāt', ĭ lŭs' trāt), *v.*, -TRATED, -TRATING. (Directing the attention to something, and bringing it forward.) The right index finger points into the left palm, held facing out before the body. The left palm moves straight out. For the passive form of this

verb, *i.e.*, BE SHOWN, the movement is reversed: the left hand, palm facing in, is moved in toward the body, while the right index finger remains pointing into the left palm. Also DEMONSTRATE, DISPLAY, EVIDENCE, EXAMPLE, EXHIBIT, EXHIBITION, INDICATE, INFLUENCE 3, PRODUCE 2, REPRESENT, SHOW 1, SIGNIFY 1.

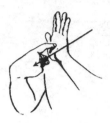

IMAGE (ĭm' ĭj), *n.* (Contours are indicated or outlined.) Both "A" hands, held about a foot apart before the face, with palms facing each other, move down simultaneously in a wavy, undulating motion. Also FIGURE 2, FORM, SCULPT, SCULPTURE, SHAPE 1, STATUE.

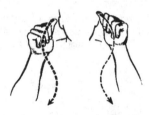

IMAGINATION 1 (ĭ măj' ə nā' shən), *n.* (A thought coming forward from the mind, modified by the letter "I" for "idea.") With the "I" position on the right hand, palm facing the body, touch the little finger to the forehead, and then move the hand up and away in a circular, clockwise motion. The hand may also be moved up and away without this circular motion. Also CONCEIVE 2, CONCEPT 1, CONCEPTION, FANCY 2, IDEA, IMAGINE 1, JUST THINK OF IT!, NOTION, POLICY 2, THEORY, THOUGHT 2.

IMAGINATION 2, *n.* (The "I" letters; thoughts wandering off into the air.) Both "I" hands are positioned near their respective temples. They move forward and up, describing a series of circles.

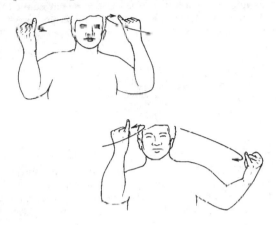

IMAGINE 1 (ĭ măj′ ĭn), v., -INED, -INING. See IMAGINATION.

IMAGINE 2, v. (Something emerges from the head and is grasped.) The index finger edge of the right "B" hand is placed in midforehead. The right hand moves straight up and then closes into the "S" position in front of the forehead, palm facing left. Also INVENT 2.

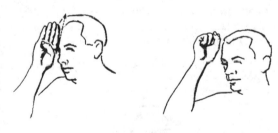

IMITATE (ĭm′ ə tāt′), v., -TATED, -TATING. (The natural sign.) The right fingers and thumb close together and move onto the upturned, open left hand, as if taking something from one place to another. Also COPY 1, DUPLICATE 1, MIMIC, MODEL.

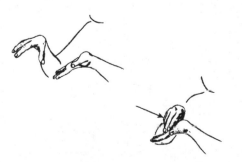

IMMEDIATELY (ĭ mē′ dĭ ĭt lĭ), adv. (A quick movement.) The thumbtip of the upright right hand is flicked quickly off the tip of the curved right index finger, as if shooting marbles. Also FAST 1, QUICK, QUICKNESS, RAPID, RATE 1, SPEED, SPEEDY, SWIFT.

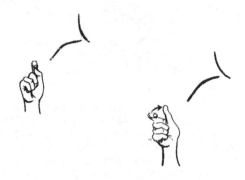

IMPAIRED (im pârd′), adj. (The letter "I"; held back or impeded.) The right little finger is brought into the space between the left thumb and index finger.

IMPEDE (ĭm pēd′), v., -PEDED, -PEDING. (Obstruct, block.) The left hand, fingers together and palm flat, is held before the body, facing somewhat down. The little finger side of the right hand, held with palm flat, makes one or several up-down chopping motions against the left hand, between its thumb and index finger. Also ANNOY 1, ANNOYANCE 1, BLOCK, BOTHER 1, CHECK 2, COME BETWEEN, DISRUPT, DISTURB, HINDER, HINDRANCE, INTERCEPT, INTERFERE, INTERFERENCE, INTERFERE WITH, INTERRUPT, MEDDLE 1, OBSTACLE, OBSTRUCT, PREVENT, PREVENTION.

IMPLORE (ĭm plōr′), v., -PLORED, -PLORING. (An act of supplication:) With the right hand clasped over the left, both hands are shaken gently before the body. The eyes often are directed upward. Also BEG 2, BESEECH, ENTREAT, PLEA, PLEAD, SUPPLICATION.

IMPLY (ĭm plī′), v., -PLIED, -PLYING. (Relative standing of one's thoughts.) A modified sign for THINK is made: the right index finger touches the middle of the forehead. The tips of the right "V" hand, palm down, are then thrust into the upturned left palm (as in STAND, q.v.). The right "V" hand is then rethrust into the upturned left palm, with right palm now facing the body. Also CONNOTE, INTEND, INTENT 1, INTENTION, MEAN 2, MEANING, MOTIVE 3, PURPOSE 1, SIGNIFICANCE 2, SIGNIFY 2, SUBSTANCE 2.

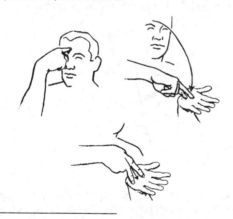

IMPORTANT 1 (ĭm pôr′ tənt), adj. Both "F" hands, palms facing each other, move apart, up, and together in a smooth elliptical fashion, coming together at the tips of the thumbs and index fingers of both hands. Also DESERVE, ESSENTIAL, MAIN, MERIT, PRECIOUS, PROMINENT 2, SIGNIFICANCE 1, SIGNIFICANT, VALUABLE, VALUE, VITAL 1, WORTH, WORTHWHILE, WORTHY.

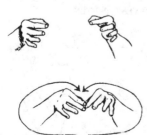

IMPORTANT 2 (arch., rare), adj. (The letter "I" is brought up to a position of prominence.) The base of the right "I" hand rests on the back of the downturned left "S" hand. The left hand moves straight up, carrying the right with it.

IMPOSSIBLE 1 (ĭm pŏs′ ə bəl), adj. (One finger encounters an unyielding quality in striking another.) The right index finger strikes the left and continues moving down. The left index finger remains in place. Also CANNOT 1, CAN'T, UNABLE.

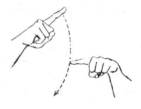

IMPOSSIBLE 2 (loc.), adj. The downturned right "Y" hand is placed in the upturned left palm a number of times. The up-down movement is very slight.

IMPOSSIBLE 3, adj. (Not able.) Both downturned fists move down simultaneously (CAN), then move apart. Meanwhile, the signer's head shakes in negation.

IMPOSTOR (ĭm pŏs′ tər), *n.* (A double face, *i.e.*, a mask covers the face.) The right hand is placed over the back of the left hand and pushes it down and a bit in toward the body. Also BLUFF, FAKE, HUMBUG, HYP-OCRITE 1.

IMPOTENCE 1 (ĭm′ pə təns), *n.* (No erection.) The sign for NO 1 is made: both "O" hands are held facing each other. They are then drawn apart while the signer's head shakes slightly in negation. This is followed by ERECTION: the left hand grasps the right arm or the crook of the right elbow as the right "S" hand moves up in an arc. Also IMPOTENT 1.

IMPOTENCE 2, *n. sl.* (The penis is limp.) The right hand is held in the downturned "X" position. Also IMPOTENT 2.

IMPOTENT 1 (ĭm′ pə tənt), *adj.* See IMPOTENCE 1.

IMPOTENT 2, *adj.* See IMPOTENCE 2.

IMPROVE (ĭm prōōv′), *v.,* -PROVED, -PROVING. (Moving up.) The little finger edge of the right hand rests on the back of the downturned left hand. It moves up the left arm in successive stages, indicating improvement or upward movement. Also MEND 2.

IN (ĭn), *prep., adv., adj.* (The natural sign.) The fingers of the right hand are thrust into the left. Also INSIDE, INTO, WITHIN.

IN A FEW DAYS, *adv. phrase.* (Several TOMORROWs ahead.) The thumb of the right "A" hand is positioned on the right cheek. One by one, the remaining fingers appear, starting with the index finger. Usually, when all five fingers have been presented, the hand moves forward a few inches to signify the concept of the future.

IN A FEW YEARS, *adv. phrase.* (Few, years, future.) The sign for FEW, as in IN A FEW MONTHS, is made. This is followed by the sign for YEAR: the right "S" hand, palm facing left, is positioned atop the left "S" hand, whose palm faces right. The right "S" hand describes a complete circle around the left and comes to rest in its original position. Finally, the sign for FUTURE, as in IN A FEW MONTHS, is made.

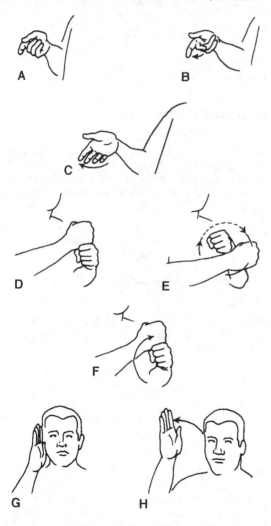

IN A WEEK, *adv. phrase.* (A week around the corner.) The upright right "D" hand is placed palm to palm against the left "5" hand, whose palm faces right. The right "D" hand moves along the left palm from base to fingertips and then curves to the left, around the left fingertips.

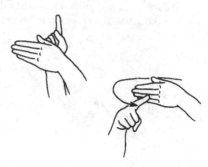

INCH 1 (ĭnch), *n.* (A small part of a sentence, *i.e.,* a word.) The tips of the right index finger and thumb, about an inch apart, are placed on the side of the outstretched left index finger, which represents the length of a sentence. Also VERBAL 2, WORD.

INCH 2, *n.* (The length of the thumb's first joint.) The upturned left thumb is crooked. The thumb and index finger of the right hand rest on the tip and first joint of the left thumb to indicate its length.

INCIDENT (ĭn′ sə dənt), *n.* (A befalling.) Both "D" hands, index fingers pointing away from the body, are simultaneously pivoted over so that the palms face down. Also ACCIDENT, BEFALL, CHANCE, COINCIDE 1, COINCIDENCE, EVENT, HAPPEN 1, OCCUR, OPPORTUNITY 4.

INCLINATION (ĭn′ klə nā′ shən), *n.* (The feelings of the heart move toward a specific object.) The tip of the right middle finger touches the heart. The open right hand, palm facing the body, then moves away from the heart toward the palm of the open left hand. Also DISPOSE, DISPOSED TO, DISPOSITION, INCLINE, INCLINED, TEND, TENDENCY.

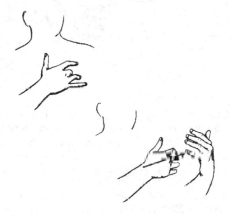

INCLINE (ĭn klīn′), *v.*, -CLINED, -CLINING. See INCLINATION.

INCLINED (ĭn klīnd′), *adj.* See INCLINATION.

INCLUDE (ĭn klōōd′), *v.*, -CLUDED, -CLUDING. (All; the whole.) The left hand is held in the "C" position, fingers pointing right. The right hand, in the "5" position, fingers facing out from the body, palm down, is held above the left. With a horizontal swing to the right, the right hand describes an arc as the fingers close and are thrust into the left "C" hand, which closes over it. Also ALL 2, ALTOGETHER, INCLUSIVE, WHOLE (THE).

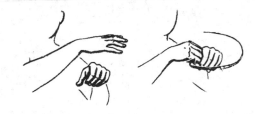

INCLUSIVE (ĭn klōō′ sĭv), *adj.* See INCLUDE.

INCOME 1 (ĭn′ kŭm), *n.* (A regular taking in.) The outstretched open left hand, held palm facing right, moves in toward the body, assuming the "A" position, palm still facing right. This is repeated several times. Also DIVIDEND, INTEREST 4, SUBSCRIBE, SUBSCRIPTION.

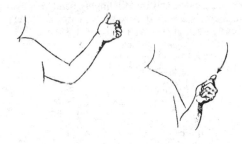

INCOME 2, *n.* (Money earned.) The sign for MONEY 1: the upturned right hand, grasping some imaginary bills, is brought down into the upturned left palm a number of times. This is followed by EARN: the right "5" hand, its little finger edge touching the left upturned palm, is drawn in a counterclockwise arc toward the body, closing into the "S" position as it sweeps over the base of the left hand.

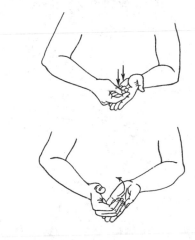

INCREASE (*n.* ĭn′ krēs; *v.* ĭn krēs′), -CREASED, -CREASING. (Adding on.) The index and middle fingers of the right "H" hand, palm up, are swung up and over until they come to rest on the index and middle fingers of the left "H" hand, held palm down. Also ADD 3, ADDITION, EXTEND 1, EXTRA, GAIN 1, ON TO, RAISE 2.

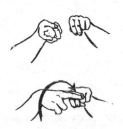

INCREDULITY (ĭn′ krə dū′ lə tĭ, -dōō′-), *n.* (The nose is wrinkled in disbelief.) The right "V" hand faces the nose. The index and middle fingers bend as a cynical expression is assumed. Also CYNIC, CYNICAL, DISBELIEF 1, DON'T BELIEVE, DOUBT 1, SKEPTIC 1, SKEPTICAL 1.

INCURABLE (in kyŏŏr′ ə bəl) *adj.* (CAN'T and WELL.) The sign for CAN'T: one index finger strikes the tip of the other index finger and moves beyond. Meanwhile the signer negates. The sign for WELL follows: both "5" hands, fingers curved and forming cups, are placed on the chest with palms facing the body. Both hands move forward and slightly upward simultaneously, closing into the "S" position.

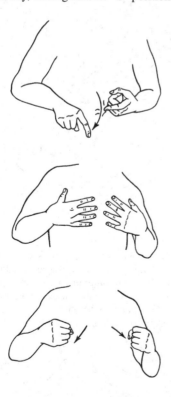

INDECISION (ĭn′ dĭ sĭzh′ ən), *n.* (On a fence.) The index and middle fingers of the right hand, palm down, straddle the index finger edge of the left "B"

hand, which is held palm facing right. In this position the right hand rocks deliberately back and forth, from left to right. Also UNCERTAIN.

INDEED (ĭn dēd′), *adv., interj.* (Coming forth directly from the lips; true.) The index finger of the right "D" hand, palm facing left, is placed against the lips. It moves up an inch or two and then describes a small arc forward and away from the lips. Also ABSOLUTE, ABSOLUTELY, ACTUAL, ACTUALLY, AUTHENTIC, CERTAIN, CERTAINLY, FAITHFUL 3, FIDELITY, FRANKLY, GENUINE, POSITIVE 1, POSITIVELY, REAL, REALLY, SINCERE 2, SURE, SURELY, TRUE, TRULY, TRUTH, VALID, VERILY.

INDEPENDENCE (ĭn′ dĭ pĕn′ dəns), *n.* (Breaking the bonds.) The "S" hands, crossed in front of the body, swing apart and face out. Also DELIVER 1, EMANCIPATE, FREE 1, INDEPENDENT, LIBERATION, REDEEM 1, RELIEF, RESCUE, SAFE, SALVATION, SAVE 1.

INDEPENDENT 1 (ĭn′ dĭ pĕn′ dənt), *adj.* See INDEPEN-DENCE.

INDEPENDENT 2, *adj.* (Initialized version.) As in INDEPENDENCE, the hands swing apart and face out, but here both hands form the letter "I."

INDIA (in′ dē ə) *n.* (The mark on the forehead, called a *bindi* or sometimes a *kumkum.*) The thumbtip of the "A" hand touches midforehead twice.

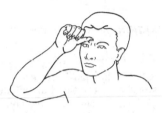

INDIAN 1 (ĭn′ dĭ ən), *n., adj.* (The feathered head-dress.) The right thumb and index fingers, holding an imaginary feather, are placed first on the tip of the nose and then under the right ear or on the right side of the head. Indicates Native American.

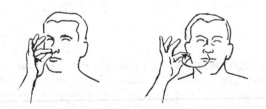

INDIAN 2, *n., adj.* (The characteristic motions during dancing.) The right "5" hand is placed behind the head, fingers pointing upward to indicate the feathers. The left hand touches the open lips repeatedly. Indicates Native American.

INDICATE (ĭn′ də kāt′), v., -CATED, -CATING. (Directing the attention to something and bringing it forward.) The right index finger points into the left palm, held facing out before the body. The left palm moves straight out. For the passive form of this verb, *i.e.,* BE SHOWN, the movement is reversed: the left hand, palm facing in, is moved in toward the body while the right index finger remains pointing into the left palm. Also DEMONSTRATE, DISPLAY, EVIDENCE, EXAMPLE, EXHIBIT, EXHIBITION, ILLUSTRATE, INFLUENCE 3, PRODUCE 2, REPRESENT, SHOW 1, SIGNIFY 1.

INDIFFERENCE (ĭn dĭf′ ər əns), *n.* Both hands, in the "5" position, are held before the chest, fingertips facing each other. With an alternate back-forth movement, the fingertips are made to strike each other. Also ANYHOW, ANYWAY, DESPITE, DOESN'T MATTER, HOWEVER 2, INDIFFERENT, IN SPITE OF, MAKE NO DIFFERENCE, NEVERTHELESS, NO MATTER, WHEREVER.

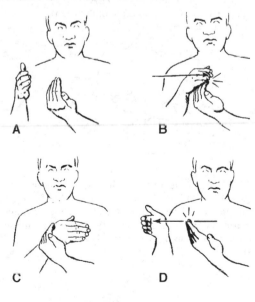

A   B

C   D

INDIFFERENT (ĭn dĭf′ ər ənt), *adj.* See INDIFFERENCE.

INDIGNANT (ĭn dĭg′ nənt), *adj.* (A violent welling up of the emotions.) The curved fingers of the right hand are placed in the center of the chest, flying up suddenly and violently. An expression of anger is worn. Also ANGER, ANGRY 2, ENRAGE, FURY, INDIGNATION, IRE, MAD 1, RAGE.

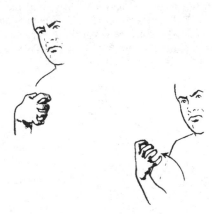

INDIGNATION (ĭn′ dĭg nā′ shən), *n.* See INDIGNANT.

INDIVIDUAL 1 (ĭn′ də vĭj′ ŏŏ əl), *n.* (The shape of an individual.) Both open hands, palms facing each other, move down the sides of the body, tracing its outline to the hips. This is an important suffix sign that changes a verb to a noun (*e.g.,* TEACH, *v.,* becomes TEACHER, *n.,* by the addition of this sign).

INDIVIDUAL 2, *n.* (The "I" hands; the outline of a person.) The "I" hands, palms facing and little fingers pointing out, are held before the body. They are drawn down a few inches, outlining the shape of an imaginary person standing before the signer.

INDOCTRINATE (ĭn dŏk′ trĭ nāt′), *v.,* -NATED, -NATING. (Giving forth from the mind.) The fingertips of each hand are placed on the temples. They then swing out and into the "5" position. Also EDUCATE, INDOCTRINATION, INSTRUCT, INSTRUCTION, TEACH.

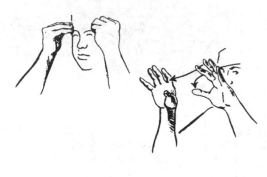

INDOCTRINATION, *n.* See INDOCTRINATE.

INDULGENCE (ĭn dŭl′ jəns) (*eccles.*), *n.* (The "P" refers to "purgatory.") The tip of the middle finger of the right "P" hand executes a continuous clockwise circle on the upturned left palm.

INDUSTRIOUS (ĭn dŭs′ trĭ əs), *adj.* (Rubbing the hands together in zeal or ambition.) The open hands are rubbed vigorously back and forth against each other. Also AMBITIOUS 1, ANXIOUS 1, ARDENT, DILIGENCE 1, DILIGENT, EAGER, EAGERNESS, EARNEST, ENTHUSIASM, ENTHUSIASTIC, METHODIST, ZEAL, ZEALOUS.

INEXPENSIVE (ĭn′ ĭk spĕn′ sĭv), *adj.* (A small amount of money.) The sign for MONEY is made: the upturned right hand, grasping some imaginary bills, is brought down into the upturned left palm a number of times. The downturned cupped right hand is then positioned over the upturned cupped left hand. The right hand descends a short distance but does not touch the left. Also CHEAP 1.

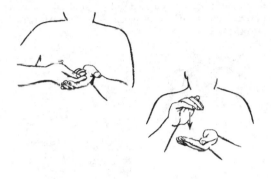

INFANT (ĭn′ fənt), *n.* (The rocking of the baby.) The arms are held with one resting on the other, as if cradling a baby. They rock from side to side. Also BABY, DOLL 2.

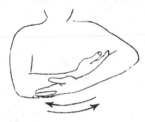

INFECTION (in fek′ shən) *n.* (The spreading.) The fingertips of the right "O" hand, palm facing the signer, rest on the back of the downturned left hand. The right fingertips spread open as the right hand moves slightly toward the signer. Also CONTAGIOUS.

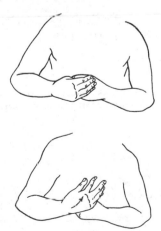

INFERIOR (in fir′ ē ər), *adj.* (The letter "I"; underneath.) The right little finger executes a clockwise circle underneath the downturned left palm.

INFINITE (ĭn′ fə nĭt), *adj.* (A large amount.) The "5" hands face each other, fingers curved and touching. They move apart rather quickly. Also EXPAND, GREAT 2, LOT, MUCH.

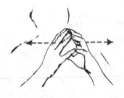

INFLATION (in flā′ shən), *n.* (The letter "I"; spiraling upward.) The base of the right "I" hand rests on the left hand. It spirals upward.

INFLUENCE 1 (ĭn′ floo əns), *n., v.,* -ENCED, -ENCING. (Swaying one to one's side.) The "A" hands, palms facing each other and the right positioned above the left, swing over simultaneously to the left side of the body. Also EFFECT 2.

INFLUENCE 2, *n., v.* (Rays of influence emanating from a given source.) All the right fingertips, including the thumb, are positioned on the tip of the upturned thumb of the left "A" hand. The right hand, opening into the downturned "5" position, moves forward from its initial position. Instead of its initial position on the left thumb, the right hand is frequently placed on the back of the downturned left "S" hand, moving forward as described above. Also BASIS 1, CAUSE, EFFECT 1, INTENT 2, LOGIC, PRODUCE 4, REASON 2.

INFLUENCE 3, *n., v.* (Directing the attention to something, and bringing it forward.) The right index finger points into the left palm, held facing out before the body. The left palm moves straight out. For the passive form of this verb, *i.e.,* BE SHOWN, the movement is reversed: the left hand, palm facing in, is moved in toward the body while the right index finger remains pointing into the left palm. Also DEMONSTRATE, DISPLAY, EVIDENCE, EXAMPLE, EXHIBIT, EXHIBITION, ILLUSTRATE, INDICATE, PRODUCE 2, REPRESENT, SHOW 1, SIGNIFY 1.

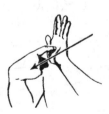

INFLUENCE 4, *n., v.* (Take something, *influence,* and disseminate it.) The left hand, held limp in front of the body, has its fingers pointing down. The fingers of the right hand, held all together, are placed on the top of the left hand and then move forward off the left hand, assuming a "5" position, palm down. Essentially similar to second part of INFLUENCE 2. Also ADVICE, ADVISE, COUNSEL, COUNSELOR.

INFORM 1 (ĭn fôrm'), *v.,* -FORMED, -FORMING. (Taking knowledge from the mind and giving it out to all.) The fingertips are positioned on either side of the forehead. Both hands then swing down and out, opening into the upturned "5" position. Also INFORMATION 1, LET KNOW 1, NOTIFY 1.

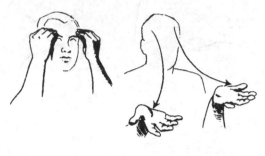

INFORM 2, *v.* The fingertips of the right "5" hand are positioned on the forehead. Both hands then swing forward and up, opening into the upturned "5" position. Also INFORMATION 2, LET KNOW 2, NOTIFY 2.

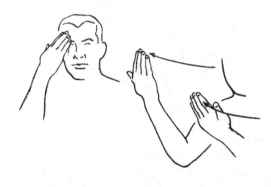

INFORMATION 1 (ĭn fər mā' shən), *n.* See INFORM 1.

INFORMATION 2, *n.* See INFORM 2.

INJECTION (ĭn jĕk' shən), *n.* (The natural sign.) The right hand goes through the motions of injecting a substance into the upper left arm. Also SHOT 1, SHOT IN THE ARM.

INJURE 1 (ĭn′ jər), v., -JURED, -JURING. (A stabbing pain.) The "D" hands, index fingers pointing to each other, are rotated in elliptical fashion before the chest—simultaneously but in opposite directions. Also ACHE, HARM 1, HURT 1, INJURY, MAR 1, OFFEND, OFFENSE, PAIN, SIN, WOUND.

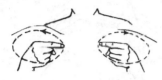

INJURE 2, v. (An encroachment; parrying a knife thrust.) The left "A" hand is held palm toward the body, knuckles facing right. The extended thumb of the right "A" hand is brought sharply over the back of the left. Also DANGER 2, DANGEROUS 2, PERIL, TRESPASS, VIOLATE.

INJURY (ĭn′ jə rĭ), n. See INJURE 1.

INJUSTICE (ĭn jŭs′ tĭs), n. (Not, justice.) The sign for NOT 1 is made: the downturned open hands are crossed; they are drawn apart rather quickly. This is followed by the sign for JUSTICE: the two "F" hands, palms facing each other, move alternately up and down.

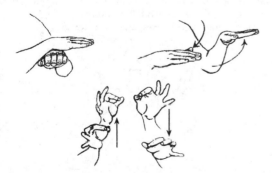

INK 1 (ĭngk), n. (The letter "I"; dipping the pen and shaking off the excess ink.) The little finger of the right "I" hand is dipped into the hole formed by the left "O" hand, held thumb side up. The right hand then emerges and shakes off the imaginary ink from the little finger.

INK 2, n. (The letter "I"; dipping the pen; writing.) The little finger of the right "I" hand is drawn along the right eyebrow from left to right. This is a modified sign for BLACK, q.v. The same finger is then dipped into the inkwell, as explained in INK 1. Finally the right hand, holding an imaginary pen, writes on the upturned left palm.

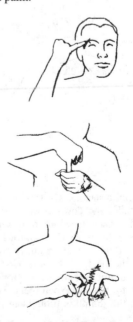

IN-LAW (ĭn′ lô′), *n.* (See material pertaining to each word.) The sign for IN is made: the fingers of the right hand are thrust into the left. This is followed by the sign for LAW: the upright right "L" hand, resting palm against palm on the upright left "5" hand, moves down in an arc a short distance, coming to rest on the base of the left palm.

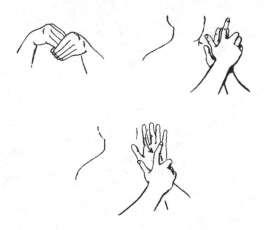

INNER FEELINGS, *n.* (Things within.) The left "C" hand is held near the base of the throat, palm facing the body. The right hand, fingers closed, is stuffed into the left. This sign should be made a bit slowly and deliberately.

INNOCENCE (ĭn′ ə səns), *n.* (Not to blame.) The sign for NOT is made: the downturned open hands are crossed at the wrists; they are drawn apart rather quickly. This is followed by the sign for BLAME: the right "A" hand, thumb pointing up, is brought down firmly against the back of the left hand, held palm down; the right thumb is then directed toward the person or object to blame. When personal blame is acknowledged, the thumb is brought in to the chest.

The two signs are sometimes presented in reverse order. Also INNOCENT.

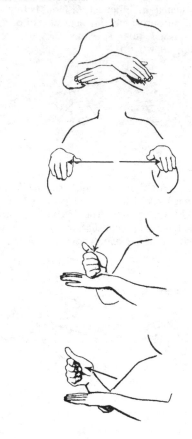

INNOCENT 1 (ĭn′ ə sənt), *adj.* See INNOCENCE.

INNOCENT 2, *adj., n.* Both open hands, palms facing out, are held in front of the mouth with the ring fingers bent against the palm. Both hands move out and away from the mouth, describing arcs. Also NAIVE 2.

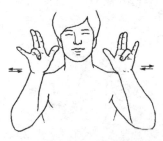

INOCULATE (ĭ nŏk′ yə lāt′) (*colloq.*), *v.*, -LATED, -LATING. (A shot in the arm.) The right index finger is thrust into the left upper arm and the thumb wiggles back and forth a number of times, as if implanting a shot in the arm. Also COCA-COLA, COKE, DOPE, MOR-PHINE, NARCOTICS.

INPUT (in′po͝ot) *n.*, *v. Computer term.* (Stuffing in.) The right fingertips stuff something into the cupped left hand. The movement is repeated.

INQUIRE 1 (ĭn kwīr′), *v.*, -QUIRED, -QUIRING. (Pray tell.) Both hands, held upright about a foot in front of the chest, with palms facing and fingers pointing straight up, are positioned about a foot apart. Moving toward the chest, they come together until they touch, as if in prayer. Also ASK 1, CONSULT, REQUEST 1.

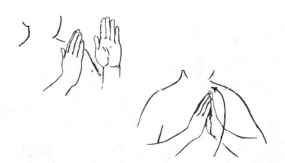

INQUIRE 2 (*colloq.*), *v.* (Fire a question.) The right hand, held in a modified "S" position with palm facing out, assumes a position with the thumb resting on the fingernail of the index finger. The index finger is flicked out and forward, usually directed at the person being asked a question. Also ASK 2, EXAMINATION 2, INTERROGATE 2, INTERROGATION 2, QUERY 2, QUESTION 2, QUIZ 2.

INQUIRE 3, *v.* (Firing questions.) The index fingers of both "D" hands repeatedly curve and straighten out as the hands are alternately flung forward and back as if firing questions. Also ASK 3, EXAMINATION 3, INTERROGATE 1, INTERROGATION 1, QUERY 1, QUESTION 3, QUIZ 3.

INSANE (ĭn sān′), *adj.* (Turning of wheels in the head.) The open right hand is held palm down before the face, fingers spread, bent, and pointing toward the forehead. The fingers move in circles before the forehead. Also CRAZY 1, INSANITY, MAD 2, NUTS 1.

INSANITY (ĭn săn′ ə tĭ), *n.* See INSANE.

INSECT 1 (ĭn′ sĕkt), *n.* (The moving legs.) The down-turned hands are crossed and interlocked at the little fingers. As they move forward, the fingers wiggle. Also SPIDER.

INSECT 2 (*sl.*), *n.* (The quivering antennae.) The thumb of the "3" hand rests against the nose, and the index and middle fingers bend slightly and straighten again a number of times. Also BUG.

INSENSATE (ĭn sĕn′ sāt), *adj.* (The slapping indicates the feelings of the heart are being tested.) The right hand rests on the heart. It then swings off and down, palm upturned, its fingertips slapping against the left palm as it moves down. An expression of contempt is often assumed.

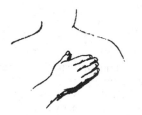

INSIDE (*prep., adv.* ĭn′ sīd′; *adj.* ĭn′ sīd′). (The natural sign.) The fingers of the right hand are thrust into the left. Also IN, INTO, WITHIN.

INSIST (ĭn sĭst′), *v.,* -SISTED, -SISTING. (Something specific is moved in toward oneself.) The palm of the left "5" hand faces right. The right index finger is thrust into the left palm, and both hands are drawn sharply in toward the chest. Also DEMAND, REQUEST 2, REQUIRE.

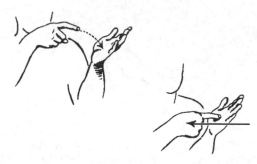

INSOMNIA (in som′ nē ə) *n.* (The eyes are wide open.) Both "C" hands are positioned against the wide-open eyes.

INSPIRE (ĭn spīr′), *v.,* INSPIRED, INSPIRING. (The feelings well up.) Both hands, fingers touching thumbs, are placed against the chest, with palms facing the body. They slide up the chest, opening into the "5" position.

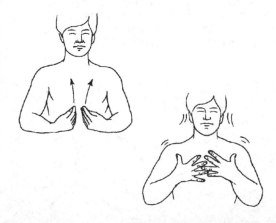

IN SPITE OF (spīt), *prep. phrase.* Both hands, in the "5" position, are held before the chest, fingertips facing each other. With an alternate back-forth movement, the fingertips are made to strike each other. Also ANYHOW, ANYWAY, DESPITE, DOESN'T MATTER, HOWEVER 2, INDIFFERENCE, INDIFFERENT, MAKE NO DIFFERENCE, NEVERTHELESS, NO MATTER, WHEREVER.

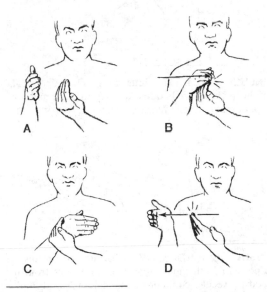

A   B

C   D

INSTALL (ĭn stôl'), *v.*, -STALLED, -STALLING. (Placing into.) The right hand, fingers touching the thumb, is placed into the left "C" hand, whose palm faces out or toward the right.

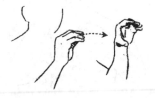

INSTEAD OF 1 (ĭn stĕd'), *prep. phrase.* (Exchanging places.) The right "A" hand, positioned above the left "A" hand, swings down and under the left, coming up a bit in front of it. Also EXCHANGE, REPLACE, SUBSTITUTE, TRADE.

INSTEAD OF 2, *prep. phrase.* This is the same sign as for INSTEAD OF 1, except that the "F" hands are used.

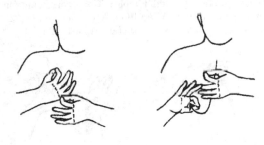

INSTITUTE 1 (ĭn' stə tūt', -to͞ot'), *n.* (The letter "I"; establishment on a firm base.) The right "I" hand is placed so that its base rests on the back of the down-turned left "S" hand. The movement is repeated, involving a slight up-down motion. Sometimes the right hand executes a small clockwise circle before coming to rest on the left. In this case the motion is not repeated. Also INSTITUTION.

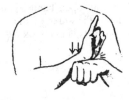

INSTITUTE 2, *v.* -TUTED, -TUTING. (Turning a key to open up a new venture.) The right index finger, resting between the left index and middle fingers, executes a half turn, once or twice. Also BEGIN, COMMENCE, INITIATE, ORIGIN 1, ORIGINATE 1, START.

INSTITUTION (ĭn' stə tū' shən), *n.* See INSTITUTE 1.

INSTRUCT (ĭn strŭkt′), *v.*, -STRUCTED, -STRUCTING. (Giving forth from the mind.) The fingertips of each hand are placed on the temples. They then swing out and open into the "5" position. Also EDUCATE, INDOCTRINATE, INDOCTRINATION, INSTRUCTION, TEACH.

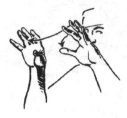

INSTRUCTION (ĭn strŭk′ shən), *n.* See INSTRUCT.

INSTRUCTOR (ĭn strŭk′ tər), *n.* The sign for INSTRUCT is made. This is followed by the sign for INDIVIDUAL: both open hands, palms facing each other, move down the sides of the body, tracing its outline to the hips. Also EDUCATOR, TEACHER.

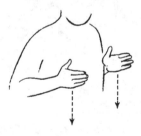

INSULT 1 (*n.* ĭn′ sŭlt; *v.* ĭn sŭlt′) -SULTED, -SULTING. (A puncturing.) The right index finger is thrust quickly and deliberately between the index and middle fingers of the left "V" hand, which is held palm facing right.

INSULT 2, *v.* (A slap in the face.) The right hand slaps the back of the left a glancing blow, and its momentum continues it beyond the left hand. Also BANISH.

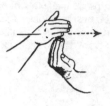

INSULT 3, *n., v.* (The thrust of a foil or épée.) The right index finger is thrust quickly forward and a bit up, in imitation of a fencing maneuver. Also RIPOSTE.

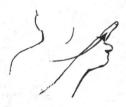

INSULT 4, *v.* (Directing a barrage of insults or ripostes.) Both index fingers, pointing out from the body, execute continuous alternate forward movements.

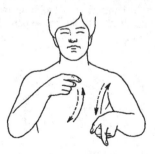

INSURANCE (ĭn shŏŏr′ əns), *n.* (The letter "I.") The right "I" hand, palm out, is shaken slightly.

INTELLIGENT (ĭn tĕl′ ə jənt), *adj.* (The mind is bright.) The middle finger is placed at the forehead, and then the hand, with an outward flick, turns around so that the palm faces outward. This indicates a brightness flowing from the mind. Also BRIGHT 3, BRILLIANT 1, CLEVER 1, SMART.

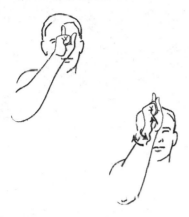

INTEND (ĭn tĕnd′), v., -TENDED, -TENDING. (Relative standing of one's thoughts.) A modified sign for THINK is made: the right index finger touches the middle of the forehead. The tips of the right "V" hand, palm down, are then thrust into the upturned left palm (as in STAND, q.v.). The right "V" hand is then rethrust into the upturned left palm, with right palm now facing the body. Also CONNOTE, IMPLY, INTENT 1, INTENTION, MEAN 2, MEANING, MOTIVE 3, PURPOSE 1, SIGNIFICANCE 2, SIGNIFY 2, SUBSTANCE 2.

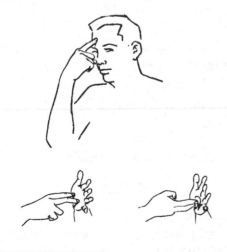

INTENT 1 (ĭn tĕnt′), n. See INTEND.

INTENT 2, n. (Rays of influence emanating from a given source.) All the right fingertips, including the thumb, are positioned on the tip of the upturned thumb of the left "A" hand. The right hand, opening into the downturned "5" position, moves forward from its initial position. Instead of its initial position on the left thumb, the right hand is frequently placed on the back of the downturned left "S" hand, moving forward as described above. Also BASIS 1, CAUSE, EFFECT 1, INFLUENCE 2, LOGIC, PRODUCE 4, REASON 2.

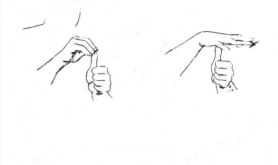

INTENTION (ĭn tĕn′ shən), n. See INTEND.

INTERCEPT (ĭn′ tər sĕpt′), v., -CEPTED, -CEPTING. (Obstruct, block.) The left hand, fingers together and palm flat, is held before the body, facing somewhat down. The little finger side of the right hand, held with palm flat, makes one or several up-down chopping motions against the left hand, between its thumb and index finger. Also ANNOY 1, ANNOYANCE 1, BLOCK, BOTHER 1, CHECK 2, COME BETWEEN, DISRUPT, DISTURB, HINDER, HINDRANCE, IMPEDE, INTERFERE, INTERFERENCE, INTERFERE WITH, INTERRUPT, MEDDLE 1, OBSTACLE, OBSTRUCT, PREVENT, PREVENTION.

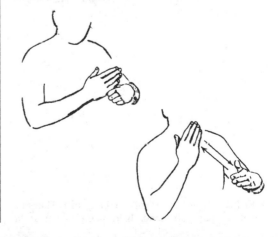

INTEREST 1 (ĭn′ tər ĭst, -trĭst), *n., v.,* -ESTED, -ESTING. (Drawing one out.) The index and middle fingers of both hands, one above the other, are placed on the middle part of the chest. Both hands move forward simultaneously. As they do, the index and middle fingers of each hand come together. Also FASCINATE 1, INTERESTED 1, INTERESTING 1.

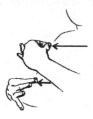

INTEREST 2, *n.* (A modification of INTEREST 1.) The same movements are employed, except that one of the hands is positioned in front of the mouth. Also ENGROSS, FASCINATE 2.

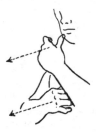

INTEREST 3, *n., v.* (The tongue is pulled out, causing the mouth to gape.) The curved open right hand is placed at the mouth, with index finger and thumb poised as if to grasp the tongue. The hand moves straight out, assuming the "A" position. Also INTERESTED 2, INTERESTING 2.

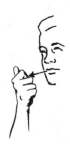

INTEREST 4, *n.* (A regular taking in.) The outstretched open left hand, held palm facing right,

moves in toward the body, assuming the "A" position, palm still facing right. This is repeated several times. Also DIVIDEND, INCOME, SUBSCRIBE, SUBSCRIPTION.

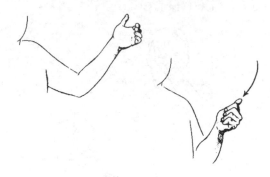

INTEREST 5, *n.* (The letter "I"; same rationale as for EARN.) The little finger edge of the right "I" hand rests on the upturned left palm. The right hand sweeps in an arc across the left palm, from right to left.

INTERESTED 1 (ĭn′ tər ĭs tĭd, -trĭs tĭd, -tə rĕs′ tĭd), *adj.* See INTEREST 1.

INTERESTED 2, *adj.* See INTEREST 3.

INTERESTING 1 (ĭn′ tər ĭs tĭng, -trĭs tĭng, -tə rĕs′ tĭng), *adj.* See INTEREST 1.

INTERESTING 2, *adj.* See INTEREST 3.

INTERFACE (in′ tər fās′) *v., n.* (Interconnectedness.) Both "5" hands, palms facing the signer, move together so the fingers interlock.

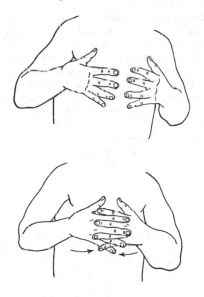

INTERFERE (ĭn′ tər fîr′), *v.,* -FERED, -FERING. (Obstruct, block.) The left hand, fingers together and palm flat, is held before the body, facing somewhat down. The little finger side of the right hand, held with palm flat, makes one or several up-down chopping motions against the left hand, between its thumb and index finger. Also ANNOY 1, ANNOYANCE 1, BLOCK, BOTHER 1, CHECK 2, COME BETWEEN, DISRUPT, DISTURB, HINDER, HINDRANCE, IMPEDE, INTERCEPT, INTERFERENCE, INTERFERE WITH, INTERRUPT, MEDDLE 1, OBSTACLE, OBSTRUCT, PREVENT, PREVENTION.

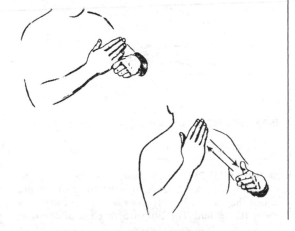

INTERFERENCE (ĭn′ tər fîr′ əns), *n.* See INTERFERE.

___

INTERFERE WITH, *v. phrase.* See INTERFERE.

___

INTERN (in′ tûrn) *n.* (The letter "I"; practicing.) The right "I" hand, palm facing out, moves back and forth rhythmically on the back of the downturned left "S" hand. Also INTERNSHIP.

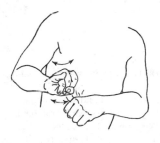

INTERNATIONAL SIGN LANGUAGE, *n. phrase.* (The gesturing of hands.) Both "5" hands are positioned with palms facing each other. They move in alternate counterclockwise circles.

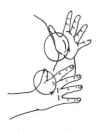

INTERNET (in′ tər net′) *n.* (Computer terminology; in touch around the globe.) Both "5" hands, palms facing each other, touch repeatedly at the middle fingertips as the two hands travel around in a horizontal or vertical circle.

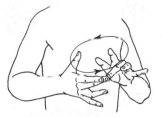

INTERPRET (ĭn tûr′ prĭt), *v.,* -PRETED, -PRETING. (Changing one language to another.) The "F" hands are held palms facing and thumbs and index fingers in contact with each other. The hands swing around each other, reversing their relative positions.

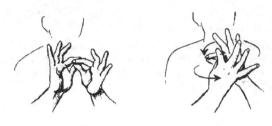

INTERROGATE 1 (ĭn tĕr′ ə gāt′), *v.,* -GATED, -GATING. (Firing questions.) The index fingers of both "D" hands repeatedly curve and straighten out as the hands are alternately flung forward and back, as if firing questions. Also ASK 3, EXAMINATION 3, INQUIRE 3, INTERROGATION 1, QUERY 1, QUESTION 3, QUIZ 3.

INTERROGATE 2 (*colloq.*), *v.* (Fire a question.) The right hand, held in a modified "S" position with palm facing out, assumes a position with the thumb resting on the fingernail of the index finger. The index finger is flicked out and forward, usually directed at the person being asked a question. Also ASK 2, EXAMINATION 2, INQUIRE 2, INTERROGATION 2, QUERY 2, QUESTION 2, QUIZ 2.

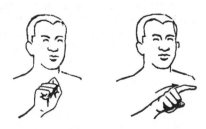

INTERROGATION 1 (ĭn tĕr′ ə gā′ shən), *n.* See INTER-ROGATE 1

INTERROGATION 2 (*colloq.*), *n.* See INTERROGATE 2.

INTERRUPT (ĭn′ tə rŭpt′), *v.,* -RUPTED, -RUPTING. (Obstruct, block.) The left hand, fingers together and palm flat, is held before the body, facing somewhat down. The little finger side of the right hand, held with palm flat, makes one or several up-down chopping motions against the left hand between its thumb and index finger. Also ANNOY 1, ANNOYANCE 1, BLOCK, BOTHER 1, CHECK 2, COME BETWEEN, DISRUPT, DISTURB, HINDER, HINDRANCE, IMPEDE, INTERCEPT, INTERFERE, INTERFERENCE, INTERFERE WITH, MEDDLE 1, OBSTACLE, OBSTRUCT, PREVENT, PREVENTION.

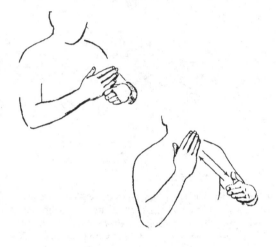

INTERSECT (ĭn′ tər sĕkt′), *v.,* -SECTED, -SECTING. (Intersecting lines.) The extended index fingers move toward each other at right angles and cross. Also CROSS 4, CROSSING, INTERSECTION.

INTERSECTION (ĭn′ tər sĕk shən), *n.* See INTERSECT.

IN THE FIELD OF, *prep. phrase.* (A straight, *i.e.,* special, path.) The hands are held in the "B" position, one above the other, with left palm facing right and right palm facing left. The little finger edge of the right hand moves straight forward along the index finger edge of the left. Also FIELD 3, SPECIALIZE, SPECIALTY.

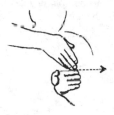

IN THE FUTURE, *adv. phrase.* (Something ahead or in the future.) The upright, open right hand, palm facing left, moves straight out and slightly up from a position beside the right temple. Also BY AND BY, FUTURE, LATER 2, LATER ON, SHALL, WILL 1, WOULD.

INTO (ĭn′ tōo), *prep.* (The natural sign.) The fingers of the right hand are thrust into the left. Also IN, INSIDE, WITHIN.

INTOXICATE (ĭn tŏk′ sə kāt′), *v.,* -CATED, -CATING. (The act of drinking.) The thumbtip of the right "Y" hand is tilted toward the mouth, as if it were a drinking glass or bottle. The signer tilts his head back slightly, as if drinking. Also DRINK 2, DRUNK, DRUNKARD, DRUNKENNESS, INTOXICATION, LIQUOR 2.

INTOXICATION (ĭn tŏk′ sə ka′ shən), *n.* See INTOXICATE.

IN TWO WEEKS, *adv. phrase.* (In a week, two.) The upright, right "2" hand is placed palm to palm against the left "5" hand, whose palm faces left. The right hand moves along the left palm from base to fingertips and then curves to the left, around the left fingertips. (This is the same sign as for IN A WEEK, except the "2" hand is used here.)

INVESTIGATE 1 (ĭn vĕs′ tə gāt′), *v.,* -GATED, -GATING. (Directing the vision from place to place.) The right "C" hand, palm facing left, moves from right to left across the line of vision in a series of counterclockwise circles. The signer's gaze remains concentrated and his head turns slowly from right to left. Also CURIOUS 1, EXAMINE, LOOK FOR, PROBE 1, QUEST, SEARCH, SEEK.

INVESTIGATE 2, *v.* (The eye is directed in a probing operation.) The right index finger is placed just below the right eye. With palm down, the same finger then moves slowly and deliberately along the upturned left palm from its base to its fingertips. Instead of the slow, deliberate movement, the finger may move along the left palm in a series of short, stabbing motions. Also INSPECT.

INVITE (ĭn vīt′), *v.,* -VITED, -VITING. (Opening or leading the way toward something.) The open right hand, held up before the body, sweeps down in an arc and over toward the left side of the chest, ending in the palm-up position. Reversing the movement gives the passive form of the verb, except that the hand does not arc upward but rather simply moves outward in a small arc from the body. Also ADMIT 2, INVITATION, INVITED, USHER, WELCOME.

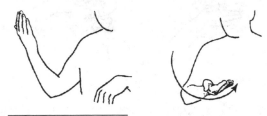

INVITED, *passive voice of the verb* INVITE. The upturned right hand, touching the chest, moves straight forward and away from the body.

INVOLVE (ĭn vŏlv′), *v.,* -VOLVED, -VOLVING. (Immersed in something.) The downturned right "5" hand moves in a clockwise circle above the cupped left "C" hand. Then the right fingers are thrust into the cupped left "C" hand, which closes over the right fingers.

ION (ī′ ən), *n.* (The letter "I"; circling.) The right "I" hand makes a clockwise circle around the left fist.

IRAN (i ran′, i rän′, ī ran′) *n.* (The gas pump. Iran is an oil-producing nation.) The downturned thumb of the right "A" hand (the pump's nozzle) is placed on the upturned palm of the left.

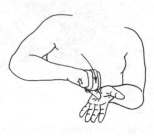

IRE (īr), *n.* (A violent welling up of the emotions.) The curved fingers of the right hand are placed in the center of the chest and fly up suddenly and violently. An expression of anger is worn. Also ANGER, ANGRY 2, ENRAGE, FURY, INDIGNANT, INDIGNATION, MAD 1, RAGE.

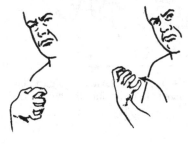

IRELAND (īr′ lənd), *n.* (A modified version of the sign for POTATO, *i.e.,* IRISH potato.) The downturned right "V" hand, poised over the downturned left "S" hand, executes a clockwise circle; then the "V" fingers stab the back of the left "S" hand. Also IRISH.

IRISH (ī′ rĭsh), *n., adj.* See IRELAND.

IRON 1 (ī′ ərn), *n.* (Striking an anvil with a hammer.) The left index finger, pointing forward from the body, represents the anvil. The right hand, grasping an imaginary hammer, swings down against the left index finger and glances off. This may be repeated. Also BLACKSMITH, STEEL.

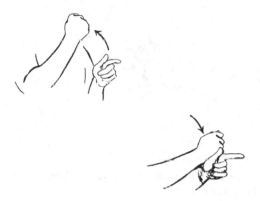

IRON 2, *n.*, IRONED, IRONING. (The act of pressing with an iron.) The right hand goes through the motion of swinging an iron back and forth over the upturned left palm. Also FLATIRON, PRESS 1.

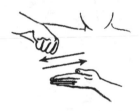

IRONY (ī′ rə nē), *n.* (Masking, or in an underhanded way.) Both downturned hands are held in front of the face, the right above the left, both hands displaying index and little fingers only. The right hand, with a flourish, descends, crossing the left arm. Meanwhile the left arm has moved to the right.

IRRITABLE (ĭr′ ə tə bəl), *adj.* (Wrinkling the brow.) The "5" hand is held palm toward the face. The fingers open and close partly, several times, while an angry expression is worn on the face. Also ANGRY 1, CROSS 1, CROSSNESS, FIERCE, ILL TEMPER.

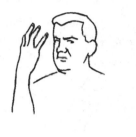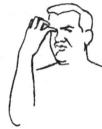

ISRAEL 1 (ĭz′ rĭ əl), *n.* (The Jewish people.) The sign for HEBREW, ISRAELITE, or JEW is made: the fingers and thumb of each hand are placed at the chin and stroke an imaginary beard. This is followed by the sign for PEOPLE: the "P" hands, held a few inches apart and palms facing, rotate in toward the body in alternate counterclockwise circles. Also HEBREWS, ISRAELITES. Also ISRAELI.

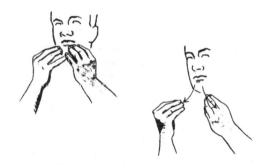

ISRAEL 2, *n.* (The letter "I"; the beard worn by many Jewish males.) The right little finger, pointing straight up, moves down the left side of the mouth and then makes the same movement down the right side of the mouth.

ISSUES (ish′ ōōz) *n., pl.* (Quotation marks used to delineate different topics or issues.) Both upright hands, palms facing each other, twist repeatedly as they move down in unison, outlining a series of quotation marks.

IT 1 (ĭt), *pron.* (A simple pointing.) The right index finger points at an object, either imaginary or real. This sign is understood mainly in context.

IT 2, *pron.* (Something specific.) The downturned right "Y" hand is placed on the upturned left palm. Also THAT 1, THESE, THIS, THOSE, WHICH 2.

IT 3 (*rare*), *pron.* (The letter "I.") The right "I" hand wiggles slightly as it moves from left to right.

IT 4, *pron.* The right little finger is thrust into the upturned left palm.

ITALY 1 (ĭt′ ə lĭ), *n.* (The letter "I"; the cross, signifying the Vatican.) The right "I" finger traces a small cross on the forehead. See ITALIAN.

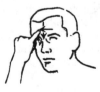

ITALY 2 (*loc.*), *n.* (A characteristic Italian gesture.) The thumb and index finger of the right "F" hand are placed against the right cheek while the hand trembles.

ITALY 3, *n.* (The shape on the map.) The thumb and index finger open and close as the hand moves down, tracing the outline of the Italian peninsula on the map.

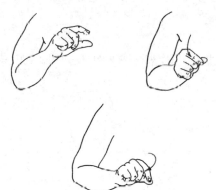

J

JAIL (jāl), *n., v.,* JAILED, JAILING. (The crossed bars.) The "4" hands, palms facing the body, are crossed at the fingers. Also IMPRISON, PENITENTIARY, PRISON.

JAM (jăm), *n.* (Spreading the letter "J.") The little finger of the right "J" hand moves twice across the upturned left palm, toward the base of the left hand. Also JELLY.

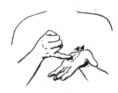

JAMAICA (jə mā′ kə), *n.* (The shape of the island.) The left hand is held downturned at chest level. The right hand, fingers together, runs along the right side of the left hand, around the fingertips and along the little finger edge.

JAPAN 1, (jə păn′), *n.* (The letter "J"; the slanting eyes.) The right little finger is placed at the corner of the right eye, pulling it back slightly into a slant. Both little fingers may also be used, involving both eyes. Also JAPANESE.

JAPAN 2, *n.* (The shape of the islands on the map.) With hands facing the body, the index fingers and thumbs form a triangle. They come apart, moving in a slight upward arc, and close, so that the index fingers now touch their respective thumbs.

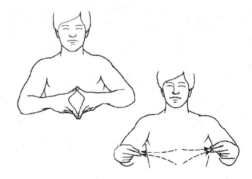

JEALOUS (jĕl′ əs), *adj.* (Biting the finger to suppress the feelings.) The tip of the index finger is bitten. The tip of the little finger is sometimes used. Also COVET 2, ENVIOUS, ENVY, JEALOUSY.

JEALOUSY (jĕl′ ə sĭ), *n.* See JEALOUS.

JEANS (jēnz), *n.* (The letters and position.) Both "J" hands are placed at the waist and outline a "J" as they move up slightly.

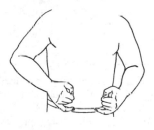

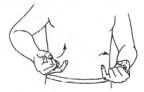

JELL-O (jel′ ō), *n.* (*trademark*). (The shaking as it is held on a plate.) The downturned right claw hand is held over the upturned left palm. The right hand shakes or trembles. Also GELATIN.

JELLY (jĕl′ ĭ), *n.* See JAM.

JERUSALEM (jĭ rōō′ sə ləm) (*eccles.*) (*rare*), *n.* (The holy city.) The sign for HOLY is made: the right "H" hand moves in a small clockwise circle several times; the right palm then wipes the upturned left palm. This is followed by the sign for CITY: the fingertips of both hands are joined, the hands and arms forming a pyramid; the fingertips separate and rejoin a number of

times; both arms may move a bit from left to right each time the fingertips separate and rejoin.

JERUSALEM 2, *n.* (The mezuzah is kissed at the portals.) The right fingertips are kissed, and then the outstretched right hand touches an imaginary mezuzah or scroll on a doorpost.

JESUS (jē′ zəs), *n.* (The marks of the crucifixion.) Both "5" hands are used. The left middle finger touches the right palm, and then the right middle finger touches the left palm.

JEW (jōō), *n.* (The beard of the old Jewish patriarchs.) The fingers and thumb of each hand are placed at the chin and stroke an imaginary beard. Also HEBREW, ISRAELITE, JEWISH.

JEWISH (jōō′ ĭsh), *adj.* See JEW.

JOB (jŏb), *n.* (Striking an anvil.) Both "S" hands are held palms down. The right hand strikes against the back of the left a number of times. Also LABOR, OCCUPATION, TASK, TOIL, TRAVAIL, VOCATION, WORK.

JOIN 1 (join), *v.,* JOINED, JOINING. (Joining together.) Both hands, held in the modified "5" position, palms out, move toward each other. The thumbs and index fingers of both hands then connect. Also AFFILIATE 1, ANNEX, ASSOCIATE 2, ATTACH, BELONG, COMMUNION OF SAINTS, CONCERN 2, CONNECT, ENLIST, ENROLL, PARTICIPATE, RELATIVE 2, UNION, UNITE.

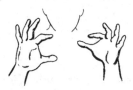 

JOIN 2, *v.* (A grouping together.) Both "C" hands, palms facing, are held a few inches apart at chest height. They are swung around in unison so that the palms now face the body. Also ASSOCIATION, AUDIENCE 1, CASTE, CIRCLE 2, CLASS, CLASSED 1, CLUB, COMPANY, FAMILY 2, GANG, GROUP 1, ORGANIZATION 1.

JOIN 3, *v.* (To enter into.) The index and middle fingers of the right "U" hand are thrust into the hole formed by the left "O" hand, held palm out. The two fingers represent the legs.

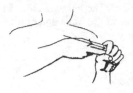

JOLLY (jŏl′ ĭ), *adj.* (A crinkling up of the face.) Both hands, in the "5" position, palms facing back, are placed on either side of the face. The fingers wiggle back and forth while a pleasant, happy expression is worn. Also AMIABLE, CHEERFUL, CORDIAL, FRIENDLY, PLEASANT.

JOURNEY 1 (jûr′ nĭ), *n., v.,* -NEYED, -NEYING. (Moving around from place to place.) Both "D" hands are held palms facing, the index fingers pointing to each other. In this position the hands describe a series of small counterclockwise circles as they move in random fashion from right to left. Also TRAVEL 1, TRIP 1.

JOURNEY 2, *n., v.* A variation of JOURNEY 1, but using only the right hand. Also TRAVEL 2, TRIP 2.

JOURNEY 3, *n., v.* A variation of JOURNEY 1 and JOURNEY 2, but using the downturned curved "V" fingers. Also TRANSIENT, TRAVEL 3, TRIP 3.

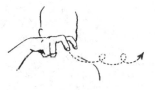

JOY (joi), *n.* (The heart is stirred; the spirits bubble up.) The open right hand, palm facing the body, strikes the heart repeatedly, moving up and off the heart after each strike. Also DELIGHT, GAIETY 1, GAY, GLAD, HAPPINESS, HAPPY, MERRY.

JOY STICK, *n. Computer term.* (The manipulation.) The little finger edge of the right fist rests in the upturned left flat palm. It rocks at random from left to right and forward and back.

JUDGE 1 (jŭj), *n., v.,* JUDGED, JUDGING. (The scales move up and down.) The two "F" hands, palms facing each other, move alternately up and down. Also CONSIDER 3, COURT, EVALUATE 1, IF, JUDGMENT, JUSTICE 1.

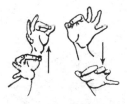

JUDGE 2, *n.* (Judge, individual.) The sign for JUDGE 1 is made. This is followed by the sign for INDIVIDUAL: both open hands, palms facing each other, move down the sides of the body, tracing its outline to the hips. Also REFEREE, UMPIRE.

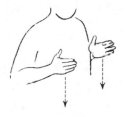

JUDGMENT (jŭj' mənt), *n.* See JUDGE 1.

JUGGLE (jug' əl), *v.,* JUGGLED, JUGGLING. (The natural movement.) The signer mimes juggling several objects.

JUMP 1 (jŭmp), *v.,* JUMPED, JUMPING. (The natural sign.) The bent right index and middle fingers rest on the upturned left palm. The right hand rises suddenly, as if the fingers have jumped up. The fingers usually remain bent, but they may also straighten out as the hand rises. The motion may also be repeated. Also HOP 1, LEAP.

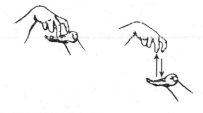

JUMP 2, *v.* One finger is used here, the middle or the index, to represent a single leg. Also HOP 2.

JUMP OVER, *v. phrase.* (The movement.) The curved index and middle fingers of the right hand, palm facing down, are brought up and over the index finger edge of the left, whose palm faces right.

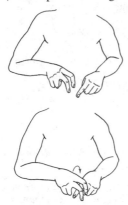

JUMP ROPE (jump rōp) *v. phrase.* (The natural movement.) The signer mimes jumping rope.

JUMP-START, *v. phrase.* (Placing the cables on the battery terminals.) Using the downturned "V" hands, the signer mimes clamping them on the terminals of a car battery.

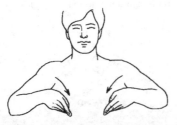

JUNIOR (jōōn′ yər), *n.* (College student.) The left index finger taps the palm of the right hand.

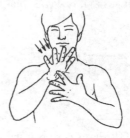

JUST A MOMENT AGO, *adv. phrase.* (Time moved backward a bit.) The right "D" hand, palm facing the body, is placed in the palm of the left hand, which is facing right. The right hand swings back a bit toward the body, with the index finger describing an arc. Also FEW SECONDS AGO, WHILE AGO, A 3.

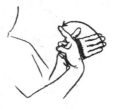

JUSTICE 1 (jŭs′ tĭs), *n.* (The scales move up and down.) The two "F" hands, palms facing each other, move alternately up and down. Also CONSIDER 3, COURT, EVALUATE 1, IF, JUDGE 1, JUDGMENT.

JUSTICE 2, *n.* (Fairness or equality; the scales of justice.) The hands are held palms facing and fingers pointing straight forward. The thumb and index finger of each hand form circles, and the hands move together until these circles touch.

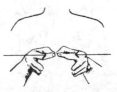

K

KANGAROO (kang gə roo′), *n.* (The shape and movement.) The vertical right arm represents the kangaroo's body; the index and little fingers, the ears; and the thumb touching the middle and ring fingers, the snout. With the upturned cupped left hand resting on the right arm near the elbow to represent the pouch, the signer executes a series of short forward jumping motions.

KARATE (kä rä′ tä), *n.* (The chopping motions.) Using both hands and arms, the signer mimes the chopping motions of karate.

KEEP (kēp), *v.,* KEPT, KEEPING. (Slow, careful movement.) The "K" hands are crossed, the right above the left, little finger edges down. In this position the hands are moved up and down a short distance. Also CARE 2, CAREFUL 2, MAINTAIN 1, MIND 3, PRESERVE, RESERVE 2, TAKE CARE OF 2.

KEEP A SECRET, *colloq. phrase.* (Squeezing the mouth shut.) The right "S" hand is placed thumb side against the lips. It swings to the palm-down position, held tightly against the lips.

KEEP QUIET 1, *v. phrase.* (The natural sign.) The index finger is placed forcefully against the closed lips. The signer frowns or looks stern. Also KEEP STILL 1.

KEEP QUIET 2, *v. phrase.* (The mouth is sealed; the sign for QUIET.) The downturned open hands are crossed at the lips with the left in front of the right. Both hands are drawn apart and down rather forcefully while the signer frowns or looks stern. Also KEEP STILL 2.

KEEP STILL 1, *v. phrase.* See KEEP QUIET 1.

KEEP STILL 2, *v. phrase.* See KEEP QUIET 2.

KERCHIEF (kûr′ chif), *n.* (Tying the kerchief over the head.) The signer mimes placing a kerchief over the head and tying it under the chin.

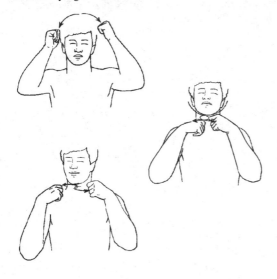

KETCHUP (kech′ əp, kach′-), *n.* (Hitting the bottom of the ketchup bottle.) The left hand grasps an imaginary bottle of ketchup while the downturned flat right hand strikes the bottom repeatedly to dislodge the contents.

KEY (kē), *n.* (The turning of the key.) The right hand, holding an imaginary key, twists it in the open left palm, which is facing right. Also LOCK 1.

KEYBOARD 1 (kē′ bôrd), *n.* (The shape and function.) The signer types on an imaginary keyboard, and then the downturned index fingers trace a rectangle, indicating the shape of the keyboard.

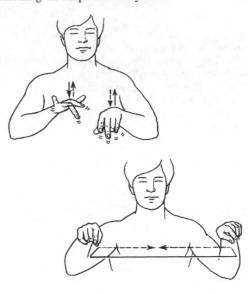

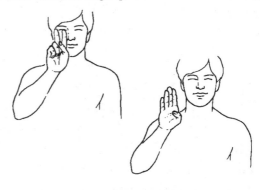

KEYBOARD 2, *n.* (A fingerspelled loan sign.) The letters "K-B" are fingerspelled.

KEYHOLE (kē′ hōl′), *n.* (Manipulating a key in a hole.) Grasping an imaginary key with the right fingers, the signer twists it forward and back in front of a small hole formed by the left hand.

KICK 1 (kĭk), *n., v.,* KICKED, KICKING. (The natural sign.) The right "B" hand, palm facing the body and fingers pointing down, swings in an arc to the left, striking the side of the left "S" hand, held palm facing up. Also KICK OUT, SOCCER.

KICK 2 (*sl.*), *v.* (Kicking.) Both "S" hands are held before the chest. Then the hands move sharply to the side, opening into a modified "V" position, palms down, as if kicking. Also COMPLAIN 2, OBJECT 3.

KID 1 (kĭd) (*colloq.*), *n.* (The running nose.) The index and little fingers of the right hand, held palm down, are extended, pointing to the left. The index finger is placed under the nose, and the hand trembles somewhat.

KID 2, *v.,* KIDDED, KIDDING. The knuckles of the right "X" hand move sharply forward along the thumb edge of the left "X" hand. Also TEASE 2.

KIDNEY (kĭd' nē), *n.* (The location in the body.) The open right hand, palm up, repeatedly taps a spot on the right middle rib cage.

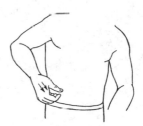

KIKE (kĭk) *n., sl.* (A disparaging and offensive sign for a person of Jewish descent.) The heel of the open right hand rests on the chin and the hand swivels forward and back, pivoted at the wrist.

KILL (kĭl), *v.,* KILLED, KILLING. (Thrusting a dagger and twisting it.) The outstretched right index finger is passed under the downturned left hand. As it moves under the left hand, the right wrist twists in a clockwise direction. Also MURDER, SLAY.

KILOGRAM (kĭl' ə gram), *n.* (The letter "K"; weighing.) The right "K" hand is balanced back and forth as it rests on the index finger of the left "G" hand.

KILOMETER (kil′ ə mē tər), *n.* (The "K" and the "M.") Both hands are first held in the "K" position. They change to the "M" position, side by side, and move apart.

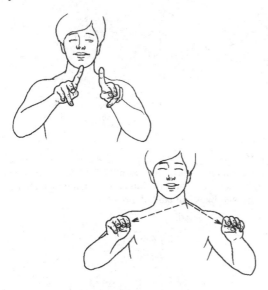

KIND 1 (kīnd), *adj.* (The heart rolls out.) Both right-angle hands roll over each other as they move down and away from their initial position at the heart. Also BENEVOLENT, GENEROUS 1, GENTLE 1, GENTLENESS, GRACIOUS, HUMANE, KINDNESS, MERCY 1, TENDER 3.

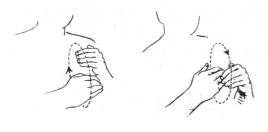

KIND 2, *n.* (The letter "K"; the wholeness or global characteristic.) The right "K" hand revolves once around the left "K" hand. This is used to describe a class or group.

KINDERGARTEN (kin′ dər gär tən), *n.* (The letter "K"; SCHOOL.) The right hand makes a "K" and

shakes it back and forth. The right open hand then comes down on the left palm, clapping several times.

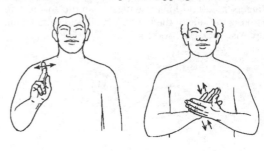

KING (kĭng), *n.* (The letter "K"; the royal sash.) The right "K" hand moves from the left shoulder to the right hip.

KISS 1 (kĭs), *n., v.,* KISSED, KISSING. (The natural sign.) The right fingertips are placed on the lips and then on the right cheek. This latter movement is often omitted.

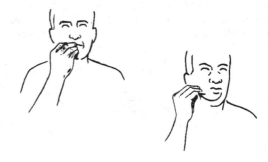

KISS 2, *n., v.* (The natural sign.) The right "A" hand, palm facing the body, is placed on the mouth so that the backs of the fingers rest against the lips. The hand, in this same position, is then placed on the right cheek, although this latter movement is often omitted.

KISS 3, *n., v.* (Lips touch lips.) With fingers touching their thumbs, both hands are brought together. They tremble slightly, indicating the degree of intensity of the kiss.

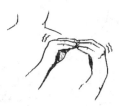

KITCHEN 1 (kĭch′ ən), *n.* (Turning over a pancake.) The open right hand rests on the upturned left palm. The right hand flips over and comes to rest with its back on the left palm. This is the action of turning over a pancake. Then the sign for ROOM is made: the open hands, palms facing and fingers pointing out, are dropped an inch or two simultaneously. They then shift their relative positions so that both palms face the body, with one hand in front of the other. In this new position they again drop an inch or two simultaneously. Also CHEF, COOK, PANCAKE.

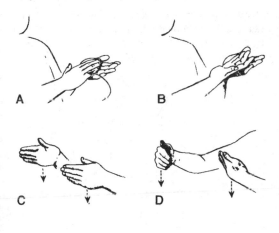

A   B

C   D

KITCHEN 2, *n.* (The letter "K.") The right "K" hand is placed palm down on the upturned left palm. It flips over to the palm-up position and comes to rest again on the upturned left palm, as if flipping over a pancake.

KITE (kīt), *n.* (Holding the kite string.) Looking up, the signer pulls on an imaginary string several times. Both hands may be used. Also FLY A KITE.

KNEE (nē), *n.* (The anatomy.) The signer points to a knee.

KNEEL (nēl), *v.,* KNELT or KNEELED, KNEELING. (Kneeling in church.) The knuckles of the right index and middle fingers are placed in the upturned left palm. The action may be repeated. Also PROTESTANT.

KNIFE 1 (nīf), *n.* (Shaving or paring.) The edge of the right "H" hand, resting on the edge of its left counterpart, moves forward several times, as if shaving layers of flesh.

KNIFE 2, *n.* (A variation of KNIFE 1.) The index fingers are used here, in the same manner as above.

KNIFE 3, *n.* (The cutting.) The right index finger cuts back and forth across the midpoint of its left counterpart.

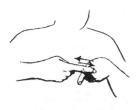

KNIT (nĭt), *n., v.,* KNITTED or KNIT, KNITTING. (The knitting.) The index fingers, pointing forward, are rubbed back and forth against each other. Also HOSE 1, SOCK(S) 1, STOCKING(S) 1.

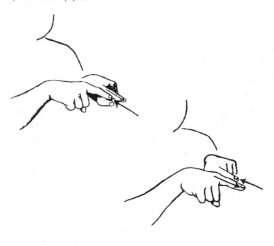

KNOCK (nŏk), *v.,* KNOCKED, KNOCKING. (The natural sign.) The right knuckles knock against the palm of the left hand, which is facing right. Also RAP.

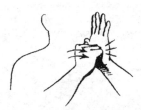

KNOT (nŏt), *n., v.,* KNOTTED, KNOTTING. (The act of tying.) Both hands, in the "A" position, go through the natural hand-over-hand motions of tying and drawing out a knot. Also BIND, FASTEN, TIE 1.

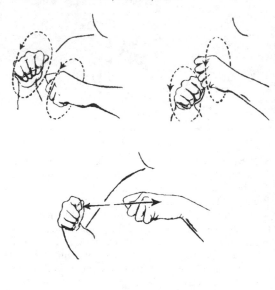

KNOW (nō), *v.,* KNEW, KNOWN, KNOWING. (Patting the head to indicate something of value inside.) The right fingers pat the forehead several times. Also INTELLIGENCE, KNOWLEDGE, RECOGNIZE.

KNOWING (nō′ ĭng), *adj.* See KNOW.

KNOWLEDGE (nŏl′ ĭj), *n.* See KNOW.

KNOW NOTHING 1 (nuth′ ĭng) (*colloq.*), *v. phrase.* (KNOW and ZERO.) The sign for KNOW is made. The little finger edge of the right "O" hand is brought sharply into the upturned left palm, emphasizing the "nothingness." This is an emphatic sign, indicating a complete lack of knowledge.

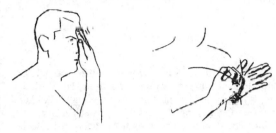

KNOW NOTHING 2, *phrase.* (Zero in the head.) The right "O" hand, palm facing left, is brought up sharply to the forehead.

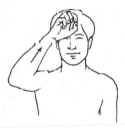

KNOW NOTHING 3, *phrase.* (A variation of above.) The right "O" hand swings back and forth at the forehead.

KNOW WELL, *phrase.* (Tapping the mind emphatically.) The fingertips strike the forehead repeatedly as the signer assumes an expression of intensity.

KOSHER (kō′ shər), *adj. n.* (The letter "K"; CLEAN.) The base of the right "K" hand sweeps forward across the open left hand, from base to fingertips.

L

LABEL (lā′ bəl), *n., v.,* LABELED, LABELING. (A label is affixed.) The right "H" hand, palm facing the signer, moves across the left breast pocket, from left to right.

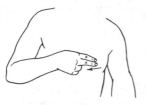

LABOR (lā′ bər), *n., v.,* -BORED, -BORING. (Striking an anvil.) Both "S" hands are held palms down. The right hand strikes against the back of the left a number of times. Also JOB, OCCUPATION, TASK, TOIL, TRAVAIL, VOCATION, WORK.

LADDER 1 (lăd′ ər), *n.* (Rising.) The right open hand, palm up, moves slowly up. Also ASCEND, CLIMB 2.

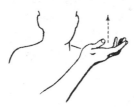

LADDER 2, *n.* (The action.) The right index and middle fingers walk up the left index finger.

LADY (lā′ dĭ), *n.* (A female with a ruffled bodice; *i.e.,* an elegantly dressed woman, a lady.) The FEMALE root sign is made: the thumb of the right "A" hand moves down along the right jaw, from ear almost to chin. The thumbtip of the right "5" hand, palm facing left, is then placed on the chest, with the other fingers pointing up. Pivoted at the thumb, the hand swings down a bit so that the other fingers are now pointing out somewhat. Also MADAM.

LAMP (lămp), *n.* (The rays come out.) The down-turned "8" hand, positioned at the chin, flicks open a number of times. Also LIGHT 3.

LAND 1 (lănd), *n.* (An expanse of ground.) The sign for SOIL 1 is made: both hands, held upright before the body, finger imaginary pinches of soil. The down-turned open right "5" hand then sweeps in an arc from right to left. Also FIELD 1.

LAND 2, *n.* (An established area.) The right "N" hand, palm down, executes a clockwise circle above the downturned prone left hand. The tips of the "N" fingers then move straight down and come to rest on the back of the left hand. Also COUNTRY 2, NATION.

LANGUAGE 1 (lăng′ gwĭj), *n.* (A series of letters spelled out on the printed page.) The downturned "F" hands are positioned with thumbs and index fingertips touching. The hands move straight apart to either side in a wavy motion. Also SENTENCE.

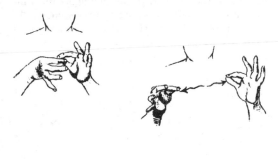

LANGUAGE 2, *n.* (The letter "L.") The sign for LANGUAGE 1 is made, but with the "L" hands.

LANGUAGE OF SIGNS, *n.* (LANGUAGE 1 and hand/arm movements.) The "D" hands, palms facing and index fingers pointing back toward the face, describe a series of continuous counterclockwise circles toward and away from the face, imitating the foot motions in

bicycling. This is followed by the sign for LANGUAGE 1. Also SIGN LANGUAGE, SIGNS.

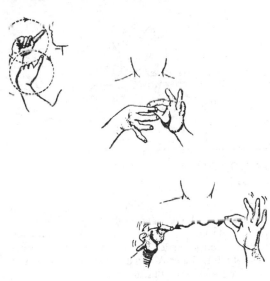

LAP (lap), *n.* (The anatomy.) The signer slaps the upper thigh twice.

LARGE (lärj), *adj.* (A delineation of something big, modified by the letter "L," which stands for LARGE.) Both "L" hands, palms facing out, are placed before the face and separate rather widely. Also BIG 1, ENORMOUS, GREAT 1, HUGE, IMMENSE.

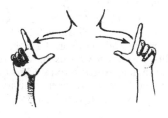

LARIAT (lar′ ē ət), *n.* (Twirling a lariat.) The signer twirls an imaginary lariat and pulls back. For added effect, the body may bounce up and down slightly, as if on horseback. Also COWBOY 2, LASSO.

LASSO (lăs′ ō), *n.* See LARIAT.

LAST 1 (lăst), *adj.* (The little, *i.e.,* LAST, fingers are indicated.) With the hands in the "I" position, the tip of the right little finger strikes the tip of its left counterpart. The right index finger may be used instead of the right little finger. Also END 1, EVENTUALLY, FINAL 1, FINALLY 1, ULTIMATE, ULTIMATELY.

LAST 2, *adj.* (A single little, *i.e.,* LAST, finger is indicated.) The tip of the index finger of the right "D" hand strikes the tip of the little finger of the left "I" hand. Also END 2, FINAL 2, FINALLY 2.

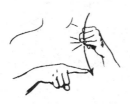

LAST 3, *v.,* LASTED, LASTING. (Steady, uninterrupted movement.) The "A" hands are held with palms out, thumbs extended and touching, the right behind the left. In this position the hands move forward in a straight, steady line. Also CONTINUE 1, ENDURE 2, EVER 1, LASTING, PERMANENT, PERPETUAL, PERSERVERE 3, PERSIST 2, REMAIN, STAY 1, STAY STILL.

LASTING (lăs′ tǐng), *adj.* See LAST 3.

LASTLY (lăst′ lǐ), *adv.* See LAST 1 or 2.

LATE (lāt), *adj.* (Hanging back.) The "5" hand and forearm, hanging loosely and straight down from the elbow, move back and forth under the armpit. Also BEHIND TIME, NOT DONE, NOT YET, TARDY.

LATER 1, *adj.* (A moving on of the minute hand of the clock.) The right "L" hand, its thumb thrust into the palm of the left and acting as a pivot, moves forward a short distance. Also AFTER A WHILE, AFTERWARD, SUBSEQUENT, SUBSEQUENTLY.

LATER 2, *adj., adv.* (Something ahead or in the future.) The upright, open right hand, palm facing left, moves straight out and slightly up from a position beside the right temple. Also BY AND BY, FUTURE, IN THE FUTURE, LATER ON, SHALL, WILL 1, WOULD.

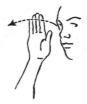

LATER ON, *adv. phrase.* See LATER 2.

LATIN 1 (lăt′ ən), *n., adj.* (The Roman nose.) The index and middle fingertips of the right "N" hand, palm facing the body, move down in an arc from the bridge of the nose to its tip. Also ROMAN, ROME.

describing short arcs. The signer meanwhile laughs. Also HYSTERICAL.

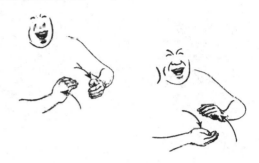

LATIN 2 (*rare*), *n., adj.* (Same rationale as in LATIN 1 with the "L" initial.) The thumbtip of the right "L" hand, palm facing left, moves down in an arc from midforehead to the tip of the nose.

LAUGHTER 3 (*colloq.*), *n.* (Literally, rolling in the aisles; the legs are doubled up and the body rolls on the floor.) With index and middle fingers crooked and its little finger edge or back resting on the upturned left palm, the right hand moves in a continuous counterclockwise circle in the left palm. The signer meanwhile laughs. Also HYSTERICAL LAUGH.

LAUGH (lăf), *n., v.,* LAUGHED, LAUGHING. (The natural sign.) The fingers of both "D" hands move repeatedly up along the jawline or up from the corners of the mouth. The signer meanwhile laughs. Also LAUGHTER 1.

LAW (lô), *n.* (A series of LAWS as they appear on the printed page.) The upright right "L" hand, resting palm against palm on the upright left "5" hand, moves down in an arc a short distance, coming to rest on the base of the left palm. Also DECREE 2, LAWYER, LEGAL, PRECEPT.

LAUGHTER 1 (lăf′ tər), *n.* See LAUGH.

LAUGHTER 2 (*colloq.*), *n.* (The shaking of the stomach.) The cupped hands, held at stomach level, palms facing the body, move alternately up and down,

LAWYER (lô′ yər), *n.* The sign for LAW is made. The sign for INDIVIDUAL is then added: both hands, fingers together, are placed at either side of the chest and are moved down to waist level.

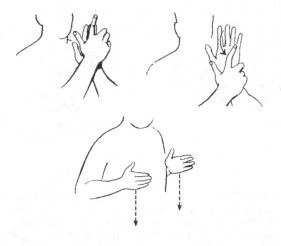

LAZINESS (lā′ zĭ nĭs), *n.* (The initial "L" rests against the body; the concept of inactivity.) The right "L" hand is placed against the left shoulder once or a number of times. The palm faces the body. Also LAZY 1, SLOTH.

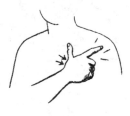

LAZY 1 (lā′ zĭ), *adj.* See LAZINESS.

LAZY 2 (*rare*), *adj.* The thumbtip of the right "L" hand rests against the left shoulder, palm facing the body. The hand moves in a wavy manner down across the chest, from the left shoulder to the right side of the body.

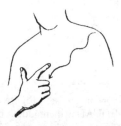

LEAD 1 (lēd), *n., v.,* LEAD, LEADING. (One hand leads the other.) The right hand grasps the tips of the left fingers and pulls the left hand forward. Also CONDUCT 2, GUIDE.

LEAD 2 (lĕd), *n.* (Heavy and hard substance.) The sign for HEAVY is made: the upturned "5" hands, held before the chest, suddenly drop a short distance. The back of the downturned right "S" hand then strikes the underside of the chin a number of times.

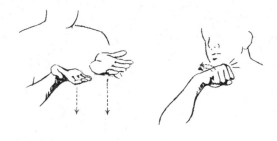

LEAF 1 (lēf), *n.* (The rustling.) This sign is used for the leaf of a tree. The right "5" hand, held straight up, represents the tree. The fingertips of the left hand are placed on the right wrist, and the right fingertips wiggle slightly.

LEAF 2, *n.* (The edge of the leaf of a book.) The sign for BOOK is made: the open hands, palms touching, open in imitation of the opening of a book. The right fingertips then run along the index finger edge of the left "B" hand, which is held with fingers pointing to the right.

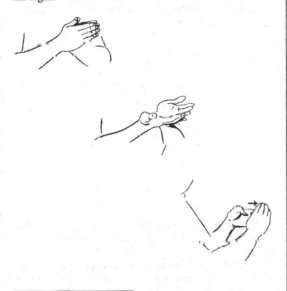

LEAF 3, *n.* The left "5" hand, palm out, is the tree. The right thumb and index finger trace the shape of a leaf from one of the outstretched left fingers.

LEAGUE (lēg), *n.* (The "L" letters; forming a circle.) Both "L" hands, palms out, move apart and together again, forming a circle.

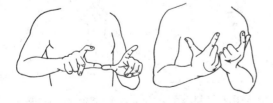

LEAK (lēk), *n., v.,* LEAKED, LEAKING. (The natural sign.) The right "4" hand, palm facing the body and fingers pointing left, moves down repeatedly from its

position below the right "S" hand, whose palm faces the body with thumb edge up. Also DRIP.

LEAK 2, *n., v.* (Slow dripping.) The closed right index and thumb are positioned beneath the downturned left "S" hand. The two right fingers open slowly and deliberately. The movement is repeated.

LEAN 1 (lēn), *adj.* (The drawn face.) The thumb and index finger run down the cheeks, which are drawn in. Also POOR 2, THIN 1.

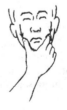

LEAN 2, *adj.* (The sunken cheeks.) The fingertips of both hands run down either side of the face. The cheeks meanwhile are sucked in a bit.

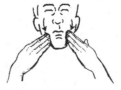

LEARN (lûrn), *v.,* LEARNED, LEARNING. (Taking knowledge from a book and placing it in the head.) The downturned fingers of the right hand are placed on the upturned left palm. They close, and then the hand rises and the right fingertips are placed on the forehead. Also EDUCATION.

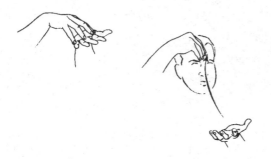

LEAST 1 (lēst), *adj., n.* The sign for LESS is made: with palms facing, the right hand is held above the left; the right hand moves slowly down toward the left but does not touch it. This is followed by the sign for FIRST: the right index finger touches the upturned left thumb. Instead of the sign for FIRST, the right thumb may be drawn straight up, to a position above the head. Also SMALLEST.

LEAST 2, *adj.* (A small amount; the superlative degree.) The slightly cupped hands, palms facing, are brought together until they almost touch, and then the right thumb is brought up sharply to a position above the head.

LEATHER (leth′ ər), *n., adj.* (The letter "L"; worn on or covering the body.) The thumb of the right "L" hand is placed on the chest and moves down an inch or two several times.

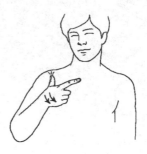

LEAVE 1 (lēv), *v.,* LEFT, LEAVING. (Pulling away.) The downturned open hands are held in a line, with fingers pointing to the left, the right hand behind the left. Both hands move in unison toward the right. As they do so, they assume the "A" position. Also DEPART, EVACUATE, FORSAKE 1, GRADUATE 2, RETIRE 1, WITHDRAW 1.

LEAVE 2, *v.* (To throw something aside.) Both "S" hands are held with palms facing at chest level and then thrown down and to the left, opening into the "5" position. Also ABANDON 1, CAST OFF, DEPOSIT 2, DISCARD 1, FORSAKE 3, LET ALONE, NEGLECT.

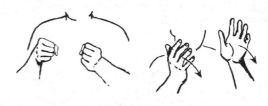

LEAVE COLLEGE, *phrase.* (A form of escaping.) The right index finger is positioned on the tip of any of the five fingers of the upturned left hand, from the little finger to the thumb. The right index moves suddenly forward and out. From the thumb, the leaving occurs at the senior year; from the ring finger, at the freshman level. The little finger is reserved for the so-called prep year in some schools designed to admit a heterogeneous student body needing extensive pre-freshman orientation.

LECTURE (lek′ chər), *n., v.,* -TURED, -TURING. (A gesture of an orator.) The right open hand, palm facing left, is held above and to the right of the head. It pivots on the wrist, forward and backward, several times. Also ADDRESS 1, ORATE, SPEECH 2, TALK 2, TESTIMONY.

LEFT 1 (lĕft), *adj., adv.* (The letter "L"; to the left side.) The left "L" hand, palm out, moves to the left.

LEFT 2, *adj.* (The remainder is left behind.) The "5" hands, palms facing each other and fingers pointing forward, are dropped simultaneously a few inches, as if dropping something on the table. Also REMAINDER, RESERVE 4, REST 3.

LEFT TURN, *phrase.* (The left "L" hand swings around.) The left "L" hand, palm facing the signer, swings around so that its palm now faces out. Also TURN LEFT.

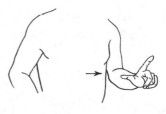

LEGAL (lē′ gəl), *adj.* (A series of LAWS as they appear on the printed page.) The upright right "L" hand, resting palm against palm on the upright left "5" hand, moves down in an arc a short distance, coming to rest on the base of the left palm. Also DECREE 2, LAW, LAWYER, PRECEPT.

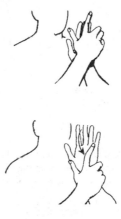

LEGISLATURE (lĕj′ ĭs lā′ chər), *n.* (The letter "L"; possibly the Roman toga.) The thumb of the right "L" hand moves from the left shoulder to the right shoulder.

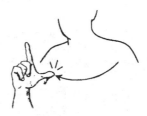

LEISURE (lē′ zhər, lĕzh′ ər), *n.* (A position of idleness.) With thumbs tucked in the armpits, the remaining fingers of both hands wiggle. Also HOLIDAY, IDLE, RETIRE 3, VACATION.

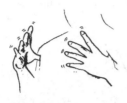

LEMON 1 (lĕm′ ən), *n.* (Yellow and sour.) The sign for YELLOW, is made: the right "Y" hand shakes back and forth, pivoted at the wrist. The sign for SOUR is then made: the right index finger is brought sharply up against the lips, while the mouth is puckered up as if tasting something sour. Also ACID, BITTER, DISAPPOINTED 1, SOUR.

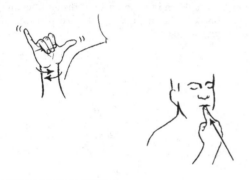

LEMON 2, *n.* (Sucking the lemon.) The right hand, grasping an imaginary lemon, is placed at the lips. It may rotate slightly. A sour expression is assumed.

LEMON 3, *n.* (The letter "L"; sour.) The index finger (or thumb) of the right "L" hand is placed on the lips, which are puckered. A sour expression is assumed.

LEMONADE (lĕm ən ād′), *n.* (The "L" for LEMON; something sour is brought to the lips.) The thumbtip of the right "L" hand is brought sharply up to the lips, and then the signer mimes drinking from a glass.

LEND 1 (lĕnd), *v.,* LENT, LENDING. (Something kept, *i.e.,* in one's custody, is moved forward to other, temporary, ownership.) The crossed "K" hands, for KEEP, *q.v.,* are moved forward simultaneously in a short arc. Also LOAN 1.

LEND 2, *v.* The side of the right index finger is brought up against the right side of the nose. Also LOAN 2.

LENGTH (lengkth), *n.* (The distance is traced.) The right index finger traces a long line along the upturned left arm from wrist almost to shoulder. Also LONG.

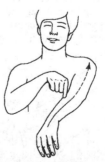

LENS (lenz), *n.* (Focusing a lens, as a camera or telescope lens.) Both "C" hands, palms facing each other, are positioned on the eye, with the right against the eye and the left in front of it. Both "C" hands, pivoting on the wrists, move in opposite circles as if focusing a lens.

LEOTARDS (lē′ ə tärdz), *n.* (Drawing up the tight garment.) The signer mimes struggling into a very tight garment. Also TIGHTS.

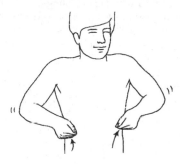

LESBIAN (lez′ bē ən), *n., adj.* (The letter "L.") The right "L" hand is held palm facing the body, index finger pointing left. In this position the hand is placed against the chin.

LESS 1 (lĕs), *adj.* (The diminishing size or amount.) With palms facing, the right hand is held above the

left. The right hand moves slowly down toward the left but does not touch it. Also DECREASE, REDUCE.

LESS 2, *adv.* (Removing.) The right "A" hand, resting in the palm of the left "5" hand, moves slightly up and away, describing a small arc. It is then cast downward, opening into the "5" position, palm down, as if removing something from the left hand and casting it down. Also ABOLISH 2, ABSENCE 2, ABSENT 2, ABSTAIN, CHEAT 2, DEDUCT, DEFICIENCY, DELETE 1, MINUS 3, OUT 2, REMOVE 1, SUBTRACT, SUBTRACTION, TAKE AWAY FROM, WITHDRAW 2.

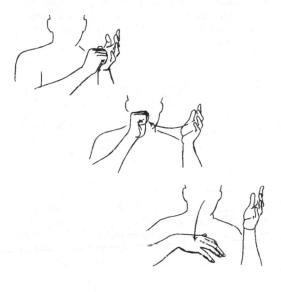

LESSON (lĕs′ ən), *n.* (A section of a page.) The upturned open left hand represents the page. The little finger edge of the right-angle hand is placed on the left palm near the fingertips. It moves up and over in an arc to the base of the left palm. Also EXERCISE 2.

LESS THAN, *adj. phrase.* (Something below.) Both downturned open hands are positioned with right below left. The right hand moves down a few inches, and the left remains stationary.

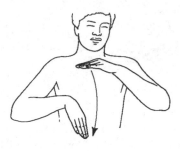

LET (lět), *v.,* LET, LETTING, *n.* (A permissive upswinging of the hands, as if giving in.) Both hands, palms facing and fingers pointing away from the body, are held at chest level almost a foot apart. With an upward movement, using their wrists as pivots, the hands sweep up until the fingers point almost straight up. Also ALLOW, GRANT 1, LET'S, LET US, MAY 3, PERMISSION 1, PERMIT 1, TOLERATE 1.

LET ALONE, *v. phrase.* (To throw something aside.) Both "S" hands are held with palms facing at chest level and then thrown down and to the left, opening into the "5" position. Also ABANDON 1, CAST OFF, DEPOSIT 2, DISCARD 1, FORSAKE 3, LEAVE 2, NEGLECT.

LET KNOW 1, *v. phrase.* (Taking knowledge from the mind and giving it out to all.) The fingertips are positioned on either side of the forehead. Both hands then

swing down and out, opening into the upturned "5" position. Also INFORM 1, INFORMATION 1, NOTIFY 1.

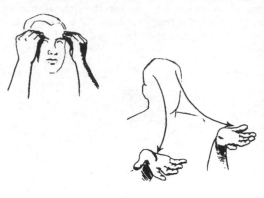

LET KNOW 2, *v. phrase.* The fingertips of the right "5" hand are positioned on the forehead. Both hands then swing forward and up, opening into the upturned "5" position. Also INFORM 2, INFORMATION 2, NOTIFY 2.

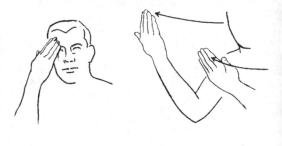

LET'S (lěts); **LET US,** *v. phrase.* See LET.

LET'S SEE, *phrase.* (Sign for SEE.) The right "V" hand, palm facing the signer, is positioned with the index finger on the corner of the right eye. It taps this corner twice.

LETTER (lĕt′ ər), *n.* (The stamp is affixed.) The right thumb is placed on the tongue, and is then pressed into the open left palm. Also EPISTLE, MAIL 1.

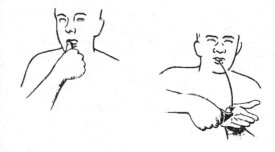

LETTUCE 1 (lĕt′ ĭs), *n.* (A head of lettuce; the upturned fingers represent the leaves.) The base of the right "5" hand strikes the right side of the head a number of times.

LETTUCE 2 (*rare*), *n.* (The downturned leaves.) The prone right hand is draped over the prone left. The right hand moves slightly back and forth, fingers hanging down.

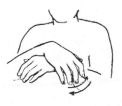

LEVEL (lĕv′ əl), *adj., n., v.,* -ELED, -ELING. (Sameness is stressed.) The downturned "B" hands, held at chest height, are brought together repeatedly so that the index finger edges or fingertips come into contact. Also EQUAL, EQUIVALENT, EVEN, FAIR 1, IMPARTIAL, JUST 1.

LIAR (lī′ ər), *n.* (Words diverted instead of coming straight, or truthfully, out.) The index finger of the right "D" hand, pointing to the left, moves along the lips from the right to left. Also FALSE, FALSEHOOD, FRAUDULENT 2, LIE 1, PREVARICATE, UNTRUTH.

LIBERATION (lĭb′ ər ā′ shən), *n.* (Breaking the bonds.) The "S" hands, crossed in front of the body, swing apart and face out. Also DELIVER 1, EMANCIPATE, FREE 1, INDEPENDENCE, INDEPENDENT, REDEEM 1, RELIEF, RESCUE, SAFE, SALVATION, SAVE 1.

LIBRARY (lī′ brĕr′ ĭ), *n.* (The initial "L.") The right "L" hand, palm out, describes a small clockwise circle, as in LIBERTY.

LICENSE 1 (lī′ səns), *n., v.,* -CENSED, -CENSING. (Affixing a seal.) The little finger edge of the right "S" hand strikes the palm of the upturned left "5" hand.

LICENSE 2 (*loc.*), *n.* (The "L" hands outline the dimensions of the license form.) The "L" hands, palms out, touch at the thumbtips several times.

LICK (lĭk), *n., v.*, LICKED, LICKING. (The action of the tongue.) The right index and middle fingers, held together, sweep up and down twice on the outstretched left palm.

LIE 1 (lī), *n., v.*, LIED, LYING. (Words diverted instead of coming straight, or truthfully, out.) The index finger of the right "D" hand, pointing to the left, moves along the lips from right to left. Also FALSE 1, FALSEHOOD, FRAUDULENT 2, LIAR, PREVARICATE, UNTRUTH.

LIE 2, *n., v.* (Same rationale as in LIE 1 but more emphatic, as indicated by several fingers.) The index finger edge of the downturned "B" hand moves along the lips (or under the chin) from right to left.

LIE 3, *v.*, LAY, LAIN, LYING. (The prone position of the legs, in lying down.) The index and middle fingers of the right "V" hand, palm facing up, are placed in the upturned left palm. Also LIE DOWN, RECLINE.

LIE DOWN, *v. phrase.* See LIE 3.

LIFE 1 (līf), *n.* (The fountain [of LIFE] wells up from within the body.) The upturned thumbs of the "A" hands move in unison up the chest. Also ADDRESS 3, ALIVE, DWELL, EXIST, LIVE 1, LIVING, MORTAL, RESIDE.

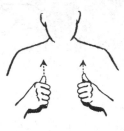

LIFE 2, *n.* (Same rationale as for LIFE 1 with the initial "L.") The upturned thumbs of the "L" hands move in unison up the chest.

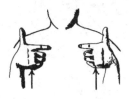

LIFT (lĭft), *v.*, LIFTED, LIFTING. (Raising something up.) Both upturned open hands move up simultaneously.

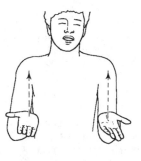

LIGHT 1 (līt), *n.* (The candle flame and the rays of light.) The index finger of the "D" hand is placed on the pursed lips as if blowing out a candle. The right hand is then raised above the head, with the fingertips and thumbtip touching and palm facing out. The hand then moves down and a bit forward, opening into the

"5" position, palm down. (The candle part of this sign is frequently omitted.) Also EPIPHANY, RAY.

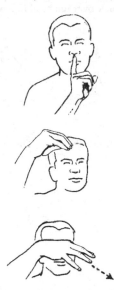

LIGHT 2, *adj.* (Easily lifted.) The open hands, palms up, move up and down together in front of the body as if lifting something very light.

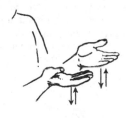

LIGHT 3, *n.* (The rays come out.) See LAMP.

LIKE 1 (līk), *v.,* LIKED, LIKING. (Drawing out the feelings.) The thumb and index finger of the right open hand, held an inch or two apart, are placed at mid-

chest. As the hand moves straight out from the chest the two fingers come together. Also ADMIRE 1, REVERE 1.

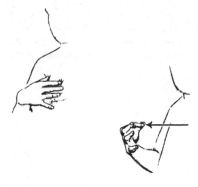

LIKE 2, *adj., n.* (Matching fingers are brought together.) The outstretched index fingers are brought together either once or several times. Also ALIKE, IDENTICAL, SAME 1, SIMILAR, SUCH.

LIKE 3, *v.* (A pleasurable feeling on the heart.) The open right hand is circled on the chest over the heart. Also APPRECIATE, ENJOY, ENJOYMENT, GRATIFY 1, PLEASE, PLEASURE, WILLING 2.

LIMIT (lĭm′ ĭt), *n., v.,* LIMITED, LIMITING. (The upper and lower limits are defined.) The right-angle hands, palms facing, are held before the body, the right above the left. They swing out 45° simultaneously, pivoted from their wrists. Also CAPACITY, QUANTITY 1, RESTRICT.

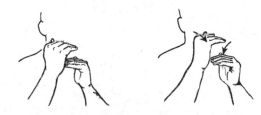

LIMOUSINE (lĭm′ ə zēn′), *n.* (The elongated chassis.) The "C" hands, left palm facing right and right palm facing left, are joined as if holding a telescope, with the right hand in front of the left. The right hand moves straight forward about 6 inches. The left hand remains in position. Sometimes both hands close into the "S" position as the right hand moves forward.

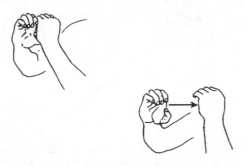

LINCOLN (lĭng′ kən), *n.* (The initial "L" at the head, probably to denote the head of the country—the president.) The right "L" hand, palm facing out, is placed with the thumbtip resting on the right temple.

LINGUISTICS (ling gwis′ tiks), *n.* (The letters "L" and "S"; stretching out words.) The downturned "L" hands, thumbtips touching, move apart in a wavy motion, ending with both hands in the "S" position.

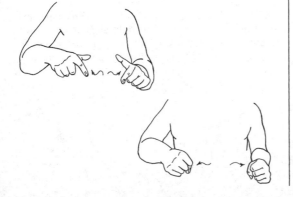

LION (lī′ ən), *n.* (The mane.) The downturned "C" hand (or "5" hand with fingers somewhat curved) moves straight back over the head in a wavy motion.

LIP (lip), *n.* (Outline the lips.) The index draws an outline around the lips.

LIPREADING (lĭp′ rēd′ ĭng), *n.* (Reading the lips—the lines of vision, represented by the two fingers, scan the lips.) The right "V" hand, palm facing the body, is placed in front of the face, with slightly curved index and middle fingers directly in front of the lips. The right hand moves in a small counterclockwise circle around the lips. Also ORAL, READ LIPS, SPEECHREADING.

LIQUOR 1 (lĭk′ ər), *n.* (The size of the jigger is indicated.) The right hand, with index and little fingers extended and the remaining fingers held against the palm by the thumb, strikes the back of the downturned "S" hand several times. Also WHISKEY 1.

LIQUOR 2, *n.* (The act of drinking.) The thumbtip of the right "Y" hand is tilted toward the mouth, as if it were a drinking glass or bottle. The signer tilts his head back slightly, as if drinking. Also DRINK 2, DRUNK, DRUNKARD, DRUNKENNESS, INTOXICATE, INTOXICATION.

LISTEN 1 (lĭs' ən), *n.*, -TENED, -TENING. (Cupping the hand at the ear.) The right hand is placed, usually slightly cupped, behind the right ear. Also HARK, HEAR, HEARKEN.

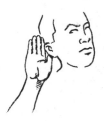

LISTEN 2, *v.* (Drawing in sound.) The thumb of the right "3" hand is placed on the right ear and the bent index and middle fingers open and close. Also HEAR 2.

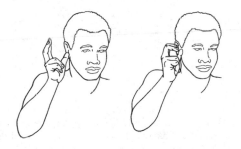

LITTLE 1 (lĭt' əl), *adj.* (Indicating a small size or amount.) The open hands are held facing each other, one facing down and the other facing up. In this position the top hand moves down toward the bottom hand but does not quite touch it. The space between the hands shows the small size or amount.

LITTLE 2, *adj., adv., n.* (A small or tiny movement.) The right thumbtip is flicked off the index finger several times as if shooting marbles, although the movement is not so pronounced. Also MINUTE 2, TINY 1.

LITURGY (lĭt' ər jē), *n.* (*eccles.*). (The raising of the Host to the lips.) Both "L" hands, palms out, touch at the tips of the thumbs. They move up simultaneously toward the lips.

LIVE 1 (lĭv), *v.*, LIVED, LIVING. (The fountain [of LIFE] wells up from within the body.) The upturned thumbs of the "A" hands move in unison up the chest. Also ADDRESS 3, ALIVE, DWELL, EXIST, LIFE 1, LIVING, MORTAL, RESIDE.

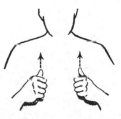

LIVE 2, *v.* See LIFE 2.

LIVER (lĭv′ ər), *n.* (The liver is indicated.) The middle finger of the right "5" hand, palm facing the body, is brought against the body a number of times in the area of the liver.

LIVING (lĭv′ ĭng), *adj.* See LIVE 1.

LIVING ROOM 1, *n.* (Life, room.) The sign for LIFE 2 is made: the upturned thumbs of the "L" hands move in unison up the chest. This is followed by the sign for ROOM: the "R" hands, palms facing and fingers pointing forward, are dropped an inch or two simultaneously. Then they shift positions so that both palms face the body, with one hand in front of the other. In this new position they again drop an inch or two simultaneously.

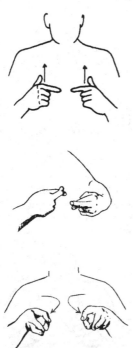

LIVING ROOM 2, *n.* (Fine room.) The downturned "5" hand is placed with the thumb touching the chest. It moves repeatedly up and out an inch or two, returning each time to its initial position. This is followed by the sign for ROOM: the open hands, palms facing and fingers pointing out, are dropped an inch or two simultaneously. They then shift their relative positions so that both palms face the body, with one hand in front of the other. In this new position they again drop an inch or two simultaneously. The "R" hands may be substituted for the open hands.

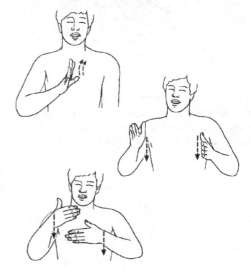

LOAF (lōf), *v.,* LOAFED, LOAFING. (Sit back with nothing to do.) The thumbs of both "5" hands are tucked in the armpits as the signer sits back.

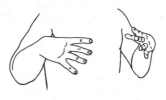

LOAN 1 (lōn), *n.* (Something kept, *i.e.,* in one's custody, is moved forward to other, temporary, ownership.) The crossed "K" hands, for KEEP, *q.v.,* are moved forward simultaneously in a short arc. Also LEND 1.

LOAN 2 (*loc.*) (*colloq.*), *n., v.,* LOANED, LOANING. The side of the right index finger is brought up against the right side of the nose. Also LEND 2.

LOATHE (lōth), *v.,* LOATHED, LOATHING. (To push away and recoil from; avoid.) The two open hands, palms facing left, are pushed deliberately to the left as if pushing something away. An expression of disdain or disgust is worn. Also ABHOR, AVOID 2, DESPISE 1, DETEST 1, HATE 1.

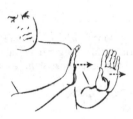

LOCAL (lō' kəl), *adj.* (In a small area.) The down-turned right "5" hand makes a continuous small counterclockwise circle in front of the chest.

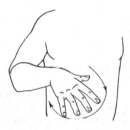

LOCATION (lō ka' shən), *n.* (The letter "P"; a circle or square is indicated to show the locale or place.) The "P" hands are held side by side before the body, with middle fingertips touching. From this position, the hands separate and outline a circle (or a square) before coming together again closer to the body. Also PLACE 1, POSITION 1, SCENE, SITE.

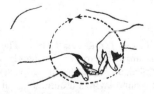

LOCK 1 (lŏk), *n., v.,* LOCKED, LOCKING. (The turning of the key.) The right hand, holding an imaginary key, twists it in the open left palm, which is facing right. Also KEY.

LOCK 2 (*loc.*), *v.* (Bind down.) The right "S" hand, palm down, makes a clockwise circle and comes down on the back of the left "S" hand, also held palm down.

LOCKED (*loc.*), *adj.* (Bound down to custom or habit.) Both "S" hands, palms down, are crossed and brought down in unison before the chest. Also ACCUSTOM, BOUND, CUSTOM, HABIT, PRACTICE 3.

LOCK HORNS, *sl. phrase.* (Clashing or banging together.) Both downturned "Y" hands, representing horns, come together forcefully.

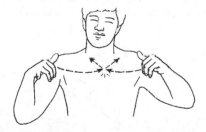

LOGIC 1 (lŏj′ ĭk), *n.* (Rays of influence emanating from a given source.) All the right fingertips, including the thumb, are positioned on the tip of the upturned thumb of the left "A" hand. The right hand, opening into the downturned "5" position, moves forward from its initial position. Instead of its initial position on the left thumb, the right hand is frequently placed on the back of the downturned left "S" hand, moving forward as described above. Also BASIS 1, CAUSE, EFFECT 1, INFLUENCE 2, INTENT 2, PRODUCE 4, REASON 2.

LOGIC 2, *n.* (The letter "L" on the head.) The thumb of the right "L" hand makes a small counterclockwise circle around the forehead.

LONE (lōn), *adj.* (One wandering around in a circle.) The index finger, pointing straight up, palm facing the body (the number *one*), is rotated before the face in a counterclockwise direction. Also ALONE, ONE 2, ONLY, SOLE, UNITY.

LONELY 1 (lōn′ lĭ), *adj.* (Oneness; quietness.) The index finger of the right "1" hand moves straight down across the lips once or twice. Also LONESOME.

LONELY 2 (*colloq.*), *adj.* ("I" signs, *i.e.,* alone with oneself.) Both "I" hands are held facing the body, the little fingers upright and held an inch or two apart. The little fingers come together and separate repeatedly.

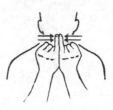

LONESOME (lōn′ səm), *adj.* See LONELY 1.

LONG 1 (lông, lŏng), *adj., n., adv.* (The distance is traced.) The right index finger traces a long line along the upturned left arm from wrist almost to shoulder.

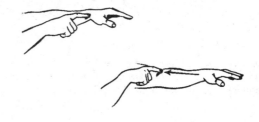

LONG 2, *v.,* LONGED, LONGING. (Grasping something and pulling it in.) The upturned "5" hands, held side by side before the chest, close slightly into a grasping position as they move in toward the body. Also COVET 1, DESIRE 1, NEED 2, WANT, WILL 2, WISH 1.

LOOK 1 (lŏŏk), *v.,* LOOKED, LOOKING. (The eyesight is directed forward.) The right "V" hand, palm facing the body, is placed so that the fingertips are just under the eyes. The hand swings around and out so that the fingertips are now pointing forward. Also PERCEIVE 1, PERCEPTION, SEE, SIGHT, WATCH 2.

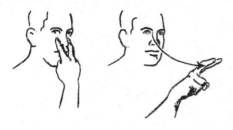

LOOK 2 (lōōk), *v.* (Something presented before the eyes.) The open right hand, palm flat and facing out, with fingers together and pointing up, is positioned at shoulder level. Pivoting from the wrist, the hand is swung around so that the palm now faces the eyes. Sometimes the eyes glance at the newly presented palm. Also APPARENT, APPARENTLY, APPEAR 1, SEEM.

LOOK AT, *v. phrase.* (The vision is directed forward.) The tips of the right "V" fingers point to the eyes. The right hand is then swung around and forward a bit. Also GAZE, OBSERVE 1, WITNESS.

LOOK DOWN, *v. phrase.* (The gaze is cast downward.) Both "V" hands, side by side and palms facing out, are

swept downward so that the fingertips now point down. A haughty expression, or one of mild contempt, is sometimes assumed. Also CONTEMPT 1, SCORN 1.

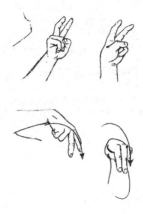

LOOK FOR, *v. phrase.* (Directing the vision from place to place; the French *chercher.*) The right "C" hand, palm facing left, moves from right to left across the line of vision in a series of counterclockwise circles. The signer's gaze remains concentrated and his head turns slowly from right to left. Also CURIOUS 1, EXAMINE, INVESTIGATE 1, PROBE 1, QUEST, SEARCH, SEEK.

LOOK UP, *v.,* LOOKED, LOOKING. (Thumbing through pages.) The downturned right thumb digs into the upturned left palm a number of times. Also PAGE.

LOOK UP TO, *phrase.* (Looking up.) Both forward pointing "V" hands are positioned before the eyes. They move forward and up.

LOOSE TOOTH, *n. phrase.* (The natural sign.) The signer grasps a tooth and shakes it.

LOPSIDED (lop′ sī′ did), *adj.* (Not on an even keel.) Both downturned open hands are held with one hand lower than the other; and the signer leans toward the lower hand. Also UNEVEN KEEL.

LORD 1 (lôrd), *n.* (The ribbon worn across the chest by nobles; the initial "L.") The right "L" hand, palm facing out, moves down across the chest from left shoulder to right hip.

LORD 2, *n.* (A motion indicating the One above.) The right open hand, palm facing left, swings up above the head and is then moved down about an inch. The signer looks up while making the sign. Also GOD.

LOSE (lōōz), *v.,* LOST, LOSING. (Dropping something.) Both hands, with fingers touching their respective thumbs, are held palms up and with the backs of the fingers almost touching or in contact with one another. The hands drop into an open position, with fingers pointing down. Also LOST.

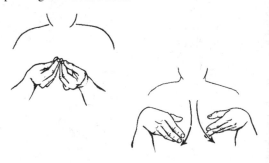

LOSE COMPETITION, *v. phrase.* (Being pinned down to the mat, as in a wrestling match.) The downturned right "3" or "V" hand is slapped into the upturned left palm.

LOST (lôst, löst), *adj.* See LOSE.

LOT (lŏt), *n.* (A large amount.) The "5" hands face each other, fingers curved and touching. They move apart rather quickly. Also EXPAND, GREAT 2, INFINITE, MUCH.

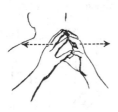

LOTION (lō' shən), *n.* (Pouring and rubbing in.) The thumbtip of the right hand is held over the upturned left palm, either motionless or turning in a small counterclockwise circle. The left hand then rubs the back of the downturned right hand, as if spreading lotion on it.

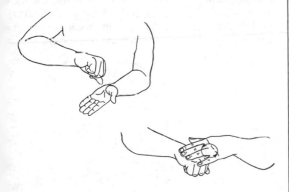

LOUD (loud), *adj.* (Something heard that shakes the surrounding area.) The right index finger touches the

car. The "5" hands, palms down, then move sharply in front of the body in quick alternate motions, first away from and then back to the body. Also LOUDLY, LOUD NOISE.

LOUDLY (loud' lĭ), *adv.* See LOUD.

LOUD NOISE, *n. phrase.* See LOUD.

LOUSY (lou' zĭ) (*sl.*), *adj.* (A modification of the sign for spitting or thumbing the nose.) The right "3" hand is held with thumbtip against the nose. Then it is thrown sharply forward and an expression of contempt is assumed. Also ROTTEN.

LOVE (lŭv), *n., v.,* LOVED, LOVING. (Clasping the heart.) The "5" hands are held one atop the other over the heart. Sometimes the "S" hands are used, in which case they are crossed at the wrists. Also BELOVED, CHARITY, DEVOTION, REVERE 2.

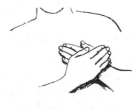

LOVER (lŭv' ər) (*colloq.*), *n.* (Heads nodding toward each other.) The "A" hands are placed together before the body with thumbs up. The thumbs wiggle up and down. Also BEAU, COURTING, COURTSHIP, MAKE LOVE 1, SWEETHEART 1.

LOW 1 (lō), *adj.* (Motion downward.) The "A" hand is held in front of the body, thumb pointing upward. The hand then moves straight downward several inches. Both hands may be used. Also BASE 1.

LOW 2, *adj., n.* (Motion downward.) The right-angle hands are held up before the head, fingertips pointing toward each other. From this position, the hands move down in an arc. Also BASE 2, DEMOTE, LOWER.

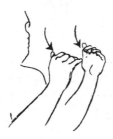

LOWER (lō′ ər), *v.,* -ERED, -ERING. See LOW 2.

LOYAL (loi′ əl), *adj.* (The arm is raised.) The right index finger is placed at the lips. The right arm is then raised, palm out and elbow resting on the back of the

left hand. Also GUARANTEE 1, OATH, PLEDGE, PROMISE 1, SWEAR 1, SWORN, TAKE OATH, VOW.

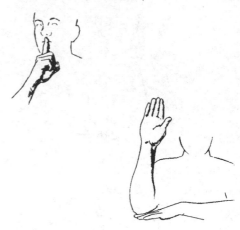

LUGGAGE (lŭg′ ĭj), *n.* (The natural sign.) The downturned right "S" hand grasps an imaginary piece of luggage and shakes it up and down slightly as if testing its weight. Also BAGGAGE, SUITCASE, VALISE.

LYRIC (lir′ ik), *n.* (The letter "L"; rhythmic movement to represent music.) The left hand is held in a downturned horizontal position. The right hand, in the "L" position, moves rhythmically back and forth over the left. Alternatively, the back-and-forth movement may be in the shape of a continuous figure eight.

M

MACHINE (mə shēn'), *n.* (The meshing gears.) With the knuckles of both hands interlocked, the hands pivot up and down, imitating the meshing of gear teeth. Also ENGINE, FACTORY, MACHINERY, MECHANIC 1, MECHANISM, MOTOR.

MACHINERY (mə shē' nə rǐ), *n.* (The meshing gears.) With the knuckles of both hands interlocked, the hands pivot up and down, imitating the meshing of gear teeth. Also ENGINE, FACTORY, MACHINE, MECHANIC 1, MECHANISM, MOTOR.

MACRO (mak' rō), *n., adj.* (*Computer terminology.*) (The "M"; spreading out instructions to a computer.) Both "M" hands, palms facing each other, are held with fingertips touching. The hands separate, moving to their respective sides.

MAD 1 (măd), *adj.* (A violent welling up of the emotions.) The curved fingers of the right hand are placed in the center of the chest and fly up suddenly and violently. An expression of anger is worn. Also ANGER, ANGRY 2, ENRAGE, FURY, INDIGNANT, INDIGNATION, IRE, RAGE.

MAD 2, *adj.* (Turning of wheels in the head.) The open right hand is held palm down before the face, fingers spread, bent, and pointing toward the forehead. The fingers move in circles before the forehead. Also CRAZY 1, INSANE, INSANITY, NUTS 1.

MAGAZINE (măg' ə zēn', măg' ə zēn'), *n.* (A book with a narrow spine.) The left hand, fingers together, is held upright, palm facing right. The right hand wraps around the lower edge of the left and travels up to the little finger. This denotes a narrow object. The sign for BOOK is then made: the hands are placed together, palm to palm, and then opened, as if opening a book. Sometimes this latter sign is omitted. Also BOOKLET, CATALOG, MANUAL, PAMPHLET.

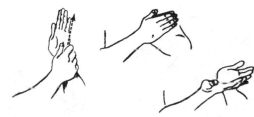

MAGNETIC (mag net′ ik), *adj.* (Drawn together.) Both downturned "M" hands, slightly apart, pivot quickly together until fingertips touch.

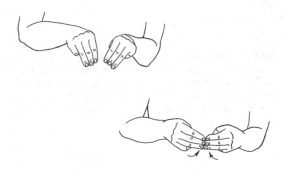

MAGNIFYING GLASS, *n.* (Focusing the glass.) Holding the handle of an imaginary magnifying glass in the right hand, the signer focuses it forward and back, using the upturned left palm as the subject of scrutiny.

MAID (mād), *n.* (Passing the dishes one by one.) The upturned "5" hands move alternately toward and away from the chest. Also SERVANT, SERVE 2, SERVICE, WAITER 2, WAIT ON 2, WAITRESS 2.

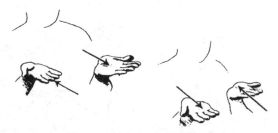

MAIL 1 (māl), *n.* (The stamp is affixed.) The right thumb is placed on the tongue and is then pressed into the open left palm. Also EPISTLE, LETTER.

MAIL 2, *v.,* MAILED, MAILING. (Sending a letter.) The sign for LETTER is made: the right thumbtip is licked and placed against the upturned left palm. The right hand, palm out and fingers touching thumb, is then thrown forward, opening into the "5" position, palm out. Also POST.

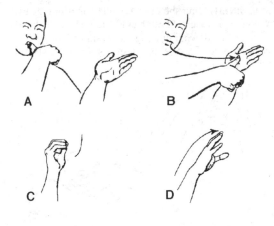

A   B

C   D

MAINSTREAM (mān′ strēm′), *adj., v.,* -STREAMED, -STREAMING. (Blending in or melding.) Both downturned "5" hands move forward as the fingers interlock.

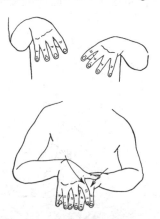

MAINTAIN 1 (mān tān′), *v.,* -TAINED, -TAINING. (Slow, careful movement.) The "K" hands are crossed, the right above the left, little finger edges down. In this position the hands are moved up and down a short distance. Also CARE 2, CAREFUL 2, KEEP, MIND 3, PRESERVE, RESERVE 2, TAKE CARE OF 2.

MAINTAIN 2, *v.* (Words tumbling from the mouth.) The right index finger, pointing left, describes a continuous small circle in front of the mouth. Also BID 3, DISCOURSE, HEARING, MENTION, REMARK, SAID, SAY, SPEAK, SPEECH 1, STATE, STATEMENT, TALK 1, TELL, VERBAL 1.

MAINTENANCE (mān′ tə nəns), *n.* (Holding up.) The right "S" hand pushes up the left "S" hand. Also ENDORSE 1, FAVOR, INDORSE 1, SUPPORT 1, SUSTAIN, SUSTENANCE, UPHOLD, UPLIFT.

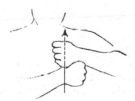

MAKE (māk), *v.,* MADE, MAKING, *n.* (Fashioning something with the hands.) The right "S" hand, palm facing left, is placed on top of its left counterpart, whose palm faces right. The hands are twisted back and forth, striking each other slightly after each twist. Also COMPOSE, CONSTITUTE, CONSTRUCT 2, CREATE,

DEVISE 2, FABRICATE, FASHION, FIX, MANUFACTURE, MEND 1, PRODUCE 3, RENDER 1, REPAIR.

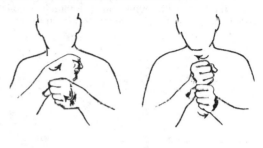

MAKE BRIEF, *v. phrase.* (To squeeze or condense into a small space.) The "C" hands face each other, with the right hand nearer to the body than the left. Both hands draw together and close deliberately, squeezing an imaginary object. Also ABBREVIATE 1, BRIEF 2, CONDENSE, SUMMARIZE 1, SUMMARY 1.

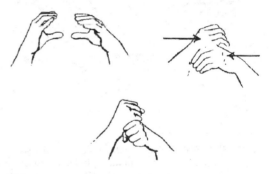

MAKE FUN OF, *v. phrase.* (Derision; poking or prodding.) Both hands are held closed except for index and little fingers, which extend straight out from the body. The right hand is brought up, and its index fingertip pulls the right corner of the mouth into a slight smile. Both hands then move forward simultaneously in a series of short jabbing motions, the right somewhat behind the left. An expression of disdain is assumed during this sign. The first part of the sign, pulling the mouth into a smile, is frequently omitted. Also MOCK, RIDICULE.

MAKE LOVE 1 (*colloq.*), *v. phrase.* (Heads nodding toward each other.) The "A" hands are placed together before the body with thumbs up. The thumbs wiggle up and down. Also BEAU, COURTING, COURTSHIP, LOVER, SWEETHEART 1.

MAKE LOVE 2 (*sl.*), *v. phrase.* (Necks interlocked.) The "S" hands, palms facing, are crossed at the wrists. They swing up and down while the wrists remain in contact. Also NECKING, PETTING.

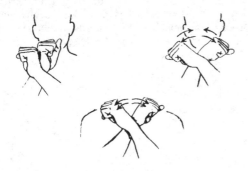

MAKE ME DISGUSTED, *v. phrase.* (Turning the stomach.) The fingertips of the curved right hand describe a continuous circle on the stomach. The signer assumes an exaggerated expression of disgust. Also DISGUST, DISGUSTED, DISGUSTING, DISPLEASED, MAKE ME SICK, NAUSEA, NAUSEATE, NAUSEOUS, OBNOXIOUS, REVOLTING.

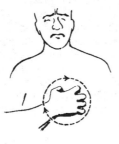

MAKE ME SICK, *v. phrase.* See MAKE ME DISGUSTED.

MAKE NO DIFFERENCE, *v. phrase.* Both hands, in the "5" position, are held before the chest, fingertips facing each other. With an alternate back-forth movement, the fingertips are made to strike each other. Also ANYHOW, ANYWAY, DESPITE, DOESN'T MATTER, HOWEVER 2, INDIFFERENCE, INDIFFERENT, IN SPITE OF, NEVERTHELESS, NO MATTER, WHEREVER.

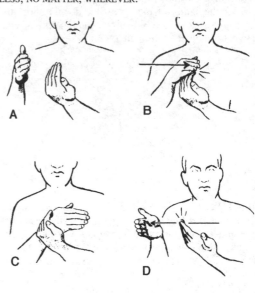

MAKE RESPONSE, *v. phrase.* (Directing a reply from the mouth to someone.) The tip of the right index finger, held in the "D" position, palm facing the body, is placed on the lips, while the left "D" hand, palm also facing the body, is held about a foot in front of the right hand. The right index finger, swinging around, moves toward and stops in a pointing position a few inches from the left index fingertip. Also ANSWER 1, REPLY 1, RESPOND, RESPONSE 1.

MAKEUP (māk′ ŭp), *n.* (Applying something to the face.) The thumbtip and fingertips of each hand are held together and rotated in small counterclockwise circles on both cheeks simultaneously. Also COSMETICS.

MAKE UP ONE'S MIND, *v. phrase.* (The mind stops wavering, and the pros and cons are resolved.) The right index finger touches the forehead, the sign for THINK, *q.v.* Both "F" hands, palms facing each other and fingers pointing straight out, then drop down simultaneously. The sign for JUDGE, *q.v.,* explains the rationale behind the movement of the two hands here. Also DECIDE, DECISION, DECREE 1, DETERMINE, MIND 5, RENDER JUDGMENT, RESOLVE, VERDICT.

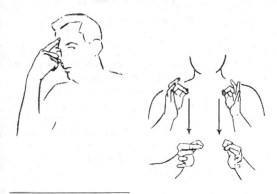

MALE (māl), *n., adj.* (The man's cap.) The thumb and extended fingers of the right hand are brought up to grasp an imaginary cap brim, representing the tipping of caps by men in olden days. This is a root sign used to modify many others. *Viz.* MALE plus BABY: SON; MALE plus SAME: BROTHER; etc. Also HUMAN, MAN, MANKIND.

MAMA (mä′ mə), *n.* (Familiar derivation of the more formal MOTHER, *q.v.*) The thumb of the right "5" hand touches the right cheek repeatedly.

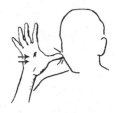

MAN (măn), *n.* See MALE.

MANAGE (măn′ ĭj), *v.,* -AGED, -AGING. (Holding the reins over all.) The "A" hands, palms facing, move alternately back and forth as if grasping and manipu-

lating reins. The left "A" hand, still in position, swings over so that its palm now faces down. The right hand opens to the "5" position, palm down, and swings over the left, which moves slightly to the right. Also AUTHORITY, CONTROL 1, DIRECT 1, GOVERN, MANAGEMENT, MANAGER, OPERATE, REGULATE, REIGN, RULE 1.

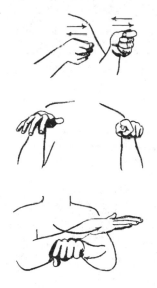

MANAGEMENT (măn′ ĭj mənt), *n.* The sign for MANAGE is made. This is followed by the sign for -MENT: the downturned right "M" hand moves down along the left palm, which is facing away from the body.

MANAGER (măn′ ĭj ər), *n.* The sign for MANAGE, *q.v.,* is made. This is followed by the sign for INDIVIDUAL: both open hands, palms facing each other, move down the sides of the body, tracing its outline to the hips.

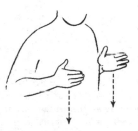

MANICURE (man′ i kyo͞or′), *n.* (Act of painting the fingernails.) With the left hand held open in the palm down position, the right index and middle fingers, forming a brush, paint one or more of the left fingernails.

MANIPULATE (mə nip′ yə lāt′), *n.* (Pulling the reins.) Both hands, holding imaginary reins, move alternately forward and back.

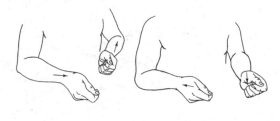

MANKIND (măn′ kīnd′), *n.* See MALE.

MANNER 1 (măn′ ər), *n.* (The hands come into view to reveal the "how" of something.) The right-angle hands, palms down and knuckles touching, swing up and open to the palms-up position. Also HOW.

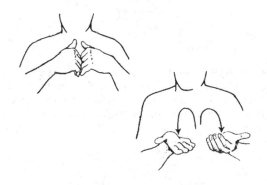

MANNER 2, *n.* (The movement.) Both hands, palms facing and fingers together and extended straight out, move in unison away from the body in a straight or winding manner. Also CORRIDOR, HALL, HALLWAY,

METHOD, OPPORTUNITY 3, PATH, ROAD, STREET, TRAIL, WAY 1.

MANUAL (măn′ yo͝o əl), *n.* (A book with a narrow spine.) The left hand, fingers together, is held upright, palm facing right. The right hand wraps around the lower edge of the left and travels up to the little finger. This denotes a narrow object. The sign for BOOK is then made: the hands are placed together, palm to palm, and then opened, as if opening a book. Sometimes this latter sign is omitted. Also BOOKLET, CATALOG, MAGAZINE, PAMPHLET.

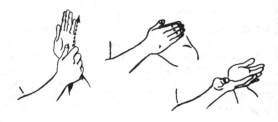

MANUAL ALPHABET (The movement of the fingers in fingerspelling.) The right hand, palm out, is moved from left to right, with the fingers wriggling up and down. Also ALPHABET, DACTYLOLOGY, FINGERSPELLING, SPELL, SPELLING.

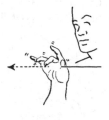

MANUFACTURE (măn′ yə făk′ chər), *n., v.,* -TURED, -TURING. (Fashioning something with the hands.) The right "S" hand, palm facing left, is placed on top of its left counterpart, whose palm faces right. The hands are twisted back and forth, striking each other slightly

after each twist. Also COMPOSE, CONSTITUTE, CONSTRUCT 2, CREATE, DEVISE 2, FABRICATE, FASHION, FIX, MAKE, MEND 1, PRODUCE 3, RENDER 1, REPAIR.

MANY (měn′ ĭ), *adj.* (*Many* fingers are indicated.) The upturned "S" hands are thrown up, opening into the "5" position, palms up. This may be repeated. Also MULTIPLE, NUMEROUS, PLURAL, QUANTITY 2.

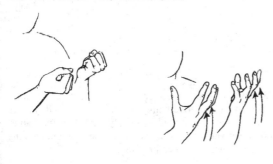

MARBLE (mär′ bəl), *n.* (Flicking a marble ball, as in a child's game.) The signer uses the thumb to flick a marble ball forward. The action is repeated. This sign is used for both the ball and the stone used in building and sculpture.

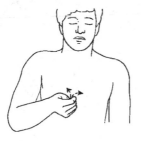

MARCH 1 (märch), *v.*, MARCHED, MARCHING. (A column of marchers, one behind the other.) The downturned open hands, fingers pointing down, are held

one behind the other. Pivoted from the wrists, they move rhythmically forward and back in unison. Also PARADE 2.

MARCH 2, *n.* The same sign as MARCH 1 except that the downturned "V" hands are used.

MARE (mâr), *n.* (A female horse.) The sign for FEMALE: the right thumb moves down the right jaw, tracing a line from ear to chin. This is followed by HORSE: the right hand, palm out, index and middle fingers extended, is placed with the right thumb touching the right temple. The index and middle fingers shake back and forth.

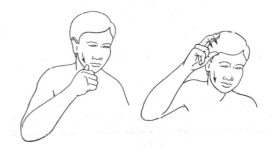

MARIJUANA (mar ə wä′ nə), *n.* (The act of smoking marijuana.) The signer mimes holding the marijuana cigarette to the lips and inhaling deeply. Also POT.

MARIONETTE (mar′ ē ə net′), *n.* (Manipulating the strings.) Both "F" hands, palms down, move up and down alternately.

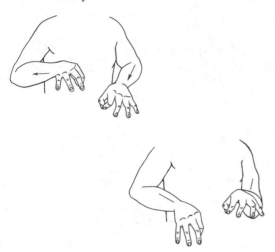

MARRIAGE (măr′ ĭj), *n.* (A clasping of hands, as during the wedding ceremony.) The hands are clasped together, the right on top of the left. Also MARRY.

MARRY (măr′ ĭ), *v.,* -RIED, -RYING. See MARRIAGE.

MASK (mask), *n., v.,* MASKED, MASKING. (Covering the face.) The cupped hands, palms facing the body and fingers pointing up, shield the eyes and then move back to cover the rest of the face.

MASSACRE (mas′ ə kər), *n., v.,* -CRED, -CRING. (KILL and HORDE.) The outstretched right index finger is

passed under the downturned left hand as if stabbing someone. Both downturned claw hands, side by side, then move forward slowly and deliberately, signifying many people stretched out in the distance.

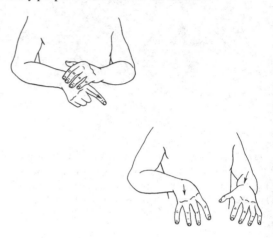

MASSAGE (mə säzh′, -säj′), *n., v.,* -SAGED, -SAGING. (The natural movement.) Both downturned hands touch respective shoulders briefly, and then the hands come forward, palms down, in an opening and closing motion much like kneading dough.

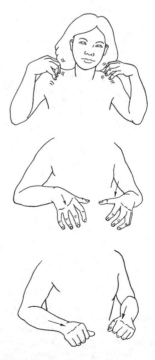

MATCH 1 (măch), *n.* (The natural sign.) The right hand, grasping an imaginary match, strikes it against the open left palm, which is facing right. Also KINDLE.

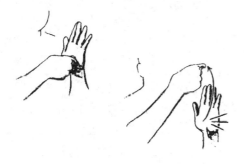

MATCH 2, *n., v.,* MATCHED, MATCHING. (Things fit together.) Both "5" or claw hands, palms facing the chest, come together so that the fingers interlock.

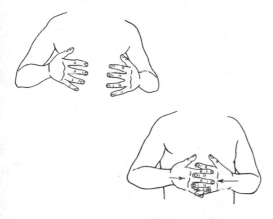

MATHEMATICS (măth′ ə măt′ ĭks), *n.* (Calculation; the "X" movement, with the letter "M.") Both "M" hands, fingertips facing and palms facing the body, are crossed repeatedly.

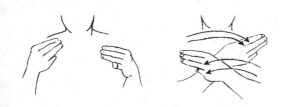

MATTRESS (ma′ tris), *n.* (SLEEP and SOFT.) The sign for SLEEP: The right cheek rests against the open right hand, whose palm faces left. Both upturned hands then open and close repeatedly, as if squeezing something SOFT.

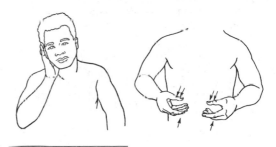

MATURE 1 (mə tyŏŏr′, -tŏŏr′), *v.,* -TURED, -TURING. (Flowers or plants emerge from the ground.) The right fingers, pointing up, emerge from the closed left hand, and they spread open as they do. Also BLOOM, DEVELOP 1, GROW, GROWN, PLANT 1, RAISE 3, REAR 2, SPRING 1,

MATURE 2, *adj., n.* (Growing up.) The index finger edge of the right "M" hand, palm facing down, moves up the outstretched upright left palm.

MAXIMUM (mak′ sə məm), *adj.* Both hands, in the "M" position, are held palms down, fingertips touching. The right hand rises above the left.

MAY 1 (mā), *aux. v.,* MIGHT. (Weighing one thing against another.) The upturned open hands move alternately up and down. Also GUESS 4, MAYBE, MIGHT 2, PERHAPS, POSSIBILITY, POSSIBLY, PROBABLE, PROBABLY, SUPPOSE.

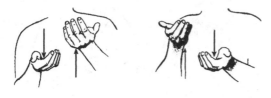

MAY 2, *aux. v.* (An affirmative movement of the hands, likened to a nodding of the head, to indicate ability or power to accomplish something.) Both "A" hands, held palms down, move down in unison a short distance before the chest. Also ABILITY, ABLE, CAN 1, CAPABLE, COMPETENT, COULD, FACULTY, POSSIBLE.

MAY 3, *aux. v.* (A permissive upswinging of the hands, as if giving in.) Both hands, palms facing and fingers pointing away from the body, are held at chest level, almost a foot apart. With an upward movement, using their wrists as pivots, the hands sweep up until the fingers point almost straight up. Also ALLOW, GRANT 1, LET, LET'S, LET US, PERMISSION 1, PERMIT 1, TOLERATE 1.

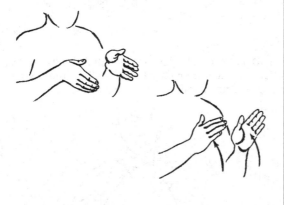

MAYBE (mā′ bǐ, -bē), *adv.* See MAY 1.

MAYONNAISE (mā ə nāz′), *n.* (The letter "M"; spreading.) The downturned right "M" hand spreads the mayonnaise on the upturned left palm.

MCDONALD'S (mək don′ əldz), *loc.* (The letter "M"; the arches of the well-known hamburger place.) The right "M" hand describes one or two arches along the back of the downturned left hand.

ME (mē; *unstressed* mǐ), *pron.* (The natural sign.) The signer points to himself. Also I 2.

MEADOW (med′ ō), *n.* (Outlining the space.) Both downturned "M" hands, index fingers touching, are held several inches in front of the chest. They describe a circle as they separate and move in toward the chest.

MEAL (mēl), *n.* (The natural sign.) The closed right hand goes through the natural motion of placing food in the mouth. This movement is repeated. Also CONSUME 1, CONSUMPTION, DEVOUR, DINE, EAT, FEED 1, FOOD 1.

MEAN 1 (mēn), *adj.* (Striking down against.) Both "A" or "X" hands are held before the chest, the right above the left. The right hand strikes down and out, hitting the left thumb and knuckles with force. Also BACKBITE, BASE 3, CRUEL 1, HARM 2, HURT 2, MAR 2, SPOIL.

MEAN 2, *v.,* MEANT, MEANING. (Relative standing of one's thoughts.) A modified sign for THINK is made: the right index finger touches the middle of the forehead. The tips of the right "V" hand, palm down, are then thrust into the upturned left palm (as in STAND, *q.v.*). The right "V" hand is then rethrust into the upturned left palm, with right palm now facing the body. Also CONNOTE, IMPLY, INTEND, INTENT 1, INTENTION, MEANING, MOTIVE 3, PURPOSE 1, SIGNIFICANCE 2, SIGNIFY 2, SUBSTANCE 2.

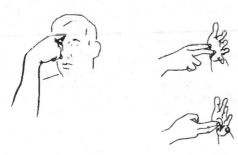

MEAN 3, *n., adj.* (Halfway between top and bottom.) The right open hand, held upright, palm facing left, rests its little finger edge across the index finger edge of the downturned open left hand. In this position the right hand moves back and forth several times, rub-

bing the base of the little finger along the edge of the left hand. Also AVERAGE.

MEANING (mē' nĭng), *n.* See MEAN 2.

MEANTIME (mēn' tīm'), *n., adv.* (Parallel time.) Both "D" hands, palms down, move forward in unison, away from the body. They may move straight forward or may follow a slight upward arc. Also DURING, IN THE MEANTIME, IN THE PROCESS OF, WHILE.

MEASURE (mĕzh' ər), *n., v.,* -URED, -URING. (The act of measuring a short distance.) Both "Y" hands, palms out, move alternately a short distance back and forth, away from and toward each other. Also GAUGE, SCALE 1.

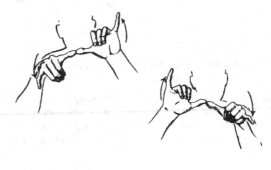

MEAT (mēt), *n.* (The fleshy part of the hand.) The right index finger and thumb squeeze the fleshy part of the open left hand between thumb and index finger. Also BEEF, FLESH.

MECHANIC 1 (mə kăn′ ĭk), *n.* (The meshing gears.) With the knuckles of both hands interlocked, the hands pivot up and down, imitating the meshing of gear teeth. This may be followed by the sign for INDIVIDUAL 1, *q.v.* Also ENGINE, FACTORY, MACHINE, MACHINERY, MECHANISM, MOTOR.

MECHANIC 2, *n.* (The natural movement.) The index finger of the right hand is grasped by the outstretched index and middle fingers of the left hand. The left hand executes a series of up-and-down movements, as if manipulating a wrench. This is followed by the sign for INDIVIDUAL: both open hands, palms facing each other, move down the sides of the body, tracing its outline to the hips. Also PIPE FITTING, PLUMBER, STEAM FITTER, WRENCH.

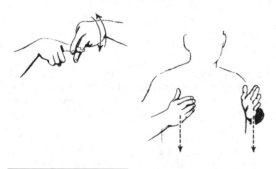

MECHANISM (mĕk′ ə nĭz′ əm), *n.* See MECHANIC 1.

MEDAL (mĕd′ əl), *n.* (The medal hanging from the left side of the chest.) The right index and middle fingers, held together and pointing straight down, are brought against the left side of the chest, either once or twice.

MEDDLE 1 (mĕd′ əl), *v.,* -DLED, -DLING. (Obstruct, block.) The left hand, fingers together and palm flat, is held before the body, facing somewhat down. The little

finger side of the right hand, held with palm flat, makes one or several up-down chopping motions against the left hand between its thumb and index finger. Also ANNOY 1, ANNOYANCE 1, BLOCK, BOTHER 1, CHECK 2, COME BETWEEN, DISRUPT, DISTURB, HINDER, HINDRANCE, IMPEDE, INTERCEPT, INTERFERE, INTERFERENCE, INTERFERE WITH, INTERRUPT, OBSTACLE, OBSTRUCT, PREVENT, PREVENTION.

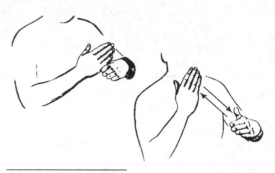

MEDDLE 2 (med′ ′l), *v.* (The nose is poked into something.) The sign for NOSE is formed by touching the tip of the nose with the index finger. The sign for IN, INTO follows: the right hand, fingertips touching the thumb, is thrust into the left "C" hand, which closes a bit over the right fingers as they enter. Also BUTT IN.

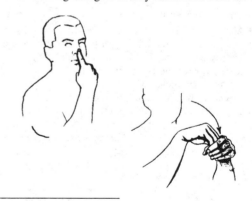

MEDICAID 1 (med′ i kād′), *n.* (Peeling off a label.) The right thumb and index finger peel off an imaginary label from the upturned left palm. This is supposed to be a label to attach to the requisite Medicaid form. An East Coast (especially New York) sign.

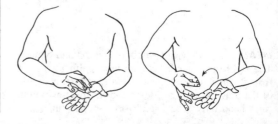

MEDICAID 2, *n.* (The letters "M" and "D"; holding up or helping.) The tips of the right "M" fingers are placed against the upturned left wrist. The hand then changes into a "D" shape, resting on the upturned left palm, which moves up very slightly. This is a West Coast sign, especially California.

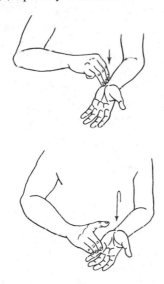

MEDICINE (měd′ ə sən), *n.* (Mixing of medicine; rolling a pill.) The ball of the middle fingertip of the right "5" hand describes a small counterclockwise circle in the upturned left palm. Also DRUG, POISON 1, PRESCRIPTION.

MEDITATE 1 (měd′ ə tāt′), *v.,* -TATED, -TATING. (Thinking and holding the brow.) The sign for THINK is made: the right index finger describes a small counterclockwise circle in midforehead. The open right hand is then placed at the brow, holding it as if in deep thought. Also MEDITATION.

MEDITATE 2 (měd′ ə tāt), *v.* (Think deep.) The sign for THINK is made: the right index finger describes a small continuous counterclockwise circle on the forehead. This is followed by DEEP; the downturned right index finger moves straight down the left palm, which is held forward or to the right.

MEDITATE 3, *v.* (The letter "M"; THINK.) The right "M" hand executes a continuous counterclockwise circle on the forehead.

MEET (mēt), *v.,* MET, MEETING. (A coming together of two persons.) Both "D" hands, palms facing each other, are brought together. Also ENCOUNTER.

MEETING 1 (mē′ tǐng), *n.* (Assemble all together.) Both "5" hands, palms facing, are held with fingers pointing out from the body. With a sweeping motion they are brought in toward the chest, and all fingertips come together. This is repeated. Also ACCUMULATE 3, ASSEMBLE, ASSEMBLY, CONFERENCE, CONVENE, CONVENTION, GATHER 2, GATHERING.

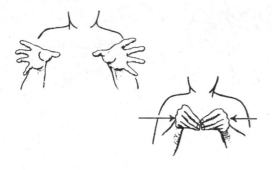

MELANCHOLY (měl′ ən kŏl′ ĭ), *n.* (The facial features drop.) Both "5" hands, palms facing the eyes and fingers slightly curved, drop simultaneously to a level with the mouth. The head drops slightly as the hands move down, and an expression of sadness is assumed. Also DEJECTED, DEPRESSED, GLOOM, GLOOMY, GRAVE 3, GRIEF 1, MOURNFUL, SAD, SORROWFUL 1.

MEETING 2 (*loc.*), *n.* (A random coming together of different persons.) The "D" hands, facing each other and touching at the thumbs, are held with right palm facing the body and left palm facing away from the body. They pivot around so that their relative positions are now reversed. This may be done several times. In addition, the hands may be separated slightly during the pivoting, but they must come together at the end of this movement.

MELBOURNE (mel′ bərn), *n.* (The "M"; a city in southeastern Australia.) The downturned right "M" hand is swept quickly and repeatedly across the chin from right to left. A local sign.

MEGABYTE (meg′ ə bīt′), *n. Computer term.* (The initials.) The signer fingerspells "M-B."

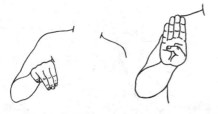

MELON (měl′ ən), *n.* (Sounding for ripeness.) The right middle finger is flicked once or twice against the back of the downturned left hand.

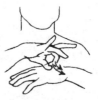

MELT (mĕlt), *v.,* MELTED, MELTING. (Fingering the small pieces resulting from the breaking up of something.) The thumbs rub slowly across the fingertips of the upturned hands, from the little fingers to the index fingers, and then continue to the "A" position, palms up. Also DECAY, DIE OUT, DISSOLVE, FADE, ROT.

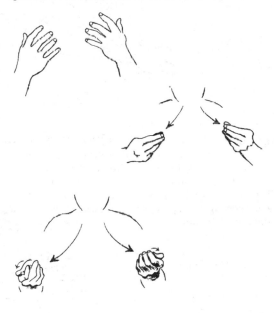

MEMBER 1 (mĕm′ bər), *n.* (Linked together.) The sign for JOIN is made: both hands, held in the modified "5" position, palms out, move toward each other. The thumbs and index fingers of both hands then connect. This is followed by the sign for INDIVIDUAL: both open hands, palms facing each other, move down the sides of the body, tracing its outline to the hips.

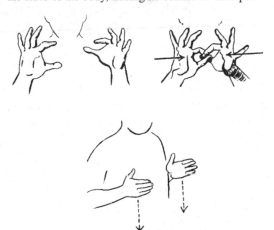

MEMBER 2, *n.* The right "M" hand, palm facing the body and fingers pointing left, moves from the left shoulder to the right. Also GALLAUDET, EDWARD MINER.

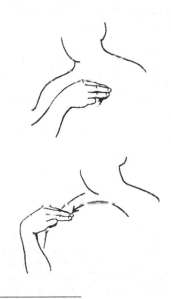

MEMORIAL (mə môr′ ē əl), *n.* (Looking back.) The right "M" hand, positioned near the right temple, moves straight back over the shoulder.

MEMORIZE 1 (mĕm′ ə rīz′), *v.,* -RIZED, -RIZING. (Holding onto knowledge.) The open right hand is placed on the forehead. Then as it is removed straight forward, it is clenched into a fist.

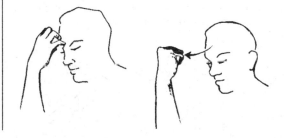

MEMORIZE 2, *v.* (Grasping a thought.) The index fingertip of the right hand touches the forehead, as in THINK, *q.v.* The right hand then swings outward from the forehead, opening as it does. Finally, the right hand closes into the "S" position before the face, as if grasping something.

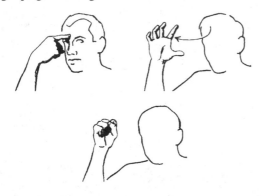

MEMORY (mĕm′ ə rĭ), *n.* (Knowledge that remains.) The sign for KNOW is made: the right fingertips are placed on the forehead. The sign for REMAIN then follows: the "A" hands are held with palms toward the body, thumbs extended and touching, the right behind the left. In this position the hands move forward in a straight, steady line or straight down. Also RECALL 2, RECOLLECT 2, REMEMBER.

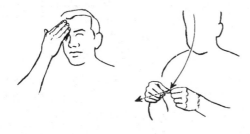

MEND 1 (mĕnd), *v.,* MENDED, MENDING. (Fashioning something with the hands.) The right "S" hand, palm facing left, is placed on top of its left counterpart, whose palm faces right. The hands are twisted back and forth, striking each other slightly after each twist. Also COMPOSE, CONSTITUTE, CONSTRUCT 2, CREATE, DEVISE 2, FABRICATE, FASHION, FIX, MAKE, MANUFACTURE, PRODUCE 3, RENDER 1, REPAIR.

MEND 2, *v.* (Moving up.) The little finger edge of the right hand rests on the back of the downturned left hand. It moves up the left arm in successive stages, indicating improvement or upward movement. The implication here is "mending one's ways." Also IMPROVE.

MENOPAUSE (men′ ə pôz), *n.* (OLD; MENSTRUATION; STOP.) The sign for OLD: the hand pulls down on an imaginary beard. For MENSTRUATION, the right "A" hand, palm facing left, is brought against the right cheek twice. For STOP, the little finger edge of the open right hand is brought sharply down on the upturned left palm.

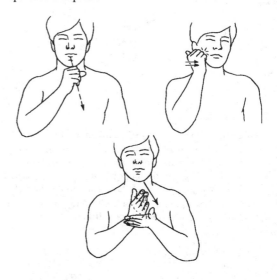

MENSTRUATE (mĕn′ strŏŏ āt′), *v.,* -ATED, -ATING. (Blotting the brow.) The knuckle edge of the right "A" hand is pressed twice against the right cheek.

-MENT, *condition. suffix.* The downturned right "M" hand moves down along the left palm, which is facing away from the body.

MENTAL (měn′ təl), *adj.* (Patting the head to indicate something of value inside.) The right fingers pat the forehead several times. Also INTELLECT, INTELLIGENCE, MIND 1, SENSE 1.

MENTALLY LIMITED, *adj.* (The limits, upper and lower, of the mind.) The signer touches the forehead with the right index finger. The two hands are then held palms facing down, the right positioned an inch or so above the left. Both hands move straight forward a short distance.

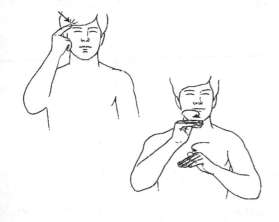

MENTALLY RETARDED, *adj. phrase.* (The "M" and the "R" at the mind.) The signer places the fingertips

of the right "M" hand at the forehead. This is followed by the "R" hand placed the same way.

MENTION (měn′ shən), *v.,* -TIONED, -TIONING. (Words tumbling from the mouth.) The right index finger, pointing left, describes a continuous small circle in front of the mouth. Also BID 3, DISCOURSE, HEARING, MAINTAIN 2, REMARK, SAID, SAY, SPEAK, SPEECH 1, STATE, STATEMENT, TALK 1, TELL, VERBAL 1.

MENU (men′ yōō, mā′ nyōō), *n.* (A list of things to eat.) The right fingertips, closed over the thumb, touch the mouth twice. The right fingertips then move down the outstretched left palm in short movements, starting at the fingertips and moving down to the base of the left hand.

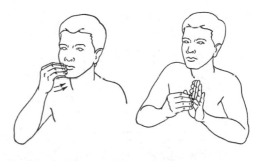

MERCHANT (mûr´ chənt), *n.* (Transferring owner-ship.) The sign for SALE is formed: the downturned hands, each with fingers grasping an imaginary object, pivot out from the wrists, away from the body. The sign for INDIVIDUAL is then made: both open hands, palms facing each other, move down the sides of the body, tracing its outline to the hips. Also SALESMAN, SELLER, VENDER.

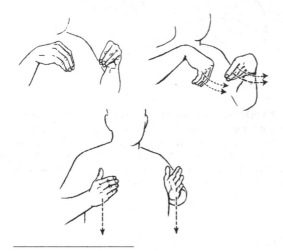

MERCY 1 (mûr´ sĭ), *n.* (The heart rolls out.) Both right-angle hands roll over each other as they move down and away from their initial position at the heart. Also BENEVOLENT, GENEROUS 1, GENTLE 1, GENTLE-NESS, GRACIOUS, HUMANE, KIND 1, KINDNESS, TENDER 3.

MERCY 2, *n.* (Feelings from the heart conferred on others.) The middle fingertip of the open right hand touches the chest over the heart. The same open hand then moves in a small, clockwise circle before the right shoulder, with palm facing forward and fingers pointing up. Also PITY, POOR 3, SYMPATHY 2.

MERGE (mûrj), *v.,* MERGED, MERGING. (The natural sign.) Both open hands are held with palms toward the chest, fingertips pointing toward each other, thumbs pointing up. The hands then move toward each other until their fingers merge.

MERRY (mĕr´ ĭ), *adj.* (The heart is stirred; the spirits bubble up.) The open right hand, palm facing the body, strikes the heart repeatedly, moving up and off the heart after each strike. Also DELIGHT, GAIETY 1, GAY, GLAD, HAPPINESS, HAPPY, JOY.

MERRY-GO-ROUND (mer´ ē gō round), *n.* (Seated and riding in a circle.) The right curved index and middle fingers are placed atop their left counterparts, and both hands make a horizontal counterclockwise circle.

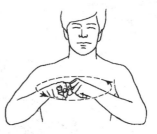

MESSAGE (mĕs´ ĭj) (*rare*), *n.* (Word, carry.) The sign for WORD is formed: the right index fingertip and thumbtip are held about an inch apart and placed on the side of the outstretched left index finger, which represents the length of a sentence. This is followed by the sign for CARRY: both open hands, palms up, move in an arc from left to right, as if carrying something from one point to another.

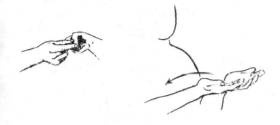

MESSIAH 1 (mə sī′ ə), *n., eccles.* (The letter "M"; one who sees ahead.) The right "M" hand, fingers pointing forward, moves under an arc formed by the downturned left hand. This is followed by the sign for INDIVIDUAL 1.

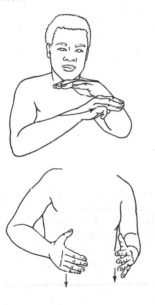

MESSIAH 2, *n.* (The letter "M"; from the heart.) The right "M" hand, placed at the heart, moves down and out, away from the chest, or down to the right hip.

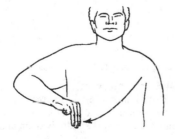

METAL 1 (mĕt′ əl), *n.* (Hammering on metal.) The little finger edge of the right "S" hand is brought down forcefully against the back of the prone, open left hand several times.

METAL 2, *n.* (A hard substance.) The right "S" hand moves up from the chest to strike the bottom of the chin several times and continues forward in a short arc after each blow.

METER (mē′ tər), *n.* (Measuring.) Both "M" hands, palms out and hands touching, move apart a short distance.

METHOD (mĕth′ əd), *n.* (The movement.) Both hands, palms facing and fingers together and extended straight out, move in unison away from the body in a straight or winding manner. Also CORRIDOR, HALL, HALLWAY, MANNER 2, OPPORTUNITY 3, PATH, ROAD, STREET, TRAIL, WAY 1.

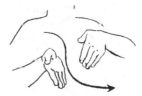

METHODIST (mĕth′ əd ĭst), *n., adj.* (Rubbing the hands together in zeal or ambition.) The open hands are rubbed vigorously back and forth against each other. Also AMBITIOUS 1, ANXIOUS 1, ARDENT, DILIGENCE 1, DILIGENT, EAGER, EAGERNESS, EARNEST, ENTHUSIASM, ENTHUSIASTIC, INDUSTRIOUS, ZEAL, ZEALOUS.

ME TOO (*colloq.*). (Two figures are compared, back and forth.) The right "Y" hand, palm facing left, is moved alternately toward and away from the body. Also SAME 2.

MEXICO (mĕk′ sə kō), *n.* (The sombrero.) Both index fingers describe the wide brim of a sombrero.

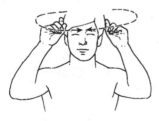

MICKEY MOUSE, *n.* (The ear.) The curved index and thumb, forming a "C," are placed atop the head, toward the side, to outline the shape of the ear. Both hands may be used.

MICROPHONE 1 (mī′ krə fōn), *n.* (Holding a microphone.) The signer mimes holding a microphone in front of the face.

MICROPHONE 2, *n.* (The earpiece and mouthpiece of the headset.) With the right thumb placed in the ear, the curved right index finger is positioned directly in front of the mouth.

MICROSCOPE (mī′ krə skōp′), *n.* (The focusing.) Both "C" or "O" hands, one behind the other, are placed at the signer's left or right eye, looking down. The hands rotate repeatedly in opposite directions as if focusing the lens. Alternatively, the more distant hand moves down to adjust the specimen platform.

MICROWAVE (mī′ krō wāv′), *n.* (The rays are emphasized.) Both hands, fingers resting on respective thumbs, are positioned side by side, with palms facing each other. The fingers suddenly open and the two hands move an inch or so together before the fingers snap shut in their former position.

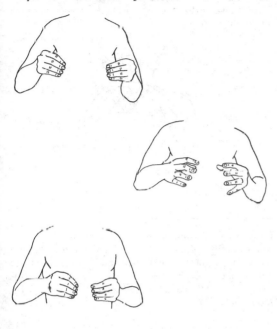

MIDDAY (mĭd′ dā′), *n.* (The sun is directly overhead.) The right "B" hand, palm facing left, is held upright in a vertical position, its elbow resting on the back of the open left hand. Also NOON.

MIDDLE (mĭd′ əl), *adj.* (The natural sign.) The down-turned right fingers describe a small clockwise circle and come to rest in the center of the upturned left palm. Also CENTER, CENTRAL.

MIDNIGHT (mĭd′ nīt′), *n.* (The sun is directly opposite the NOON position, *q.v.*) The right "B" hand is held fingers pointing straight down and palm facing left. The left hand, representing the horizon, is held open and fingers together, palm down, its little finger edge resting against the right arm near the crook of the elbow.

MIGHT 1 (mīt), *n.* (Flexing the muscles.) With fists clenched, palms facing back, the signer raises both arms and shakes them once, with force. Also MIGHTY 1, POWER 1, POWERFUL 1, STRONG 1, STURDY, TOUGH 1.

MIGHT 2, *aux. v.* (Weighing one thing against another.) The upturned open hands move alternately up and down. Also GUESS 4, MAY 1, MAYBE, PERHAPS, POSSIBIL-ITY, POSSIBLY, PROBABLE, PROBABLY, SUPPOSE.

MIGHT 3, *n.* (The curve of the flexed biceps is indicated.) The left hand, clenched into a fist, is held up, palm facing the body. The index finger of the right "D" hand moves in an arc over the left biceps muscle, from shoulder to crook of the elbow. Also POWER 2, POWERFUL 2.

MIGHTY 1 (mī′ tĭ), *adj.* See MIGHT 1.

MIGHTY 2, *adj.* (Strength emanating from the body.) Both "5" hands are placed palms against the chest. They move out and away, forcefully, closing and assuming the "S" position. Also BRAVE, BRAVERY, COURAGE, COURAGEOUS, FORTITUDE, HALE, HEALTH, HEALTHY, STRENGTH, STRONG 2, WELL 2.

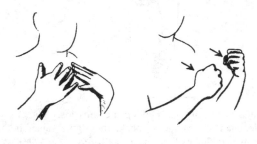

MILK (mĭlk), *n., v.,* MILKED, MILKING. (The act of milking a cow.) Both hands, alternately grasping and releasing imaginary teats, move alternately up and down before the body.

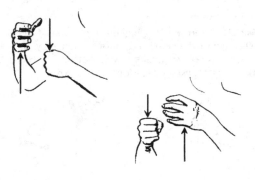

MILLIGRAM (mil′ ə gram), *n.* (The letters "M" and "G"; weighing on a beam balance.) The right "M" hand, positioned on the knuckle of the left index finger, moves forward toward the left index fingertip, while changing to the "G."

MILLIMETER (mil′ ə mē tər), *n.* (The letters "M.") Both "M" hands are held with index fingers touching. They move apart a short distance, dropping down slightly as they do.

MILLION (mĭl′ yən), *n., adj.* (A thousand thousands.) The fingertips of the right "M" hand, palm down, are thrust twice into the upturned left palm, first at the base of the palm and then near the base of the left fingers. (The "M" stands for *mille,* the Latin word for *thousand.*)

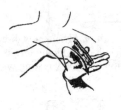

MIMIC (mĭm′ ĭk), *n., v.,* -ICKED, -ICKING. (The natural sign.) The right fingers and thumb close together and move onto the upturned, open left hand, as if taking something from one place to another. Also COPY 1, DUPLICATE 1, IMITATE, MODEL.

MINCE (mins), *v.*, MINCED, MINCING. (Chopping up into small pieces.) The little finger edge of the right "B" hand, palm facing left, chops vigorously against the upturned left palm.

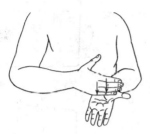

MIND 1 (mīnd), *n.* (Patting the head to indicate something of value inside.) The right fingers pat the forehead several times. Also INTELLECT, INTELLIGENCE, MENTAL, SENSE 1.

MIND 2, *n.* (Directing one's attention forward; applying oneself; concentrating.) Both hands, fingers pointing up and together, are held at the sides of the face. They move straight out from the face. Also APPLY 2, ATTEND (TO), ATTENTION, CONCENTRATE, CONCENTRATION, FOCUS, GIVE ATTENTION (TO), PAY ATTENTION (TO).

MIND 3, *v.*, MINDED, MINDING. (Slow, careful movement.) The "K" hands are crossed, the right above the left, little finger edges down. In this position the hands are moved up and down a short distance. Also CARE 2, CAREFUL 2, KEEP, MAINTAIN 1, PRESERVE, RESERVE 2, TAKE CARE OF 2.

MIND 4, *v.* (The hands are thrown open as an act of obeisance.) Both "A" hands, palms facing, are positioned at either side of the head. They are thrown open and out, ending in the "5" position, palms up. The head is bowed slightly at the same time. Also OBEDIENCE, OBEDIENT, OBEY.

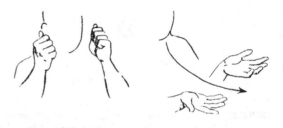

MIND 5, *n.* (The mind stops wavering, and the pros and cons are resolved.) The right index finger touches the forehead, the sign for THINK, *q.v.* Both "F" hands, palms facing each other and fingers pointing straight out, then drop down simultaneously. The sign for JUDGE, *q.v.*, explains the rationale behind the movement of the two hands here. Also DECIDE, DECISION, DECREE 1, DETERMINE, MAKE UP ONE'S MIND, RENDER JUDGMENT, RESOLVE, VERDICT.

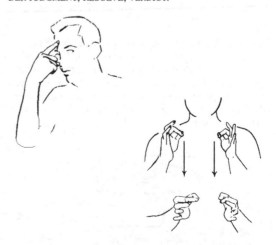

MINE 1 (mīn), *pron.* (Pressing something to one's bosom.) The "5" hand is brought up against the chest. Also MY, OWN.

MINE 2, *n.* (The action of a pick on the mine wall.) The right "X" finger digs repeatedly against the left palm, which faces right.

MINGLE 1 (mĭng′ gəl), *v.,* -GLED, -GLING. (Scrambling or mixing up.) The downturned right hand is positioned above the upturned left. The fingers of both are curved. Both hands move in opposite horizontal circles. Also CLUTTER, COMPLICATE, CONFUSE, CONFUSED, CONFUSION, DISORDER, MIX, MIXED, MIX UP, SCRAMBLE.

MINGLE 2, *v.* (Mingling with.) Both hands are held in modified "A" positions, thumbs out. The left hand is positioned with its thumb pointing straight up, and the right hand, with its thumb pointing down, revolves above the left thumb in a counterclockwise direction. Also ASSOCIATE 1, EACH OTHER, FELLOWSHIP, MUTUAL 1, ONE ANOTHER.

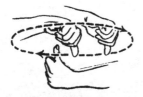

MINIMUM (min′ ə məm), *adj., n.* (The space limitations; the letter "M.") Both "M" hands are held one above the other, palms facing down. The top hand moves down to rest on the back of the bottom hand.

MINISTER (mĭn′ ĭs tər), *n.* (Placing morsels of wisdom, or food for thought, into the mind.) The right hand, palm out, with thumb and index finger touching, is moved forward and slightly downward a number of times from its initial position near the right temple. This is followed by the sign for INDIVIDUAL: both open hands, palms facing each other, move down the sides of the body, tracing its outline to the hips. Also PASTOR, PREACHER.

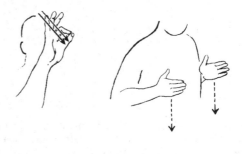

MINNEAPOLIS (min′ ē ap′ ə lis), *n.* The right "D" palm, facing the signer, is tapped twice against the left part of the chest.

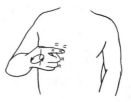

MINUTE 1 (mĭn′ ĭt), *n.* (The minute hand of a clock.) The right "D" hand is held with its index finger edge against the palm of the left "5" hand, which faces right. The right index finger moves forward in a short arc. Also MOMENT.

MINUTE 2, *adj*. (A small or tiny movement.) The right thumbtip is flicked off the index finger several times as if shooting marbles, although the movement is not so pronounced. Also LITTLE 2, TINY 1.

MIRROR (mĭr′ ɔr), *n*. (A glass object through which one views oneself.) The sign for GLASS is made: the tip of the right index finger is brought up against the exposed front teeth. The open curved right hand is then held palm opposite the face. The hand, pivoting from the wrist, moves back and forth a bit as if focusing the facial image in its center. Meanwhile, the eyes are directed to the center of the palm. (The sign for GLASS is frequently omitted.) Also LOOKING GLASS.

MISGUIDED (mis gī′ did), *adj*. (Lead the wrong way.) The sign for WRONG: the right "Y" hand, palm facing the body, is brought up against the chin. The sign for LEAD: the right fingers grasp their left counterparts and pull forward.

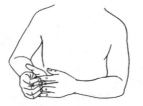

MISJUDGE (mis juj′), *v.*, -JUDGED, -JUDGING. (Judge wrongly.) The sign for WRONG, as above, is followed by the sign for JUDGE: both "F" hands, palms facing each other, move alternately up and down.

MISSING 1 (mĭs′ ĭng), *adj*. (A disappearance.) The right open hand, palm facing the body, is held by the left hand and is drawn down and out, ending in a position with fingers drawn together. The left hand, meanwhile, may close into a position with fingers also drawn together. Also ABSENCE 1, ABSENT 1, DEPLETE, DISAPPEAR, EMPTY 1, EXTINCT, FADE AWAY, GONE 1, OMISSION 1, OUT 3, OUT OF, VANISH.

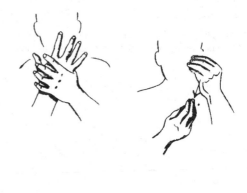

MISSING 2, *adj*. The extended right index finger strikes against the downturned middle finger of the left hand, which is held with palm down and other fingers pointing right. Also DEARTH, LACK.

MISSION 1 (mĭsh′ ən) (*eccles.*), *n.* (The letter "M" at the heart; God.) The right "M" hand, palm facing the body, is brought up against the heart. The sign for GOD is then made: the open right hand, palm facing left, swings up above the head and is then moved down about an inch. The signer looks up while making the sign. Also MISSIONARY 1.

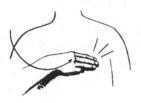

MISSION 2 (*eccles.*), *n.* (The letter "M"; set up or established.) The right "M" hand moves in a small clockwise circle and comes down to rest on the back of the downturned left "A" or "S" hand. Also MISSIONARY 2.

MISSION 3, *n.* (The letter "M.") The right downturned "M" hand swings from the right shoulder to the left.

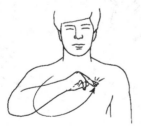

MISSTATEMENT (mis stāt′ ment), *n.* (Words twisted around as they are uttered.) The right "V" fingers are placed on the lips, palm facing the signer. They twist around so that the palm now faces out.

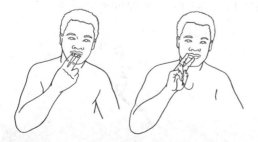

MISTAKE (mĭs tāk′), *n.* (Rationale obscure; the thumb and little finger are said to represent, respectively, right and wrong, with the head poised between the two.) The right "Y" hand, palm facing the body, is brought up to the chin. Also ERROR, FAULT 2, SACRILEGIOUS, WRONG 1.

MISUNDERSTAND (mĭs′ ŭn dər stănd′), *v.,* -STOOD, -STANDING. (The thought is twisted around.) The right "V" hand is positioned with index and middle fingers touching the right side of the forehead. The hand swings around so that the palm now faces out, with the two fingers still on the forehead.

MITTEN (mit′ n), *n.* (The shape is outlined.) The upright left hand is outlined by the right index finger, which moves along the edge from thumb to below the little finger. The outline may also start at the little finger edge and move along to the thumb.

MIX (mĭks), *n., v.,* MIXED, MIXING. (Scrambling or mixing up.) The downturned right hand is positioned above the upturned left. The fingers of both are curved.

Both hands move in opposite horizontal circles. Also CLUTTER, COMPLICATE, CONFUSE, CONFUSED, CONFUSION, DISORDER, MINGLE 1, MIXED, MIX UP, SCRAMBLE.

MIXED (mĭkst), *adj.* See MIX.

MIXED UP, *adj. phrase.* See MIX.

MIX-UP (mĭks′ ŭp′), *n.* See MIX.

MNEMONIC (ni mon′ ik), *adj.* (Initials, with MEMORY.) The fingertips of the right "M" hand touch the forehead, and then the fingertips of the right "N" hand follow suit.

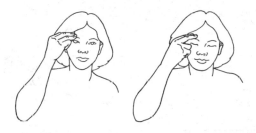

MOB (mob), *n.* (Many people spread out.) The downturned claw hands move straight forward. Also CROWD.

MOCCASIN (mok′ ə sin, -zən), *n.* (Indian shoes.) The sign for INDIAN: the index and thumb of the right

"F" hand moves from the mouth to the temple, tracing the war paint. SHOES follows: both downturned "S" hands strike each other repeatedly.

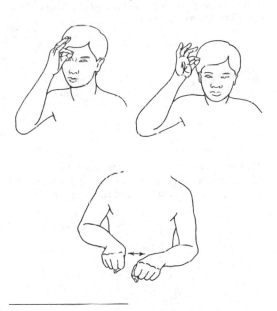

MOCK (mŏk), *v.,* MOCKED, MOCKING. (Derision; poking or prodding.) Both hands are held closed except for index and little fingers, which extend straight out from the body. The right hand is brought up and its index fingertip pulls the right corner of the mouth into a slight smile. Both hands then move forward simultaneously in a series of short jabbing motions, the right somewhat behind the left. An expression of disdain is assumed during this sign. The first part of the sign, pulling the mouth into a smile, is frequently omitted. Also MAKE FUN OF, RIDICULE.

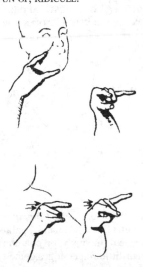

MODEL (mŏd′ əl), n., adj., v., -ELED, -ELING. (The natural sign.) The right fingers and thumb close together and move onto the upturned, open left hand, as if taking something from one place to another. Also COPY 1, DUPLICATE 1, IMITATE, MIMIC.

MODERN (mod′ ərn), adj. (A new leaf is turned.) With both hands held palm up before the body, the right hand sweeps in an arc into the left and continues up a bit.

MODIFY (mŏd′ ə fī′), v., -FIED, -FYING. (To change positions.) Both "A" hands, thumbs up, are held before the chest, several inches apart. The left hand is pivoted over so that its thumb points to the right. Simultaneously, the right hand is moved up and over the left, describing a small arc, with its thumb pointing to the left. Also ADJUST, ALTER, ALTERATION, CHANGE 1, CONVERT, REVERSE 2, TRANSFER 1.

MODULAR (moj′ ə lər), adj. Computer term. (The outlines of a unit.) Both "C" hands, palms facing out, held at either side of the body, pivot around simultaneously, until their little finger edges come together. The

hands meanwhile have moved over to the other side of the body. Also MODULE.

MOIST (moist), adj. (The wetness.) The right fingertips touch the lips, and then the fingers of both hands open and close against the thumbs a number of times. Also CERAMICS, CLAY, DAMP, WET.

MOLECULE (mol′ ə kyōol), n. (The letter "M"; around the world.) The right "M" hand makes a circle around the left fist.

MOMENT (mō′ mənt), n. (The minute hand of a clock.) The right "D" hand is held with its index finger edge against the palm of the left "5" hand, which faces right. The right index finger moves forward in a short arc. Also MINUTE 1.

MONEY 1 (mŭn′ ĭ), *n.* (Slapping of paper money in the palm.) The upturned right hand, grasping some imaginary bills, is brought down into the upturned left palm a number of times. Also CAPITAL 2, CURRENCY, FINANCES, FUNDS.

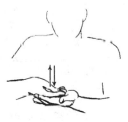

MONEY 2 (*rare*), *n.* (Jiggling coins.) The cupped hands jiggle imaginary coins.

MONEY 3, *n.* (Fingering the money.) The thumb rubs over the index and middle fingers of the upturned hand as if fingering money.

MONITOR (mon′ i tər), *n., v.,* -TORED, -TORING. (Eyes everywhere.) Both downturned "V" hands, side by side, move back and forth together.

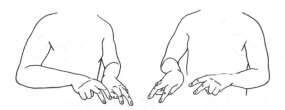

MONK (mungk), *n.* (The hood.) The downturned cupped or "M" hands outline the shape of a hood as it comes up over the head.

MONKEY (mŭng′ kĭ), *n.* (The scratching of apes.) Both hands go through the natural motion of scratching the sides of the chest. Also APE.

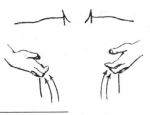

MONOTONOUS 1 (mə nŏt′ ə nəs), *adj.* (The nose is pressed, as if to a grindstone wheel.) The right index finger touches the tip of the nose as a bored expression is assumed. The right hand is sometimes pivoted back and forth slightly as the fingertip remains against the nose. Also BORING, TEDIOUS.

MONOTONOUS 2, *adj.* (The grindstone wheel is indicated here.) The sign for MONOTONOUS 1 is made. The thumb edge of the right "S" hand is then placed in the left palm, which is facing right. The right hand describes a rather slow, continuous, clockwise circle in the left palm. Also GRIND 2.

MONOTONOUS 3, *adj.* (Identical hand positions, indicating sameness, emphasized over and over again.) Both downturned "Y" hands simultaneously describe small ellipses, the right hand in a counterclockwise and the left in a clockwise direction. Emphasis is given to the downward portions of the movements.

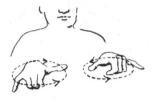

MONSTER (mon′ stər), *n.* (The characteristic gestures of children trying to frighten others.) Both claw hands are held palms out in a threatening way. The signer grimaces and shows the teeth.

MONTH (mŭnth), *n.* (The tip and three joints represent the four weeks of a month.) The extended right index finger moves down along the upturned, extended left index finger.

MONTHLY (mŭnth′ lĭ), *adj., adv.* (Month after month.) The sign for MONTH is made several times.

MOON 1 (mōōn), *n.* (The face in the moon; the rays.) The right "C" hand is placed over the right side of the face. The right fingers then close over the thumb as the hand is raised above the head, palm out. The hand

moves down and out, opening into the "5" position as it does.

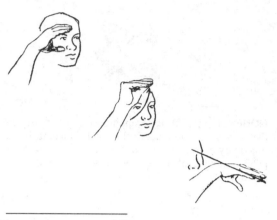

MOON 2, *n.* (The face only.) The right "C" hand indicates the face of the moon, as in MOON 1. The second part of the sign, however, is omitted.

MOOSE (mōōs), *n.* (The branching of the antlers from the head.) Both hands, in the "5" position, palms up, are placed at the head, thumbs resting on the head above the temples. Also ANTLERS, DEER, ELK.

MORE (mōr), *adj., n., adv.* (One hand is added to the other; an addition.) Both hands, palms facing, are held fingers together, the left a bit above the right. The right hand is brought up to the left until their fingertips touch. Also ADD 4, BESIDES, FURTHER 2, MOREOVER 2.

MORE THAN (mor than), *adj.* (Above the limit.) Both downturned hands are held horizontally, right above left. The right hand, with a slight flourish, moves up above the left.

MORNING (môr´ nĭng), *n.* (The sun comes over the horizon.) The little finger edge of the left hand rests in the crook of the right elbow. The left arm, held horizontally, represents the horizon. The open right hand, fingers together and pointing up, with palm facing the body, rises slowly to an almost upright angle. Also FORENOON.

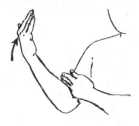

MORON (môr´ ŏn) (*colloq.*), *n.* (The thickness of the skull is indicated to stress intellectual density.) With the thumb of the right "C" hand grasped by the closed left hand, the right hand is swung in toward the body, describing a small arc as it moves. The space between the curved right fingers and the closed left hand indicates the thickness of the skull. Also CLUMSY 2, DUMB 2, STUPID 2, THICKSKULLED, UNSKILLED.

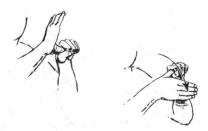

MORPHINE (môr´ fēn), *n.* (A shot in the arm.) The right index finger is thrust into the left upper arm and the thumb wiggles back and forth a number of times, as if implanting a shot in the arm. Also COCA-COLA, COKE, DOPE, INOCULATE, NARCOTICS.

MORTIFICATION (môr´ tə fə kā´ shən), *n.* (The red rises in the cheeks.) The sign for RED is made: the tip of the right index finger of the "D" hand moves down over the lips, which are red. Both hands are then placed palms facing the cheeks and move up along the face to indicate the rise of color. Also BLUSH, EMBARRASS, EMBARRASSED, FLUSH.

MOSCOW (mos´ kou), *n.* The knuckles of the right "A" hand slap the right cheek twice. A native sign.

MOSES 1 (mō´ zis), *n.* (The letter "M"; the Ten Commandments.) The downturned right "M" hand is positioned with index finger edge against the outstretched left palm, near the fingertips. The "M" moves down in an arc to the heel of the left hand.

MOSES 2, *n.* (*arch*). (The veil said to have been worn by Moses to shield the populace from the brilliant rays of light surrounding his face upon his return from talking with God.) The two "F" hands mime lifting up a veil and placing it in front of the face and fastening it behind. This sign, rarely seen today, is often mistaken for a pair of horns, implying that Moses was a horned and therefore evil man.

MOSQUITO (mə skē′ tō), *n.* (The biting and slapping.) The index and thumb of either hand pinch an area of the body such as the throat or the back of the other hand. The signer then slaps the spot where it was bitten.

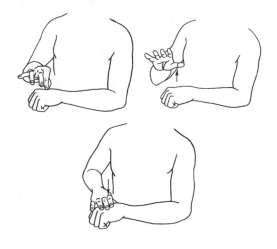

MOTH (môth, moth), *n.* (The "M"s; the motion of the wings.) Both "M" hands, crossed and palms facing the signer, imitate a moth's flapping wings.

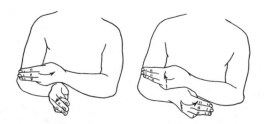

MOTHER 1 (mŭth′ ər), *n.* (A female who carries a baby.) The FEMALE root sign is made: the thumb of the right "A" hand moves down along the line of the right jaw from ear almost to chin. Both hands are then held open and palms facing up, as if holding a baby. This is the formal sign.

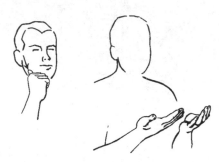

MOTHER 2 (*colloq.*), *n.* (Derived from the FEMALE root sign.) The thumb of the right "5" hand rests on the right cheek or on the right chinbone. The other fingers wiggle slightly. Or the thumb is thrust repeatedly into the right side of the face, and the rest of the hand remains open and in the "5" position, palm facing out. This latter modification is used for MAMA.

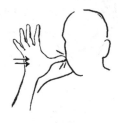

MOTION 1 (mō′ shən), *n.* (An offering; a presenting.) Both hands, slightly cupped, palms up, are held close to the chest. They move up and out in unison, describing a very slight arc. Also BID 2, OFFER 1, OFFERING 1, PRESENT 1, PROPOSE, SUGGEST, TENDER 2.

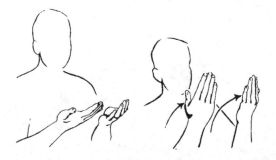

MOTION 2, *n.* (Continuous movement.) The down-turned right index finger moves in a continuous clockwise direction.

MOTION PICTURE (The frames of the film speeding through the projector.) The left "5" hand, palm facing right and thumb pointing up, is the projector. The right "5" hand is placed against the left and moves back and forth quickly. Also CINEMA, FILM, MOVIE(S), MOVING PICTURE.

MOTIVATE (mō′ tə vāt′), *v.*, -VATED, -VATING. (Pushing forward.) Both "5" hands are held, palms out, the right fingers facing right and the left fingers left. The hands move straight forward in a series of short movements. Also ENCOURAGE, MOTIVATION, URGE 1.

MOTIVATION (mō′ tə vā′ shən), *n.* See MOTIVATE.

MOTIVE 1 (mō′ tĭv), *n.* (A thought is turned over in the mind.) The index finger makes a small circle on the forehead. Also CONSIDER 1, RECKON, SPECULATE 1, SPECULATION 1, THINK, THOUGHT 1, THOUGHTFUL.

MOTIVE 2, *n., adj.* (The welling up of feelings or emotions in the heart.) The right middle finger, touching the heart, moves up an inch or two a number of times. Also EMOTION 1, FEEL 2, FEELING, SENSATION, SENSE 2.

MOTIVE 3, *n., adj.* (Relative standing of one's thoughts.) A modified sign for THINK is made: the right index finger touches the middle of the forehead. The tips of the right "V" hand, palm down, are then thrust into the upturned left palm (as in STAND, *q.v.*). The right "V" hand is then rethrust into the upturned left palm, with right palm now facing the body. Also CONNOTE, IMPLY, INTEND, INTENT 1, INTENTION, MEAN 2, MEANING, PURPOSE 1, SIGNIFICANCE 2, SIGNIFY 2, SUBSTANCE 2.

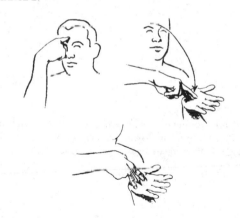

MOTOR 1 (mō′ tər), *n.* (The meshing gears.) With the knuckles of both hands interlocked, the hands pivot up and down, imitating the meshing of gear teeth. Also ENGINE, FACTORY, MACHINE, MACHINERY, MECHANIC 1, MECHANISM.

MOTOR 2, *n*. (The pistons moving.) Both upturned fists move alternately up and down.

MOTORCYCLE (mō′ tər sī′ kəl), *n*. (Manipulating the handles.) The "S" hands, spread apart, grasp and manipulate the handlebars of an imaginary motorcycle.

MOUNT (mount), *v*., MOUNTED, MOUNTING. (Getting on the saddle.) The downturned right "V" fingers are placed on the index finger edge of the left "B" hand.

MOUNTAIN (moun′ tən), *n*. (An undulating pile of rocks.) The sign for ROCK is made: the back of the upturned right "S" hand strikes the back of the down-turned left "S" hand twice. The downturned "5"

hands then move from left to right in wavy, up-down movements.

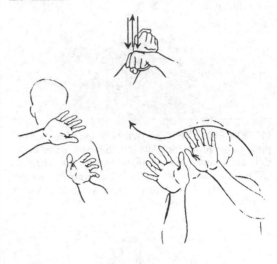

MOURNFUL (mōrn′ fəl), *adj*. (The facial features drop.) Both "5" hands, palms facing the eyes and fingers slightly curved, drop simultaneously to a level with the mouth. The head drops slightly as the hands move down, and an expression of sadness is assumed. Also DEJECTED, DEPRESSED, GLOOM, GLOOMY, GRAVE 3, GRIEF 1, MELANCHOLY, SAD, SORROWFUL 1.

MOUSE 1 (mous), *n*. (The twitching nose.) The index finger brushes across the tip of the nose several times.

MOUSE 2, *n.* (A variation of MOUSE 1.) Both index fingers simultaneously brush the tip of the nose.

MOVE (mōōv), *n., v.,* MOVED, MOVING. (Moving from one place to another.) The downturned hands, fingers touching their respective thumbs, move in unison from left to right. Also MIGRATE, PLACE 3, PUT, REMOVE 2, TRANSFER 2.

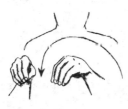

MOVIE(S) (mōō′ vǐ), *n.* (The frames of the film speeding through the projector.) The left "5" hand, palm facing right and thumb pointing up, is the projector. The right "5" hand is placed against the left and moves back and forth quickly. Also CINEMA, FILM, MOTION PICTURE, MOVING PICTURE.

MOVIE CAMERA, *n.* (Using the old-fashioned hand crank.) The left "B" is held at the left side of the face, palm facing right. The right hand, positioned next to the left and holding an imaginary crank, rotates forward repeatedly in a clockwise direction.

MOVING PICTURE, *n.* See MOVIE(S).

MOW 1 (mō) *v.,* MOWED, MOWING. (Threshing by hand.) The signer manipulates an imaginary scythe with both hands. Also SCYTHE.

MOW 2, *v.* (The action of manipulating a lawn mower.) The signer, grasping a pair of imaginary handles, mimes moving forward and pushing a lawn mower. Also LAWN MOWER 2.

MOW 3, *v.* (The clipping blades.) The downturned right "5" hand rests on its downturned left counterpart. Both hands move quickly back and forth over each other, imitating opposite moving blades for cutting grass or hair.

MUCH (mŭch), *adj., adv.* (A large amount.) The "5" hands face each other, fingers curved and touching. They move apart rather quickly. Also EXPAND, GREAT 2, INFINITE, LOT.

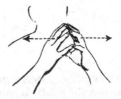

MUG (mug), *n.* (Holding the handle and tipping the mug to the mouth.) The little finger of the right "Y" hand rests on the upturned left palm. The "Y" hand moves up to the mouth, as if tipping the contents of the mug into the mouth.

MULE (mūl), *n.* (The donkey's broad ear; the animal is traditionally a stubborn one.) The open hand, or the "B" hand, is placed at the side of the head, with palm out and fingers pointing straight up. The hand moves forward and back, pivoting at the wrist, as in the case of a donkey's ears flapping. Both hands may also be used, at either side of the head. Also DONKEY, MULISH, OBSTINATE, STUBBORN.

MULISH (mū′ lǐsh), *adj.* See MULE.

MULL OVER, *v. phrase.* (Many thoughts turn over in the mind.) The right hand makes a continuous counterclockwise circle in front of the head. Meanwhile, the fingers wriggle continuously.

MULTIPLE (mŭl′ tə pəl), *adj.* (Many fingers are indicated.) The upturned "S" hands are thrown up, open-

ing into the "5" position, palms up. This may be repeated. Also MANY, NUMEROUS, PLURAL, QUANTITY 2.

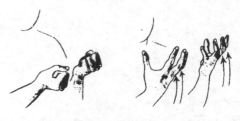

MULTIPLY 1 (mŭl′ tə plī′), *v.,* -PLIED, -PLYING. (A multiplying.) The "V" hands, palms facing the body, alternately cross and separate several times. Also ARITHMETIC, CALCULATE, ESTIMATE, FIGURE 1.

MULTIPLY 2, *v.* (A variation of MULTIPLY 1.) The same sign as MULTIPLY 1 except that the index fingers are used instead of the "V" fingers. Also TIMES.

MUMMY (mum′ ē), *n.* (The crossed hands in the coffin.) The signer, with eyes closed, crosses the arms on the chest.

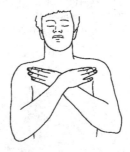

MURDER (mûr′ dər), *n.* (Thrusting a dagger and twisting it.) The outstretched right index finger is passed under the downturned left hand. As it moves under the left hand, the right wrist twists in a clockwise direction. Also KILL, SLAY.

MUSCLE (mus′ əl), *n.* (Pointing to the muscle.) The signer flexes the left arm and points to the biceps muscle.

MUSEUM (myoo zē′ əm), *n.* (The letter "M"; a house or building.) With both hands forming the letter "M," the signer traces the outline of the roof and walls.

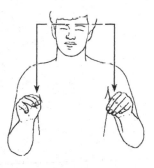

MUSHROOM (mush′ room), *n.* (The stem and cap.) The downturned right claw hand is positioned on top of the left index finger.

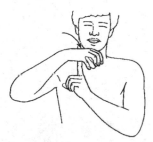

MUSIC (mū′ zĭk), *n.* (A rhythmic, wavy movement of the hand to indicate a melody; the movement of a conductor's hand in directing a musical performance.) The right "5" hand, palm facing left, is waved back and forth over the downturned left hand in a series of elongated figure eights. Also CHANT, HYMN 1, MELODY, SING, SONG.

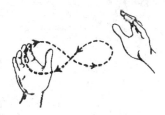

MUST (mŭst), *aux. v.* (Being pinned down.) The right hand, in the "X" position, palm down, moves forcefully up and down once or twice. An expression of determination is frequently assumed. Also HAVE TO, IMPERATIVE, NECESSARY 1, NECESSITY, NEED 1, OUGHT TO, SHOULD, VITAL 2.

MUTUAL 1 (mū′ choo əl), *adj.* (Mingling with.) Both hands are held in modified "A" positions, thumbs out. The left hand is positioned with its thumb pointing straight up, and the right hand, with its thumb pointing down, revolves above the left thumb in a counterclockwise direction. Also ASSOCIATE 1, EACH OTHER, FELLOWSHIP, MINGLE 2, ONE ANOTHER.

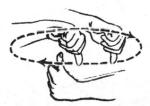

MUTUAL 2, *adj.* (The fingers are drawn together.) The right "2" hand, palm facing the body, is drawn down through the left "C" hand. As it moves, the right index and middle fingers come together. Also BOTH, PAIR.

MY (mī), *pron.* (Pressing something to one's bosom.) The "5" hand is brought up against the chest. Also MINE 1, OWN.

MYSELF (mī sĕlf'), *pron.* (The thumb represents the self.) The upturned thumb of the right "A" hand is brought up against the chest.

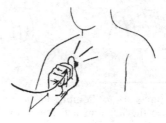

N

NAG (năg), *v.*, NAGGED, NAGGING. (The hen's beak pecks.) The index finger and thumb of the right hand, held together, are brought against the index finger of the left "D" hand a number of times. Also HENPECK, PECK, PICK ON.

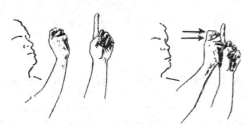

NAIL POLISH (pŏl′ ĭsh), *n.* (The natural sign.) The fingertips of the right "U" hand, held palm down, are brushed repeatedly over the fingernail of the left middle or index finger.

NAIVE 1 (nä ĕv′), *adj.* Both "N" hands are placed at the lips. They move forward and out, away from the lips.

NAIVE 2, *adj.* Both open hands, palms facing out, are held in front of the mouth, with the ring fingers bent against the palm. Both hands move out and away from the mouth, describing arcs. Also INNOCENT 2.

NAIVE 3, *adj.* (Clumsy in gait; all thumbs.) The "3" hands, palms down, move alternately up and down before the body. Also AWKWARD, AWKWARDNESS, CLUMSINESS, CLUMSY 1, GREEN 2, GREENHORN 2.

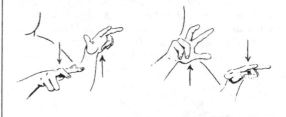

NAKED (nā′ kĭd), *adj.* (Devoid of everything on the surface.) The middle finger of the downturned right "5" hand sweeps over the back of the downturned left "A" or "S" hand, from wrist to knuckles, and continues beyond a bit. Also BARE 2, EMPTY 2, NUDE, OMISSION 2, VACANCY, VACANT, VOID.

NAME (nām), *n., v.,* NAMED, NAMING. (The "X" used by illiterates in writing their names. This sign is indicative of widespread illiteracy when the language of signs first began to evolve as an instructional medium in deaf education.) The right "H" hand, palm facing left, is brought down on the left "H" hand, palm facing right.

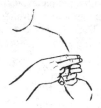

NAMED, *v.* (NAME, indicating who is named.) The sign for NAME is made: the right "H" hand, palm facing left, is brought down on the left "H" hand, palm facing right. The hands, in this position, move forward a few inches. Also CALLED.

NAP 1 (năp), *v.,* NAPPED, NAPPING, *n.* (The eyes are closed.) The fingers of the right open hand, facing the forehead, are placed on the forehead. The hand moves down and away from the head, with the fingers closing so that they all touch. The eyes meanwhile close, and the head bows slightly, as in sleep. Also ASLEEP, DOZE, SLEEP 1.

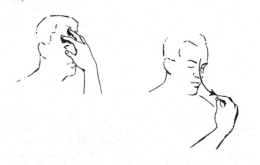

NAP 2, *n., v.* (A short sleep.) The sign for SLEEP is made: the open hand, palm facing the signer, is placed in front of the eyes. It moves down a bit while the fingers come together. The eyes close as the hand moves down. The sign for SHORT follows: the index and middle fingers of the right "H" hand are placed across the top of the index and middle fingers of the left "H"

hand and move a short distance back and forth along the length of the left index finger.

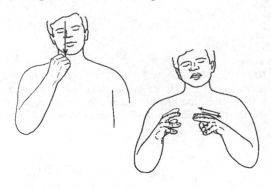

NARCOTICS (när kŏt′ iks), *n. pl.* (A shot in the arm.) The right index finger is thrust into the left upper arm and the thumb wiggles back and forth a number of times, as if implanting a shot in the arm. Also COCA-COLA, COKE, DOPE, INOCULATE, MORPHINE.

NARRATE (nă rāt′, năr′, āt), *v.,* -RATED, -RATING. (The unraveling or stretching out of words or sentences.) Both open hands are held close to each other, with fingers open and palms facing and almost touching. As the hands are drawn apart, the thumb and index finger of each hand come together to form circles. This is repeated several times. Also DESCRIBE 2, EXPLAIN 2, FABLE, FICTION, GOSPEL 1, NARRATIVE, STORY 1, TALE, TELL ABOUT.

NARRATIVE (năr′ ə tĭv), *n.* See NARRATE.

NATION (nā′ shən), *n.* (An established area.) The right "N" hand, palm down, executes a clockwise circle above the downturned prone left hand. The tips of the

"N" fingers then move straight down and come to rest on the back of the left hand. Also COUNTRY 2, LAND 2.

NATIVE AMERICAN 1 (nāt′ iv ə měr′ i kən), *n., adj.* (The feathered headdress.) The right thumb and index fingers, holding an imaginary feather, are placed first on the tip of the nose and then under the right ear or on the right side of the head. Also INDIAN 1.

NATIVE AMERICAN 2, *n., adj.* (The characteristic motions during dancing.) The right "5" hand is placed behind the head, fingers pointing upward to indicate the feathers. The left hand touches the open lips repeatedly. Also INDIAN 2.

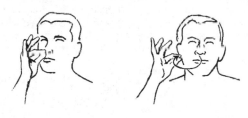

NAUGHT 1 (nôt), *n.* (The zeros.) Both "O" hands, palms facing, are thrown out and down into the "5" position. Also NONE 1, NOTHING 1.

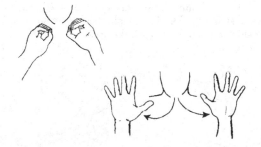

NAUGHT 2, *n.* (The zeros.) Both "O" hands, palms facing, move back and forth a number of times, the right hand to the right and the left hand to the left. Also NOTHING 2.

NAUGHT 3 (*sl.*), *n.* (An emphatic movement of the "0," *i.e.,* ZERO hand.) The little finger edge of the right "0" hand is brought sharply into the upturned left palm. Also NONE 4, NOTHING 4, ZERO 1.

NAUSEA (nô′ shə, -shĭ ə, -sĭ ə), *n.* (Turning the stomach.) The fingertips of the curved right hand describe a continuous circle on the stomach. The signer assumes an exaggerated expression of disgust. Also DISGUST, DISGUSTED, DISGUSTING, DISPLEASED, MAKE ME DISGUSTED, MAKE ME SICK, NAUSEATE, NAUSEOUS, OBNOXIOUS, REVOLTING.

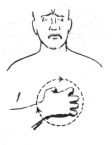

NAUSEATE, *v.*, -ATED, -ATING. See NAUSEA.

NAUSEOUS (nô′ shəs, -shĭ əs), *adj.* See NAUSEA.

NAVY (nā′ vē), *n.* (The bell-bottoms.) Both down-pointing open hands move down along one leg and then the other, widening as they move down.

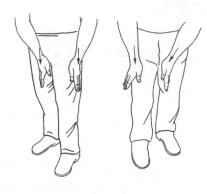

NEAR 1 (nĭr), *adv., prep.* (One hand is near the other.) The left hand, cupped, fingers together, is held before the chest, palm facing the body. The right hand, also cupped, fingers together, moves a very short distance back and forth as it is held in front of the left. Also ADJACENT, BESIDE, BY 1, CLOSE (TO) 2, NEIGHBOR, NEIGHBORHOOD, VICINITY.

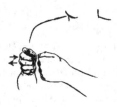

NEAR 2, *adv., prep.* (Coming close to.) Both hands are held in the right-angle position, fingers facing each other, with the right hand held between the left hand and the chest. The right hand slowly moves toward the left. Also APPROACH, TOWARD 2.

NEARLY (nĭr′ lĭ), *adv.* The left hand is held at chest level in the right-angle position, with fingers pointing up and the back of the hand facing right. The right fin-

gers are swept up along the back of the left hand. Also ABOUT 2, ALMOST.

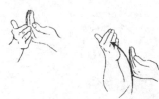

NECESSARY 1 (nĕs′ ə sĕr′ ĭ), *adj.* (Being pinned down.) The right hand, in the "X" position, palm down, moves forcefully up and down once or twice. An expression of determination is frequently assumed. Also HAVE TO, IMPERATIVE, MUST, NECESSITY, NEED 1, OUGHT TO, SHOULD, VITAL 2.

NECESSARY 2, *adj.* (The letter "N"; a forceful movement of the hand.) The "N" hand is thrust straight down a few inches.

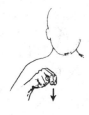

NECESSITY (nə sĕs′ ə tĭ), *n.* See NECESSARY 1.

NECKING (nĕk′ ĭng) (*sl.*), *n.* (Necks interlocked.) The "S" hands, palms facing, are crossed at the wrists. They swing up and down while the wrists remain in contact. Also MAKE LOVE 2, PETTING.

NECKTIE (nĕk′ tī′), *n*. (The natural motion.) The "H" hands go through the natural hand-over-hand motions of tying a knot in a necktie at the throat. The right "H" hand then moves down the front of the chest to indicate the tail of the tie. Also TIE 2.

NÉE (nā), *adj*. (Presenting the baby from womb to hand; a coming out from the womb to the waiting hand. Referring to birth name.) The upturned right hand is brought forward from the stomach to the upturned left palm. Also BIRTH 1, BORN 1.

NEED 1 (nēd), *n., v.,* NEEDED, NEEDING. (Being pinned down.) The right hand, in the "X" position, palm down, moves forcefully up and down once or twice. An expression of determination is frequently assumed. Also HAVE TO, IMPERATIVE, MUST, NECESSARY 1, NECESSITY, OUGHT TO, SHOULD, VITAL 2.

NEED 2, *n*. (Grasping something and pulling it in.) The upturned "5" hands, held side by side before the chest, close slightly into a grasping position as they move in toward the body. Also COVET 1, DESIRE 1, LONG 2, WANT, WILL 2, WISH 1.

NEED 3, *n., v*. (The letter "N"; a forceful movement of the hand.) The "N" hand is twice thrust down a few inches.

NEEDLE 1 (nē′ dəl), *n*. (The sewing; the length is indicated.) The sign for SEW is made: the right hand, grasping an imaginary needle, goes through the natural motion of hand-stitching on the open left palm. The thumb and index finger of the right hand are then placed on the side of the left index finger at the tip and third knuckle to indicate the length of the needle.

NEEDLE 2, *n*. (The natural sign.) The signer mimes threading a needle and pulling the thread through the hole.

NEGLECT (nĭ glĕktʹ), *v.*, -GLECTED, -GLECTING. (To throw something aside.) Both "S" hands are held with palms facing at chest level and then thrown down and to the left, opening into the "5" position. Also ABANDON 1, CAST OFF, DEPOSIT 2, DISCARD 1, FORSAKE 3, LEAVE 2, LET ALONE.

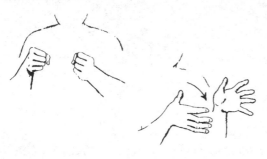

NEGOTIATE (ni gōʹ shē ātʹ), *v.*, -TIATED, -TIATING. (The "N"s; back and forth.) Both downturned "N" hands, fingers facing each other, move alternately back and forth. Also NEGOTIATION.

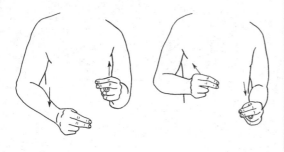

NEIGHBOR (nāʹbər), *n.* (One who is near.) The sign for NEAR is made: the left hand, cupped, fingers together, is held before the chest, palm facing the body. The right hand, also cupped, fingers together, moves a very short distance back and forth as it is held in front of the left. This is followed by the sign for INDIVIDUAL: both open hands, palms facing each other, move down the sides of the body, tracing its outline to the hips.

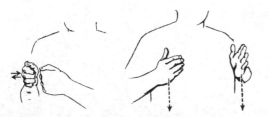

NEIGHBORHOOD (nāʹ bər hŏŏdʹ), *n.* See NEIGHBOR. The sign is repeated on both sides of the body, and the sign for INDIVIDUAL 1 is omitted.

NEPHEW (nĕfʹ ū), *n.* (The initial "N"; the upper or masculine portion of the head.) The right "N" hand, held near the right temple, shakes slightly or pivots at the wrist.

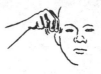

NERVE 1 (nûrv) (*colloq.*), *n.* (The cheek is indicated.) The knuckles of the right index and middle fingers are thrust or twisted against the right cheek. Also CHEEK, NERVY.

NERVE 2, *n.* (Tracing a nerve along the arm.) The right "N" moves along the outstretched left arm from elbow to wrist.

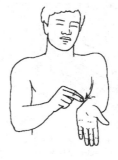

NERVOUS (nûrʹ vəs), *adj.* (The trembling fingers.) Both "5" hands, held palm down, tremble noticeably.

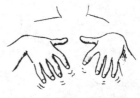

NEST 1 (nest), *v.*, NESTED, NESTING. (Computer terminology; placing a command into the computer.) The thumb and index fingers of the right "G" hand are thrust into the space created by the "C" shape of the left hand.

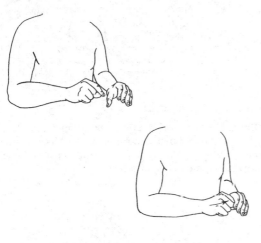

NEST 2, *n.* (A bowl-shaped dwelling for birds.) Both upturned "N" hands, somewhat curved, move up, forming the shape of a bowl.

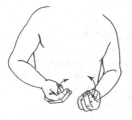

NEST 3, *n.* (The natural sign.) The upturned cupped hands form an imaginary nest. They separate and swing in toward the body, outlining the contours of the nest.

NET (net), *n.* (The shape.) The upturned cupped hands are held with fingertips interlocked. They move apart and up, outlining a net.

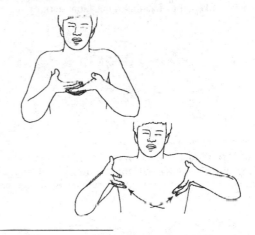

NETWORK(ING) (net' wûrk), *n., v.* (Remaining in contact.) The middle fingers of both "5" hands touch, and both hands move together in a large counterclockwise circle.

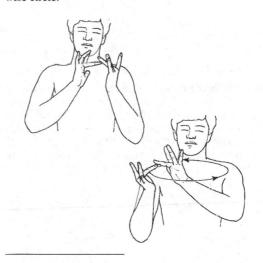

NEUROTIC (nŏŏ rot' ik), *adj.* (The letter "N"; something to do with the mind.) The tips of the right "N" hand are placed against the right temple. The hand may shake very slightly.

NEVER (nĕv′ ər), *adv.* The open right hand, fingers together and palm facing out, moves in a short arc from left to right and then straight down. The movement is likened to forming a question mark or an "S" in the air.

NEVER AGAIN, *phrase.* (Avoid touching something.) The right downturned middle finger touches the upturned left palm quickly a number of times. The signer is frowning.

NEVERTHELESS (nĕv′ ər tʰə lĕs′), *adv.* Both hands, in the "5" position, are held before the chest, fingertips facing each other. With an alternate back-forth movement, the fingertips are made to strike each other. Also ANYHOW, ANYWAY, DESPITE, DOESN'T MATTER, HOWEVER 2, INDIFFERENCE, INDIFFERENT, IN SPITE OF, MAKE NO DIFFERENCE, NO MATTER, WHEREVER.

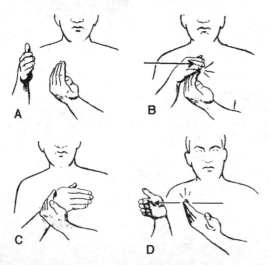

A

B

C

D

NEW (nū, nōō), *adj.* (Turning over a new leaf.) With both hands held palm up before the body, the right hand sweeps in an arc into the left and continues up a bit. Also NEWS, NOVELTY, ORIGINAL 2, TIDINGS.

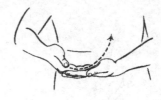

NEW ORLEANS (ôr′ lĭ ənz; *older:* ôr lēnz′), *n.* (The letter "O"; a modified sign for NEW, *q.v.*) The thumb side of the downturned right "O" hand brushes down twice across the left palm, which is facing right.

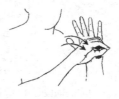

NEWS (nūz, nōōz), *n.* See NEW.

NEWSPAPER (nūz′ pā′ pər, nōōz′ -, nŭs,′ -nōōs′ -), *n.* (The action of the press.) The right "5" hand, held palm down, fingers pointing left, is brought down twice against the upturned left "5" hand, whose fingers point right. Also PAPER, PUBLISH 1.

NEW ZEALAND 1 (nōō zē′ lənd), *n.* (The "N" and "Z.") The signer fingerspells "N" and "Z."

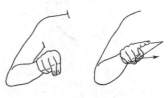

NEW ZEALAND 2, *n.* (The sign for NEW is followed by the British two-handed alphabet letter "Z." New

Zealand is part of the British commonwealth.) With both hands held palm up before the body, the right hand sweeps in an arc into the left and continues up a bit. The British letter "Z" then follows: the fingertips of the right hand, palm down, are thrust into the upturned left palm. A local sign.

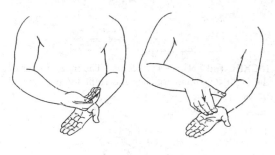

NEXT 1 (někst), *adj.* The index finger of the right hand is placed across the index finger of the left "L" hand. The right hand then flips over around the tip of the left index finger and up against its underside. Also SERIES, THENCE.

NEXT 2, *adj.* The extended right index finger is placed across the back of the thumb of the left "L" hand. The right hand then moves up over the left thumb and curves down, ending with its index fingertip touching the left index fingertip.

NEXT 3, *adj., adv.* The left hand is lifted over the right and placed down in front of the right palm.

NEXT 4, *adj., adv.* The right open hand is held with palm toward the body, fingers pointing left. In this position the right hand moves forward and back against the back of the left open hand, which is also held with palm toward the body, fingers pointing right.

NEXT WEEK 1, *adv. phrase.* The right "L" hand is placed against the base of the open left palm, which faces right, fingers pointing forward. The right hand moves forward toward the left fingertips, its thumb and index finger coming together as it goes. Finally, the right index finger is extended as the hand curves to the left around the left fingertips.

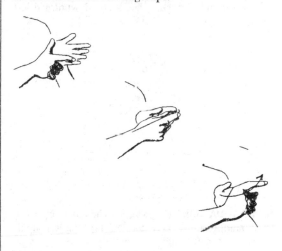

NEXT WEEK 2, *adv. phrase.* (A modification of NEXT WEEK 1.) The upright, right "D" hand is placed palm to palm against the left "5" hand, whose palm faces right. The right "D" hand moves along the left palm from base to fingertips and then beyond in an arc. Also WEEK 2.

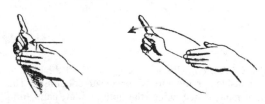

NEXT YEAR, *adv. phrase.* (A year in the future.) The right "S" hand, palm facing left, is brought forcefully down to rest on the upturned thumb edge of the left "S" hand, which is held with palm facing right. (See YEAR.) From this position the right hand moves forward with index finger extended and pointing ahead.

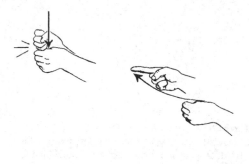

NIBBLE (nib′ əl), *n., v.,* -BLED, -BLING. (Small bites.) The right fingertips make a series of small bites against the index finger edge of the downturned left hand.

NICARAGUA (nik ə rä′ gwə), *n.* (The letter "N.") The right hand, forming the letter "N," taps the left shoulder twice. A native sign.

NICE (nīs), *adj.* (Everything is wiped off the hand to emphasize an uncluttered or clean condition.) The right hand slowly wipes the upturned left palm from wrist to fingertips. Also CLEAN 1, IMMACULATE, NEAT, PLAIN 2, PURE 1, PURITY, SIMPLE 2.

NICKEL (nik′ əl), *n.* (Five cents.) The index finger of the right "5" hand touches the right temple several times.

NIECE (nēs), *n.* (The initial "N"; the lower or feminine portion of the head.) The right "N" hand, held near the right side of the jaw, shakes slightly or pivots at the wrist.

NIGHT (nīt), *n.* (The sun drops beneath the horizon.) The left hand, palm down, is positioned at chest height. The downturned right hand, held an inch or so above the left, moves over the left hand in an arc, as the sun setting beneath the horizon. Also EVENING.

NIGHTMARE (nīt′ mâr), *n.* (Bad dream.) The sign for BAD is made: the tips of the right "B" hand are placed at the lips and then the hand is thrown down. This is followed by the sign for DREAM: the right curved index finger opens and closes quickly and continuously as it leaves its initial position on the forehead and moves up into the air.

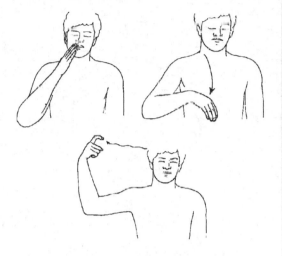

NIPPLES 1 (nip′ əlz), *n.* (The shape and position.) The right "F" hand is placed first at the right nipple and then at the left.

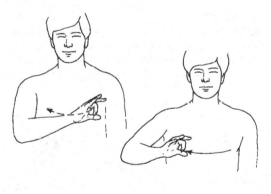

NIPPLES 2, *n.* (The nipples stand out.) Both down-turned "S" hands are placed at the respective nipples. The index fingers flick straight out.

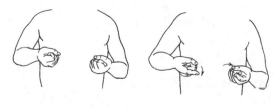

NITWIT (nit′ wit′), *n., sl.* (A tiny brain occupies the skull.) The right thumb and index finger, half an inch

apart, are placed on the forehead, palm facing the signer. The two fingers move counterclockwise, covering 90°, coming to rest still on the forehead. Also PEABRAIN.

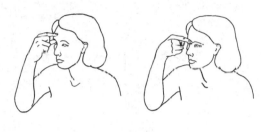

NO 1 (nō), *adv., adj.* (The letter "O.") Both "O" hands are held facing each other in front of the face. They are then drawn apart slowly, the right hand moving to the right and the left hand moving to the left.

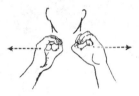

NO 2, *interj.* (The letters "N" and "O.") The index and middle fingers of the right "N" hand are held raised and are then lowered against the extended right thumb in a modified "O" position.

NOBODY (nō′ bod′ ē, -bud′ ē, -bə dē), *n.* (The zero is emphasized.) The right "O" hand, representing a zero, is held palm out and shakes back and forth from left to right. Both hands may be used instead of one.

NO FEAR *phrase.* (Minimal or no regard for feelings of the heart.) The right fingertips are placed against the heart, and then the right hand swings down in an arc so that the right fingertips brush down against the left palm. Also BRASH.

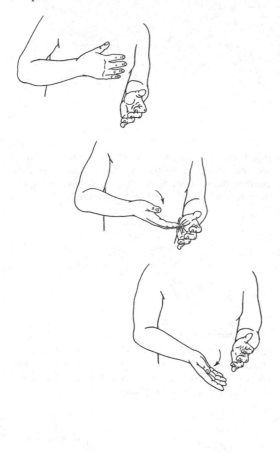

NO GOOD 1 (nō go͝od′), *adj. phrase.* (Of no worth.) The "F" hands face each other, the right above the left. The right hand swings down in an arc, passing the left. As it does so, the thumb and index finger of the right hand strike the corresponding fingers of the left rather sharply. An expression of disdain is assumed. Also WORTHLESS 2.

NO GOOD 2, *phrase.* (A fingerspelled loan sign.) The letters "N-G" are fingerspelled.

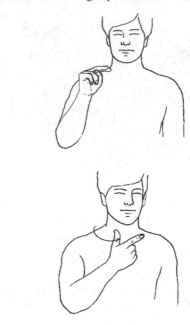

NOISE (noiz), *n.* (A shaking that disturbs the ear.) After placing the index finger on the ear, both hands assume the "S" position, palms down. They move alternately back and forth, forcefully. Also DIN, NOISY, RACKET, SOUND, THUNDER.

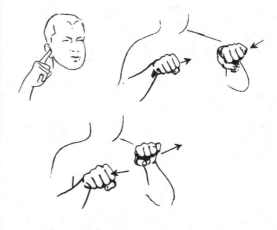

NOISY (noi′ zĭ), *adj.* See NOISE.

NO MATTER, *phrase.* Both hands, in the "5" position, are held before the chest, fingertips facing each other. With an alternate back-forth movement, the fingertips are made to strike each other. Also ANYHOW, ANYWAY, DESPITE, DOESN'T MATTER, HOWEVER 2, INDIFFERENCE, INDIFFERENT, IN SPITE OF, MAKE NO DIFFERENCE, NEVERTHELESS, WHEREVER.

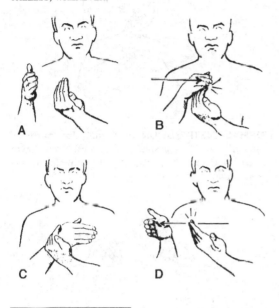

A   B

C   D

NOMINATE (nom′ ə nāt), *v.*, -NATED, -NATING. (The "N" letters; offering something up front.) The "N" hands, palms up, move forward alternately, tracing continuous elliptical paths.

NONE 1 (nŭn), *adj.* (The zeros.) Both "O" hands, palms facing, are thrown out and down into the "5" position. Also NAUGHT 1, NOTHING 1.

NONE 2, *adj.* (The "O" hands.) Both "O" hands are crossed at the wrists before the chest, thumb edges toward the body. From this position the hands draw apart, the right hand moving to the right and the left hand to the left.

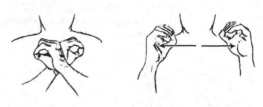

NONE 3, *n., adj.* (Blowing away.) The thumb and index finger of each hand come together to form circles in front of the mouth, as if holding something. The signer then blows on the hands, whereupon they move abruptly away from the face and open into the "5" position, palms out, showing that whatever they held is gone.

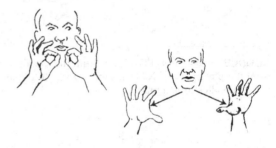

NONE 4 (*sl.*), *pron.* (An emphatic movement of the "O," *i.e.*, ZERO hand.) The little finger edge of the right "O" hand is brought sharply into the upturned left palm. Also NAUGHT 3, NOTHING 4, ZERO 1.

NONSENSE (nŏn′ sĕns), *n.* (Thoughts flickering back and forth.) The right "Y" hand, thumb almost touching the forehead, is shaken back and forth across the forehead several times. Also ABSURD, DAFT, FOLLY, FOOLISH, RIDICULOUS, SILLY, TRIFLING.

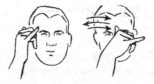

NONSTOP (non′ stop′), *adj., n.* (NONE and STOP.) Both "O" hands, palms out, are held side by side at the chest. They separate a few inches. The sign for STOP: the little finger edge of the right open hand is brought down sharply on the upturned left palm.

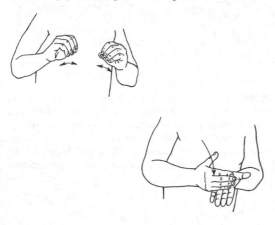

NOODLE (nōōd′ l), *n.* (The "N"; lifting the noodles from the plate.) Both "N" hands mime forks lifting a pile of noodles from a plate.

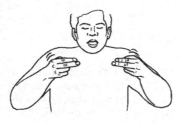

NOON (nōōn), *n.* (The sun is directly overhead.) The right "B" hand, palm facing left, is held upright in a vertical position, its elbow resting on the back of the open left hand. Also MIDDAY.

NORM (nôrm), *n.* (The letter "N"; going through the range, from top to bottom.) The right "N" hand is positioned against the fingertips of the outstretched left palm. It moves down to the base of the left hand.

NORMAL DISTRIBUTION (nôr′ məl dis trə byŏŏ′ shən), *n.* (The typical statistical curve.) Both downturned "N" hands, held side by side, move apart and down, tracing a curve in the air.

NORWAY 1 (nôr′ wā), *n.* (The letter "N"; the upper or "northern" part of the head indicates the geographical location of the country, *i.e.,* in the northern part of Europe.) The right "N" hand, palm down, describes a small counterclockwise circle on the forehead. Also NORWEGIAN.

NORWAY 2, *n.* (The letter "N"; the streaming of the flag.) The right hand, forming an "N" (or a modified "H") makes a wavy movement across the chest, from left to right.

NOSTRIL (nŏs′ trəl), *n.* (The shape.) The index finger circles the edge of the nostril.

NOSY 1 (nō′ zĭ) (*sl.*), *adj.* (A big nose.) The right index finger, after resting on the tip of the nose, moves forward and then back to the nose, in an oval, as if tracing a long extension of the nose.

NOSY 2 (*sl.*), *adj.* (An elongated nose.) The index finger and thumb, held slightly apart, rest on the tip of the nose. As they move forward from the nose they come together.

NOSY 3 (*sl.*), *adj.* (The nose is emphasized.) The index finger taps the tip of the nose a number of times.

NOSY 4, *adj.* (Poking one's nose into the affairs of others.) The right index fingertip touches the nose.

The hand then swings around and the index finger, now curved, with palm out, is thrust into a cup formed by the left "O" hand.

NOT 1 (not), *adv.* (Crossing the hands—a negative gesture.) The downturned open hands are crossed. They are drawn apart rather quickly. Also NEGATIVE 1, UN-.

NOT 2, *adv.* The right "A" hand is placed with the tip of the upturned thumb under the chin. The hand draws out and forward in a slight arc. Also NEGATION, NEGATIVE 2.

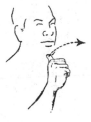

NOT DONE, *phrase.* (Hanging back.) The "5" hand and forearm, hanging loosely and straight down from the elbow, move back and forth under the armpit. Also BEHIND TIME, LATE, NOT YET, TARDY.

NOTHING 1 (nŭth′ ĭng), *n.* (The zeros.) Both "O" hands, palms facing, are thrown out and down into the "5" position. Also NAUGHT 1, NONE 1.

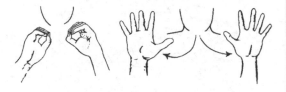

NOTHING 2, *n.* (The zeros.) Both "0" hands, palms facing, move back and forth a number of times, the right hand to the right and the left hand to the left. Also NAUGHT 2.

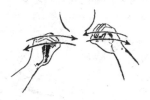

NOTHING 3 (*sl.*), *adv.* (Blowing something away so that it no longer remains.) The signer blows into the upturned palm. Also BLOW AWAY.

NOTHING 4 (*sl.*), *n.* (An emphatic movement of the "0," *i.e.,* ZERO hand.) The little finger edge of the right "O" hand is brought sharply into the upturned left palm. Also NAUGHT 3, NONE 4, ZERO 1.

NOTICE (nō′ tis), *n.* (Posted on the wall.) The thumbs mime pinning thumbtacks into the wall to hold up a four-cornered sheet of paper.

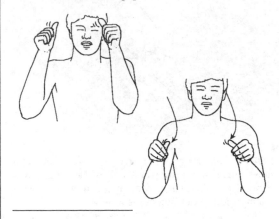

NOTIFY 1 (nō′ tə fī′), *v.,* -FIED, -FYING. (Taking knowledge from the mind and giving it out to all.) The fingertips are positioned on either side of the forehead. Both hands then swing down and out, opening into the upturned "5" position. Also INFORM 1, INFORMATION 1, LET KNOW 1.

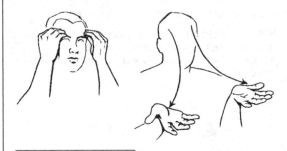

NOTIFY 2, *v.* The fingertips of the right "5" hand are positioned on the forehead. Both hands then swing forward and up, opening into the upturned "5" position. Also INFORM 2, INFORMATION 2, LET KNOW 2.

NOT RESPONSIBLE 1, *phrase.* (Flicking responsibility from the shoulders.) Both hands, palms facing back, are positioned at the respective shoulders, with thumbs resting on middle fingers. Both middle fingers flick out once or twice simultaneously. This sign may also be made with one hand.

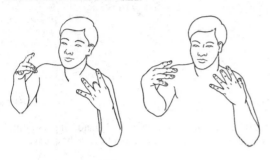

NOT RESPONSIBLE 2, *phrase.* As above, but the arms are crossed so that the right hand rests on the left shoulder and the left on the right.

NOT YET, *phrase.* (Hanging back.) The "5" hand and forearm, hanging loosely and straight down from the elbow, move back and forth under the armpit. Also BEHIND TIME, LATE, NOT DONE, TARDY.

NOUN (noun), *n.* The signer moves the "N" hand back and forth in very small left-right movements.

NOW (nou), *adv.* (Something right in front of you.) The upturned right-angle hands drop down rather sharply. The "Y" hands may also be used. Also CURRENT, IMMEDIATE, PRESENT 3.

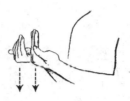

NOW AND THEN, *adv. phrase.* (Forward in slow, deliberate movements.) The right hand, palm facing the signer, fingers pointing left, makes a series of small forward movements, describing a small arc each time. Also FROM TIME TO TIME, ONCE IN A WHILE 2.

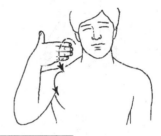

NUCLEAR (noo' klē ər), *adj.* (The letter "N"; around the world.) The right "N" hand makes a circle around the left "S" hand.

NUDE (nūd, nŏŏd), *adj.* (Devoid of everything on the surface.) The middle finger of the downturned right "5" hand sweeps over the back of the downturned left "A" or "S" hand from wrist to knuckles and continues beyond a bit. Also BARE 2, EMPTY 2, NAKED, OMISSION 2, VACANCY, VACANT, VOID.

NUMEROUS (nū′ mər əs, nōō′ -), *adj.* (Many fingers are indicated.) The upturned "S" hands are thrown up, opening into the "5" position, palms up. This may be repeated. Also MANY, MULTIPLE, PLURAL, QUANTITY 2.

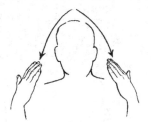

NUN (nŭn), *n.* (The veil.) Both open hands, palms facing the head and fingers pointing up, are moved down along either side of the head, as if tracing the outline of a nun's hood. Also SISTER 2.

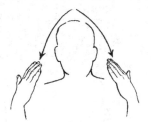

NURSE 1 (nûrs), *n.* (The letter "N"; taking the pulse.) The index and middle fingers of the right "N" hand are placed against the upturned left wrist.

NURSE 2, *n. arch.* The right "R" hand, fingers pointing up, is drawn down the side of the right cheek.

O

OATH (ōth), *n.* (The arm is raised.) The right index finger is placed at the lips. The right arm is then raised, palm out and elbow resting on the back of the left hand. Also GUARANTEE 1, LOYAL, PLEDGE, PROMISE 1, SWEAR 1, SWORN, TAKE OATH, VOW.

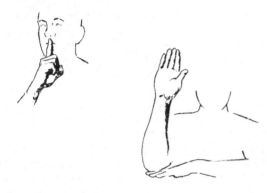

OBEDIENCE (ō bē′ dǐ əns), *n.* (The hands are thrown open as an act of obeisance.) Both "A" hands, palms facing, are positioned at either side of the head. They are thrown open and out, ending in the "5" position, palms up. The head is bowed slightly at the same time. Also MIND 4, OBEY, OBEDIENT.

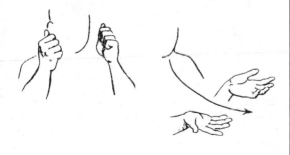

OBEDIENT (ō bē′ dǐ ənt), *adj.* See OBEDIENCE.

OBEY (ō bā′), *v.,* OBEYING, OBEYED. See OBEDIENT.

OBJECT 1 (ŏb′ jǐkt), *n.* (Something shown in the hand.) The outstretched right hand, palm up and held before the chest, is dropped slightly and brought over a bit to the right. Also ANYTHING, APPARATUS, INSTRUMENT, MATTER, SUBSTANCE 1, THING.

OBJECT 2 (əb jĕkt′), *v.,* -JECTED, -JECTING. (The hand is thrust into the chest to force a complaint out.) The curved fingers of the right hand are thrust forcefully into the chest. Also COMPLAIN 1, COMPLAINT, OBJECTION, PROTEST.

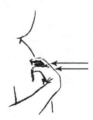

OBJECT 3 (*sl.*), *v.* (Kicking.) Both "S" hands are held before the chest. Then the hands move sharply to the side, opening into a modified "V" position, palms down, as if "kicking." Also COMPLAIN 2, KICK 2.

OBJECTION (əb jĕk′ shən), *n.* See OBJECT 2.

OBJECTIVE (əb jĕk′ tĭv), *n.* (A thought directed upward toward a goal.) The left "D" hand, palm facing the body, is held above the head to represent the goal. The index finger of the right "D" hand, after touching the forehead (modified sign for THINK, *q.v.*), moves slowly and deliberately up to the tip of the left index finger. Also AIM, AMBITION, ASPIRE, GOAL, PERSEVERE 4, PURPOSE 2.

OBLIGATION 1 (ŏb′ lə gā′ shən), *n.* (Something that weighs down or burdens one with responsibility.) The fingertips of both hands, placed on the right shoulder, bear down. Also ATTRIBUTE 1, BEAR 4, BURDEN, RELY 1, RESPONSIBILITY 1, RESPONSIBLE 1.

OBLIGATION 2, *n.* (The letter "D"; bound down.) The base of the right "D" hand repeatedly strikes the back of the downturned left "S" hand. Also DUTY 1.

OBLIGATION 3, *n.* (Pointing to the palm where the money should be placed.) The index finger of one hand is thrust into the upturned palm of the other several times. Also ARREARS, DEBIT, DEBT, DUE, OWE.

OBNOXIOUS (əb nŏk′ shəs), *adj.* (Turning the stomach.) The fingertips of the curved right hand describe a continuous circle on the stomach. The signer assumes an exaggerated expression of disgust. Also DISGUST, DISGUSTED, DISGUSTING, DISPLEASED, MAKE ME DISGUSTED, MAKE ME SICK, NAUSEA, NAUSEATE, NAUSEOUS, REVOLTING.

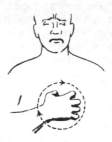

OBSERVE 1 (əb zûrv′), *v.,* -SERVED, -SERVING. (The vision is directed forward.) The tips of the right "V" fingers point to the eyes. The right hand is then swung around and forward a bit. Also GAZE, LOOK AT, WITNESS.

OBSERVE 2, *v.* (The eye is directed to something specific.) The right index finger touches the base of the right eye and is then thrust into the upturned left palm. Also DETECT, NOTE, NOTICE.

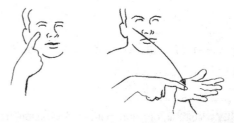

OBSERVE 3, *v.* (The vision is directed all over.) Both "V" hands, pointing out, are moved alternately in circular directions.

OBSOLETE (ob′ sə lēt′, ob′ sə lēt′) *adj.* (OLD.) The right hand pulls down a very long imaginary beard.

OBSTACLE (ŏb′ stə kəl), *n.* (Obstruct, block.) The left hand, fingers together and palm flat, is held before the body, facing somewhat down. The little finger side of the right hand, held with palm flat, makes one or several up down chopping motions against the left hand between its thumb and index finger. Also ANNOY 1, ANNOYANCE 1, BLOCK, BOTHER 1, CHECK 2, COME BETWEEN, DISRUPT, DISTURB, HINDER, HINDRANCE, IMPEDE, INTERCEPT, INTERFERE, INTERFERENCE, INTERFERE WITH, INTERRUPT, MEDDLE 1, OBSTRUCT, PREVENT, PREVENTION.

OBSTINATE (ŏb′ stə nĭt), *adj.* (The donkey's broad ear; the animal is traditionally a stubborn one.) The open hand, or the "B" hand, is placed at the side of the head with palm out and fingers pointing straight up.

The hand moves forward and back, pivoting at the wrist, as in the case of a donkey's ears flapping. Both hands may also be used, at either side of the head. Also DONKEY, MULE, MULISH, STUBBORN.

OBSTRUCT (əb strŭkt′), *v.,* -STRUCTED, -STRUCTING. See OBSTACLE.

OBTAIN (əb tān′), *v.,* -TAINED, -TAINING. (A grasping and bringing forward to oneself.) Both hands, in the "5" position, fingers curved, are crossed at the wrists, with the left palm facing right and the right palm facing left. They are brought in toward the chest while closing into a grasping "S" position. Also ACQUIRE, GET, PROCURE, RECEIVE.

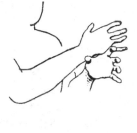

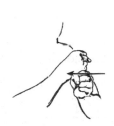

OBVIOUS (ŏb′ vĭ əs), *adj.* (Rays of light clearing the way.) Both hands are held at chest height, palms out, all fingertips together. They open into the "5" position in unison, the right hand moving toward the right and the left toward the left. The palms of both hands remain facing out. Also BRIGHT 1, BRILLIANCE 1, BRILLIANT 2, CLEAR, EXPLICIT 2, PLAIN 1.

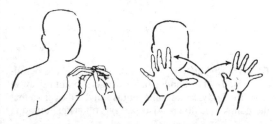

OCCASIONAL 1 (ə kā′ zhən əl), *adj.* (The "1" finger is brought up very slowly.) The right index finger, resting in the open left palm, which is facing right, swings up slowly from its position to one in which it is pointing straight up. The movement is repeated slowly after a pause. Also OCCASIONALLY, ONCE IN A WHILE, SELDOM, SOMETIME(S).

OCCASIONAL 2, *adv., adj.* (From time to time; in stages.) The right-angle hand, fingers closed and thumb pointing up, is held with palm facing the body. The hand moves forward in arcs, indicating successive stages.

OCCASIONALLY (ə kā′ zhən ə lĭ), *adv.* See OCCASIONAL.

OCCUPATION (ŏk′ yə pā′ shən), *n.* (Striking an anvil.) Both "S" hands are held palms down. The right hand strikes against the back of the left a number of times. Also JOB, LABOR, TASK, TOIL, TRAVAIL, VOCATION, WORK.

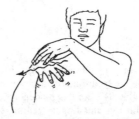

OCCUR (ə kûr′), *v., -*CURRED, -CURRING. (A befalling.) Both "D" hands, index fingers pointing away from the body, are simultaneously pivoted over so that the palms face down. Also ACCIDENT, BEFALL, CHANCE, COINCIDE 1, COINCIDENCE, EVENT, HAPPEN 1, INCIDENT, OPPORTUNITY 4.

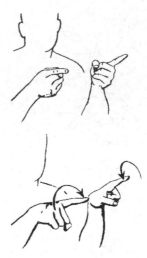

OCTOPUS 1 (ŏk′ tə pəs), *n.* (The natural sign.) The downturned "5" hands, crossed at the arms, writhe and wiggle in imitation of the random movements of an octopus.

OCTOPUS 2, *n.* (The shape and swimming motion.) The left downturned cupped hand rests on the back of the downturned right hand. The right hand makes a series of undulating up-down motions, with fingers wriggling all the time.

ODD (ŏd), *adj.* (Something that distorts the vision.) The "C" hand describes a small arc in front of the face. Also CURIOUS 2, GROTESQUE, PECULIAR, QUEER 1, STRANGE 1, WEIRD.

ODOR (ō′ dər), *n.* (Bringing something up to the nose.) The upturned right hand moves slowly up to and past the nose, and the signer breathes in as the hand sweeps by. Also FRAGRANT, SCENT, SMELL.

OF 1 (ŏv, ŭv; *unstressed* əv), *prep.* (Revolving about.) The left hand is held at chest height, all fingers extended and touching the thumb and all pointing to the right. The right index finger circles about the left fingers several times. Also ABOUT 1, CONCERNING, ELECTRIC MOTOR.

OF 2, *adj.* (Connected, and therefore pertaining to.) The index fingers and thumbs interlock.

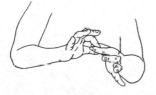

OFF 1 (ôf), *adv., prep.* The fingers of the downturned, open right hand rest on the back of the fingers of the downturned, open left hand. Then the right hand moves up and forward, turning so that its palm faces the body. Also AWAY.

OFF 2, *adv.* (Moving beyond, *i.e.,* the concept of distance or "farness.") The "A" hands are held together, thumbs pointing up or away from the body. The right hand moves straight ahead in a slight arc. The left hand does not move. Also DISTANCE, DISTANT, FAR, REMOTE.

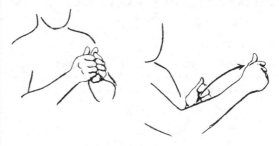

OFFER 1 (ôf′ ər), *v.,* -FERED, -FERING. (An offering; a presenting.) Both hands, slightly cupped, palms up, are held close to the chest. They move up and out in unison, describing a very slight arc. Also BID 2, MOTION 1, OFFERING 1, PRESENT 1, PROPOSE, SUGGEST, TENDER 2.

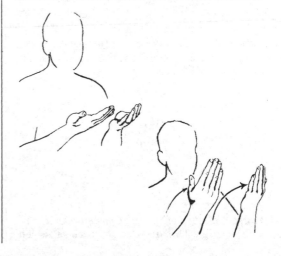

OFFER 2, *v., n.* (Bringing oneself forward.) The right index finger and thumb grasp the clothing near the right shoulder (often the lapel of a suit or the collar of a dress) and tug it up and down gently several times. Sometimes one tug only is used. Also APPLY 1, CANDIDATE, RUN FOR OFFICE, VOLUNTEER.

OFFERING 1 (ôf′ ər ĭng), *n.* See OFFER 1.

OFFERING 2 (*eccles.*), *n.* (Offering upward.) The upturned hands, led by the right, move up and forward in unison as the signer looks upward. Also OBLATION.

OFFICER (ôf′ ə sər, ŏf′ ə-), *n.* (The epaulets.) The fingertips of the downturned right "5" hand strike the right shoulder twice. Also CAPTAIN.

OFFLINE (ôf′ līn′, of′-), *adj. Computer term.* The downfacing right hand rests on the back of its left

counterpart and moves up and off. The little fingertips, palms in and facing the body, then separate.

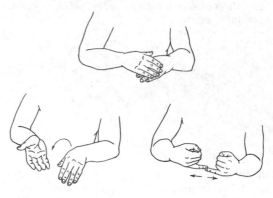

OFF THE SUBJECT, *phrase.* (Deviating.) The left index finger is held either straight up or pointing forward. The right index finger moves sharply off to the left, striking the left index finger as it does.

OFTEN (ôf′ ən, ŏf′ ən), *adv.* The left hand, open in the "5" position, palm up, is held before the chest. The right hand, in the right-angle position, fingers pointing up, arches over and into the left palm. This is repeated several times. Also FREQUENT.

OH 1 (ō) (*rare*), *interj*. The right "O" hand, palm facing left, moves in front of the face, from left to right.

OH! 2, *interj*. (A fingerspelled loan sign.) The signer, assuming an expression of surprise or sudden understanding, fingerspells "O-H" in a slow and deliberate manner, throwing the hand out for the "H."

OIL 1 (oil) (*colloq.*), *v.*, OILED, OILING. (The oil can.) The curved right "V" fingers grasp the crown of an imaginary oil can, and the right thumb moves in and out repeatedly, as if pressing the bottom of the can.

OIL 2, *n.* (The drippings from a fleshy, *i.e.,* animal, substance. Used, however, to indicate both organic and inorganic types of oil.) The right thumb and middle finger grasp the fleshy part of the open left hand. The right hand moves straight down. This is repeated once or twice. Also FAT 3, FATTY, GRAVY, GREASE, GREASY, OILY.

OILY (oi′ lĭ), *adj.* See OIL 2.

OINTMENT (oint′ mənt), *n.* (Rubbing on the skin.) The signer mimes taking a dab of ointment from a jar and rubbing it on the back of the hand.

O.K. 1 (ō′ kā′), *adj., adv.* (A straightening out.) The right hand, fingers together and palm facing left, is placed in the upturned left palm, whose fingers point away from the body. The right hand slides straight out along the left palm, over the left fingers, and stops with its heel resting on the left fingertips. Also ALL RIGHT, PRIVILEGE, RIGHT 1, RIGHTEOUS 1, YOU'RE WELCOME 2.

O.K. 2 (*adj., adv.* ō′ kā′; *v., n.* ō′ kā′), *colloq. phrase.* The letters "O" and "K" are fingerspelled.

OLD (ōld), *adj.* (The beard of an old man.) The right hand grasps an imaginary beard at the chin and pulls it downward. Also AGE 1, ANTIQUE.

OLD-FASHIONED (ōld′ fash′ ənd), *adj*. Use the sign for OLD, and then the downturned right "F" hand makes a short downward thrust and moves to the right in a slight arc, where it makes a second downward thrust.

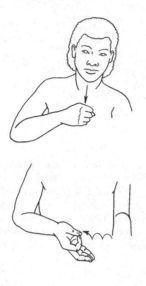

OLYMPICS (ō lim′ pikz), *n*. (The interlocking circles of the Olympic logo.) The thumbs and index fingers of both hands interlock several times.

OMISSION 1 (ō mĭsh′ ən), *n*. (A disappearance.) The right open hand, palm facing the body, is held by the left hand and is drawn down and out, ending in a posi-

tion with fingers drawn together. The left hand, meanwhile, may close into a position with fingers also drawn together. Also ABSENCE 1, ABSENT 1, DEPLETE, DISAPPEAR, EMPTY 1, EXTINCT, FADE AWAY, GONE 1, MISSING 1, OUT 3, OUT OF, VANISH.

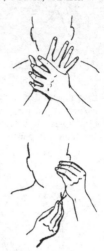

OMISSION 2, *n*. (Devoid of everything on the surface.) The middle finger of the downturned right "5" hand sweeps over the back of the downturned left "A" or "S" hand from wrist to knuckles and continues beyond a bit. Also BARE 2, EMPTY 2, NAKED, NUDE, VACANCY, VACANT, VOID.

ON (ŏn, ôn), *prep*. (Placing one hand on the other.) The right hand is placed on the back of the downturned left hand.

ONCE (wŭns), *adv*. (The "1" finger jumps up.) The right index finger (the "1" finger) touches the left palm, which is facing right. It is then brought up sharply so that it points straight up.

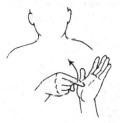

ONCE IN A WHILE, 1 *adv. phrase.* (The "1" finger is brought up very slowly.) The right index finger, resting in the open left palm, which is facing right, swings up slowly from its position to one in which it is pointing straight up. The movement is repeated slowly after a pause. Also OCCASIONAL, OCCASIONALLY, SELDOM, SOMETIME(S).

ONCE IN A WHILE 2, *phrase.* (Forward in slow, deliberate movements.) The right hand, palm facing the signer, fingers pointing left, makes a series of small forward movements, describing a small arc each time. Also FROM TIME TO TIME, NOW AND THEN.

ONCE UPON A TIME, *adv. phrase.* (Something past, behind.) The upraised right hand, in the "5" position with palm facing the body, is held just above the right

shoulder and is thrown back over it. Also AGO, FORMERLY, PAST, PREVIOUS, PREVIOUSLY, WAS, WERE.

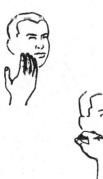

ONE ANOTHER, *pron. phrase.* (Mingling with.) Both hands are held in modified "A" positions, thumbs out. The left hand is positioned with its thumb pointing straight up, and the right hand, with its thumb pointing down, revolves above the left thumb in a counterclockwise direction. Also ASSOCIATE 1, EACH OTHER, FELLOWSHIP, MINGLE 2, MUTUAL 1.

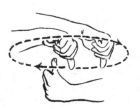

ONE MORE, *colloq. phrase.* (One finger beckons.) The right hand is held palm up, with the index finger making very small and rapid beckoning movements.

ONE-TO-ONE, *phrase.* (The natural sign.) The "D" hands, palms facing, are brought together a number of times.

ONE-YEAR-OLD, *adj. phrase.* (OLD, ONE) The sign for OLD is followed by the sign for ONE. Simple age combinations are made likewise: with OLD followed by the number.

ONION 1 (ŭn′ yən), *n.* (The rubbing of the eye, which is irritated by the onion.) The knuckle of the right "X" finger is placed just beside the right eye. The right hand pivots back and forth at the wrist.

ONION 2, *n.* (Same rationale as in ONION 1.) The knuckles of the right "S" hand, positioned as in ONION 1, execute the same pivoting movement.

ONLINE (on′ līn′, ôn′-), *adj. Computer term.* The downfacing right hand is brought to rest on the back of its left counterpart. The little fingertips, palms in and facing the body, then separate.

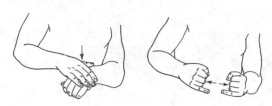

ONLY (ōn′ lĭ), *adv.* (One wandering around in a circle.) The index finger, pointing straight up, palm facing the body (the number *one*), is rotated before the face in a counterclockwise direction. Also ALONE, LONE, ONE 2, SOLE, UNITY.

ONLY ONE, *phrase.* (Emphasizing the "1" finger.) The "1" hand, palm out, swings around emphatically, moving slightly upward at the same time.

ON THE CONTRARY 1, *adv. phrase.* (A divergence or a difference; the opposite of SAME.) The index fingers of both "D" hands, palms facing down, are crossed near their tips. The hands are drawn apart. Also ALTHOUGH, BUT, HOWEVER 1.

ON THE CONTRARY 2, *adv. phrase.* (Opposites.) With index fingertips touching initially, both hands move away from each other.

ON TO (too), *phrase.* (Adding on.) The index and middle fingers of the right "H" hand, palm up, are swung up and over until they come to rest on the index and middle fingers of the left "H" hand, held palm down. Also ADD 3, ADDITION, EXTEND 1, EXTRA, GAIN 1, INCREASE, RAISE 2.

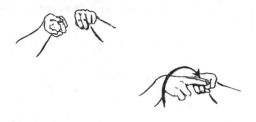

OPEN 1 (ō′ pən), *adj., v.,* OPENED, OPENING. (The natural sign.) The "B" hands, palms out, are held with index finger edges touching. They swing apart so that the palms now face each other.

OPEN 2, *adj., v.* (The natural sign.) Here the "B" hands move straight apart, with palms still facing out. See OPEN 1.

OPEN 3, *v.* (Opening a jar.) The signer mimes struggling with and then opening a jar.

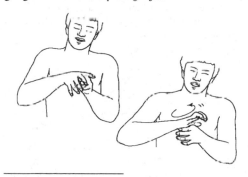

OPEN-EYED (ō′ pən īd′) (*colloq.*), *adj.* (The eyes pop open.) The "S" hands, palms facing each other, are held before the eyes. They suddenly open into the "C" position, with the eyes wide open. Also SHOCKED 2, SURPRISED.

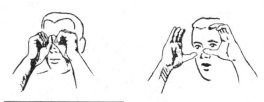

OPENMOUTHED (ō′ pən mouthd′, -moutht′) (*colloq.*), *adj.* (The mouth drops open.) The fingertips of both "V" hands are held curved and touching before the body, one hand above the other. Then the hands are suddenly drawn apart, and at the same instant the mouth drops open and the eyes open wide. Also DUMFOUNDED 2, FLABBERGASTED, SPEECHLESS, SURPRISE 2.

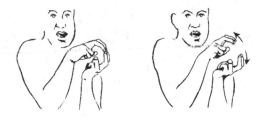

OPEN THE DOOR, *v. phrase.* (The opening and closing of the door.) The "B" hands, palms out and edges touching, are drawn apart and then come together again. Also DOOR, DOORWAY.

OPEN THE WINDOW, *phrase.* (The opening of the window.) With both palms facing the body, the little finger edge of the right hand rests atop the index finger edge of the left hand. The right hand then moves straight up. Also WINDOW.

OPERA 1 (op′ ər ə), *n.* (The rhythmic movement.) The right "5" hand, palm facing left, is waved back and forth over the downturned left hand. The mouth may be held open in song. Also SING, SONG.

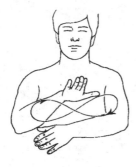

OPERA 2, *n.* (A variation of OPERA 1, above.) The letter "O" is substituted for the "5."

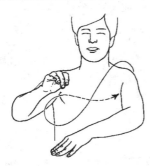

OPERATE (ŏp′ ə rāt′), *v.,* -ATED, -ATING. (Holding the reins over all.) The "A" hands, palms facing, move alternately back and forth as if grasping and manipulating reins. The left "A" hand, still in position, swings over so that its palm now faces down. The right hand opens to the "5" position, palm down, and swings over the left, which moves slightly to the right. Also

AUTHORITY, CONTROL 1, DIRECT 1, GOVERN, MANAGE, MANAGEMENT, MANAGER, REGULATE, REIGN, RULE 1.

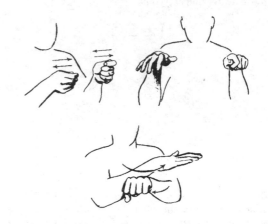

OPERATION 1 (ŏp′ ə rā′ shən), *n.* (The action of the scalpel.) The thumb of the right "A" hand is drawn straight down across the upright left palm. Also SURGERY.

OPERATION 2, *n.* (The action of a scalpel.) The thumbtip of the right "A" hand, palm facing down, moves a short distance across the lower chest or stomach region.

OPINION (ə pǐn′ yən), *n.* (The "O" hand, circling in the head.) The right "O" hand circles before the forehead several times.

OPOSSUM (ə pos′ əm, pos′ əm), *n.* (The prehensile tail used for hanging from a tree.) The two little fingers are interlocked, one hanging from the other.

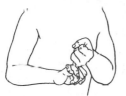

OPPONENT (ə pō′ nənt), *n.* (At sword's point.) The two index fingers, after pointing to each other, are drawn sharply apart. This is followed by the sign for INDIVIDUAL: both open hands, palms facing each other, move down the sides of the body, tracing its outline to the hips. Also ENEMY, FOE, RIVAL 1.

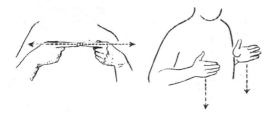

OPPORTUNITY 1 (ŏp′ ər tū′ nə tĭ), *n.* Both hands, slightly cupped, palms up, are held close to the chest. They move up and out in unison, describing an arc. Also OCCASION, TIME 4.

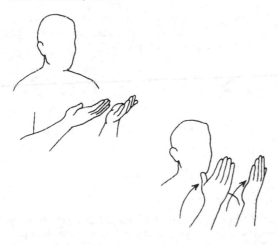

OPPORTUNITY 2, *n.* (Two individuals pitted against each other.) The hands are held in the "A" position,

thumbs pointing straight up, palms facing the body. They come together forcefully, moving down a bit as they do, and the knuckles of one hand strike those of the other. Also CHALLENGE, GAME 1, VERSUS.

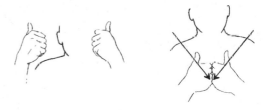

OPPORTUNITY 3, *n.* (The movement.) Both hands, palms facing and fingers together and extended straight out, move in unison away from the body in a straight or winding manner. Also CORRIDOR, HALL, HALLWAY, MANNER 2, METHOD, PATH, ROAD, STREET, TRAIL, WAY 1.

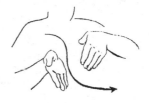

OPPORTUNITY 4, *n.* (A befalling.) Both "D" hands, index fingers pointing away from the body, are simultaneously pivoted over so that the palms face down. Also ACCIDENT, BEFALL, CHANCE, COINCIDE 1, COINCIDENCE, EVENT, HAPPEN 1, INCIDENT, OCCUR.

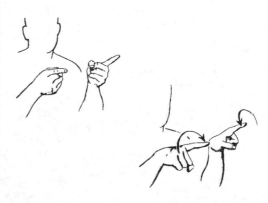

OPPORTUNITY 5, *n.* (The letters "O" and "P"; pushing through.) Both "O" hands are held palms down, side by side. They swing up a bit as they assume the "P" position.

OPPOSE (ə′ pōz), *v.,* OPPOSED, OPPOSING. (Opposed to; restraint.) The tips of the right fingers, held together, are thrust purposefully into the open left palm, whose fingers are also together and pointing forward. Also AGAINST.

OPPOSITE (ŏp′ ə zĭt), *adj., n.* (Separateness.) The tips of the extended index fingers touch before the chest, the right finger pointing left and the left finger pointing right. The fingers then draw apart sharply to either side. Also CONTRAST 2, REVERSE 1.

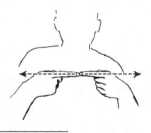

OPPRESS (ə pres′), *v.,* -PRESSED, -PRESSING. (Pushing someone down.) The downturned right "5" hand pushes down on the left "D" hand, whose index finger points straight out.

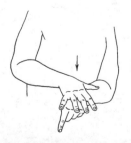

OPTION (op′ shən), *n.* (Selecting from among choices.) The right thumb and index finger pluck the tip of the left index and then the tip of the left middle finger. Also CHOOSE.

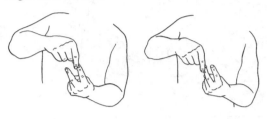

OR 1 (ôr; *unstressed* ər), *conj.* (Selection between two or among multiple choices.) The left "L" hand is held palm facing the body and thumb pointing straight up. The right index finger touches the left thumbtip and then the left index fingertip. Also EITHER 1.

OR 2, *conj.* (Considering one thing against another.) The "A" hands, palms facing and thumbs pointing straight up, move alternately up and down before the chest. Also EITHER 3, WHETHER, WHICH 1.

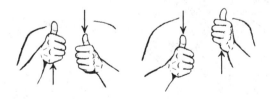

ORAL 1 (ōr′ əl), *adj.* (Reading the lips—the lines of vision, represented by the two fingers, scan the lips.) The right "V" hand, palm facing the body, is placed in front of the face, with slightly curved index and middle fingers directly in front of the lips. The right hand moves in a small counterclockwise circle around the lips. Also LIPREADING, READ LIPS, SPEECH-READING.

ORAL 2, *adj.* (The letter "O.") Same as ORAL 1, but the signer uses the "O" hand.

ORANGE 1 (ôr′ ĭnj, ŏr′-), *n., adj.* (The action of squeezing an orange to get its juice into the mouth.) The right "C" hand is held at the mouth. It opens and closes deliberately, as if squeezing an orange.

ORANGE 2, *n.* (The peeling of the fruit.) The thumbtip of the right "Y" hand moves over the back of the left "S" hand, which is held palm down or palm facing the body.

ORANGE 3, *n., adj.* Both "Y" hands are held before the body, palms facing each other. In this position the hands alternate in drawing imaginary circles in the air with the little fingers. This sign is used for both the color and the fruit.

ORANGUTAN (ô rang′ ŏŏ tan′, ō rang′-, ə rang′), *n.* (The unique gait of the animal.) The signer mimes the gait of the animal, using the little finger edges of both hands as support and alternately moving them forward to support the forward gait.

ORATE (ō rāt′, ōr′ āt), *v.,* ORATED, ORATING. (A gesture of an orator.) The right open hand, palm facing left, is held above and to the right of the head. It pivots on the wrist, forward and backward, several times. Also ADDRESS 1, LECTURE, SPEECH 2, TALK 2, TESTIMONY.

ORATOR (ôr′ ə tər, ŏr′ -), *n.* (The characteristic waving of the speaker's hand as he makes his point.) The sign for ORATE is made. This is followed by the sign for INDIVIDUAL: both open hands, palms facing each other, move down the sides of the body, tracing its outline to the hips. Also SPEAKER.

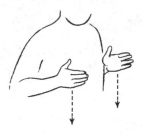

ORBIT 1 (ôr′ bĭt), *n., v.,* -BITED, -BITING. (Encircling the planet.) The left hand, in the "S" position, knuckles facing right, is encircled by the right index finger, which travels in a clockwise direction. It makes one revolution and comes to rest atop the left hand. Also ALL YEAR, ALL YEAR ROUND, AROUND THE WORLD.

ORBIT 2, *n., v.* The same movement as in ORBIT 1, except that the right "O" hand (for "orbit") is used.

ORCHESTRA (ôr′ kə strə, -kes trə), *n.* (The conductor leading.) The signer waves an imaginary baton rhythmically. The free hand may or may not accompany this movement.

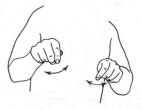

ORDER 1 (ôr′ dər), *n., v.,* -DERED, -DERING. (An issuance from the mouth.) The tip of the index finger of the "D" hand, palm facing the body, is placed at the closed lips. It moves around and out rather forcefully. Also BID 1, COMMAND, DIRECT 2.

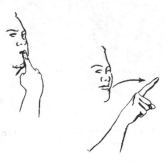

ORDER 2 (*rare*), *n.* (Something you write and give to someone.) The sign for WRITE is made: the right index finger and thumb, grasping an imaginary pen, write across the open left palm. This is followed by the sign for GIVE: both hands are held, palms down, about a foot apart, thumbs resting on fingertips. The hands are extended forward in a slight arc, opening to the "5" position as they do.

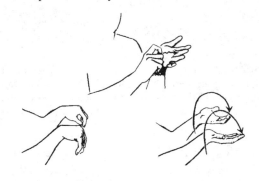

ORDER 3, *n., v.* (Placing things in order.) The hands, palms facing, fingers together and pointing away from the body, are positioned at the left side and held about a foot apart. With a slight up-down motion, as if describing waves, the hands travel in unison from left to right. Also ARRANGE, ARRANGEMENT, CLASSED 2, DEVISE 1, PLAN 1, POLICY 1, PREPARE 1, PROGRAM 1, PROVIDE 1, PUT IN ORDER, READY 1, SCHEME, SYSTEM.

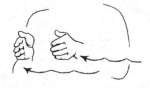

ORDERLY (ôr′ dər lĭ), *adj.* (In order, *i.e.,* equally spaced or arranged.) Both open hands, palms facing each other and fingers pointing away from the body, move in unison, in a series of short arcs, from left to right. This is essentially the same as ORDER 3.

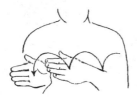

ORGANIZATION 1 (ôr′ gən ə zā′ shən), *n.* (A grouping together.) Both "C" hands, palms facing, are held a few inches apart at chest height. They are swung around in unison so that the palms now face the body. Also ASSOCIATION, AUDIENCE 1, CASTE, CIRCLE 2, CLASS, CLASSED 1, CLUB, COMPANY, FAMILY 2, GANG, GROUP 1, JOIN 2.

ORGANIZATION 2, *n.* (The letter "O"; a group or class.) Both "O" hands are held with palms facing out and thumb edges touching. The hands swing apart, around, and come together again with little finger edges touching.

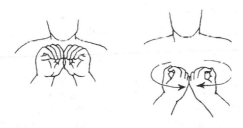

ORIENTATION 1 (ôr′ ĭ ĕn tā′ shən), *n.* (The letter "O"; polishing up.) The fingertips of the right "O" hand brush back and forth over the left index finger. This is a modification of the sign for PRACTICE 1, *q.v.*

ORIENTATION 2, *n.* (The surroundings are explored.) The right "O" hand circles the left upright index finger.

ORIGIN 1 (ôr′ ə jĭn, ŏr′ -), *n.* (Turning a key to open up a new venture.) The right index finger, resting between the left index and middle fingers, executes a half turn once or twice. Also BEGIN, COMMENCE, INITIATE, INSTITUTE 2, ORIGINATE 1, START.

ORIGIN 2, *n.* (The first finger is indicated.) The right index finger touches the upturned left thumb. Also FIRST 1, INITIAL, PRIMARY.

ORIGIN 3, *n.* (First to be grasped from the mind.) The right "D" hand moves straight up against the forehead and then closes into the "S" position, still against the forehead. Also INVENT 1, ORIGINAL 1, ORIGINATE 2.

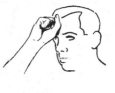

468

ORPHAN (ôr′ fən), *n.* (The letter "O"; female and male.) The right "O" hand is placed first at the chin and then at the temple.

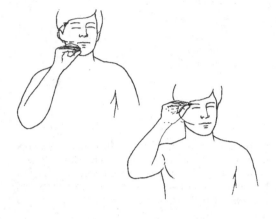

ORTHODOX 1 (ôr′ thə doks), *adj.* (Adhering to a strict and straight line.) The right index and thumb, forming an "F," move forward along the upturned left palm.

ORTHODOX 2, *adj.* (The *pais,* or earlocks, worn by ultra-Orthodox Jewish males.) The signer twirls an imaginary curl hanging down the side of the head. Also HASIDIC.

OSAKA (ō′ sä kä), *n.* The right "U" hand, palm facing out, is placed at the forehead, like a salute. It moves very slightly back and forth. A native sign.

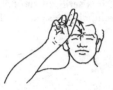

OSTRICH (ô′ strich, os′ trich), *n.* (The "O"; the long neck is raised and lowered.) The elbow of the right "O" hand is placed on the back of the downturned left hand. The right swings up and down in an arc, like an ostrich's neck.

OTHER (ŭth′ ər), *adj.* (Moving over to another position.) The right "A" hand, thumb up, is pivoted from the wrist and swung over to the right so that the thumb now points to the right. Also ANOTHER.

OUGHT TO (ôt), *v. aux.* (Being pinned down.) The right hand, in the "X" position, palm down, moves forcefully up and down once or twice. An expression of determination is frequently assumed. Also HAVE TO, IMPERATIVE, MUST, NECESSARY 1, NECESSITY, NEED 1, SHOULD, VITAL 2.

OUR (our), *pron.* (An encompassing including one-self and others.) The right "C" hand, palm facing left, is placed at the right shoulder. It swings around to the left shoulder, its palm now facing right.

OURSELVES (our sĕlvz′), *pron. pl.* (An encompassing; the thumb representing *self, i.e.,* oneness.) The right "A" hand, thumb held straight up, is placed at the right shoulder. It executes the same movement as in OUR.

OUT 1 (out), *adv.* (The natural motion of withdrawing, *i.e.,* taking *out* of the hand.) The downturned open right hand, grasped loosely by the left, is drawn up and out of the left hand's grasp. Simultaneously, the fingers come together with the thumb. The left hand, meanwhile, closes into the "O" position, palm facing right. Also EXIT.

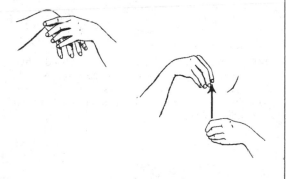

OUT 2, *adv.* (Removing.) The right "A" hand, resting in the palm of the left "5" hand, moves slightly up and

away, describing a small arc. It is then cast downward, opening into the "5" position, palm down, as if removing something from the left hand and casting it down. Also ABOLISH 2, ABSENCE 2, ABSENT 2, ABSTAIN, CHEAT 2, DEDUCT, DEFICIENCY, DELETE 1, LESS 2, MINUS 3, REMOVE 1, SUBTRACT, SUBTRACTION, TAKE AWAY FROM, WITHDRAW 2.

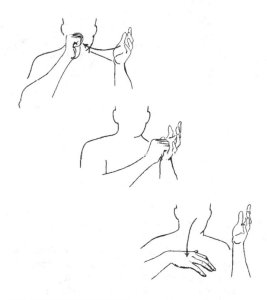

OUT 3, *adv.* (A disappearance.) The right open hand, palm facing the body, is held by the left hand and is drawn down and out, ending in a position with fingers drawn together. The left hand, meanwhile, may close into a position with fingers also drawn together. Also ABSENCE 1, ABSENT 1, DEPLETE, DISAPPEAR, EMPTY 1, EXTINCT, FADE AWAY, GONE 1, MISSING 1, OMISSION 1, OUT OF, VANISH.

OUTFIT (out′ fit), *n*. (Matching top and bottom.) The thumb of the right "Y" hand is placed at midchest, and then the hand travels down so that the little finger of the same "Y" hand touches the trousers or skirt.

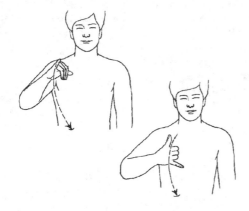

OUTPUT (out′ poŏt′), *n. Computer term*. (Coming out of something; withdrawing.) The downturned open right hand, grasped loosely by the left, is drawn up and out of the left hand's grasp. At the same time, the fingers come together with the thumb. The left hand, meanwhile, closes into the "O" position, palm facing right. Also OUT.

OUTSPOKEN (out′ spō′ kən), *adj*. (Talking straight out.) The index finger of the right "4" hand, whose palm faces left, is placed on the lips. The whole hand moves sharply forward.

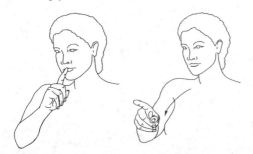

OVARIES (ō′ və rēz), *n*. (The location of the ovaries.) Both downturned "F" hands are placed against the abdomen, on either side of the body.

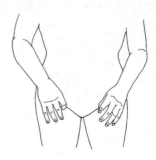

OVEN (ŭv′ ən), *n*. (Placing the bread in the oven.) The downturned right "B" hand, representing the bread, is thrust slowly forward under the downturned left hand, representing the oven. Also BAKE.

OVER 1 (ō′ vər), *prep*. (One hand moves above the other.) Both hands, palms flat and facing down, are held before the chest. The right hand circles horizontally above the left in a counterclockwise direction. Also ABOVE.

OVER 2, *prep*. (A crossing over.) The left hand is held before the chest, palm down and fingers together. The right hand, fingers together, glides over the left, with the right little finger touching the top of the left hand. Also ACROSS, CROSS 3.

OVER AGAIN, *phrase.* (Turning over a new leaf.) The left hand, in the "5" position, palm up, is held before the chest. The right hand, in the right-angle position, fingers pointing up, arches up and over into the left palm.

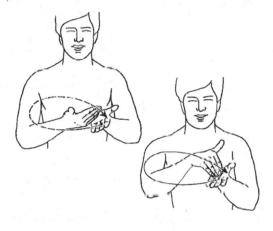

OVERALLS (ō′ vər ôlz), *n.* (The clips at the shoulders, holding up the garment.) Both hands are positioned with index and middle fingers and thumbs all pointing down. The hands trace a pair of imaginary suspenders up along the chest, and the fingers close against their respective thumbs.

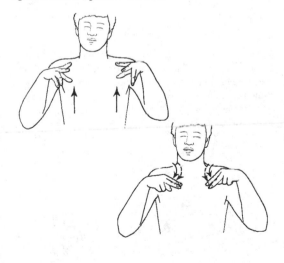

OVERCOME (ō′ vər kŭm′), *v.,* -CAME, -COME, -COMING. (Forcing the head into a bowed position.) The right "S" hand, placed across the left "S" hand, moves over and down a bit. Also BEAT 2, CONQUER, DEFEAT, SUBDUE.

OVERHEAD PROJECTOR *n.* (Projecting something behind a speaker.) The right hand, thumb resting against all the other fingers, moves over the right shoulder as all fingers open into the "5" position.

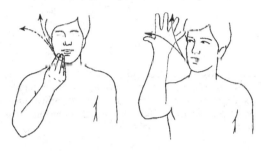

OVERLAP (ō′ vər lap′, ō′ vər lap′), *n., v.,* -LAPPED, -LAPPING. (One on top of the other.) Both flat, downturned hands are placed one atop the other. The bottom hand is withdrawn and placed on top of the other. This continues, with the hands rising slightly each time.

OVERLOOK (ō′ vər lŏŏk′), *v.,* -LOOKED, -LOOKING. (Something that eludes observation by slipping past the eyes.) The right hand, fingers together and palm facing the face, moves down in an arc from right to left. The eyes may close at the same time.

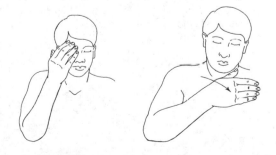

OVER MY HEAD, *sl. phrase.* Both index fingers flick out as the "S" hands, palms facing backward, are thrown over the head.

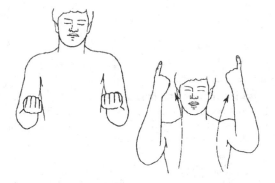

OVERSPEND (ō vər spend′), *v.,* -SPENT, -SPENDING. (Throwing money randomly into the air.) Both hands, closed into fists, palms facing the chest, move alternately up into the air, index fingers flicking out. Also SPEND 2, SQUANDER 2.

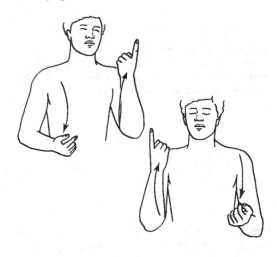

OVERWHELM (ō′ vər hwelm′, -welm′), *v.,* -WHELMED, -WHELMING. (Slipping past one.) Both curved open hands, palms facing the signer, are swept up and over the head or shoulders, moving back a bit toward the rear.

OVERWHELMED (ō vər hwelmd′), *adj.* (Over one's head.) Both downturned hands, fingers pointing back, move backward over the head.

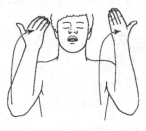

OWE (ō), *v.,* OWED, OWING. (Pointing to the palm where the money should be placed.) The index finger of one hand is thrust into the upturned palm of the other several times. Also ARREARS, DEBIT, DEBT, DUE, OBLIGATION 3.

OWN (ōn), *adj., v.,* OWNED, OWNING. (Holding something to oneself.) The downturned right hand, fingers open, is brought up to the chest, where the fingers come together.

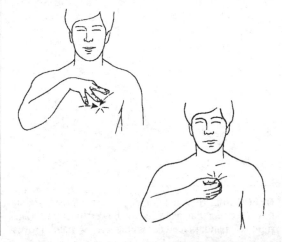

OXYGEN 1 (ok′ si jən), *n.* (The oxygen mask.) The cupped right hand is placed over the mouth and nose.

OXYGEN 2, *n.* (The symbol for oxygen.) The signer fingerspells "O-2," dropping the hand a bit for the "2."

OYSTER 1 (ois′ tər), *n.* (The shucking action.) The open hands, palms facing, are held with right above left. The right hand swings down into sharp contact with the left palm and continues downward, as if having split open the shell.

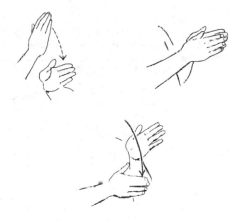

OYSTER 2, *n.* (The shucking movement.) The upturned right open hand's little finger edge is wedged between the downturned left thumb and index. The right hand rocks back and forth, attempting to gain entry into the shell.

PACK (pak), *v.,* PACKED, PACKING. (Putting pieces into place.) With both downturned hands holding imaginary objects and thrusting down alternately, the signer mimes placing these objects into a box or package. Also ASSEMBLE.

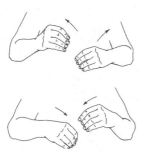

PACKAGE (păk′ ĭj), *n., v.,* -AGED, -AGING. (The dimensions are indicated.) The open hands, palms facing and fingers pointing out, are dropped an inch or two simultaneously. They then shift their relative positions so that both palms face the body, with one hand in front of the other. In this new position they again drop an inch or two simultaneously. Also BOX 1, ROOM 1, SQUARE 1, TRUNK.

PAGE 1 (pāj), *n.* (Act of turning over a page.) The right "F" hand, grasping an imaginary page, goes through the motion of turning it over.

PAGE 2, *n.* (Thumbing through pages.) The downturned right thumb digs into the upturned left palm a number of times. Also LOOK UP.

PAGE 3, *n.* The letter "P." The middle finger of the right "P" hand moves down the left hand, whose palm faces out.

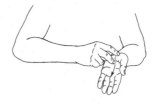

PAGEANT (paj′ ənt), *n.* (The sash worn by a contestant.) The curved thumb and index finger of the right hand trace an imaginary ribbon from the left shoulder to the right side of the waist. The letter "P" may be substituted for the thumb and index.

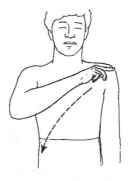

PAIL (pāl), *n.* (The shape and grasping the handle.) The left hand holds an imaginary pail. the right index finger describes a downturned arc as it moves from the left wrist to the elbow.

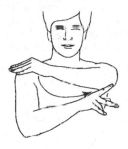

PAIN (pān), *n.* (A stabbing pain.) The "D" hands, index fingers pointing to each other, are rotated in elliptical fashion before the chest—simultaneously but in opposite directions. Also ACHE, HARM 1, HURT 1, INJURE 1, INJURY, MAR 1, OFFEND, OFFENSE, SIN, WOUND.

PAINT 1 (pānt), *n., v.,* PAINTED, PAINTING. (The action of the brush.) The hands are held open with palms facing each other. The right hand, representing a wide brush, sweeps back and forth over the left palm, as if spreading paint on it. (This sign is used in the sense of painting a large area such as a wall.)

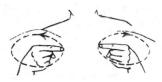

PAINT 2, *n., v.* (The action of a small brush.) The tips of the fingers of the right "H" hand are swept back and forth repeatedly over the left palm, as if spreading paint on it with a small or narrow brush. (This sign is used in reference to fine-art painting.)

PAINTER 1 (pān′ tər), *n.* The sign for PAINT 1 is made, followed by the sign for INDIVIDUAL 1: both open hands, palms facing each other, move down the sides of the body, tracing its outline to the hips.

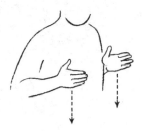

PAINTER 2, *n.* The sign for PAINT 2 is made, followed by the sign for INDIVIDUAL 1, as in PAINTER 1.

PAJAMAS 1 (pə jä′ məz), *n.* (A fingerspelled loan sign.) The signer fingerspells "P-J."

PAJAMAS 2, *n.* (The "P"; slipping on clothes.) The "P" hands, palms facing the chest, move twice down the chest.

PAL (pal), *n.* The right index finger and thumb form a "C." The right thumbtip moves across the chin from left to right.

PALACE (pal′ is), *n.* (The elaborate roofline.) The downturned "P" hands trace an elaborate roofline, moving in stages down and apart.

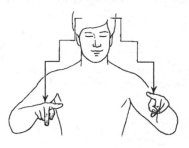

PALE (pāl) *adj., v.,* PALED, PALING. The sign for WHITE is made: the fingertips of the "5" hand are placed against the chest. The hand moves straight out from the chest while the fingers and thumb all come together. Then both hands, fingers spread, rise up and over the cheeks.

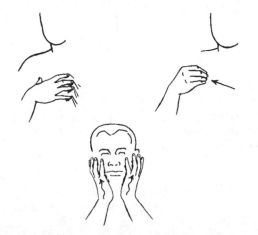

PALERMO (pä ler′ mō), *n.* (Stealing something.) The downturned right "3" or claw-shaped hand, held near the right hip, swivels twice in a clockwise manner, as if picking up something surreptitiously. This sign is highly derogatory, for it implies that all natives of this city are thieves. It should not normally be used. Also SICILY.

PAMPHLET (pam′ flit), *n.* (A book with a narrow spine.) The left hand, fingers together, is held upright, palm facing right. The right hand wraps around the lower edge of the left and travels up to the little finger. This denotes a narrow object. The sign for BOOK is then made: the hands are placed together, palm to palm, and then opened as if opening a book. Sometimes this latter sign is omitted. Also BOOKLET, CATALOG, MAGAZINE, MANUAL.

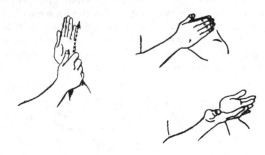

PAN (pan), *n.* (Manipulating the handle.) The signer grasps the handle of an imaginary pan and moves it forward and back quickly a number of times.

PANAMA (pan′ ə mä, *n.* (The letter "P"; the crossing of the canal.) The right "P" hand crosses over the back of the loosely held downturned left hand.

PANCAKE (păn′ kāk′), *n.* (Turning over a pancake.) The open right hand rests on the upturned left palm. The right hand flips over and comes to rest with its back on the left palm. This is the action of turning over a pancake. Also CHEF, COOK, KITCHEN 1.

PANDA (pan′ də), *n.* (The letter "P"; emphasizing the panda's markings.) The right "P" hand makes a counterclockwise circle around the face.

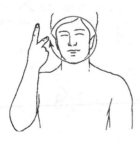

PANEL (pan′ l), *n.* (A group of people sitting side by side in a row.) Both hands, palms out, are held with curved downturned indexes and thumbs. The hands move apart. Also JURY.

PANT (pant), *v.,* PANTED, PANTING. (The action of the chest.) Both hands on the chest move in and out quickly and repeatedly.

PANTIES (pan′ tēz), *n.* (The elastic waist.) Grasping an imaginary waistline, the signer mimes stretching it open and closed.

PANTS (pănts), *n. pl.* (The natural sign.) The open hands are drawn up along the thighs, starting at the knees. Also TROUSERS.

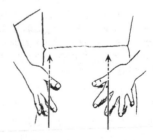

PANTYHOSE (pan′ tē hōz′), *n.* (Pulling up the garment.) Both hands, positioned on the thighs, mime pulling up a pair of pantyhose.

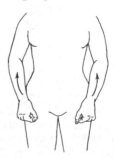

PAPA (pä′ pə), *n*. (Derived from the formal sign for FATHER 1, *q.v.*) The thumbtip of the right "5" hand touches the right temple a number of times. The other fingers may also wiggle. Also DAD, DADDY, FATHER 2, POP 2.

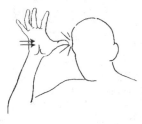

PAPER (pā′ pər), *n*. (The action of the press.) The right "5" hand, held palm down, fingers pointing left, is brought down twice against the upturned left "5" hand, whose fingers point right. Also NEWSPAPER, PUBLISH 1.

PAPER BAG (pā′ pər bag), *n*. (The material and the shape.) The sign for PAPER: the heels of both hands come together several times. The signer next traces the bottom and sides of a paper bag, using the "C" hands, palms facing.

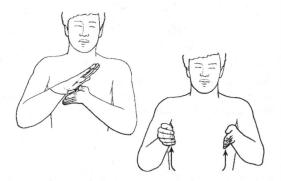

PAPER CLIP (pā′ pər klĭp), *n*. (The natural sign.) The right thumb plus index and middle fingers are clamped over the middle of the index and middle fingers of the left "U" hand, whose palm faces right. The

right fingers may also be slipped over the left fingers instead of being clamped over them.

PARADE 1 (pə rād′), *n., v.,* -RADED, -RADING. (Rows of people marching.) Both "V" hands, palms out and the left behind the right, move forward in unison in a series of short upward-arced motions. Also FUNERAL, PROCESSION.

PARADE 2, *n., v*. (A column of marchers, one behind the other.) The downturned open hands, fingers pointing down, are held one behind the other. Pivoted from the wrists, they move rhythmically forward and back in unison. Also MARCH 1.

PARAGUAY (par′ ə gwī′, -gwā′), *n*. The right hand reaches under the left elbow to withdraw an imaginary sword. A native sign.

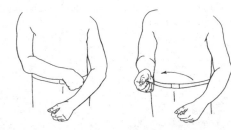

PARAKEET (par′ ə kēt′), *n.* (The curved beak.) The bent thumb and index fingers open and close at the corner of the mouth.

PARALLELOGRAM (par ə lel′ ɔ gram), *n.* With the left hand in the "P" position and the right in the "R" position, the signer traces a rectangle in the air.

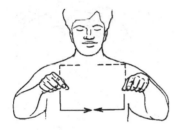

PARAMEDIC (par′ ə med′ ik), *n.* (The "P" and "M" at the wrist, taking a pulse.) The right "P" hand is placed on the upturned left wrist, where it changes to an "M."

PARANOID (par′ ə noid′), *adj.* (The letter "P"; picking at the mind.) The middle finger of the right "P" hand scratches repeatedly against the right temple.

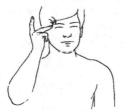

PARASITE (păr′ ə sīt′), *n.* (Attaching to something and tugging on it.) The extended right thumb, index, and middle fingers grasp the extended left index and middle fingers. In this position the right hand pulls at the left several times. Also LEECH, MOOCH, MOOCHER, TAKE ADVANTAGE OF 2.

PARDON (păr′ dən), *n.* (A wiped-off and cleaned slate.) The right hand wipes off the left palm several times. Also APOLOGIZE 2, APOLOGY 2, EXCUSE, FORGIVE 2, PAROLE.

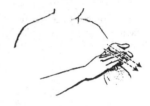

PARENTHESES (pə ren′ thə sēz′), *n.* (The shape.) Both index fingers, pointing forward, trace a pair of parentheses in the air.

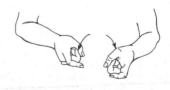

PARENTS 1 (pâr′ əntz), *n.* (Mother and father.) Using the right "5" hand, the right thumbtip first touches the right side of the chin, then moves up to touch the right temple.

PARENTS 2, *n.* Same as for PARENTS 1 above, but the letter "P" is used.

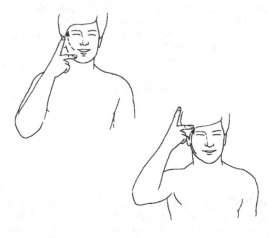

PARIS (par′ is), *n.* (The Eiffel Tower.) Both "V" hands, palms facing, move up above the head, fingertips coming in contact. Also EIFFEL TOWER, TOWER.

PARK 1 (pärk), *v.*, PARKED, PARKING. (A vehicle is brought to a distinct stop.) The right "3" hand, palm facing left, moves down an inch or two in front of the body. It may also, in so doing, be placed in the upturned open left palm.

PARK 2, *arch., loc.* (The windows in the head of the Statue of Liberty.) The curved fingers of the right hand repeatedly touch the forehead as the hand moves from left to right. This sign was once popular with New York City deaf children since a class outing to

the Statue of Liberty was considered a treat, on a par with a visit to the local park or zoo.

PARLIAMENT (pär′ lə mənt), *n.* (The letter "P"; the Roman toga fastened at the shoulders.) The right "P" hand moves from left shoulder to right.

PAROLE (pə rōl′), *n., v.,* -ROLED, -ROLING. See PARDON.

PARROT (par′ ət), *n.* (The curved beak.) The curved index finger moves away from and down from the nose.

PART 1 (pärt), *n., adj.* (Cutting off or designating a part.) The little finger edge of the open right hand moves straight down the middle of the upturned left palm. Also PIECE, PORTION, SECTION, SHARE 1, SOME.

PART 2, *n., adj.* (Separating to classify.) Both hands, in the right-angle position, are placed palms down before the body, knuckles to knuckles. They pull apart or separate once or a number of times. Also ASSORT, SEPARATE 2.

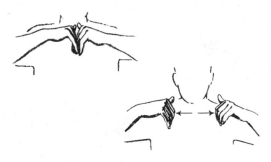

PART 3, *n., adj.* (The hands are moved apart.) Both hands, in the "A" position, thumbs up, are held together with knuckles touching. With a deliberate movement they come apart. Also APART, DIVORCE 1, SEPARATE 1.

PART 4, *n.* (The letter "P.") This is the same sign as for PART 1, except that the middle finger of the right "P" hand touches the upturned left palm as the sign is made.

PART FROM, *v. phrase.* (An unlocking.) With thumbs and index fingers interlocked initially (the links of a chain), the hands draw apart, showing the break in the chain. Also DETACH, DISCONNECT.

PARTICIPATE 1 (pär tĭs′ ə pāt′), *v.,* -PATED, -PATING. (Joining together.) Both hands, held in the modified "5" position, palms out, move toward each other. The thumbs and index fingers of both hands then connect. Also AFFILIATE 1, ANNEX, ASSOCIATE 2, ATTACH, BELONG, COMMUNION OF SAINTS, CONCERN 2, CONNECT, ENLIST, ENROLL, JOIN 1, RELATIVE 2, UNION, UNITE.

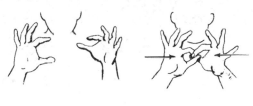

PARTICIPATE 2, *v.* (The letter "P"; jumping into an endeavor.) The right "P" hand is thrust into a cup formed by the left "O" or "C" hand.

PARTNER (pärt′ nər), *n.* (Sharing.) The little finger edge of the right hand sweeps back and forth over the index finger edge of the left hand. This is followed by the sign for INDIVIDUAL.

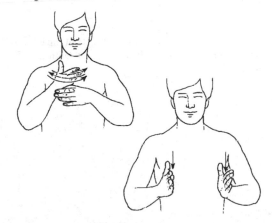

PARTY 1 (pär′ tĭ), *n.* (The swinging of tambourines.) Both open hands, held somewhat above the head, are pivoted back and forth repeatedly as if swinging a pair of tambourines. Also GAIETY 2.

PARTY 2, *n.* (The rhythmic swaying of the feet.) The downturned index and middle fingers of the right "V" hand swing rhythmically back and forth over the upturned left palm. Also BALL 1, DANCE.

PARTY 3 (*loc.*), *n.* The right "O" hand, palm facing the rear, is placed with knuckles touching the right cheek. The hand is thrown out and down a bit into the palm-down "5" position. Both hands, placed at either cheek, may also be used.

PARTY 4, *n., v.,* PARTIED, PARTYING. (Initialized version of PARTY 1.) As in PARTY 1, but with the "P" hands.

PASS 1 (păs), *v.,* PASSED, PASSING. (One hand passes the other.) Both "A" hands, palms facing each other, are held before the body, the right behind the left. The right hand moves forward, its knuckles brushing those of the left, and continues forward a bit beyond the left. Also ELAPSE, GO BY.

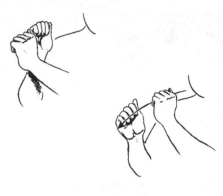

PASS 2 (*sports*), *v.* (The action of passing a football.) The left hand goes through the natural motion of passing an imaginary football. (The right hand may also be used.)

PASS BY (păs bī), *v. phrase.* (The fingers pass each other.) The right "D" hand, palm facing away from the body, moves forward a bit. At the same time the left "D" hand, palm facing the body, moves toward the body a bit. The action involves both hands passing each other as they move in opposite directions.

PASSENGER (pas′ ən jər), *n.* (One who rides.) The curved index and middle fingers of the right hand, palm facing down, are inserted into a cup formed by the left "O" or "C" hand. Both hands move forward together. This is followed by the sign for INDIVIDUAL 1.

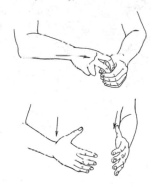

PASSION 1 (păsh′ ən), *n.* (The alimentary canal—the area of hunger and hunger gratification—is indicated.) The fingertips of the right "C" hand move slowly and deliberately down the middle of the chest once or twice. The eyes are usually narrowed and the teeth clenched. Also LUST.

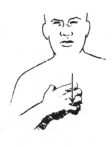

PASSION 2, *v.* (A clenching of the fists; the rise and fall of pain.) Both "S" hands, tightly clenched, revolve about each other, slowly and deliberately, while a pained expression is worn. Also AGONY, BEAR 3, DIFFICULT 3, ENDURE 1, SUFFER 1, TOLERATE 2.

PASS OUT 1, *v. phrase.* (An animal's legs sticking up in the air, in death.) Both hands are held with palms facing each other and curved index and middle fingers presented. The hands pivot up a bit simultaneously, assuming the "V" position as they do. Also DEAD 2, DIE 2.

PASS OUT 2, *v.* (To faint; attempting to grab something as one falls.) The downturned open hands, fingers somewhat curved, suddenly separate and close into the "S" position. The head, meanwhile, falls back a bit and the eyes close. Also FAINT 2.

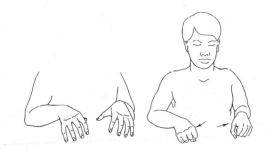

PASSOVER (pas′ ō vər), *n.* (The letter "P"; passing over.) The right "P" hand passes over the downturned left hand.

PAST (păst), *adj., n., adv.* (Something past, behind.) The upraised right hand, in the "5" position with palm facing the body, is held just above the right shoulder and is thrown back over it. Also AGO, FORMERLY, ONCE UPON A TIME, PREVIOUS, PREVIOUSLY, WAS, WERE.

PASTE (pāst), *n., v.*, PASTED, PASTING. (Spreading the paste.) The downturned "H" hand spreads the paste over the thumb and index fingers of the left fist or "O" hand.

PASTE UP, *v.* (Spreading out or taping something on a surface or piece of paper.) Both downturned thumbs, tips touching, move apart simultaneously. The movement is usually repeated.

PASTOR (păs′ tər), *n.* (Placing morsels of wisdom, or food for thought, into the mind.) The right hand, palm out, with thumb and index finger touching, is moved forward and slightly downward a number of times from its initial position near the right temple. This is followed by the sign for INDIVIDUAL 1: both open

hands, palms facing each other, move down the sides of the body, tracing its outline to the hips. Also MINISTER, PREACHER.

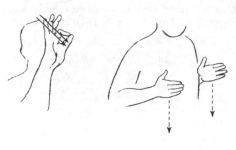

PAT (pat), *n., v.*, PATTED, PATTING. (The natural sign.) The signer's right hand pats the left shoulder several times.

PATH (păth), *n.* (The winding movement.) Both hands, palms facing and fingers together and extended straight out, move in unison away from the body in a winding manner. Also CORRIDOR, HALL, HALLWAY, MANNER 2, METHOD, OPPORTUNITY 3, ROAD, STREET, TRAIL, WAY 1.

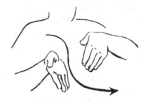

PATIENCE 1 (pā′ shəns), *n.* The thumb of the right "A" hand is drawn down across the lips. This is frequently followed by the sign for SUFFER 1: both "S"

hands, tightly clenched, revolve about each other, slowly and deliberately, while a pained expression is worn. Also PATIENT 1.

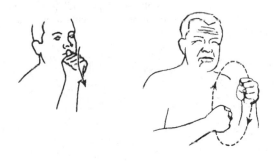

PATIENCE 2, *n.* (Silence; an avoidance of an outcry or impatience.) The index finger of the right "D" hand, palm facing left, is placed at the scaled lips. The head is held slightly bowed. Also HURT 3, PATIENT 2.

PATIENT 1 (pā′ shənt), *n.* See PATIENCE 1.

PATIENT 2, *adj.* See PATIENCE 2.

PATIENT 3, *n.* (The letter "P"; the red cross on the hospital gown's sleeve.) The thumb and middle fingers of the right "P" hand trace a small cross on the upper left arm.

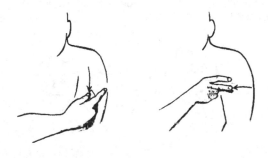

PATRONIZE (pā′ trən īz), *v.*, -RONIZED, -RONIZING. (Offering unwanted sympathy.) The middle fingers of

both "5" hands move forward in small circles together. The signer's expression is one of condescension. This sign indicates patronizing someone. To be patronized, the hands swing around so that the middle fingers point to the signer. The same expression is used.

PAY 1 (pā), *v.*, PAID, PAYING. (Giving forth of money.) The right index finger, resting in the upturned left palm, swings forward and up a bit.

PAY 2, *v.* (Releasing coins from the grasp.) The right hand, palm up, holds some imaginary coins, with the thumb resting on the tips of the fingers. The hand moves forward, and the thumb meanwhile glides over the fingertips and assumes the "A" position, palm still up.

PAY 3, *v.* (A modification of PAY 1, with the letter "P.") The middle finger of the right "P" hand is placed in the upturned left palm, and the right "P" hand executes the same movement as in PAY 1.

PAY ATTENTION (TO), *v. phrase.* (Directing one's attention forward; applying oneself; concentrating.) Both hands, fingers pointing up and together, are held at the sides of the face. They move straight out from the face. Also APPLY 2, ATTEND (TO), ATTENTION, CONCENTRATE, CONCENTRATION, FOCUS, GIVE ATTENTION (TO), MIND 2.

PEACE (pēs), *n.* (The hands are clasped as a gesture of harmony or *peace;* the opening signifies quiet or calmness.) The hands are clasped both ways, and then they open and separate, assuming the "5" position, palms down.

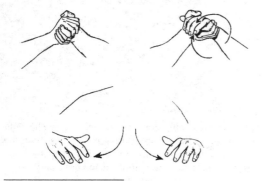

PEACOCK (pē′ kok), *n.* (The letter "P"; the fantail.) The right "P" hand is first positioned at the left elbow; then it moves down the arm, opening into a wide fan, with fingers spread apart.

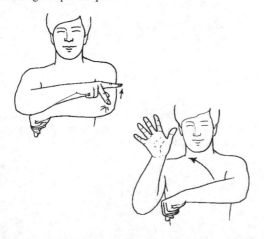

PEARLS (pûrlz), *n.* (White beads around the neck.) The sign for WHITE: the right "5" hand, palm against the chest, moves away from the body as the fingers close to touch the thumb. The right "F" hand then makes a series of successive movements around the neck, from right to left.

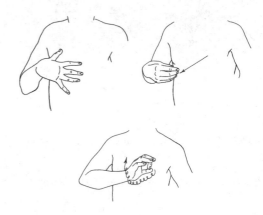

PECAN (pi kän′, -kan′, pē′ kan), *n.* (Biting into the nut.) The upturned thumb of the right "A" hand, held in the teeth, is thrust out, and then the thumb is brought up into a cup formed by the left closed hand.

PECULIAR (pǐ kūl′ yər), *adj.* (Something that distorts the vision.) The "C" hand describes a small arc in front of the face. Also CURIOUS 2, GROTESQUE, ODD, QUEER 1, STRANGE 1, WEIRD.

PEEK 1 (pēk), *v.,* PEEKED, PEEKING. (The eye is alternately hidden and uncovered.) The right "B" hand, palm facing left, is held against the face so that it covers the right eye. The hand moves alternately an inch to the left and right, covering and uncovering the right eye. Also SPY 1.

PEEK 2, *n., v.* (The eye looks through a narrow aperture.) The right "V" hand, palm facing out, is held at the face, with the right eye looking out between the index and middle fingers. Also SPY 2.

PEEK 3, *n., v.* (Looking through a keyhole.) The signer closes the left eye and, with the right eye, looks though a hole formed by the right index finger and thumb.

PEER (pĭr), *n.* (Equal in height or status.) The right-angle hands, palms down, are held at about eye level, one in front of the other. The hand in front moves straight forward a short distance, away from the face, while the other hand remains stationary. This sign is used to indicate an equal, never a member of the nobility.

PENALTY 1 (pĕn′ əl tĭ), *n.* (A striking movement.) The right index finger makes a striking movement below the left "S" hand, which is held up as if grasping a culprit. Also DISCIPLINE 3, PUNISH 1.

PENALTY 2, *n.* (A modification of the striking movement.) The right index finger strikes the left elbow with a glancing blow. Also DISCIPLINE 2, PENANCE 1, PUNISH 3.

PENALTY 3, *n.* (Nicking into one.) The knuckle of the right "X" finger is nicked against the palm of the left hand, held in the "5" position, palm facing right. Also ADMISSION 2, CHARGE 1, COST, DUTY 2, EXCISE, EXPENSE, FEE, FINE 2, IMPOST, PRICE 2, TAX 1, TAXATION 1, TOLL.

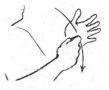

PENCIL SHARPENER, *n.* (The action of sharpening a pencil.) The sign for PENCIL, above, is followed by the left index finger pointing to the right. The right hand, grasping an imaginary lever, rotates forward in a clockwise direction.

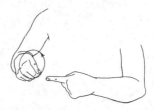

PENDANT (pen′ dənt), *n.* (The shape hanging from a chain.) Both index fingers move down, tracing a chain hanging around the throat. The left or right "F" hand, forming a circle, is then placed flat against the chest. The hanging chain sign may be omitted.

PENDULUM (pen′ jə ləm, pen′ dyə-, -də-), *n.* (The swinging.) The left downturned arm is placed horizontally across the chest. The right arm, hanging down, then swings from left to right in a series of broad arcs.

PENGUIN (pen′ gwin), *n.* (The characteristic gait.) Both downturned hands, fingers touching, are held at the sides of the body. The signer rocks alternately back and forth.

PENIS 1 (pē′ nĭs), *n.* (The shape is indicated.) Both "C" hands, palms up, are held in front of the body, the little finger edge of the right hand touching the index finger edge of the left. The right hand moves forward a short distance, in a slight arc, while the left remains stationary.

PENIS 2, *n.* (The letter "P" for "pee.") The middle finger of the right "P" hand is placed on the tip of the nose.

PENITENT (pĕn′ ə tənt), *adj.* (The heart is circled to indicate feeling, modified by the letter "S" for SORRY.) The right "S" hand, palm facing the body, is rotated several times over the area of the heart. Also APOLOGIZE 1, APOLOGY 1, CONTRITION, REGRET, REGRETFUL, REPENT, REPENTANT, RUE, SORROW, SORROWFUL 2, SORRY.

PENNANT (pen′ ənt), *n.* (The shape.) The right index and thumb, representing an "L," are placed on the upright left index finger, representing the staff. They move off to the right, tracing a pyramid as they come together.

PENNILESS 1 (pen′ i lis), *adj.* (The head is chopped off, perhaps reminiscent of pauper's prison. Also a play on words: "broke" indicating a broken neck.) The little finger edge of the downturned right hand is thrust forcefully into the right side of the neck.

Alternatively, both hands may be used, on either side of the neck. Also BANKRUPT, BROKE.

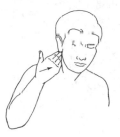

PENNILESS 2, *adj.* (Turning the pockets inside out.) The signer mimes turning the pockets inside out. This may be preceded by MONEY 1: the upturned right hand, grasping a number of bills, is brought down into the upturned left palm a number of times.

PENNILESS 3, *adj.* (Blowing on the palm to indicate there is nothing there.) The sign for MONEY 1 is followed by a blowing on the upturned palm.

PENNILESS 4, *adj.* (Turning up the hands to indicate there is nothing there.) The sign for MONEY 1 is made. Then both "L" hands, side by side with palms down, are rapidly and repeatedly swiveled at the wrists to the palms-up position. The signer assumes a look of inner distress.

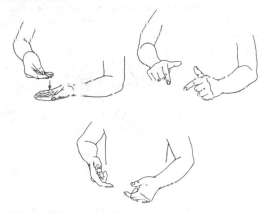

PENNY (pen' ē), *n.* (The Lincoln head.) The right index finger touches the right temple and moves up and away quickly. This is one cent. For two cents, the "2" hand is used, etc. Also CENT, CENTS.

PENNY-PINCHING (pen' ē pinch ing), *adj.* (Holding onto money tightly.) The signer makes a tight fist, shaking it slightly. Also TIGHTFISTED.

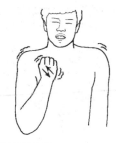

PENSION (pen' shən), *n.* (A regular income.) The upturned right "A" hand opens and closes repeatedly each time it pulls down an imaginary object from the right.

PEOPLE (pē′ pəl), *n. pl.* (The letter "P" in continuous motion to indicate plurality.) The "P" hands, side by side, are moved alternately in continuous counterclockwise circles. Also AUDIENCE 2, HUMANITY, PUBLIC.

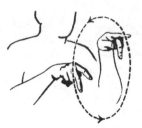

PEPPER 1 (pĕp′ ər), *n.* (Something black that is shaken on food.) The sign for BLACK is made: the right index finger is drawn over the right eyebrow from left to right. The right hand, grasping an imaginary shaker, then shakes the pepper on some unseen food. The sign for BLACK is frequently omitted.

PEPPER 2, *n.* (The "P"; sprinkling.) The right "P" hand shakes up and down slightly, as if sprinkling something.

PEPPER 3, *n.* (Sprinkling a pinch of pepper.) The right "F" hand, holding an imaginary pinch of pepper, shakes up and down slightly.

PEPPER 4, *n.* (The pepper mill.) Both hands, forming fists, one atop the other, mime grinding pepper from a pepper mill.

PERCEIVE 1 (pər sēv′), *v.,* -CEIVED, -CEIVING. (The eyesight is directed forward.) The right "V" hand, palm facing the body, is placed so that the fingertips are just under the eyes. The hand swings around and out so that the fingertips are now pointing forward. Also LOOK 1, PERCEPTION, SEE, SIGHT, WATCH 2.

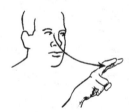

PERCEIVE 2, *v.* (The vision is directed forward into the distance.) The right "V" fingertips are placed under the eyes, with palm facing the body. The hand is then swung around and forward, moving under the downturned prone left hand and continuing forward and upward. Also FORECAST, FORESEE, FORETELL, PREDICT, PROPHECY, PROPHESY, PROPHET, VISION 2.

PERCENT (pər sĕnt′), *n.* (Drawing a percent symbol in the air.) The right "O" hand traces the percent symbol (%) in the air. Also RATE 2.

PERCEPTION (pər sĕp′ shən), *n.* See PERCEIVE 1.

PERFECT (*adj., n.* pûr′ fĭkt; *v.* pər fĕkt′), -FECTED, -FECTING. (The letter "P"; the hands come into precise contact.) The "P" hands face each other. The right executes a clockwise circle above the stationary left and then moves down so that the thumb and middle fingers of each hand come into precise contact.

PERFORM 1 (pər fôrm′), *v.,* -FORMED, -FORMING. (An activity.) Both open hands, palms down, are swung right and left before the chest. Also ACT 2, ACTION, ACTIVE, ACTIVITY, BUSY 2, CONDUCT 1, DEED, DO, PER-FORMANCE 1, RENDER 2.

PERFORM 2, *v.* (Motion or movement, modified by the letter "A" for "act.") Both "A" hands, palms out, are held at shoulder height and rotate alternately toward the head. Also ACT 1, ACTOR, ACTRESS, DRAMA, PERFORMANCE 2, PLAY 2, SHOW 2.

PERFORMANCE 1 (pər fôr′ məns), *n.* See PERFORM 1.

PERFORMANCE 2, *n.* See PERFORM 2.

PERFUME 1 (pûr′ fūm, pər fūm′), *n.* (Act of smelling and pouring.) The right "A" hand, holding the neck of an imaginary bottle, is placed at the nose. The hand is then tipped over slightly against the chest. Also COLOGNE.

PERFUME 2, *n.* (Touching the perfume to the throat.) The middle finger delicately touches one side of the throat, then the other.

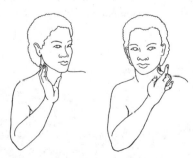

PERHAPS (pər hăps′), *adv.* (Weighing one thing against another.) The upturned open hands move alternately up and down. Also GUESS 4, MAY 1, MAYBE, MIGHT 2, POSSIBILITY, POSSIBLY, PROBABLE, PROBABLY, SUPPOSE.

PERIL (pĕr′ əl), *n.* (An encroachment; parrying a knife thrust.) The left "A" hand is held palm toward the body, knuckles facing right. The extended thumb of the right "A" hand is brought sharply over the back of the left. Also DANGER 2, DANGEROUS 2, INJURE 2, TRESPASS, VIOLATE.

PERIPHERAL (pə rif′ ər əl), *adj.* (The "P"; surrounding.) The downturned right "P" hand makes a circle around the upturned left right-angle hand.

PERISCOPE 1 (per′ ə skōp′), *n.* (The action from below deck.) The signer mimes grasping the handles of a periscope and swinging them slightly back and forth, while focusing into the lens.

PERMANENT (pûr′ mə nənt), *adj.* (Steady, uninterrupted movement.) The "A" hands are held with palms out, thumbs extended and touching, the right behind the left. In this position the hands move forward in a straight, steady line. Also CONTINUE 1, ENDURE 2, EVER 1, LAST 3, LASTING, PERPETUAL, PERSEVERE 3, PERSIST 2, REMAIN, STAY 1, STAY STILL.

PERMANENT WAVE, *n.* (The old electric curlers or the newer plastic rollers in the hair.) Both open "C" hands, palms facing forward, are positioned at either side of the head. They close into fists and move alternately forward and back as if pulling the hair.

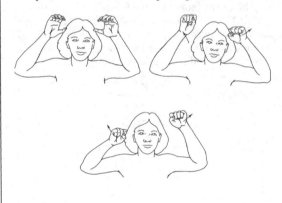

PERMISSION 1 (pər mĭsh′ ən), *n.* (A permissive upswinging of the hands, as if giving in.) Both hands, palms facing and fingers pointing away from the body, are held at chest level, almost a foot apart. With an upward movement, using their wrists as pivots, the hands sweep up until the fingers point almost straight up. Also ALLOW, GRANT 1, LET, LET'S, LET US, MAY 3, PERMIT 1, TOLERATE 1.

PERMISSION 2, *n.* (The "P" hands are used.) The same sign as in PERMISSION 1 is used, except with the "P" hands. Also PERMIT 2.

PERMIT 1 (par mit′), *v.*, -MITTED, -MITTING. See PERMISSION 1.

PERMIT 2, *n., v.* See PERMISSION 2.

PERPENDICULAR 1 (pûr pan dik′ ya lar), *adj.* (The letter "P.") The right index finger touches the middle finger of the left "P" hand.

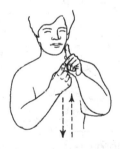

PERPENDICULAR 2, *adj.* (The shape.) The little finger edge of the right hand rests upright and perpendicular in the upturned left palm. It may wave back and forth slightly, as if achieving balance.

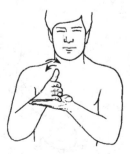

PERPETUAL (par pĕch′ ŏŏ al), *adj.* (Steady, uninterrupted movement.) The "A" hands are held with palms out, thumbs extended and touching, the right behind the left. In this position the hands move forward in a straight, steady line. Also CONTINUE 1, ENDURE 2, EVER 1, LAST 3, LASTING, PERMANENT, PERSEVERE 3, PERSIST 2, REMAIN, STAY 1, STAY STILL.

PERSEVERE 1 (pûr′ sa vĭr′), *v.*, -VERED, -VERING. (Trying to push through.) The "A" hands, palms facing before the body, are swung around and a bit down so that the palms now face out. The movement indicates an attempt to push through a barrier. Also ATTEMPT 1, EFFORT 1, ENDEAVOR, PERSIST 1, TRY 1.

PERSEVERE 2, *v.* (Trying to push through, using the "T" hands, for "try.") This is the same sign as PERSEVERE 1, except that the "T" hands are employed. Also ATTEMPT 2, EFFORT 2, TRY 2.

PERSEVERE 3, *v.* (Steady, uninterrupted movement.) The "A" hands are held with palms out, thumbs extended and touching, the right behind the left. In this position the hands move forward in a straight, steady line. Also CONTINUE 1, ENDURE 2, EVER 1, LAST 3, LASTING, PERMANENT, PERPETUAL, PERSIST 2, REMAIN, STAY 1, STAY STILL.

PERSEVERE 4, *v.* (A thought directed upward toward a goal.) The left "D" hand, palm facing the body, is held above the head to represent the goal. The index finger of the right "D" hand, after touching the forehead (modified sign for THINK, *q.v.*), moves slowly and deliberately up to the tip of the left index finger. Also AIM, AMBITION, ASPIRE, GOAL, OBJECTIVE, PURPOSE 2.

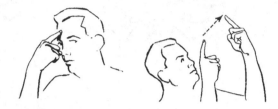

PERSIST 1 (pər sĭst′, -zĭst′), *v.,* -SISTED, -SISTING. (Trying to push through.) The "A" hands, palms facing before the body, are swung around and a bit down so that the palms now face out. The movement indicates an attempt to push through a barrier. Also ATTEMPT 1, EFFORT 1, ENDEAVOR, PERSEVERE 1, TRY 1.

PERSIST 2, *v.* (Steady, uninterrupted movement.) The "A" hands are held with palms out, thumbs extended and touching, the right behind the left. In this position the hands move forward in a straight, steady line. Also CONTINUE 1, ENDURE 2, EVER 1, LAST 3, LASTING, PERMANENT, PERPETUAL, PERSEVERE 3, REMAIN, STAY 1, STAY STILL.

PERSON 1 (pûr′ sən), *n.* (The letter "P"; an individual is indicated.) The "P" hands, side by side, move straight down a short distance, as if outlining the sides of an unseen individual.

"PERSON" 2 (*ending*). Both open hands, palms facing each other, move down the sides of the body, tracing its outline to the hips.

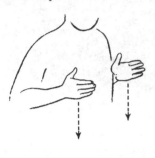

PERSONAL (pûr′ sən əl), *adj.* (The lips are sealed, as in a secret or something personal.) The back of the right thumb is pressed against the lips.

PERSONAL COMPUTER *n.* (A fingerspelled loan sign.) The signer fingerspells "P-C."

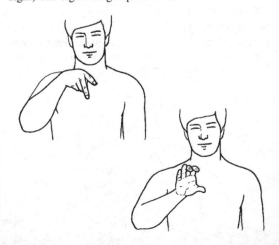

PERSPECTIVE (pər spek′ tiv), *n.* (Directing the vision to something specified.) The right "V" hand is held under the right eye, with palm facing the body. It swings around and away toward the left upright index finger.

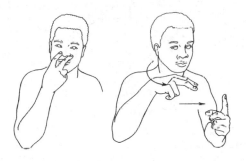

PERSPIRATION 1 (pûr′ spə rā′ shən), *n.* See PERSPIRE 1.

PERSPIRATION 2, *n.* See PERSPIRE 2.

PERSPIRE 1 (pər spīr′), *v.,* -SPIRED, -SPIRING. (Wiping the brow.) The bent right index finger is drawn across the forehead from left to right and then shaken to the side as if getting rid of the sweat. Also PERSPIRATION 1, SWEAT 1.

PERSPIRE 2, *v.* (Perspiration dripping from the brow.) The index finger edge of the open right hand wipes across the brow, and the same open hand then continues forcefully downward off the brow, its fingers wiggling as if shaking off the perspiration gathered. Also PERSPIRATION 2, SWEAT 2.

PERSUADE (pər swād′), *v.,* -SUADED, -SUADING. (The karate chop to the neck wins the prize, *i.e.,* convinces the victim.) One hand or both upturned open hands mimes a karate chop to the neck. This sign, especially for PERSUASIVE (see below) may be preceded by the fingertips of the right hand stroking back and forth against the upright left index finger.

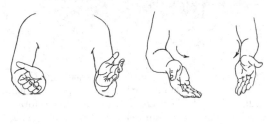

PERSUASION (pər swā′ zhən), *n.* See PERSUADE.

PERSUASIVE (pər swā′ siv, -ziv), *adj.* See PERSUADE, above. Also, CONVINCE.

PERU (pə rōō′), *n.* (Possibly to do with native head-dress.) The middle finger of the right "P" hand taps the forehead several times. A native sign.

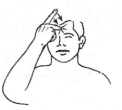

PET (pĕt), *n., adj., v.,* PETTED, PETTING. (Stroking a person or the head of a pet.) The right hand strokes the back of the left several times. Also DEAR 1, FOND 1, STROKE 2, TAME.

PETTING (pĕt′ ĭng) (*sl.*), *v.* (Necks interlocked.) The "S" hands, palms facing, are crossed at the wrists. They swing up and down while the wrists remain in contact. Also MAKE LOVE 2, NECKING.

PETTY (pĕt′ ĭ), *adj.* (Indicating a small mass.) The extended right thumb and index finger are held slightly spread. They are then moved slowly toward each other until they almost touch. Also SLIGHT, SMALL 1, TINY 2.

PHARAOH (fâr′ ō), *n.* (The "P"; the headdress.) Both "P" hands trace the shape of the headdress down the sides of the head.

PHEASANT (fez′ ənt), *n.* (Tracing the neck markings.) The right thumb and index fingers move across the right side of the neck.

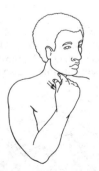

PHEW! *interj.* The "5" hand, palm facing the body, is shaken up and down several times.

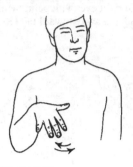

PHILADELPHIA (fĭl′ ə dĕl′ fĭ ə), *n.* The right "P" hand moves down in a quick, curved, right-left-right manner.

PHILANTHROPY (fi lan′ thrə pē), *n.* (Giving money.) The sign for MONEY: the upturned right hand, grasping some imaginary bills, is brought down into the upturned left palm once or twice. The modified right "A" hand, palm facing left, and thumb tucked beneath the curved right index finger, moves out and back several times in different directions as if distributing something.

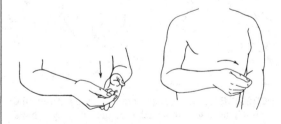

PHILIPPINES (fil′ ə pēnz′, fil′ ə pēnz′), *n.* (The "P" on an island.) The right downturned "P" hand, touching the back of the downturned left hand, makes a counterclockwise circle around it.

PHONE 1 (fōn), *n.*, *v.*, PHONED, PHONING. (The natural sign.) The left "S" hand represents the mouthpiece and is placed at the mouth with palm facing right. Its right counterpart represents the earpiece and is placed at the right ear with palm facing forward. This is the old-fashioned two-piece telephone. Also TELEPHONE 1.

PHONE 2, *n.*, *v.* (The natural sign.) The right "Y" hand is placed at the right side of the head with the thumb touching the ear and the little finger touching the lips. This is the more modern telephone receiver. Also TELEPHONE 2.

PHONOGRAPH 1 (fō' nə graf', -gräf), *n.* (The needle in contact.) The left "C" hand, palm facing right, represents the revolving record or disk. The downturned right "X" finger makes a continuous counterclockwise circle above the "C."

PHONOGRAPH 2, *n.* A variant of the above, using the downturned right "P" hand instead of the right "X" finger.

PHOOEY! *interj.* (A look of derision.) With a look of derision, the signer throws one hand down and out, as if ridding himself of something. Also BAH!

PHOTOGRAPH 1 (fō' tə gräf'), *n.*, *v.*, -GRAPHED, -GRAPHING. (Recording an image.) The right "C" hand is held in front of the face, with thumb edge near the face and palm facing left. The hand is then brought sharply around in front of the open left hand and is struck firmly against the left palm, which is held facing forward with fingers pointing up. Also PICTURE 1.

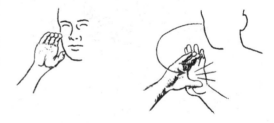

PHOTOGRAPH 2, *n.* (Recording an image.) The right "C" hand or crooked index finger is drawn down over the face. The hand is then brought sharply around in front of the open left hand and is struck firmly against the left palm, which is held facing forward with fingers pointing up. (In step 1, the right "C" hand or index finger may simply touch the bridge of the nose instead of moving down over the face.) Also PICTURE 2.

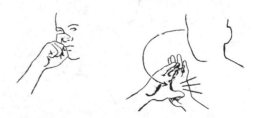

PHOTOGRAPH 3, *v.* (Capturing an image) Both open hands are held before the body, fingers pointing upward, the right hand positioned in front of the left. The right hand then moves forcefully backward against the left palm, closing into the "AND" position as it does. Also TAKE A PICTURE.

PHYSICAL 1 (fĭz′ ə kəl), *adj.* (The body is indicated.) One or both hands are placed against the chest and then are removed and replaced at a point a bit below the first. Also BODY.

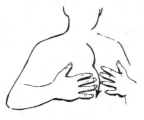

PHYSICAL 2, *adj.* (The "P" letters; indicating the body.) The downturned "P" hands are positioned at chest height on the body. They move down in an arc to the waist.

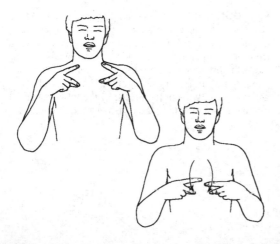

PHYSICAL 3, *adj.* (The "Ps"; the body is outlined.) Both downturned "P" hands, placed at either side of the chest, move down simultaneously.

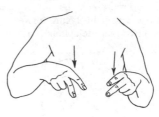

PHYSICS 1 (fĭz′ ĭks), *n.* (The points of the electrodes.) The "X" hands are held palms facing the body, thumb edges up. The knuckles of the index fingers touch each other repeatedly. Also ELECTRIC, ELECTRICITY.

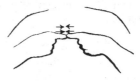

PHYSICS 2, *n.* Same as PHYSICS 1, above, but using the bent "V" hands instead of the "X" hands.

PIANO (pĭ ăn′ ō), *n.* (The natural sign.) The downturned hands go through the natural movements involved in manipulating a piano keyboard.

PICK 1 (pĭk), *v.,* PICKED, PICKING. (The natural motion of selecting something from the hand.) The thumb and index fingers of the outstretched right hand grasp an imaginary object on the upturned left palm. The right hand then moves straight up. Also CHOOSE 2, DIS-COVER, FIND, SELECT 1.

PICK 2, *v.* (The natural sign.) The fingertips and thumbtip of the downturned open right hand come together, and the hand moves up a short distance, as if picking something. Also PICK UP 2, SELECT 3.

PICKLE (pĭk′ əl), *n., v.* -LED, -LING. (Something sour or bitter.) The right index finger is brought sharply up against the lips, while the mouth is puckered up as if tasting something sour. The thumb and index finger may then indicate the length of the pickle. Also ACID, BITTER, DISAPPOINTED 1, LEMON 1, SOUR.

PICK ON (pĭk), *v. phrase.* (The hen's beak pecks.) The index finger and thumb of the right hand, held together, are brought against the index finger of the left "D" hand a number of times. Also HENPECK, NAG, PECK.

PICKPOCKET (pĭk′ pok′ it), *n.* (Pulling something out of a pocket.) The right "F" hand quickly and surreptitiously removes an item from an imaginary right back pocket.

PICK UP 1, *v. phrase.* (To take up.) Both hands, held palms down in the "5" position, are at chest level. With a grasping upward movement, both close into "S" positions before the face. Also ASSUME, TAKE UP.

PICK UP 2, *v. phrase.* See PICK 2.

PICTURE 1 (pĭk′ chər), *n., v.,* -TURED, -TURING. (Recording an image.) The right "C" hand is held in front of the face with thumb edge near the face and palm facing left. The hand is then brought sharply around in front of the open left hand and is struck firmly against the left palm, which is held facing forward with fingers pointing up. Also PHOTOGRAPH 1.

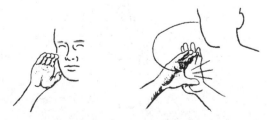

PICTURE 2, *n*. (Recording an image.) The right "C" hand or crooked index finger is drawn down over the face. The hand is then brought sharply around in front of the open left hand and is struck firmly against the left palm, which is held facing forward with fingers pointing up. (In step 1, the right "C" hand or index finger may simply touch the bridge of the nose instead of moving down over the face.) Also PHOTO-GRAPH 2.

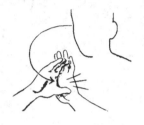

PIE 1 (pī), *n*. (Slicing a wedge-shaped piece of pie.) The upturned left hand represents the pie. The little finger edge of the open right hand goes through the motions of slicing a wedge-shaped piece from the pie.

PIE 2 (*loc.*), *n*. (The letter "K," the last initial of an instructor of baking at a school for the deaf.) The middle finger of the right "K" hand touches the right cheek twice. Also CAKE 2.

PIECE (pēs), *n., v.,* PIECED, PIECING. (Cutting off or designating a part.) The little finger edge of the open right hand moves straight down the middle of the upturned left palm. Also PART 1, PORTION, SECTION, SHARE 1, SOME.

PIG 1 (pĭg), *n*. (The snout digs into the trough.) The downturned right prone hand is placed under the chin, fingers pointing forward. The hand, in this position, swings alternately up and down. Also HOG 1.

PIG 2, *n*. (Same rationale as for PIG 1.) The sign for PIG 1 is repeated, except that the fingers point to the left. Also HOG 2.

PILGRIM 1 (pil′ grim), *n*. (The letter "P"; the wide collar.) Both "P" hands trace a wide collar around the neck, beginning in the back and moving around to the front.

PILGRIM 2, *n.* (The bow on the hat.) The signer mimes tightening a bow in front of a hat.

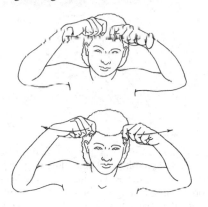

PILLAGE (pil′ ij), *v.,* -AGED, -AGING. (Grabbing things all over.) Both downturned claw hands move alternately up and down, closing into fists each time they move down.

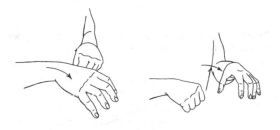

PILLAR 1 (pil′ ər), *n.* (The shape and function.) The elbow of the upright fist-shaped right arm is placed on the downturned open left hand. The signer has the option of doing the same with the upright left arm and downturned right hand, in which case the plural is indicated.

PILLAR 2, *n.* (The shape.) Both "C" hands, palms facing and thumbs up, move upward in unison, tracing a tall column rising above the head.

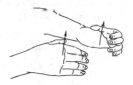

PILOT (pī′ lot), *n.* (An individual who flies a plane.) The sign for either AIRPLANE 1 or AIRPLANE 2 is made, and this is followed by the sign for INDIVIDUAL 1: both open hands, palms facing each other, move down the sides of the body, tracing its outline to the hips. Also AVIATOR, FLIER.

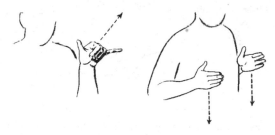

PIMPLES (pim′ pəlz), *n.* (Marks on the face.) The index finger touches the face repeatedly and at random, indicating the presence of pimples on the skin.

PINCH (pinch), *n., v.,* PINCHED, PINCHING. (The natural sign.) The index finger and thumb pinch the skin.

PINEAPPLE 1 (pīn′ ap əl), *n.* (The "P"; chewing.) The middle fingertip of the right "P" hand is placed against the cheek. The hand swivels back and forth. Alternately, the "P" may move in a continuous counterclockwise circle against the cheek.

PINEAPPLE 2, *n.* (The slicing and coring.) The right thumb is thrust into the cup of the downturned left hand. Swiveling on the right thumb, the curved right index finger moves clockwise.

PINWHEEL (pin′ hwēl), *n.* (The whirling around.) With the index finger thrust into the palm of the other "5" hand, the "5" hand moves very rapidly back and forth, imitating a spinning pinwheel.

PIONEER (pī ə nir′), *n.* (The first finger, *i.e.,* first explorers.) The middle finger of the right "P" hand touches the tip of the left thumb, the hand's first finger.

PIRATE (pī′ rət), *n.* (The patch over the eye.) The right "U" hand faces and covers the right eye.

PITY (pĭt′ ĭ), *n., v.,* PITIED, PITYING. (Feelings from the heart conferred on others.) The middle fingertip of the open right hand touches the chest over the heart. The same open hand then moves in a small, clockwise circle before the right shoulder, with palm facing forward and fingers pointing up. Also MERCY 2, POOR 3, SYMPATHY 2.

PIZZA 1 (pēt′ sə), *n.* (Eating a slice.) The signer mimes eating a slice of pizza.

PIZZA 2, *n.* (The letter "P"; the drawing of a "Z" in the air.) The right "P" hand draws a "Z" in the air.

PIZZA 3, *n*. (The double "Z" in the spelling.) The curved index and middle fingers draw a "Z" in the air.

PLACE 1 (plās), *n*. (The letter "P"; a circle or square is indicated to show the locale or place.) The "P" hands are held side by side before the body with middle fingertips touching. From this position, the hands separate and outline a circle (or a square) before coming together again closer to the body. Also LOCATION, POSITION 1, SCENE, SITE.

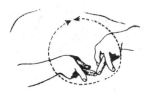

PLACE 2, *n*. (An area is outlined.) With the "I" hands held palms up and the tips of the little fingers touching, the hands separate as they move in toward the body. As they do, the tips of the little fingers come together again. Also POSITION 2.

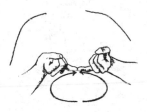

PLACE 3, *v*., PLACED, PLACING. (Moving from one place to another.) The downturned hands, fingers touching their respective thumbs, move in unison from left to right. Also MIGRATE, MOVE, PUT, REMOVE 2, TRANSFER 2.

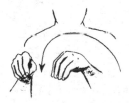

PLACEMENT (plās' mənt), *n*. (Putting an object firmly in place.) The right hand, held in a fist, moves firmly forward and down.

PLAGIARISM (plā' jə riz em), *n*. (The letter "P"; steal.) The right hand, forming a "P," makes a small clockwise circle, and then the curved index and middle fingers close over an imaginary object under the left elbow and move up toward the right.

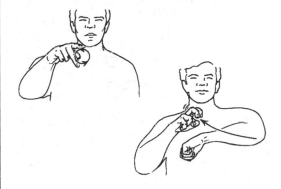

PLAID (plad), *n*. (The distinctive markings.) The right "4" hand, palm facing the chest or left arm, moves across, turns over, and then moves down.

PLAIN 1 (plān), *adj.* (Rays of light clearing the way.) Both hands are held at chest height, palms out, all fingertips together. They open into the "5" position in unison, the right hand moving toward the right and the left toward the left. The palms of both hands remain facing out. Also BRIGHT 1, BRILLIANCE 1, BRILLIANT 2, CLEAR, EXPLICIT 2, OBVIOUS.

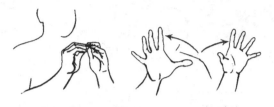

PLAIN 2, *adj.* (Everything is wiped off the hand to emphasize an uncluttered or clean condition.) The right hand slowly wipes the upturned left palm from wrist to fingertips. Also CLEAN 1, IMMACULATE, NEAT, NICE, PURE 1, PURITY, SIMPLE 2.

PLAIN 3, *n.* (The letters "P"; the space.) Both "P" hands draw a circle toward the chest.

PLAINTIFF (plān' tif), *n.* (Voicing one's feelings or objections.) The sign for COMPLAIN is made: the right claw hand, palm facing the body, is thrust twice into midchest. The sign for INDIVIDUAL 1 then follows.

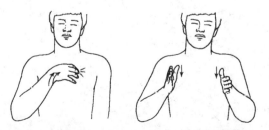

PLAN 1 (plăn), *n., v.,* PLANNED, PLANNING. (Placing things in order.) The hands, palms facing, fingers together and pointing away from the body, are positioned at the left side and held about a foot apart. With a slight up-down motion, as if describing waves, the hands travel in unison from left to right. Also ARRANGE, ARRANGEMENT, CLASSED 2, DEVISE 1, ORDER 3, POLICY 1, PREPARE 1, PROGRAM 1, PROVIDE 1, PUT IN ORDER, READY 1, SCHEME, SYSTEM.

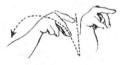

PLAN 2, *n., v.* (The initial "P.") PLAN 1 is repeated, except the "P" hands are palms down.

PLANE 1 (plān), *n.* (The wings of the airplane.) The "Y" hand, palm down and drawn up near the shoulder, moves forward several times, up and away from the body. Either hand may be used. Also AIRPLANE 1, FLY 1.

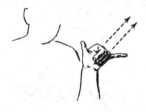

PLANE 2, *n.* (The wings and fuselage of the airplane.) The hand assumes the same position as in PLANE 1, but the index finger is also extended to represent the fuselage of the airplane. Either hand may be used, and the movement is the same as in PLANE 1. Also AIRPLANE 2, FLY 2.

PLANE 3 (*voc.*), *n., v.,* PLANED, PLANING. (The natural motion.) The left "S" hand moves forward forcefully over the open right palm from wrist to fingertips. The movement is repeated. This is the carpenter's plane.

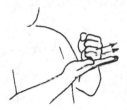

PLANET 1 (plăn′ ĭt), *n.* (The earth and its axes are indicated.) The downturned left "S" hand indicates the earth. The thumb and index finger of the downturned right "5" hand are placed at each edge of the left. In this position the right hand swings back and forth while maintaining contact with the left. Also EARTH 1, GEOGRAPHY, GLOBE 1.

PLANET 2, *n.* (The letter "P"; around the world.) The right "P" hand moves around the left fist.

PLANT 1 (plănt), *n.* (Flowers or plants emerge from the ground.) The right fingers, pointing up, emerge from the closed left hand, and they spread open as they do. Also BLOOM, DEVELOP 1, GROW, GROWN, MATURE, RAISE 3, REAR 2, SPRING 1.

PLANT 2, *v.,* PLANTED, PLANTING. (Placing the seed into the ground.) The right hand, holding some imaginary seeds, is thrust into the cupped left hand.

PLANT 3, *v.* (Sprinkling seeds.) The downturned right fingers sprinkle imaginary seeds in a row.

PLASTIC (plăs′ tik), *n., adj.* (Pliable.) The right hand grasps the middle finger of the left "P" hand and bends it back and forth.

PLATE 1 (plāt), *n.* (The material and shape.) The sign for GLASS or PORCELAIN is made: the index finger is brought up to touch the exposed front teeth. The downturned index fingers then describe the circular shape of the plate.

PLATE 2, *n.* (The shape.) The downturned thumbs and index fingers are held in a curve as they outline the edge of a plate.

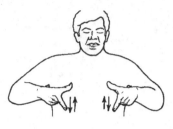

PLATEAU (pla tō′), *n.* (The flatness.) The right "P" hand, palm down, moves in a counterclockwise circle.

PLATTER (plat′ ər), *n.* (The shape and function.) Both upturned hands, side by side, describe a circle as they move outward from the body.

PLAY 1 (plā), *v.*, PLAYED, PLAYING. (Shaking tambourines.) The "Y" hands, held aloft, are shaken back and forth, pivoted at the wrists. Also FROLIC, RECREATION.

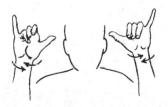

PLAY 2, *n.* (Motion or movement, modified by the letter "A" for "act.") Both "A" hands, palms out, are held at shoulder height and rotate alternately toward the head. Also ACT 1, ACTOR, ACTRESS, DRAMA, PERFORM 2, PERFORMANCE 2, SHOW 2.

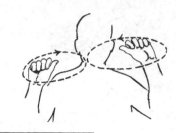

PLAYER (plā′ ər), *n.* The sign for PLAY 1 is made, followed by the sign for INDIVIDUAL 1: both open hands, palms facing each other, move down the sides of the body, tracing its outline to the hips.

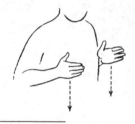

PLAYHOUSE (plā′ hous′), *n.* (PLAY and HOUSE.) The sign for PLAY: both "A" hands, palms out, are held at shoulder height and rotate alternately toward the head. This is followed by HOUSE: both hands, fingertips touching, form a sloping roof. They move down, separate, and indicate the walls. The sign for PLAY 1 may also be made by shaking both "Y" hands back and forth.

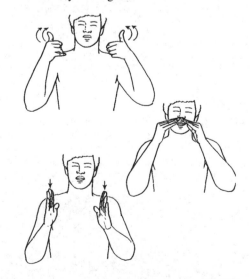

PLAYING CARDS, *n. pl.* (The action of dealing out cards.) The signer goes through the motions of dealing out imaginary playing cards. Also CARD PLAYING, CARDS, DISTRIBUTE 2.

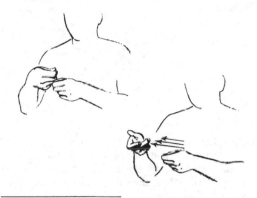

PLAYWRIGHT (plā′ rīt), *n.* (One who writes plays.) The sign for PLAY 1, as above, is made, followed by the sign for WRITE: the right hand moves an imaginary pencil over the upturned left palm. Optionally, the sign for INDIVIDUAL 1 may be added.

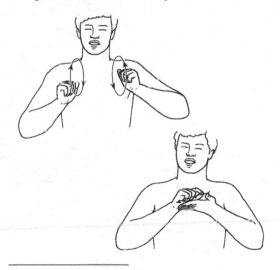

PLEA (plē), *n.* (An act of supplication.) With the right hand clasped over the left, both hands are shaken gently before the body. The eyes often are directed upward. Also BEG 2, BESEECH, ENTREAT, IMPLORE, PLEAD, SUPPLICATION.

PLEAD (plēd), *v.,* PLEADED, PLEADING. See PLEA.

PLEASANT (plĕz′ ənt), *adj.* (A crinkling up of the face.) Both hands, in the "5" position, palms facing back, are placed on either side of the face. The fingers wiggle back and forth while a pleasant, happy expression is worn. Also AMIABLE, CHEERFUL, CORDIAL, FRIENDLY, JOLLY.

PLEASE (plēz), *v.,* PLEASED, PLEASING. (A pleasurable feeling on the heart.) The open right hand is circled on the chest over the heart. Also APPRECIATE, ENJOY, ENJOYMENT, GRATIFY 1, LIKE 3, PLEASURE, WILLING 2.

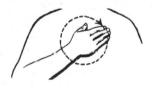

PLEASURE (plĕzh′ ər), *n.* See PLEASE.

PLEDGE (plĕj), *n., v.,* PLEDGED, PLEDGING. (The arm is raised.) The right index finger is placed at the lips. The right arm is then raised, palm out and elbow resting on the back of the left hand. Also GUARANTEE 1, LOYAL, OATH, PROMISE 1, SWEAR 1, SWORN, TAKE OATH, VOW.

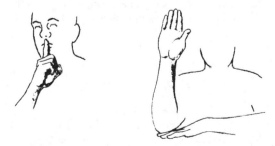

PLENTY (plĕn′ tĭ), *n., adj., adv.* (A full cup.) The left hand, in the "S" position, is held palm facing right. The right "5" hand, palm down, is brushed outward several times over the top of the left, indicating a wiping off of the top of a cup. Also ABUNDANCE, ABUNDANT, ADEQUATE, AMPLE, ENOUGH, SUBSTANTIAL, SUFFICIENT.

PLOT (plot), *v.,* PLOTTED, PLOTTING. *Computer term.* (The "P" draws a graph.) The middle finger of the right "P" hand makes up-down zigzag movements on the left palm as it moves from the heel of the hand to the fingertips.

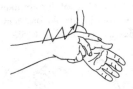

PLOW (plou), *n.* (The action of the plow's blade in making a furrow.) The open right hand is placed upright in a perpendicular position on the upturned left palm, with the little finger edge resting in the palm. The right hand moves forward along the left palm. As it does so, it swings over to a palm-down position and moves off a bit to the right. Also FARM 1.

PLOWER (plou′ ər), *n.* The sign for PLOW is made. This is followed by the sign for INDIVIDUAL 1: both open hands, palms facing each other, move down the sides of the body, tracing its outline to the hips.

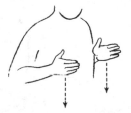

PLUG (plug), *n., v.,* PLUGGED, PLUGGING. (The plug is inserted in the socket.) The downturned right "V" hand is thrust against the upturned left index finger so that the finger is impaled between the right index and middle fingers.

PLUM (plum), *n.* (The texture, likened to a smooth cheek.) The thumb and index and middle fingers, held apart, are placed at the cheek. They move away and back repeatedly. Each time they move off, the three fingers come together.

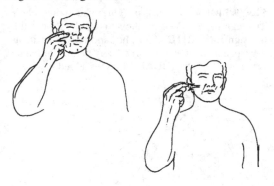

PLURAL (plŏŏr′ əl), *adj.* (Many fingers are indicated.) The upturned "S" hands are thrown up, opening into the "5" position, palms up. This may be repeated. Also MANY, MULTIPLE, NUMEROUS, QUANTITY 2.

PLUS (plŭs), *prep., n.* (A mathematical symbol.) The two index fingers are crossed at right angles. Also ADD 2, ADDITION, POSITIVE 2.

POCKET CALCULATOR, *n.* (The action of the fingers.) The right fingers wriggle up and down over the upturned left palm, as if manipulating the keys of a calculator.

POEM 1 (pō′ əm), *n.* (The letter "P"; the waving hand denotes rhythm.) The right "P" hand swings back and forth rhythmically over the open left hand, whose palm faces the body. The right hand may also describe a figure-eight movement instead of the back-and-forth movement. Also POETRY, PSALM.

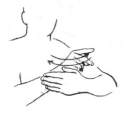

POEM 2, *n.* (Taking from the heart.) The signer grasps at the heart and throws the hand forward and open, with the palm up.

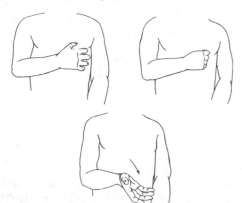

POISON 1 (poi′ zən), *n.* (Mixing of medicine; rolling a pill.) The ball of the middle fingertip of the right "5" hand describes a small counterclockwise circle in the upturned left palm. Also DRUG, MEDICINE, PRESCRIPTION.

POISON 2, *n.* (The letter "P"; something taken by mouth.) The middle finger and thumb of the right "P" hand touch the lips repeatedly.

POISON 3, *n.* (The crossed bones.) Both "S" hands are crossed and held against the chest. The signer bares the teeth, in imitation of a skull.

POKER (pō′ kər), *n.* The slightly curved left index finger, pointing slightly up and out, moves in and out from the body, an inch or so.

POLAR BEAR *n.* (A white bear.) The sign for BEAR is made: both claw hands, crossed, scratch the shoulders several times. This is followed by WHITE: the right "5" hand is placed against the chest, palm facing the body. The hand moves forward once or twice; each time the fingertips come together.

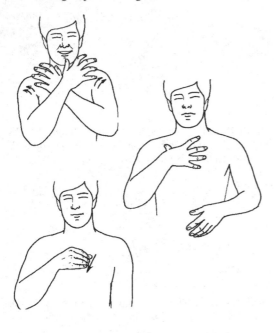

POLICE (pə lēs′), *n., v.,* -LICED, -LICING. (The letter "C" for "cop"; the shape and position of the badge.) The right "C" hand, palm facing left, is placed against the heart. Also COP, POLICEMAN, SHERIFF.

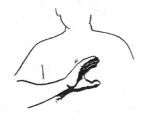

POLICEMAN (pə lēs′ mən), *n.* See POLICE.

POLICY 1 (pŏl′ ə sē), *n.* (Placing things in order.) The hands, palms facing, fingers together and pointing away from the body, are positioned at the left side and

held about a foot apart. With a slight up-down motion, as if describing waves, the hands travel in unison from left to right. Also ARRANGE, ARRANGEMENT, CLASSED 2, DEVISE 1, ORDER 3, PLAN 1, PREPARE 1, PROGRAM 1, PROVIDE 1, PUT IN ORDER, READY 1, SCHEME, SYSTEM.

POLICY 2, *n.* (A thought coming forward from the mind, modified by the letter "I" for "idea.") With the "I" position on the right hand, palm facing the body, touch the little finger to the forehead, and then move the hand up and away in a circular, clockwise motion. The hand may also be moved up and away without this circular motion. Also CONCEIVE 2, CONCEPT 1, CONCEPTION, FANCY 2, IDEA, IMAGINATION, IMAGINE 1, JUST THINK OF IT!, NOTION, THEORY, THOUGHT 2.

POLICY 3, *n.* (The letter "P"; the law, as spelled out on the outstretched page.) The right "P" hand rests on the fingertips of the outstretched left palm. The right hand moves down to the heel of the left palm.

POLISH 1 (pŏl′ ĭsh) (*voc.*), *n., v.,* -ISHED, -ISHING. (The act of rubbing.) The right knuckles rub briskly

against the outstretched left palm. Also RUB, SANDPA-
PER, SHINE SHOES.

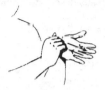

POLISH 2 (pō′ lĭsh), *adj*. See POLAND.

POLITE (pə līt′), *adj*. (The ruffled shirtfront of a gentleman of old.) The thumb of the right "5" hand is thrust
into the chest. The hand then pivots down, with thumb
remaining in place. This latter part of the sign, however,
is optional. Also COURTEOUS, COURTESY, FINE 4.

POLITICAL (pə lit′ i kəl), *adj*. (The letter "P"; at the
head.) The right "P" hand, held facing the side of the
head, makes a clockwise circle and comes to rest with
the little finger touching the right temple.

POLKA DOTS (pō′ kə), *n*. (The shape.) With the right
"F" hand forming a circle, the hand moves at random
around the chest.

POLLUTE 1 (pə lōōt′), *v.*, -LUTED, -LUTING. (Spreading poison.) The middle finger of the right "P" hand
makes a small clockwise circle in the upturned left
palm. This is a sign for POISON. The downturned
hands then spread out in a counterclockwise arc.

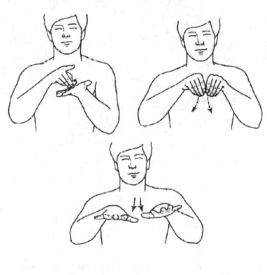

POLLUTE 2, *v*. (Spreading dirt.) The downturned
open hand is placed under the chin, where the fingers
wriggle. This is the sign for DIRT. The downturned
hand then spreads out in a counterclockwise arc.

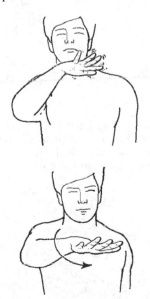

POLO (pō′ lō), *n.* (The polo playing.) The signer, holding a pair of imaginary reins and moving as if on horseback, swings an imaginary polo mallet, hitting a ball on the ground.

PONCE (pôn′ sā), *n.* (The letter "P"; the Arawak Indian headdress.) The right "P" hand is placed at the forehead and moves back over the head. A native sign in Puerto Rico.

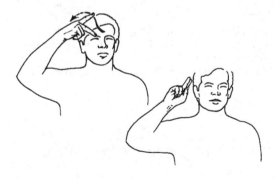

POND (pŏnd), *n.* (The letter "P"; the space and shimmering water.) The right "P" hand describes a counterclockwise circle, while the hand trembles slightly, as if reflecting the shimmering water.

PONDER (pŏn′ dər), *v.,* -DERED, -DERING. (Turning thoughts over in the mind.) Both index fingers, pointing to the forehead, describe continuous alternating circles. Also CONSIDER 2, CONTEMPLATE, SPECULATE 2, SPECULATION 2, WEIGH 2, WONDER 1.

POOL 1 (pōōl), *v.,* POOLED, POOLING. (Paying in.) The "AND" hands are held about a foot apart in front of the body, with fingertips facing each other and palms toward the chest. From this position the hands move downward and toward each other in an arc. At the same time, both thumbs slide forward along the index fingers. Also CHIP IN.

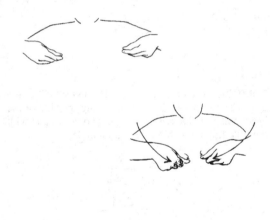

POOL 2, *n.* (The game of pool.) The signer, hunched over an imaginary cue stick, mimes striking the ball. Also BILLIARDS.

POOR 1 (pŏŏr), *adj.* (Ragged elbows.) The open right hand is placed at the left elbow. It moves down and off, closing into the "O" position. Also POVERTY 1.

POOR 2, *adj.* (The drawn face.) The thumb and index finger run down the cheeks, which are drawn in. Also LEAN 1, THIN 1.

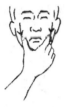

POOR 3, *adj.* (Feelings from the heart conferred on others.) The middle fingertip of the open right hand touches the chest over the heart. The same open hand then moves in a small, clockwise circle before the right shoulder, with palm facing forward and fingers pointing up. Also MERCY 2, PITY, SYMPATHY 2.

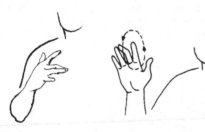

POP 1 (pŏp), *n.* (Corking a bottle.) The left "O" hand is held with thumb edge up, representing a bottle. The thumb and index finger of the right "5" hand, representing a cork, are inserted into the circle formed by the "O" hand. The palm of the open right hand then strikes down on the upturned edge of the "O" hand as if forcing the cork into the bottle. Also SODA POP, SODA WATER.

POP 2 (*informal*), *n.* (Derived from the formal sign for FATHER 1, *q.v.*) The thumbtip of the right "5" hand touches the right temple a number of times. The other fingers may also wiggle. Also DAD, DADDY, FATHER 2, PAPA.

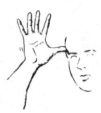

POPCORN (pŏp′ kôrn), *n.* (The popping.) The index fingers alternately flick up.

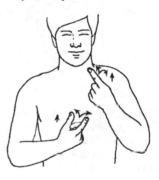

POPSICLE (pŏp′ si kəl), *n.* (Licking the popsicle.) The index and middle fingers of either hand, held together, are brought up repeatedly to the outstretched tongue.

POPULAR 1 (pop′ yǝ lǝr), *adj., arch.* (Known widely.) The downturned "5" hand is placed on the right forehead with index finger at the temple. The hand swings out in an arc, moving over to the left side.

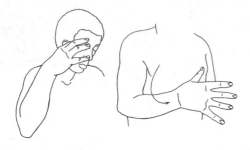

POPULAR 2, *adj.* (Surrounded on all sides.) The downturned right claw hand rests on the tip of the upturned left index finger.

POPULATION 1 (pŏp′ yǝ lā′ shǝn), *n.* (The letter "P"; an encompassing movement.) The "P" hands are held side by side, palms facing out. They swing out and around, describing a circle, and come together with little finger edges touching.

POPULATION 2, *n.* (Running through many individuals.) The left "5" hand is held palm facing the body. The right "P" hand sweeps over the outstretched left fingers, starting at the little finger.

POP UP (*colloq.*), *v.* (Popping up before the eyes.) The right index finger, pointing up, pops up between the index and middle fingers of the left hand, whose palm faces down. Also APPEAR 2, RISE 2.

PORCELAIN (pōr′ sǝ lǐn, pōrs′ lǐn), *n.* (The finger touches a brittle substance.) The index finger is brought up to touch the exposed front teeth. Also BONE, CHINA 2, DISH, GLASS 1, PLATE.

PORCUPINE (pôr′ kyǝ pīn), *n.* (The outstretched quills.) The right "S" hand rests on the back of the left "S" hand. The right hand, moving down to the fingers of the left, opens wide, the fingers representing outstretched quills.

PORTION (pōr′ shǝn), *n.* (Cutting off or designating a part.) The little finger edge of the open right hand moves straight down the middle of the upturned left palm. Also PART 1, PIECE, SECTION, SHARE 1, SOME.

PORTUGAL (pôr′ chə gəl), *n.* (The coastline looks like a human profile.) The right index finger moves down the face, from forehead to chin, tracing the outline of the features. A native sign.

POSITION 1 (pə zĭsh′ ən), *n.* (The letter "P"; a circle or square is indicated to show the locale or place.) The "P" hands are held side by side before the body, with middle fingertips touching. From this position, the hands separate and outline a circle (or a square), before coming together again closer to the body. Also LOCATION, PLACE 1, SCENE, SITE.

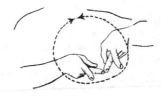

POSITION 2, *n.* (An area is outlined.) With the "I" hands held palms up and the tips of the little fingers touching, the hands separate as they move in toward the body. As they do, the tips of the little fingers come together again. Also PLACE 2.

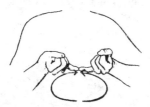

POSITION 3, *n.* (The feet planted on the ground.) The downturned right "V" fingers are thrust into the upturned left palm. Also STAND 1, STANDING.

POSITIVE 1 (pŏz′ ə tĭv), *adj.* (Coming forth directly from the lips; true.) The index finger of the right "D" hand, palm facing left, is placed against the lips. It moves up an inch or two and then describes a small arc forward and away from the lips. It moves up an inch or two and then describes a small arc forward and away from the lips. Also ABSOLUTE, ABSOLUTELY, ACTUAL, ACTUALLY, AUTHENTIC, CERTAIN, CERTAINLY, FAITHFUL 3, FIDELITY, FRANKLY, GENUINE, INDEED, POSITIVELY, REAL, REALLY, SINCERE 2, SURE, SURELY, TRUE, TRULY, TRUTH, VALID, VERILY.

POSITIVE 2, *adj.* (A mathematical symbol.) The two index fingers are crossed at right angles in the sign for PLUS. Also ADD 2, ADDITION, PLUS.

POSITIVELY, *adv.* See POSITIVE 1.

POSSESS 1 (pə zĕs′), *v.*, -SESSED, -SESSING. (A modification of HAVE 1.) The hands are crossed over each other as they rest on the chest. Also HAVE 3.

POSSESS 2, *v.* (The act of bringing something over to oneself.) The right-angle hands, palms facing and thumbs pointing up, are swept toward the body until the fingertips come to rest against the middle of the chest. Also HAVE 1.

POSSIBILITY (pŏs′ ə bĭl′ ə tĭ), *n.* (Weighing one thing against another.) The upturned open hands move alternately up and down. Also GUESS 4, MAY 1, MAYBE, MIGHT 2, PERHAPS, POSSIBLY, PROBABLE, PROBABLY, SUPPOSE.

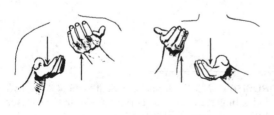

POSSIBLE (pŏs′ ə bəl), *adj.* (An affirmative movement of the hands, likened to a nodding of the head, to indicate ability or power to accomplish something.) Both "A" hands, held palms down, move down in unison a short distance before the chest. Also ABILITY, ABLE, CAN 1, CAPABLE, COMPETENT, COULD, FACULTY, MAY 2.

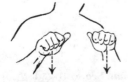

POSSIBLY (pŏs′ ə blĭ), *adv.* See POSSIBILITY.

POST- 2, *prefix* (The letter "P"; something afterward.) The left open hand, held horizontally, is positioned facing the chest. The right "P" hand, placed against the back of the left, moves straight forward a short distance.

POST OFFICE *n.* (A fingerspelled loan sign.) The signer fingerspells "P-O."

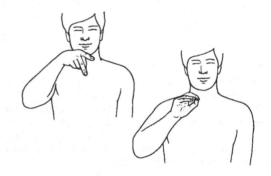

POSTPONE (pōst pōn′), *v.*, -PONED, -PONING. (Putting off; moving things forward repeatedly.) The "F" hands, palms facing and fingers pointing out from the body, are moved forward simultaneously in a series of short movements. Also DEFER, DELAY, PROCRASTINATE, PUT OFF.

POT 1 (pŏt), *n.* (The natural shape.) The cupped hands form a bowl and move up a bit to indicate the height. Also BOWL 1.

POT 2, *n. sl.* (The act of smoking marijuana.) The signer mimes holding the marijuana cigarette to the lips and inhaling deeply. Also MARIJUANA.

POTATO (pə tā′ tō), *n.* (The fork is thrust into the potato.) The downturned left "S" hand represents the potato. The slightly bent fingers of the right "V" hand are thrust repeatedly against the back of the left hand.

POTATO CHIP (pə tā′ tō chĭp) *n.* (Breaking a chip with the teeth.) The sign for POTATO is made: the downturned right index and middle fingers are thrust repeatedly onto the left fist. The signer then mimes breaking a potato chip with the teeth.

POUND 1 (pound), *n.* (The balancing of the scale is described.) The fingers of the right "H" hand are centered on the left index finger and rocked back and forth. Also SCALE 2, WEIGH 1, WEIGHT.

POUND 2 (*rare*), *n.* (A small amount of weight.) The slightly curved right index finger exerts a small amount of downward pressure as it rests on the down-turned left index finger.

POUND 3, *v.,* POUNDED, POUNDING. (The natural sign.) The right "S" hand strikes its knuckles forcefully against the open left palm, which is held facing right. Also HIT 1, PUNCH 1, STRIKE 1.

POVERTY 1 (pŏv′ ər tĭ), *n.* (Ragged elbows.) The open right hand is placed at the left elbow. It moves down and off, closing into the "O" position. Also POOR 1.

POVERTY 2, *n.* (The knuckles are rubbed to indicate a condition of being worn down.) The knuckles of the curved index and middle fingers of both hands are rubbed up and down against each other. Instead of the up-down rubbing, they may rub against each other in an alternate clockwise/counterclockwise manner. Also DIFFICULT 1, DIFFICULTY, HARD 1, HARDSHIP, PROBLEM 2.

POWDER 1 (pou′ dər) *n., v.,* -DERED, -DERING. (Sprinkling powder or talc on the body.) The signer shakes an imaginary powder container on the chest.

POWDER 2 (pou′ dər), *n. v.* (The natural sign.) The open right hand pats the right cheek several times, as if applying face powder.

POWDER 3, *n.* (White material blown off the hand.) The sign for WHITE is made: the fingertips of the "5" hand are placed against the chest. The hand moves straight out from the chest while the fingers and thumb all come together. The right fingertips then feel the texture of an imaginary pinch of powder. The right hand is then opened and brought up to the mouth, which blows the powder away. The sign for WHITE is often omitted.

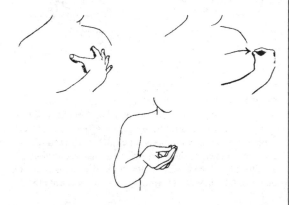

POWER 1 (pou′ ər), *n.* (Flexing the muscles.) With fists clenched, palms facing back, the signer raises

both arms and shakes them, once, with force. Also MIGHT 1, MIGHTY 1, POWERFUL 1, STRONG 1, STURDY, TOUGH 1.

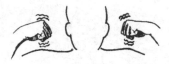

POWER 2, *n.* (The curve of the flexed biceps is indicated.) The left hand, clenched into a fist, is held up, palm facing the body. The index finger of the right "D" hand moves in an arc over the left biceps muscle from shoulder to crook of the elbow. Also MIGHT 3, POWERFUL 2.

POWERFUL 1 (pou′ ər fəl), *adj.* See POWER 1.

POWERFUL 2, *adj.* See POWER 2.

PRACTICE 1 (prăk′ tĭs), *n., v.,* -TICED, -TICING. (Polishing or sharpening up.) The knuckles of the downturned right "A" hand are rubbed briskly back and forth over the side of the hand and index finger of the left "D" hand. Also DISCIPLINE 1, DRILL 3, TRAIN 2, TRAINING 1.

PRACTICE 2 (*rare*), *v.* (Same rationale as for PRAC-TICE 1.) The knuckles of both "A" hands, palms facing, sweep past each other repeatedly, coming in contact each time they do.

PRACTICE 3, *n., v.* (Bound down to custom or habit.) Both "S" hands, palms down, are crossed and brought down in unison before the chest. Also ACCUSTOM, BOUND, CUSTOM, HABIT, LOCKED.

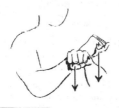

PRAISE (prāz), *n., v.,* PRAISED, PRAISING. (Good words coming from the mouth; clapping hands.) The fingertips of the right hand, palm flat and facing the body, are brought up to the lips so that they touch (part of the sign for GOOD, *q.v.*). The hands are then clapped together several times. Also ACCLAIM 2, APPLAUD, APPLAUSE, APPROBATION, APPROVAL, APPROVE, CLAP, COMMEND, CONGRATULATE 1, CONGRATULATIONS 1.

PRAM (pram), *n.* (Rocking back and forth.) The signer mimes grasping a pram's handle and rocking it back and forth. Also CARRIAGE.

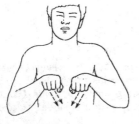

PRANCE (prans, präns), *n., v.,* PRANCED, PRANCING. (The high stepping of a horse.) Both downturned hands are held with curved index and middle fingers. The hands move alternately up and down while the signer's body moves slightly up and down, keeping time with the rhythm of the moving hands. The index fingers alone may also be used.

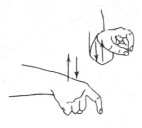

PRE- (prē), *adv. prefix.* (The letter "P.") The right "P" hand, placed behind the open left hand, moves straight back toward the body.

PREACH (prēch), *v.,* PREACHED, PREACHING. (Placing morsels of wisdom or food for thought into the mind.) The right hand, palm out, with thumb and index finger touching, is moved forward and slightly downward a number of times from its initial position near the right temple. Also SERMON.

PREACHER (prē′ chər), *n.* The sign for PREACH is made. This is followed by the sign for INDIVIDUAL 1: both open hands, palms facing each other, move down the sides of the body, tracing its outline to the hips. Also MINISTER, PASTOR.

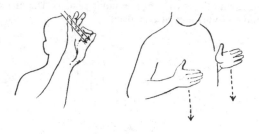

PRECIOUS 1 (prĕsh′ əs), *adj.* Both "F" hands, palms facing each other, move apart, up, and together in a smooth elliptical fashion, coming together at the tips of the thumbs and index fingers of both hands. Also DESERVE, ESSENTIAL, IMPORTANT 1, MAIN, MERIT, PROMINENT 2, SIGNIFICANCE 1, SIGNIFICANT, VALUABLE, VALUE, VITAL 1, WORTH, WORTHWHILE, WORTHY.

PRECIOUS 2, *adj.* The right claw hand, palm facing the signer, is placed against the chin and closes into a fist. This sign originally denoted a Jew, particularly a bearded Eastern Jew or Shylock, one who is selfish, conniving, manipulative. It is thus, on the face of it, a highly derogatory and disparaging sign. In its present form, PRECIOUS 2 actually refers to covetousness, unwillingness to share, and keeping things exclusively for oneself. Also TREASURE.

PRECISE (prĭ sīs′), *adj.* (The fingers come together precisely.) The thumb and index finger of each hand, palms facing, the right above the left, form circles. They are brought together with a deliberate movement so that the fingers and thumbs now touch. Sometimes the right hand, before coming together with the left, executes a slow clockwise circle above the left. Also ACCURATE 1, EXACT 1, EXACTLY, EXPLICIT 1, SPECIFIC.

PREDECESSOR (pred′ ə ses′ ər), *n.* (One who is behind or before.) Both open hands, palms facing the body, are held over the right breast, the right in front of the left. The right hand swings up and over the right shoulder, leaving the left behind.

PREDICT (prĭ dĭkt′), *v.,* -DICTED, -DICTING. (The vision is directed forward into the distance.) The right "V" fingertips are placed under the eyes, with palm facing the body. The hand is then swung around and forward, moving under the downturned prone left hand and continuing forward and upward. Also FORECAST, FORESEE, FORETELL, PERCEIVE 2, PROPHECY, PROPHESY, PROPHET, VISION 2.

PREFER 1 (prĭ fûr′), *v.,* -FERRED, -FERRING. (More good.) The fingertips of one hand are placed at the lips, as if tasting something (*vide,* GOOD). Then the hand is moved up to a position just above the head, where it assumes the "A" position, thumb up. Also BETTER.

PREFER 2, *v.* (To the taste.) The middle finger of the right "5" hand, palm facing the body, touches the lip once or twice.

PREFER 3, *v.* (A variant of PREFER 1.) Instead of the right fingertips resting on the lips initially, they rest on the middle of the chest. The hand then moves up as before.

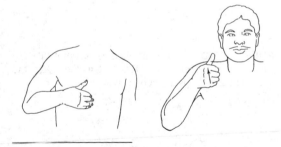

PREGNANT 1 (preg′ nənt), *adj.* One or both open hands are placed on the stomach and move forward an inch or two to indicate the swollen belly.

PREGNANT 2, *adj.* (Same as PREGNANT 1.) The hands interlock.

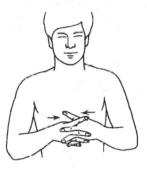

PREGNANT 3, *adj.* (Impaled by a forklike implement, *i.e,* stuck.) The index and middle fingers are thrust quickly into the throat. This would refer to an unwanted pregnancy, *i.e.,* "stuck with it."

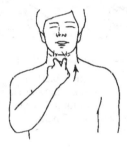

PREPARE 1 (prĭ pâr′), *v.,* -PARED, -PARING. (Placing things in order.) The hands, palms facing, fingers together and pointing away from the body, are positioned at the left side and held about a foot apart. With a slight up-down motion, as if describing waves, the hands travel in unison from left to right. Also ARRANGE, ARRANGEMENT, CLASSED 2, DEVISE 1, ORDER 3, PLAN 1, POLICY 1, PROGRAM 1, PROVIDE 1, PUT IN ORDER, READY 1, SCHEME, SYSTEM.

PREPARE 2, v. (The "R" hands, for READY.) The "R" hands are held side by side before the body, palms up and fingers pointing outward. The hands then turn toward each other and over, so that the palms face down and fingers point toward each other. Also READY 2.

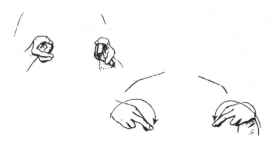

PREPARE 3, v. (Set out.) The hands are crossed, with the right resting on top of the left. The right palm faces left and the left palm faces right. Both hands suddenly open and swing apart to the palm-down position. Also READY 4.

PRESBYTERIAN 1 (prĕz′ bə tĭr′ ĭ ən, prĕs′-) (eccles.), n., adj. (The act of standing and singing in church.) The tips of the downturned, right "V" fingers are placed in the upturned left palm.

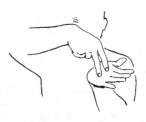

PRESBYTERIAN 2, n., adj. Like PRESBYTERIAN 1, but using the middle finger of the right "P" hand.

PRESCHOOL (prē′ sko͞ol′, prē′ sko͞ol′), n., adj. (The prefix PRE- followed by SCHOOL.) The prefix PRE- is followed by a clapping of the hands, the sign for SCHOOL.

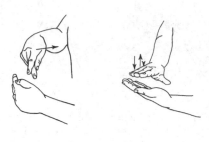

PRESCRIPTION 1 (prĭ skrĭp′ shən), n. (Mixing of medicine; rolling a pill.) The ball of the middle finger-tip of the right "5" hand describes a small counter-clockwise circle in the upturned left palm. Also DRUG, MEDICINE, POISON 1.

PRESCRIPTION 2, n. (The medical symbol "R-X.") The signer fingerspells "R-X." On the "X," the spelling hand drops an inch or two.

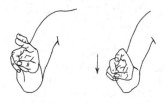

PRESENCE (prĕz′ əns), n. (Face-to-face.) The left hand, fingers together, palm flat and facing the eyes, is held a bit above eye level. The right hand, fingers also together, is held in front of the mouth with palm facing the left hand. With a sweeping upward movement the right hand moves toward the left, which moves straight up an inch or two at the same time. Also

APPEAR 3, APPEARANCE, BEFORE 3, CONFRONT, FACE 2, FACE-TO-FACE.

PRESENT 1 (prĕz′ ənt), *n.* (An offering; a presenting.) Both hands, slightly cupped, palms up, are held close to the chest. They move up and out in unison, describing a very slight arc. Also BID 2, MOTION 1, OFFER 1, OFFERING 1, PROPOSE, SUGGEST, TENDER 2.

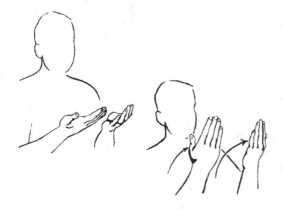

PRESENT 2 (*n.* prĕz′ ənt; *v.* prĭ zĕnt′), -SENTED, -SENT-ING. (A giving of something.) Both "A" hands, with index fingers somewhat draped over the tips of the thumbs, are held palms facing in front of the chest. They are pivoted forward and down in unison from the wrists. Also AWARD, BEQUEATH, BESTOW, CONFER, CONSIGN, CONTRIBUTE, GIFT.

PRESENT 3, *adj.* (Something right in front of you.) The upturned right-angle hands drop down rather

sharply. The "Y" hands may also be used. Also CURRENT, IMMEDIATE, NOW.

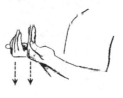

PRESERVE (prĭ zûrv′), *v.,* -SERVED, -SERVING. (Slow, careful movement.) The "K" hands are crossed, the right above the left, little finger edges down. In this position the hands are moved up and down a short distance. Also CARE 2, CAREFUL 2, KEEP, MAINTAIN 1, MIND 3, RESERVE 2, TAKE CARE OF 2.

PRESIDENT (prĕz′ ə dənt), *n.* The "C" hands, held palms out at either temple, close over imaginary horns and move up a bit to either side, tracing the shape of the horns. Also HORNS, SUPERINTENDENT.

PRESS 1 (prĕs), *v.,* PRESSED, PRESSING. (The act of pressing with an iron.) The right hand goes through the motion of swinging an iron back and forth over the upturned left palm. Also FLATIRON, IRON 2.

PRESS 2, v. (The act of pressing clothes.) The downturned "S" hands swing down in unison as if manipulating a tailor's steam press.

PRESS 3, v. (The act of pressing something together with the hands.) The ball of the right "5" hand is pressed against the upturned left palm. The right hand may turn back and forth, maintaining its pressure against the left. Also SQUASH 2.

PRESSURE (presh′ ər), n. (Pushing down.) The left index finger, pointing forward, is pushed down by the downturned right hand. The signer assumes an expression of intensity.

PRETEND (pri tend′), v., -TENDED, -TENDING. (Changing the face.) The right "5" hand is placed palm out against the nose. It moves forward, and the fingers come together against the thumb and touch their left counterparts.

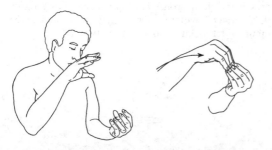

PRETTY (prĭt′ ē), adj. (Literally, a good face.) The right hand, fingers closed over the thumb, is placed at or just below the lips (indicating a tasting of something GOOD, q.v.). It then describes a counterclockwise circle around the face, opening into the "5" position, to indicate the whole face. At the completion of the circling movement the hand comes to rest in its initial position, at or just below the lips. Also ATTRACTIVE 2, BEAUTIFUL, BEAUTY, EXQUISITE, SPLENDID 3.

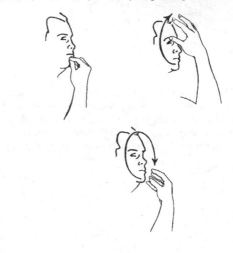

PRETZEL (pret′ səl), n. (The shape.) Both "R" hands trace the twisted shape of a pretzel.

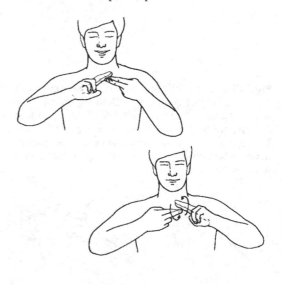

PREVENT (prĭ vĕnt′), v., -VENTED, -VENTING. (Obstruct, block.) The left hand, fingers together and palm flat, is held before the body, facing somewhat down. The little finger side of the right hand, held with palm flat, makes one or several up-down chopping motions against the left hand between its thumb and index finger. Also ANNOY 1, ANNOYANCE 1, BLOCK, BOTHER 1, CHECK 2, COME BETWEEN, DISRUPT, DISTURB, HINDER, HINDRANCE, IMPEDE, INTERCEPT, INTERFERE, INTERFERENCE, INTERFERE WITH, INTERRUPT, MEDDLE 1, OBSTACLE, OBSTRUCT, PREVENTION.

PREVENTION (prǐ věn′ shən), *n.* See PREVENT.

PREVIOUS (prē′ vǐ əs), *adj.* (Something past, behind.) The upraised right hand, in the "5" position with palm facing the body, is held just above the right shoulder and is thrown back over it. Also AGO, FORMERLY, ONCE UPON A TIME, PAST, PREVIOUSLY, WAS, WERE.

PREVIOUSLY, *adv.* See PREVIOUS.

PRICE 1 (prīs), *n., v.,* PRICED, PRICING. (Amount of money is indicated.) The sign for MONEY is made: the upturned right hand, grasping some imaginary

bills, is brought down into the upturned left palm a number of times. The right hand then moves straight up, opening into the "5" position, palm up. Also HOW MUCH MONEY?, WHAT IS THE PRICE?

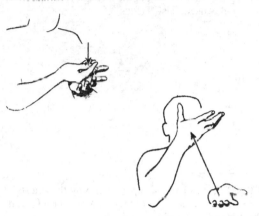

PRICE 2, *n., v.* (Nicking into one.) The knuckle of the right "X" finger is nicked against the palm of the left hand, held in the "5" position, palm facing right. Also ADMISSION 2, CHARGE 1, COST, DUTY 2, EXCISE, EXPENSE, FEE, FINE 2, IMPOST, PENALTY 3, TAX 1, TAXATION 1, TOLL.

PRIDE (prīd), *n., v.,* PRIDED, PRIDING. (The feelings rise up.) The thumb of the right "A" hand, palm down, moves up along the right side of the chest. A haughty expression is assumed. Also HAUGHTY, PROUD.

PRIEST 1 (prēst), *n.* (The ecclesiastical collar.) The thumbs and index fingers of both hands indicate the shape of the collar as they move around the neck, coming together in front of the throat. Sometimes only one hand is used. Also FATHER 3.

PRIEST 2, *n.* (The breastplate worn by the priests of the Old Testament.) The index fingers, placed on the chest, describe the shape of the breastplate.

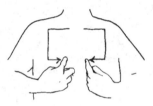

PRIEST 3, *n.* (Modified sign of the cross.) The right "4" hand, palm facing the body, is drawn down the middle of the chest, almost to the waist. The same hand is then drawn across the chest, from the left shoulder to the right shoulder.

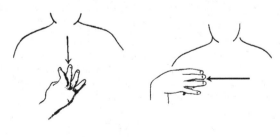

PRIEST 4, *n.* (The sign of the Oremus at Mass.) The "F" hands, palms facing and thumb sides facing up, are joined at their respective fingertips. They separate, move apart and toward the body in half circles, and

come together again in their initial position, closer to the body than before. Also RECTOR, REVEREND.

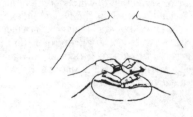

PRINCE (prĭns), *n.* (The letter "P"; the sash worn by royalty.) The MALE root sign is made: the thumb and extended fingers of the right hand are brought up to grasp an imaginary cap brim, representing the tipping of caps by men in olden days. The right "P" hand then moves from the left shoulder to the right waist.

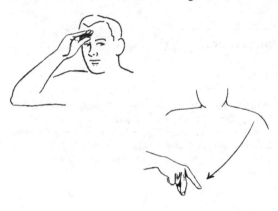

PRINCESS (prĭn′ sĭs), *n.* (The letter "P"; the sash worn by royalty.) The FEMALE root sign is made: the thumb of the right "A" hand moves down along the line of the right jaw from ear almost to chin. The right "P" hand then moves from the left shoulder to the right waist.

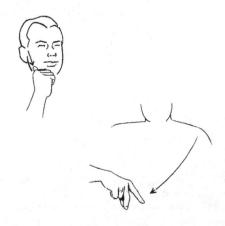

PRINCIPAL 1 (prĭn′ sə pəl), *n.* (The letter "P"; one who rules over others.) The downturned, right "P" hand is swung from right to left over the back of the prone left hand.

PRINCIPAL 2, *adj.* (The largest or greatest amount.) The sign for MUCH is made: the "5" hands, palms facing, fingers curved and thumbs pointing up, draw apart. The sign for the superlative suffix, "-EST," is then made: the right "A" hand, thumb pointing up, quickly moves straight upward until it is above the head. The MUCH sign may be omitted. Also CHIEF, MAINLY, MOST, MOST OF ALL.

PRINCIPLE (prĭn′ sə pəl), *n.* (A collection or listing is indicated by the open palm, representing a page.) The right "P" hand is placed against the upper part of the open left hand, which faces right, fingers pointing upward. The right "P" hand swings down to the lower part of the left palm. Also DOCTRINE 1.

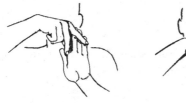

PRINT 1 (prĭnt), *v.*, PRINTED, PRINTING. (Placing type in a printer's stick.) The upturned, left "5" hand represents the printer's stick. The right index finger and thumb close over an imaginary piece of type and place it in the left palm. Also PUBLISH 2.

PRINT 2, *v.* (The act of printing block letters.) The right index finger traces letters in the upturned left palm.

PRIORITY 1 (prī ôr′ ə tē), *n.* (The letter "P"; touching the first finger.) The middle finger of the right "P" hand touches the left thumbtip.

PRIORITY 2, *n.* (The letter "P"; scanning things to see which is first.) The middle finger of the right "P" hand travels over the fingertips of the left open hand, from little finger to thumb. The left palm faces right or straight up.

PRISON (prĭz′ ən), *n.* (The crossed bars.) The "4" hands, palms facing the body, are crossed at the fingers. Also IMPRISON, JAIL, PENITENTIARY.

PRIVACY (prī′ və sĭ), *n.* (The sealing of the lips; keeping the words back.) The back of the thumb of the right "A" hand is placed firmly against the closed lips. The thumb, in this position, may move off the lips slightly and return again to the lips. As an optional addition, the thumb may swing down under the down-turned cupped left hand after being placed on the lips as above. Also DON'T TELL, PRIVATE 1, SECRET.

PRIVATE 1 (prī′ vĭt), *adj.* See PRIVACY.

PRIVATE 2 (*colloq.*), *adj.* (Closed.) Both open hands are held before the body, fingers pointing out, right palm facing left and left facing right. The right hand, held above the left, comes down against the index finger edge of the left a number of times.

PRIVATE 3, *n.* (The stripe on the uniform sleeve.) The right index finger traces the shape of the private's stripe on the left sleeve.

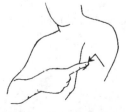

PRIVATE CONVERSATION (*colloq. phrase*). (Small give-and-take from the mouth.) The index and middle fingers of the right or left "V" hand move alternately back and forth on the lips.

PRIVILEGE (prĭv′ ə lĭj), *n.* (A straightening out.) The right hand, fingers together and palm facing left, is placed in the upturned left palm, whose fingers point away from the body. The right hand slides straight out along the left palm, over the left fingers, and stops with its heel resting on the left fingertips. Also ALL RIGHT, O.K. 1, RIGHT 1, RIGHTEOUS 1, YOU'RE WELCOME 2.

PRIZE (prīz), *n.* (Giving something.) Both "X" hands, palms facing, swing forward in an arc and somewhat down.

PRO (prō), *adj.* (Supporting.) The right fist pushes up its left counterpart.

PROBABLE (prŏb′ ə bəl), *adj.* (Weighing one thing against another.) The upturned open hands move alternately up and down. Also GUESS 4, MAY 1, MAYBE, MIGHT 2, PERHAPS, POSSIBILITY, POSSIBLY, PROBABLY, SUPPOSE.

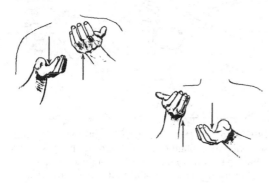

PROBABLY (prŏ′ ə blĭ), *adv.* See PROBABLE.

PROBE 1 (prōb), *v.,* PROBED, PROBING, *n.* (Directing the vision from place to place.) The right "C" hand, palm facing left, moves from right to left across the line of vision in a series of counterclockwise circles. The signer's gaze remains concentrated and his head turns slowly from right to left. Also CURIOUS 1, EXAMINE, INVESTIGATE 1, LOOK FOR, QUEST, SEARCH, SEEK.

PROBE 2, *v.* (Drilling.) The "S" hands revolve around each other in front of the chest, as if drilling a hole with a hand brace. Also PRY, PUMP 2.

PROBLEM 1 (prŏb′ ləm), *n.* (A clouding over; a troubling.) Both "B" hands, palms facing each other, are

rotated alternately before the forehead. Also ANNOY 2, ANNOYANCE 2, ANXIOUS 2, BOTHER 2, CONCERN 1, FRET, TROUBLE, WORRIED, WORRY 1.

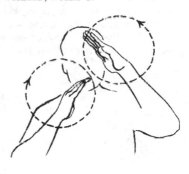

PROBLEM 2, *n.* (The knuckles are rubbed to indicate a condition of being worn down.) The knuckles of the curved index and middle fingers of both hands are rubbed up and down against each other. Instead of the up-down rubbing, they may rub against each other in an alternate clockwise/counterclockwise manner. Also DIFFICULT 1, DIFFICULTY, HARD 1, HARDSHIP, POVERTY 2.

PROBLEM 3, *n.* (Coming to grips.) The curved index and middle fingers of both hands, palms facing the body, are brought sharply into an interlocking position. The action may be repeated, this time with the wrists first twisted slightly in opposite directions.

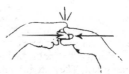

PROCEDURE (prə sē′ jər), *n.* (Step by step.) Both right-angle hands are placed in overlapping positions in front of the body, left fingers pointing right and right fingers pointing left. The right hand, located behind the left, jumps over the left and is now in front. The left hand does the same thing, ending up in front of the right. This is done two or three times.

PROCEED (prə sēd′), *v.,* -CEEDED, -CEEDING. (Moving forward.) Both right-angle hands, palms facing each other and knuckles facing forward, move forward simultaneously. Also FORWARD, GO AHEAD, MOTION FORWARD, ONWARD, PROGRESS 2, RESUME.

PROCRASTINATE (prō krăs′ tə nāt′), *v.,* -NATED, -NATING. (Putting off; moving things forward repeatedly.) The "F" hands, palms facing and fingers pointing out from the body, are moved forward simultaneously in a series of short movements. Also DEFER, DELAY, POSTPONE, PUT OFF.

PROCURE (prō kyŏŏr′), *v.,* -CURED, -CURING. (A grasping and bringing forward to oneself.) Both hands, in the "5" position, fingers curved, are crossed at the wrists, with the left palm facing right and the right palm facing left. They are brought in toward the chest while closing into a grasping "S" position. Also ACQUIRE, GET, OBTAIN, RECEIVE.

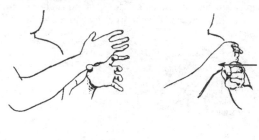

PROD (prŏd), *v.,* PRODDED, PRODDING. (Shaking someone to implant one's will into another.) Both "A" hands, palms facing, are held before the chest, the left slightly in front of the right. In this position the hands move back and forth a short distance. Also COAX, CONVINCE, INDUCE, PERSUADE, PERSUASION, URGE 2.

PRODUCE 1 (*n.* prŏd′ ūs; *v.* prə dūs′), -DUCED, -DUCING. (Carrying something over.) Both open hands, palms up, move in an arc from left to right as if carrying something from one point to another. Also BRING, CARRY 2, DELIVER 2, FETCH, TRANSPORT.

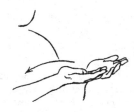

PRODUCE 2, *n., v.* (Directing the attention to something and bringing it forward.) The right index finger points into the left palm, held facing out before the body. The left palm moves straight out. For the passive form of this verb, *i.e.,* BE SHOWN, the movement is reversed: the left hand, palm facing in, is moved in toward the body, while the right index finger remains pointing into the left palm. Also DEMONSTRATE, DISPLAY, EVIDENCE, EXAMPLE, EXHIBIT, EXHIBI-

TION, ILLUSTRATE, INDICATE, INFLUENCE 3, REPRESENT, SHOW 1, SIGNIFY 1.

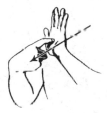

PRODUCE 3, *v.* (Fashioning something with the hands.) The right "S" hand, palm facing left, is placed on top of its left counterpart, whose palm faces right. The hands are twisted back and forth, striking each other slightly after each twist. Also COMPOSE, CONSTITUTE, CONSTRUCT 2, CREATE, DEVISE 2, FABRICATE, FASHION, FIX, MAKE, MANUFACTURE, MEND 1, RENDER 1, REPAIR.

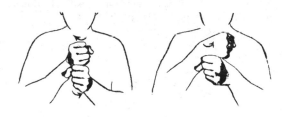

PRODUCE 4, *n., v.* (Rays of influence emanating from a given source.) All the right fingertips, including the thumb, are positioned on the tip of the upturned thumb of the left "A" hand. The right hand, opening into the downturned "5" position, moves forward from its initial position. Instead of its initial position on the left thumb, the right hand is frequently placed on the back of the downturned left "S" hand, moving forward as described above. Also BASIS 1, CAUSE, EFFECT 1, INFLUENCE 2, INTENT 2, LOGIC, REASON 2.

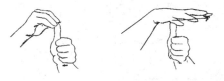

PRODUCER (prə dōō′ sər), *n.* (One who makes.) Both "P" hands are crossed, the right above the left. The hands are twisted back and forth, striking each

other after each twist. The sign for INDIVIDUAL 1 then follows.

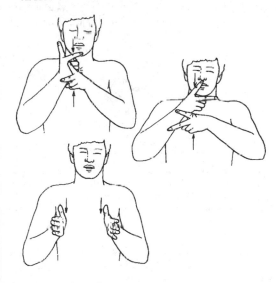

PRODUCT (prŏd′ əkt), *n.* The same sign as PRODUCER, but the INDIVIDUAL 1 sign is omitted.

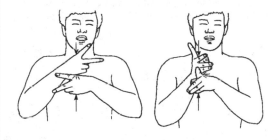

PRODUCTION (prə duk′ shən), *n.* The "P"s; making or fashioning something.) Both "P" hands are held one on top of the other, palms facing the signer, with the right fingertips pointing left and left fingertips pointing right. They turn forward repeatedly so that the fingertips are now facing forward. The movement is repeated several times.

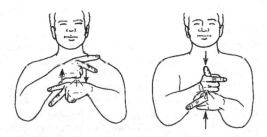

PROFESSION 1 (prə fĕsh′ ən), *n.* (The letter "F" for FIELD; straight line denotes a specific line or area of pursuit.) The thumb edge of the right "F" hand moves forward along the outstretched left index finger. Also FIELD 4.

PROFESSION 2 (prə fĕsh′ ən), *n.* (The letter "P"; the field or line.) The middle finger of the right "P" hand moves forward along the line of the outstretched, left index finger.

PROFILE (prō′ fīl), *n.* (Indicating a profile on the face.) The index finger slides down the face from the forehead, over the nose and down to the lips and chin. Also PORTUGAL.

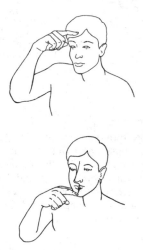

PROFIT (prŏf′ ĭt), *n., v.,* -FITED, -FITING. (To get a profit; a coin popped into the vest pocket.) The sign for GET is made: both outstretched hands, held in a grasping "5" position, close into "S" positions, with the right on top of the left. At the same time both hands are drawn in to the body. The thumb and index finger of the right hand, holding an imaginary coin,

are then popped into an imaginary vest or breast pocket. *Note:* the sign for GET is sometimes omitted. Also BENEFIT 2, GAIN 2.

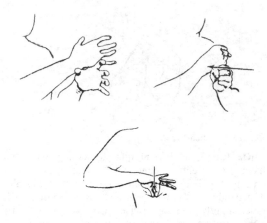

PROFOUND (prə found′), *adj.* (Something deep.) The downturned right index finger moves straight down the outfacing left palm. Also INTENSIVE.

PROGRAM 1 (prō′ grăm, -grəm), *n.* (Placing things in order.) The hands, palms facing, fingers together and pointing away from the body, are positioned at the left side and held about a foot apart. With a slight up-down motion, as if describing waves, the hands travel in unison from left to right. Also ARRANGE, ARRANGEMENT, CLASSED 2, DEVISE 1, ORDER 3, PLAN 1, POLICY 1, PREPARE 1, PROVIDE 1, PUT IN ORDER, READY 1, SCHEME, SYSTEM.

PROGRAM 2, *n.* (The letter "P"; a listing on both sides of the page.) The thumb side of the right "P" hand is placed against the palm of the open left hand, which is facing right. The right "P" hand moves down the left palm. The left hand then swings around so that its palm faces the body. The right "P" hand then moves down the back of the left hand.

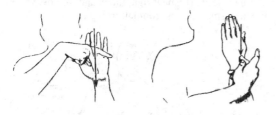

PROGRESS 1 (*n.* prŏg′ rĕs; *v.* prə grĕs′), -GRESSED, -GRESSING. (Moving forward step by step.) Both hands, in the right-angle position, palms facing, are held before the chest, a few inches apart, with the right hand slightly behind the left. The right hand is brought up, over, and forward so that it is now ahead of the left. The left hand then follows suit so that it is now ahead of the right. Also ADVANCE.

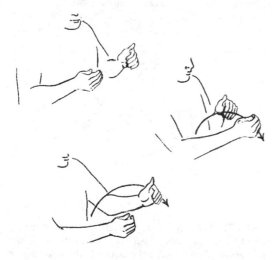

PROGRESS 2, *n.* See PROCEED.

PROHIBIT (prō hĭb′ ĭt), *v.*, -ITED, -ITING. (A modification of LAW, *q.v.;* "against the law.") The downturned right "D" or "L" hand is thrust forcefully into the left palm. Also BAN, FORBID 1, FORBIDDEN 1.

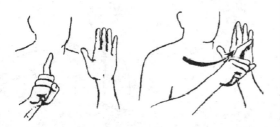

PROJECT (proj′ ekt), *n.* (The letters "P" and "J.") The middle finger of the right "P" hand moves down the left palm, held facing the body. Then the right "J" hand moves down the back of the left hand.

PROJECTOR (prə jek′ tər), *n.* (The image moves out.) The left hand is held upright, palm facing forward. The right fingers, resting on the right thumb, are placed on the left palm, which also faces forward. The right fingers move forward, away from the left palm, and open into the "5" shape.

PROLOGUE (prō′ lôg), *n.* (The "P"s; bringing together or introducing.) Both "P" hands are held side by side, palms up and fingertips facing each other. The hands are swung toward each other, stopping just before they touch.

PROMINENT 1 (prŏm′ ə nənt), *adj.* (One's fame radiates far and wide.) The extended index fingers rest on the lips (or on the temples). Moving in small, continuous spirals, they move up and to either side of the head. Also CELEBRATED, FAME, FAMOUS, RENOWNED.

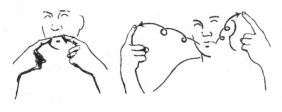

PROMINENT 2, *adj.* Both "F" hands, palms facing each other, move apart, up, and together in a smooth elliptical fashion, coming together at the tips of the thumbs and index fingers of both hands. Also DESERVE, ESSENTIAL, IMPORTANT 1, MAIN, MERIT, PRECIOUS, SIGNIFICANCE 1, SIGNIFICANT, VALUABLE, VALUE, VITAL 1, WORTH, WORTHWHILE, WORTHY.

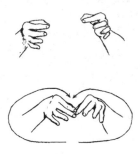

PROMINENT 3, *adj.* (Indicating height.) The right "A" hand, held with thumb pointing upward, moves straight up above the right shoulder. Also HIGH 2, SUPERIOR.

PROMISCUOUS 1 (prə mis′ kyōō əs), *adj.* (Traveling from one person to the next.) The left "5" hand faces down or right. The bent right index and middle fingers move in small jumps from left to right.

PROMISCUOUS 2, *adj., sl.* (One whose legs are separated.) Both "X" hands, palms down, move up to the palms-out position. This sign is used only for a female.

PROMISE 1 (prŏm′ ĭs), *n., v.,* -ISED, -ISING. (The arm is raised.) The right index finger is placed at the lips. The right arm is then raised, palm out and elbow resting on the back of the left hand. Also GUARANTEE 1, LOYAL, OATH, PLEDGE, SWEAR 1, SWORN, TAKE OATH, VOW.

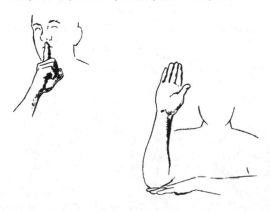

PROMISE 2, *n., v.* (Sealing the word.) The right index finger is placed at the lips, as in PROMISE 1. The open right hand is then brought down against the upturned left hand.

PROMISE 3, *n., v.* (A variation of PROMISE 2.) The right index finger is placed at the lips, as in PROMISE 1. The open right hand is then brought down against the thumb side of the left "S" hand.

PROMOTE (prə mōt′), *v.,* -MOTED, -MOTING. (Something high up.) Both hands, in the right-angle position, are held before the face, about a foot apart, palms facing. They are raised abruptly about a foot, in a slight outward curving movement. Also ADVANCED, HIGH 1, PROMOTION.

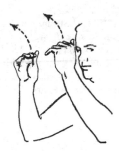

PROMOTION (prə mō′ shən), *n.* See PROMOTE.

PROOF (proof), *n.* (Laying out the proof for all to see.) The back of the open right hand is placed with a

flourish on the open left palm. The index finger may first touch the lips. Also PROVE.

PROPER (prŏp′ ər), *adj.* The right index finger, held above the left index finger, comes down rather forcefully so that the bottom of the right hand comes to rest on top of the left thumb joint. Also ACCURATE 2, CORRECT 1, DECENT, EXACT 2, JUST 2, RIGHT 3, SUITABLE

PROPHECY (prŏf′ ə sĭ), *n.* (The vision is directed forward into the distance.) The right "V" fingertips are placed under the eyes, with palm facing the body. The hand is then swung around and forward, moving under the downturned prone left hand and continuing forward and upward. Also FORECAST, FORESEE, FORETELL, PERCEIVE 2, PREDICT, PROPHESY, PROPHET, VISION 2.

PROPHESY (prŏf′ ə sī), *v.,* -SIED, -SYING. See PROPHECY.

PROPHET (prŏf′ ĭt), *n.* See PROPHECY.

PROPORTION (prə pōr′ shən), *n.* (In proportion.) Both "D" or "P" hands, palms facing down, are held before the body. They describe a short arc from right to left and, while unnecessary, they may return to their original position. Also HENCE, RATIO, THEREFORE 1, THUS.

PROPOSE (prə pōz′), *v.,* -POSED, -POSING. (An offering; a presenting.) Both hands, slightly cupped, palms up, are held close to the chest. They move up and out in unison, describing a very slight arc. Also BID 2, MOTION 1, OFFER 1, OFFERING 1, PRESENT 1, SUGGEST, TENDER 2.

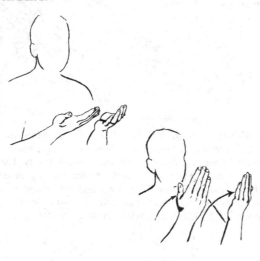

PROSE (prōz), *n.* (The letter "P"; writing.) The right "P" hand, held above the upturned left, moves toward the right. Optionally, the right hand may wriggle slightly as it moves toward the right.

PROSPER (prŏs′ pər), *v.,* -PERED, -PERING. (Penetrating the heights.) The "D" hands, palms back, are held at each side of the head near the temples. With a pivoting motion of the wrists, the hands swing up and around simultaneously to a position above the head, with palms facing out. Also ACCOMPLISH 1, ACHIEVE 1, ATTAIN, SUCCEED, SUCCESS, SUCCESSFUL, TRIUMPH 2.

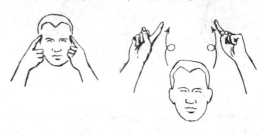

PROSTITUTE (prŏs′ tə tūt′), *n.* (The blood rushes up the cheek in shame—several times for emphasis.) The curved back of the right hand, placed against the right cheek, moves up and off the cheek several times. Also HARLOT, STRUMPET, WHORE.

PROTECT (prə tĕkt′), *v.,* -TECTED, -TECTING. (Hold down firmly; cover and strengthen.) The "S" hands, downturned, are held side by side in front of the body, the arms almost horizontal and the left hand in front of the right. Both arms move a short distance forward and slightly downward. Also DEFEND, DEFENSE, FORTIFY, GUARD, PROTECTION, SHIELD 1.

PROTECTION (prə tĕk′ shən), *n.* See PROTECT.

PROTEST 1 (*n.* prō′ tĕst; *v.* prə tĕst′), -TESTED, -TEST-ING. (The hand is thrust into the chest to force a complaint out.) The curved fingers of the right hand are thrust forcefully into the chest. Also COMPLAIN 1, COMPLAINT, OBJECT 2, OBJECTION.

PROTEST 2, *n., v.* (Turning one's head away in protest.) The right "S" hand, palm facing back, is held at forehead level. It swings forcefully around to the palm-forward position. This sign is used to indicate organized activity, as in "protesting the company's new policy."

PROTESTANT (prŏt′ ĭs tənt), *n., adj.* (Kneeling in church.) The knuckles of the right index and middle fingers are placed in the upturned left palm. The action may be repeated. Also KNEEL.

PROTON (prō′ ton), *n.* (The letter "P"; around the world.) The right "P" hand makes a circle around the left fist.

PROUD (proud), *adj.* (The feelings rise up.) The thumb of the right "A" hand, palm down, moves up along the right side of the chest. A haughty expression is assumed. Also HAUGHTY, PRIDE.

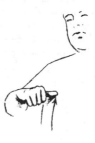

PROVE (pro͞ov), *v.,* PROVED, PROOVED or PROVEN, PROVING. See PROOF.

PROVIDE 1 (prə vīd′), *v.,* -VIDED, -VIDING. (Placing things in order.) The hands, palms facing, fingers together and pointing away from the body, are positioned at the left side and held about a foot apart. With a slight up-down motion, as if describing waves, the hands travel in unison from left to right. Also ARRANGE, ARRANGEMENT, CLASSED 2, DEVISE 1, ORDER 3, PLAN 1, POLICY 1, PREPARE 1, PROGRAM 1, PUT IN ORDER, READY 1, SCHEME, SYSTEM.

PROVIDE 2, *v.* (Handing over.) The "AND" hands are held upright with palms toward the body. From this position they swing forward and down, opening up as if giving something out.

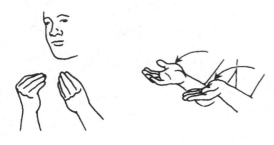

PRUNE 1 (pro͞on) (*loc.*), *n.* (The shape.) The "Q" hands, palms facing each other, are held before the body, respective thumbs and index fingers in contact. The hands then draw apart a few inches, and their thumbs and index fingers come together.

PRUNE 2, *v.*, PRUNED, PRUNING. (Trimming branches.) The left arm and open hand are held upright, like a tree. The right index and middle fingers, imitating scissors, snip the left arm and hand randomly, as if trimming outgrowths.

PSEUDONYM (so͞o′ də nim), *n.* (False name.) The right hand is held in the "P" position. The upturned right index finger then brushes the tip of the nose (FALSE). Optionally, the sign for NAME is then

made: the index and middle fingers of the right "H" hand come down on top of their left counterparts.

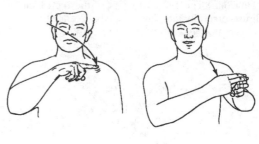

PSYCHIATRIST (sī kī′ ə trĭst), *n.* (The letter "P"; the pulse, which the doctor feels.) The thumb and middle finger of the right "P" hand twice touch the pulse of the upturned left hand.

PSYCHOLOGY 1 (sī kŏl′ ə jĭ), *n.* (The Greek letter psi (ψ), symbol of psychology.) The little finger edge of the open right hand is thrust into the open left hand, between thumb and index finger. The action is usually repeated.

PSYCHOLOGY 2, *n.* (The letter "P"; the mind.) The thumb and middle finger of the right "P" hand twice tap the right temple.

PSYCHOSIS (sī kō′ sis), *n.* (The mind collapses or breaks down.) The right index touches the forehead, and then both hands, palms down, fingers slightly interlocked, collapse downward.

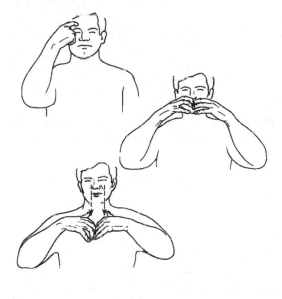

PUBLIC 1 (pŭb′ lĭk), *adj., n.* (People, indicated by the rotating "P" hands.) The "P" hands, side by side, are moved alternately in continuous counterclockwise circles. Also AUDIENCE 2, HUMANITY, PEOPLE.

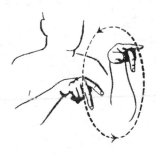

PUBLIC 2, adj., *n.* The right index finger, pointing left, describes a continuous small circle in front of the mouth. This is the sign for HEARING, *q.v.* This culturally oriented sign defines the difference between going to a school for the Deaf, where signing is used, and a so-called public school, *i.e.,* a mainstream school program that caters mainly to the needs of children with hearing. Thus the term *public* is erroneously equated with the term *hearing.*

PUBLIC RELATIONS, *n.* (The abbreviation; a fingerspelled loan sign.) The letters "P" and "R" are fingerspelled. This may be confused with "Puerto Rico," so one must rely on context.

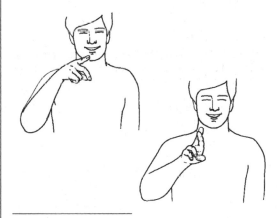

PUBLISH 1 (pŭb′ lĭsh), *v.,* -LISHED, -LISHING. (The action of the press.) The right "5" hand, held palm down, fingers pointing left, is brought down twice against the upturned left "5" hand, whose fingers point right. Also NEWSPAPER, PAPER.

PUBLISH 2, *v.* (Placing type in a printer's stick.) The upturned, left "5" hand represents the printer's stick. The right index finger and thumb close over an imaginary piece of type and place it in the left palm. Also PRINT.

PUDDLE (pud′ l), *n.* (A small area of water or other liquid.) The right "W" is brought to the lips. Both indexes and thumbs, in the "C" shape, palms facing, then indicate a small area of water.

PUERTO RICO (pwer′ tō rē′ kō), *n.* (The letters.) The signer makes the letters "P" and "R" on the back of the downturned left hand. A native sign.

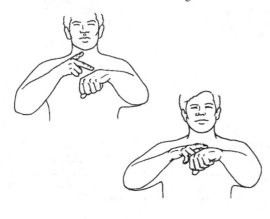

PULL 1 (pŏŏl), *v., PULLED, PULLING.* (The natural action.) Both open hands, the right palm up and the left palm down, grasp an imaginary pole and pull it toward the body Also DRAG, DRAW 2.

PULL 2, *v.* (Hooking on to something and pulling.) With index fingers interlocked, the right hand pulls the left hand from left to right. Also HITCH, HOOK, TOW.

PULSE (pŭls), *n.* (The natural action of feeling the pulse.) The right fingertips are placed against the left pulse.

PUMPKIN 1 (pŭmp′ kĭn), *n.* (Thumping a yellow sphere.) The sign for YELLOW is made: the right "Y" hand, palm facing the body, shakes slightly, pivoting at the wrist. The downturned, left "S" hand represents the pumpkin. The middle finger of the right hand is then flicked against the back of the left. Also SQUASH 1.

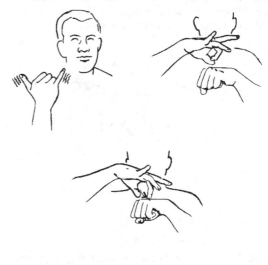

PUMPKIN 2, *n.* (The yellow object is defined.) The sign for YELLOW, as in PUMPKIN 1, *q.v.,* is made. Then the open "5" hands, fingers curved and palms facing, are held before the body to define the shape of the pumpkin.

PUNCH 1 (pŭnch), *n., v.,* PUNCHED, PUNCHING. (The natural sign.) The right "S" hand strikes its knuckles forcefully against the open left palm, which is held facing right. Also HIT 1, POUND 3, STRIKE 1.

PUNCH 2, *n., v.* (The natural sign.) The right fist strikes the chin.

PUNISH 1 (pŭn′ ĭsh), *v.,* -ISHED, -ISHING. (A striking movement.) The right index finger makes a striking movement below the left "S" hand, which is held up as if grasping a culprit. Also DISCIPLINE 3, PENALTY 1.

PUNISH 2, *v.* (The natural sign.) The left hand is held in a fist before the face, as if grasping something or someone. The right hand, at the same time, is held as if grasping a stick or whip; it strikes repeatedly at the

imaginary object or person dangling from the left hand. Also BEAT 1, WHIP.

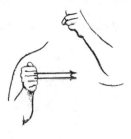

PUNISH 3, *v.* (A modification of the striking movement.) The right index finger strikes the left elbow with a glancing blow. Also DISCIPLINE 2, PENALTY 2, PENANCE 1.

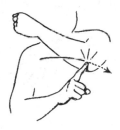

PUPIL 1 (pū′ pəl), *n.* (One who learns.) The sign for LEARN is made: the downturned fingers of the right hand are placed on the upturned left palm; they close, and then the hand rises and the right fingertips are placed on the forehead. This is followed by the sign for INDIVIDUAL 1: both open hands, palms facing each other, move down the sides of the body, tracing its outline to the hips. Also LEARNER, SCHOLAR, STUDENT 1.

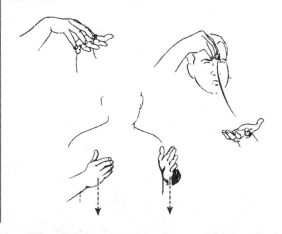

PUPIL 2, *n.* (One who studies.) The sign for STUDY is made: the upturned left hand represents a page; the right fingers wiggle as they move back and forth a short distance above the left hand. This is followed by the sign for INDIVIDUAL 1, as in PUPIL 1.

PUPIL 3, *n.* (The letter "P.") The middle finger of the right "P" hand is placed in the upturned left palm and moved from little finger edge to thumb edge a number of times.

PURCHASE (pûr′ chəs), *n., v.,* -CHASED, -CHASING. (Giving out money.) The sign for MONEY is made: the upturned right hand, grasping some imaginary bills, is brought down into the upturned left palm, and then the right hand moves forward and up in a small arc, opening up as it does. Also BUY.

PURE 1 (pyŏŏr), *adj.* (Everything is wiped off the hand to emphasize an uncluttered or clean condition.) The right hand slowly wipes the upturned left palm from wrist to fingertips. Also CLEAN 1, IMMACULATE, NEAT, NICE, PLAIN 2, PURITY, SIMPLE 2.

PURE 2, *n.* (The letter "P" for PURE, passed over the palm to denote CLEAN.) The right "P" hand moves forward along the palm of the upturned left hand, which is held flat, with fingers pointing forward. Also CHASTITY.

PURITAN (pyŏŏr′ ə tən), *n.* (The letter "P"; wiping off the hand.) The right "P" hand sweeps over the upturned left palm. The sign for INDIVIDUAL 1 then follows.

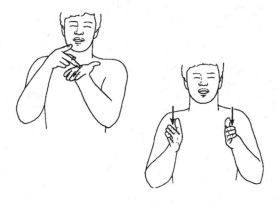

PURITY (pyŏŏr′ ə tĭ), *n.* See PURE 1.

PURPOSE 1 (pûr′ pəs), *n.* (Relative standing of one's thoughts.) A modified sign for THINK is made: the right index finger touches the middle of the forehead. The tips of the right "V" hand, palm down, are then thrust into the upturned left palm (as in STAND, *q.v.*). The right "V" hand is then rethrust into the upturned left palm, with right palm now facing the body. Also CONNOTE, IMPLY, INTEND, INTENT 1, INTENTION, MEAN 2, MEANING, MOTIVE 3, SIGNIFICANCE 2, SIGNIFY 2, SUBSTANCE 2.

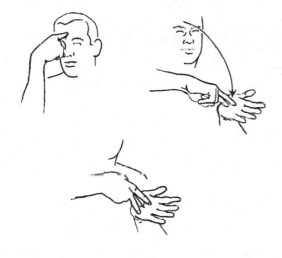

PURPOSE 2, *n.* (A thought directed upward, toward a goal.) The left "D" hand, palm facing the body, is held above the head to represent the goal. The index finger of the right "D" hand, after touching the forehead (modified sign for THINK, as in PURPOSE 1), moves slowly and deliberately up to the tip of the left index finger. Also AIM, AMBITION, ASPIRE, GOAL, OBJECTIVE, PERSEVERE 4.

PURPOSE 3, *n.* (The letter "P"; the mind, seat of thought.) The middle finger of the right "P" hand describes a small, counterclockwise circle on the middle of the forehead.

PURSUE (pər sōō'), *v.*, -SUED, -SUING. (The natural sign.) The "A" hands are held in front of the body, with the thumbs facing forward, the right palm facing left and the left palm facing right. The left hand is held slightly ahead of the right, it then moves forward in a straight line while the right hand follows after, executing a circular motion or swerving back and forth, as if in pursuit. Also CHASE 1.

PUSHCART (pŏŏsh' kärt), *n.* (Holding the handles and moving forward.) Grasping an imaginary pair of handles and lifting with effort, the signer moves slightly forward. Also WHEELBARROW.

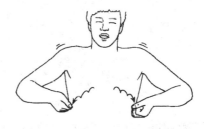

PUT (pŏŏt), *v.*, PUT, PUTTING. (Moving from one place to another.) The downturned hands, fingers touching their respective thumbs, move in unison from left to right. Also MIGRATE, MOVE, PLACE 3, REMOVE 2, TRANSFER 2.

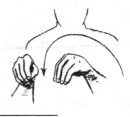

PUT DOWN, *v. phrase.* (The natural motion.) The downturned "O" hands are brought down and to the left simultaneously from an initial side-by-side position near the right shoulder. Also DEPOSIT 1.

PUT IN ORDER, *v. phrase.* (Placing things in order.) The hands, palms facing, fingers together and pointing away from the body, are positioned at the left side and held about a foot apart. With a slight up-down motion, as if describing waves, the hands travel in unison from left to right. Also ARRANGE, ARRANGEMENT, CLASSED 2, DEVISE 1, ORDER 3, PLAN 1, POLICY 1, PREPARE 1, PROGRAM 1, PROVIDE 1, READY 1, SCHEME, SYSTEM.

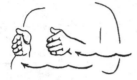

PUT OFF, *v. phrase.* (Putting off; moving things forward repeatedly.) The "F" hands, palms facing and fingers pointing out from the body, are moved forward simultaneously in a series of short movements. Also DEFER, DELAY, POSTPONE, PROCRASTINATE.

PUT SOMEONE DOWN (*colloq*), *v. phrase.* (Giving someone a stamp of disapproval.) The right "U" hand, palm out, is brought forward quickly, as if placing a stamp on someone's forehead. Also "ZAP" SOMEONE, PUT SOMEONE IN HIS/HER PLACE.

PUT SOMEONE IN HER/HIS PLACE (*colloq.*), *v. phrase.* See above.

PUTT (put), *n., v.,* PUTTED, PUTTING. (Manipulating a golf club.) The signer mimes using a golf club to drive a golf ball a short distance.

PUZZLE (puz′ əl), *n.* (Manipulating the pieces.) The downturned fingers of both hands manipulate the pieces of a jigsaw puzzle.

PUZZLED (puz′ əld), *adj.* (A question mark above the head, as in cartoons.) The upright index finger is placed on top of the head. It suddenly bends or curves in while the signer maintains an expression of puzzlement.

PYRAMID (pir′ ə mid), *n.* (The shape.) Both downturned "B" hands, held far apart, move up toward the head, describing a pyramid.

QUAKE (kwāk) (*colloq.*), *v.*, QUAKED, QUAKING. (The legs tremble.) Both "D" hands, index fingers pointing down, are held side by side to represent the legs. The hands tremble.

QUALIFICATIONS (kwŏl′ ə fĭ kā′ shənz), *n.* (The "Q" letter; on the heart.) The right "Q" hand, palm down, is placed with a flourish on the heart.

QUANTITY 1 (kwŏn′ tə tĭ), *n.* (The upper and lower limits are defined.) The right-angle hands, palms facing, are held before the body, the right above the left. They swing out 45° simultaneously, pivoted from their wrists. Also CAPACITY, LIMIT, RESTRICT.

QUANTITY 2, *n.* (Many fingers are indicated.) The upturned "S" hands are thrown up, opening into the

"5" position, palms up. This may be repeated. Also MANY, MULTIPLE, NUMEROUS, PLURAL.

QUARREL (kwôr′ əl, kwŏr′ -), *n., v.* -RELED, -RELING. (Repeated rejoinders.) Both "D" hands are held with index fingers pointing toward each other. The hands move up and down alternately, each pivoting in turn at the wrist. Also ROW 2.

QUART (kwôrt), *n.* The "Q" hand, palm down, shakes slightly.

QUEEN (kwēn), *n.* (The letter "Q"; the royal sash.) The right "Q" hand, palm down, moves from left shoulder to right hip, tracing the sash worn by royalty.

QUEER 1 (kwĭr), *adj.* (Something that distorts the vision.) The "C" hand describes a small arc in front of the face. Also CURIOUS 2, GROTESQUE, ODD, PECULIAR, STRANGE 1, WEIRD.

QUEER 2, *adj., sl.* (An effeminate gesture.) The right fingertips slap the back of the limply held left wrist.

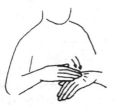

QUERY 1 (kwĭr′ ĭ), *n., v.,* -RIED, -RYING. (Firing questions.) The index fingers of both "D" hands repeatedly curve and straighten out as the hands are alternately flung forward and back, as if firing questions. Also ASK 3, EXAMINATION 3, INQUIRE 3, INTERROGATE 1, INTERROGATION 1, QUESTION 3, QUIZ 3.

QUERY 2 (*colloq.*), *n.* (Fire a question.) The right hand, held in a modified "S" position with palm facing out, assumes a position with the thumb resting on the fingernail of the index finger. The index finger is flicked out and forward, usually directed at the person being asked a question. Also ASK 2, EXAMINATION 2, INQUIRE 2, INTERROGATE 2, INTERROGATION 2, QUESTION 2, QUIZ 2.

QUESTION 1 (kwĕs′ chən), *n.* (The natural sign.) The right index finger draws a question mark in the air. Also QUESTION MARK.

QUESTION 2, *n.* See QUERY 2

QUESTION 3, *n.* See QUERY 1

QUESTION MARK, *n.* See QUESTION 1

QUEUE 1 (kū), *n., v.,* QUEUED, QUEUING. (The fingers indicate a row of people, all in a line.) Both "4" or "5" hands are held before the chest, with both palms facing left and little fingertips touching. The right hand moves straight back from the left a short distance. The same sign may also be made with right hand facing left and left hand facing right and the initial position involving the right little fingertip touching the tip of the left index finger. Also LINEUP, SINGLE FILE.

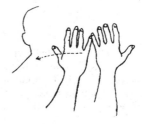

QUEUE 2, *n., v. Computer term.* (Lined up.) The right "4" hand, palm facing its left counterpart, draws in toward the chest.

QUICK (kwĭk), *adj.* (A quick movement.) The thumbtip of the upright right hand is flicked quickly off the tip of the curved right index finger as if shooting marbles. Also FAST 1, IMMEDIATELY, QUICKNESS, RAPID, RATE 1, SPEED, SPEEDY, SWIFT.

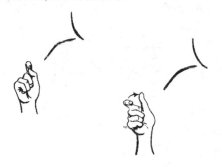

QUICKNESS, *n.* See QUICK

QUICK-WITTED *adj.* (Quick mind.) The right index finger taps the right temple, followed by the sign for QUICK, above.

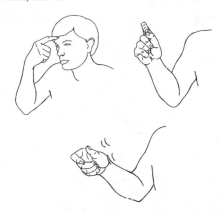

QUIET 1 (kwī′ ət), *n., adj., interj., v.,* QUIETED, QUIETING. (The natural sign.) The index finger is brought up against the pursed lips. Also BE QUIET 1, CALM 2, HUSH, NOISELESS, SILENCE 1, SILENT, STILL 2.

QUIET 2, *n., adj., interj., v.* (Quiet and peace.) The open hands are crossed before the mouth, the right palm facing left, left facing right. Then both hands, held palms down, move down from the mouth, curving outward to either side of the body. Also BE QUIET 2, BE STILL, CALM 1, SILENCE 2.

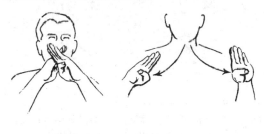

QUIT (kwĭt), *v.,* QUIT, QUITTING. (Pulling out.) The index and middle fingers of the right "H" hand are grasped by the left hand. The right hand pulls out of the left. Also RESIGN, WITHDRAW 3.

QUIZ 1 (kwĭz), *v.,* QUIZZED, QUIZZING, *n.* (A series of questions spread out on a page.) Both "D" hands, palms down, simultaneously execute a single circle, the right hand moving in a clockwise direction and the left in a counterclockwise direction. Upon completion of the circle, both hands open into the "5" position and move straight down a short distance. (The hands actually draw question marks in the air.) Also EXAMINATION 1, TEST.

QUIZ 2 (*colloq.*), *n. v.* (Fire a question.) The right hand, held in a modified "S" position with palm facing out, assumes a position with the thumb resting on the fingernail of the index finger. The index finger is flicked out and forward, usually directed at the person being asked a question. Also ASK 2, EXAMINATION 2,

INQUIRE 2, INTERROGATE 2, INTERROGATION 2, QUERY 2, QUESTION 2.

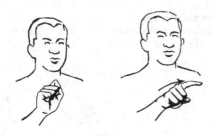

QUIZ 3, *n., v.* (Firing questions.) The index fingers of both "D" hands repeatedly curve and straighten out as the hands are alternately flung forward and back, as if firing questions. Also ASK 3, EXAMINATION 3, INQUIRE 3, INTERROGATE 1, INTERROGATION 1, QUERY 1, QUESTION 3.

QUOTATION (kwō tā′ shən), *n.* (The quotation marks are indicated.) The curved index and middle fingers of both hands, held palms out, move slightly to either side of the body, as if drawing quotation marks in the air. Also CAPTION, CITE, QUOTE, SO-CALLED, SUBJECT, THEME, TITLE, TOPIC.

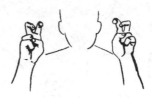

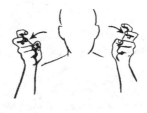

QUOTE (kwōt), *n., v.*, QUOTED, QUOTING. See QUOTATION

R

RABBI 1 (răb′ ī), *n.* (A Jewish minister or preacher.) The sign for JEW is made: the fingers and thumb of each hand are placed at the chin and stroke an imaginary beard. This is followed by the sign for MINISTER or PREACHER: the right hand, palm out, with thumb and index finger touching, is moved forward and slightly downward a number of times from its initial position near the right temple. This is followed by the sign for INDIVIDUAL 1: both open hands, palms facing each other, move down the sides of the body, tracing its outline to the hips.

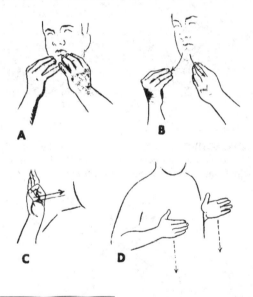

RABBI 2, *n.* (The letter "R"; the prayer shawl or talis.) Both upright "R" hands trace the fall of the shawl down the sides of the chest.

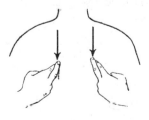

RABBIT 1 (răb′ ĭt), *n.* (The movement of the ears.) Both "U" hands are placed at either side of the head,

palms facing back. The index and middle fingers, joined together, move forward and back repeatedly, imitating a rabbit's ears.

RABBIT 2, *n.* (Same rationale as for RABBIT 1.) The "H" hands are crossed at the wrists, palms facing the body. The index and middle fingers of both hands move up and down repeatedly.

RACE 1 (rās), *n., v.,* RACED, RACING. (Two opponents come together.) Both hands are closed, with thumbs pointing straight up and palms facing the body. From their initial position about a foot apart, the hands are brought together sharply so that the knuckles strike. The hands, as they are drawn together, also move down a bit so that they describe a "V." Also COMPETE 1, COMPETITION 1, CONTEND 1, CONTEST 1, RIVAL 2, RIVALRY 1, VIE 1.

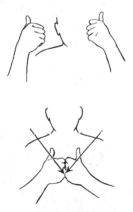

RACE 2, *n., v.* (Opposing objects.) The "A" hands are held side by side before the chest, palms facing each other and thumbs pointing forward. In this position the hands move alternately back and forth, toward and away from the body. Also COMPETE 2, COMPETITION 2, CONTEND 2, CONTEST 2, RIVAL 3, RIVALRY 2, VIE 2.

RACE 3, *n., v.* (The changing fortunes of competitors.) The "A" hands are held facing each other, thumbs pointing up in front of the body. Both hands are moved alternately backward and forward past each other several times. Also COMPETE 3, COMPETITION 3, CONTEND 3, CONTEST 3, RIVAL 4, RIVALRY 3, VIE 3.

RACKET 1 (răk′ ĭt), *n.* (A shaking that disturbs the ear.) After placing the index finger on the ear, both hands assume the "S" position, palms down. They move alternately back and forth, forcefully. Also DIN, NOISE, NOISY, SOUND, THUNDER, VIBRATION.

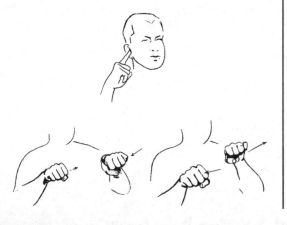

RACKET 2, *n.* (Holding the racket.) The signer goes through the motions of manipulating a tennis racket. Also TENNIS.

RADAR (rā′ där), *n.* (The revolving radar screen.) The base of the right "C" hand rests on the tip of the upright left index finger. The right hand revolves around the left finger in a counterclockwise direction.

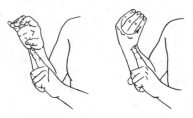

RADIOACTIVE (ra′ dē ō ak′ tiv), *adj.* (The "R" and "A" letters; moving away.) The right "R" hand moves away from the left "A" hand, as if tracing the rays.

RAFT (raft), *n.* (Floating along on top of a support.) With the right hand resting on the left, both hands float away.

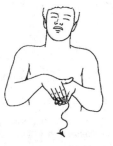

RAGE (rāj), *n., v.,* RAGED, RAGING. (A violent welling up of the emotions.) The curved fingers of the right hand are placed in the center of the chest, and they fly up suddenly and violently. An expression of anger is worn. Also ANGER, ANGRY 2, ENRAGE, FURY, INDIGNANT, INDIGNATION, IRE, MAD 1.

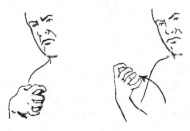

RAILROAD 1 (rāl′ rōd′), *n.* (Running along the tracks.) The "V" hands are held palms down. The right "V" fingers move over the backs of the downturned left "V" fingers from base to tips. Also CARS, TRAIN 1.

RAILROAD 2, *n.* (The letter "R.") The right "R" hand, palm down, moves down an inch or two and moves to the right in a small arc.

RAINBOW (rān′ bō′), *n.* (Tracing the colors across the sky.) The right "4" hand, palm facing the signer, describes an arc in the air, from left to right.

RAISE 1 (rāz), *v.,* RAISED, RAISING, *n.* (Getting onto one's feet.) The upturned index and middle fingers of the right hand, representing the legs, are swung up and over in an arc, coming to rest in the upturned left palm. Also ARISE 2, ELEVATE, GET UP, RISE 1, STAND 2, STAND UP.

RAISE 2, *n., v.* (Adding on.) The index and middle fingers of the right "H" hand, palm up, are swung up and over until they come to rest on the index and middle fingers of the left "H" hand, held palm down. Also ADD 3, ADDITION, EXTEND 1, EXTRA, GAIN 1, INCREASE, ON TO.

RAISE 3, *n., v.* (Flowers or plants emerge from the ground.) The right fingers, pointing up, emerge from the closed left hand, and they spread open as they do. Also BLOOM, DEVELOP 1, GROW, GROWN, MATURE, PLANT 1, REAR 2, SPRING 1.

RAISE 4, *v.* (To bring up, say, a child.) The downturned, open left hand slowly rises straight up, indicating the growth of a child. The right hand may also be used.

RAISINS (rā′ zənz), *n.* (The letter "R"; a cluster of grapes.) The right "R" fingers move down the back of the prone left hand, tapping as they go.

RAMP (ramp), *n.* (The incline.) The downturned right hand, fingers pointing forward, moves up an imaginary incline. Both hands may also be used, with one leading the other.

RAM'S HORN, *n.* (The shape of the horn and its blowing.) The left "S" hand, palm facing right, is placed on the lips, with the right "C" hand placed in front of it. The right "C" hand moves forward and arcs to the right. This indicates the shape and blowing of the ram's horn or shofar at the celebration of Rosh Hashanah, the Jewish New Year. Also SHOFAR.

RANCH (ranch), *n.* (The letter "R"; the stubbled chin of a rough cowboy.) The right "R" hand, palm facing left, slides from the left chin to the right.

RANDOM (ran′ dəm), *adj.* (Here and there.) Both "D" hands, palms down, move alternately up and down as

they move apart slightly. The "R" hands may be substituted.

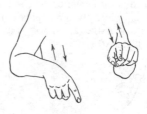

RAPE 1 (rāp), *n., v.,* RAPED, RAPING, *vulg.* (Pulling the legs apart and penetrating the victim.) The signer mimes pulling a victim's legs apart forcefully. The right "S" hand then moves down and forward in an arc. This rather coarse sign is not used in polite conversation. The first part of the sign, involving the legs, is often omitted.

RAPE 2, *n., v.* (An assault involving wringing the neck.) Both "S" hands are held palms facing forward. The right "S" brushes against the left "S" as it twists and moves forward. This is a more socially acceptable sign than RAPE 1.

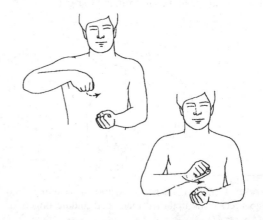

RASH (rash), *n.* (Spots on the body.) Both claw hands make dots all over the chest and/or face.

RAT (răt), *n.* (The twitching nose.) The tips of the right "R" fingers brush the tip of the nose several times.

RATE 1 (rāt), *n., v.*, RATED, RATING. See RAPID.

RATE 2, *n., v.* (Drawing a percent symbol in the air.) The right "O" hand traces the percent symbol (%) in the air. Also PERCENT.

RE- (rē-), *adj. prefix* (The "R"; "AGAIN.") The right "R" hand arcs over toward the left, coming to rest on the upturned left palm. Also AGAIN.

REACTION 1 (rĭ ăk′ shən), *n.* (The letter "R"; coming out of the mouth.) Both "R" hands are held before the face, with the right "R" hand at the lips and behind the left "R" hand. Both hands move forward simultaneously, describing a small upward arc. Also ANSWER 2, REPLY 2, REPORT, RESPONSE 2.

REACTION 2, *n.* (The "R"; moving apart.) Both "R" hands, fingers touching at the tips, move apart.

READ 1 (rēd), *v.*, READ, READING. (The eyes scan the page.) The left hand is held before the body, palm up and fingers pointing to the right. This represents the page. The right "V" hand then moves down as if scanning the page.

READ 2, *v.* (The eyes scan a page.) The index and middle fingers of the right "V" hand represent the eyes and follow imaginary lines on the left palm, which represents the page of a book.

READ 3, *v.* (Reading a book.) The open hands support an imaginary book. The signer, looking at the book, moves his head repeatedly from left to right as if reading.

READ LIPS, *v. phrase.* (Reading the lips—the lines of vision, represented by the two fingers, scan the lips.) The right "V" hand, palm facing the body, is placed in front of the face, with slightly curved index and middle fingers directly in front of the lips. The right hand moves in a small counterclockwise circle around the lips. Also LIPREADING, ORAL, SPEECHREADING.

READ THE MIND, *phrase.* (READ and scanning the forehead.) The right "V" hand, representing the vision, is positioned with fingertips facing the forehead. The hand moves back and forth across the forehead from right to left.

READY 1 (rĕd′ ĭ), *adj., v.,* READIED, READYING. (Placing things in order.) The hands, palms facing, fingers together and pointing away from the body, are positioned at the left side and held about a foot apart. With a slight up-down motion, as if describing waves, the hands travel in unison from left to right. Also ARRANGE, ARRANGEMENT, CLASSED 2, DEVISE 1, ORDER

3, PLAN 1, POLICY 1, PREPARE 1, PROGRAM 1, PROVIDE 1, PUT IN ORDER, SCHEME, SYSTEM.

READY 2, *adj.* (The "R" hands.) The "R" hands are held side by side before the body, palms up and fingers pointing outward. The hands then turn toward each other and over, so that the palms face down and fingers point toward each other. Also PREPARE 2.

READY 3, *adj., adv.* (The "R" hands.) The same sign as for READY 1, *q.v.,* is made, except that the "R" hands are used. With palms facing down, they move simultaneously from left to right. Also GET READY.

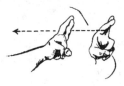

READY 4, *adj., v.* (Set out.) The hands are crossed, with the right resting on top of the left. The right palm faces left and the left palm faces right. Both hands suddenly open and swing apart to the palm-down position. Also PREPARE 3.

REAL (rē′ əl, rēl), *adj.* (Coming forth directly from the lips; true.) The index finger of the right "D" hand, palm facing left, is placed against the lips. It moves up an inch or two and then describes a small arc forward and away from the lips. Also ABSOLUTE, ABSOLUTELY,

ACTUAL, ACTUALLY, AUTHENTIC, CERTAIN, CERTAINLY, FAITHFUL 3, FIDELITY, FRANKLY, GENUINE, INDEED, POSITIVE 1, POSITIVELY, REALLY, SINCERE 2, SURE, SURELY, TRUE, TRULY, TRUTH, VALID, VERILY.

REALIZE (rē′ ə līz′), v., -IZED, -IZING. (Knowing and understanding.) The sign for KNOW is made: the right fingers pat the forehead several times. This is followed by the sign for UNDERSTAND: the curved index finger of the right hand, palm facing the body, is placed with the fingernail resting on the middle of the forehead. It suddenly flicks up into the "D" position.

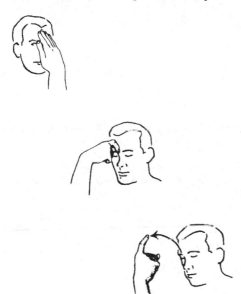

REALLY (rē′ ə lĭ, rē′ lĭ), adv. See REAL.

REAP 1 (rēp), v., REAPED, REAPING. (Cutting the stalks.) The left hand holds an imaginary bunch of stalks, and the right hand, holding an imaginary sickle, sweeps under the left as if cutting the stalks. The right "X"

hand may also be used. Here the curved finger represents the blade. Also HARVEST 1.

REAP 2, v. (Gathering in the harvest.) The right open hand sweeps across the upturned left palm and closes into the "A" position, as if gathering up some stalks. Also HARVEST 2.

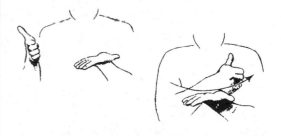

REAP 3, v. (The cutting.) The left hand grasps the heads of imaginary wheat stalks. The upturned right hand, imitating a sickle blade, then swings in to cut the stalks. Also HARVEST 3.

REAR 1 (rĭr), n. (The natural sign.) The right hand moves over the right shoulder to tap the back. Also BACK 2.

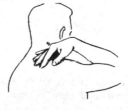

REAR 2, *v.*, REARED, REARING. (Flowers or plants emerge from the ground.) The right fingers, pointing up, emerge from the closed left hand, and they spread open as they do. Also BLOOM, DEVELOP 1, GROW, GROWN, MATURE, PLANT 1, RAISE 3, SPRING 1.

REASON 1 (rē′ zən), *n.* (The letter "R"; the thought.) The fingertips of the right "R" hand describe a small counterclockwise circle in the middle of the forehead.

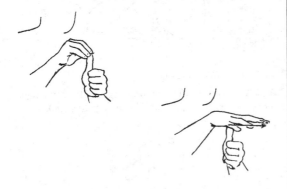

REASON 2, *n.* (Rays of influence emanating from a given source.) All the right fingertips, including the thumb, are positioned on the tip of the upturned thumb of the left "A" hand. The right hand, opening into the downturned "5" position, moves forward from its initial position. Instead of its initial position on the left thumb, the right hand is frequently placed on the back of the downturned left "S" hand, moving forward as described above. Also BASIS 1, CAUSE, EFFECT 1, INFLUENCE 2, INTENT 2, LOGIC, PRODUCE 4.

REBEL (*adj., n.* rĕb′ əl; *v.* rĭ bel′), -BELLED, -BELLING. (Turning the head.) The right "S" hand, held up with its palm facing the body, swings sharply around to the palm-out position. The head meanwhile moves slightly toward the left. Also DISOBEDIENCE, DISOBEY.

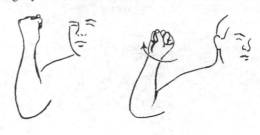

REBUTTAL (ri but′ l), *n.* (Pushing one's words back against the lips.) The "U" hand, palm facing the signer, is brought up sharply against the lips.

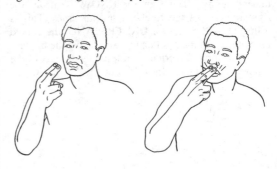

RECALL 1 (rĭ kôl′), *v.*, -CALLED, -CALLING. (Bringing something back from the past.) The right open hand reaches back over the right shoulder as if to grasp something and then brings the imaginary thing before the face with the closed "AND" hand. Also RECOLLECT 1.

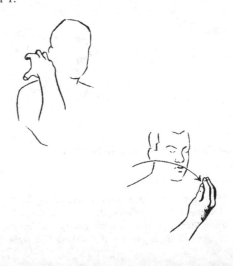

RECALL 2, *v.* (Knowledge that remains.) The sign for KNOW is made: the right fingertips are placed on the forehead. The sign for REMAIN then follows: the "A" hands are held with palms toward the body, thumbs extended and touching, the right behind the left. In this position the hands move forward in a straight, steady line or straight down. Also MEMORY, RECOLLECT 2, REMEMBER.

RECEIVE (rǐ sēv′), *v.,* -CEIVED, -CEIVING. (A grasping and bringing forward to oneself.) Both hands, in the "5" position, fingers curved, are crossed at the wrists, with the left palm facing right and the right palm facing left. They are brought in toward the chest while closing into a grasping "S" position. Also ACQUIRE, GET, OBTAIN, PROCURE.

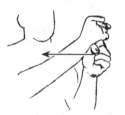

RECEIVE REGULARLY, *phrase.* (Pulling in repeatedly.) The right claw hand, held above the side of the head, palm facing left, is pulled down repeatedly, closing into the "S" shape each time. This is an appropriate sign for "subscription," "benefits" such as Social Security, and "earnings" or "salary."

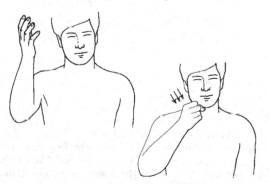

RECENT (rē′ sənt), *adj.* (The slight movement represents a slight amount of time.) With the closed right hand held with knuckles against the right cheek, the thumbtip flicks off the tip of the curved index finger a number of times. The eyes squint a bit and the lips are drawn out in a slight smile. The hand remains against the cheek during the flicking movement. Sometimes, instead of the flicking movement, the tip of the curved index finger scratches slightly up and down against the cheek. In this case, the palm faces back toward the shoulder. The same expression is used as in the flicking movement. Also JUST NOW 2, RECENTLY, WHILE AGO, A 2.

RECENTLY, *adv.* See RECENT.

RECEPTION (ri sep′ shən), *n.* (The "R" letters; eating continuously.) Both "R" hands are brought up to the mouth continuously, forming alternate ellipses.

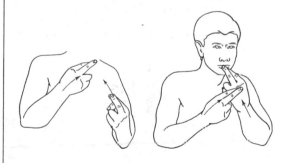

RECESS (ri ses′, rē′ ses), *n.* (Suspending activity.) The curved index finger, hanging down like a hook, pulls up the other curved index finger.

RECITATION (rĕs′ ə tā′ shən), *n.* (Studying back and forth.) This sign is derived from the sign for STUDY, *q.v.* The right-angle hands face each other, with the right hand facing left and the left hand facing right. They move alternately forward and back, with fingers wiggling.

RECKLESS (rĕk′ lĭs), *adj.* (The vision is sidetracked, causing one to lose sight of the object in view.) The right "V" hand, representing the vision, is held in front of the face, palm facing left. The hand, pivoted at the wrist, moves back and forth a number of times. Also CARELESS, HEEDLESS, THOUGHTLESS.

RECKON (rĕk′ ən), *v.,* -ONED, -ONING. (A thought is turned over in the mind.) The index finger makes a small circle on the forehead. Also CONSIDER 1, MOTIVE 1, SPECULATE 1, SPECULATION 1, THINK, THOUGHT 1, THOUGHTFUL.

RECLINE (rĭ klīn′), *v.,* -CLINED, -CLINING. (The prone position of the legs in lying down.) The index and middle fingers of the right "V" hand, palm facing up, are placed in the upturned left palm. Also LIE 3, LIE DOWN.

RECOGNIZE (rĕk′ əg nīz′), *v.,* -NIZED, -NIZING. (Patting the head to indicate something of value

inside.) The right fingers pat the forehead several times. Also INTELLIGENCE, KNOW, KNOWLEDGE.

RECOIL (ri koil′), *v.,* -COILED, -COILING. (Drawing back and away from something.) The signer's body suddenly moves backward, while both upraised arms, with palms facing outward, also move backward with the body. An expression of horror or annoyance is assumed.

RECOLLECT 1 (rĕk ə lĕkt′), *v.,* -LECTED, -LECTING. (Bringing something back from the past.) The right open hand reaches back over the right shoulder as if to grasp something and then brings the imaginary thing before the face with the closed "AND" hand. Also RECALL 1.

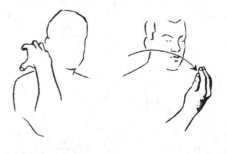

RECOLLECT 2, *v.* (Knowledge that remains.) The sign for KNOW is made: the right fingertips are placed on the forehead. The sign for REMAIN then follows: the "A" hands are held with palms toward the body, thumbs extended and touching, the right behind the left. In this position the hands move forward in a straight, steady line or straight down. Also MEMORY, RECALL 2, REMEMBER.

RECORD (rek′ ərd), *n.* (The letter "P"; revolving record table.) The right "R" hand, fingers pointing down, makes a series of large clockwise circles in the upturned left palm.

RECOVER (ri kuv′ ər), *v.*, -ERED, -ERING. (The body is strong again.) The sign for AGAIN: the upturned left hand is held before the chest. The right hand, in the right-angle position, fingers pointing up, arches over and into the left palm. Both palms are then placed on the chest. They move forward strongly, closing into fists. Also RECOVERY.

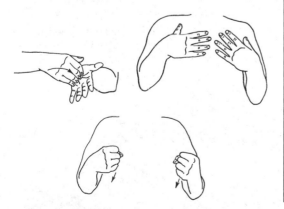

RECOVERY (ri kuv′ ə rē), *n.* See RECOVER.

RECRUIT (ri kroot′), *v.*, -CRUITED, -CRUITING. (Hooking someone.) The curved right index finger is suddenly hooked around the left upturned index finger, pulling it to the right.

RECTANGLE (rek′ tang′ gəl), *n.* (The letter "R"; the shape.) Both "R" hands describe a rectangle in the air.

RED (rĕd), *adj., n.* (The lips, which are red, are indicated.) The tip of the right index finger moves down across the lips. The "R" hand may also be used.

REDEEM 1 (rĭ dēm′), *v.*, -DEEMED, -DEEMING. (Breaking the bonds.) The "S" hands, crossed in front of the body, swing apart and face out. Also DELIVER 1, EMANCIPATE, FREE 1, INDEPENDENCE, INDEPENDENT, LIBERATION, RELIEF, RESCUE, SAFE, SALVATION, SAVE 1.

REDEEM 2, *v.* (The "R" hands.) The sign for RE-DEEM 1 is made with the "R" hands.

 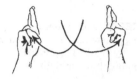

REDEEMER (rĭ dē′ mər), *n.* (One who redeems.) The sign for REDEEM 1 or 2 is made. This is followed by the sign for INDIVIDUAL 1: both open hands, palms facing each other, move down the sides of the body, tracing its outline to the hips.

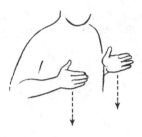

REDHEAD (red′ hed′), *n.* (RED; hair.) The sign for RED, above, is made, and then the signer fingers a lock of hair.

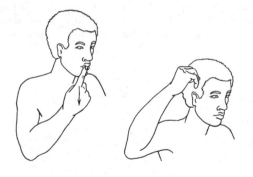

REDUCE 1 (rĭ dūs′, -do͞os′), *v.,* -DUCED, -DUCING. (The diminishing size or amount.) With palms facing, the right hand is held above the left. The right hand moves slowly down toward the left but does not touch it. Also DECREASE, LESS 1.

REDUCE 2, *v.* Same as REDUCE 1, but using the "R"s.

REFER (rĭ fûr′), *v.,* -FERRED, FERRING. (The letter "R," transferring.) The fingertips of the right "R" hand touch the palm of the open left hand, which is held with palm facing right, fingers pointing upward. From this position the right hand moves backward off the left palm.

REFEREE 1 (rĕf′ ə rē′), *n.* (Judge, individual.) The sign for JUDGE is formed: the two "F" hands, palms facing each other, move alternately up and down. This is followed by the sign for INDIVIDUAL 1: both open hands, palms facing each other, move down the sides of the body, tracing its outline to the hips. Also JUDGE 2, UMPIRE.

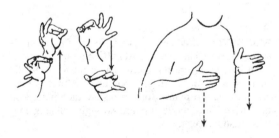

REFEREE 2, *n., v.,* -REED, -REEING. (Blowing the whistle.) The curved index and middle fingers are inserted in the mouth, and the signer mimes whistling.

REFILL (rē′ fil′ rē fil′), *n., v.,* -FILLED, -FILLING. (The "R"; moving up to the top of a container.) The right "R" hand, palm down, moves straight up until it comes in contact with the downturned left palm.

REFLECT (ri flekt′), *v.,* -FLECTED, -FLECTING. (The image reflects back.) The right "R" fingers, held up, touch the outstretched left palm, and move forward slowly and deliberately. The signer may cause the right hand to tremble slightly as it moves forward.

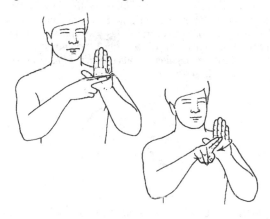

REFORM 1 (ri fôrm′), *v.,* -FORMED, -FORMING. (Change; the "R" hands.) Both "R" hands are positioned with fingers pointing up, palms facing each other. The hands are twisted around each other. This is an appropriate sign for *"We need to reform."*

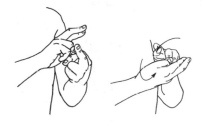

REFORM 2, *adj.* (Breaking the bonds; the "R" hands.) The "R" hands, crossed at the wrists, swing apart and around so that their palms face out. This is an appropriate sign for *Reform Judaism.*

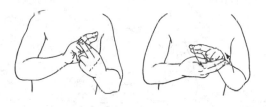

REFRIGERATOR 1 (ri frij′ ə rā′ tər), *n.* (ELECTRIC, *i.e.,* an icebox operated by electricity.) Both bent index fingers strike each other repeatedly at the knuckles. The movement pertains to the contact between the electrodes. This sign, though archaic in concept, is still widely used today.

REFRIGERATOR 2, *n.* (A fingerspelled loan word.) The signer fingerspells "R-E-F."

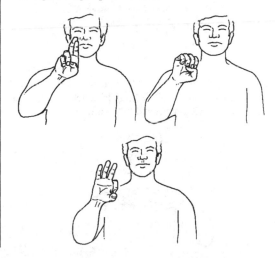

REFRIGERATOR 3, *n.* (Initialized version of COLD 1.) Both "R" hands, palms facing, shiver at the sides of the body.

REFUGE (rĕf′ ūj), *n.* (A shield.) The "S" hands are held before the chest, the left behind the right, and are pushed slightly away from the body. Then the right hand opens, palm facing out, and moves clockwise as if shielding the left fist. Also SHELTER, SHIELD 2.

REFUSE (rĭ fūz′), *v.,* -FUSED, -FUSING. (Holding back.) The right "A" hand, palm facing left, moves up sharply to a position above the right shoulder. Also WON'T.

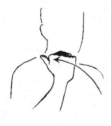

REGION (rē′ jən), *n.* (The "R" letters; a space is outlined.) Both downturned "R" hands, touching, execute a circle by moving apart and in toward the chest.

REGRESSION (ri gresh′ ən), *n.* The letter "R"; declining or going down.) The right "R" hand runs down the outstretched, downturned left arm in a series of small steps.

REGRET (rĭ grĕt′), *v.,* -GRETTED, -GRETTING, *n.* (The heart is circled to indicate feeling, modified by the letter "S" for SORRY.) The right "S" hand, palm facing the body, is rotated several times over the area of the heart. Also APOLOGIZE 1, APOLOGY 1, CONTRITION, PENITENT, REGRETFUL, REPENT, REPENTANT, RUE, SORROW, SORROWFUL 2, SORRY.

REGRETFUL (rĭ grĕt′ fəl), *adj.* See REGRET.

REGULAR (rĕg′ yə lər), *adj.* (Coming together with regular frequency.) Both "D" hands are held with index fingers pointing forward, the right hand above the left. The right "D" hand is brought down on the left several times in rhythmic succession as both hands move forward. Also CONSISTENT, FAITHFUL 1.

REGULATE (rĕg′ yə lāt′), *v.,* LATED, -LATING. (Holding the reins over all.) The "A" hands, palms facing, move alternately back and forth as if grasping and manipulating reins. The left "A" hand, still in position, swings over so that its palm now faces down. The right hand opens to the "5" position, palm down, and swings over the left, which moves slightly to the right. Also AUTHORITY, CONTROL 1, DIRECT 1, GOVERN, MANAGE, MANAGEMENT, MANAGER, OPERATE, REIGN, RULE 1.

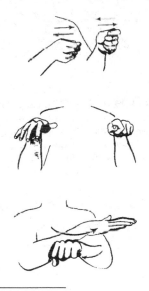

REGULATION(S) (rĕg′ yə lā′ shən), n. (The letter "R"; the listing.) The upright, open left hand, fingers together and palm facing out, represents a piece of paper on which are listed the rules or regulations. The right "R" hand is placed upright against the tips of the left fingers, and then it moves down in an arc to a position against the base of the left hand. Also RULE(S) 2.

REHABILITATION (rē′ hə bĭl′ ə tā′ shən), n. (The letter "R"; one hand helps or supports the other.) The right "R" hand rests with its base or side in the upturned left palm. The left hand pushes up the right hand a short distance.

REIGN (rān), n. See REGULATE.

REINFORCE (rē′ ĭn fōrs′), v., -FORCED, -FORCING. (The letter "R"; pushing up, i.e., assisting or reinforcing.) The right "R" hand, palm facing down, pushes up the left "S" hand, which is facing right.

REINS (rānz), n. pl. (Holding the reins.) The hands grasp and manipulate imaginary reins.

REJECT (n. rē′ jĕkt; v. rĭ jĕkt′), -JECTED, -JECTING. (The act of rejecting or sending off.) The downturned, right right-angle hand is positioned just above the base of the upturned, open left hand. The right hand sweeps forward in an arc over the left, and its fingertips brush sharply against the left palm. Also REJECTION.

REJECTION (rĭ jĕk′ shən), n. See REJECT.

REJOICE (rĭ jois′), v., -JOICED, -JOICING. (Waving of flags.) Both upright hands, grasping imaginary flags, wave them in small circles. Also CELEBRATE, CELEBRATION, CHEER, VICTORY 1, WIN 1.

RELAPSE 1 (rĭ lăps′), *n., v.,* -LAPSED, -LAPSING. (Going down.) The little finger edge of the open right hand is placed at the elbow of the downturned left arm. The right hand travels down the left arm in one sweeping movement or in short stages. This is the opposite of IMPROVE, *q.v.*

RELAPSE 2, *n., v.* (AGAIN; SICK.) The sign for AGAIN: the left hand, open in the "5" position, palm up, is held before the chest. The right hand, in the right-angle position, fingers pointing up, arches over and into the left palm. SICK: the middle fingers of each "5" hand are used, the right on the forehead and the left on the stomach. The order can be reversed.

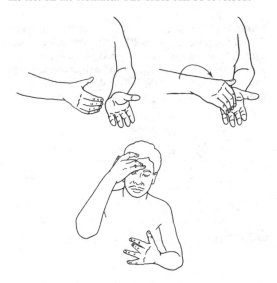

RELATION (rĭ lā′ shən) (*rare*), *n.* (A variation of the COUSIN sign, *q.v.*) The right "C" hand, held near the right temple, wiggles down to shoulder level.

RELATIONSHIP 1 (rĭ lā′ shən shĭp′), *n.* (The fingers are connected.) The index fingers and thumbs of both hands interlock, and the hands move back and forth from right to left. Also CONNECTION.

RELATIONSHIP 2, *n.* (The "R" hands.) The fingertips of the "R" hands move toward each other and touch. This is followed by the -SHIP suffix sign: the down-turned right "S" hand moves down along the left palm, which is facing away from the body.

RELATIVE 1 (rĕl′ ə tĭv), *n.* (Touching one another, as members of a family.) The "D" hands, palms facing the body and index fingers pointing toward each other, swing alternately up and down. Each time they pass each other, the index fingertips come into mutual contact. Also KIN.

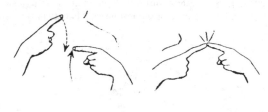

RELATIVE 2, *adj.* (Joining together.) Both hands, held in the modified "5" position, palms out, move toward each other. The thumbs and index fingers of both hands then connect. Also AFFILIATE 1, ANNEX, ASSOCIATE 2, ATTACH, BELONG, COMMUNION OF SAINTS, CONCERN 2, CONNECT, ENLIST, ENROLL, JOIN 1, PARTICIPATE, UNION, UNITE.

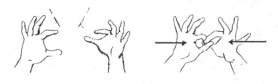

RELATIVE 3, *n.* (The "R"s) The sign for RELATIVE 1 is made, using both "R" hands.

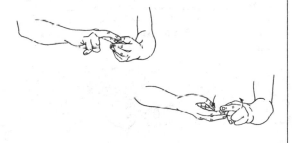

RELAX 1 (rĭ lăks′), *v.*, -LAXED, -LAXING. (The folded arms; a position of rest.) With palms facing the body, the arms are folded across the chest. Also LIMBO, REST 1, RESTFUL 1.

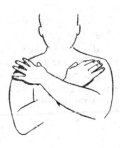

RELAX 2, *n.* (The "R" hands.) The sign for REST 1, *q.v.,* is made, but with the crossed "R" hands. Also REST 2, RESTFUL 2.

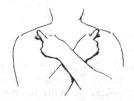

RELAY (rē′ lā), *n., v.,* -LAYED, LAYING. (Back-and-forth movement.) Both "R" hands pass each other repeatedly as they move back and forth.

RELEASE 1 (ri lĕs′), *n., v.,* -LEASED, -LEASING. (Opening up.) The interlocked "F" hands spring apart.

RELEASE 2, *n., v.* (The "R" hands; breaking the bonds.) Both crossed "R" hands, palms facing each other, are swung apart so that they now face out.

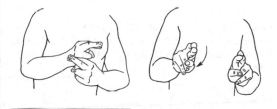

RELIEF (rĭ lēf′), *n.* (Breaking the bonds.) The "S" hands, crossed in front of the body, swing apart and face out. Also DELIVER 1, EMANCIPATE, FREE 1, INDEPENDENCE, INDEPENDENT, LIBERATION, REDEEM 1, RESCUE, SAFE, SALVATION, SAVE 1.

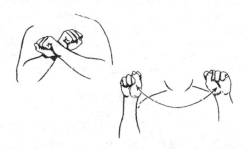

RELINQUISH (rĭ lĭng′ kwĭsh), *v.,* -QUISHED, -QUISHING. (Throwing up the hands in a gesture of surrender.) Both "A" hands are held palms down before the chest and then thrown up in unison, ending in the "5" position. Also ABDICATE, CEDE, DISCOURAGE 1, FORFEIT, GIVE UP, LOSE HOPE, RENOUNCE, RENUNCIATION, SURRENDER 1, YIELD 1.

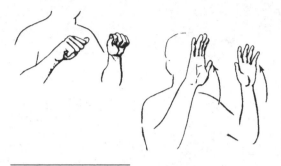

RELY 1 (rĭ lī′), *v.,* -LIED, -LYING. (Something that weighs down or burdens one with responsibility.) The fingertips of both hands, placed on the right shoulder, bear down. Also ATTRIBUTE 1, BEAR 4, BURDEN, OBLIGATION 1, RESPONSIBILITY 1, RESPONSIBLE 1.

RELY 2, *v.* (Hanging onto.) With the right index finger resting across its left counterpart, both hands drop down a bit. Also DEPEND 1, DEPENDABLE, DEPENDENT, HINGE 2.

REMAIN (rĭ mān′), *v.,* -MAINED, -MAINING. (Steady, uninterrupted movement.) The "A" hands are held with palms out, thumbs extended and touching, the right behind the left. In this position the hands move forward in a straight, steady line or down. Also CONTINUE 1, ENDURE 2, EVER 1, LAST 3, LASTING, PERMANENT, PERPETUAL, PERSEVERE 3, PERSIST 2, STAY 1, STAY STILL.

REMAINDER (rĭ mān′ dər), *n.* (The remainder is left behind.) The "5" hands, palms facing each other and fingers pointing forward, are dropped simultaneously a few inches, as if dropping something on the table. Also LEFT 2, RESERVE 4, REST 3.

REMARK (rĭ märk′), *v.,* -MARKED, -MARKING. (Words tumbling from the mouth.) The right index finger, pointing left, describes a continuous small circle in front of the mouth. Also BID 3, DISCOURSE, HEARING, MAINTAIN 2, MENTION, SAID, SAY, SPEAK, SPEECH 1, STATE, STATEMENT, TALK 1, TELL, VERBAL 1.

REMEMBER (rĭ mĕm′ bər), *v.,* -BERED, -BERING. (Knowledge that remains.) The sign for KNOW is made: the right fingertips are placed on the forehead. The sign for REMAIN then follows: the "A" hands are held with palms toward the body, thumbs extended and touching, the right behind the left. In this position the hands move forward in a straight, steady line or straight down. Also MEMORY, RECALL 2, RECOLLECT 2.

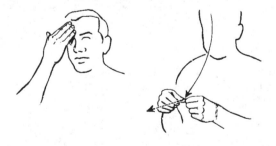

REMIND 1 (rĭ mīnd′) (*colloq.*) *v.,* -MINDED, -MINDING. (Bring up to mind.) The index finger swings up quickly to the forehead. As it touches the forehead, the head tilts back. The eyes are sometimes opened wide for emphasis.

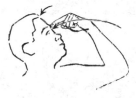

REMIND 2, *v.* (Tapping someone.) The signer taps the right shoulder with the right hand.

REMIND 3, *v.* (Tap for attention.) One hand taps either shoulder twice.

REMOTE (rĭ mōt′), *adj.* (Moving beyond, *i.e.,* the concept of distance or "farness.") The "A" hands are held together, thumbs pointing away from the body. The right hand moves straight ahead in a slight arc. The left hand does not move. Also DISTANCE, DISTANT, FAR, OFF 2.

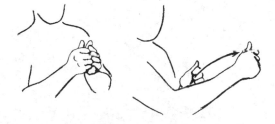

REMOVE 1 (rĭ mōŏv′), *v.,* -MOVED, -MOVING. (Removing.) The right "A" hand, resting in the palm of the left "5" hand, moves slightly up and away, describing a small arc. It is then cast downward, opening into the "5" position, palm down, as if removing something from the left hand and casting it down. Also ABOLISH 2, ABSENCE 2, ABSENT 2, ABSTAIN, CHEAT 2, DEDUCT, DEFICIENCY, DELETE 1, LESS 2, MINUS 3, OUT 2, SUBTRACT, SUBTRACTION, TAKE AWAY FROM, WITHDRAW 2.

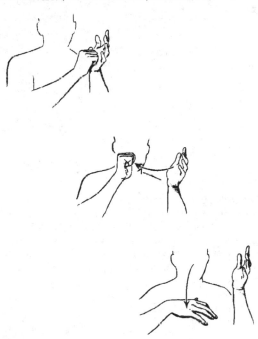

REMOVE 2, *v.* (Moving from one place to another.) The downturned hands, fingers touching their respective thumbs, move in unison from left to right. Also MIGRATE, MOVE, PLACE 3, PUT, TRANSFER 2.

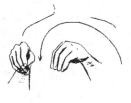

REMOVE 3, *v.* (Wiping off.) The left "5" hand, palm up, is held slightly below the right "5" hand, held palm down. The right hand swings up, just brushing over the left palm. Both hands close into the "S" position, and the right is brought back with force to its initial position, striking a glancing blow against the left knuckles as it returns. Also ABOLISH 1, ANNIHILATE, CORRUPT, DEFACE, DEMOLISH, DESTROY, HAVOC, PERISH 2, RUIN.

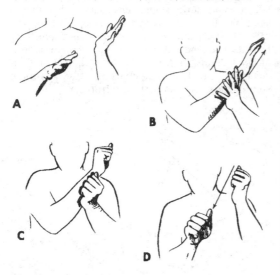

RENOUNCE (rĭ nouns'), v., -NOUNCED, -NOUNCING. (Throwing up the hands in a gesture of surrender.) Both "A" hands are held palms down before the chest and then thrown up in unison, ending in the "5" position. Also ABDICATE, CEDE, DISCOURAGE 1, FORFEIT, GIVE UP, LOSE HOPE, RELINQUISH, RENUNCIATION, SURRENDER 1, YIELD.

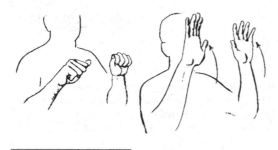

RENOWNED (rĭ nound'), adj. (One's fame radiates far and wide.) The extended index fingers rest on the lips (or on the temples). Moving in small, continuous spirals, they move up and to either side of the head. Also CELEBRATED, FAME, FAMOUS, PROMINENT 1.

RENT (rent), n., v., RENTED, RENTING. (Monthly.) The sign for MONTH is made: the extended right index finger moves down along the upturned extended left index finger. This movement is repeated several times. Also MONTHLY.

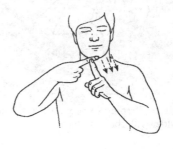

RENUNCIATION (rĭ nŭn' sĭ ā' shən, -shĭ-), n. See RENOUNCE.

REPAIR (rĭ pâr'), v., -PAIRED, -PAIRING. (Fashioning something with the hands.) The right "S" hand, palm facing left, is placed on top of its counterpart, whose palm faces right. The hands are twisted back and forth, striking each other slightly after each twist. Also COMPOSE, CONSTITUTE, CONSTRUCT 2, CREATE, DEVISE 2, FABRICATE, FASHION, FIX, MAKE, MANUFACTURE, MEND 1, PRODUCE 3, RENDER 1.

REPAIR WHAT WAS SAID (Grammatical device in ASL.) The right index finger is brought firmly up against the tightly closed lips. The eyes may be closed and the head may shake slightly. The English gloss here may be "Excuse me, I didn't mean that," "Let me correct myself." Also known as "repairs" in ASL grammar.

REPEAT (rǐ pēt′), *v.,* -PEATED, -PEATING. The left hand, open in the "5" position, palm up, is held before the chest. The right hand, in the right-angle position, fingers pointing up, arches over and into the left palm. Also AGAIN, ENCORE.

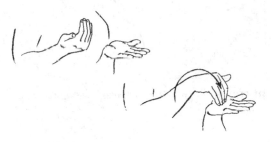

REPEATEDLY, *adv.* (Repeating over and over again.) The sign for REPEAT is made several times.

REPENT (rǐ pěnt′), *v.,* -PENTED, -PENTING. (The heart is circled to indicate feeling, modified by the letter "S" for SORRY.) The right "S" hand, palm facing the body, is rotated several times over the area of the heart. Also APOLOGIZE 1, APOLOGY 1, CONTRITION, PENITENT, REGRET, REGRETFUL, REPENTANT, RUE, SORROW, SORROWFUL 2, SORRY.

REPENTANCE (ri pen′ təns), *n.* (The "R" letters, twisting the heart.) Both "R" hands, fingers touching, execute a twisting motion at the heart.

REPENTANT (rǐ pěn′ tənt), *adj.* See REPENT.

REPLACE (rǐ plās′), *v.,* -PLACED, -PLACING. (Exchanging places.) The right "A" hand, positioned above the left "A" hand, swings down and under the left, coming up a bit in front of it. Also EXCHANGE, INSTEAD OF 1, SUBSTITUTE, TRADE.

REPLY 1 (rǐ plī′), *n., v.,* -PLIED, -PLYING. (Directing a reply from the mouth to someone.) The tip of the right index finger, held in the "D" position, palm facing the body, is placed on the lips, while the left "D" hand, palm also facing the body, is held about a foot in front of the right hand. The right index finger, swinging around, moves toward and stops in a pointing position a few inches from the left index fingertip. Also ANSWER 1, MAKE RESPONSE, RESPOND, RESPONSE 1.

REPLY 2, *v.* (The letter "R"; coming out of the mouth.) Both "R" hands are held before the face, with the right "R" hand at the lips and behind the left "R" hand. Both hands move forward simultaneously, describing a small upward arc. Also ANSWER 2, REACTION, REPORT, RESPONSE 2.

REPORT (rǐ pōrt′), *v.,* -PORTED, -PORTING. See REPLY 2.

REPRESENT (rĕp′ rĭ zĕnt′), *v.,* -SENTED, -SENTING. (Directing the attention to something and bringing it forward.) The right index finger points into the left palm, held facing out before the body. The left palm moves straight out. For the passive form of this verb, *i.e.,* BE SHOWN, the movement is reversed: the left hand, palm facing in, is moved in toward the body, while the right index finger remains pointing into the left palm. Also DEMONSTRATE, DISPLAY, EVIDENCE, EXAMPLE, EXHIBIT, EXHIBITION, ILLUSTRATE, INDICATE, INFLUENCE 3, PRODUCE 2, SHOW 1, SIGNIFY 1.

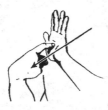

REPRESENTATIVE 1 (rĕp′ rĭ zĕn′ tə tĭv), *n.* (The letter "R"; perhaps the drape of the Roman toga about the shoulders.) The right "R" hand, palm facing left, swings from the right shoulder to the left shoulder.

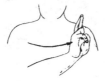

REPRESENTATIVE 2, *n.* (The letter "R"; to show.) The right "R" hand, placed in the left palm, is pushed forward by the palm. The sign for INDIVIDUAL 1 usually then follows.

REPRIMAND (rĕp′ rə mănd′), *n., v.,* -MANDED, -MANDING. (A scolding with the finger.) The right

index finger shakes back and forth in a natural scolding movement. Also ADMONISH 2, REPROVE, SCOLD 1.

REPROVE (rĭ prōōv′), *v.,* -PROVED, -PROVING. See REPRIMAND.

REPUBLIC (ri pub′ lik), *n.* (The letter "R"; NATION.) The tips of the right "R" fingers make a clockwise circle above the downturned left hand and come down to rest on the back of the left fist. Also COUNTRY 2, LAND 2, NATION.

REQUEST 1 (rĭ kwĕst′), *n., v.,* -QUESTED, -QUESTING. (Pray tell.) Both hands, held upright about a foot in front of the chest, with palms facing and fingers pointing straight up, are positioned about a foot apart. Moving toward the chest, they come together until they touch, as if in prayer. Also ASK 1, CONSULT, INQUIRE 1.

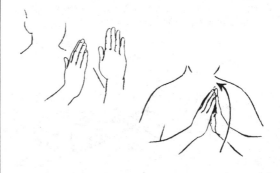

REQUEST 2, *n., v.* (Something specific is moved in toward oneself.) The palm of the left "5" hand faces right. The right index finger is thrust into the left palm, and both hands are drawn sharply in toward the chest. Also DEMAND, INSIST, REQUIRE.

REQUIRE (rǐ kwīr′), v., -QUIRED, -QUIRING. See RE-QUEST 2.

RESCUE (rĕs′ kū), v., -CUED, -CUING, n. (Breaking the bonds.) The "S" hands, crossed in front of the body, swing apart and face out. Also DELIVER 1, EMANCIPATE, FREE 1, INDEPENDENCE, INDEPENDENT, LIBERATION, REDEEM 1, RELIEF, SAFE, SALVATION, SAVE 1.

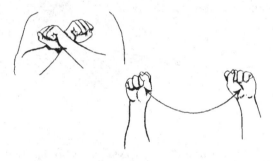

RESERVATION 1 (rĕz′ ər vā′ shən), n. (Binding the hands down.) The downturned right "S" hand makes a single, clockwise circle and comes down to rest on the back of the downturned left "S" hand. Also RESERVE 1

RESERVATION 2, n. (The letter "R"; an area.) Both "R" hands, palms down and fingers pointing forward, describe a circle by simultaneously moving apart, in toward the body, and together. This is the sign for a Native American reservation.

RESERVE 1 (rǐ zûrv′), v., -SERVED, -SERVING. See RESERVATION.

RESERVE 2, v. (Slow, careful movement.) The "K" hands are crossed, the right above the left, little finger edges down. In this position the hands are moved up and down a short distance. Also CARE 2, CAREFUL 2, KEEP, MAINTAIN 1, MIND 3, PRESERVE, TAKE CARE OF 2.

RESERVE 3, v. (Holding back.) The right "V" fingers are tapped once or twice across the back of their left counterparts. Both palms face the chest. Also SAVE 2, STORE 2.

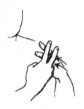

RESERVE 4, n. (The remainder is left behind.) The "5" hands, palms facing each other and fingers pointing forward, are dropped simultaneously a few inches, as if dropping something on the table. Also LEFT 2, REMAINDER, REST 3.

RESIDE (rǐ zīd′), v., -SIDED, -SIDING. (A place where one lives.) The "A" hands, thumbs up, are placed on either side of the body at waist level. They slide up the body in unison to chest level. This is the sign for LIFE or LIVE, indicating an upsurging of life. Also ADDRESS 3, ALIVE, DWELL, EXIST, LIFE 1, LIVE 1, LIVING, MORTAL.

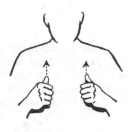

RESIDENCE 1 (rĕz′ ə dəns), *n.* (A place where one eats and sleeps.) The closed fingers of the right hand are placed against the lips (the sign for EAT) and then, opening into a flat palm, against the right cheek (resting the head on a pillow, as in SLEEP). The head leans slightly to the right, as if going to sleep in the right palm, during this latter movement. Also ADDRESS 2, HOME.

RESIDENCE 2, *n.* (The shape of the building.) The open hands are held with fingertips touching so that they form a pyramid a bit above eye level. From this position, the hands separate and move diagonally downward for a short distance; then they continue straight down a few inches. This movement traces the outline of a roof and walls. Also BARN, DOMICILE, HOUSE.

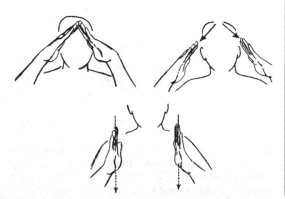

RESIDENCE 3, *n.* (The letter "R"; LIVE.) Both "R" hands move up together against the body. This is an initialized version of LIVE.

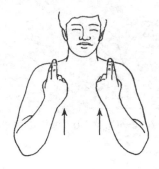

RESIGN (rĭ zīn′), *v.,* -SIGNED, -SIGNING. (Pulling out.) The index and middle fingers of the right "H" hand are grasped by the left hand. The right hand pulls out of the left. Also QUIT, WITHDRAW 3.

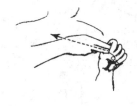

RESOLVE (rĭ zŏlv′), *v.,* -SOLVED, -SOLVING, *n.* (The mind stops wavering, and the pros and cons are resolved.) The right index finger touches the forehead, the sign for THINK, *q.v.* Both "F" hands, palms facing each other and fingers pointing straight out, then drop down simultaneously. The sign for JUDGE, *q.v.* explains the rationale behind the movement of the two hands here. Also DECIDE, DECISION, DECREE 1, DETERMINE, MAKE UP ONE'S MIND, MIND 5, RENDER JUDGMENT, VERDICT.

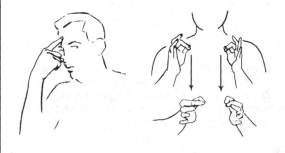

RESPECT (rĭ spĕkt′), *n., v.,* -SPECTED, -SPECTING. (The letter "R"; bowing the head.) The right "R" hand swings up in an arc toward the head, which bows somewhat as the hand moves up toward it. The hand's movement is sometimes reversed, moving down and away from the head in an arc while the head bows,

RESPIRATION (rĕs' pə rā' shən), n. (The rise and fall of the chest in respiration.) The hands, folded over the chest, move forward and back to the chest to indicate the breathing. Also BREATH, BREATHE.

RESPOND (rĭ spŏnd'), v., -PONDED, -PONDING. (Directing a reply from the mouth to someone.) The tip of the right index finger, held in the "D" position, palm facing the body, is placed on the lips, while the left "D" hand, palm also facing the body, is held about a foot in front of the right hand. The right index finger, swinging around, moves toward and stops in a pointing position a few inches from the left index fingertip. Also ANSWER 1, MAKE RESPONSE, REPLY 1, RESPONSE 1.

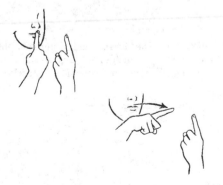

RESPONSE 1 (rĭ spŏns'), n. See RESPOND.

RESPONSE 2, n. (The letter "R"; coming out of the mouth.) Both "R" hands are held before the face, with the right "R" hand at the lips and behind the left "R" hand. Both hands move forward simultaneously, describing a small upward arc. Also ANSWER 2, REACTION, REPLY 2, REPORT.

RESPONSIBILITY 1 (rĭ spŏn' sə bĭl' ə tĭ), n. (Something that weighs down or burdens one with responsibility.) The fingertips of both hands, placed on the right shoulder, bear down. Also ATTRIBUTE 1, BEAR 4, BURDEN, OBLIGATION 1, RELY 1, RESPONSIBLE 1.

RESPONSIBILITY 2, n. (Something that weighs down or burdens, modified by the letter "R" for "responsibility.") The "R" hands bear down on the right shoulder in the same manner as RESPONSIBILITY 1. Also ATTRIBUTE 2, RESPONSIBLE 2.

RESPONSIBLE 1 (rĭ spŏn' sə bəl), adj. See RESPONSIBILITY 1.

RESPONSIBLE 2, adj. See RESPONSIBILITY 2.

REST 1 (rĕst), *n.* (The folded arms; a position of rest.) With palms facing the body, the arms are folded across the chest. Also LIMBO, RELAX 1, RESTFUL 1.

REST 2, *n.* (The "R" hands.) The sign for REST 1 is made, but with the crossed "R" hands. Also RELAX 2, RESTFUL 2.

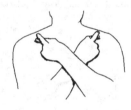

REST 3, *n.* (The remainder is left behind.) The "5" hands, palms facing each other and fingers pointing forward, are dropped simultaneously a few inches, as if dropping something on the table. Also LEFT 2, REMAINDER, RESERVE 4.

RESTFUL 1 (rĕst′ fəl), *adj.* See REST 1.

RESTFUL 2, *adj.* See REST 2.

RESTRAIN (ri strān′), *v.,* -STRAINED, -STRAINING. (Hold down one's feelings.) The right claw hand closes as it moves down the throat.

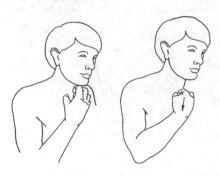

RESTRICT (rĭ strĭkt′), *v.,* -STRICTED, -STRICTING. (The upper and lower limits are defined.) The right-angle hands, palms facing, are held before the body, the right above the left. They swing out 45° simultaneously, pivoted from their wrists. Also CAPACITY, LIMIT, QUANTITY 1.

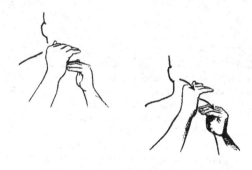

REST ROOM *n.* (The "R"s). The downturned right "R" hand moves down an inch or so, arcs over to the right slightly, and then again moves down an inch or so.

RESULT (ri zult′), *n.* (The "R"; dropping off the end; a conclusion.) The downturned right "R" hand moves along the index finger edge of the left open hand and drops down after reaching the fingertips.

RESUME (rĭ zōōm′), v., -SUMED, -SUMING. (Moving forward.) Both right-angle hands, palms facing each other and knuckles facing forward, move forward simultaneously. Also FORWARD, GO AHEAD, MOTION FORWARD, ONWARD, PROCEED, PROGRESS 2.

RÉSUMÉ (rez′ ŏŏ mā), n. (The letter "R"; the shape of a piece of paper.) Both "R" hands trace the top and sides of an imaginary piece of paper.

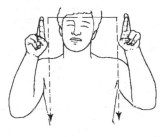

RETALIATE 1 (rĭ tăl′ ĭ āt′), v., -ATED, -ATING. (Birds pecking back and forth at each other.) The right index finger and thumb, pressed together, strike their counterparts with force. Also RETALIATION 1, REVENGE.

RETALIATE 2, v. (An exchange.) The downturned "O" hands are positioned one in front of the other. They then exchange places. Also RETALIATION 2.

RETALIATION 1 (rĭ tăl′ ĭ ā′ shən), n. See RETALIATE 1.

RETALIATION 2, n. See RETALIATE 2.

RETARDED 1 (ri tär′ did), adj. (The mind is slow.) The index finger taps the forehead twice, followed by the sign for SLOW: the downturned open right hand is drawn slowly over the back of the downturned left hand from fingertips to wrist.

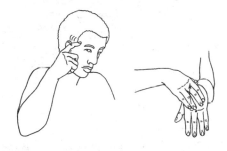

RETARDED 2, adj. (The "R"; the mind is indicated.) The right "R" fingers rock slowly up and down from their position against the forehead or right temple.

RETARDED 3, adj. Same as RETARDED 2, except that the bent index and middle fingers of the right hand repeatedly open and close against the forehead or temple.

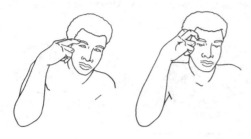

RETARDED 4, *adj.* (The MIND is LIMITED.) The index finger taps the forehead or temple once or twice, and then the sign for LIMIT is made, giving the upper and lower limits: the right-angle hands, palms facing, are held before the body, the right above the left. They swing out 45° simultaneously, pivoted from their wrists.

RETARDED 5, *sl.* (A pea brain.) The mind is tapped by the index finger, and then the thumb is flicked off the tip of the little finger. This sign is of course derogatory and should be used only in a joking situation among friends.

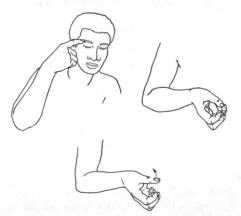

RETIRE 1 (rǐ tīr′), *v.*, -TIRED, -TIRING. (Pulling away.) The downturned open hands are held in a line, with fingers pointing to the left, the right hand behind the left. Both hands move in unison toward the right. As they do so, they assume the "A" position. Also DEPART, EVACUATE, FORSAKE 1, GRADUATE 2, LEAVE 1, WITHDRAW 1.

RETIRE 2 (*colloq.*), *v.* (Tucking the legs beneath the covers.) The index and middle fingers of the right "U" hand, held either palm down or palm up, are thrust into the downturned left "O" hand. Also GO TO BED 2.

RETIRE 3, *v.* (A position of idleness.) With thumbs tucked in the armpits, the remaining fingers of both hands wiggle. Also HOLIDAY, IDLE, LEISURE, VACATION.

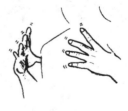

REVENGE (rǐ věnj′), *n.*, *v.*, -VENGED, -VENGING. (Birds pecking back and forth at each other.) The right index finger and thumb, pressed together, strike their left counterparts with force. Also RETALIATE 1, RETALIATION 1.

REVERBERATE (ri vûr′ bə rāt′), v., -ATED, -ATING, (A sound comes back.) The right index touches the right ear and then changes to a fist, striking the left palm. The right fingers then open up and the right hand moves back toward the body, away from the left palm, with the right fingers wriggling and the right hand itself swiveling back and forth very slightly. Also ECHO.

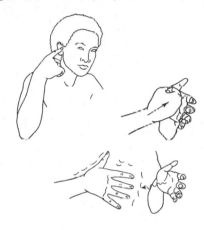

REVERE 1 (rǐ vǐr′), v., -VERED, -VERING. (Drawing out the feelings.) The thumb and index finger of the right open hand, held an inch or two apart, are placed at midchest. As the hand moves straight out from the chest the two fingers come together. Also ADMIRE 1, REVERE 1.

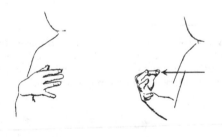

REVERE 2, v. (Clasping the heart.) The "5" hands are held one atop the other over the heart. Sometimes the "S" hands are used, in which case they are crossed at the wrists. Also BELOVED, CHARITY, DEVOTION, LOVE.

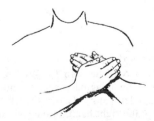

REVERSE 1 (rǐ vûrs′), adj., n., v., -VERSED, -VERSING. (Separateness.) The tips of the extended index fingers touch before the chest, the right finger pointing left and the left finger pointing right. The fingers then draw apart sharply to either side. Also CONTRAST 2, OPPOSITE.

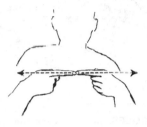

REVERSE 2, adj., n., v. (To change positions.) Both "A" hands, thumbs up, are held before the chest several inches apart. The left hand is pivoted over so that its thumb points to the right. Simultaneously, the right hand is moved up and over the left, describing a small arc, with its thumb pointing to the left. Also ADJUST, ALTER, ALTERATION, CHANGE 1, CONVERT, MODIFY, TRANSFER 1.

REVERSE 3, v. (The "R"s.) The sign for REVERSE 2, is made with the "R" hands.

REVERSE 4, n., v. (Like REVERSE ROLES, but using both "V" hands, palms in and fingertips facing each other.) This is often used to indicate a switch in polarity or voltage.

REVERSE INTERPRET *v.* (Combined "R" and "I.") With the left hand making an "I" and the right an "R," both hands, crossed, swing around each other.

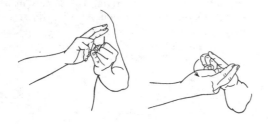

REVERSE ROLES, *phrase.* (Changing places.) The right "V" hand, palm up, fingers pointing left, turns over to the palm-down position.

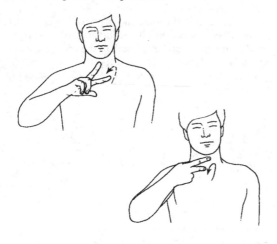

REVIEW (ri vyōō'), *v.,* -VIEWED, -VIEWING. (Backward in time.) The right "R" hand, palm facing in, is placed with its little finger edge on the open left hand, whose palm faces right. The "R" hand arcs backward until it is over the left wrist.

REVOLTING (rĭ vōl' tĭng), *adj.* (Turning the stomach.) The fingertips of the curved right hand describe a continuous circle on the stomach. The signer assumes an exaggerated expression of disgust. Also DISGUST, DISGUSTED, DISGUSTING, DISPLEASED, MAKE ME DISGUSTED, MAKE ME SICK, NAUSEA, NAUSEATE, NAUSEOUS, OBNOXIOUS.

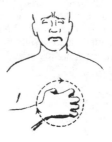

REVOLUTION 1 (rev' ə lōō' shən), *n.* (The letter "R"; a whirlwind.) Both "R" hands, fingertips pointing at each other, are held with the right above the left. The "R" fingers spin around each other in a sudden and dramatic movement.

REVOLUTION 2, *n.* (The letter "R"; turning around or rebelling.) The upturned right "R" hand, held palm back at shoulder height, twists around suddenly with a dramatic flourish to the palm-out position.

REWRITE (rē rīt', rē' rīt'), *v.,* -WROTE, -WRITING. (WRITE; AGAIN.) The sign for WRITE: the right hand, grasping an imaginary pencil, mimes writing across the open left palm. AGAIN: the left "5" hand is held palm up; the right hand, in the right-angle position, fingers pointing up, arches over and into the left palm.

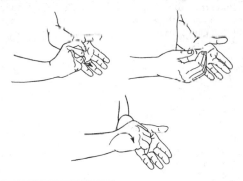

RHINOCEROS (rī nos′ ər əs), *n.* (The horn.) The right "I" hand, palm facing left and thumb tucked under the fingers, is placed on the nose. The hand moves forward and up in an arc, tracing the characteristic shape of the horn.

RHYME (rīm), *n., v.,* RHYMED, RHYMING. (The "R"; a rhythmic movement.) The right "R" hand makes a series of figure-eight movements over the left arm, held either palm up or palm down. The body usually sways back and forth slightly, keeping time.

RHYTHM (rith′ əm), *n.* (The letter "R"; the rhythmic beat.) The right "R" hand taps the left wrist in a rhythmic fashion.

RIBBON (rib′ ən), *n.* (The "R"s; tying a ribbon in the hair.) Both "R" hands mime tying a ribbon's bow in the hair.

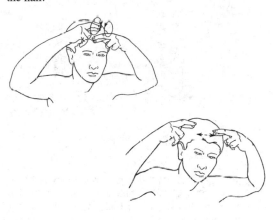

RICE 1 (rīs), *n.* The tips of the four right fingers move up and down simultaneously as they move along the left index finger from knuckle to tip. This sign is used generally for different grains. Also BEAN(S), GRAIN, OATMEAL.

RICE 2, *n.* (The "R"; picking up the grain with chopsticks. The signer, using the "R" hand, mimes bringing rice up to the mouth.

RICH (rĭch), *adj.* (A pile of money.) The sign for MONEY is made: the back of the upturned right hand, whose thumb and fingertips are all touching, is placed in the upturned left palm. The right hand then moves straight up as it opens into the "5" position, palm facing down and fingers somewhat curved. Also WEALTH, WEALTHY.

RIDICULE (rĭd′ ə kūl′), *n., v.,* -CULED, -CULING. (Derision; poking or prodding.) Both hands are held closed except for index and little fingers, which extend straight out from the body. The right hand is brought up and its index fingertip pulls the right corner of the mouth into a slight smile. Both hands then move forward simultaneously in a series of short jabbing motions, the right somewhat behind the left. An expression of disdain is assumed during this sign. The first part of the sign, pulling the mouth into a smile, is frequently omitted. Also MAKE FUN OF, MOCK.

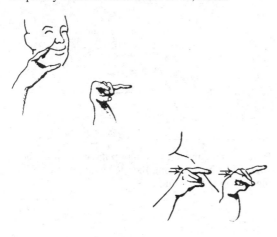

RIDICULOUS (rĭ dĭk′ yə ləs), *adj.* (Thoughts flickering back and forth.) The right "Y" hand, thumb almost touching the forehead, is shaken back and forth across the forehead several times. Also ABSURD, DAFT, FOLLY, FOOLISH, NONSENSE, SILLY, TRIFLING.

RIFLE (rī′ fəl), *n.* (Shooting a gun.) The left "S" hand is held above the head as if holding a gun barrel. At the same time the right "L" hand is held below the left hand, its index finger moving back and forth as if pulling a trigger. Also GUN, PISTOL, SHOOT 2, SHOT 2.

RIGHT 1 (rīt), *adj.* (A straightening out.) The right hand, fingers together and palm facing left, is placed in the upturned left palm, whose fingers point away from the body. The right hand slides straight out along the left palm, over the left fingers, and stops with its heel resting on the left fingertips. Also ALL RIGHT, O.K. 1, PRIVILEGE, RIGHTEOUS 1, YOU'RE WELCOME 2.

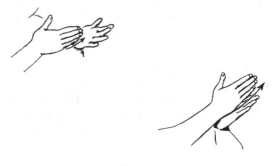

RIGHT 2, *adj., adv.* (The letter "R"; the movement.) The right "R" hand moves toward the right. Also RIGHT-HAND.

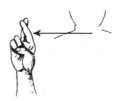

RIGHT 3, *adj., adv.* The right index finger, held above the left index finger, comes down rather forcefully so that the bottom of the right hand comes to rest on top of the left thumb joint. Also ACCURATE 2, CORRECT 1, DECENT, EXACT 2, JUST 2, PROPER, SUITABLE.

RIGHTEOUS 1 (rī′ chəs), *adj.* See RIGHT 1.

RIGHTEOUS 2, *adj.* (The letter "R"; the wiping signifies cleanliness or purity.) The right "R" hand moves in a small, clockwise circle, and then the right palm wipes across its upturned left counterpart.

RIGID (rĭj′ ĭd), *adj.* (The stiff fingers.) The fingers of the "5" hands, held palms down, stiffen and contract. Also FREEZE, FROZEN, ICE.

RING 1 (rĭng), *n.* (The natural sign.) The index finger and thumb of the open right hand go through the motions of slipping a ring on the left ring finger.

RING 2, *n., v.,* RANG, RUNG, RINGING. (The bell's reverberations.) The right fist strikes the front of the left hand and then opens and moves away from the left in an undulating manner to indicate the sound waves. Also BELL 1.

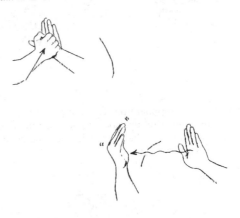

RIP OFF (rĭp′ ôf′), *v., sl.* (A magician's trick of flipping a coin into the sleeve, and thus cheating someone.) The middle finger of the right downturned hand rests on the upturned left palm. The finger makes a swift backward movement, closing against the right palm. The movement is sometimes repeated. Also TAKE ADVANTAGE OF.

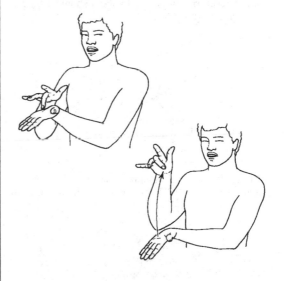

RISE 1 (rīz), *v.,* ROSE, RISEN, RISING, *n.* (Getting onto one's feet.) The upturned index and middle fingers of the right hand, representing the legs, are swung up and over in an arc, coming to rest in the upturned left palm. Also ARISE 2, ELEVATE, GET UP, RAISE 1, STAND 2, STAND UP.

RISE 2, *v., n.* (Popping up before the eyes.) The right index finger, pointing up, pops up between the index and middle fingers of the left hand, whose palm faces down. Also APPEAR 2, POP UP.

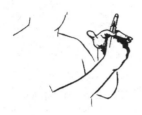

RISE 3, *v., n.* (Rising up.) Both upturned hands, held at chest level, rise in unison to about shoulder height. Also ARISE 1, STAND 3.

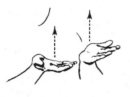

RISK (risk), *n., v.,* RISKED, RISKING. (Cutting the throat.) The right "R" is drawn across the throat from left to right.

RITUAL (rich′ ŏŏ əl), *n., adj.* (The letter "R"; bound down by custom.) The right "R" hand, palm down, is placed on top of the left fist. It pushes the fist down.

RIVAL 1 (rī′ vəl), *n., adj., v.,* -VALED, -VALING. (At sword's point.) The two index fingers, after pointing to each other, are drawn sharply apart. This is followed by the sign for INDIVIDUAL 1: both open hands, palms facing each other, move down the sides of the body, tracing its outline to the hips. Also ENEMY, FOE, OPPONENT.

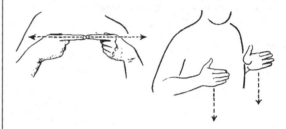

RIVAL 2, *v.* (Two opponents come together.) Both hands are closed, with thumbs pointing straight up and palms facing the body. From their initial position about a foot apart, the hands are brought together sharply so that the knuckles strike. The hands, as they are drawn together, also move down a bit so that they describe a "V." Also COMPETE 1, COMPETITION 1, CONTEND 1, CONTEST 1, RACE 1, RIVALRY 1, VIE 1.

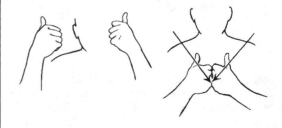

RIVAL 3, *n., v.* (Opposing objects.) The "A" hands are held side by side before the chest, palms facing each other and thumbs pointing forward. In this position the hands move alternately back and forth, toward and away from the body. Also COMPETE 2, COMPETITION 2, CONTEND 2, CONTEST 2, RACE 2, RIVALRY 2, VIE 2.

RIVAL 4, *n., v.* (The changing fortunes of competitors.) The "A" hands are held facing each other, thumbs pointing up in front of the body. Both hands are moved alternately backward and forward past each other several times. Also COMPETE 3, COMPETITION 3, CONTEND 3, CONTEST 3, RACE 3, RIVALRY 3, VIE 3.

RIVALRY 1 (rī′ vəl rĭ), *n.* See RIVAL 2.

RIVALRY 2, *n.* See RIVAL 3.

RIVALRY 3, *n.* See RIVAL 4.

ROAD (rōd), *n.* (The winding movement.) Both hands, palms facing and fingers together and extended straight out, move in unison away from the body in a winding manner. Also CORRIDOR, HALL, HALLWAY, MANNER 2, METHOD, OPPORTUNITY 3, PATH, STREET, TRAIL, WAY 1.

ROAM (rōm), *v.,* ROAMED, ROAMING. (Random movement.) The right "D" hand, palm facing left, moves to and fro from right to left. Also WANDER 2.

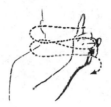

ROAR (rôr), *n., v.,* ROARED, ROARING. (Miming making a roar.) Both claw hands, palms facing and one on top of the other, open up in front of the mouth. Meanwhile the signer makes a silent roar, baring the teeth.

ROB 1 (rŏb), *v.,* ROBBED, ROBBING. (The hand, partly concealed, takes something surreptitiously.) The index and middle fingers of the right hand, somewhat curved, are placed under the left elbow. As they move slowly along the left forearm toward the left wrist, they close a bit. Also ABDUCT, EMBEZZLE, EMBEZZLEMENT, KIDNAP, ROBBERY 1, STEAL 1, SWIPE, THEFT 1, THIEF 1, THIEVERY.

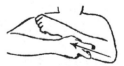

ROB 2 (*colloq.*), *v.* (A sly, underhanded movement.) The right open hand, palm down, is held a bit behind the body at waist level. Beginning with the little finger, the hand closes finger by finger into the "A" position, as if wrapping itself around something. Also ROBBERY 1, STEAL 2, THEFT 2.

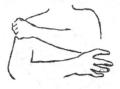

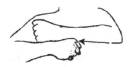

ROB 3, *v.* (A mustachioed thief.) The fingertips of both "H" hands, palms facing the body, are placed above the lips and are drawn slowly apart, describing a mustache. Sometimes one hand only is used. Also BANDIT, BURGLAR, BURGLARY, CROOK, ROBBER 1, ROBBERY 1, STEAL 3, THEFT 3, THIEF 2.

ROB 4, *v.* (Brandishing handguns.) The signer mimes brandishing a pair of guns.

ROBBER 1 (rŏb′ ər), *n.* See ROB 3. This is followed by the sign for INDIVIDUAL: both open hands,

palms facing each other, move down the sides of the body, tracing its outline to the hips.

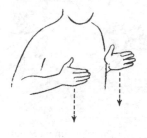

ROBBER 2, *n.* The sign, ROB 1, 2, or 3 is used. It is followed by the sign, INDIVIDUAL, as in ROBBER 1.

ROBBERY 1 (rŏb′ ə rĭ), *n.* See ROB 1, 2, 3.

ROBBERY 2 (*colloq.*), *n.* (The guns.) Both "L" hands, palms facing each other, thumbs pointing straight up, are thrown forward slightly, as if presenting a pair of revolvers. Also HOLDUP.

ROBE (rōb), *n.* (The drape of the garment.) Both open hands are placed palm side against the chest. They slide down to waist level, and the right then goes across to cover the left.

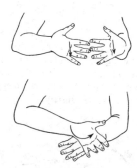

ROBOT (rō′ bət), *n.* (The robot's mechanical gait.) The signer mimes the mechanical walk of a fiction-type robot, with the stiff movements of the hands, arms and legs.

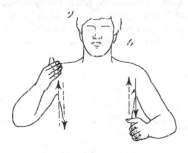

ROCK 1 (rŏk), *n.* (The hardness is indicated by the striking of the fists.) The back of the right "S" hand is struck several times against the back of the left "S" hand. Also STONE 1.

ROCK 2, *n.* (A hard object.) The right "S" hand swings downward before the body, striking its knuckles against the knuckle of the index finger of the left "S" hand, which is held palm down. The right hand continues downward and away from the body in a short curve. Also ROCKY, STONE 2.

ROCK 3, *n.* (A hard, unyielding substance.) The back of the right "S" hand strikes the bottom of the chin twice. Also STONE 2.

ROCKET (rŏk′ ĭt), *n.* (A rocket takes off from its pad.) The downturned right "R" hand (for ROCKET) is placed so that its index and middle fingers rest on the back of the downturned left "S" hand. The right hand moves quickly forward off the left hand. The "R" hand may also point up and move off the left hand from this position. Also MISSILE.

ROCKING CHAIR 1, *n.* (A rocking chair.) The "L" hands, palms facing each other and about two feet apart, are held before the chest. They arc up and down toward the shoulders a number of times. The body is sometimes rocked back and forth in time with the movement of the hands. Also CHAIR 3.

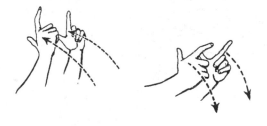

ROCKING CHAIR 2, *n.* (The natural sign.) The extended left index and middle fingers are draped over the thumb of the right "C" hand. In this position, both hands rock alternately forward and back a number of times, in imitation of the motion of the rocking chair. The body may also swing forward and back to emphasize the motion.

ROCKING CHAIR 3, *n.* (The "R" hands; retire or loaf.) The thumbs of both "R" hands are tucked into the armpits, and the signer imitates the forward-backward motion of a rocking chair.

RODEO (rō′ dē ō′, rō dā′ ō), *n*. (Bumping along on horseback.) The downturned right "V" hand straddles the index finger edge of the left "B" hand, whose palm faces right. The right hand moves repeatedly off its perch on the left hand, with the left pushing up each time, as if it were throwing off the right hand.

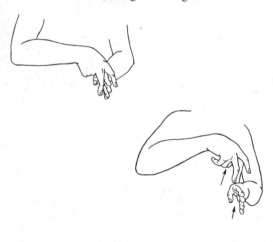

ROLE (rōl), *n*. (The "R"; placing someone in the center of a frame.) The right "R" hand makes a counterclockwise circle in front of the forward-facing left palm and comes to rest in the palm's center.

ROLE MODEL, *n*. (The "R" and "M.") The right "R" hand, palm facing the signer, makes a clockwise circle in front of the outstretched left palm and comes to rest in the center of the palm. The "R" hand changes to the "M" shape, is placed palm down against the left palm, and both hands move forward simultaneously.

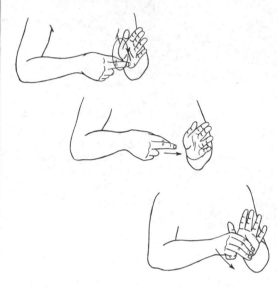

ROLLER COASTER (rō′ lər kō′ stər), *n*. (The undulating movement.) The downturned right hand mimes the movement of a roller coaster, climbing to the top, speeding down, and veering off suddenly to change direction.

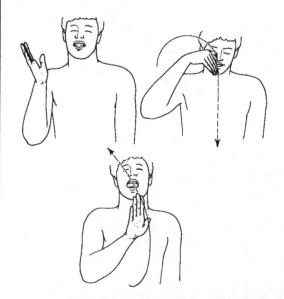

ROM (rom), *n. Computer acronym.* ("Read-only memory.") The signer fingerspells "R-O-M."

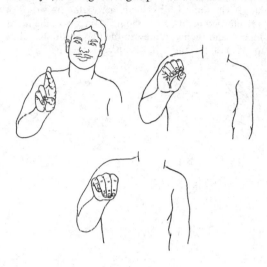

ROMANIA 1 (rō mā′ nē ə, mān′ yə), *n.* Both open hands, palms facing, are drawn apart in a slight upward arc. As they move apart, the fingers close so that they touch their respective thumbs.

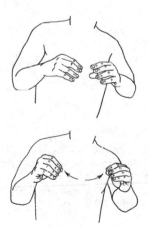

ROMANIA 2, *n.* (The sash, a holdover from royalty.) The right thumb and index finger, forming a "C," are drawn down from left shoulder to right hip.

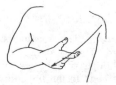

ROOM 1 (rōōm, rŏŏm), *n.* (The dimensions are indicated.) The open hands, palms facing and fingers pointing out, are dropped an inch or two simultaneously. They then shift their relative positions so that both palms face the body, with one hand in front of the other. In this new position they again drop an inch or two simultaneously. Also BOX 1, PACKAGE, SQUARE 1, TRUNK.

ROOM 2, *n.* (The "R" hands.) This is the same sign as for ROOM 1, except that the "R" hands are used. Also OFFICE 1.

ROOMY (rōō′ mē), *adj.* (Lots of elbow room.) The "S" hands, palms facing, are positioned at chest height. As the elbows move apart the palms move down.

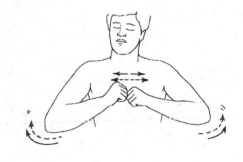

ROOSTER (rōōs′ tər), *n.* (The pecking beak and the comb of the cock.) The "Q" hand's back is placed against the lips, and the thumb and index fingers open and close, representing a beak. The thumb of the right "3" hand is then thrust against the forehead a couple of times, representing the comb. Also COCK.

ROSE (rōz), *n.* (The "R"; smelling the rose.) The right "R" hand moves from one nostril to the other.

ROSH HASHANAH 1 (rŏsh hə shä′ nə, rōsh) (*eccles.*), *n.* (The New Year.) The sign for NEW is made: with both hands held palm up before the body, the right hand sweeps in an arc into the left and continues up a bit. This is followed by the sign for YEAR: the right "S" hand, palm facing left, represents the earth; it is positioned atop the left "S" hand, whose palm faces right, and represents the sun; the right "S" hand describes a clockwise circle around the left, coming to rest in its original position. Also NEW YEAR.

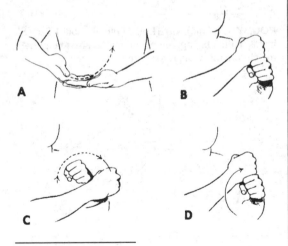

A B

C D

ROSH HASHANAH 2, *n.* (Blowing the shofar or ram's horn.) The thumb of the "Y" hand touches the lips, and the signer pretends to blow.

ROT (rŏt), *v.,* ROTTED, ROTTING, *n.* (Fingering the small pieces resulting from the breaking up of something.) The thumbs rub slowly across the fingertips of the upturned hands, from the little fingers to the index fingers, and then continue to the "A" position, palms up. Also DECAY, DIE OUT, DISSOLVE, FADE, MELT.

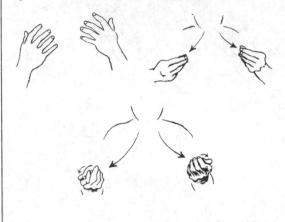

ROTATE (rō′ tāt), *v.,* -TATED, TATING. (The "R" hands; the movement.) Both "R" hands, palms facing and one above the other, move in an alternate clockwise fashion.

ROTTEN (rŏt′ ən), *adj.* (A modification of the sign for spitting or thumbing the nose.) The right "3" hand is held with thumbtip against the nose. Then it is thrown sharply forward, and an expression of contempt is assumed. Also LOUSY.

ROUGH 1 (rŭf), *adj.* (The "roughness," in the form of ridges, described.) The tips of the curved right fingers trace imaginary ridges over the upright left palm, from the base of the hand to the fingertips. The action is repeated several times. Also ROUGHNESS, RUDE 1, SCOLD 2.

ROUGH 2, *adj.* (Same rationale as for ROUGH 1.) The little finger edge of the open right hand passes along the back of the downturned, open left hand, from wrist to fingertips, making a waving motion as if passing over a rough surface.

ROUGH 3, *adj.* (Rationale the same as for ROUGH 1.) The right palm is placed against the left palm and moved forward with a wavy motion as if moving over a rough surface. Also RUGGED.

ROUND 1 (round), *adj.* (The shape.) The curved open hands are held with fingertips touching, as if holding a ball. Also BALL 2, ORB, SPHERE.

ROUND 2, *adj.* (The circle is described.) The index finger, pointing down or out, describes a circle. Also CIRCLE 1.

ROUTINE (roo̅ tēn′), *n., adj.* The right "R" hand moves up the left palm, over the fingertips, and down along the back of the left hand. Also PROGRAM 2.

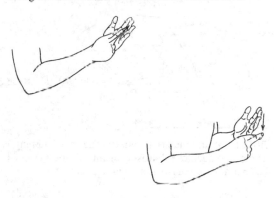

ROW 1 (rō), *v.*, ROWED, ROWING. (The natural sign.) The signer manipulates a pair of imaginary oars, as if rowing a boat.

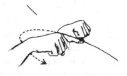

ROW 2 (rou), *n.* (Repeated rejoinders.) Both "D" hands are held with index fingers pointing toward each other. The hands move up and down alternately, each pivoting in turn at the wrist. Also QUARREL.

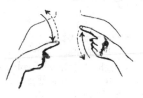

ROW 3, *n.* (A row of chairs.) The hands, palms down, are held side by side, both with bent index and middle fingers. The hands separate, tracing an imaginary line or row of chairs.

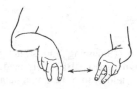

ROYAL (roi′ əl), *adj*. (The "R"; the sash worn by royalty.) The right "R" hand traces a line from the left shoulder to the right waist.

RUB (rŭb), *v.*, RUBBED, RUBBING. (The act of rubbing.) The right knuckles rub briskly against the outstretched left palm. Also POLISH 1, SANDPAPER, SHINE SHOES.

RUBBER 1 (rŭb′ ər), *n*. (The pliability.) The side of the right "X" finger moves up and down on the right cheek. The mouth is held open and may engage in a chewing motion, keeping time with the right "X" finger. Also GUM.

RUBBER 2, *n*. (Snapping a rubber band.) The thumbtip of the right "A" hand is placed behind the tips of the upper front teeth and is then snapped out and forward, away from the mouth.

knuckles facing forward. The hands move apart slowly, as if grasping the ends of a rubber band and stretching it.

RUDE 1 (rōōd), *adj*. (The "roughness" of words is described.) The tips of the curved right fingers trace imaginary ridges over the upright left palm from the base of the hand to the fingertips. The action is repeated several times. Also ROUGH 1, ROUGHNESS, SCOLD 2.

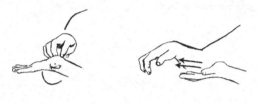

RUDE 2, *adj*. The left hand is held palm down, with index finger pointing forward. The right hand is held in the same way, but slightly above and to the right of the left hand. The right hand then moves down and forward repeatedly, striking against the base of the left index finger at each pass. Also RUDENESS.

RUDENESS (rōōd′ nĭs), *n*. See RUDE 2.

RUE (rōō), *v.*, RUED, RUING, *n*. (The heart is circled to indicate feeling, modified by the letter "S" for SORRY.) The right "S" hand, palm facing the body, is rotated several times over the area of the heart. Also APOLOGIZE 1, APOLOGY 1, CONTRITION, PENITENT, REGRET, REGRETFUL, REPENT, REPENTANT, SORROW, SORROWFUL 2, SORRY.

RUBBER 3, *n*. (Snapping and stretching a rubber band.) The sign for RUBBER 2 is made. Then both "A" hands are held before the body, palms down and

RUG (rug), *n.* (The "R"; covering a flat surface.) The right "R" hand is placed on the upturned left palm, with the right thumb underneath the left hand. The right hand moves straight forward from the heel.

RUIN 1 (rōō′ ĭn), *n.* (Wiping off.) The left "5" hand, palm up, is held slightly below the right "5" hand, held palm down. The right hand swings up, just brushing over the left palm. Both hands close into the "S" position, and the right is brought back with force to its initial position, striking a glancing blow against the left knuckles as it returns. Also ABOLISH 1, ANNIHILATE, CORRUPT, DEFACE, DEMOLISH, DESTROY, HAVOC, PERISH 2, REMOVE 3.

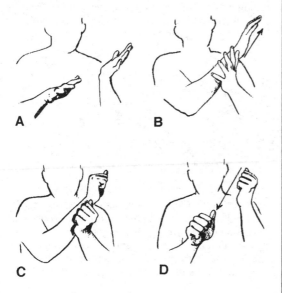

RUIN 2, *v.,* RUINED, RUINING. (Defacing or damaging.) Both "X" hands are held palms facing, with the right slightly above and behind the left. The right "X" hand moves forward abruptly, striking the left "X" finger and continuing beyond.

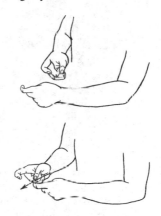

RULE 1 (rōōl), *n., v.,* RULED, RULING. (Holding the reins over all.) The "A" hands, palms facing, move alternately back and forth as if grasping and manipulating reins. The left "A" hand, still in position, swings over so that its palm now faces down. The right hand opens to the "5" position, palm down, and swings over the left, which moves slightly to the right. Also AUTHORITY, CONTROL 1, DIRECT 1, GOVERN, MANAGE, MANAGEMENT, MANAGER, OPERATE, REGULATE, REIGN.

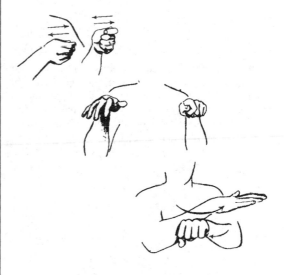

RULE(S) 2, *n.* (The letter "R"; the listing.) The upright, open left hand, fingers together and palm facing out, represents a piece of paper on which are listed the rules or regulations. The right "R" hand is placed upright against the tips of the left fingers, and then it moves down in an arc to a position against the base of the left hand. Also REGULATION(S).

RUMOR (rōō′ mər), *n.* (Mouths chattering.) Both hands are held before the face, their index fingers and thumbs extended. The fingers open and close rapidly several times. The hands sometimes move back and forth. Also GOSSIP.

RUN 1 (rŭn), *v.*, RAN, RUN, RUNNING. The open left hand is held pointing out, palm down. The open right hand is held beneath it, facing up. The right hand is thrown forward rather quickly so the palm brushes repeatedly across the palm of the left.

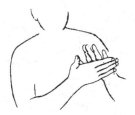

RUN 2, *v.* The "L" hands are held side by side, palms down. The left index finger rests across the right thumb, and in this position the two index fingers wiggle back and forth. The hands may move forward simultaneously.

RUN 3, *v.* (A turning wheel, as in a machine that is running.) The upturned, open right hand moves in a counterclockwise circle on the palm of the down-turned, open left hand.

RUN 4, *v.* (The nose is running.) The index finger of the right "4" hand moves down several times from its position at the nose. This sign is used for a running or a bleeding nose. Also NOSEBLEED.

RUN AWAY, *v. phrase.* (Slipping out and away.) The right index finger is held pointing upward between the index and middle fingers of the prone left hand. From this position the right index finger moves to the right, slipping out of the grasp of the left fingers and away from the left hand. Also LEAVE CLANDESTINELY 2, SLIP AWAY.

 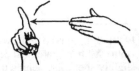

RUNNER-UP (run′ ər up′), *n.* (In second position, indicated by the "2.") The right "2" hand, fingers pointing straight forward, moves back an inch or two toward the body. Also SECOND 4,

RUN OFF (rŭn′ ôf′), *v.* (Moving forward suddenly and quickly.) The upturned right palm slaps against the downturned left palm and shoots forward.

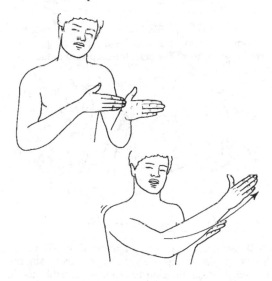

RUN OUT (OF), *v. phrase.* (A wiping-off motion to indicate a condition of no longer present.) The little finger edge of the right "5" hand, palm facing the body, rests either on the palm or the back of the left hand. The right hand moves straight forward sud-

denly, closing into the "S" position, palm still facing the body. Also GONE 2, EXHAUSTED.

RUSSIA 1 (rŭsh′ ə), *n.* (The characteristic Cossack dance.) The downturned "5" hands swing repeatedly in toward the hips. The hands come in contact with the hips at the midpoints between thumbs and index fingers. Also RUSSIAN.

RUSSIA 2, *n.* The right index fingertip travels across the lips from left to right and is then thrown down. This is a native sign.

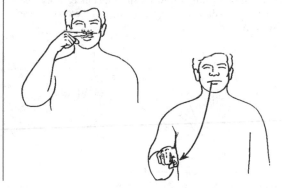

S

SABBATH 1 (săb′ əth), *n.* (Day of rest.) The sign for REST 1 is made: with palms facing the body, the arms are folded across the chest. This is followed by the sign for DAY: the left arm, held horizontally, palm down, represents the horizon. The right elbow rests on the back of the left hand, with the right arm in a perpendicular position. The right "D" hand, palm facing left, moves in an arc to the left until it is just above the left elbow. This latter movement may be reversed.

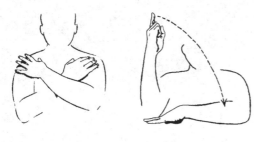

SABBATH 2, *n.* (A day of quiet, of rest.) The "5" hands, held side by side and palms out before the body, move straight down a short distance. They may also move slightly outward as they move down. Also SUNDAY 1.

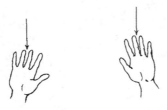

SABBATH 3, *n.* (The letter "S.") The right "S" hand, palm facing out, moves straight down a few inches.

SABBATH 4, *n.* (The Jewish Sabbath; the sun going down.) The downturned left arm, held horizontally, represents the horizon. The right thumb and index

form a circle, moving down in front of the downturned left hand. The circle may also be formed with the right "O" hand. Also SHABBAT, SUNSET.

SACRIFICE (săk′ rə fīs′), *n., v.,* -FICED, -FICING. (An offering.) The outstretched hands, palms up, move upward gracefully. The head turns upward at the same time.

SAD (săd), *adj.* (The facial features drop.) Both "5" hands, palms facing the eyes and fingers slightly curved, drop simultaneously to a level with the mouth. The head drops slightly as the hands move down, and an expression of sadness is assumed. Also DEJECTED, DEPRESSED, GLOOM, GLOOMY, GRAVE 3, GRIEF 1, MELANCHOLY, MOURNFUL, SORROWFUL 1.

SAFE (sāf), *adj., n.* (Breaking the bonds.) The "S" hands, crossed in front of the body, swing apart and

face out. Also DELIVER 1, EMANCIPATE, FREE 1, INDE-
PENDENCE, INDEPENDENT, LIBERATION, REDEEM 1,
RELIEF, RESCUE, SALVATION, SAVE 1.

SAFETY PIN (sāf' tē pin), *n.* (Closing the pin.) The
right index and thumb come together against the left
chest.

SAID (sĕd), *v.* (Words tumbling from the mouth.)
The right index finger, pointing left, describes a con-
tinuous small circle in front of the mouth. Also BID 3,
DISCOURSE, HEARING, MAINTAIN 2, MENTION, REMARK,
SAY, SPEAK, SPEECH 1, STATE, STATEMENT, TALK 1, TELL,
VERBAL 1.

SAILBOAT 1 (sāl' bōt), *n.* (The rocking of the masts.)
The right "3" hand, palm facing left, rocks back and
forth. Also SAILING.

SAILBOAT 2, *n.* (The ballooning spinnaker.) The left
"3" hand, palm facing the signer and fingers pointing
right, represents the boat. The right cupped hand,
positioned in front of the left and also facing the
signer, moves forward together with the left. This is
the spinnaker pulling the boat ahead with the wind
following. Instead of the "3" hand, the "1" or "D"
hand may be used.

SAILOR 1 (sā' lər), *n.* (The three stripes on the
sailor's blouse.) The middle finger of the right "3"
hand brushes against the right shoulder several times.
Also SEAMAN.

SAILOR 2, *n.* (The bell-bottoms.) Both hands, fingers
pointing straight down, indicate the flare of bell bottom pants, first above the left leg and then the right.

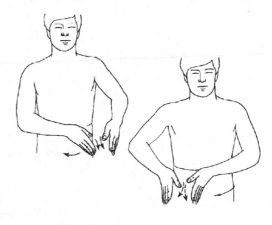

SAINT 1 (sānt) (*eccles.*), *n.* (Cleanliness or purity,
defined by the letter "S.") The right hand wipes off the

left palm. As it moves across the left palm, it assumes the "S" position.

SAINT 2 (*eccles.*), *n.* (See SAINT 1 for rationale.) The right "S" hand is wiped across the open left palm.

SALAD 1 (săl′ əd), *n.* (The letter "G.") The right "G" hand is shaken slightly. The movement involves a slight pivoting action at the wrist. The hands may also go through the motions of tossing a salad. Also GREEN 1, GREENHORN 1.

SALAD 2, *n.* (The tossing.) Both upturned claw hands mime tossing up pieces of salad in a bowl.

SALAD DRESSING *n.* (The pouring.) Using SALAD 2, the signer then tips the right thumb down and mimes pouring dressing over the salad.

SALAMI (sə lä′ mē), *n.* (The shape and length.) Both downturned "C" hands, palms facing out, separate about a foot or more, and then the "C" hands close into the "S" shape.

SALARY 1 (săl′ ə rĭ), *n.* (Gathering in.) The right "5" hand, its little finger edge touching the upturned left palm, is drawn in an arc toward the body, closing into the "S" position as it sweeps over the base of the left hand. Also ACCUMULATE 1, COLLECT, EARN, WAGES.

SALARY 2, *n.* (EARN, MONEY.) The sign for EARN is made: the right "5" hand, its little finger edge resting on the upturned left palm, moves toward the left and closes into the "S" position. This is followed by MONEY: the upturned right fingertips, grasping a wad of imaginary dollar bills, slap down on the left palm.

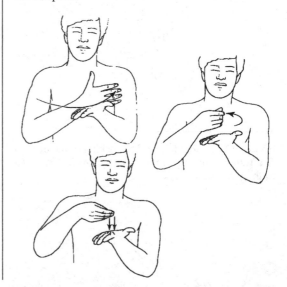

SALE (sāl), *n.* (Transferring ownership of an object.) Both "AND" hands, fingers touching their respective thumbs, are held palms down before the body. The hands are pivoted simultaneously outward and away from the body, once or several times. Also SELL, VEND.

SALIVA (sə lī' və), *n.* (The dripping or drooling.) The right "4" hand, palm facing the lips, moves down repeatedly.

SALOON (sə lōōn'), *n.* (Raising the beer stein or mug.) The thumb of the right "A" or "Y" hand is brought up to the mouth. Also BAR.

SALT 1 (sôlt), *n.* (The act of tapping the salt from a knife edge.) Both "H" hands, palms down, are held before the chest. The fingers of the right "H" hand tap those of the left several times.

SALT 2, *n.* (Tasting the salt.) The tips of the right "H" hand are placed against the lips. The rest of this sign is exactly like SALT 1.

SALVATION (săl vā' shən), *n.* (Breaking the bonds.) The "S" hands, crossed in front of the body, swing apart and face out. Also DELIVER 1, EMANCIPATE, FREE 1, INDEPENDENCE, INDEPENDENT, LIBERATION, REDEEM 1, RELIEF, RESCUE, SAFE, SAVE 1.

SAME 1 (sām), *adj.* (Matching fingers are brought together.) The outstretched index fingers are brought together, either once or several times. Also ALIKE, IDENTICAL, LIKE 2, SIMILAR, SUCH.

SAME 2 (*colloq.*), *adj.* (Two figures are compared, back and forth.) The right "Y" hand, palm facing left, is moved alternately toward and away from the body. Also ME TOO.

SAME 3, *adj.* (Parallel movement.) Both downturned "Y" hands, held a few inches apart, move simultaneously from left to right. Also UNIFORM, UNIFORMLY.

SAME AS, *phrase.* (A likeness; a sameness.) Both index fingers, held together at one side of the body near waist level, point forward. As they travel to the other side of the body they separate an inch or two and come together again. Also ACCORDING (TO), ALSO 1, AS, DUPLICATE 2, TOO.

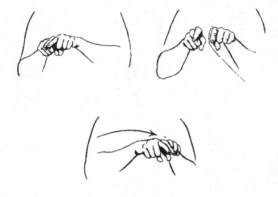

SAME TIME, *adv. phrase.* (Time is the same.) The downturned curved right index finger taps the back of the left wrist, and then both hands, in the downturned "Y" position, separate quickly. Also SIMULTANEOUSLY.

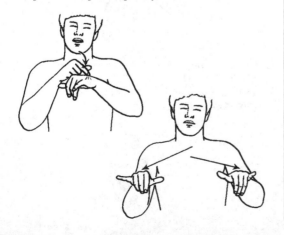

SAMPLE (săm′ pəl), *n.* (The letter "S"; something shown or pushed forward.) The left "5" hand pushes the right "S" hand forward.

SAN ANTONIO (san′ an tō′ nē ō), *n.* The right "G" hand twice strikes the right cheek.

SANCTUARY (sangk′ chōō er′ ē), *n.* (The letter "S"; describing an area.) Both downturned "S" hands describe a circle as they are drawn in toward the chest.

SAND 1 (sand), *n.* (Trickling.) The right fist is held above the upturned left palm and, trembling slightly, pretends to trickle sand on it.

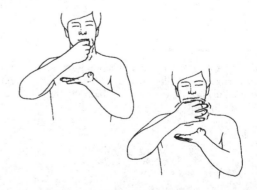

SAND 2, *n.* (The "S"; grinding against a hard substance to produce sand.) The back of the upturned "S" hand makes a continuous counterclockwise circle against the back of the downturned "S" hand.

SANDALS 1 (săn' dəlz), *n.* (The crossed straps or thongs.) The downturned right "4" hand crosses the downturned left hand from little finger edge to thumb. It then turns around to the palm-up position and crosses the left hand from wrist to fingertips.

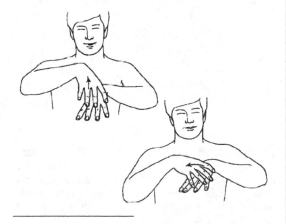

SANDALS 2, *n. pl.* (The thong between the toes.) The left "5" hand is held palm down. The index finger traces the course of an imaginary thong between the left index and middle fingers.

SANDPAPER (sănd' pā' pər) (*voc.*), *n.* (The act of rubbing.) The right knuckles rub briskly against the outstretched left palm. Also POLISH 1, RUB, SHINE SHOES.

SANDWICH 1 (sănd' wĭch, săn' -), *n.* (The two pieces of bread.) With the fingertips of both hands facing the body, one hand is placed atop the other and both are brought up to the mouth, which opens slightly.

SANDWICH 2, *n.* (In between slices.) The fingers of the upturned right hand are tucked between the middle and third fingers of the left hand, whose palm faces the signer. The motion may be repeated.

SAN FRANCISCO (săn' frən sĭs' kō). The initials "S" and "F" are formed. During the formation of the "F," the hand may be moved slightly to the right.

SAN JUAN (săn hwän'), *n.* (The letters.) The right "J" hand makes a series of quick clockwise movements.

SANTA CLAUS *n.* (The beard.) Both "C" hands, palms up, outline the large rounded beard as they move from jawline to chest.

SANTO DOMINGO *n.* The right thumb is pressed twice into the upturned left palm. A native sign.

SARCASM (sär′ kaz əm), *n.* (Twisting the meaning of something said.) Both downturned hands are held near the face, with index and little fingers exposed and the right hand resting on the tip of the nose or the lips. The right hand moves down sharply, going under the left. Also IRONY.

SATAN (sā′ tən), *n.* (The horns.) With the thumbs resting on the temples, the index and middle fingers of both hands open and close repeatedly. Also DEMON, DEVIL, DEVILMENT, HELL 1.

SATIRE (sat′ īr), *n.* (The letter "S"; going under or around that which would point out the truth or the actual.) The right "S" hand makes a small clockwise circle, and then both hands assume a shape involving the outstretched index and little fingers. The right hand goes under the left.

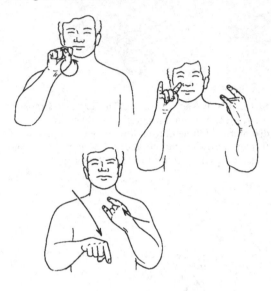

SATISFACTION (săt′ ĭs făk′ shən), *n.* (The inner feelings settle down.) Both "B" hands (or "5" hands, fingers together) are placed palms down against the chest, the right above the left. Both move down simultaneously a few inches. Also CONTENT, CONTENTED, GRATIFY 2, SATISFIED, SATISFY 1.

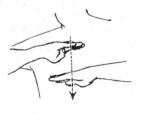

SATISFIED, *adj.* See SATISFACTION.

SATISFY 1 (săt′ ĭs fī), *v.,* -FIED, -FYING. See SATISFACTION.

SATISFY 2, *v.* This is the same sign as for SATISFY 1 but with only one hand used.

SATURDAY (săt′ ər dĭ), *n.* The "S" hand, held before the body, is rotated clockwise.

SAUSAGE (sô′ sij), *n.* (The links.) Both downturned "C" hands are positioned almost touching. They open and close repeatedly into the "S" position as they move apart.

SAVE 1 (sāv), *v.,* SAVED, SAVING. (Breaking the bonds.) The "S" hands, crossed in front of the body, swing apart and face out. Also DELIVER 1, EMANCIPATE, FREE 1, INDEPENDENCE, INDEPENDENT, LIBERATION, REDEEM 1, RELIEF, RESCUE, SAFE, SALVATION.

SAVE 2, *v.* (Holding back.) The right "V" fingers are tapped once or twice across the back of their left counterparts. Both palms face the chest. Also RESERVE 3, STORE 2.

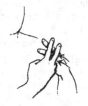

SAW 1 (sô), *n., v.,* SAWED, SAWN, SAWING. (The sawing of wood.) The little finger edge of the open right hand moves back and forth in a sawing motion over the back of the downturned left hand. Also LUMBER 1, WOOD.

SAW 2 (*voc.*), *n., v.* (Act of holding a saw.) The right hand grasps an imaginary saw and moves back and forth over the downturned left hand. Also HANDSAW.

SAY (sā), *v.,* SAID, SAYING. (Words tumbling from the mouth.) The right index finger, pointing left, describes a continuous small circle in front of the mouth. Also BID 3, DISCOURSE, HEARING, MAINTAIN 2, MENTION, REMARK, SAID, SPEAK, SPEECH 1, STATE, STATEMENT, TALK 1, TELL, VERBAL 1.

SCAFFOLD (skăf′ əld, -ōld), *n.* (Hanging by the throat.) The thumb of the right "Y" hand is placed at the right side of the neck, and the head hangs toward the left as if it were caught in a noose. Also HANG 2.

SCALE 1 (skāl) (*voc.*), *n.* (The act of measuring a short distance.) Both "Y" hands, held side by side palms out, move alternately a short distance back and forth, away from and toward each other. Also GAUGE, MEASURE.

SCALE 2, *n.* (The balancing of the scale is described.) The fingers of the right "H" hand are centered on the left index finger and rocked back and forth. Also POUND 1, WEIGH 1, WEIGHT.

SCALE 3, *n., v.,* SCALED, SCALING. (The scales.) Both open hands, held palms down in front of the body, move alternately up and down, imitating a pair of scales. Also BALANCE 2.

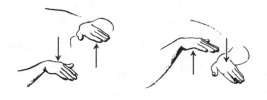

SCAPULAR (skăp′ yələr) (*eccles.*), *n.* (The garment is described.) The index fingers are drawn from the shoulders to a point where they come together at the center of the chest.

SCARE(D) (skâr), *v.,* SCARED, SCARING, *n.* (The heart is suddenly covered with fear.) Both hands, fingers together, are placed side by side, palms facing the

chest. They quickly open and come together over the heart, one on top of the other. Also AFRAID, COWARD, FEAR 1, FRIGHT, FRIGHTEN, TERROR 1.

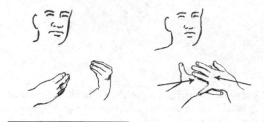

SCARF (skärf), *n.* (Tying the scarf.) The signer mimes placing a scarf over the head and tying it in a knot at the throat.

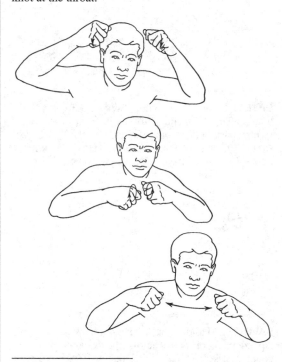

SCENE 1 (sēn), *n.* (The letter "P"; a circle or square is indicated to show the locale or place.) The "P" hands are held side by side before the body with middle fingertips touching. From this position, the hands separate and outline a circle (or a square), before coming together again closer to the body. Also LOCATION, PLACE 1, POSITION 1, SITE.

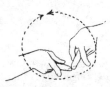

SCENE 2, *n.* (The letter "S"; a portion of a play-script.) The right "S" hand is placed at the top of the outstretched left palm. It moves down to the base of the palm.

SCENT (sĕnt), *n.* (Bringing something up to the nose.) The upturned right hand moves slowly up to and past the nose, and the signer breathes in as the hand sweeps by. Also FRAGRANT, ODOR, SMELL.

SCHEDULE (skej' ōōl), *n.* (Making boxes to indicate dates on a calendar.) The right "4" hand, palm facing the left palm, moves down, turns over, and moves forward along the left palm, from the heel to the fingertips.

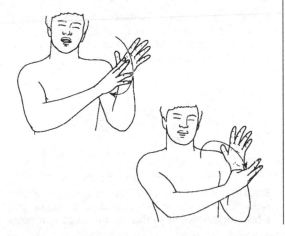

SCHIZOPHRENIA (skit' sō frē' nē ə), *n.* (The letter "S"; the zigzag movement depicts the splitting of the head, *i.e.*, a split personality.) The right "S" hand is placed on the upturned open left palm or on the forehead. The "S" hand opens into the "B" position, little finger edge resting on the left palm. It moves down the palm in a zigzag manner.

SCHOLAR (skŏl' ər), *n.* (One who learns.) The sign for LEARN is made: the downturned fingers of the right hand are placed on the upturned left palm. They close, and then the hand rises and the right fingertips are placed on the forehead. This is followed by the sign for INDIVIDUAL 1: both open hands, palms facing each other, move down the sides of the body, tracing its outline to the hips. Also LEARNER, PUPIL 1, STUDENT 1.

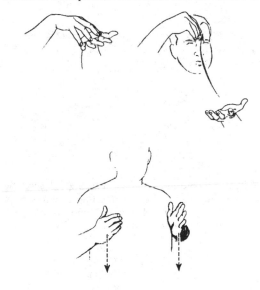

SCHOOL (skōōl), *n.* (The teacher's hands are clapped for attention.) The hands are clapped together several times.

SCIENCE 1 (sī′ əns), *n.* (Deep wisdom.) The right index fingertip touches the forehead and is then moved down and thrust between the extended and loosely parted fingers of the downturned left hand to indicate that wisdom goes deep.

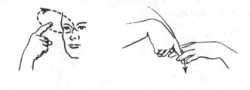

SCIENCE 2, *n.* (Pouring alternately from test tubes.) The upright thumbs of both "A" hands swing over alternately as if pouring out the contents of a pair of test tubes. Also CHEMISTRY.

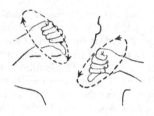

SCISSORS (sĭz′ ərz), *n., pl.* or *sing.* (The natural sign.) The index and middle fingers, forming a "V," open and close like scissors.

SCOLD 1 (skōld), *v.,* SCOLDED, SCOLDING. (A scolding with the finger.) The right index finger shakes back and forth in a natural scolding movement. Also ADMONISH 2, REPRIMAND, REPROVE.

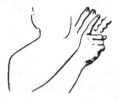

SCOLD 2 (*colloq.*), *v.* (Rough language.) The tips of the curved right fingers trace imaginary ridges over the upright left palm from the base of the hand to the

fingertips. The action is repeated several times. Also ROUGH 1, ROUGHNESS, RUDE 1.

SCOLD 3, *v., sl.* (The opening and closing of the barking dog's mouth.) The hands are positioned palm against palm before the body, with the fingertips pointing forward. With the bases of the hands always touching and serving as a hinge, the hands open and close repeatedly, with the stress on the opening movement, which is sudden and abrupt. Also BARK.

SCOLD 4, *v., sl.* (Big, *i.e.,* curse, words tumble out.) The right "Y" hand moves forward in a wavy manner along the left index finger, which is pointing forward. The action is repeated several times. The wide space between the thumb and little finger of the "Y" hand represents the length of the words, and the forward movement is the tumbling out of the words in anger.

SCORE (skôr, skōr), *v.,* SCORED, SCORING, *basketball term.* (The ball goes into the hoop.) The curved downturned right index finger moves in an arc into a circle formed by the left hand.

SCORN 1 (skôrn), *n.* (The gaze is cast downward.) Both "V" hands, side by side and palms facing out, are swept downward so that the fingertips now point down. A haughty expression or one of mild contempt is sometimes assumed. Also CONTEMPT 1, LOOK DOWN.

SCORN 2 (*rare*), *n., v.,* SCORNED, SCORNING. (The finger is flicked to indicate something petty, small, *i.e.,* to be scorned as inconsequential.) The right index finger and thumb are used to press the lips down into an expression of contempt. The right thumb is then flicked out from the closed hand. Also CONTEMPT 2, DESPISE 2, DETEST 2, DISLIKE, HATE 2.

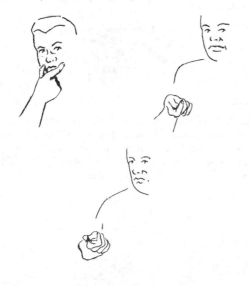

SCORPION (skôr′ pē ən), *n.* (The walking legs and the stinger.) The left hand is held in the "X" position, palm facing forward, its base resting on the back of the downturned right claw hand. The fingers of the right hand wriggle as they move forward, carrying the left "X" finger along with it.

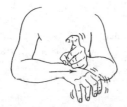

SCOT 1 (skŏt), *n.* (The crossing of the plaid pattern is indicated on the hand.) The outstretched fingers of the open right hand, palm down, are brought over the back of the downturned left hand, from the little finger side to the thumb side. The right hand then turns to the palm-up position and is drawn along the left hand, back to back, from wrist to fingertips. Also SCOTCH 1, SCOTLAND 1, SCOTTISH 1.

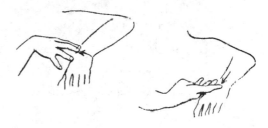

SCOT 2, *n.* (The plaid.) The "5" hands are held with palms toward the chest, the right fingers resting across the back of the left fingers to represent "plaid." The hands then drop away toward either side. Also SCOTCH 2, SCOTLAND 2, SCOTTISH 2.

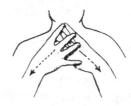

SCOT 3, *n.* (Plaid.) The four fingers of the right "B" hand, held slightly spread, trace a set of imaginary parallel lines across the left arm just below the shoulder. The hand is then turned over, and the backs of the fingers trace another set of parallel lines downward across the first set, completing an imaginary plaid pattern. Also SCOTCH 3, SCOTLAND 3, SCOTTISH 3.

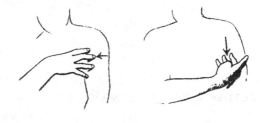

SCOTCH 1 (skŏch), *n., adj.* See SCOT 1.

SCOTCH 2, *n., adj.* See SCOT 2.

SCOTCH 3, *n., adj.* See SCOT 3.

SCOTCH TAPE, *n., v.,* TAPED, TAPING. (Spreading the tape.) Both downturned thumbs, tips touching, move apart in opposite directions, as if smoothing on a piece of tape.

SCOTLAND 1 (skŏt′ lənd), *n.* See SCOT 1.

SCOTLAND 2, *n.* See SCOT 2.

SCOTLAND 3, *n.* See SCOT 3.

SCOTLAND 4, *n.* (The bagpipes.) With the signer miming blowing the pipes, the left elbow moves in repeatedly against the left ribs. (A native sign.)

SCOTTISH 1 (skŏt′ ish), *adj.* See SCOT 1.

SCOTTISH 2, *adj.* See SCOT 2.

SCOTTISH 3, *adj.* See SCOT 3.

SCOUT (skout), *n.* (The traditional Scout salute.) The signer gives a three-fingered salute, using the thumb to hold back the little finger.

SCRAMBLE (skrăm′ bəl), *v.,* -BLED, -BLING. (Scrambling or mixing up.) The downturned right hand is positioned above the upturned left. The fingers of both are curved. Both hands move in opposite horizontal circles. Also CLUTTER, COMPLICATE, CONFUSE, CONFUSED, CONFUSION, DISORDER, MINGLE 1, MIX, MIXED, MIX UP.

SCRAPE (skrāp) (*voc.*), *v.,* SCRAPED, SCRAPING, *n.* (The natural motion of using a scraper.) The tips of the right "B" hand move along the upturned left palm, from midpalm to fingertips. The motion is repeated several times.

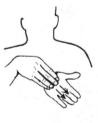

SCRATCH (skrach), *n., v.,* SCRATCHED, SCRATCHING. (The natural movement.) The signer, with curved index finger, mimes making a quick scratch on the back of the left hand.

SCREAM (skrēm), v., SCREAMED, SCREAMING. (Harsh words thrown out.) The right hand, as in CURSE 1, appears to claw words out of the mouth. This time, however, it turns and throws them out, ending in the "5" position. Also BLASPHEME 2, CALL OUT, CRY 3, CRY OUT, CURSE 2, SHOUT, SUMMON 1, SWEAR 3.

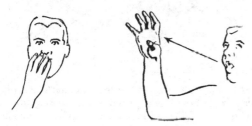

SCREEN (skrēn), n. (The mesh.) Both "4" hands, palms facing the body, are placed one over the other. They separate, moving down and tracing the lines of the wire mesh. The movement may be repeated.

SCREW 1 (skrōō), n., v., SCREWED, SCREWING. (The movement.) The right index finger makes a clockwise turn in the left palm.

SCREW 2, n. (The length of the screw is indicated.) The thumb and index finger of the right hand, held an inch or two apart, are placed on the left index finger to indicate the length of the screw.

SCRIPTURE (skrip' chər), n. (The letter "S"; writing.) The downturned right "S" hand rests on the upturned left palm. Pivoted by the wrist, it moves slightly in a wavy manner as it goes from the ball of the left palm to the tips of the left fingers.

SCROLL (skrōl), v., SCROLLED, SCROLLING. *Computer terminology.* Both "4" hands, one above the other and both palms facing the signer, move up simultaneously, imitating the upward movement, or scrolling, of material on a computer screen. The movement may be repeated.

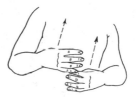

SCRUB (skrub), v., SCRUBBED, SCRUBBING. (The action.) Both "A" hands, palms facing each other, scrub back and forth on the knuckles.

SCULPT (skŭlpt), v., SCULPTED, SCULPTING. (Contours are indicated or outlined.) Both "A" hands, held about a foot apart before the face, with palms facing each other, move down simultaneously in a wavy, undulating motion. Also FIGURE 2, FORM, IMAGE, SCULPTURE, SHAPE 1, STATUE.

SCULPTOR (skŭlp′ tər), *n.* (An individual who carves.) The thumb of the right "A" hand, placed in the upturned left palm, is twisted up and down several times as if gouging out material from the left palm. This is followed by the sign for INDIVIDUAL 1: both open hands, palms facing each other, move down the sides of the body, tracing its outline to the hips.

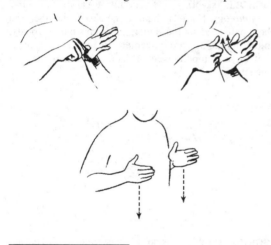

SCULPTURE (skŭlp′ chər), *n., v.,* -TURED, -TURING. See SCULPT.

SEAL 1 (sēl), *n.* (The natural sign.) The right hand grasps an imaginary rubber stamp and presses it against the upturned left palm. Also GUARANTEE 2, STAMP 2.

SEAL 2, *n.* (Squeezing the embossing seal.) The right hand grips the arms of an imaginary seal held at the

little finger edge of the upturned left hand. The right hand squeezes the seal once or twice.

SEAL 3, *n.* (The flapping of the mammal's rear flippers.) With both hands joined at their bases, fingers pointing forward, the hands open and close repeatedly.

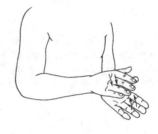

SEAMAN (sē′ mən), *n.* (The three stripes on the sailor's blouse.) The middle finger of the right "3" hand brushes against the right shoulder several times. Also SAILOR 1.

SEARCH (sûrch), *v.,* SEARCHED, SEARCHING. (Directing the vision from place to place.) The right "C" hand (the French *chercher*), palm facing left, moves from right to left across the line of vision in a series of counterclockwise circles. The signer's gaze remains concentrated and his head turns slowly from right to left. Also CURIOUS 1, EXAMINE, INVESTIGATE 1, LOOK FOR, PROBE 1, QUEST, SEEK.

SEAT (sēt), *n., v.,* SEATED, SEATING. (The act of sitting.) The extended right index and middle fingers are draped across the back of the same two fingers of the down-turned left hand. The hands then move straight downward a short distance. Also BE SEATED, CHAIR 1, SIT 1.

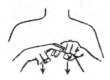

SEAT BELT, *n.* (The shape and function.) The sign for SEAT is made: the extended right index and middle fingers are draped across the back of the same two fingers of the downturned left hand. The hands move straight down together an inch or two. The right thumb and curved index finger, forming a "C," then move from the left shoulder to the right hip.

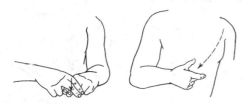

SECOND 1 (sĕk′ ənd), *adj.* (The second finger is indicated.) The tip of the index finger of the right "D" hand is placed on the tip of the middle finger of the left "V" hand. The right hand then executes a short pivotal movement in a clockwise direction. The left "L" hand may be substituted for the left "V" hand, with the right index fingertip placed on the left index fingertip. Also SECONDARY, SECONDLY.

SECOND 2, *v.,* -ONDED, -ONDING. ("Second"—two fingers.) The right "L" hand, held somewhat above the head, index finger pointing straight up, pivots forward a bit so that the index finger now points forward. Used in parliamentary procedure. Also ENDORSE 3, INDORSE 3, SUPPORT 3.

SECOND 3, *n.* (The ticking off of seconds on the clock.) The index finger of the right "D" hand executes a series of very short movements in a clockwise manner as it rests against the left "S" hand, which is facing right.

SECOND 4, *adj.* (In second position, indicated by the "2.") The right "2" hand, fingers pointing straight forward, moves back an inch or two toward the body. Also RUNNER-UP.

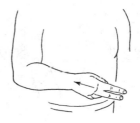

SECONDARY (sĕk′ ən dĕr′ ĭ), *adj.* See SECOND 1.

SECONDLY (sĕk′ ənd lĭ), *adv.* See SECOND 1.

SECRECY (sē′ krə sē), *n.* (Secret after secret.) Both "A" hands, palms facing, are brought alternately up to the sealed lips.

SECRET 1 (sē′ krĭt), *n., adj.* (The sealing of the lips; keeping the words back.) The back of the thumb of the right "A" hand is placed firmly against the closed lips. The thumb, in this position, may move off the lips slightly and return again to the lips. As an optional addition, the thumb may swing down under the down-turned cupped left hand after being placed on the lips as above. Also DON'T TELL, PRIVACY, PRIVATE 1.

SECRET 2, *n.* (The lips are sealed.) The thumb edge of the right "S" hand is placed against the tightly closed lips. It swings from right to left, never losing contact with the lips. Also SEAL ONE'S LIPS.

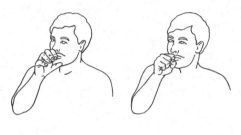

SECRETARY (sĕk′ rə tĕr′ ĭ), *n.* (Taking a pencil from behind the ear.) An imaginary pencil is taken from the right ear and then is used to go through the motions of writing on the upturned left palm.

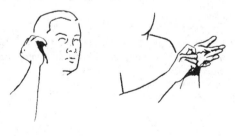

SECTION (sĕk′ shən), *n.* (Cutting off or designating a part.) The little finger edge of the open right hand moves straight down the middle of the upturned left palm. Also PART 1, PIECE, PORTION, SHARE 1, SOME.

SECURITY (si kyo͝or′ i tē), *n.* (Guarding or protecting.) Both arms, fists clenched, are held in a crossed position. They move forward about half an inch.

SEE (sē), *v.,* SAW, SEEN, SEEING. (The eyesight is directed forward.) The right "V" hand (the French *voir*), palm facing the body, is placed so that the fingertips are just under the eyes. The hand swings around and out so that the fingertips are now pointing forward. The hand often moves straight out without turning around. Also LOOK 1, PERCEIVE 1, PERCEPTION, SIGHT, WATCH 2.

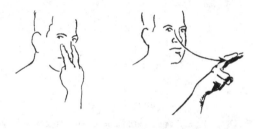

SEEK (sēk), *v.,* SOUGHT, SEEKING. (Directing the vision from place to place.) The right "C" hand (the French *chercher*), palm facing left, moves from right to left across the line of vision in a series of counterclockwise circles. The signer's gaze remains concentrated and his head turns slowly from right to left. Also CURIOUS 1, EXAMINE, INVESTIGATE 1, LOOK FOR, PROBE 1, QUEST, SEARCH.

SEEM (sēm), *v.,* SEEMED, SEEMING. (Something presented before the eyes.) The open right hand, palm flat and facing out, with fingers together and pointing up, is positioned at shoulder level. Pivoting from the wrist, the hand is swung around so that the palm now faces the eyes. Sometimes the eyes glance at the newly presented palm. Also APPARENT, APPARENTLY, APPEAR 1, LOOK 2.

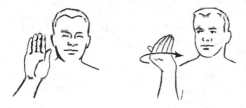

SEESAW (sē′ sô′), *n.* (The up-and-down movement.) Both downturned "H" hands are held with index and middle fingers touching. They move alternately up and down, always maintaining contact.

SEETHE (sēth), *v.*, SEETHED, SEETHING. (A slow boil.) The right hand, palm up, is placed beneath the palm down left hand. The right fingers wriggle under the left palm.

SEIZE (sēz), *v.*, SEIZED, SEIZING. (Grasping something and holding it down.) Both hands, palms down, quickly close into the "S" position, the right on top of the left. Also CAPTURE, CATCH 2, GRAB, GRASP.

SEIZURE (sē′ zhər), *n.* (The body shakes in a fit.) The right hand, palm up, index and middle fingers curved, is placed in the upturned left palm. The right hand's index and middle fingers open and close slightly as the two fingers tremble. Also EPILEPSY, FIT.

SELDOM (sĕl′ dəm), *adv.* (The "1" finger is brought up very slowly.) The right index finger, resting in the open left palm, which is facing right, swings up slowly from its position to one in which it is pointing straight up. The movement is repeated slowly after a pause. Also OCCASIONAL, OCCASIONALLY, ONCE IN A WHILE, SOMETIME(S).

SELECT 1 (sĭ lĕkt′), *v.*, -LECTED, -LECTING. (The natural motion of selecting something from the hand.) The thumb and index fingers of the outstretched right hand grasp an imaginary object on the upturned left palm. The right hand then moves straight up. Also CHOOSE 2, DISCOVER, FIND, PICK 1.

SELECT 2, *v.* (Taking unto oneself.) The right hand, palm out, is extended before the chest, index finger and thumb in an open position, the other fingers separated and pointing up. The hand is drawn in toward the chest, and the index and thumb close at the same time, indicating something taken to oneself. Also ADOPT, APPOINT, CHOOSE 1, TAKE.

SELECT 3, *v.* (The natural sign.) The fingertips and thumbtip of the downturned open right hand come together, and the hand moves up a short distance as if picking something. Also PICK 2, PICK UP 2.

-SELF 1 (sĕlf), *n. used with a gender prefix as a reflexive and intensive pronoun; adj.* (The individual is indicated with the thumb.) The right hand, held in the "A" position, thumb up, moves several times in the direction of the person indicated: *myself, yourself, himself, herself, itself, oneself, ourselves, yourselves, themselves.*

SELF 2, *n.* (The self is carried uppermost.) The right "A" hand, thumb up, is brought up against the chest, from waist to breast. Also AMBITIOUS 2, EGOTISM 1.

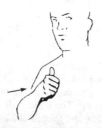

SELF-CENTERED (self' sen' tərd), *adj. phrase.* (SELF and CENTER.) The sign for SELF is made: the right "A" hand, thumb pointing up, is brought against the chest. The sign for CENTER follows: the downturned right fingers describe a small clockwise circle and come to rest in the upturned left palm.

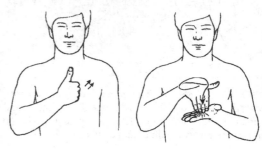

SELFISH 1 (sĕl' fĭsh), *adj.* (Pulling things toward oneself.) Both prone open or "V" hands are held in front of the body with fingers bent. The hands are then drawn quickly and forcefully inward as if raking things toward oneself. Also GREEDY 1, STINGY 1, TIGHTWAD 1.

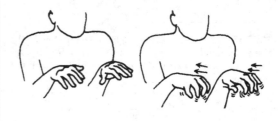

SELFISH 2, *adj.* (Scratching the palm in greed.) The right fingers scratch the upturned left palm several times. A frowning expression is often used. Also AVARICIOUS, GREEDY 2, STINGY 2, TIGHTWAD 2.

SELFISH 3, *adj.* (Scratching in greed.) The downturned "3" hands, held side by side, make a scratching motion as they move in toward the body. Also GREEDY 3, STINGY 3.

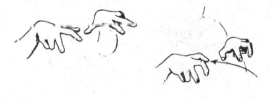

SELL (sĕl), v., SOLD, SELLING. (Transferring owner-ship of an object.) Both "AND" hands, fingers touch-ing their respective thumbs, are held palms down before the body. The hands are pivoted simultaneously outward and away from the body, once or several times. Also SALE, VEND.

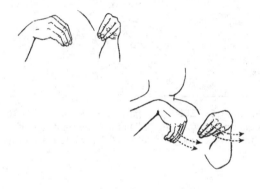

SELLER (sĕl' ər), n. (Transferring ownership.) The sign for SELL is formed. The sign for INDIVIDUAL 1 is then made: both open hands, palms facing each other, move down the sides of the body, tracing its out-line to the hips. Also MERCHANT, SALESMAN, VENDER.

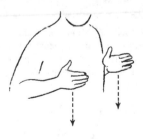

SEMEN (sē' mən), n. (The pulsing of the penis during release.) The left index finger, representing the penis, is positioned at the base of the right "E" hand, whose palm faces left. The fingers of the right hand open and

close twice, as the two hands, connected, move forward an inch or so. Also EJACULATE 1, EJACULATION 1, SPERM.

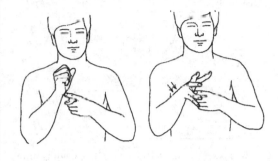

SEMESTER (si mes' tər), n. (The "S.") The right "S" hand, palm out, moves to the right and then down, in a continuous sweep.

SEMINARY 1 (sĕm' ə nĕr' ĭ) (eccles.), n. (A college dedicated to Christianity.) The sign for JESUS is made: both "5" hands are used. The left middle finger touches the right palm, and then the right middle finger touches the left palm. This is followed by the sign for COLLEGE: the sign for SCHOOL, q.v., is made, but without the clapping of hands. The upper hand swings up in an arc above the lower. The upper hand may form a "C" instead of assuming a clapping position.

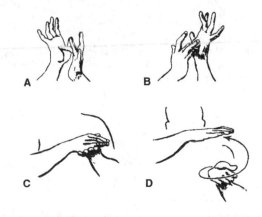

A   B

C   D

SEMINARY 2, n. (The letter "S"; a college.) The downturned, right "S" hand rests on the upturned left palm. The right hand moves up toward the right and then over toward the left, describing an arc, as in COLLEGE, *q.v.*

SEND 1 (sĕnd), *v.*, SENT, SENDING. (Sending away from.) The right fingertips tap the back of the down-turned, left "S" hand and then swing forward away from the hand.

SEND 2, *v.* (Sending something forth.) The right "AND" hand is held palm out. It then opens and moves forcefully outward in a throwing motion.

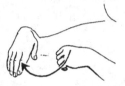

SEND AWAY 1, *v. phrase.* (Moving away from.) The fingertips of the right hand move off the top of the left hand. Also DISPATCH.

SEND AWAY 2, *v. phrase.* (Forcing something away.) The left open hand is held with fingers pointing forward. The extended right index finger points forward. In this position the right index finger moves forcefully

across the left palm, from wrist to fingertips, and continues upward in an arc. The left hand may be omitted.

SENIOR (sēn′ yər), *n., adj.* (College student.) The right index finger touches the thumbtip of the left hand. Also, the open "5" hand, palm down, may rest on the left thumbtip. Also TOP DOG.

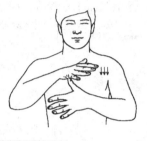

SENIOR CITIZEN, *n.* (The letters "S" and "C.") The signer places the right "S" hand at the right side of the chin and then moves it into a "C" at the left side of the chin.

SENSATION (sĕn sā′ shən), *n.* (The welling up of feelings or emotions in the heart.) The right middle finger, touching the heart, moves up an inch or two a number of times. Also EMOTION 1, FEEL 2, FEELING, MOTIVE 2, SENSE 2.

SENSE 1 (sĕns), *n.* (Patting the head to indicate something of value inside.) The right fingers pat the forehead several times. Also INTELLECT, INTELLIGENCE, MENTAL, MIND 1.

SENSE 2, *n.*, *v.*, SENSED, SENSING. See SENSATION.

SENSELESS 1 (sens' lis), 1 *adj.* (A speck of brain, the total capacity one has, is blown away, indicating how small it is.) The forehead is tapped, and then the signer blows on the upturned palm.

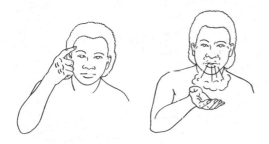

SENSELESS 2, *adj.* (A pea-brain.) The forehead is tapped as above, and then the thumb flicks off the tip of the little finger.

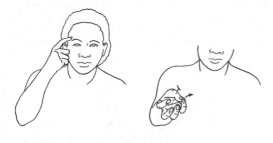

SENSITIVE (sĕn' sə tĭv), *adj.* (A nimble touch.) The middle finger of the right hand touches the chest over

the heart very briefly and lightly and is then flicked off. Also SENSITIVITY.

SENSITIVITY (sĕn' sə tĭv' ə tĭ), *n.* See SENSITIVE.

SENTENCE (sĕn' təns), *n.*, *v.*, -TENCED, -TENCING. (A series of letters spelled out on the printed page.) The downturned "F" hands are positioned with thumbs and index fingertips touching. The hands move straight apart to either side in a wavy or straight motion. Also LANGUAGE.

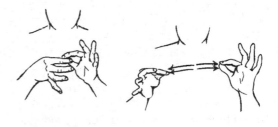

SEPARATE 1 (*adj., n.* sĕp' ə rĭt; *v.* sĕp' ə rāt'), RATED, -RATING. (The hands are moved apart.) Both hands, in the "A" position, thumbs up, are held together with knuckles touching. With a deliberate movement they come apart. Also APART, DIVORCE 1, PART 3.

SEPARATE 2, *adj.*, *n.*, *v.* (Separating to classify.) Both hands, in the right-angle position, are placed palms down before the body, knuckles to knuckles. They pull apart or separate, once or a number of times. Also ASSORT, PART 2.

SEQUEL (sē′ kwəl), *n.* (One hand follows the other.) The "A" hands are used, thumbs pointing up. The right is positioned a few inches behind the left. The left hand moves straight forward, while the right follows behind in a series of wavy movements. Also CONSECUTIVE, FOLLOW, FOLLOWING.

SEQUELAE (si kwē′ lē), *n., pl., rare med. term* (Things backing up or following others, to form a string of events resulting from an original event, such as an illness or accident.) Both "A" hands, thumbs up, palms facing each other, are held before the chest. The left hand does not move, but the right moves back toward the chest in a series of short arcs.

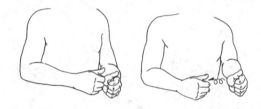

SEQUENCE (sē′ kwəns), *n.* (Indicating the order.) Both open hands, palms facing and fingers pointing out, are positioned almost touching. The right hand moves away toward the right in a series of short, jumpy movements. Also SERIAL.

SERIOUS (sēr′ ē əs), *adj.* The tip of the right index finger is placed on the chin and is twisted a bit counterclockwise. The signer assumes a serious expression.

SERMON (sûr′ mən), *n.* (Placing morsels of wisdom or food for thought into the mind.) The right hand, palm out, with thumb and index finger touching, is moved forward and slightly downward a number of times from its initial position near the right temple. Also PREACH.

SERVANT (sûr′ vənt), *n.* (Passing the dishes, one by one.) The upturned "5" hands move alternately toward and away from the chest. This may be followed by the INDIVIDUAL 1 sign, *q.v.* Also MAID, SERVE 2, SERVICE, WAITER 2, WAIT ON 2, WAITRESS 2.

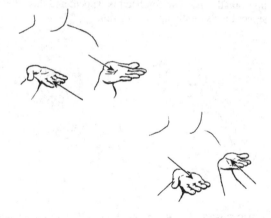

SERVE 1 (sûrv), *v.,* SERVED, SERVING, *n.* (Passing out dishes of food, one by one.) The upturned hands are held before the chest as if bearing dishes of food. The left moves alternately to the left and back to the right, as if extending the dishes to a diner. Also WAIT ON 1.

SERVE 2, *v.* See SERVANT.

SERVICE (sûr′ vĭs), *n., v.,* -VICED, -VICING. See SERVANT.

SETTLE (sct′ l), *v.,* SETTLED, SETTLING. (Settle down.) Both open hands are held palms down and fingers pointing forward. The hands move straight down a short distance. Also SIT DOWN.

SEVERAL (sĕv′ ər əl), *adj.* (The fingers are presented, in order, to convey the concept of "several.") The right "A" hand is held palm facing up. One by one the fingers open, beginning with the index finger and ending with the little finger. Some use only the index and middle fingers. Also FEW, RARE, SCARCE, SUNDRY.

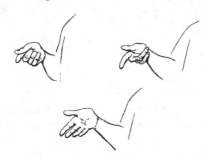

SEVERE (sə vēr′), *adj.* See SERIOUS.

SEWING MACHINE, *n.* (The needle moves over the cloth.) The left index finger points straight forward. The right thumb and index, forming a somewhat elongated circle, move forward repeatedly over the left index, from knuckle to tip, imitating the up-down movement of the needle.

SEX (seks), *n.* (The gender signs with the letter "X.") The right "X" finger is placed first at the right jawline and then at the right temple.

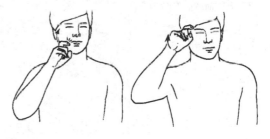

SEXUAL INTERCOURSE, *n. phrase.* (The motions of the legs during the sexual act.) The upturned left "V" hand remains motionless, while the downturned right "V" hand comes down repeatedly on the left. Also COPULATE, FORNICATE.

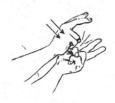

SHADE (shād), *n.* (The natural sign.) The signer mimes pulling down a window shade.

SHAKE 1 (shāk), *v.,* SHAKEN, SHAKING. (The natural sign.) Both "5" hands, grasping an imaginary object, go through the motions of shaking it several times.

SHAKE 2, *v.* (Rumbling and shaking of the environment.) Both downturned "S" hands move alternately forward and back. This sign would be appropriate for EARTHQUAKE and THUNDER.

SHAKESPEARE (shāk′ spir), *n.* (Shaking and throwing a spear; a play on signs.) The right fist shakes a bit, and then the right arm mimes throwing a spear.

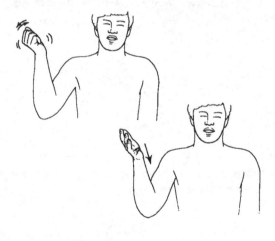

SHAKING KNEES, phrase. Both curved downturned index fingers move rapidly away from and toward each other, imitating shaking knees. Also TREMBLE 2.

SHALL (shăl, *unstressed* shəl), *v., future tense of the verb* TO BE. (Something ahead or in the future.) The upright, open right hand, palm facing left, moves

straight out and slightly up from a position beside the right temple. Also BY AND BY, FUTURE, IN THE FUTURE, LATER 2, LATER ON, WILL 1, WOULD.

SHAME 1 (shām), *n., v.,* SHAMED, SHAMING. (The color rises in the cheek; an attempt is made to hide the head.) The backs of the fingers of the right hand, held in the right-angle position, are placed against the right cheek. The hand moves up along the cheek, pivoting at the wrist, so that the fingers finally point to the rear. Also ASHAMED 1, BASHFUL 1, IMMODEST, IMMORAL, SHAMEFUL, SHAME ON YOU, SHY 1.

SHAME 2, *n.* Similar to SHAME 1, but both hands are used, at either cheek. Also ASHAMED 2, BASHFUL 2, SHY 2.

SHAMEFUL (shām′ fəl), *adj.* See SHAME 1.

SHAME ON YOU, *phrase.* See SHAME 1.

SHAMPOO (sham pōō′), *v., n.* (Stirring up suds on the scalp.) Both downturned claw hands give the scalp an imaginary lathering as they move rapidly forward and backward.

SHAPE 1 (shāp), *n., v.,* SHAPED, SHAPING. (Contours are indicated or outlined.) Both "A" hands, held about a foot apart before the face, with palms facing each other, move down simultaneously in a wavy, undulating motion. Also FIGURE 2, FORM, IMAGE, SCULPT, SCULPTURE, STATUE.

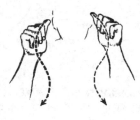

SHAPE 2 (*voc.*), *v.* The downturned, open right hand rubs across the back of the downturned left "S" hand from wrist to knuckles.

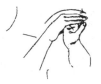

SHARE 1 (shâr), *n., v.,* SHARED, SHARING. (Cutting off or designating a part.) The little finger edge of the open right hand moves straight down the middle of the upturned left palm. Also PART 1, PIECE, PORTION, SECTION, SOME.

SHARE 2, *n., v.* (A splitting apart or dividing.) The two hands are crossed, with the right little finger resting on the left index finger. Both hands are dropped

down and separated simultaneously so that the palms face down. Also APPORTION, DIVIDE 1.

SHARK (shärk), *n.* (The dorsal fin.) The upturned fingers of the right "B" hand protrude straight up between the left middle and ring fingers. The right fingers move off and away in a wavy, meandering path.

SHARP 1 (shärp), *adj.* (The finger feels a sharp edge.) The index finger of the right "D" hand, palm facing down, moves quickly over the index finger of the left "D" hand, striking a glancing blow on it.

SHARP 2, *adj.* (A tapering or sharp point is indicated.) The index finger and thumb of the left hand grasp the tip of the index finger of the right "D" hand. The left hand then moves away a short distance, and its index finger and thumb come together. Also POINT 2, TIP.

SHARP 3, *adj.* (The mind is bright.) The right "5" hand, palm facing the signer, is placed with the tip of the middle finger touching the forehead. The hand swings quickly out and around, moving up an inch or two as it does so. Also CLEVER 2.

SHARP 4, *adj.* (A sharp-edged hand.) The right hand grasps the little finger edge of the left firmly. As it leaves this position, moving down and out, it assumes the "A" position, palm facing left. Also ADEPT, EXPERIENCE 1, EXPERT, SHREWD, SKILL, SKILLFUL.

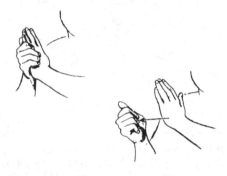

SHARPEN (shär' pən), *v.*, -PENED, -PENING. (Mime a pencil sharpener.) The left index finger points right. The right thumb and index finger, holding the lever of an imaginary pencil sharpener, make a continuous clockwise rotation at the tip of the left index. Also PENCIL SHARPENER.

SHE (shē), *pron.* (Pointing at a female.) The FEMALE prefix sign is made: the right "A" hand's thumb moves down along the line of the right jaw from ear almost to chin. The right index finger then points at an imaginary female. If in context the gender is clear, the prefix sign is usually omitted. Also HER.

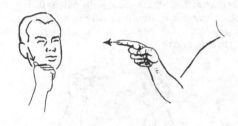

SHED RESPONSIBILITY, *phrase.* (Flicking off what would weigh you down.) With one or both hands resting on their respective shoulders, the middle fingers are flicked off the thumb.

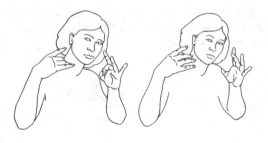

SHELTER (shĕl' tər), *n.* (A shield.) The "S" hands are held before the chest, the left behind the right, and are pushed slightly away from the body. Then the right hand opens, palm facing out, and moves clockwise as if shielding the left fist. Also REFUGE, SHIELD 2.

SHIELD 1 (shēld), *n., v.,* SHIELDED, SHIELDING. (Hold down firmly; cover and strengthen.) The "S" hands, downturned, are held side by side in front of the body, the arms almost horizontal and the left hand in front of the right. Both arms move a short distance forward and slightly downward. Also DEFEND, DEFENSE, FORTIFY, GUARD, PROTECT, PROTECTION.

SHIELD 2, *n., v.* See SHELTER.

SHIELD 3, *n., v.* (Warding off danger: the shape.) The sign for SHIELD 1 is made. The thumbs then trace the outline of an imaginary shield.

SHINE (shīn), *v.,* SHINED, SHINING, SHONE. (Reflected glistening of light rays.) The left hand, held supinely before the chest, palm down, represents the object from which the rays glisten. The right hand, in the "5" position, touches the back of the left lightly and moves up toward the right, pivoting slightly at the wrist, with fingers wiggling. Also BRIGHT 2, GLISTEN, SHINING.

SHINE SHOES, *v. phrase.* (The act of rubbing.) The right knuckles rub briskly against the outstretched left palm. Also POLISH 1, RUB, SANDPAPER.

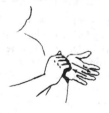

SHINING, *adj.* See SHINE.

SHIP (shĭp), *n.* (The ship is transported over the waves; its masts are indicated.) The right "3" hand,

palm facing left and resting on the upturned left palm, is moved forward by the left hand in a series of undulating movements.

SHIRK (shûrk), *v.,* SHIRKED, SHIRKING. (Ducking back and forth, away from something.) Both "A" hands, thumbs pointing straight up, are held some distance before the chest, with the left hand in front of the right. The right hand, swinging back and forth, moves away from the left and toward the chest. Also AVOID 1, EVADE, EVASION, SHUN.

SHIRT (shûrt), *n.* (Draping the clothes on the body.) With fingertips resting on the chest, both hands move down simultaneously. The action is repeated. Also CLOTHES, CLOTHING, DRESS, FROCK, GARMENT, GOWN, SUIT, WEAR 1.

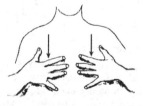

SHIVER 1 (shĭv′ ər), *v.,* -ERED, -ERING. (The trembling from cold.) Both "S" hands, palms facing, are placed at the sides of the body. In this position the arms and hands shiver. Also CHILLY, COLD 1, FRIGID, WINTER 1.

SHIVER 2 (*colloq.*), *n., v.* (The chattering of the teeth.) The extended and curved index and middle fingers of both hands are placed together, almost touching, with the right hand above the left, palms facing. Both hands shake back and forth in opposing directions a number of times.

SHOCKED 1 (shŏkt), *v.* (The mind is frozen; the thought is frozen.) The index finger of the right "D" hand, palm facing the body, touches the forehead (modified THINK sign, *q.v.*). Both hands, in the "5" position, palms down, are then suddenly and deliberately dropped down in front of the body. A look of surprise is assumed at this point, and the head jerks back slightly. Also AT A LOSS, DUMFOUNDED 1, JOLT, STUMPED.

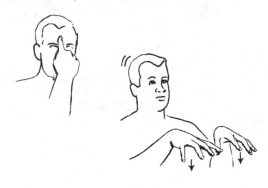

SHOCKED 2 (*colloq.*), *adj.* (The eyes pop open.) The "S" hands, palms facing each other, are held before the eyes. They suddenly open into the "C" position, with the eyes wide open. Also OPEN-EYED, SURPRISED.

SHOE(S) 1 (shōō), *n.* Both "S" hands, palms facing down, are brought together sharply twice.

SHOE(S) 2, *n.* (Slipping the foot into the shoe.) The downturned right "B" hand is slipped into the upturned left "C" hand.

SHOFAR (shō′ fər), *n., eccles.* (The shape of the ram's horn and its blowing.) The left "S" hand, palm facing right, is placed on the lips, with the right "C" hand placed in front of it. The right "C" hand moves forward and arcs to the right. This indicates the blowing of the ram's horn or shofar at the celebration of Rosh Hashanah, the Jewish New Year. Also RAM'S HORN.

SHOOT 1 (shōōt), *v.,* SHOT, SHOOTING. (Firing a gun.) The right "L" hand is pointed forward, palm facing left. The right thumb is then moved down as in the movement of the pistol's hammer. The index or trigger finger may also move.

SHOOT 2, *v.* (Shooting a gun.) The left "S" hand is held above the head as if holding a gun barrel. At the same time the right "L" hand is held below the left hand, its index finger moving back and forth as if pulling a trigger. Also GUN, PISTOL, RIFLE, SHOT 2.

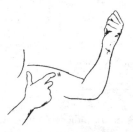

SHOP 1 (shŏp), *n., v.,* SHOPPED, SHOPPING. (Paying out money.) The right hand, palm up and all fingertips touching the thumb, is placed in the upturned left hand. From this position it moves forward and off the left hand a number of times. The right fingers usually remain against the thumb, but they may be opened very slightly each time the right hand moves forward. Also GROCERIES, SHOPPING.

SHOP 2, *n.* (A house where things are sold.) The sign for SELL is made: both "AND" hands, fingertips touching their respective thumbs, are held palms down before the body. The hands are pivoted outward and away from the body once or several times. This is followed by the sign for HOUSE: the hands form a pyramid a bit above eye level and then separate, moving diagonally downward and then straight down a few inches. It may also be followed by the sign for PLACE: the "P" hands are held side by side before the body, with middle fingertips touching. From this position the hands separate and outline a circle (or a square) before coming together again closer to the body. Also STORE 1.

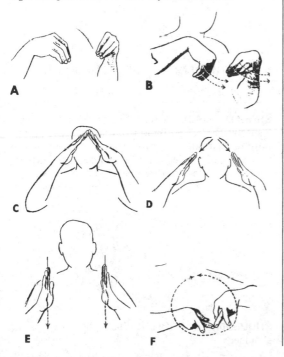

SHOPLIFT (shop' lift'), *v.,* -LIFTED, LIFTING. (Taking surreptitiously.) Both downturned "V" hands are crossed. As they come apart, they move to their respective sides of the body, and the "V"s bend in, as if grasping.

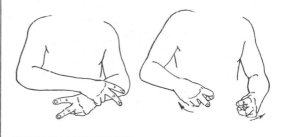

SHOPPING (shŏp' ĭng), *n.* See SHOP 1.

SHOPPING CENTER, *n.* (SHOP, CENTER.) The sign for SHOPPING is made: the right hand, palm up and all fingertips touching the thumb, is placed in the upturned left hand. The right hand moves forward and off the left hand several times. This is followed by CENTER: the downturned right fingers make a clockwise circle over the upturned open left hand, coming down to stand on the left palm.

SHORT 1 (shôrt), *adj.* (To make short; to measure off a short space.) The index and middle fingers of the right "H" hand are placed across the top of the index and middle fingers of the left "H" hand and move a short distance back and forth along the length of the left index finger. Also ABBREVIATE 2, BRIEF 1, SHORTEN.

SHORT 2, *adj.* (A shortness of height is indicated.) The right hand, in right-angle position, pats an imaginary head at approximately chest level. Also MINOR, SMALL 2.

SHORTEN (shôr′ tən), *v.,* -ENED, -ENING. See SHORT 1.

SHORT HAIR, *n.* (Indicating the length.) Both right-angle hands, palms down, are positioned at either side of the head, near the cheeks. They move up an inch or two.

SHORTS (shôrtz), *n.* (The length is indicated.) The signer indicates the hem of a pair of shorts on the legs. Indicate the length of the shorts by crossing the thighs.

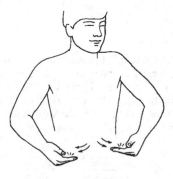

SHOT 1 (shŏt) (*colloq.*), *n.* (The natural sign.) The right hand goes through the motions of injecting a

substance into the upper left arm. Also INJECTION, SHOT IN THE ARM.

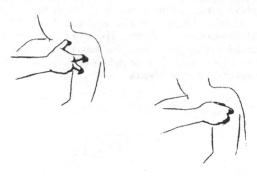

SHOT 2, *n.* (Shooting a gun.) The left "S" hand is held above the head as if holding a gun barrel. At the same time the right "L" hand is held below the left hand, its index finger moving back and forth as if pulling a trigger. Also GUN, PISTOL, RIFLE, SHOOT 2.

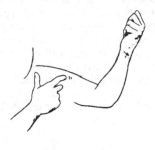

SHOT IN THE ARM, *n., sl. phrase.* See SHOT 1.

SHOULD (shŏŏd), *v.* (Being pinned down.) The right hand, in the "X" position, palm down, moves forcefully up and down once or twice. An expression of determination is frequently assumed. Also HAVE TO, IMPERATIVE, MUST, NECESSARY 1, NECESSITY, NEED 1, OUGHT TO, VITAL 2.

SHOULDER (shōl′ dər), *n.* The right hand taps the shoulder.

SHOULDN'T HAVE TOUCHED IT, *phrase.* (Touch and quickly remove hand.) Both open hands, palms down, middle fingers pointing straight down, are positioned with the right middle finger touching the back of the left hand. Both hands suddenly move up, the middle fingers snapping back to touch their respective palms. Also WON'T TOUCH IT.

SHOUT (shout), *v.,* SHOUTED, SHOUTING. (Harsh words thrown out.) The right hand, as in CURSE 1, appears to claw words out of the mouth. This time, however, it turns and throws them out, ending in the "5" position. Also BLASPHEME 2, CALL OUT, CRY 3, CRY OUT, CURSE 2, SCREAM, SUMMON 1, SWEAR 3.

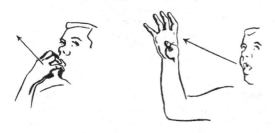

SHOVEL 1 (shŭv′ əl), *n., v.,* -ELED, -ELING. (The natural motion.) Both hands, in the "A" position, right hand facing up and left hand facing down, grasp an imaginary shovel. They go through the natural movements of shoveling earth—first digging in and then tossing the earth aside. Also DIG 2, SPADE.

SHOVEL 2, *v.,* -ELED, -ELING. (Turning over the earth.) The upturned right palm, cupped, acts like a

scoop for the earth, turning it over to the left. The upturned left palm may act as a foil.

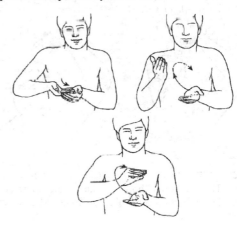

SHOW 1 (shō), *n., v.,* SHOWED, SHOWN, SHOWING. (Directing the attention to something and bringing it forward.) The right index finger points into the left palm, held facing out before the body. The left palm moves straight out. For the passive form of this verb, *i.e.,* BE SHOWN, the movement is reversed: the left hand, palm facing in, is moved in toward the body, while the right index finger remains pointing into the left palm. Also DEMONSTRATE, DISPLAY, EVIDENCE, EXAMPLE, EXHIBIT, EXHIBITION, ILLUSTRATE, INDICATE, INFLUENCE 3, PRODUCE 2, REPRESENT, SIGNIFY 1.

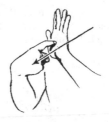

SHOW 2, *n.* (Motion or movement, modified by the letter "A" for "act.") Both "A" hands, palms out, are held at shoulder height and rotate alternately toward the head. Also ACT 1, ACTOR, ACTRESS, DRAMA, PERFORM 2, PERFORMANCE 2, PLAY 2.

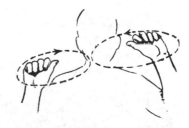

SHOWER (shou′ ər), *n.* (The sprinkling of water on the head.) The right hand sprinkles imaginary water on the head. Also BAPTISM.

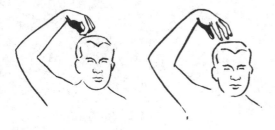

SHOW OFF 1 (shō ôf′), *v.* (Indicating the self repeatedly.) The thumbs of both "A" hands are alternately thrust into the chest a number of times. Also BOAST, BRAG.

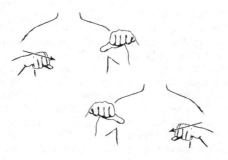

SHOW-OFF 2, *n., loc.* The right "P" hand, palm facing down, is swung several times into the open left hand, whose palm is facing right.

SHRIMP 1 (shrimp), *n.* (The movement in the water.) Both hands, palms out, are held side by side with the thumbs touching their respective index fingers. The fingers open and close quickly a number of times.

SHRIMP 2, *n.* (The swimming motion.) The curved right index finger, representing the tail, points left. It moves to the right in a succession of small movements, each one accompanied by an opening and closing of the index finger.

SHRIMP 3, *n.* (The method of locomotion.) The downturned crossed "I" hands move forward simultaneously as the little fingers wriggle open and closed.

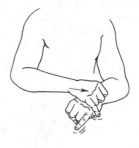

SHRIVEL (shriv′ əl), *v.*, -VELED, VELLING. (The natural sign.) The right claw hand, palm down or facing forward, slowly shrivels into the "S." The sign is sometimes made with the upright index finger simply waving back and forth in front of the lips.

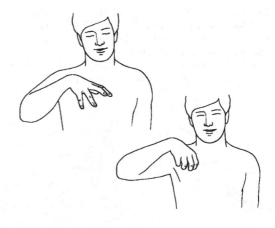

SHUN (shŭn), *v.*, SHUNNED, SHUNNING. (Ducking back and forth away from something.) Both "A" hands, thumbs pointing straight up, are held some distance before the chest, with the left hand in front of the right. The right hand, swinging back and forth, moves away from the left and toward the chest. Also AVOID 1, EVADE, EVASION, SHIRK.

SHUT (shŭt), *adj., v.,* SHUT, SHUTTING. (The act of closing.) Both "B" hands, held palms out before the body, come together with some force. Also CLOSE 1.

SHUT UP 1 (shŭt ŭp'), *interj.* (Closing of the mouth.) The open right hand, fingers together and pointing left, palm toward the face, is placed so that the back of the thumb rests against the lips. The hand snaps shut so that all fingers now also rest on the lips. An angry expression is assumed.

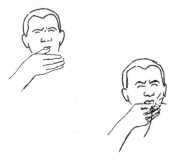

SHUT UP 2, *interj.* (The natural motion of "shushing.") The index finger of the right "D" hand is brought up forcefully against the lips. An angry expression is assumed.

SHY 1 (shī), *adj.* (The color rises in the cheek; an attempt is made to hide the head.) The backs of the fingers of the right hand, held in the right-angle position, are placed against the right cheek. The hand moves up along the cheek, pivoting at the wrist, so that the fingers finally point to the rear. Also ASHAMED 1, BASHFUL 1, IMMODEST, IMMORAL, SHAME 1, SHAMEFUL, SHAME ON YOU.

SHY 2, *adj.* Similar to SHY 1, but both hands are used, at either cheek. Also ASHAMED 2, BASHFUL 2, SHAME 2.

SICILY (sis' ə lē), *n.* (Stealing something.) The downturned right "3" or claw-shaped hand, held near the right hip, swivels twice in a clockwise manner as if picking up something surreptitiously. This sign is highly derogatory, for it implies that all Sicilians are thieves. It should not normally be used. Also PALERMO.

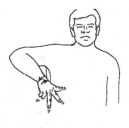

SICK (sĭk), *adj., adv.* (The sick parts of the anatomy are indicated.) The right middle finger rests on the forehead and its left counterpart is placed against the stomach. The signer assumes an expression of sadness or physical distress. Also DISEASE 1, ILL, ILLNESS, SICKNESS.

SIDEBURNS (sīd′ bûrnz′), *n.* (The outline and shape.) Both curved index fingers and thumbs, forming a modified "C," trace a pair of sideburns down either side of the face. The action is repeated.

SIGHT (sīt), *n., SAW, SEEN, SEEING.* (The eyesight is directed forward.) The right "V" hand, palm facing the body, is placed so that the fingertips are just under the eyes. The hand swings around and out so that the fingertips are now pointing forward. Also LOOK 1, PERCEIVE 1, PERCEPTION, SEE, WATCH 2.

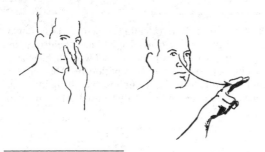

SIGNIFICANCE 1 (sĭg nĭf′ ə kəns), *n.* Both "F" hands, palms facing each other, move apart, up, and together in a smooth, elliptical fashion, coming together at the tips of the thumbs and index fingers of both hands. Also DESERVE, ESSENTIAL, IMPORTANT 1, MAIN, MERIT, PRECIOUS, PROMINENT 2, SIGNIFICANT, VALUABLE, VALUE, VITAL 1, WORTH, WORTHWHILE, WORTHY.

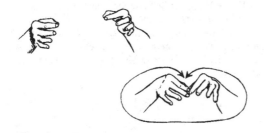

SIGNIFICANCE 2, *n.* (Relative standing of one's thoughts.) A modified sign for THINK is made: the right index finger touches the middle of the forehead. The tips of the right "V" hand, palm down, are then thrust into the upturned left palm (as in STAND, *q.v.*).

The right "V" hand is then rethrust into the upturned left palm, with right palm now facing the body. Also CONNOTE, IMPLY, INTEND, INTENT 1, INTENTION, MEAN 2, MEANING, MOTIVE 3, PURPOSE 1, SIGNIFY 2, SUBSTANCE 2.

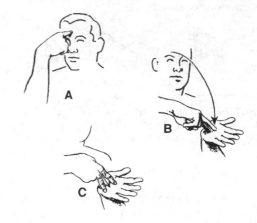

SIGNIFICANT (sĭg nĭf′ ə kənt), *adj.* See SIGNIFICANCE 1.

SIGNIFY 1 (sĭg′ nə fī′), *v.,* -FIED, -FYING. (Directing the attention to something and bringing it forward.) The right index finger points into the left palm, held facing out before the body. The left palm moves straight out. For the passive form of this verb, *i.e.,* BE SHOWN, the movement is reversed: the left hand, palm facing in, is moved in toward the body, while the right index finger remains pointing into the left palm. Also DEMONSTRATION, DISPLAY, EVIDENCE, EXAMPLE, EXHIBIT, EXHIBITION, ILLUSTRATE, INDICATE, INFLUENCE 3, PRODUCE 2, REPRESENT, SHOW 1.

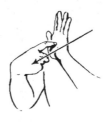

SIGNIFY 2, *n.* See SIGNIFICANCE 2.

SIGN LANGUAGE, *n.* (LANGUAGE 1, *q.v.,* and hand/arm movements.) The "D" hands, palms facing and index fingers pointing back toward the face, describe a series of continuous counterclockwise circles toward and away from the face, imitating the foot motions in bicycling. This is followed by the sign for LANGUAGE: the downturned "F" hands are positioned with thumbs and index fingertips touching. The hands move straight apart to either side in a wavy motion. The LANGUAGE part is often omitted. Also LANGUAGE OF SIGNS, SIGNS.

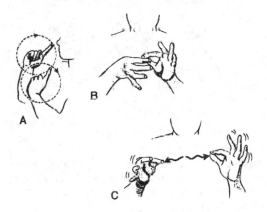

SIGN OFF, *v. Phrase in computer terminology.* (SIGN and DISCONNECT.) The outstretched right index and middle fingers, palm facing down, are slapped into the upturned left palm. The interlocked right and left thumbs and index fingers then break apart.

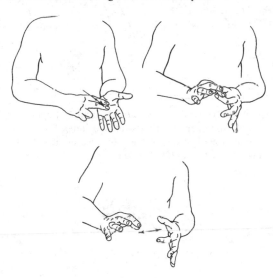

SIGN ON, *v. Phrase in computer terminology.* (SIGN and CONNECT.) As in SIGN OFF, above, but the right and left thumbs and index fingers interconnect.

SIGNS (sīnz), *n., pl.* See SIGN LANGUAGE.

SILENCE 1 (sī′ ləns), *interj., n., v.,* -LENCED, LENCING. (The natural sign.) The index finger is brought up against the pursed lips. Also BE QUIET 1, CALM 2, HUSH, NOISELESS, QUIET 1, SILENT, STILL 2.

SILENCE 2, *n., interj., v.* (Quiet and peace.) The open hands are crossed before the mouth, the right palm facing left, left facing right. Then both hands, held palms down, move down from the mouth, curving outward to either side of the body. Also BE QUIET 2, BE STILL, CALM 1, QUIET 2.

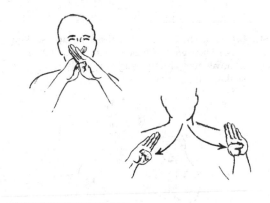

SILENT (sī′ lənt), *adj.* See SILENCE 1.

SILLY (sĭl′ ĭ), *adj.* (Thoughts flickering back and forth.) The right "Y" hand, thumb almost touching the forehead, is shaken back and forth across the forehead several times. Also ABSURD, DAFT, FOLLY, FOOLISH, NONSENSE, RIDICULOUS, TRIFLING.

SILVER 1 (sĭl′ vər) (*rare*), *n.* (Jiggling coins.) The sign for WHITE is formed: the fingertips of the "5" hand are placed against the chest. The hand moves straight out from the chest, while the fingers and thumb all come together. Then the left open hand grasps the right fingers and shakes them several times. The sign for WHITE is often omitted.

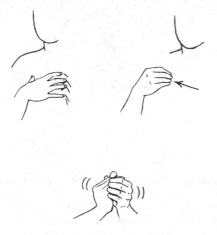

SILVER 2, *n.* (Sparkling from the eyes and shaking the coins.) The right "S" hand is positioned at the right eye. It moves forward, pivoting repeatedly at the wrist as if shaking imaginary coins.

SILVER 3 (*loc.*), *n., adj.* Both "5" hands are held before the face with palms facing each other, thumb edges up, and fingers somewhat bent. From this position, the hands turn palms downward and move away from each other to either side.

SILVER 4, *n., adj.* (Sparkling before the eyes.) The fingers of one or both hands wriggle before the eyes.

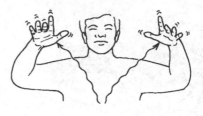

SILVER 5, *n., adj.* (A silver earring.) The right index finger touches the right earlobe, then the hand, changing to the "S" position, trembles slightly as it moves off to the right.

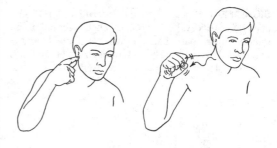

SIMILAR 1 (sĭm′ ĭ lər), *adj.* (Matching fingers are brought together.) The outstretched index fingers are brought together either once or several times. Also ALIKE, IDENTICAL, LIKE 2, SAME 1, SUCH.

SIMILAR 2, *adj.* (Matching back and forth.) The downturned "Y" hand moves quickly back and forth from left to right.

SIMPLE 1 (sĭm′ pəl), *adj.* (The fingertips are easily moved.) The right fingertips brush repeatedly over their upturned left counterparts, causing them to move. Also EASY 1, FACILITATE.

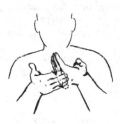

SIMPLE 2, *adj.* (Everything is wiped off the hand to emphasize an uncluttered or clean condition.) The right hand slowly wipes the upturned left palm from wrist to fingertips. Also CLEAN 1, IMMACULATE, NEAT, NICE, PLAIN 2, PURE 1, PURITY.

SIMPLE 3, *adj.* Both hands are held in the "F" position, fingers pointing out and palms facing each other. The right hand comes down past the left, its index finger and thumb smartly striking their left counterparts. The signer often assumes a pursed-lips expression.

SIMULTANEOUS COMMUNICATION, *n.* (The "S" and the "C," back and forth. Both hands, one in the "C" position and the other in the "S," move alternately back and forth from the mouth. This is also the acronym SIMCOM.

SIMULTANEOUSLY (sī′ məl tā′ nē əs lē), *adv.* (Time is the same.) The downturned curved right index finger taps the back of the left wrist, and then both hands, in the downturned "Y" position, separate quickly. Also SAME TIME.

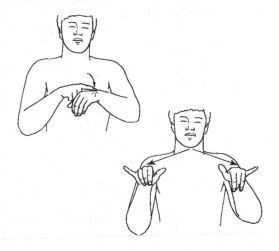

SIN (sĭn), *n., v.,* SINNED, SINNING. (A stabbing.) The "D" hands, index fingers pointing to each other, are rotated in elliptical fashion before the chest—simultaneously but in opposite directions. Also ACHE, HARM 1, HURT 1, INJURE 1, INJURY, MAR 1, OFFEND, OFFENSE, PAIN, WOUND.

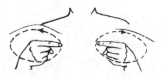

SINCE 1 (sĭns), *adv., prep., conj.* (From a point up and over.) In the "D" position, palms down, both index fingers touch the right shoulder and then are brought up and over, ending in a palm-up position, pointing straight ahead of the body. Also ALL ALONG, ALL THE TIME, EVER SINCE, SO FAR, THUS FAR.

SINCE 2, *conj.* (A thought or knowledge uppermost in the mind.) The fingers of the right hand, or the index finger, are placed on the center of the forehead, and then the hand is brought strongly up above the head, assuming the "A" position, thumb pointing up. Also BECAUSE, FOR 2.

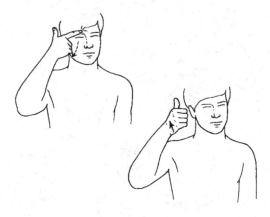

SINCERE 1 (sĭn sîr′), *adj.* (The letter "H" for HONEST; a straight and true path.) The index and middle fingers of the right "H" hand, whose palm faces left, move straight forward along the upturned left palm. Also FRANK, HONEST, HONESTY.

SINCERE 2, *adj.* (Coming forth directly from the lips; true.) The index finger of the right "D" hand, palm facing left, is placed against the lips. It moves up an inch or two and then describes a small arc forward and away from the lips. Also ABSOLUTE, ABSOLUTELY, ACTUAL, ACTUALLY, AUTHENTIC, CERTAIN, CERTAINLY, FAITHFUL 3, FIDELITY, FRANKLY, GENUINE, INDEED, POSITIVE 1, POSITIVELY, REAL, REALLY, SURE, SURELY, TRUE, TRULY, TRUTH, VALID, VERILY.

SING (sĭng), *n., v.,* SANG or SUNG, SUNG, SINGING. (A rhythmic, wavy movement of the hand to indicate a melody; the movement of a conductor's hand in directing a musical performance.) The right "5" hand, palm facing left, is waved back and forth near the open left hand in a series of elongated figure eights. Also CHANT, HYMN 1, MELODY, MUSIC, SONG.

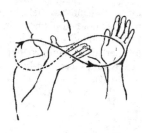

SINGLE 1 (sing′ gəl), *adj.* (The "1" indicates "alone" or "single.") The right "1" hand, palm facing the signer, moves in rhythmic fashion from left to right as it moves forward from the body.

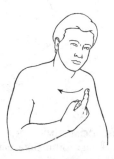

SINGLE 2, *adj.* (Based on BACHELOR.) The right "S" hand, palm out, moves from the right side of the chin to the left side.

SINK 1 (sǐngk), *v.*, SANK or SUNK, SUNK or SUNKEN, SINKING. (The natural sign.) The thumb of the right "3" hand protrudes upward between the index and middle fingers of the downturned left hand. The right hand then slips out from between the left fingers and moves straight downward.

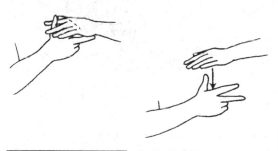

SINK 2, *v.* (Movement downward.) The index and middle fingers of the right "V" hand, held pointing down, move downward through the spread middle and ring fingers of the downturned open left hand.

SINK 3, *n.* (The faucets and the shape.) Both downturned hands mime turning a pair of faucets. The upturned open hands then trace the outline of a sink, from the bottom to the sides.

SIREN (sī′ rən), *n.* (An emergency vehicle being heard.) Touch the index to the ear; then, with upturned cupped or claw hand held above the head, the hand moves in a continuous clockwise rotation.

SISSY (sis′ ē), *n.* (An effeminate gesture.) The right hand lightly taps the back of the limp left hand.

SISTER 1 (sǐs′ tər), *n.* (Female root sign; SAME. Meaning a female from the same family.) The FEMALE root sign is made: the thumb of the right "A" hand moves down along the right jawbone, almost to the chin. This is followed by the sign for SAME: the outstretched index fingers are brought together either once or several times.

SISTER 2, *n.* (The hood.) Both open hands, palms facing the head and fingers pointing up, are moved down along either side of the head as if tracing the outline of a nun's hood. Also NUN.

SISTER 3, *n.* (A variant of SISTER 1.) The right "L" hand is placed so that the thumb rests on the right cheek. The "L" hand then moves down so that the little finger edge comes to rest on the back of the downturned left "S" hand.

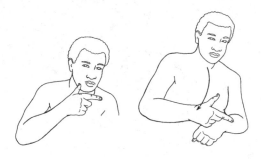

SIT 1 (sĭt), *v.,* SAT, SITTING. (The act of sitting.) The extended right index and middle fingers are draped across the back of the same two fingers of the downturned left hand. The hands then move straight downward a short distance. The movement is repeated. Also BE SEATED, CHAIR 1, SEAT.

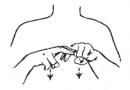

SIT 2, *v.* (Act of sitting down; the legs of the chair.) Both hands, palms down, are held before the chest, and they move down a short distance in unison. The downturned index fingers are then thrust downward a few inches, moved in toward the body, and thrust

downward once again to represent the four legs of the chair. Also CHAIR 2.

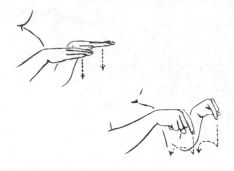

SITUATION (sich′ ōō ā′ shən), *n.* (The letter "S"; an encircling environment.) The right "S" hand makes a counterclockwise circle around the upturned left index finger.

SIZE (sīz), *n.* (Measuring space between the hands.) Both downturned "Y" hands, thumbs touching, separate and come together several times.

SKATEBOARD (skāt′ bôrd), *n.* The right index and middle fingers stand on the tips of their left counterparts. Both hands, thus connected, move forward in a swaying motion, imitating the rhythms of riding on a skateboard.

SKELETON (skel′ ə tən), *n.* (The crossed bones.) Both "V" hands, fingers bent and palms facing the body, are crossed at the chest. The two "V"s make scratching movements repeatedly as they rest on the biceps.

SKEPTIC 1 (skĕp′ tĭk), *n.* (The nose is wrinkled in disbelief.) The right "V" hand faces the nose. The index and middle fingers bend as a cynical expression is assumed. This is followed by the sign for INDIVID-UAL 1: both open hands, palms facing each other, move down the sides of the body, tracing its outline to the hips. Also CYNIC, CYNICAL, DISBELIEF 1, DON'T BELIEVE, DOUBT 1, INCREDULITY, SKEPTICAL 1.

SKEPTIC 2, *n.* (Warding off.) The sign for SKEPTI-CAL 2 is formed. This is followed by the sign for INDIVIDUAL 1, as in SKEPTIC 1.

SKEPTICAL 1 (skĕp′ tə kəl), *adj.* See SKEPTIC 1.

SKEPTICAL 2, *adj.* (Warding off.) The right "S" hand is held before the right shoulder, elbow bent out to the side. The hand is then thrown forward several times as if striking at someone. Also SUSPICION 3.

SKETCH (skech), *n., v.,* SKETCHED, SKETCHING. (A piece of charcoal describes lines on a piece of paper.) The right little finger represents the charcoal. It is placed on the upturned left palm and moves down in random wavy fashion, describing the drawing process.

SKI 1 (skē), *v.,* SKIED, SKIING. (The ski poles.) The signer, holding an imaginary pair of ski poles, pushes down on them in order to create forward motion.

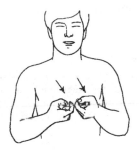

SKI 2, *v.* (Downhill movement.) Both "X" hands, palms up, move downward as if sliding downhill.

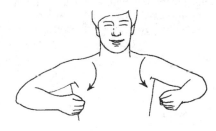

SKID 1 (skĭd), *n., v.,* SKIDDED, SKIDDING. (The natural movement.) The sign for STAND is made: the down-turned right "V" fingers are thrust into the upturned left palm. The fingers then skid forward across the left palm from wrist to fingertips.

SKID 2, *n., v.* (The movement of a vehicle in skidding.) The right "3" or so-called vehicle shape is placed with the little finger edge on the upturned left palm. It curves in a zigzag manner as it slides forward off the left palm.

SKILL (skĭl), *n.* (A sharp-edged hand.) The right hand grasps the little finger edge of the left firmly. As it leaves this position, moving down and out, it assumes the "A" position, palm facing left. Also ADEPT, EXPERIENCE 1, EXPERT, SHARP 4, SHREWD, SKILLFUL.

SKILLFUL (skĭl′ fəl), *adj.* See SKILL.

SKIN DIVING, *n.* (The snorkel tube.) With the right cheek puffed out, the right index and thumb form a circle at the right corner of the mouth, moving straight up to outline a tube emerging from the mouth.

SKINNY (skĭn′ ĭ), *adj., sl.* (A thin, tapering object is described with the little fingers, the thinnest of all.) The tips of the little fingers, touching, one above the other, are drawn apart. The cheeks may also be drawn in for emphasis. Also BEANPOLE, THIN 2.

SKIP (skip), *v.,* SKIPPED, SKIPPING. (Something is missing.) The extended right index finger strikes against the downturned middle finger of the left hand, which is held palm down and other fingers pointing right or forward.

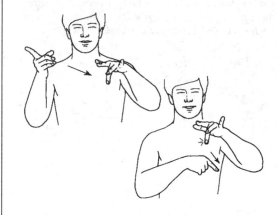

SKULLCAP (skul′ kap′), *n.* (Its placement on the head.) The downturned right claw hand is placed squarely on top of the head. Also YARMULKE.

SKY 1 (skī), *n.* (Entering heaven through a break in the clouds.) Both open hands, fingers straight and pointing up, move upward in an arc on either side of the head. Just before they touch above the head, the right hand, palm down, sweeps under the left and moves up, its palm now facing out. Also HEAVEN.

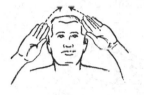

SKY 2, *n.* (Blue overhead.) The "B" hand is drawn in a wavy motion over the head.

SKYSCRAPERS (skī′ skrā′ pərz), *n., pl.* (The tall buildings are indicated.) Both index fingers move alternately up and down.

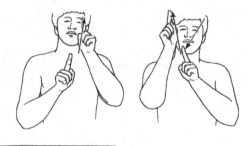

SLANG (slang), *n., adj.* (The "S" letters; quotation marks.) Both "S" hands, palms out, are drawn apart an inch or two. The curved "V" hands, palms also out, then draw quotation marks in the air.

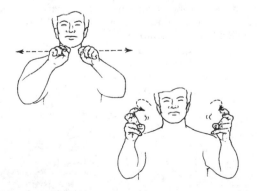

SLAY (slā), *v.,* SLEW, SLAIN, SLAYING. (Thrusting a dagger and twisting it.) The outstretched right index finger is passed under the downturned left hand. As it moves under the left hand, the right wrist twists in a clockwise direction. Also KILL, MURDER.

SLED 1 (sled), *n.* (The handlebars.) The signer mimes manipulating a sled's handlebars back and forth. The head should be hanging down, as if the body were belly down on a sled.

SLED 2, *n.* (The shape and movement.) The right hand, in the curved "V" position, palm up, moves straight forward on the back of the downturned left hand.

SLEEP 1 (slēp), *v.,* SLEPT, SLEEPING, *n.* (The eyes are closed.) The fingers of the right open hand, facing the forehead, are placed on the forehead. The hand moves down and away from the head with the fingers closing so that they all touch. The eyes meanwhile close, and the head bows slightly, as in sleep. Also ASLEEP, DOZE, NAP.

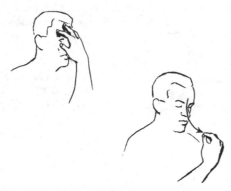

SLEEP 2, *n., v.* (The natural sign.) The signer's head leans to the right and rests in the upturned palm of the open right hand.

SLEEP TOGETHER, *v. phrase.* (Both sets of legs are tucked under the same cover.) Both downturned "H" hands, held at chest level and fingers pointing forward, are brought close and move forward together. Also GO TO BED TOGETHER.

SLEEPY (slē' pĭ), *adj.* (Drooping eyelids.) The right fingers are wiggled in front of the face and the head is bowed forward.

SLEEVE (slēv), *n.* (Indicating the sleeve.) The thumb and index fingers of either hand move up and down the opposite arm.

SLIDE 1 (slīd), *v.*, SLID, SLIDING. (The natural sign.) The right crooked "V" hand slides forward on the upturned left palm.

SLIDE 2, *n., v.* (The natural sign.) The index and middle fingertips of the downturned right "V" hand slide forward over the upturned left palm from wrist to fingertips.

SLIDE 3, *n.* (Slide being inserted in projector.) The right "H" hand, palm facing the signer and fingertips pointing left, moves into the left palm.

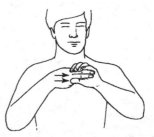

SLIGHT (slīt), *adj.* (Indicating a small mass.) The extended right thumb and index finger are held slightly spread. They are then moved slowly toward each other until they almost touch. Also PETTY, SMALL 1, TINY 2.

SLING (sling), *n.* (The shape and function.) Both arms, held horizontally and close to the chest, are positioned with the right arm above the left. The right arm executes a circle around the left, coming back to its initial position.

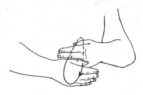

SLINGSHOT (sling′ shot′), *n.* (The shape and movement.) The left "V" hand, palm facing the signer, is the slingshot. The signer pulls back on an imaginary rubber band or elastic and lets go.

SLIP AWAY, *v. phrase.* (Slipping out and away.) The right index finger is held pointing upward between the index and middle fingers of the prone left hand. From this position the right index finger moves to the right, slipping out of the grasp of the left fingers and away from the left hand. Also LEAVE CLANDESTINELY 2, RUN AWAY.

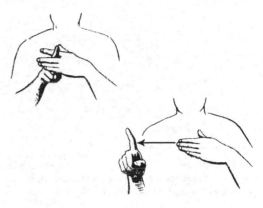

SLIPPER (slĭp′ ər), *n.* The downturned right open hand moves back and forth across the upturned cupped left palm.

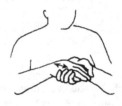

SLOPPY (slop′ ē), *adj.* (Food all over the mouth.) The downturned "4" hand, positioned on the chin, wriggles as it slides from left to right.

SLOW 1 (slō), *adj.* (The movement indicates the slowness.) The right hand is drawn slowly over the back of the downturned left hand from fingertips to wrist.

SLOW 2, *adv., adj. (loc.)* The right "Y" hand moves slowly down the right cheek.

SLUMP (slump), *n., v.,* SLUMPED, SLUMPING. (The direction; going down.) The downturned right arm moves forward and then rather sharply downward.

SMALL 1 (smôl), *adj.* (Indicating a small mass.) The extended right thumb and index finger are held slightly spread. They are then moved slowly toward each other until they almost touch. Also PETTY, SLIGHT, TINY 2.

SMALL 2, *adj.* (A shortness of height is indicated.) The right hand, in right-angle position, pats an imaginary head at approximately chest level. Also MINOR, SHORT 2.

SMART 1 (smärt), *adj.* (The mind is bright.) The middle finger is placed at the forehead, and then the hand, with an outward flick, turns around so that the palm faces outward. This indicates a brightness flowing from the mind. Also BRIGHT 3, BRILLIANT 1, CLEVER 1, INTELLIGENT.

SMART 2, *adj.* (A large brain.) The right "C" hand, palm facing left, is positioned with thumb touching the forehead. Also SCHOLARLY.

SMASHED IN, *v. phrase.* (Collapsing inward.) With fingers interlocked and palms facing the signer, both hands, using the interconnected fingers as hinges, move in toward the chest.

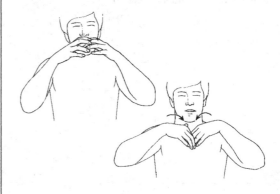

SMELL (směl), *v.,* SMELLED, SMELLING, *n.* (Bringing something up to the nose.) The upturned right hand moves slowly up to and past the nose, and the signer breathes in as the hand sweeps by. Also FRAGRANT, ODOR, SCENT.

SMILE (smīl), *v.*, SMILED, SMILING, *n.* (Drawing the lips into a smile.) The right index finger is drawn back over the lips toward the ear. As the finger moves back, the signer breaks into a smile. (Both index fingers may also be used.)

SMOKESTACK (smōk' stak'), *n.* (The shape.) The open hands, palms facing each other, are held a few inches apart. They move up together a short distance, come together an inch or two, and then continue their upward movement. Also CHIMNEY.

SNAIL (snāl), *n.* (The shape and function.) The down-turned bent right "V" hand is concealed by the down-turned cupped left hand. The right "V" fingers protrude from the left as both hands move slowly forward.

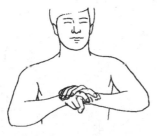

SNAKE 1 (snāk), *n.* (The movement.) The left hand is held up with palm down. The right index finger imitates the weaving movement of a snake, as it passes under the left palm.

SNAKE 2, *n.* (The slithering movement.) The right index finger, pointing outward, moves in a corkscrew motion along the outer left forearm, from wrist to elbow, while the left arm is held against the chest and the left hand assumes the "S" position, palm down.

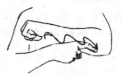

SNAKE 3, *n.* (The movement.) The right "G" hand, palm facing left, is held with its elbow resting on the upturned open left palm. In this position the hand spirals forward.

SNAKE 4, *n.* (The head and fangs gyrating.) The right elbow rests on the palm of the left hand, while the right hand gyrates in imitation of a snake's head, the thumb and first two fingers extended forward to represent fangs.

SNAKE 5, *n.* (The fangs and the slithering movement.) The right "V" hand is held palm forward before the face, with the index and middle fingers bending forward in imitation of fangs. The right elbow then rests on the palm of the left hand, while the right forearm and "G" hand move forward in a wavy movement, imitating a SNAKE.

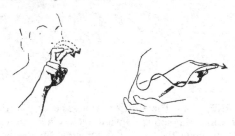

SNAKE 6, *n.* (The fangs and forward movement.) The backs of the right index and middle fingers are held to the mouth. In this position, the fingers are drawn in and extended quickly, in imitation of a snake's fangs. Then the fingers move forward in a rapid, spiraling motion.

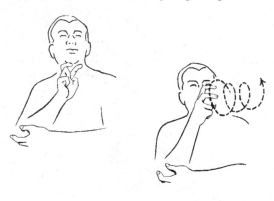

SNAP (snap), *v.,* SNAPPED, SNAPPING. (Snapping the fingers.) The fingers are snapped.

SNAPS (snapz), *n.* (Fastening snaps on clothes.) The signer mimes closing snaps on the shirt.

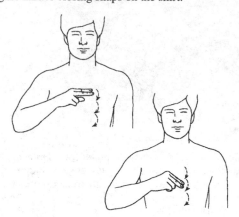

SNATCH UP (*colloq.*), *v.* (Sleight of hand.) The downturned open hand is positioned at chest height, with the middle finger hanging farther down than the rest of the fingers. With a quick and sudden movement, the hand moves up into the "A" position. For maximum impact, the signer's tongue is visible, sticking out from the pursed lips. As the hand moves up, the tongue is suddenly sucked into the mouth.

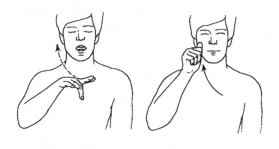

SNEEZE 1 (snēz), *n., v.,* SNEEZED, SNEEZING. (The natural motion.) The signer goes through the motions of covering his nose and sneezing: the head is tossed back while the thumb and index finger are placed over the nose. The head then moves abruptly forward and down, the hand still covering the nose.

SNEEZE 2, *n., v.* (Stifling a sneeze.) The index finger is pressed lengthwise under the nose.

SNIFF (snif), *n., v.* (Drawing into the nose.) The right hand, fingers open and extended forward, moves in toward the nose while the fingers come together.

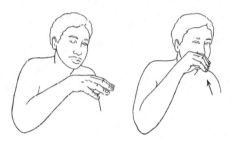

SNITCH (snich), *n., sl., v.* (A word escapes from the corner of the mouth.) The right "S" hand, palm facing the body, is placed on the mouth, knuckles facing left. The right index finger suddenly flicks out. The signer may jerk the head slightly to the left as the finger springs out.

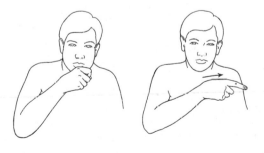

SNOB 1 (snŏb), *n.* (Turning up the nose.) The tip of the extended right index finger is held against the right side of the nose. The signer raises his chin and assumes a haughty air.

SNOB 2, *n.* (The upturned nose.) The right thumb and index finger, slightly open, are placed at the tip of the nose, and move up, coming together as they do.

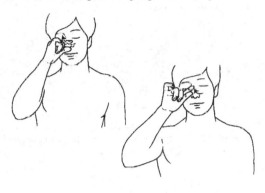

SNOWFLAKE (snō′ flāk′), *n.* (Descending and settling.) The sign for SNOW is made: the fingers wriggle repeatedly as the downturned hands move slowly down. The right thumb and index, forming a circle, then settle gently on the back of the downturned left hand.

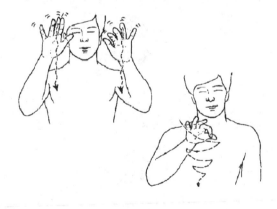

SO (sō), *interj.* (The natural sign, accompanied by a sigh.) With palms facing up, the signer heaves a distinct sigh, causing the shoulders to rise slightly. Also WELL 3.

SOAP 1 (sōp), *n., v.,* SOAPED, SOAPING. (Working up a lather in the hand.) The fingertips of the right hand move back and forth on the upturned left palm in small downturned arcs.

SOAP 2, *n., v.* (Same rationale as for SOAP 1.) The fingertips of the right hand move straight back and forth across the upturned left palm.

SOAP 3, *n., v.* (Same rationale as for SOAP 1.) The base of the right hand moves around in small circles against the open left palm, which is facing right.

SOAP 4, *n., v.* (Same rationale as for SOAP 1.) The fingertips of the right hand move straight up and down against the upturned left palm.

SO-CALLED (sō′ kôld′), *adj.* (The quotation marks are indicated.) The curved index and middle fingers of both hands, held palms out, move slightly to either side of the body, as if drawing quotation marks in the air. Also CAPTION, CITE, QUOTATION, QUOTE, SUBJECT, THEME, TITLE, TOPIC.

SOCIAL SECURITY, *n.* (The "S" letters.) The signer fingerspells the letters "S-S."

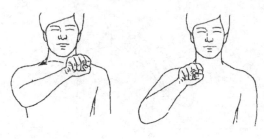

SOCIAL STUDIES, *n.* The right hand makes the letter "S" twice, moving slightly to the right after the first time.

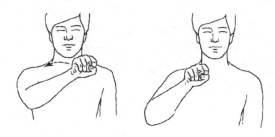

SOCIAL WORK, *n.* (The "S" and "W"; WORK.) The right "S" hand, palm facing left, is thrust down into the upturned left palm. This is followed by the right "W" hand doing the same movement. For SOCIAL WORKER, add the INDIVIDUAL 1 sign.

SOCK(S) 1 (sŏk), *n.* (The knitting.) The index fingers, pointing forward, are rubbed back and forth against each other. Also HOSE 1, KNIT, STOCKING(S) 1.

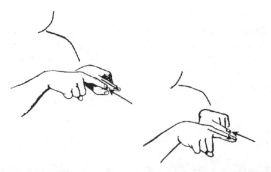

SOCK(S) 2, *n.* (Pulling on hose.) The downturned, open right hand grasps its left counterpart at the fingertips and slides over the back of the hand and up the arm as if pulling on hose. Also HOSE 2, STOCKING(S) 2.

SODA POP, *n.* (Corking a bottle.) The left "O" hand is held with thumb edge up, representing a bottle. The thumb and index finger of the right "5" hand represent a cork and are inserted into the circle formed by the "O" hand. The palm of the open right hand then strikes down on the upturned edge of the "O" hand, as if forcing the cork into the bottle. Also POP 1, SODA WATER.

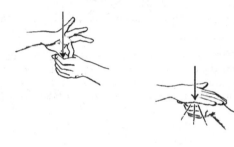

SODA WATER, *n. phrase.* See SODA POP.

SOFA (sō′ fə), *n.* (An elongated seat.) The sign for SIT; the downturned right "H" hand is placed on its left counterpart. The downturned "C" hands then move apart from each other, describing a long object. Also COUCH.

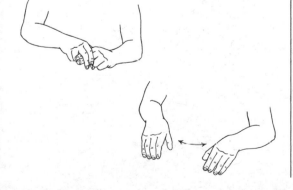

SO FAR, *adv. phrase.* (From a point up and over.) In the "D" position, palms down, both index fingers touch the right shoulder and then are brought up and over, ending in a palm-up position, pointing straight ahead of the body. Also ALL ALONG, ALL THE TIME, EVER SINCE, SINCE, THUS FAR.

SOFT (sôft, sŏft), *adj.* (Squeezing for softness.) The hands slowly and deliberately squeeze an imaginary object or substance. Also RIPE, TENDER 1.

SOIL 1 (soil), *n.* (Fingering the soil.) Both hands, held upright before the body, finger imaginary pinches of soil. Also DIRT, EARTH 2, GROUND.

SOIL 2, *v.,* SOILED, SOILING. (A modification of the pig's snout groveling in a trough.) The downturned right hand is placed under the chin. Its fingers, pointing left, wiggle repeatedly. Also DIRTY, FILTHY, FOUL, IMPURE, NASTY, STAIN.

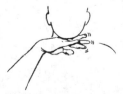

SOLAR SYSTEM, *n.* (The movement of the planets.) The right "S" hand makes a clockwise circle around its left counterpart. Both "S" hands, palms forward, then separate and draw "Z"'s in the air. This latter sign means SYSTEM.

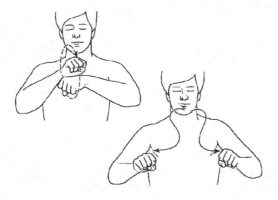

SOLDER (sŏd′ ər), *n., v.,* -DERED, -DERING. (The welder's torch.) The right "L" hand, thumb straight up, moves in a circle with the index finger pointing to the left palm. Also WELD.

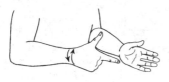

SOLDIER (sōl′ jər), *n.* (Bearing arms.) Both "A" hands, palms facing the body, are placed at the left breast, with the right hand above the left, as if holding a rifle against the body. The sign for INDIVIDUAL 1 follows: both open hands, palms facing each other, move down the sides of the body, tracing its outline to the hips. Also ARMS.

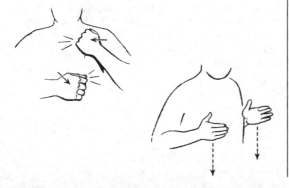

SOLE (sōl), *adj.* (One wandering around in a circle.) The index finger, pointing straight up, palm facing the body (the number *one*), is rotated before the face in a counterclockwise direction. Also ALONE, LONE, ONE 2, ONLY, UNITY.

SO LONG, *interj.* (A wave of the hand.) The right open hand waves back and forth several times. Also FAREWELL 2, GOODBYE 2, HELLO 2.

SOME (sŭm; *unstressed* səm), *adj.* (Cutting off or designating a part.) The little finger edge of the open right hand moves straight down the middle of the upturned left palm. Also PART 1, PIECE, PORTION, SECTION, SHARE 1.

SOMERSAULT (sum′ ər sôlt), *n., v.,* -SAULTED, -SAULTING. (The natural sign.) The signer mimes a somersault: the right bent "V" hand, palm facing forward, executes a somersault, twisting into a palm-up position.

SOMETIME(S) (sŭm′ tīmz′), *adv.* (The "1" finger is brought up very slowly.) The right index finger, resting in the open left palm, which is facing right, swings up slowly from its position to one in which it is pointing straight up. The movement is repeated slowly, after a pause. Also OCCASIONAL, OCCASIONALLY, ONCE IN A WHILE, SELDOM.

SON (sŭn), *n.* (Male, baby.) The sign for MALE is made: the thumb and extended fingers of the right hand are brought up to grasp an imaginary cap brim. This is followed by the sign for BABY: the arms are held with one resting on the other, as if cradling a baby.

SONG (sông, sŏng), *n.* (A rhythmic, wavy movement of the hand to indicate a melody; the movement of a conductor's hand in directing a musical performance.) The right "5" hand, palm facing left, is waved back and forth near the open left hand in a series of elongated figure eights. Also CHANT, HYMN 1, MELODY, MUSIC, SING.

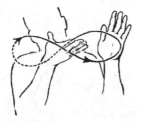

SOPHISTICATED (sə fis′ ti kā′ tid), *adj.* (Nose in the air.) The right "3" hand is placed with thumb under chin, head held high. The hand moves slightly forward and up. Alternatively, the index and little fingers are used, with the index moving up off the chin as before.

SOPHOMORE (sof′ ə môr), *n.* (College student.) The right index finger touches the middle finger of the left hand.

SORE THROAT, *n.* (The area is indicated.) The index and thumb move up and down on the throat.

SORROW (sŏr′ ō, sôr′ ō), *n.* (The heart is circled to indicate feeling, modified by the letter "S" for SORRY.) The right "S" hand, palm facing the body, is rotated several times over the area of the heart. Also APOLOGIZE 1, APOLOGY 1, CONTRITION, PENITENT, REGRET, REGRETFUL, REPENT, REPENTANT, RUE, SORROWFUL 2, SORRY.

SORROWFUL 1 (sŏr′ ə fəl, sôr′ -), *adj.* (The facial features drop.) Both "5" hands, palms facing the eyes and fingers slightly curved, drop simultaneously to a level with the mouth. The head drops slightly as the hands move down, and an expression of sadness is assumed. Also DEJECTED, DEPRESSED, GLOOM, GLOOMY, GRAVE 3, GRIEF 1, MELANCHOLY, MOURNFUL, SAD.

SORROWFUL 2, *adj.* See SORROW.

SORRY (sŏr′ ĭ, sôr′ ĭ), *adj.* See SORROW.

SORT (sôrt), *v.,* SORTED, SORTING. (Separating into different groups.) The downturned right-angle hands, knuckles touching, move apart repeatedly as both hands travel from left to right.

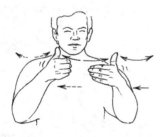

SO-SO (sō′ sō′), *phrase.* (Neither this way nor that.) The downturned "5" hand flips over and back several times.

SOUL (sōl), *n.* (Something thin and filmy, *i.e.,* ephemeral.) The hands are held palms facing, with one above the other and index fingers and thumbs touching and almost connected. As the upper hand moves straight up, the index fingers and thumbs of both hands slowly come together, giving the impression of drawing out a thread or other thin substance. Also GHOST, SPIRIT.

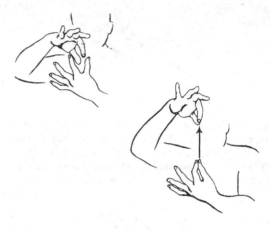

SOUP (sōōp), *n.* (The natural sign.) The upturned open left hand represents the bowl of soup. The index and middle fingers of the right "H" hand form a small scoop to represent the spoon and move from the left palm to the lips. The movement is usually repeated.

SOUR (sour), *adj.* (Something sour or bitter.) The right index finger is brought sharply up against the lips, while the mouth is puckered up as if tasting something sour. Also ACID, BITTER, DISAPPOINTED 1, LEMON 1, PICKLE.

SO WHAT? *exclam.* The right right-angle hand, palm down, is placed under the chin. It moves smartly forward in an arc so that the palm now faces up. This sign is used in the sense *"It's your problem, not mine,"* or *"I don't care."* Also TOUGH 4.

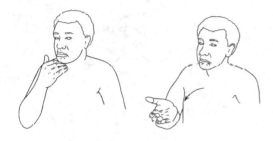

SPACE 1 (spās), *n.* (Area high above earth.) The sign for EARTH 1 is made: the thumb and index finger of the downturned right "5" hand are placed at each edge of the downturned left "S" hand. In this position the right hand swings back and forth. Then the open right hand, held upright with palm out, moves in an upward arc from left to right above the head, indicating an area high overhead.

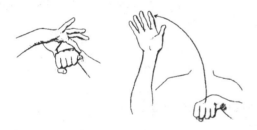

SPACE 2, *n.* (The movement upward and outward.) Both "A" hands, palms facing forward and thumbs touching, open to the "5" position as they move upward and outward, with the signer looking up.

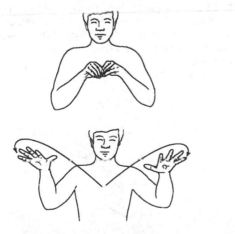

SPAGHETTI (spə gĕt′ ĭ), *n.* (Unraveling a thin string, as indicated by the little fingers.) With palms facing the body, the tips of the extended little fingers touch. As they are drawn slowly apart, they describe very small spirals. Also STRING, THREAD, TWINE.

SPEAK (spēk), *v.,* SPOKE, SPOKEN, SPEAKING. (Words tumbling from the mouth.) The right index finger, pointing left, describes a continuous small circle in front of the mouth. Also BID 3, DISCOURSE, HEARING, MAINTAIN 2, MENTION, REMARK, SAID, SAY, SPEECH 1, STATE, STATEMENT, TALK 1, TELL, VERBAL 1.

SPEAKER (spē′ kər), *n.* (The characteristic waving of the speaker's hand as he makes his point.) The right hand is held above the head, palm facing left. The hand, pivoting at the wrist, swings forward and back repeatedly. This is followed by the sign for INDIVIDUAL 1: both open hands, palms facing each other, move down the sides of the body, tracing its outline to the hips. Also ORATOR.

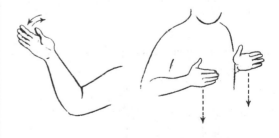

SPECIAL (spĕsh′ əl), *adj.* (Selecting a particular item from among several.) The index finger and thumb of the right hand grasp and pull up the left index finger. Also ESPECIAL, EXCEPT, EXCEPTION.

SPECIALIZE (spĕsh′ ə līz′), *v.*, -IZED, -IZING. (A straight, *i.e.*, special, path.) The hands are held in the "B" position, one above the other, with left palm facing right and right palm facing left. The little finger edge of the right hand moves straight forward along the index finger edge of the left. Also FIELD 3, IN THE FIELD OF, SPECIALTY.

SPECIALTY (spĕsh′ əl tĭ), *n., pl.* -TIES. See SPECIALIZE.

SPECIFIC 1 (spĭ sĭf′ ĭk), *adj.* (The fingers come together precisely.) The thumb and index finger of each hand, palms facing, the right above the left, form circles. They are brought together with a deliberate movement, so that the fingers and thumbs now touch. Sometimes the right hand, before coming together with the left, executes a slow clockwise circle above the left. Also ACCURATE 1, EXACT 1, EXACTLY, EXPLICIT 1, PRECISE.

SPECIFIC 2, *adj.* (Pointing.) The signer points to the index finger.

SPECULATE 1 (spĕk′ yə lāt′), *v.*, -LATED, -LATING. (A thought is turned over in the mind.) The index finger makes a small circle on the forehead. Also CONSIDER 1, MOTIVE 1, RECKON, SPECULATION 1, THINK, THOUGHT 1, THOUGHTFUL.

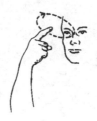

SPECULATE 2, *v.* (Turning thoughts over in the mind.) Both index fingers, pointing to the forehead, describe continuous alternating circles. Also CONSIDER 2, CONTEMPLATE, PONDER, SPECULATION 2, WEIGH 2, WONDER 1.

SPECULATION 1 (spĕk′ yə lā′ shən), *n.* See SPECULATE 1.

SPECULATION 2, *n.* See SPECULATE 2.

SPEECH 1 (spēch), *n.* (Words tumbling from the mouth.) The right index finger, pointing left, describes a continuous small circle in front of the mouth. Also BID 3, DISCOURSE, HEARING, MAINTAIN 2, MENTION, REMARK, SAID, SAY, SPEAK, STATE, STATEMENT, TALK 1, TELL, VERBAL 1.

SPEECH 2, *n.* (A gesture of an orator.) The right open hand, palm facing left, is held above and to the right of the head. It pivots, forward and backward, on the wrist several times. Also ADDRESS 1, LECTURE, ORATE, TALK 2, TESTIMONY.

SPEECHLESS (spēch′ lĭs) (*colloq.*), *adj.* (The mouth drops open.) The fingertips of both "V" hands are held curved and touching before the body, one hand above the other. Then the hands are suddenly drawn apart, and at the same instant the mouth drops open and the eyes open wide. Also DUMFOUNDED 2, FLABBER-GASTED, OPEN-MOUTHED, SURPRISE 2.

SPEECHREADING, *n.* (Reading the lips—the lines of vision, represented by the two fingers, scan the lips.) The right "V" hand, palm facing the body, is placed in front of the face, with slightly curved index and middle fingers directly in front of the lips. The right hand moves in a small counterclockwise circle around the lips. Also LIPREADING, ORAL, READ LIPS.

SPEED (spēd), *n., v.,* SPED or SPEEDED, SPEEDING. (A quick movement.) The thumbtip of the upright right hand is flicked quickly off the tip of the curved right index finger as if shooting marbles. Also FAST 1, IMMEDIATELY, QUICK, QUICKNESS, RAPID, RATE 1, SPEEDY, SWIFT.

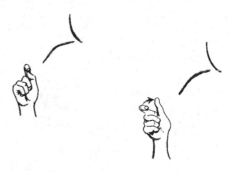

SPEEDY (spē′ dǐ), *adj.* See SPEED.

SPELL (spĕl), *v.,* SPELLED or SPELT, SPELLING. (The movement of the fingers in fingerspelling.) The right hand, palm out, is moved from left to right with the fingers wriggling up and down. Also ALPHABET, DACTYLOLOGY, FINGERSPELLING, MANUAL ALPHABET, SPELLING.

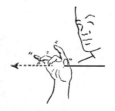

SPELLING (spĕl′ ĭng), *n.* See SPELL.

SPEND 1 (spĕnd), *v.,* SPENT, SPENDING. (Repeated giving forth.) The back of the upturned right hand, thumb touching fingertips, is placed in the upturned left palm. The right hand moves off and away from the left once or several times, each time opening into the "5" position, palm up. Also EXTRAVAGANT, SQUANDER, WASTE 1.

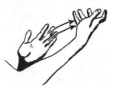

SPEND 2, *v.* (Throwing money randomly into the air.) Both hands, closed into fists, palms facing the chest, move alternately up into the air, index fingers flicking out. Also OVERSPEND, SQUANDER 2.

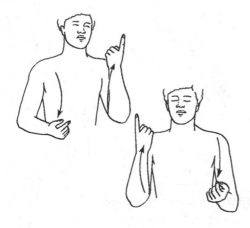

SPERM (spûrm), *n.* (The pulsing of the penis during release.) The left index finger, representing the penis, is positioned at the base of the right "E" hand, whose palm faces left. The fingers of the right hand open and close twice, as the two hands, connected, move forward an inch or so. Also EJACULATE 1, EJACULATION 1, SEMEN.

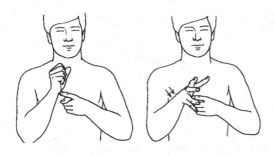

SPICE (spīs), *n.* (The mouth is on fire.) The cupped right hand, palm over the mouth, moves forward, away from the mouth, with fingers wriggling as flames. The cupped right hand may also face out, away from the mouth. Also SPICY.

SPICY (spī′ sē), *adj.* See SPICE, above.

SPILL (spil), *n., v.,* SPILLED, SPILLING. (Dropping down and spreading.) Both hands are held in the "AND" position, fingertips touching and palms down. They separate and spread open into the downturned "5" position.

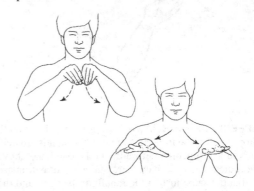

SPIRIT (spĭr′ ĭt), *n.* (Something thin and filmy, *i.e.,* ephemeral.) The hands are held palms facing, with one above the other and index fingers and thumbs touching and almost connected. As the upper hand moves straight up, the index fingers and thumbs of both hands slowly come together, giving the impression of drawing out a thread or other thin substance. Also GHOST, SOUL.

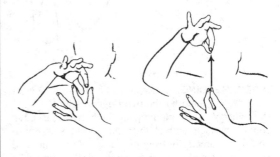

SPIT (spit), *n., v.,* SPIT OR SPAT, SPITTING. (A discharge from the mouth.) The right "S" hand, palm up, is placed against the chin. The right index flicks out suddenly, moving slightly to the left. The signer meanwhile mimes spitting.

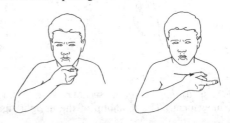

SPLENDID 1 (splĕn′ dĭd), *adj.* (The hands gesture toward the heavens.) The "5" hands, palms out and arms raised rather high, are positioned somewhat above the line of vision. The arms move abruptly forward and up once or twice. An expression of pleasure or surprise is usually assumed. Also EXCELLENT, GRAND 1, GREAT 3, MARVEL, MARVELOUS, MIRACLE, O!, SWELL 1, WONDER 2, WONDERFUL 1.

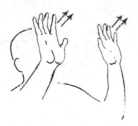

SPLENDID 2, *adj., interj.* (The feelings are titillated.) With the thumb resting on the upper part of the chest, the fingers are wiggled back and forth. Also ELEGANT, FINE 1, GRAND 2, GREAT 4, SWELL 2, WONDERFUL 2.

SPLENDID 3, *adj.* (Literally, a good face.) The right hand, fingers closed over the thumb, is placed at or just below the lips (indicating a tasting of something GOOD, *q.v.*). It then describes a counterclockwise circle around the face, opening into the "5" position to indicate the whole face. At the completion of the circling movement the hand comes to rest in its initial position at or just below the lips. Also ATTRACTIVE 2, BEAUTIFUL, BEAUTY, EXQUISITE, PRETTY.

SPLINTER (splin′ tər), *n.* (Stuck in the finger.) The right index fingertip sticks an imaginary splinter into the tip of the left index finger.

SPOIL 1 (spoil), *n., v.,* SPOILED, SPOILING, (Striking down against.) Both "A" or "X" hands are held before the chest, the right above the left. The right hand strikes down and out, hitting the left thumb and knuckles with force. Also BACKBITE, BASE 3, CRUEL 1, HARM 2, HURT 2, MAR 2, MEAN 1.

SPOIL 2, *v.* (To damage.) Both hands are in the "X" position, palms facing and knuckles pointing out. The top hand moves forward over the left, striking it as it passes.

SPOON (spōon), *n., v.,* SPOONED, SPOONING. (The shape and action.) The upturned left palm represents a dish or plate. The curved index and middle fingers of the right hand represent the spoon. They are drawn up repeatedly from the left palm to the lips. Also ICE CREAM 1.

SPOON ON, *phrase.* (The natural sign.) The signer, holding an imaginary spoon, tips it over slightly as if pouring off its contents.

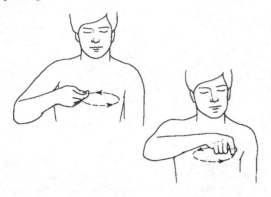

SPORTS (spôrtz), *n.* (A challenge.) Both hands are held in the "A" position, knuckles facing and thumbs standing up. They come together forcefully.

SPREAD 1 (sprĕd), *v.,* SPREAD, SPREADING. (Spreading apart.) Both "AND" hands are held before the body, palms down. They are then directed forward and toward each side while the fingers open out. Also SCATTER.

SPREAD 2, *n.* (The natural motion.) The fingers of the downturned open right hand sweep across the upturned open left hand several times, from fingertips to wrist. The right hand may also move in a circle.

SPRING 1 (sprĭng), *n.* (Flowers or plants emerge from the ground.) The right fingers, pointing up, emerge from the closed left hand, and they spread open as they do. The action may be repeated. Also BLOOM, DEVELOP 1, GROW, GROWN, MATURE, PLANT 1, RAISE 3, REAR 2.

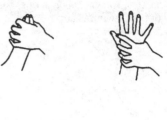

SPRING 2, *n.* (Moving upward and flowing outward.) The right "AND" hand is moved up through the left "C" hand, which is held with thumb edge up and palm facing the body. As the fingers of the right hand emerge, they wiggle to indicate a trickling of water. The action is usually repeated. Also FOUNTAIN.

SPRINKLE 1 (sprĭng′ kəl), *v.,* -KLED, -KLING. The "AND" hands touch each other at the thumbtips, palms out. The hands then separate, open, and sweep upward and to the sides several times, with fingers spread.

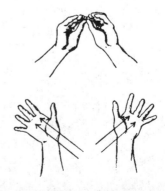

SPRINKLE 2, *v.* (The natural sign.) The signer, thumb moving against wriggling fingers, goes through the motions of sprinkling something, like salt, on food.

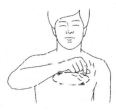

SQUANDER (skwŏn′ dər), *v.,* -DERED, -DERING. (Repeated giving forth.) The back of the upturned right hand, thumb touching fingertips, is placed in the upturned left palm. The right hand moves off and away from the left once or several times, each time opening into the "5" position, palm up. Also EXTRAVAGANT, SPEND, WASTE 1.

SQUARE 1 (skwâr), *n., v.,* SQUARED, SQUARING, *adj., adv.* (The dimensions are indicated.) The open hands, palms facing and fingers pointing out, are dropped an inch or two simultaneously. They then shift their relative positions so that both palms face the body, with one hand in front of the other. In this new position they again drop an inch or two simultaneously. Also BOX 1, PACKAGE, ROOM 1, TRUNK.

SQUARE 2 (*sl.*), *adj., n.* (A square face, *i.e.*, person.) The "B" hands outline a square in front of the face. Used to indicate an unsophisticated or naive person.

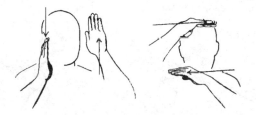

STABLE (stā′ bəl), *n.* (A house for horses.) The sign for HORSE is made: the thumbtip is placed at the temple, with the index and middle fingers extended upward. The signer then describes the roof and walls of a house: peaked fingers come apart and move down.

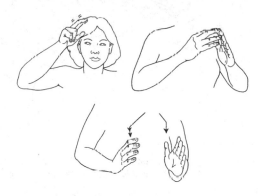

STAFF (staf, stäf), *n.* (The "S" and the "F.") The right hand, forming an "S," moves from left shoulder to right, changing to an "F" as it does. This would be used for personnel in an organization.

STAGE 1 (stāj), *n.* (The letter "S"; the flat surface.) The right "S" hand is drawn over the back of the downturned left hand, from the wrist to the fingertips.

STAGE 2, *n.* The downturned right "S" hand sweeps forward along the downturned left arm.

STAIR(S) 1 (stâr), *n.* (The natural sign.) The down-turned open hands, fingers pointing forward, move in alternate upward steps before the body. Also STEP(S) 2.

STAIR(S) 2, *n.* (The natural sign.) The right open hand, palm facing left or down, traces a series of steps upward. Also STEP(S) 3.

STALL (stôl), *n.* (A box for horses.) The sign for HORSE is made as above. The signer then describes the sides of a box.

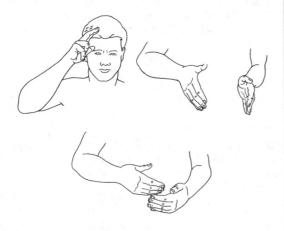

STAMP 1 (stămp), *n.* (Licking the stamp.) The tips of the right index and middle fingers are licked with the tongue, and then the fingers are pressed against the upturned left palm, as if affixing a stamp to an envelope.

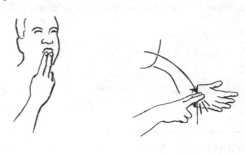

STAMP 2, *n., v.,* STAMPED, STAMPING. (The natural sign.) The right hand grasps an imaginary rubber stamp and presses it against the upturned left palm. Also GUARANTEE 2, SEAL 1.

STAND 1 (stănd), *v.,* STOOD, STANDING, *n.* (The feet planted on the ground.) The downturned right "V" fingers are thrust into the upturned left palm. Also POSITION 3, STANDING.

STAND 2, *n., v.* (Getting onto one's feet.) The upturned index and middle fingers of the right hand, representing the legs, are swung up and over in an arc, coming to rest in the upturned left palm. Also ARISE 2, ELEVATE, GET UP, RAISE 1, RISE 1, STAND UP.

STAND 3, *n.*, *v.* (Rising up.) Both upturned hands, held at chest level, rise in unison to about shoulder height. Also ARISE 1, RISE 3.

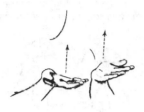

STANDARD (stan′ dərd), *adj.*, *n.* (The same all around.) Both downturned "Y" hands execute counterclockwise circles. Also COMMON.

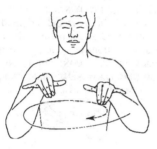

STANDING (stăn′ dĭng), *n.* See STAND 1.

STAND UP, *v. phrase.* See STAND 2.

STAPLER (stā′ plər), *n.* (The natural sign.) The signer mimes hitting a stapler with the downturned hand.

STARE (stâr), *n.*, *v.* (Eyes focused on something.) Both "V" hands, palms down and fingers facing straight ahead, are positioned side by side with one hand slightly ahead of the other. Both hands move repeatedly forward and back again an inch or so. The signer's eyes should remain wide open and focused ahead. Reversing the movement so that the fingers now point at the signer creates the sign for STARE AT ME.

START (stärt), *v.*, STARTED, STARTING. (Turning a key to open up a new venture.) The right index finger, resting between the left index and middle fingers, executes a half turn once or twice. Also BEGIN, COMMENCE, INITIATE, INSTITUTE 2, ORIGIN 1, ORIGINATE 1.

STARVATION (stär vā′ shən), *n.* (The upper alimentary tract is outlined.) The right "C" hand, palm facing the body, is placed with fingertips touching midchest. In this position it moves down a bit. Also APPETITE, CRAVE, DESIRE 2, FAMINE, HUNGARIAN, HUNGARY, HUNGER, HUNGRY, STARVE, STARVED, WISH 2.

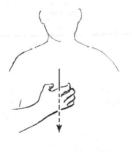

STARVE (stärv), *v.*, STARVED, STARVING. See STARVATION.

STARVED, *v.* See STARVATION.

STATE 1 (stāt), *v.*, STATED, STATING. (Words tumbling from the mouth.) The right index finger, pointing left, describes a continuous small circle in front of the mouth. Also BID 3, DISCOURSE, HEARING, MAINTAIN 2, MENTION, REMARK, SAID, SAY, SPEAK, SPEECH 1, STATEMENT, TALK 1, TELL, VERBAL 1.

STATE 2, *n.* (The letter "S"; a collection of laws.) The right "S" hand moves down the open left palm, from fingertips to base.

STATEMENT (stāt′ mənt), *n.* The sign for STATE is made. This is followed by the sign for -MENT: the downturned right "M" hand moves down along the left palm, which is facing away from the body.

STATISTICS (stə tis′ tiks), *n.* (The letter "S"; the multiplication symbol.) Both "S" hands repeatedly cross each other as in the "X" symbol for multiplication.

STATUE (stăch′ ōō), *n.* (Contours are indicated or outlined.) Both "A" hands, held about a foot apart before the face, with palms facing each other, move down simultaneously in a wavy, undulating motion. Also FIGURE 2, FORM, IMAGE, SCULPT, SCULPTURE, SHAPE 1.

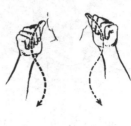

STAY 1 (stā), *n., v.*, STAYED, STAYING. (Steady, uninterrupted movement.) The "A" hands are held with palms out, thumbs extended and touching, the right behind the left. In this position the hands move forward in a straight, steady line. Also CONTINUE 1, ENDURE 2, EVER 1, LAST 3, LASTING, PERMANENT, PERPETUAL, PERSEVERE 3, PERSIST 2, REMAIN, STAY STILL.

STAY 2, *n., v.* (Duration of movement from past to present.) The right "Y" hand is held palm down in front of the right shoulder and is then moved slowly down and forward in a smooth curve. Also CONTINUE 2, STILL 1, YET 1.

STAY 3, *v.* (Remaining in place.) One "Y" hand, held palm down, drops down a few inches.

STAY 4, *v.* (A firm, steadying motion.) The down-turned open right hand is held before the right shoulder and moved down a short distance.

STAY STILL, *v. phrase.* See STAY 1.

STEAL 1 (stēl), *n., v.,* STOLE, STOLEN, STEALING. (The hand, partly concealed, takes something surreptitiously.) The index and middle fingers of the right hand, somewhat curved, are placed under the left elbow. As they move slowly along the left forearm toward the left wrist, they close a bit. Also ABDUCT, EMBEZZLE, EMBEZZLEMENT, KIDNAP, ROB 1, ROBBERY 1, SWIPE, THEFT 1, THIEF 1, THIEVERY.

STEAL 2 (*colloq.*), *v.* (A sly, underhanded movement). The right open hand, palm down, is held a bit behind the body at waist level. Beginning with the little finger, the hand closes finger by finger into the "A" position, as if wrapping itself around something. Also ROB 2, ROBBERY 1, THEFT 2.

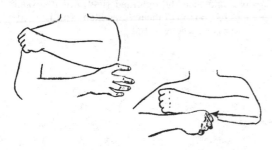

STEAL 3, *v.* (A mustachioed thief.) The fingertips of both "H" hands, palms facing the body, are placed above the lips and are drawn slowly apart, describing a mustache. Sometimes one hand only is used. Also

BANDIT, BURGLAR, BURGLARY, CROOK, ROB 3, ROBBER 1, THEFT 3, THIEF 2.

STEAM 1 (stēm), *n.* (Water, hot.) The sign for WATER is made: the right "W" hand, palm facing left, touches the lips a number of times. This is followed by the sign for HOT: the cupped hand, palm facing the body, moves up in front of the slightly open mouth. It is then flung down to the palm-down position while the signer puffs out his cheeks as if blowing out vapor.

STEAM 2, *n.* (Boiling and circling up.) The down-turned right "S" hand is held above the wriggling fingertips of the left. The right "S" hand then moves up in a wavy motion. The wavy movement may be substituted for a spiral movement up.

STEP 1 (stĕp), *n., v.,* STEPPED, STEPPING. (The movement of the feet.) The downturned "5" hands move

alternately toward and away from the chest. Also PACE, WALK.

STEP(S) 2, *n.* (The natural sign.) The downturned open hands, fingers pointing forward, move in alternate upward steps before the body. Also STAIR(S) 1.

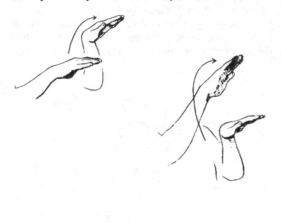

STEP(S) 3, *n.* (The natural sign.) The right open hand, palm facing left or down, traces a series of steps upward. Also STAIR(S) 2.

STEPBROTHER (stĕp′ bruth′ ər), *n.* (Second brother.) The sign for SECOND is made: the right "L" hand, palm facing left and index straight up, moves forward so that the index now faces forward. This is followed by BROTHER: the thumb of the right "L" hand is placed at the right temple. The hand moves down to

rest on top of the downturned left hand. The order of the two signs may be reversed.

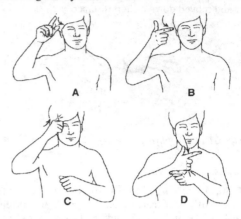

STEPCHILDREN (stĕp′ chil′ drən), *n.* (Second children.) The sign for SECOND is made, as above. This is followed by the downturned right "5" hand, or both "5" hands, miming the patting of children's heads.

STEPDAUGHTER (stĕp′ dô′ tər), *n.* (Second daughter.) The sign for SECOND is made, as in STEPBROTHER. This is followed by DAUGHTER: the thumb of the right "A" hand moves down the right jawline, and then the upturned right arm is brought down to rest on top of the upturned left arm. The order of the signs may be reversed.

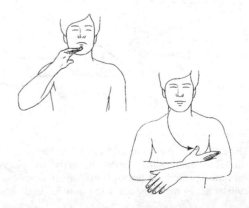

STEPFATHER 1 (stĕp' fä' thər), *n.* (Father once removed.) The right "L" hand is held with its thumbtip at the right temple; its index finger moves back and forth several times.

STEPFATHER 2, *n.* (Second father.) The sign for SECOND is made as in STEPBROTHER. This is followed by FATHER: the thumb of the right "5" hand is placed on the right temple. The FATHER sign may be made first, followed by SECOND.

STEPMOTHER 1 (stĕp' mŭth' ər), *n.* (Mother once removed.) The index finger of the right "L" hand pivots back and forth on the right thumbtip, which is held against the right side of the chin.

STEPMOTHER 2, *n.* (Second mother.) The sign for SECOND is made as in STEPBROTHER. This is followed by MOTHER: the thumb of the right "5" hand is placed on the right jawline. The MOTHER sign may be made first, followed by SECOND.

STEPSISTER (stĕp' sis' tər), *n.* (Second sister.) The sign for SECOND is made as in STEPBROTHER. This is followed by SISTER: the thumb of the right "L" hand is placed on the right jawline. The hand moves down to rest on top of the downturned left hand. The order of the two signs may be reversed.

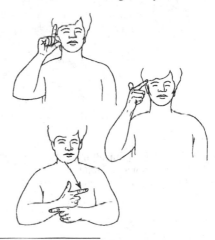

STEPSON (stĕp' sun'), *n.* (Second son.) The sign for SECOND is made as in STEPBROTHER. This is followed by SON: the right hand grasps an imaginary cap brim, and then the upturned right arm is brought down to rest on top of the upturned left arm. The order of the signs may be reversed.

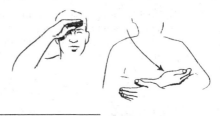

STEREO (ster' ē ō), *n.* (Sound waves.) One or both fists may be placed against their respective ears. The hand or hands then open and spread out in a wavy or wriggling movement.

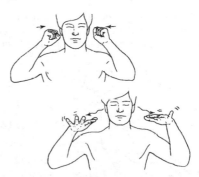

STETHOSCOPE (steth′ ə skōp), *n.* (Miming.) The earpieces are placed in the ears, and then the other end of the instrument touches different spots on the chest.

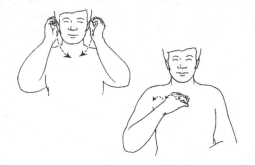

STICK SHIFT, *n.* (Manipulating a stick shift in an automobile.) The signer, grasping an imaginary stick shift with the right hand, maneuvers it forcefully forward or back.

STILL 1 (stĭl), *adv., conj.* (Duration of movement from past to present.) The right "Y" hand is held palm down in front of the right shoulder and is then moved slowly down and forward in a smooth curve. Also CONTINUE 2, STAY 2, YET 1.

STILL 2, *adj.* (The natural sign.) The index finger is brought up against the pursed lips. Also BE QUIET 1, CALM 2, HUSH, NOISELESS, QUIET 1, SILENCE 1, SILENT.

STING (sting), *n., v.,* STUNG, STINGING. (The natural sign.) The thumb and index of the right "F" hand suddenly come down on the back of the downturned left hand.

STINGY 1 (stĭn′ jĭ), *adj.* (Pulling things toward oneself.) Both prone open or "V" hands are held in front of the body with fingers bent. The hands are then drawn quickly and forcefully inward, as if raking things toward oneself. Also GREEDY 1, SELFISH 1, TIGHTWAD 1.

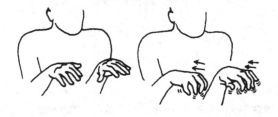

STINGY 2, *adj.* (Scratching the palm in greed.) The right fingers scratch the upturned left palm several times. A frowning expression is often used. Also AVARICIOUS, GREEDY 2, SELFISH 2, TIGHTWAD 2.

STINGY 3, *adj.* (Scratching in greed.) The downturned "3" hands, held side by side, make a scratching motion as they move in toward the body. Also GREEDY 3, SELFISH 3.

STINK (stingk), *n.*, *v.*, STANK or STUNK, STUNK, STINK-ING. (The nose is held.) The nose is pinched with the thumb and index while the signer assumes a look of strong distress.

STIR (stûr), *v.*, STIRRED, STIRRING. (Miming.) The downturned curved right index finger makes a series of rapid, stirring clockwise movements above the "C"-shaped left hand.

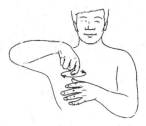

ST. LOUIS (sānt' lōo is), *n.* (The arch.) The left arm is outstretched, palm down. The right "S" hand is placed at the left elbow. It travels up and over in a distinct arch, changing to an "L" as it does and coming to rest on the back of the left hand. The left arm sometimes faces up instead of down.

STOCKING(S) 1, (stŏk' ĭng), *n.* (The knitting.) The index fingers, pointing forward, are rubbed back and forth against each other. Also HOSE 1, KNIT, SOCK(S) 1.

STOCKING(S) 2, *n.* (Pulling on hose.) The down-turned, open right hand grasps its left counterpart at the fingertips and slides over the back of the hand and up the arm, as if pulling on hose. Also HOSE 2, SOCK(S) 2.

STOMACH ACHE (stum' ək āk'), *n.* (A pain or stabbing sensation in the stomach.) The stomach is touched, and then both index fingers, pointing to each other, move in a twisting back-forth motion in front of the stomach.

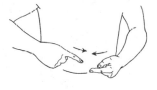

STONE 1 (stōn), *n.* (The hardness is indicated by the striking of the fists.) The back of the right "S" hand is struck several times against the back of the left "S" hand. Also ROCK 1.

STONE 2, *n.* (A hard object.) The right "S" hand swings downward before the body, striking its knuckles against the knuckle of the index finger of the left "S" hand, which is held palm down. The right hand continues downward and away from the body in a short curve. Also ROCK 2, ROCKY.

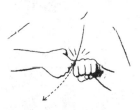

STONE 3, *n.* (A hard, unyielding substance.) The back of the right "S" hand strikes the bottom of the chin twice. Also ROCK 2.

STONEWALL (stōn′ wôl′), *n., v.,* -WALLED, -WALLING. (Something set up to block one.) Both downturned "B" hands, palms down and crossed, with right little finger edge touching left index, are brought up with a flourish to a point above the eyes. Also BRICK WALL.

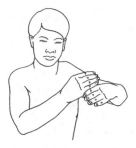

STOP (stŏp), *v.,* STOPPED, STOPPING, *n.* (A stopping or cutting short.) The little finger edge of the right hand is thrust abruptly into the upturned left palm, indicating a cutting short. Also ARREST 2, CEASE, HALT.

STOPWATCH (stop′ woch′), *n.* (Tapping the wrist and starting the watch.) The signer taps the back of the left wrist, and then the right thumb mimes pressing down to start or stop the counter.

STORE 1 (stōr), *n.* (A house where things are sold.) The sign for SELL, is made: both "AND" hands, fingertips touching their respective thumbs, are held palms down before the body; the hands are pivoted outward and away from the body once or several times. This is followed by the sign for HOUSE: the hands form a pyramid a bit above eye level and then separate, moving diagonally downward and then straight down a few inches. It may also be followed by the sign for PLACE: the "P" hands are held side by side before the body, with middle fingertips touching. From this position the hands separate and outline a circle (or a square), before coming together again closer to the body. Also SHOP 2.

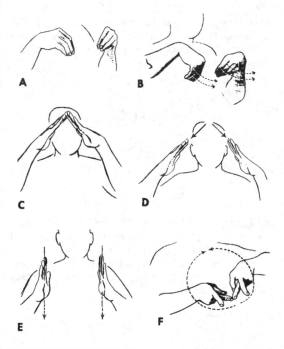

STORE 2, *v.,* STORED, STORING. (Holding back.) The right "V" fingers are tapped once or twice across the back of their left counterparts. Both palms face the chest. Also RESERVE 3, SAVE 2.

STORE 3 (*rare*), *n., v.* (The shape.) The left arm is held horizontally, and the right index finger describes an arc under it, from wrist to elbow, representing the shape of a basket as it hangs on the left arm. Also BASKET, EPISCOPAL, EPISCOPALIAN.

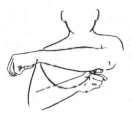

STORM (stôrm), *n.* (The blowing back and forth of the wind.) The "5" hands, palms facing and held up before the body, sway gracefully back and forth in unison. The cheeks meanwhile are puffed up and the breath is being expelled. The nature of the swaying movement—graceful and slow, fast and violent, etc.—determines the type of wind. The strength of exhalation is also a classifier. Also BLOW 1, BREEZE, GALE, WIND.

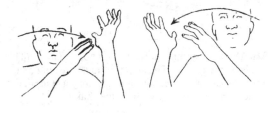

STORY 1 (stôr′ ĭ), *n.* (The unraveling or stretching out of words or sentences.) Both open hands are held close to each other, with fingers open and palms facing and almost touching. As the hands are drawn apart, the thumb and index finger of each hand come together to form circles. This is repeated several times. Also DESCRIBE 2, EXPLAIN 2, FABLE, FICTION, GOSPEL 1, NARRATE, NARRATIVE, TALE, TELL ABOUT.

STORY 2, *n.* (A level surface.) The downturned "B" hands are held side by side, with index fingers touching. Then they move apart several inches. This action is usually repeated with the hands held somewhat

higher, indicating a higher story in a building. The sign is somewhat similar to FLOOR, *q.v.*

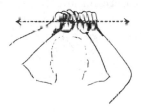

STOUT (stout), *adj.* (The swollen cheeks.) The cheeks are puffed out, and the open "C" hands, positioned at either cheek, move away to their respective sides. Also FAT 1.

STOVE (stōv), *n.* (Cooking and the shape.) The sign for COOK is made: the open right hand rests on the upturned left palm; the right hand flips over and comes to rest with its back on the left palm, as if it has turned over a pancake. The shape of the stove is then indicated: both downturned hands move apart and then, with palms facing each other, downward.

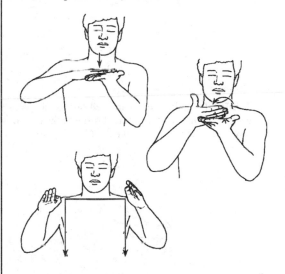

ST. PETERSBURG (sănt pē′ tərz bûrg′), *n.* (A city in the former Soviet Union.) The crossed birds in the

Straight 666 Straw

coat of arms.) Both open hands, palms facing the signer, are crossed, with thumbs interlocked and fingers slightly cupped. A native sign.

STRAIGHT 1 (strāt), *adj.* (The natural sign.) Both open hands are held with fingers pointing out from the body, the right above the left, the right palm facing left and left palm facing right. The right hand moves its little finger edge along the thumb edge of the left hand, in a straight line outward.

STRAIGHT 2, *adj., sl.* (Heterosexual.) The upright right arm, palm facing left, moves straight forward in an arc. Also HETEROSEXUAL.

STRANDED (străndəd), *adj.* (Impaled on a stick, as a snake's head.) The "V" fingers are thrust into the throat. Also CAUGHT IN THE ACT 2, CHOKE 2, STUCK 2, TRAP.

STRANGE 1 (strānj), *adj.* (Something that distorts the vision.) The "C" hand describes a small arc in

front of the face. Also CURIOUS 2, GROTESQUE, ODD, PECULIAR, QUEER 1, WEIRD.

STRANGE 2 (*rare*), *adj.* The open hands are held in front of the body, palms up, and are lifted with an apparent effort, as if they held a load.

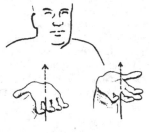

STRANGLE (strang′ gəl), *v.,* -GLED, -GLING. (The hands on the throat.) The signer mimes grasping a victim's throat and squeezing and shaking it. One hand alone may be used, but without the shaking.

STRAW (strô), *n.* (Miming.) The signer, lips pursed, sips through an imaginary drinking straw held by one or both hands.

STRAWBERRY 1 (strô′ bĕr′ ĭ), *n.* (Indicating a small, round object.) The right thumb and fingers grasp the index fingertip or thumb of the left "1" hand. In this position the right hand twists back and forth at the wrist.

STRAWBERRY 2, *n., adj.* (Wiping the lips.) The right index finger brushes down against the lips (the sign for RED), and then the right thumbtip brushes down against the lips in the same way.

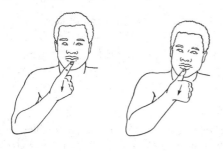

STRAY (strā), *v.,* STRAYED, STRAYING. (The natural motion.) The "G" hands are held side by side and touching, palms down, index fingers pointing forward. Then the right hand moves forward, curving toward the right side as it does. Also DEFLECT, DEVIATE 2, GO OFF THE TRACK, WANDER 1.

STREET (strēt), *n.* (The path.) Both hands, palms facing and fingers together and extended straight out, move in unison away from the body in a straight or winding manner. Also CORRIDOR, HALL, HALLWAY,

MANNER 2, METHOD, OPPORTUNITY 3, PATH, ROAD, TRAIL, WAY 1.

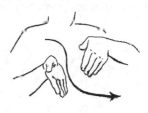

STRENGTH (strĕngkth, strĕngth), *n.* (Strength emanating from the body.) Both "5" hands are placed palms against the chest. They move out and away forcefully, closing and assuming the "S" position. Also BRAVE, BRAVERY, COURAGE, COURAGEOUS, FORTITUDE, HALE, HEALTH, HEALTHY, MIGHTY 2, STRONG 2, WELL 2.

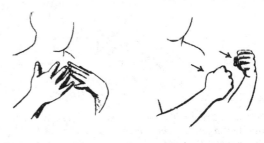

STRESS 1 (strĕs), *n., v.,* STRESSED, STRESSING. (Pressing down to emphasize.) The right thumb is pressed down deliberately against the upturned left palm. Both hands move forward a bit. Also EMPHASIS, EMPHASIZE, EMPHATIC. **STRESS** 2, *n., v.* (Pushing down.) The downturned open right hand pushes down on the left closed fist.

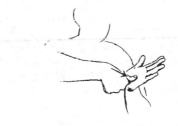

STRESS 2, *n., v.* (Pushing down.) The downturned open right hand pushes down on the left closed fist.

STRETCH (strĕch), *v.*, STRETCHED, STRETCHING. (Pulling apart.) Both "S" hands are pulled apart once or twice slowly, as if stretching something they are holding. Also ELASTIC.

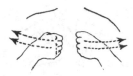

STRICT 1 (strĭkt), *adj.* (A sharp quality, indicated by pointing and jabbing.) The prone left open hand is held with fingers pointing forward and upward. Meanwhile, the extended right index finger is pushed and twisted slowly and steadily leftward under the left palm.

STRICT 2 (*colloq.*), *adj.* The extended right index and middle fingers are bent and brought up sharply so that the edge of the index finger strikes the bridge of the nose.

STRIKE 1 (strīk), *v.*, STRUCK, STRIKING. (The natural sign.) The right "S" hand strikes its knuckles forcefully against the open left palm, which is held facing right. Also HIT 1, POUND 3, PUNCH 1.

STRIKE 2, *n., v.* (Holding a picket's sign.) Both upright hands grasp the stick of an imaginary display

sign. The hands move forward and back repeatedly against the chest. This movement represents the walking back and forth of a striker or picket. Also PICKET.

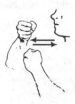

STRIKE 3, *n. v.* (Turning the head away, *i.e.,* refusing to obey.) The upraised right fist, palm left, is swung around to the palm-out position. This indicates an employee action against management.

STRIKE THAT, *phrase, interj., colloq.* (Sealing the lips to indicate something that should not have been said.) The index finger is brought up sharply against the sealed lips. The head may be shaken slightly. This is known as "repairs" in ASL.

STRING (strĭng), *n., v.,* STRUNG, STRINGING. (Unraveling a thin string, as indicated by the little fingers.) With palms facing the body, the tips of the extended little fingers touch. As they are drawn slowly apart, they describe very small spirals. Also SPAGHETTI, THREAD, TWINE.

STROKE 1 (strōk), *n.* (A blow or accident inside the head.) The right fingertips touch the forehead or the side of the head, and then the right hand forms a fist that strikes the left palm. This sign is used only for a cardiovascular accident.

STROKE 2, *n., v.,* STROKED, STROKING. (Stroking a person or the head of a pet.) The right hand strokes the back of the left several times. Also DEAR 1, FOND 1, PET, TAME.

STROKE 3, *n.* (The cerebral hemisphere is outlined.) The right "B" hand, horizontal and twisted so that its palm faces right, traces a line down the forehead to the chest.

STROLLER (strō′ lər), *n.* (The back-and-forth movement.) The hands, grasping the handlebar of an imaginary stroller, move forward and back repeatedly.

STRONG 1 (strông, strŏng), *adj.* (Flexing the muscles.) With fists clenched, palms facing down or back, the signer raises both arms and shakes them once with force. Also MIGHT 1, MIGHTY 1, POWER 1, POWERFUL 1, STURDY, TOUGH 1.

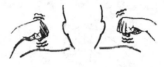

STRONG 2, *adj.* (Strength emanating from the body.) Both "5" hands are placed palms against the chest. They move out and away forcefully, closing and assuming the "S" position. Also BRAVE, BRAVERY, COURAGE, COURAGEOUS, FORTITUDE, HALE, HEALTH, HEALTHY, MIGHTY 2, STRENGTH, WELL 2.

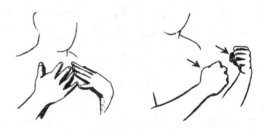

STRUCTURE (struk′ chər), *n.* The "S" letters; building something up by blocks or bricks.) Both downturned "S" hands mime placing bricks one atop the other. The hands meanwhile move up in stages. The walls, finally, are outlined.

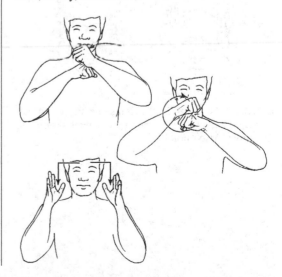

STRUGGLE 1 (strŭg′ əl), *n., v.,* -GLED, -GLING. (Two opposing forces.) Both "S" hands, held knuckle to knuckle before the body, move alternately up and down, the knuckles striking against each other as the hands pass.

STRUGGLE 2, *n., v.* (Back-and-forth movement.) Both index fingers, pointing to each other, move back and forth simultaneously.

STUBBORN (stŭb′ ərn), *adj.* (The donkey's broad ear; the animal is traditionally a stubborn one.) The open hand, or the "B" hand, is placed at the side of the head, with palm out and fingers pointing straight up. The hand moves forward and back, pivoting at the wrist, as in the case of a donkey's ears flapping. Both hands may also be used, at either side of the head. Also DONKEY, MULE, MULISH, OBSTINATE.

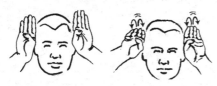

STUCK 1 (stŭk), *adj.* (Catching one by the throat.) The right hand makes a natural movement of grabbing the throat. Also CHOKE 1.

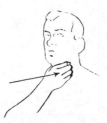

STUCK 2, *adj.* (Impaled on a stick, as a snake's head.) The "V" fingers are thrust into the throat. Also CAUGHT IN THE ACT 2, CHOKE 2, STRANDED, TRAP.

STUDENT 1 (stū′ dənt, stōō′ -), *n.* (One who learns.) The sign for LEARN is made: the downturned fingers of the right hand are placed on the upturned left palm; they close, and then the hand rises and the right fingertips are placed on the forehead. This is followed by the sign for INDIVIDUAL 1: both open hands, palms facing each other, move down the sides of the body, tracing its outline to the hips. Also LEARNER, PUPIL 1, SCHOLAR.

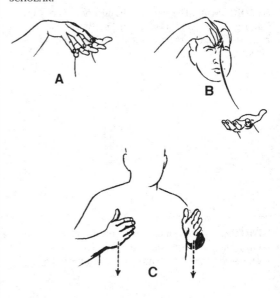

STUDENT 2, *n.* (One who studies.) The sign for STUDY is made. This is followed by the sign for INDIVIDUAL 1, as in STUDENT 1.

STUFFING (stuf′ ing), *n.* The signer goes through the motions of pushing stuffing into the open cavity of a bird.

STUMBLE (stum′ bəl), *v.,* -BLED, -BLING. (Tripping over something.) The downturned right "V" hand strikes the index finger edge of the downturned left open hand and stumbles over it to the little finger edge.

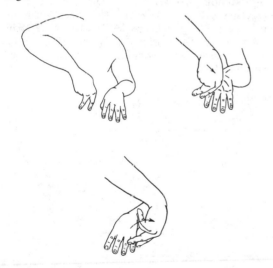

STUPID 1 (stū′ pĭd, stoō′ -), *adj.* (Knocking the head to indicate its empty state.) The "S" hand, palm facing the body, knocks against the forehead. Also DULL 1, DUMB 1, DUNCE.

STUPID 2 (*colloq.*), *adj.* (The thickness of the skull is indicated to stress intellectual density.) With the thumb of the right "C" hand grasped by the closed left hand, the right hand is swung in toward the body, describing a small arc as it moves. The space between the curved right fingers and the closed left hand indicates the thickness of the skull. Also CLUMSY 2, DUMB 2, MORON, THICK-SKULLED, UNSKILLED.

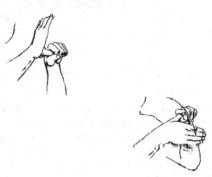

STURDY (stûr′ dĭ), *adj.* (Flexing the muscles.) With fists clenched, palms facing down or back, the signer raises both arms and shakes them once with force. Also MIGHT 1, MIGHTY 1, POWER 1, POWERFUL 1, STRONG 1, TOUGH 1.

SUBCONSCIOUS (sub kon′ shəs), *n., adj.* (The "S" and "C" letters; the mind underneath.) The left hand is held palm facing down. The right "S" hand makes a single counterclockwise circle under the left. It then changes to a "C" and makes another similar circle.

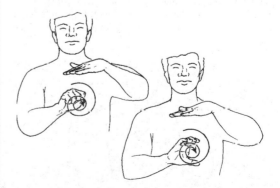

SUBDUE (səb dū′, -dōō′), *v.,* -DUED, -DUING. (Forcing the head into a bowed position.) The right "S" hand, placed across the left "S" hand, moves over and down a bit. Also BEAT 2, CONQUER, DEFEAT, OVERCOME.

SUBJECT (sŭb′ jĭkt), *n.* (The quotation marks are indicated.) The curved index and middle fingers of both hands, held palms out, move slightly to either side of the body, as if drawing quotation marks in the air. Also CAPTION, CITE, QUOTATION, QUOTE, SO-CALLED, THEME, TITLE, TOPIC.

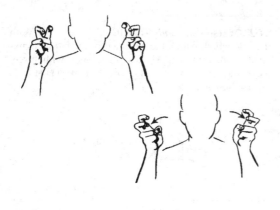

SUBMARINE (sub′ mə rēn′), *n.* (Cruising underwater.) The right "3" hand, palm facing left, moves forward under the shelter of the downturned left hand. The sign may be executed at eye level.

SUBMIT (səb mit′), *v.,* -MITTED, -MITTING. (Throwing up the hands in a gesture of surrender.) The hands move palms up in an arc.

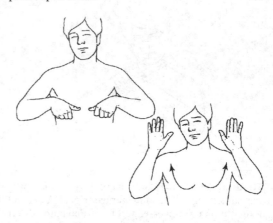

SUBSCRIBE (səb skrīb′), *v.,* -SCRIBED, -SCRIBING. (A regular taking in.) The outstretched open left hand, held palm facing right, moves in toward the body, assuming the "A" position, palm still facing right. This is repeated several times. Also DIVIDEND, INCOME, INTEREST 4, SUBSCRIPTION.

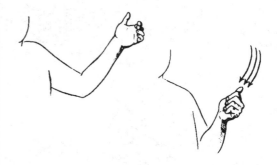

SUBSCRIPTION (səb skrĭp′ shən), *n.* See SUBSCRIBE.

SUBSEQUENT (sub′ sə kwənt), *adj.* (A moving on of the minute hand of the clock.) The right "L" hand, its thumb thrust into the palm of the left and acting as a pivot, moves forward a short distance. Also AFTER A WHILE, AFTERWARD, LATER 1, SUBSEQUENTLY.

Subsequently

673

Subway

SUBSEQUENTLY (sub′ sə kwənt ly), *adv.* See SUBSE-QUENT.

SUBSTANCE 1 (sŭb′ stəns), *n.* (Something shown in the hand.) The outstretched right hand, palm up and held before the chest, is dropped slightly and brought over a bit to the right. Also ANYTHING, APPARATUS, INSTRUMENT, MATTER, OBJECT 1, THING.

SUBSTANCE 2, *n.* (Relative standing of one's thoughts.) A modified sign for THINK is made: the right index finger touches the middle of the forehead; the tips of the right "V" hand, palm down, are then thrust into the upturned left palm (as in STAND, *q.v.*); the right "V" hand is then rethrust into the upturned left palm, with right palm now facing the body. Also CONNOTE, IMPLY, INTEND, INTENT 1, INTENTION, MEAN 2, MEANING, MOTIVE 3, PURPOSE 1, SIGNIFICANCE 2, SIGNIFY 2.

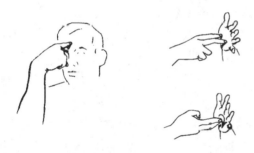

SUBSTANTIAL (səb stăn′ shəl), *adj.* (A full cup.) The left hand, in the "S" position, is held palm facing right. The right "5" hand, palm down, is brushed outward several times over the top of the left, indicating a wiping off of the top of a cup. Also ABUNDANCE, ABUNDANT, ADEQUATE, AMPLE, ENOUGH, PLENTY, SUFFICIENT.

SUBSTITUTE (sŭb′ stə tūt′), *n., v.,* -TUTED, -TUTING. (Exchanging places.) The right "A" hand, positioned above the left "A" hand, swings down and under the left, coming up a bit in front of it. Also EXCHANGE, INSTEAD OF 1, REPLACE, TRADE.

SUBTRACT (səb trăkt′), *v.,* -TRACTED, -TRACTING. (Removing.) The right "A" hand, resting in the palm of the left "5" hand, moves slightly up and away, describing a small arc. It is then cast downward, opening into the "5" position, palm down, as if removing something from the left hand and casting it down. Also ABOLISH 2, ABSENCE 2, ABSENT 2, ABSTAIN, CHEAT 2, DEDUCT, DEFICIENCY, DELETE 1, LESS 2, MINUS 3, OUT 2, REMOVE 1, SUBTRACTION, TAKE AWAY FROM, WITHDRAW 2.

SUBTRACTION (səb trăk′ shən), *n.* See SUBTRACT.

SUBWAY 1 (sub′ wā), *n.* (An underground train.) The sign for TRAIN 1 is made: the downturned right "H" hand slides back and forth on its left counterpart. The right index finger then moves forward under the cupped left hand. The TRAIN 1 sign is often omitted.

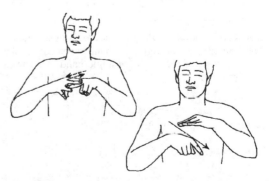

SUBWAY 2, *n.* (Underground railway.) The upturned right "Y" hand moves back and forth under the down-turned left open hand.

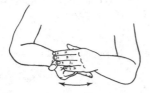

SUCCEED (sək sēd′), *v.,* -CEEDED, -CEEDING. (Penetrating the heights.) The "D" hands, palms back, are held at each side of the head near the temples. With a pivoting motion of the wrists, the hands swing up and around simultaneously to a position above the head, with palms facing out. Also ACCOMPLISH 1, ACHIEVE 1, ATTAIN, PROSPER, SUCCESS, SUCCESSFUL, TRIUMPH 2.

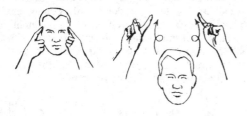

SUCCESS (sək sĕs′), *n.* See SUCCEED.

SUCCESSFUL (sək sĕs′ fəl), *adj.* See SUCCEED.

SUCH (sŭch), *adj.* (Matching fingers are brought together.) The outstretched index fingers are brought together either once or several times. Also ALIKE, IDENTICAL, LIKE 2, SAME 1, SIMILAR.

SUCKER (sŭk′ ər) (*colloq.*), *n.* (Knocking someone.) The knuckles of the right "S" hand repeatedly strike the fingertips of the left right-angle hand. Also TAKE ADVANTAGE OF 1.

SUDDENLY (sud′ n lē), *adv.* (The sign for WRONG 1, in the sense of an unexpected occurrence.) The right "Y" hand is placed on the chin, palm facing the signer. It swivels on the wrist over the chin, maintaining contact, as it moves from right to left. The signer assumes a look of sudden surprise. Also ALL OF A SUDDEN.

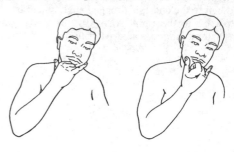

SUDDEN UNDERSTANDING, *phrase.* (A sudden awakening.) Both "S" hands are held in front of the forehead, the left in front of the right. They suddenly open into the "C" position as the hands separate. The eyes usually open wide at the same time.

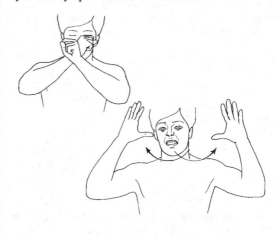

SUE (sōō), *v.,* SUED, SUING. (Against.) The tips of the right fingers, held together, are thrust purposefully into the open left palm, whose fingers are also together and pointing forward. Also AGAINST, ANTI, OPPOSE.

SUFFER 1 (sŭf′ ər), v., -FERED, -FERING. (A clenching of the fists; the rise and fall of pain.) Both "S" hands, tightly clenched, revolve about each other slowly and deliberately while a pained expression is worn. Also AGONY, BEAR 3, DIFFICULT 3, ENDURE 1, PASSION 2, TOLERATE 2.

SUFFER 2, v. (Patience, suffering.) The sign for PATIENCE is made: the thumb of the right "A" hand is drawn down across the lips. This is followed by the sign for SUFFER 1.

SUFFER 3 (rare), v. (Carrying a burden and keeping the lips sealed.) The thumb or index finger is pressed against the closed lips. Both "S" hands are then placed before the stooped left shoulder as if holding onto a heavy bag draped over the shoulder.

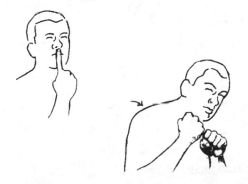

SUFFICIENT (sə fĭsh′ ənt), adj. (A full cup.) The left hand, in the "S" position, is held palm facing right. The right "5" hand, palm down, is brushed outward several times over the top of the left, indicating a wiping off of the top of a cup. Also ABUNDANCE, ABUNDANT, ADEQUATE, AMPLE, ENOUGH, PLENTY, SUBSTANTIAL.

SUGAR (shoog′ ər), n. (Titillating to the taste.) The fingertips of the right "U" hand, palm facing the body, brush against the chin a number of times, beginning at the lips. Also CANDY 1, CUTE 1, SWEET.

SUGGEST (səg jĕst′), v., -GESTED, -GESTING. (An offering; a presenting.) Both hands, slightly cupped, palms up, are held close to the chest. They move up and out in unison, describing a very slight arc. Also BID 2, MOTION 1, OFFER 1, OFFERING 1, PRESENT 1, PROPOSE, TENDER 2.

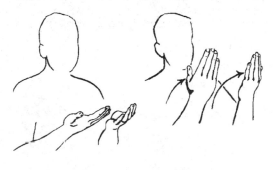

SUICIDE (soo′ ə sīd′), n. (Kill self.) The sign for KILL: the outstretched right index finger is passed under the downturned left hand; as it moves under the left hand, the right wrist twists in a clockwise direction. This is followed by the sign for SELF 2: the right "A" hand, thumb up, is brought into the chest.

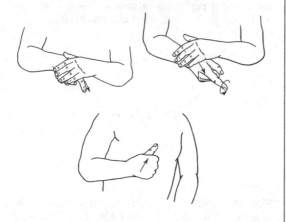

SUIT (sōōt), *n.* (Draping the clothes on the body.) With fingertips resting on the chest, both hands move down simultaneously. The action is repeated. Also CLOTHES, CLOTHING, DRESS, FROCK, GARMENT, GOWN, SHIRT, WEAR 1.

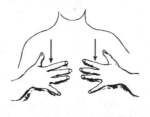

SUITABLE (sōō′ tə bəl), *adj.* The right index finger, held above the left index finger, comes down rather forcefully so that the bottom of the right hand comes to rest on top of the left thumb joint. Also ACCURATE 2, CORRECT 1, DECENT, EXACT 2, JUST 2, PROPER, RIGHT 3.

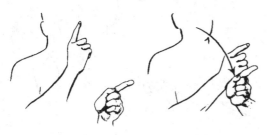

SUITCASE (sōōt′ kās′), *n.* (The natural sign.) The downturned right "S" hand grasps an imaginary piece of luggage and shakes it up and down slightly, as if testing its weight. Also BAGGAGE, LUGGAGE, VALISE.

SUM (sŭm), *n., v.,* SUMMED, SUMMING. (To bring up all together.) The two open hands, palms and fingers facing each other, with the left hand above the right, are brought together, with all fingers closing simultaneously. This sign is used mainly in the sense of adding up figures or items. Also ADD 1, ADDITION, AMOUNT 1, SUMMARIZE 2, SUMMARY 2, SUM UP, TOTAL.

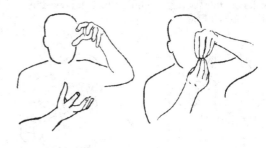

SUMMARIZE 1 (sŭm′ ə rīz′), *v.,* -RIZED, -RIZING. (To squeeze or condense into a small space.) The "C" hands face each other, with the right hand nearer to the body than the left. Both hands draw together and close deliberately, squeezing an imaginary object. Also ABBREVIATE 1, BRIEF 2, CONDENSE, MAKE BRIEF, SUMMARY 1.

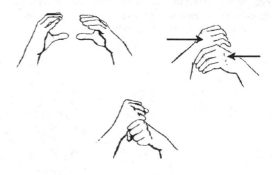

SUMMARIZE 2, *v.* See SUM.

SUMMARY 1 (sŭm′ ə rĭ), *n., adj.* See SUMMARIZE 1.

SUMMARY 2, *n.* See SUM.

SUMMER (sŭm′ ər), *n.* (Wiping the brow.) The down-turned right index finger, slightly curved, is drawn across the forehead from left to right. Also HOT WEATHER.

SUMMON 1 (sŭm′ ən), *v.,* -MONED, -MONING. (Harsh words thrown out.) The right hand appears to claw words out of the mouth as in CURSE 1. This time, however, it turns and throws them out, ending in the "5" position. Also BLASPHEME 2, CALL OUT, CRY 3, CRY OUT, CURSE 2, SCREAM, SHOUT, SWEAR 3.

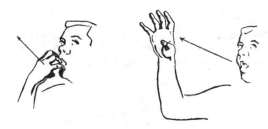

SUMMON 2, *v.* (To tap someone for attention.) The right hand is placed on the back of the left, held palm down. The right hand then moves up and in toward the body, assuming the "A" position. As an optional addition, the right hand may then assume a beckoning movement. Also CALL 1.

SUM UP, *v. phrase.* See SUM.

SUN (sŭn), *n., v.,* SUNNED, SUNNING. (The round shape and the rays.) The right index finger, pointing forward and held above the face, describes a small clockwise circle. The right hand, all fingers touching the thumb, then drops down and forward from its position above the head. As it does so, the fingers open to the "5" position. Also SUNSHINE.

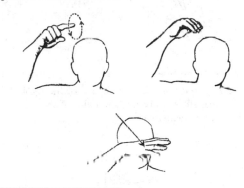

SUNBURN (sun′ bûrn′), *n.* (The signs for SUN and BURN.) The "C" hand is brought up against the eye, and then both "5" hands, palms facing the signer, wriggle as they move up.

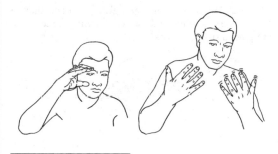

SUNDAE (sun′ dā), *n.* (The whipped cream is spiraled on.) The right thumb is held pointing down over the left "S" hand, whose palm faces right. The thumb spirals up in a counterclockwise manner.

SUNDAY 1 (sŭn′ dĭ), *n.* (A day of quiet, of rest.) The "5" hands, held side by side and palms out before the body, move straight down a short distance. They may also move slightly outward as they move down. Also SABBATH 2.

SUNDAY 2 (*loc.*), *n.* The thumb side of the right "S" hand is brought sharply into the palm of the left "5" hand, which is facing right.

SUNGLASSES (sun′ glas əz, -gläs-), *n.* (The shape.) Both hands, thumbs and indexes forming large "C"s, are placed over the eyes.

SUNRISE (sŭn′ rīz′), *n.* (The natural sign.) The downturned left arm, held horizontally, represents the horizon. The right thumb and index finger form a circle, and this circle is drawn up from a position in front of the downturned left hand.

SUNSET (sŭn′ sĕt′), *n.* (The natural sign.) The movement described in SUNRISE is reversed, with the

right hand moving down below the downturned left hand.

SUNSHINE (sŭn′ shīn′), *n.* See SUN.

SUPERB (soŏ pûrb′, sə-), *adj.* (The familiar ring sign.) With right thumb and index forming a circle, the signer moves the right hand firmly and slightly forward. A nod or a wink may accompany this.

SUPERFICIAL (soō′ pər fish′ əl), *adj.* (On the surface.) The right fingertips describe a small circle as they rub against the top of the downturned left hand.

SUPERINTENDENT (soō′ pər ĭn tĕn′ dənt, soō′ prĭn-), *n.* The "C" hands, held palms out at either temple, close over imaginary horns and move up a bit to either side, tracing the shape of the horns. Also HORNS, PRESIDENT.

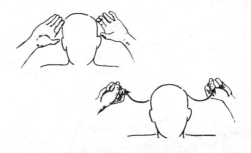

SUPERIOR 1 (sə pîr' ĭ ər, sŏo-), *adj.* (Indicating height.) The right "A" hand, held with thumb pointing upward, moves straight up above the right shoulder. Also HIGH 2, PROMINENT 3.

SUPERIOR 2, *adj.* (The letter "S"; hovering above others.) The right "S" hand makes a counterclockwise circle as it hovers over the downturned left hand.

SUPERSTITIOUS (sŏo' pər stish' əs), *adj.* (Pertaining to the imagination.) Both "I" hands, palms facing the temples, move forward in alternate clockwise circles. This may be followed by the sign for FEAR: both hands, fingers together, are placed side by side, palms facing the chest. They open quickly and move together over the heart. This is usually repeated.

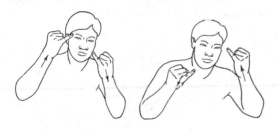

SUPERVISE (sŏo' pər vīz'), *v.*, -VISED, -VISING. (The eyes sweep back and forth.) The "V" hands, held crossed, describe a counterclockwise circle before the chest.

SUPPER (sŭp' ər), *n.* (An evening or night meal.) The sign for NIGHT is made: the left hand, palm down, is positioned at chest height; the downturned right hand, held an inch or so above the left, moves over the left hand in an arc, the sun setting beneath the horizon. This is followed by the sign for EAT: the closed right hand goes through the natural motion of placing food in the mouth. This latter movement is repeated. The NIGHT and EAT signs may be reversed.

SUPPLICATION (sŭp' lə kā' shən), *n.* (An act of supplication.) With the right hand clasped over the left, both hands are shaken gently before the body. The eyes often are directed upward. Also BEG 2, BESEECH, ENTREAT, IMPLORE, PLEA, PLEAD.

SUPPORT 1 (sə pōrt'), *n.*, *v.*, -PORTED, -PORTING. (Holding up.) The right "S" hand pushes up the left "S" hand. Also ENDORSE 1, FAVOR, INDORSE 1, MAINTENANCE, SUSTAIN, SUSTENANCE, UPHOLD, UPLIFT.

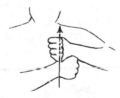

SUPPORT 2, *n.*, *v.* (One hand upholds the other.) Both hands, in the "S" position, are held palms facing the body, the right under the left. The right hand pushes up the left in a gesture of support. Also ADVOCATE, ENDORSE 2, INDORSE 2.

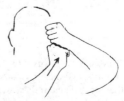

SUPPORT 3 (*rare*), *n., v.* ("Second"—two fingers.) The right "L" hand, held somewhat above the head, index finger pointing straight up, pivots forward a bit so that the index finger now points forward. Used in parliamentary procedure. Also ENDORSE 3, INDORSE 3, SECOND 2.

SUPPOSE 1 (sə pōz′), *v.*, -POSED, -POSING. (Weighing one thing against another.) The upturned open hands move alternately up and down. Also GUESS 4, MAY 1, MAYBE, MIGHT 2, PERHAPS, POSSIBILITY, POSSIBLY, PROBABLE, PROBABLY.

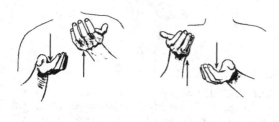

SUPPOSE 2, *v.* (To have an idea.) The little fingertip of the right "I" hand taps the right temple once or twice.

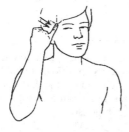

SUPPRESS FEELINGS, *v. phrase.* (Keeping the feelings down.) The curved fingertips of both hands are placed against the chest. The hands slowly move down

as the fingers close into the "S" position. One hand only may be used. Also CONTROL 2.

SURE (shŏŏr), *adj., adv.* (Coming forth directly from the lips; true.) The index finger of the right "D" hand, palm facing left, is placed against the lips. It moves up an inch or two and then describes a small arc forward and away from the lips. Also ABSOLUTE, ABSOLUTELY, ACTUAL, ACTUALLY, AUTHENTIC, CERTAIN, CERTAINLY, FAITHFUL 3, FIDELITY, FRANKLY, GENUINE, INDEED, POSITIVE 1, POSITIVELY, REAL, REALLY, SINCERE 2, SURELY, TRUE, TRULY, TRUTH, VALID, VERILY.

SURELY (shŏŏr′ lĭ), *adv.* See SURE.

SURFING (sûrf′ ing), *n.* (The position and motion.) Both hands face down. The right index and middle finger stand on their left counterparts.

SURGERY (sûr′ jə rĭ), *n.* (The action of the scalpel.) The thumb of the right "A" hand is drawn straight down across the upright left palm. Also OPERATION 1.

SURPRISE 1 (sər prīz′), *v.*, -PRISED, -PRISING, *n.* (The eyes pop open in amazement.) Both hands are held in modified "O" positions with thumb and index fingers of each hand near the eyes. These fingers suddenly flick open, and the eyes simultaneously pop open wide. Also AMAZE, AMAZEMENT, ASTONISH, ASTONISHED, ASTONISHMENT, ASTOUND.

SURPRISE 2 (*colloq.*), *adj.* (The mouth drops open.) The fingertips of both "V" hands are held curved and touching before the body, one hand above the other. Then the hands are suddenly drawn apart, and at the same instant the mouth drops open and the eyes open wide. Also DUMFOUNDED 2, FLABBERGASTED, OPENMOUTHED, SPEECHLESS.

SURPRISED (*colloq.*), *adj.* (The eyes pop open.) The "S" hands, palms facing each other, are held before the eyes. They suddenly open into the "C" position, with the eyes wide open. Also OPEN-EYED, SHOCKED 2.

SURRENDER 1 (sə rĕn′ dər), *v.*, -DERED, -DERING. (Throwing up the hands in a gesture of surrender.) Both "A" hands are held palms down before the chest and then thrown up in unison, ending in the "5" position. Also ABDICATE, CEDE, DISCOURAGE 1, FORFEIT,

GIVE UP, LOSE HOPE, RELINQUISH, RENOUNCE, RENUNCIATION, YIELD.

SURRENDER 2, *v.* (Grasping something and giving it over.) Both open hands are held palms facing inward before the body, the right hand slightly above the left, thumb edges up. In this position the hands close into the "S" position. Then they open and turn over, to lie side by side before the body, palms up, fingers pointing forward.

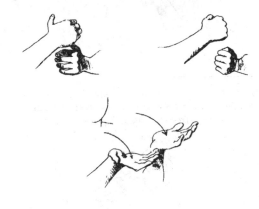

SUSPECT 1 (sə spĕkt′), *v.*, -PECTED, -PECTING. (Digging into the mind.) The right index finger scratches at the right temple several times. Also SUSPICION 1.

SUSPECT 2 (sus′ spĕkt), (*arch.*), *n.* The end of the index finger of the "V" hand is placed under and against the front teeth; then, without moving the arms, the ends of the fingers are thrown outward, the index

finger slipping away from the teeth. Also SPY 3, SUSPI-
CION 2.

SUSPEND 1 (sə spĕnd′), *v.,* -PENDED, -PENDING. (The
natural sign.) The curved right index finger hangs on
the extended left index finger. Also HANG 1.

SUSPEND 2, *v.* (The natural sign.) The extended
index fingers are hooked together, with the left hand
thus suspended from the right. Also SUSPENSION.

SUSPENDERS (sə spen′ dərz), *n.* (The shape or outline.) Both "G" hands trace a pair of braces or suspenders down the chest.

SUSPICION 1 (sə spĭsh′ ən), *n.* See SUSPECT 1.

SUSPICION 2, *n.* See SUSPECT 2.

SUSPICION 3, *n.* (Warding off.) The right "S" hand is
held before the right shoulder, elbow bent out to the
side. The hand is then thrown forward several times as
if striking at someone. Also SKEPTICAL 2.

SUSTAIN (sə stān′), *v.,* -TAINED, -TAINING. (Holding
up.) The right "S" hand pushes up the left "S" hand.
Also ENDORSE 1, FAVOR, INDORSE 1, MAINTENANCE,
SUPPORT 1, SUSTENANCE, UPHOLD, UPLIFT.

SUSTENANCE (sŭs′ tə nəns), *n.* See SUSTAIN.

SWEAR 1 (swâr), *v.,* SWORE, SWORN, SWEARING. (The
arm is raised.) The right index finger is placed at the
lips. The right arm is then raised, palm out and elbow
resting on the back of the left hand. Also GUARANTEE
1, LOYAL, OATH, PLEDGE, PROMISE 1, SWORN, TAKE OATH,
VOW.

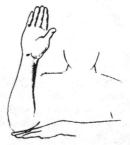

SWEAR 2, *v.* (Harsh words and a threatening hand.) The right hand appears to claw words out of the mouth. It ends in the "S" position, above the head, shaking back and forth in a threatening manner. Also BLASPHEME 1, CURSE 1.

SWEAR 3, *v.* (Harsh words thrown out.) The right hand as in SWEAR 2, appears to claw words out of the mouth. This time, however, it turns and throws them out, ending in the "5" position. Also BLASPHEME 2, CALL OUT, CRY 3, CRY OUT, CURSE 2, SCREAM, SHOUT, SUMMON 1.

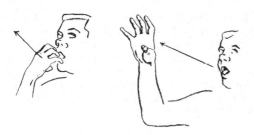

SWEAR 4 (*sl.*), *v.* (Curlicues, as one finds in cartoon-type swearwords.) The right "Y" hand, palm down, pivots at the wrist along the left "G" hand, from the wrist to the tip of the finger. Also BLASPHEME 3, CURSE 3.

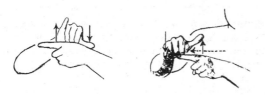

SWEAT 1 (swĕt), *n.*, *v.*, SWEAT or SWEATED, SWEATING. (Wiping the brow.) The bent right index finger is drawn across the forehead from left to right and then shaken to the side as if getting rid of the sweat. Also PERSPIRATION 1, PERSPIRE 1.

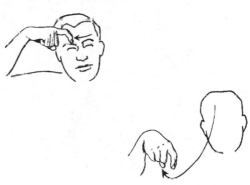

SWEAT 2, *n.*, *v.* (Perspiration dripping from the brow.) The index finger edge of the open right hand wipes across the brow, and the same open hand then continues forcefully downward off the brow, its fingers wiggling as if shaking off the perspiration gathered. Also PERSPIRATION 2, PERSPIRE 2.

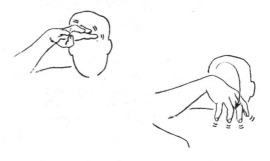

SWEDE (swēd), *n.* The right "S" hand, palm facing left, describes a small circle on the forehead. (All the Scandinavian—northern—countries are indicated at the forehead, the topmost part of the body.) Also SWEDEN, SWEDISH.

SWEDEN 1 (swēd′ n), *n.* See SWEDE.

SWEDEN 2, *n.* (A "hairy Swede," perhaps borrowed from the image of the early Swedish explorers.)

Finger the hair on back of the hand. This is a native sign, but catching on quickly in the United States.

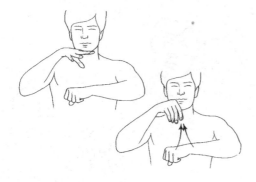

SWEEP 1 (swēp), *v.,* SWEPT, SWEEPING, *n.* (The natural sign.) The hands grasp and manipulate an imaginary broom. Also BROOM.

SWEEP 2, *v.* (Collecting dust.) The upturned left hand represents the dustpan. The little finger edge of the right hand moves over the left hand repeatedly, sweeping against the fingers from the fingertips to the palm.

SWEET (swēt), *adj., n.* (Titillating to the taste.) The fingertips of the right "U" hand, palm facing the body, brush against the chin a number of times, beginning at the lips. Also CANDY 1, CUTE 1, SUGAR.

SWEETHEART 1 (swēt' härt') (*colloq.*), *n.* (Heads nodding toward each other.) The "A" hands are placed together before the body with thumbs up. The thumbs wiggle up and down. Also BEAU, COURTING, COURTSHIP, LOVER, MAKE LOVE 1.

SWEETHEART 2 (*colloq.*), *n.* (Locked together.) With little fingers interlocked and palms facing the body, the thumbs of both hands wiggle back and forth.

SWELL 1 (swĕl), *adj.* (The hands gesture toward the heavens.) The "5" hands, palms out and arms raised rather high, are positioned somewhat above the line of vision. The arms move abruptly forward and up once or twice. An expression of pleasure or surprise is usually assumed. Also EXCELLENT, GRAND 1, GREAT 3, MARVEL, MARVELOUS, MIRACLE, O!, SPLENDID 1, WONDER 2, WONDERFUL 1.

SWELL 2, *adj., interj.* (The feelings are titillated.) With the thumb resting on the upper part of the chest, the fingers are wiggled back and forth. Also ELEGANT, FINE 1, GRAND 2, GREAT 4, SPLENDID 2, WONDERFUL 2.

SWELL 3, *v.*, SWELLED, SWELLING. (A swelling.) The palm of the right hand is placed on the back of the downturned left hand. Then the right hand is raised slowly off the left, indicating a swelling.

SWELLHEADED (*colloq.*), *adj.* (The natural sign.) Both downturned "L" hands are positioned with index fingers at the temples. They move away from the head rather slowly, indicating the size or growth of the head. The head is often moved slightly back and forth as the hands move away. An expression of superiority is assumed. Also BIGHEADED, CONCEITED, BIG SHOT.

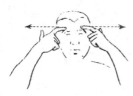

SWIFT (swĭft), *adj.* (A quick movement.) The thumbtip of the upright right hand is flicked quickly off the tip of the curved right index finger as if shooting marbles. Also FAST 1, IMMEDIATELY, QUICK, QUICKNESS, RAPID, RATE 1, SPEED, SPEEDY.

SWIMSUIT (swim' sōōt'), *n.* (Swim clothes.) The motions of swimming (usually the breast stroke) are made, followed by CLOTHES: both downturned "5" hands are posed with thumbs touching the chest. Both hands sweep down the chest repeatedly.

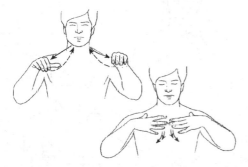

SWINDLER (swin' dlər), *n.* (Knocking someone.) The knuckles of the right "S" hand repeatedly strike the fingertips of the left right-angle hand. This may be followed by the sign for INDIVIDUAL 1. Also SUCKER.

SWITZERLAND (swit' sər lənd), *n.* (The cross in the Swiss flag.) The tips of the right "C" hand trace a cross on the signer's chest. Also SWISS.

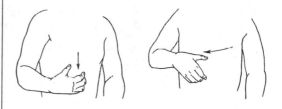

SWORN (swōrn), *adj.* (The arm is raised.) The right index finger is placed at the lips. The right arm is then raised, palm out and elbow resting on the back of the left hand. Also GUARANTEE 1, LOYAL, OATH, PLEDGE, PROMISE 1, SWEAR 1, TAKE OATH, VOW.

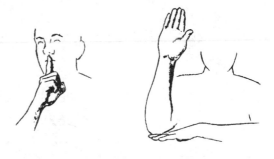

SYDNEY (sid' nē), *n.* (The shape of the landmark opera house in Sydney, Australia.) Both hands, palms down, are held with the indexes and middle fingers together. The hands draw apart quickly and repeatedly. Each time they draw apart, the indexes and middle fingers come down to touch the respective thumbs. A local sign.

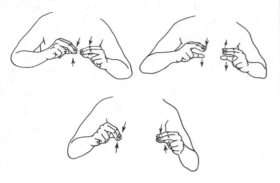

SYMBOL (sim′ bəl), *n.* (The letter "S"; showing something.) The right "S" is placed in the outstretched left palm. Both hands move forward simultaneously.

SYMPATHETIC (sĭm′ pə thĕt′ ĭk), *adj.* (Feeling with.) The tip of the right middle finger, touching the heart, moves up an inch or two on the chest. The sign for WITH is then made: both "A" hands come together, so that the thumbs are side by side. Also SYMPATHY 1.

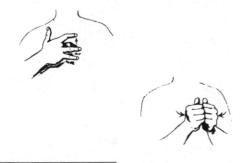

SYMPATHY 1 (sĭm′ pə thĭ), *n.* See SYMPATHETIC.

SYMPATHY 2, *n.* (Feelings from the heart conferred on others.) The middle fingertip of the open right hand touches the chest over the heart. The same open hand then moves in a small, clockwise circle before the

right shoulder, with palm facing forward and fingers pointing up. Also MERCY 2, PITY, POOR 3.

SYPHILIS (sif′ ə lis), *n.* (A fingerspelled loan sign.) The signer fingerspells "V-D," for "venereal disease."

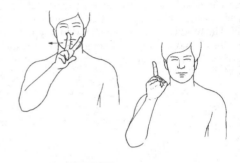

SYRUP 1 (sĭr′ əp, sûr′ -), *n.* (Wiping it from the lips.) The upturned right index finger moves across the lips from left to right. Also MOLASSES.

SYRUP 2, *n.* (Wiping the mouth and pouring.) The upturned right index sweeps across the mouth, from right to left. The hand then forms the "A" shape and pivots over so that the thumb represents a left arm.

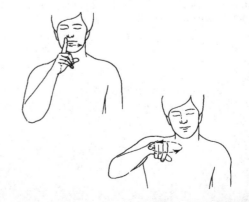

SYSTEM 1 (sĭs′ təm), *n.* (Placing things in order.) The hands, palms facing, fingers together and pointing away from the body, are positioned at the left side and held about a foot apart. With a slight up-down motion, as if describing waves, the hands travel in unison from left to right. Also ARRANGE, ARRANGEMENT, CLASSED 2, DEVISE 1, ORDER 3, PLAN 1, POLICY 1, PREPARE 1, PROGRAM 1, PROVIDE 1, PUT IN ORDER, READY 1, SCHEME.

SYSTEM 2, *n.* (An arrangement.) Both "S" hands, palms facing out, are positioned side by side. They separate, move down, and separate yet more, tracing a zigzag pattern.

T

TABLE 1 (tā′ bəl), *n.* (The shape and the legs.) The downturned open hands are held together before the chest, fingers pointing forward. From this position the hands separate and move in a straight line to either side, indicating the table top. Then the downturned index fingers are thrust downward simultaneously, moved in toward the body, and again thrust downward. These motions indicate the legs.

TABLE 2, *v.,* -BLED, -BLING. (Shelving a motion or proposal.) The right "V" hand is brought down over the upturned left index finger.

TABLECLOTH (tā′ bəl klôth′), *n.* (Laying the cloth on the table.) The closed hands go through the natural motions of flinging the cloth in the air and guiding its descent on the table. This sign may be preceded by the sign for WHITE, *q.v.*

TACKLE (tăk′ əl) (*sports*), *n.* (The natural motion.) The right open hand closes forcefully over the extended index and middle fingers of the downturned left hand.

TAIL 1 (tāl), *n.* (The shape.) The extended right thumb and index finger come together, and the hand moves away from the body in a downward arc, outlining an imaginary tail.

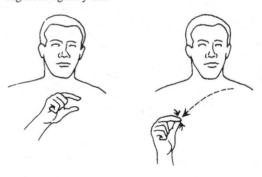

TAIL 2, *n.* (The wagging.) The downturned left arm represents the dog's body. The right "D" hand's base rests against the left fingertips, and the right index wags back and forth repeatedly.

TAKE (tāk), *v.,* TOOK, TAKEN, TAKING, *n.* (Taking unto oneself.) The right hand, palm out, is extended before the chest, index finger and thumb in an open position, the other fingers separated and pointing up. The hand is drawn in toward the chest, and the index and thumb close at the same time, indicating something taken to oneself. Also ADOPT, APPOINT, CHOOSE 1, SELECT 2.

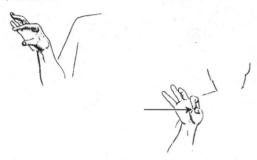

TAKE ADVANTAGE OF 1 (*colloq.*), *v. phrase.* (Knocking someone.) The knuckles of the right "S" hand repeatedly strike the fingertips of the left right-angle hand. Also SUCKER.

TAKE ADVANTAGE OF 2, *v. phrase.* (Attaching to something and tugging on it.) The extended right thumb plus index, and middle fingers grasp the extended left index and middle fingers. In this position the right hand pulls at the left several times. Also LEECH, MOOCH, MOOCHER, PARASITE.

TAKE ADVANTAGE OF 3, *phrase.* (A magician's trick of flipping a coin into the sleeve and thus cheating someone.) The middle finger of the right downturned hand rests on the upturned left palm. The finger

makes a swift backward movement, closing against the right palm. Also RIP OFF.

TAKE AWAY FROM, *v. phrase.* (Removing.) The right "A" hand, resting in the palm of the left "5" hand, moves slightly up and away, describing a small arc. It is then cast downward, opening into the "5" position, palm down, as if removing something from the left hand and casting it down. Also ABOLISH 2, ABSENCE 2, ABSENT 2, ABSTAIN, CHEAT 2, DEDUCT, DEFICIENCY, DELETE 1, LESS 2, MINUS 3, OUT 2, REMOVE 1, SUBTRACT, SUBTRACTION, WITHDRAW 2.

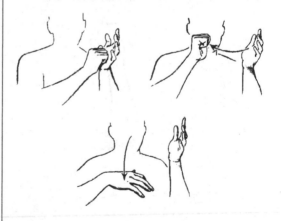

TAKE CARE OF 1, *v. phrase.* (The "K" for *keep* in the sense of *keeping carefully*.) Both "K" hands are crossed, the right atop the left. The right hand moves up and down a very short distance, several times, each time coming to rest on top of the left. Also BE CAREFUL, CAREFUL 3, CARE 2, CAREFUL 2, KEEP, MAINTAIN 1, MIND 3, PRESERVE, RESERVE 2.

TAKE CARE OF 2, *v. phrase.* (Slow, careful movement.) The "K" hands are crossed, the right above the left, little finger edges down. In this position they describe a small counterclockwise circle in front of the chest. Also CARE 1, CARE FOR, CAREFUL 1.

TAKE OATH (ōth), *v. phrase.* (The arm is raised.) The right index finger is placed at the lips. The right arm is then raised, palm out and elbow resting on the back of the left hand. Also GUARANTEE 1, LOYAL, OATH, PLEDGE, PROMISE 1, SWEAR 1, SWORN, VOW.

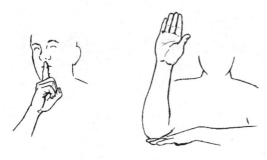

TAKEOFF; TAKE OFF (tāk′ ôf′, -of′; *v.* tāk′ ôf′), *n.* (The flight path, going up.) The right downturned hand, with thumb plus index and little fingers extended, moves up and forward from an initial position resting on the upturned left open hand.

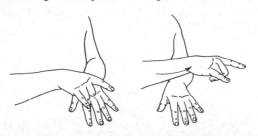

TAKE TURNS, *phrase.* (First one, then the other.) The thumb of the right "L" hand is pointed to the chest. The hand swings around so that the thumb now points out.

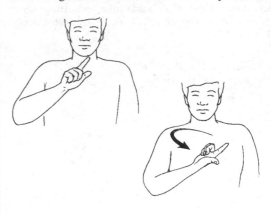

TAKE UP, *v. phrase.* (Responsibility.) Both hands, held palms down in the "5" position, are at chest level. With a grasping upward movement, both close into "S" positions before the face. Also ASSUME, PICK UP 1.

TALE (tāl), *n.* (The unraveling or stretching out of words or sentences.) Both open hands are held close to each other, with fingers open and palms facing and almost touching. As the hands are drawn apart, the thumb and index finger of each hand come together to form circles. This is repeated several times. Also DESCRIBE 2, EXPLAIN 2, FABLE, FICTION, GOSPEL 1, NARRATE, NARRATIVE, STORY 1, TELL ABOUT.

TALK 1 (tôk), *v.,* TALKED, TALKING. (Words tumbling from the mouth.) The right index finger, pointing left, describes a continuous small circle in front of the mouth. Also BID 3, DISCOURSE, HEARING, MAINTAIN 2,

MENTION, REMARK, SAID, SAY, SPEAK, SPEECH 1, STATE, STATEMENT, TELL, VERBAL 1.

TALK 2, *n., v.* (A gesture of an orator.) The right open hand, palm facing left, is held above and to the right of the head. It pivots on the wrist, forward and backward, several times. Also ADDRESS 1, LECTURE, ORATE, SPEECH 2, TESTIMONY.

TALK 3, *n., v.* (Movement forward from and back to the mouth.) The tips of both index fingers, held pointing up, move alternately forward from and back to the lips. Also COMMUNICATE WITH, CONVERSATION 1, CONVERSE.

TALL 1 (tôl), *adj.* (The height is indicated.) The index finger of the right "D" hand moves straight up against the palm of the left "5" hand. Also HEIGHT 1.

TALL 2, *adj.* (The height is indicated.) The right right-angle hand, palm facing the left, is held at the height the signer wishes to indicate. Also BIG 2, HEIGHT 2, HIGH 3.

TALL 3 (*loc.*), *adj.* (The stooped position.) The curved index finger of the right "D" hand, held up before the body, moves forward, away from the body, in a series of small bobbing motions. The head may be stooped and may also bob slightly in cadence with the hand.

TAME (tām), *adj., v.*, TAMED, TAMING. (Stroking a person or the head of a pet.) The right hand strokes the back of the left several times. Also DEAR 1, FOND 1, PET, STROKE 2.

TAPE 1 (tāp), *n., v.,* TAPED, TAPING. (The positioning and stretching out of the tape.) The "A" hands, palms facing down, touch at the thumbtips. They move apart a short distance.

TAPE 2, *n. Computer term.* (The movement of a computer tape.) Both "T" hands, facing out, simultaneously execute clockwise circles.

TAPE RECORDER, *n.* (The movement of the spools.) Both hands are held downturned, with middle fingers hanging down. Both hands move in unison in a clockwise direction.

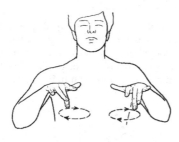

TARDY (tär′ dǐ), *adj.* (Hanging back.) The "5" hand and forearm, hanging loosely and straight down from the elbow, move back and forth under the armpit. Also BEHIND TIME, LATE, NOT DONE, NOT YET.

TASK (tăsk), *n.* (Striking an anvil.) Both "S" hands are held palms down. The right hand strikes against

the back of the left a number of times. Also JOB, LABOR, OCCUPATION, TOIL, TRAVAIL, VOCATION, WORK.

TATTLE 1 (tăt′ əl), *v.,* -TLED, -TLING. (Words moving outward from the mouth.) The right hand is held with index and middle fingertips touching the thumbtip and with its thumb edge at the mouth. The hand then moves outward from the mouth, with its extended thumb and first two fingers alternately opening and closing. Also TATTLETALE 1, TELLTALE 1.

TATTLE 2, *v.* (Words shooting out from the mouth.) The right "S" hand is held palm out before the mouth, with the knuckle of the index finger touching the lips. From this position the hand moves forward, away from the mouth. At the same time the index finger straightens and points forward. Also TATTLETALE 2, TELLTALE 2.

TATTLETALE 1 (tăt′ əl tāl′), *n.* See TATTLE 1.

TATTLETALE 2, *n.* See TATTLE 2.

TAX 1 (tăks), *n., v.,* TAXED, TAXING. (Nicking into one.) The knuckle of the right "X" finger is nicked against the palm of the left hand, held in the "5" position, palm facing right. Also ADMISSION 2, CHARGE 1,

COST, DUTY 2, EXCISE, EXPENSE, FEE, FINE 2, IMPOST, PENALTY 3, PRICE 2, TAXATION 1, TOLL.

TAX 2, *n., v.* (Making a nick, as in "nicking the pocketbook.") The tip of the right index finger, moving downward in an arc, makes a nick in the open left palm, which is facing right. Also TAXATION 2.

TAXATION 1 (tăks ā′ shən), *n.* See TAX 1.

TAXATION 2, *n.* See TAX 2.

TAXI 1 (tăk′ sĭ), *n.* (The letter "T"; the act of driving.) The "T" hands go through the motion of manipulating a steering wheel.

TAXI 2, *n. loc.* (The light on the taxi's roof.) The downturned curved fingers of the right hand tap the top of the head twice. Also CAB 1.

TEA 1 (tē), *n.* (Dipping the teabag.) The right index finger and thumb raise and lower an imaginary teabag into a cup formed by the left "C" or "O" hand, held thumb side up.

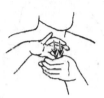

TEA 2, *n.* (Stirring the teabag.) The hand positions in TEA 1 are assumed, but the right hand executes a circular, stirring motion instead.

TEACH (tēch), *v.,* TAUGHT, TEACHING. (Giving forth from the mind.) The fingertips of each hand are placed on the temples. They then swing out and open into the "5" position. Also EDUCATE, INDOCTRINATE, INDOCTRINATION, INSTRUCT, INSTRUCTION.

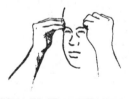

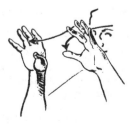

TEACHER (tē′ chər), *n.* The sign for TEACH is made. This is followed by the sign for INDIVIDUAL 1: both open hands, palms facing each other, move down the sides of the body, tracing its outline to the hips. Also EDUCATOR, INSTRUCTOR.

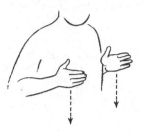

TEAR 1 (târ), *n., v.,* TORE, TORN, TEARING. (The natural motion.) Both "A" hands, held palms down before the body, grasp an imaginary object; then they move forcefully apart, as if tearing the object. Also REND, RIP 1.

TEAR 2 (tēr), *n.* (Tears streaming down the cheeks.) Both index fingers, in the "D" position, move down the cheeks, either once or several times. Sometimes one finger only is used. Also BAWL 1, CRY 1, TEARDROP, WEEP 1.

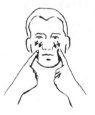

TEARDROP (tēr′ drŏp′), *n.* See TEAR 2.

TEASE 1 (tēz), *n., v.,* TEASED, TEASING. (Striking against one.) The knuckles of the right "A" hand move sharply forward along the thumb edge of the left "A" hand. Also PERSECUTE, TORMENT.

TEASE 2, *n., v.* The movements in TEASE 1 are duplicated, except that the "X" hands are used. Also KID 2.

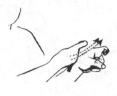

TEASE 3, *n., v.* The movements in TEASE 1 are duplicated, except that the "G" hands are used. Also CRUEL 3.

TECHNICAL (tek′ ni kəl), *adj.* (Forming a T shape with both hands.) The left open hand faces the chest. The middle finger of the right "5" hand, palm facing the signer, is placed at the little finger edge of the left.

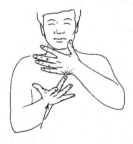

TECHNICAL REHEARSAL (tek′ ni kəl ri hûr′ səl), *n.* (Tightening a screw in the head.) The right index and middle fingers, held straight together, turn repeatedly in a clockwise manner on the right temple. This sign is reserved for stagecraft; it refers to taking care of the technical details of a stage production.

TEDDY BEAR (ted′ ē bâr), *n.* (The sign for BEAR; hugging.) Both crossed hands make a series of scratching movements against the shoulders. The signer then mimes a bear hug.

TEDIOUS (tē′ dĭ əs, tē′ jəs), *adj.* (The nose is pressed as if to a grindstone wheel.) The right index finger touches the tip of the nose as a bored expression is assumed. The right hand is sometimes pivoted back and forth slightly as the fingertip remains against the nose. Also BORING, MONOTONOUS 1.

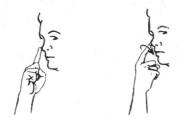

TEEN (tēn), *n.* (The letter "T"; female and male.) The right "T" hand is placed first at the jaw and then at the temple.

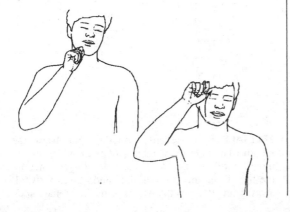

TEETH (tēth), *n. pl.* (The natural sign.) The extended right index finger passes over the exposed teeth.

TEL AVIV (tel′ ä vēv′), *n.* The right thumb and index finger, held at the right eye, open and close. A local sign.

TELEPHONE 1 (tĕl′ ə fōn′), *n., v.,* -PHONED, -PHONING. (The natural sign.) The left "S" hand represents the mouthpiece and is placed at the mouth with palm facing right. Its right counterpart represents the earpiece and is placed at the right ear with palm facing forward. This is the old-fashioned two-piece telephone. Also PHONE 1.

TELEPHONE 2, *n., v.* (The natural sign.) The right "Y" hand is placed at the right side of the head with the thumb touching the ear and the little finger touching the lips. This is the more modern telephone receiver. Also PHONE 2.

TELESCOPE (tel′ ə skōp), *n.* (Miming.) The signer mimes opening a telescope and peering through the eyepiece.

TELETYPE (tel′ ə tīp), *n., v.,* -TYPED, -TYPING. (Holding a phone and typing.) The right "Y" hand is placed at the side of the head, little finger touching the mouth and thumb touching the ear. The signer then mimes using a typewriter.

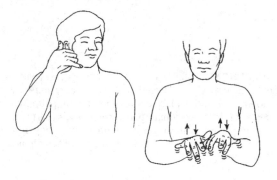

TELL (tĕl), *v.,* TOLD, TELLING. (Words tumbling from the mouth.) The right index finger, pointing left, describes a continuous small circle in front of the mouth. Also BID 3, DISCOURSE, HEARING, MAINTAIN 2, MENTION, REMARK, SAID, SAY, SPEAK, SPEECH 1, STATE, STATEMENT, TALK 1, VERBAL 1.

TELL ABOUT, *v. phrase.* (The unraveling or stretching out of words or sentences.) Both open hands are held close to each other, with fingers open and palms facing and almost touching. As the hands are drawn apart, the thumb and index finger of each hand come together to form circles. This is repeated several times. Also DESCRIBE 2, EXPLAIN 2, FABLE, FICTION, GOSPEL 1, NARRATE, NARRATIVE, STORY 1, TALE.

TELL ME, *phrase.* (The natural sign.) The tip of the index finger of the right "D" hand, palm facing the body, is first placed at the lips and then moves down to touch the chest.

TELLTALE 1 (tĕl′ tāl′), *n.* (Words moving outward from the mouth.) The right hand is held with index and middle fingertips touching the thumbtip and with its thumb edge at the mouth. The hand then moves outward from the mouth with its extended thumb and first two fingers alternately opening and closing. Also TATTLE 1, TATTLETALE 1.

TELLTALE 2, *n.* (Words shooting out from the mouth.) The right "S" hand is held palm out before the mouth with the knuckle of the index finger touching the lips. From this position the hand moves forward, away from the mouth. At the same time the index finger straightens and points forward. Also TATTLE 2, TATTLETALE 2.

TEMPERATE (tĕm′ pər ĭt), *adj.* (In between.) The little finger edge of the right "5" hand is placed between the thumb and index finger of the left "C" hand, whose palm faces the body. The right hand moves back and forth.

TEMPERATURE (tĕm′ pər ə chər, -prə chər), *n.* (The rise and fall of the mercury in the thermometer.) The index finger of the right "D" hand, pointing left, moves slowly up and down the index finger of the left "D" hand, which is held pointing up. Also FEVER, THERMOMETER.

TEMPLE (tĕm′ pəl), *n.* (The letter "T"; an establishment, *i.e.,* something placed on a foundation.) The base of the right "T" hand comes down against the back of the downturned left "S" hand. The action is repeated.

TEMPT (tĕmpt), *v.,* TEMPTED, TEMPTING. (Tapping one surreptitiously at a concealed place.) With the left arm

held palm down before the chest, the curved right index finger taps the left elbow a number of times. Also ENTICE, TEMPTATION.

TEMPTATION (tĕmp tā′ shən), *n.* See TEMPT.

TEND (tĕnd), *v.,* TENDED, TENDING. (The feelings of the heart move toward a specific object.) The tip of the right middle finger touches the heart. The open right hand, palm facing the body, then moves away from the heart toward the palm of the open left hand. Also DISPOSE, DISPOSED TO, DISPOSITION, INCLINATION, INCLINE, INCLINED, TENDENCY.

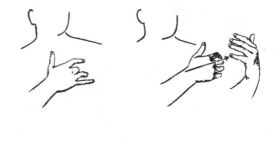

TENDENCY (tĕn′ dən sĭ), *n.* See TEND.

TEPEE (tē′ pē), *n.* (The letter "T"; the shape.) Both "T" hands, joined together, come apart as they move down, describing the sloping roof of a tent or tepee.

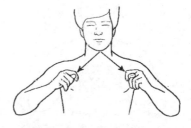

TERMINAL (tûr′ mə nl), *n. Computer term.* (The shape and the "T.") Both outfacing "T" hands, held side by side, separate and move straight down, outlining the shape of a computer terminal.

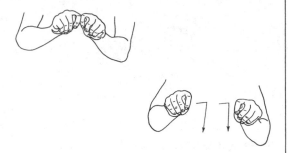

TERRIBLE (tĕr′ ə bəl), *adj.* (Throwing out the hands.) Both hands, their fingertips touching their respective thumbs, are held, palms facing each other, near the temples. They are thrown out before the face, assuming "5" positions, palms still facing. Also AWFUL, CALAMITOUS, CATASTROPHIC, DANGER 1, DANGEROUS 1, DREADFUL, FEARFUL, TRAGEDY, TRAGIC.

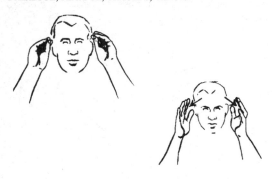

TERRITORY (ter′ ə tôr′ ē), *n.* (The letter "T"; an area.) The "T" hands are held together before the body, palms out. They separate and move back in a circle toward the chest, coming together again an inch or so from the chest.

TERROR 1 (tĕr′ ər), *n.* (The heart is suddenly covered with fear.) Both hands, fingers together, are placed side by side, palms facing the chest. They quickly open and come together over the heart, one on top of the other. Also AFRAID, COWARD, FEAR 1, FRIGHT, FRIGHTEN, SCARE(D).

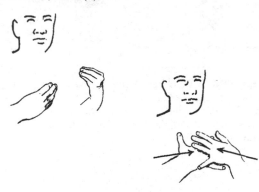

TERROR 2, *n.* (The hands attempt to ward off something that causes fear.) The "5" hands, right behind left, move downward before the body in a wavy motion. Also DREAD, FEAR 2, TIMID.

TEST (tĕst), *n., v.,* TESTED, TESTING. (A series of questions spread out on a page.) Both "D" hands, palms down, simultaneously execute a single circle, the right hand moving in a clockwise direction and the left in a counterclockwise direction. Upon completion of the circle, both hands open into the "5" position and move straight down a short distance. (The hands actually draw question marks in the air.) Also EXAMINATION 1, QUIZ 1.

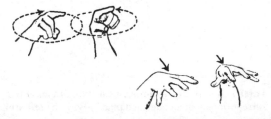

TESTES (tes′ tēz), *n.* (Holding the testes.) Both upturned cupped hands move up and down a short distance near the lower abdomen. Also TESTICLES.

TESTICLES (tes′ ti kəlz), *n.* See TESTES.

TESTIMONY 1 (tĕs′ tə mō′ nĭ), *n.* (A gesture of an orator.) The right open hand, palm facing left, is held above and to the right of the head. It pivots on the wrist, forward and backward, several times. Also ADDRESS 1, LECTURE, ORATE, SPEECH 2, TALK 2.

TESTIMONY 2, *n.* (The letter "T"; to show or indicate.) The right "T" hand is placed against the outfacing left palm. Both hands move forward in unison.

THAILAND (tī′ land′, -lənd), *n.* (The elephant's trunk.) The index finger moves out quickly from the

tip of the nose, coming together as if tracing an elephant's trunk.

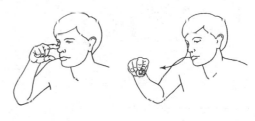

THANKS (thăngks), *n. pl., interj.* See THANK YOU.

THANK YOU, *phrase.* (Words extended politely from the mouth.) The fingertips of the right "5" hand are placed at the mouth. The hand moves away from the mouth to a palm-up position before the body. The signer meanwhile usually nods smilingly. Also FAREWELL 1, GOODBYE 1, HELLO 1, THANKS, YOU'RE WELCOME 1.

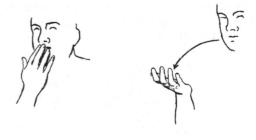

THAT 1 (that, *unstressed* thət), *pron.* (Something specific.) The downturned right "Y" hand is placed on the upturned left palm. Also IT 2, THESE, THIS, THOSE, WHICH 2.

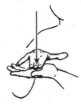

THAT 2, *pron.* (Indicating a specific item.) The right index finger touches the tip of the index finger of the left "L" hand, which is held thumb pointing up and palm facing right.

THAT 3, *pron.* (The concept of alternateness, *i.e.,* "this or *that.*") The extended right index finger touches the tip of its left counterpart and then moves over to the extended left thumbtip, describing a small arc as it does so.

THAT ONE (*colloq.*), *phrase.* The downturned "Y" hand drops down abruptly, ending with a finger pointing at the one referred to. A knowing expression is assumed, or sometimes an exaggerated grimace, as if announcing a surprising fact.

THEFT 1 (thĕft), *n.* (The hand, partly concealed, takes something surreptitiously.) The index and middle fingers of the right hand, somewhat curved, are placed under the left elbow. As they move slowly along the left forearm toward the left wrist, they close a bit. Also ABDUCT, EMBEZZLE, EMBEZZLEMENT, KIDNAP, ROB 1, ROBBERY 1, STEAL 1, SWIPE, THIEF 1, THIEVERY.

THEFT 2 (*colloq.*), *n.* (A sly, underhanded movement.) The right open hand, palm down, is held a bit behind the body at waist level. Beginning with the little finger, the hand closes finger by finger into the "A" position, as if wrapping itself around something. Also ROB 2, ROBBERY 1, STEAL 2.

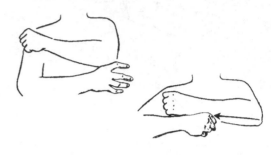

THEFT 3, *n.* (A mustachioed thief.) The fingertips of both "H" hands, palms facing the body, are placed above the lips and are drawn slowly apart, describing a mustache. Sometimes one hand only is used. Also BANDIT, BURGLAR, BURGLARY, CROOK, ROB 3, ROBBER 1, STEAL 3, THIEF 2.

THEIR(S) (thâr, *unstressed* thər), *pron.* (Belonging to; pushed toward.) The open right hand, palm facing out and fingers together and pointing up, moves out a short distance from the body. This is repeated several times, with the hand moving an inch or two toward the right each time. The hand may also be swept in a short left-to-right arc in this position.

THEM (thĕm, *unstressed* thəm), *pron.* (The natural sign.) The right index finger points in turn to a number of imaginary persons or objects. Also THEY.

THEME (thēm), *n.* (The quotation marks are indicated.) The curved index and middle fingers of both hands, held palms out, move slightly to either side of the body, as if drawing quotation marks in the air. Also CAPTION, CITE, QUOTATION, QUOTE, SO-CALLED, SUBJECT, TITLE, TOPIC.

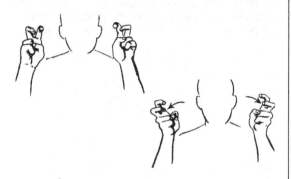

THEMSELVES (thəm sĕlvz′), *pron. pl.* (The thumb indicates an individual, *i.e.,* a *self;* several are indicated.) The right hand, in the "A" position with thumb pointing up, makes a series of short forward movements as it sweeps either from right to left or from left to right.

THEN 1 (thĕn), *adv.* (Going from one specific point in time to another.) The left "L" hand is held palm facing right and thumb pointing left. The right index finger, positioned behind the left thumb, moves in an arc over

the left thumb and comes to rest on the tip of the left index finger.

THEN 2, *adv.* (Same basic rationale as for THEN 1, but modified to incorporate the concept of nearness, *i.e.,* NEXT. The sign, then, is "one point [in time] to the next.") The left hand is held as in THEN 1. The extended right index finger rests on the ball of the thumb. The right hand then opens and arcs over, coming to rest on the back of the left hand, whose index finger has now closed.

THEORY 1 (thē′ ə rĭ, thĭr′ ĭ), *n.* (A thought coming forward from the mind, modified by the letter "I" for "idea.") With the "I" position on the right hand, palm facing the body, touch the little finger to the forehead and then move the hand up and away in a circular, clockwise motion. The hand may also be moved up and away without this circular motion. The "T" hand may be substituted. Also CONCEIVE 2, CONCEPT 1, CONCEPTION, FANCY 2, IDEA, IMAGINATION, IMAGINE 1, JUST THINK OF IT!, NOTION, POLICY 2, THOUGHT 2.

THEORY 2, *n.* (The letter "T"; turning over a thought in the mind.) The right "T" hand makes a small counterclockwise circle against the forehead.

THERAPY (ther′ ə pē), *n.* (The letter "T"; helping.) The right "T" hand is placed palm down or palm left on the left palm. The left palm pushes up the right a short distance.

THERE 1 (thâr), *adv.* (The natural sign.) The right index finger points to an imaginary object, usually at or slightly above eye level, *i.e.,* "yonder."

THERE 2, *adv.* (Something brought to the attention.) The right hand is brought forward, simultaneously opening into the palm-up position.

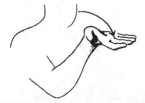

THEREABOUTS (thâr′ ə boutz), *adv.* (In the general area.) The downturned open "5" hand moves in a counterclockwise direction in front of the body. Also ABOUT 3.

THEREFORE 1 (thâr′ fōr′), *adv.* (In proportion.) Both "D" or "P" hands, palms facing down, are held before the body. They describe a short arc from right to left and, while unnecessary, they may return to their original position. Also HENCE, PROPORTION, RATIO, THUS.

THEREFORE 2, *adv.* (The mathematical symbol.) The index finger describes three dots in the air, in pyramidal arrangement. This is used in the mathematical context.

THEREFORE 3, *adv.* (A natural sign.) Both hands simultaneously open into a supine position on either side of the body. As they do so, the head nods slightly and the shoulders sink slightly.

THERMOMETER (thər mŏm′ ə tər), *n.* (The rise and fall of the mercury in the thermometer.) The index finger of the right "D" hand, pointing left, moves slowly up and down the index finger of the left "D" hand, which is held pointing up. Also FEVER, TEMPERATURE.

THERMOS (thûr′ məs), *n.* (Closing a bottle.) The sign for BOTTLE is made: the right "C" hand is held little finger edge against the upturned left palm. The right hand moves straight up, describing the shape of a bottle. The right hand then mimes tightening a bottle cap on the left hand, which now holds the imaginary bottle.

THEY (thā), *pron.* (The natural sign.) The right index finger points in turn to a number of imaginary persons or objects. Also THEM.

THICK-SKULLED (*colloq.*), *adj.* (The thickness of the skull is indicated to stress intellectual density.) With the thumb of the right "C" hand grasped by the closed left hand, the right hand is swung in toward the body, describing a small arc as it moves. The space between the curved right fingers and the closed left

hand indicates the thickness of the skull. Also CLUMSY 2, DUMB 2, MORON, STUPID 2, UNSKILLED.

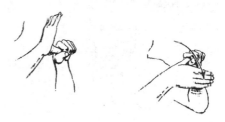

THIEF 1 (thēf), *n.* (The hand, partly concealed, takes something surreptitiously.) The index and middle fingers of the right hand, somewhat curved, are placed under the left elbow. As they move slowly along the left forearm toward the left wrist, they close a bit. This is followed by INDIVIDUAL 1, as in THIEF 2. Also ABDUCT, EMBEZZLE, EMBEZZLEMENT, KIDNAP, ROB 1, ROBBERY 1, STEAL 1, SWIPE, THEFT 1, THIEVERY.

THIEF 2, *n.* (A mustachioed thief.) The fingertips of both "H" hands, palms facing the body, are placed above the lips and are drawn slowly apart, describing a mustache. Sometimes one hand only is used. This is followed by the sign for INDIVIDUAL 1: both open hands, palms facing each other, move down the sides of the body, tracing its outline to the hips. Also BANDIT, BURGLAR, BURGLARY, CROOK, ROB 3, ROBBER 1, STEAL 3, THEFT 3.

THIEVERY (thē′və rǐ), *n.* See THIEF 1 or 2.

THIN 1 (thĭn), *adj.* (The drawn face.) The thumb and index finger run down the cheeks, which are drawn in. Also LEAN 1, POOR 2.

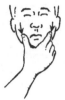

THIN 2 (*sl.*), *adj.* (A thin, tapering object is described with the little fingers, the thinnest of all.) The tips of the little fingers, touching, one above the other, are drawn apart. The cheeks may also be drawn in for emphasis. Also BEANPOLE, SKINNY.

THING (thĭng), *n.* (Something shown in the hand.) The outstretched right hand, palm up and held before the chest, is dropped slightly and brought over a bit to the right. Also ANYTHING, APPARATUS, INSTRUMENT, MATTER, OBJECT 1, SUBSTANCE 1.

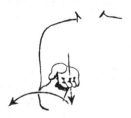

THINK (thĭngk), *v.*, THOUGHT, THINKING. (A thought is turned over in the mind.) The index finger makes a small circle on the forehead. Also CONSIDER 1, MOTIVE 1, RECKON, SPECULATE 1, SPECULATION 1, THOUGHT 1, THOUGHTFUL.

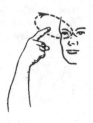

THIRST (thûrst), *n.* (The parched throat.) The index finger moves down the throat a short distance. Also SWALLOW 1, THIRSTY.

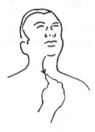

THIRSTY (thûrs′ tĭ), *adj.* See THIRST.

THIS (thĭs), *pron., adj.* (Something specific.) The downturned right "Y" hand is placed on the upturned left palm. Also IT 2, THAT 1, THESE, THOSE, WHICH 2.

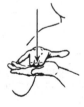

THIS MONTH, *phrase.* (Now, month.) The sign for NOW is made: the upturned right-angle hands drop down rather sharply. The "Y" hands may also be used. This is followed by the sign for MONTH: the extended right index finger moves down along the upturned, extended left index finger. The two signs are sometimes given in reverse order.

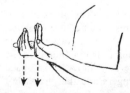

THORN 1 (thûrn), *n.* (The natural motion of the pricking of a thorn, its removal, and the rubbing of the wound.) The right index finger, representing a thorn, jabs into the back of the prone left hand. It then moves away quickly, as in a sudden extraction, and finally the right fingertips rub the back of the left hand in a circular fashion.

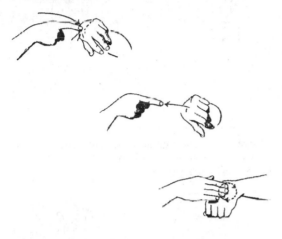

THORN 2, *n.* (The shape.) The right index and thumb rest on the upturned left index and trace the pointed shape of a thorn.

THOUGHT 1 (thôt), *n.* (A thought is turned over in the mind.) The index finger makes a small circle on the forehead. Also CONSIDER 1, MOTIVE 1, RECKON, SPECULATE 1, SPECULATION 1, THINK, THOUGHTFUL.

THOUGHT 2, *n.* (A thought coming forward from the mind, modified by the letter "I" for "idea.") With the "I" position on the right hand, palm facing the body, touch the little finger to the forehead, and then move the hand up and away in a circular, clockwise motion. The hand may also be moved up and away without this circular motion. Also CONCEIVE 2, CONCEPT 1, CONCEPTION, FANCY 2, IDEA, IMAGINATION, IMAGINE 1, JUST THINK OF IT!, NOTION, POLICY 2, THEORY.

THOUGHTFUL (thôt′ fəl), *adj.* See THOUGHT 1.

THOUGHT OF SOMETHING, *v. phrase.* (An idea pops up.) The right little or index finger touches the forehead or the area under the right eye, and then the index finger pops up through the space between the left index and middle fingers.

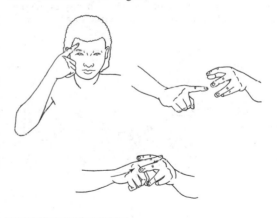

THREAD (thrĕd), *n.* (Unraveling a thin string, as indicated by the little fingers.) With palms facing the body, the tips of the extended little fingers touch. As they are drawn slowly apart, they describe very small spirals. Also SPAGHETTI, STRING, TWINE.

THREE OF US, *phrase.* (Three all around.) The right "3" hand, palm facing the body, moves in a half circle from right shoulder to left shoulder.

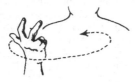

THRILL 1 (thrĭl), *n., v.,* THRILLED, THRILLING. (The heart beats violently.) Both middle fingers move up alternately to strike the heart sharply. Also EXCITE, EXCITEMENT, EXCITING.

THRILL 2 (*colloq.*), *n., v.* (The feelings well up and come out.) The open hands are placed near the chest, with middle fingers resting on the chest. Both hands move up and out simultaneously. A happy expression is assumed. Also WHAT'S NEW?, WHAT'S UP?

THROUGH (thrōō), *adv., prep., adj.* (The natural movement.) The open right hand is pushed between either the middle and index or the middle and third fingers of the open left hand.

THROW 1 (thrō), *v.,* THREW, THROWN, THROWING, *n.* (The natural sign.) The signer goes through the natural motions of throwing a ball. Also PITCH.

THROW 2, *v.* (The natural movement.) The right "S" hand is thrown forward and up a bit as it opens into the "5" position. Also TOSS.

THROW 3 (*sports*), *v.* (Pinning one's opponent in wrestling.) Both "A" or "S" hands, extended before the body, palms facing each other or held slightly to the side, move down forcefully an inch or two as if grasping someone by the ankles and forcing his shoulders to touch the ground. Also PIN 3.

THUNDER (thŭn′ dər), *n.* (A shaking that disturbs the ear.) After placing the index finger on the ear, both hands assume the "S" position, palms down. They move alternately back and forth forcefully. Also DIN, NOISE, NOISY, RACKET, SOUND, VIBRATION.

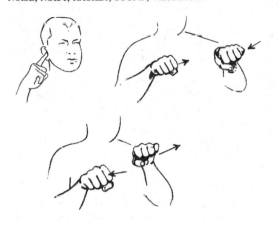

THUS (thŭs), *adv.* (In proportion.) Both "D" or "P" hands, palms facing down, are held before the body. They describe a short arc from right to left and, while unnecessary, may return to their original position. Also HENCE, PROPORTION, RATIO, THEREFORE 1.

THUS FAR, *adv. phrase.* (From a point up and over.) In the "D" position, palms down, both index fingers touch the right shoulder and then are brought up and over, ending in a palm-up position, pointing straight ahead of the body. Also ALL ALONG, ALL THE TIME, EVER SINCE, SINCE, SO FAR.

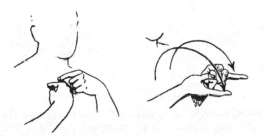

TICKET 1 (tĭk′ ĭt), *n.* (The natural sign.) The sides of the ticket are outlined with the thumb and index finger of each hand. Also CARD.

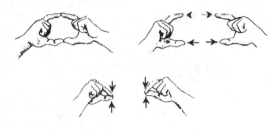

TICKET 2, *n.* (A baggage check or ticket.) The sign for TICKET 1 is made. Then the middle knuckles of the second and third fingers of the right hand squeeze the outer edge of the left palm, as a conductor's ticket punch. Also CHECK 4.

TIE 1 (tī), *v.,* TIED, TYING. (The act of tying.) Both hands, in the "A" position, go through the natural hand-over-hand motions of tying and drawing out a knot. Also BIND, FASTEN, KNOT.

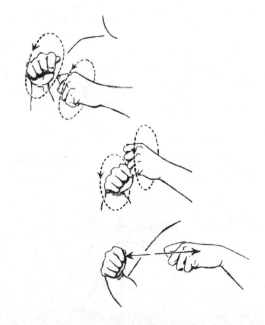

TIE 2, *n*. (The natural motion.) The "H" hands go through the natural hand-over-hand motions of tying a knot in a necktie at the throat. The right "H" hand then moves down the front of the chest to indicate the fall of the tie. Also NECKTIE.

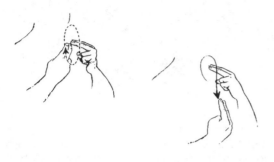

TIGER 1 (tī′ gər), *n*. (A striped cat.) The sign for CAT is made: the thumbs and index fingers of both hands stroke an imaginary pair of whiskers at either side of the face. The right thumb and index finger, held an inch apart, then trace a series of stripes down the chest, moving left with each stripe. Both hands may also be used, moving either toward or away from each other with each successive stripe. The bent fingers of both hands may also trace stripes across the face, from the edges of the mouth to the ears. The stripes on the chest are then omitted.

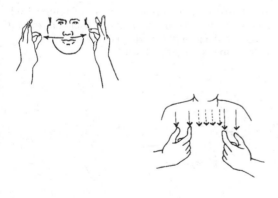

TIGER 2, *n*. (The stripes on the face.) The claw hands trace the cat's stripes on the face.

TIGHTROPE (tīt′ rōp′), *n*. (The natural activity.) The signer, arms outstretched, mimes walking a tightrope.

TIGHTS (tīts), *n*. (The natural activity of donning tights.) The signer mimes struggling into a pair of tights, pulling down the top over the chest, and showing the effort on the face. Also LEOTARDS.

TIGHTWAD 1 (tīt′ wŏd′), *n*. (Pulling things toward oneself.) Both prone open or "V" hands are held in front of the body with fingers bent. The hands are then drawn quickly and forcefully inward, as if raking things toward oneself. Also GREEDY 1, SELFISH 1, STINGY 1.

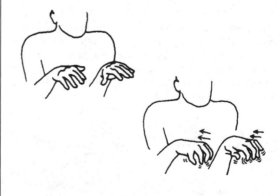

TIGHTWAD 2, *n*. (Scratching the palm in greed.) The right fingers scratch the upturned left palm several times. A frowning expression is often used. Also AVARICIOUS, GREEDY 2, SELFISH 2, STINGY 2.

TIGHTWAD 3 (*colloq.*), *n.* (Holding tightly to money.) The "S" hand, tightly clenched, is held up, and trembles a bit. A frowning expression is frequently assumed for emphasis.

TILL (tĭl), *prep.* (From one point to the next.) The extended right index finger moves forward slowly and comes to rest on the tip of the extended, upturned left index finger. Also TO 1, TOWARD 1, UNTIL, UNTO, UP TO, UP TO NOW.

TIME 1 (tīm), *n.* (Time by the clock, indicated by the ticking of the clock or watch.) The curved right index finger taps the back of the left wrist several times. Also CLOCK, WATCH 3.

TIME 2, *n.* (Time in the abstract, indicated by the rotating of the "T" hand on the face of a clock.) The

right "T" hand is placed palm to palm in the open left hand. It describes a clockwise circle and comes to rest again in the left palm. Also AGE 2, EPOCH, ERA, PERIOD 2, SEASON.

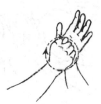

TIME 3 (*sports*), *n.* (The gesture employed in sports.) The fingertips of the right hand, pointing up, are thrust into the open left hand, whose palm is facing down. A "T" is thus formed. This movement may be repeated. Also TIME OUT.

TIME 4, *n.* Both hands, slightly cupped, palms up, are held close to the chest. They move up and out in unison, describing an arc. Also OCCASION, OPPORTUNITY 1.

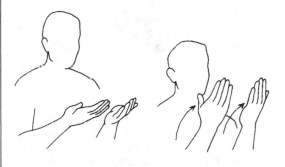

TIME OUT (*sports*), *phrase.* See TIME 3.

TIMID (tĭm′ ĭd), *adj.* (The hands attempt to ward off something that causes fear.) The "5" hands, right behind left, move downward before the body in a wavy motion. Also DREAD, FEAR 2, TERROR 2.

TINY 1 (tī′ ni), *adj.* (A small or tiny movement.) The right thumbtip is flicked off the index finger several times as if shooting marbles, although the movement is not so pronounced. Also LITTLE 2, MINUTE 2.

TINY 2, *adj.* (Indicating a small mass.) The extended right thumb and index finger are held slightly spread. They are then moved slowly toward each other until they almost touch. Also PETTY, SLIGHT, SMALL 1.

TIP 1 (tĭp), *n., v.,* TIPPED, TIPPING. (A tapering or sharp point is indicated.) The index finger and thumb of the left hand grasp the tip of the index finger of the right "D" hand. The left hand then moves away a short distance, and its index finger and thumb come together. Also POINT 2, SHARP 2.

TIP 2, *n., v.* (Putting a coin in someone's hand.) The right hand places an imaginary coin in the upturned left palm.

TIP 3, *n., v.* (Fingering a coin or a bill.) The upturned right hand holds an imaginary coin or bill. As it moves forward, the thumb rubs against the fingertips, from middle finger to index, assuming the "A" position.

TIPTOE (tip′ tō′), *n., v.,* -TOED, -TOEING. (The feet touch lightly.) With both index fingers pointing down, the signer very lightly, slowly, and deliberately moves forward first one and then the other index finger. The shoulders are a little stooped, and with each successive forward movement of the index fingers, the signer moves forward very slightly.

TIRE (tīr), *v.,* TIRED, TIRING. (The hands collapse in exhaustion.) Both "C" hands are placed either on the lower chest or at the waist. The palms face the body. They fall away into a palms-up position. At the same time, the shoulders suddenly sag in a very pronounced fashion. An expression of weariness may be used for emphasis. Also DISCOURAGE 2, EXHAUST, FATIGUE, TIRED, WEARY.

TIRED (tīrd), *adj.* See TIRE.

TIRES (tīrz), *n.* (The shape.) Both index fingers, held on either side of the chest, outline the round shape of a pair of tires or wheels.

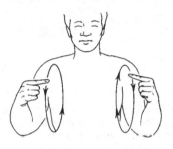

TITLE (tī′ təl), *n.* (The quotation marks are indicated.) The curved index and middle fingers of both hands, held palms out, move slightly to either side of the body, as if drawing quotation marks in the air. Also CAPTION, CITE, QUOTATION, QUOTE, SO-CALLED, SUBJECT, THEME, TOPIC.

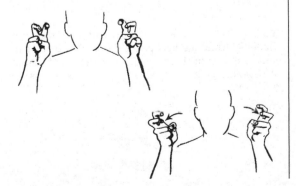

TO 1 (to͞o), *prep.* (From one point to the next.) The extended right index finger moves forward slowly and comes to rest on the tip of the extended, upturned left index finger. This sign should never be used for an infinitive; it is simply omitted in that case. Also TILL, TOWARD 1, UNTIL, UNTO, UP TO, UP TO NOW.

TO 2, *prep.* (The thoughts are directed outward toward a specific goal or purpose.) The right index finger, resting on the right temple, leaves its position and moves straight out in front of the face. Also FOR 1, TOWARD 3.

TOAST 1 (tōst), *n., v.,* TOASTED, TOASTING. (The fork is thrust into each side of the toast to turn it around.) With the left hand held upright, the tips of the right "V" fingers are thrust into the open left palm and then into the back of the same hand.

TOAST 2, *n., v.* (Bringing the glasses together.) Both hands, holding imaginary glasses, come together, knuckle to knuckle, with a flourish.

TOASTER (tōs′ tər), *n.* (Popping the bread into a box.) The downturned right fingers are thrust into the left hand. The sides of the toaster are then indicated.

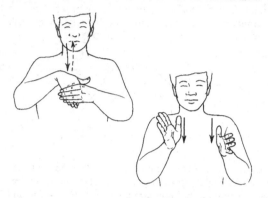

TODAY 1 (tə dā′), *n.* (Now, day.) The sign for NOW is made: the upturned right-angle hands drop down rather sharply. The "Y" hands may also be used. This is followed by the sign for DAY: the left arm, held horizontally, palm down, represents the horizon. The right elbow rests on the back of the left hand, with the right arm in a perpendicular position. The right "D" hand, palm facing left, moves in an arc to the left until it is just above the left elbow. The two signs may be reversed.

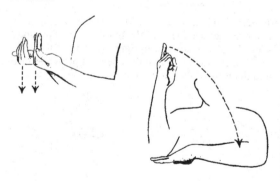

TODAY 2, *prep.* (Right before one, *i.e.*, now.) The right-angle or "Y" hands, palms up, drop down twice.

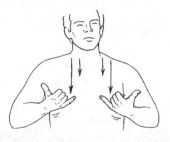

TOE(S) 1 (tō), *n.* (The wiggling and pointing.) The extended thumb is wiggled, and then the signer points to his foot. The signs may also be reversed.

TOE(S) 2, *n.* (Touching them in turn.) The downturned left "5" hand is held at chest height. The right thumb and index finger (or the right "T" hand) moves from the left thumb to the little finger, indicating the toes, one by one.

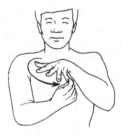

TOGETHER (tŏŏ gĕth′ ər), *adv.* (To go along with.) Both "A" hands, knuckles together and thumbs up, are moved forward in unison, away from the chest. Also ACCOMPANY, WANDER AROUND WITH, WITH.

TOIL (toil), *n., v.,* TOILED, TOILING. (Striking an anvil.) Both "S" hands are held palms down. The right hand strikes against the back of the left a number of times. Also JOB, LABOR, OCCUPATION, TASK, TRAVAIL, VOCATION, WORK.

TOILET (toi′ lĭt), *n.* (The letter "T.") The right "T" hand is shaken slightly.

TOKYO (tō′ kē ō), *n.* (The skyscrapers.) Both "L" hands, palms facing out, move alternately up and down.

TOLERATE 1 (tŏl′ ə rāt′), *v., -ATED, -ATING.* (A permissive upswinging of the hands, as if giving in.) Both hands, palms facing and fingers pointing away from the body, are held at chest level, almost a foot apart. With an upward movement, using their wrists as pivots, the hands sweep up until the fingers point almost straight up. Also ALLOW, GRANT 1, LET, LET'S, LET US, MAY 3, PERMISSION 1, PERMIT 1.

TOLERATE 2, *v.* (A clenching of the fists; the rise and fall of pain.) Both "S" hands, tightly clenched, revolve about each other slowly and deliberately while a pained expression is worn. Also AGONY, BEAR 3, DIFFICULT 3, ENDURE 1, PASSION 2, SUFFER 1.

TOLL (tōl), *n.* (Nicking into one.) The knuckle of the right "X" finger is nicked against the palm of the left hand, held in the "5" position, palm facing right. Also ADMISSION 2, CHARGE 1, COST, DUTY 2, EXCISE, EXPENSE, FEE, FINE 2, IMPOST, PENALTY 3, PRICE 2, TAX 1, TAXATION 1.

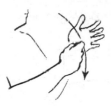

TOMATO 1 (tə mā′ tō), *n.* (The slicing is indicated.) The sign for RED is made: the tip of the right index finger moves down across the lips. The open right hand, palm facing left, is then brought down against the thumb side of the downturned left "S" hand in a slicing movement. This latter movement is repeated a number of times. The slicing may also be done with the index finger.

TOMATO 2 (*rare*), *n.* (The peeling is indicated.) After the sign for RED is made, as in TOMATO 1, the thumbtip of the right "A" hand is drawn over the back of the left "S" hand a number of times.

TOMORROW (tə môr′ ō, -mŏr′ ō), *n., adv.* (A single step ahead, *i.e.,* into the future.) The thumb of the right "A" hand, placed on the right cheek, moves straight out from the face, describing an arc.

TONIGHT (tə nīt′), *n.* (Now, night.) The sign for NOW is made: the upturned right-angle hands drop down rather sharply. The "Y" hands may also be used. This is followed by the sign for NIGHT: the left hand, palm down, is positioned at chest height. The down-turned right hand, held an inch or so above the left, moves over the left hand in an arc, as the sun setting beneath the horizon. The two signs may be reversed.

TONSILS (ton′ səlz), *n.* (Pointing to the tonsils.) The signer points to both sides of the throat.

TOO (tōō), *adv.* (A likeness; a sameness.) Both index fingers, held together at one side of the body near waist level, point forward. As they travel to the other side of the body they separate an inch or two and come together again. Also ACCORDING (TO), ALSO 1, AS, DUPLICATE 2, SAME AS.

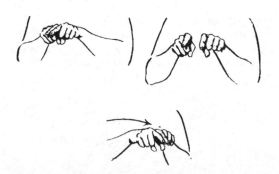

TOOTHPASTE (tōōth′ pāst′), *n.* (Squeezing the tube.) The signer mimes squeezing toothpaste onto the out-stretched left index finger.

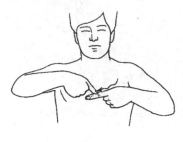

TOOTHPICK (tōōth′ pik′), *n.* (The natural motion.) The signer goes through the motions of picking the teeth with a toothpick.

TOP (top), *n.* (Winding up a top and spinning it.) The signer mimes winding up a toy top and spinning it.

TOP DOG (top′ dôg) *n.* (*sl.*) (The senior year at school.) The downturned open right palm rests on the tip of the left thumb. Also SENIOR.

TOPIC (tŏp′ ĭk), *n.* (The quotation marks are indicated.) The curved index and middle fingers of both hands, held palms out, move slightly to either side of the body, as if drawing quotation marks in the air. Also CAPTION, CITE, QUOTATION, QUOTE, SO-CALLED, SUBJECT, THEME, TITLE.

TOPPLE (top′ əl), *v.*, -PLED, -PLING. (Crashing to the ground.) The right "S" hand is placed with its elbow resting on the back of the downturned left "S" hand. It swings down in an arc so that the right "S" hand "crashes" down on the crook of the left elbow.

TORMENT (*n.* tôr′ mĕnt; *v.* tôr mĕnt′), -MENTED, -MENTING. (Striking against one.) The knuckles of the right "A" hand move sharply forward along the thumb edge of the left "A" hand. Also PERSECUTE, TEASE 1.

TOSS AND TURN, *colloq. phrase.* (The body moves around in bed.) The upturned curved index and middle fingers of the right hand, swiveled from the right wrist, move back and forth in the upturned open left palm.

TOTAL (tō′ təl), *adj., n., v.,* -TALED, -TALING. (To bring up all together.) The two open hands, palms and fingers facing each other, with the left hand above the right, are brought together, with all fingers closing simultaneously. This sign is used mainly in the sense of adding up figures or items. Also ADD 1, ADDITION, AMOUNT 1, SUM, SUMMARIZE 2, SUMMARY 2, SUM UP.

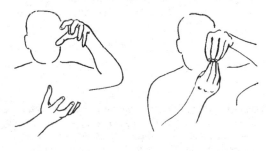

TOTAL COMMUNICATION, *n. educational term.* (The "T" and "C" back and forth.) The left "T" and the right "C" move alternately forward and back in front of the mouth. This term refers to a description of a philosophy of communication embodying all communicative modes: speech, fingerspelling, speechreading, signing, mime, writing, etc.

TOUCH (tŭch), *n., v.,* TOUCHED, TOUCHING. (The natural movement of touching.) The tip of the middle finger of the downturned right "5" hand touches the back of the left hand a number of times. Also CONTACT 1, FEEL 1, TOUCHDOWN.

TOUCHED (tŭcht), *adj.* (A piercing of the heart.) The tip of the middle finger of the right "5" hand is thrust against the heart. The head, at the same time, moves abruptly back a very slight distance. Also FEEL TOUCHED, TOUCHING.

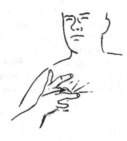

TOUCHING (tŏuch′ ĭng), *adj.* See TOUCHED.

TOUGH 1 (tŭf), *adj.* (Flexing the muscles.) With fists clenched, palms facing back, the signer raises both arms and shakes them once with force. Also MIGHT 1, MIGHTY 1, POWER 1, POWERFUL 1, STRONG 1, STURDY.

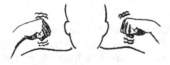

TOUGH 2 (*sl.*), *adj.* (A hard heart.) The index fingers trace a heart on the appropriate place on the chest. The knuckles of the downturned right "S" hand then come down sharply against the back of the left "S" hand. Also HARD-BOILED.

TOUGH 3 (*sl.*), *adj.* (Striking the chest to indicate toughness, *i.e.,* a "tough guy.") The little finger edge of the upturned right "S" hand strikes the chest repeatedly.

TOURIST (tŏŏr′ ist), *n.* (One who wanders around.) Using the downturned curved "V" fingers, the signer describes a series of small counterclockwise circles as the fingers move in random fashion from right to left. This is followed by the sign for INDIVIDUAL.

TOURNAMENT (tûr′ nə mənt), *n.* (First one team leads, then the other.) The curved index fingers and thumbs of both hands, palms facing, move up and down alternately.

TOW (tō), *n., v.,* TOWED, TOWING. (Hooking onto something and pulling.) With index fingers interlocked, the right hand pulls the left hand from left to right. Also HITCH, HOOK, PULL 2.

TOWARD 1 (tōrd, tə wôrd'), *prep.* (From one point to the next.) The extended right index finger moves forward slowly and comes to rest on the tip of the extended, upturned left index finger. Also TILL, TO 1, UNTIL, UNTO, UP TO, UP TO NOW.

TOWARD 2, *prep.* (Coming close to.) Both hands are held in the right-angle position, fingers facing each other, with the right hand held between the left hand and the chest. The right hand slowly moves toward the left. Also APPROACH, NEAR 2.

TOWARD 3, *prep.* (The thoughts are directed outward toward a specific goal or purpose.) The right index finger, resting on the right temple, leaves its position and moves straight out in front of the face. Also FOR 1, TO 2.

TOWEL 1 (tou' əl), *n.* (The natural sign.) The signer goes through the motions of wiping his face with a towel. Also WASH 2.

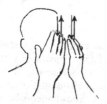

TOWEL 2, *n.* (Drying off the back.) The signer mimes using a large towel to dry off the back.

TOWN (toun), *n.* (A collection of rooftops.) The fingertips of both hands are joined, the hands and arms forming a pyramid. The fingertips separate and rejoin a number of times. Both arms may move a bit from left to right each time the fingertips separate and rejoin. Also CITY, COMMUNITY 2.

TOY (toi), *n.* (The "T"s; playing.) Both downturned "T" hands swivel alternately from their wrists. The swiveling movement is derived from the sign to PLAY.

TRADE (trād), *n., v.,* TRADED, TRADING. (Exchanging places.) The right "A" hand, positioned above the left "A" hand, swings down and under the left, coming up a bit in front of it. Also EXCHANGE, INSTEAD OF 1, REPLACE, SUBSTITUTE.

TRAGEDY 1 (trăj′ ə dĭ), *n.* (Throwing out the hands.) Both hands, their fingertips touching their respective thumbs, are held, palms facing each other, near the temples. They are thrown out before the face, assuming "5" positions, palms still facing. Also AWFUL, CALAMITOUS, CATASTROPHIC, DANGER 1, DANGEROUS 1, DREADFUL, FEARFUL, TERRIBLE, TRAGIC.

TRAGEDY 2, *n.* (The "T" letters; tears running down the cheeks.) Both "T" hands move down the side of the face. A look of sadness is assumed.

TRAGIC (trăj′ ĭk), *adj.* See TRAGEDY 1 or 2.

TRAIL (trāl), *n.* (The winding movement.) Both hands, palms facing and fingers together and extended straight out, move in unison away from the body in a winding manner. Also CORRIDOR, HALL, HALLWAY, MANNER 2, METHOD, OPPORTUNITY 3, PATH, ROAD, STREET, WAY 1.

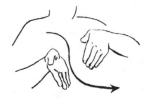

TRAILER (trā′ lər), *n.* (The rig swings back and forth.) Both downturned hands are positioned with the left fingertips against the heel of the right hand, the

cab. Both hands sway slightly back and forth as they move forward.

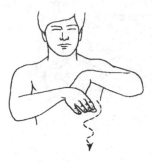

TRAIN 1 (trān), *n.* (Running along the tracks.) The "V" hands are held palms down. The right "V" moves back and forth over the left "V." Also CARS, RAILROAD 1.

TRAIN 2, *v.*, TRAINED, TRAINING. (Polishing or sharpening up.) The knuckles of the downturned right "A" hand are rubbed briskly back and forth over the side of the hand and index finger of the left "D" hand. Also DISCIPLINE 1, DRILL 3, PRACTICE 1, TRAINING 1.

TRAIN 3, *v.* The same movement as in TRAIN 2 is executed, but the right hand is held in the "T" position for the initial letter in TRAIN. Also TRAINING 2.

TRANSFER 1 (*n.* trăns′ fər; *v.* trăns fûr′), -FERRED, -FERRING. (To change positions.) Both "A" hands, thumbs up, are held before the chest, several inches apart. The left hand is pivoted over so that its thumb points to the right. Simultaneously, the right hand is moved up and over the left, describing a small arc, with its thumb pointing to the left. Also ADJUST, ALTER, ALTERATION, CHANGE 1, CONVERT, MODIFY, REVERSE 2.

TRANSFER 2, *n., v.* (Moving from one place to another.) The downturned hands, fingers touching their respective thumbs, move in unison from left to right. Also MIGRATE, MOVE, PLACE 3, PUT, REMOVE 2.

TRANSFER 3, *n., v.* (Shift position or travel.) The downturned curved right "V" fingers move forward in a horizontal arc.

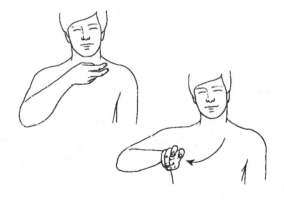

TRANSIENT (trăn′ shənt), *adj.* A variation of TRAVEL 1 and TRAVEL 2, but using the downturned curved "V" fingers. Also JOURNEY 3, TRAVEL 3, TRIP 3.

TRANSLATE (trans lāt′), *v.,* -LATED, -LATING. (The "T" letters; changing around.) Both "T" hands, palms facing and touching each other, swing around each other.

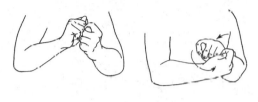

TRANSMISSION (trans mish′ ən), *n.* (The internal working of an automobile transmission.) Both claw hands are held up, palms facing each other. They rotate repeatedly from the wrists in opposite directions.

TRANSPORTATION 1 (trăns′ pər tā′ shən), *n.* (The natural sign.) The right "A" hand, palm facing left and thumb held straight up, moves back and forth repeatedly from left to right. Also BACK AND FORTH.

TRANSPORTATION 2, *n.* (Running along the tracks.) The "V" hands are held palms down. The right "V" moves back and forth over the left "V." Also RAILROAD 1, TRAIN 1.

TRAP 1 (trăp), *n., v.,* TRAPPED, TRAPPING. (Impaled on a stick, as a snake's head.) The "V" fingers are thrust into the throat. Also CAUGHT IN THE ACT 2, CHOKE 2, STRANDED, STUCK 2.

TRAP 2, *n.* (The jaws of the trap snap together.) Both "X" hands, palms out, are held a few inches apart. They suddenly snap together.

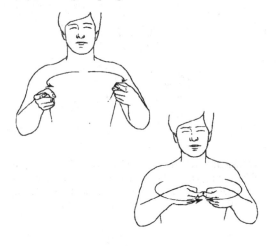

TRAP 3, *n., v.* (The trap snaps shut.) The fingers of the right hand snap shut over the fingers of the left.

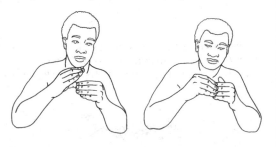

TRAPEZE ARTIST (trə pēz′ är′ tist), *n.* (The natural movements.) The outstretched left index finger represents the bar of the trapeze. The right index and mid-

dle fingers stand on the left index finger and, maintaining contact, swing back and forth.

TRAVAIL (trăv′ āl), *n.* (Striking an anvil.) Both "S" hands are held palms down. The right hand strikes against the back of the left a number of times. Also JOB, LABOR, OCCUPATION, TASK, TOIL, VOCATION, WORK.

TRAVEL 1 (trăv′ əl), *n., v.,* -ELED, -ELING. (Moving around from place to place.) Both "D" hands are held palms facing, the index fingers pointing to each other. In this position the hands describe a series of small counterclockwise circles as they move in random fashion from right to left. Also JOURNEY 1, TRIP 1.

TRAVEL 2, *n., v.* A variation of TRAVEL 1, but using only the right hand. Also JOURNEY 2, TRIP 2.

TRAVEL 3, *n., v.* A variation of TRAVEL 1 and TRAVEL 2, but using the downturned curved "V" fingers. Also JOURNEY 3, TRANSIENT, TRIP 3.

TREE (trē), *n.* (The shape.) The elbow of the upright right arm rests on the palm of the upturned left hand. This is the trunk. The right "5" fingers wiggle to imitate the movement of the branches and leaves. Also BRANCH.

TREMBLE *v.,* -BLED, -BLING. (The knees shake.) Both curved downturned index fingers move rapidly away from and toward each other, imitating shaking knees. Also SHAKING KNEES.

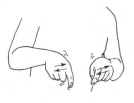

TRESPASS (trĕs′ pəs), *n., v.,* -PASSED, -PASSING. (An encroachment.) The left "A" hand is held palm toward the body, knuckles facing right. The extended thumb of the right "A" hand is brought sharply over the back of the left. Also DANGER 2, DANGEROUS 2, INJURE 2, PERIL, VIOLATE.

TRIFLING (trī′ flĭng), *adj.* (Thoughts flickering back and forth.) The right "Y" hand, thumb almost touching the forehead, is shaken back and forth across the

forehead several times. Also ABSURD, DAFT, FOLLY, FOOLISH, NONSENSE, RIDICULOUS, SILLY.

TRIP 1 (trĭp), *n.* (Moving around from place to place.) Both "D" hands are held palms facing, the index fingers pointing to each other. In this position the hands describe a series of small counterclockwise circles as they move in random fashion from right to left. Also JOURNEY 1, TRAVEL 1.

TRIP 2, *n.* A variation of TRIP 1, but using only the right hand. Also JOURNEY 2, TRAVEL 2.

TRIP 3, *n.* A variation of TRIP 1 and TRIP 2, but using the downturned curved "V" fingers. Also JOURNEY 3, TRANSIENT, TRAVEL 3.

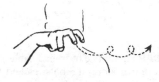

TRIUMPH 1 (trī′ əmf), *n., v.,* -UMPHED, -UMPHING. (Waving a flag.) The right "A" hand goes through the natural movement of waving a flag in circular fashion. Preceding this, the right hand may go through the motion of grabbing the flagstaff out of the left hand. Also EXULTATION, VICTORY 2, WIN 2.

TRIUMPH 2, *n.* (Penetrating the heights.) The "D" hands, palms back, are held at each side of the head, near the temples. With a pivoting motion of the wrists, the hands swing up and around, simultaneously, to a position above the head, with palms facing out. Also ACCOMPLISH 1, ACHIEVE 1, ATTAIN, PROSPER, SUCCEED, SUCCESS, SUCCESSFUL.

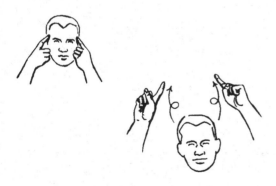

TROLLEY CAR 1 (trŏl′ ĭ), *n.* (Running along the overhead cable.) The extended index finger of the downturned left "D" hand represents the overhead cable. The knuckles of the curved right index and middle fingers, grasping the left index finger, move along its length from base to tip.

TROLLEY CAR 2, *n.* (The overhead cable.) The right "E" hand is drawn along the outstretched left index

finger, from its base to its fingertip, as if riding along a cable. This sign is also used for "el," an elevated railway.

TROUBLE (trŭb′ əl), *n., v.,* -BLED, -BLING. (A clouding over; a troubling.) Both "B" hands, palms facing each other, are rotated alternately before the forehead. Also ANNOY 2, ANNOYANCE 2, ANXIOUS 2, BOTHER 2, CONCERN 1, FRET, PROBLEM 1, WORRIED, WORRY 1.

TRUE (trōō), *adj.* (Coming forth directly from the lips; true.) The index finger of the right "D" hand, palm facing left, is placed against the lips. It moves up an inch or two and then describes a small arc forward and away from the lips. Also ABSOLUTE, ABSOLUTELY, ACTUAL, ACTUALLY, AUTHENTIC, CERTAIN, CERTAINLY, FAITHFUL 3, FIDELITY, FRANKLY, GENUINE, INDEED, POSITIVE 1, POSITIVELY, REAL, REALLY, SINCERE 2, SURE, SURELY, TRULY, TRUTH, VALID, VERILY.

TRULY (trōō′ lĭ), *adv.* See TRUE.

TRUMPET (trum′ pit), *n.* (The action of blowing.) The signer places the thumb edge of the left "S" hand at the lips and uses three fingers of the right hand, in front of the left, to work the stops of the instrument.

TRUNK (trŭngk), *n*. (The dimensions are indicated.) The open hands, palms facing and fingers pointing out, are dropped an inch or two simultaneously. They then shift their relative positions so that both palms face the body, with one hand in front of the other. In this new position they again drop an inch or two simultaneously. Also BOX 1, PACKAGE, ROOM 1, SQUARE 1.

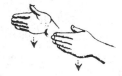 

TRUST (trŭst), *n., v.,* TRUSTED, TRUSTING. (Planting a flagpole, *i.e.,* planting one's trust.) The "S" hands grasp and plant an imaginary flagpole in the ground. This sign may be preceded by the extended index finger placed against the forehead. Also CONFIDENCE, FAITH.

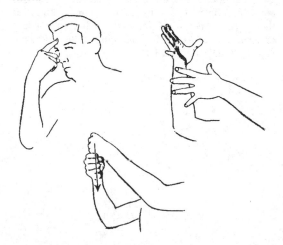

TRUSTEE (trus tē'), *n*. (The "T"; the Roman toga.) The right "T" hand moves from the left shoulder to the right shoulder.

TRUTH (trōōth), *n*. See TRUE.

TRY 1 (trī), *n., v.,* TRIED, TRYING. (Trying to push through.) The "Λ" hands, palms facing before the body, are swung around and a bit down so that the palms now face out. The movement indicates an attempt to push through a barrier. Also ATTEMPT 1, EFFORT 1, ENDEAVOR, PERSEVERE 1, PERSIST 1.

TRY 2, *n., v.* (Trying to push through, using the "T" hands, for "try.") This is the same sign as TRY 1, except that the "T" hands are employed. Also ATTEMPT 2, EFFORT 2, PERSEVERE 2.

TTY/TDD 1, *n., v.* (Phone and type.) The "Y" hand is held at the side of the face, indicating the phone's receiver. The signer then executes typing motions.

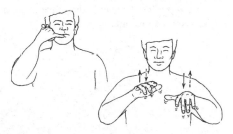

TTY/TDD 2, *n., v.* (A fingerspelled loan sign.) The signer fingerspells either "T-T-Y" or "T-D-D."

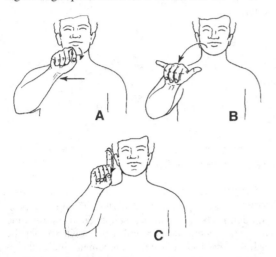

TUBA (tōō′ bə), *n.* (The shape and function.) One hand grasps the mouthpiece and holds it at the pursed lips, while the other hand, in the "5" position, facing out, traces the outline of the instrument and its sweep over the head.

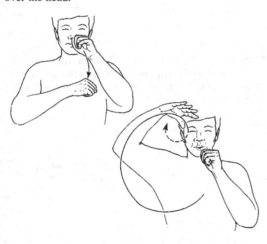

TUNNEL (tun′ l), *n., v.* (Proceeding through a tunnel.) The downturned left "C" hand is the tunnel. The right index finger spirals through.

TURKEY 1 (tûr′ kĭ), *n.* (The wattle shakes.) The "G" hand, palm down, is shaken before the nose or under the chin.

TURKEY 2, *n.* A variation of TURKEY 1. The "9" hand shakes as it moves straight down from the tip of the nose.

TURKEY 3, *n.* (The crescent on the Turkish flag is indicated.) The "C" hand is placed against the upper part of the forehead.

TUTOR (tōō′ tər), *n., v.,* -TORED, -TORING. (The letter "T"; taking knowledge from the mind and giving it to someone.) Both "T" hands, palms facing, are placed at the temples. They move forward and back again several times. Used as a noun, this sign is followed by the sign for INDIVIDUAL 1.

TWICE (twīs), *adv.* (Two fingers are brought up.) The right "V" fingers rest in the open left palm, and are then swung in an arc to an upright position. Also DOU-BLE.

TWINE (twīn), *n., v.,* TWINED, TWINING. (Unraveling a thin string, as indicated by the little fingers.) With palms facing the body, the tips of the extended little fingers touch. As they are drawn slowly apart, they describe very small spirals. Also SPAGHETTI, STRING, THREAD.

TWINS 1 (twinz), *n.* The right "T" hand moves from the left corner of the mouth to the right corner.

TWINS 2, *n.* The thumb edge of the right "T" hand is placed on the left corner of the mouth. It moves away and over to the right corner of the mouth.

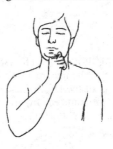

TWO MORE (*colloq.*), *phrase.* (Two fingers beckon.) The right hand is held palm up, with the index and middle fingers making very small and rapid beckoning movements.

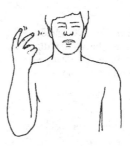

TWO WEEKS, *n. phrase.* ("2"; week.) The base of the right "2" hand is drawn across the upturned left palm from its base to its fingertips. Also WEEK 2.

U

UGLINESS 1 (ŭg′ lĭ nəs), *n.* (The facial features are distorted.) The "X" hands are moved alternately up and down in front of the face, whose features are distorted with a pronounced frown. Also GRIMACE, HOMELY 1, MAKE A FACE, UGLY 1.

UGLINESS 2, *n.* The "X" hands, palms down, move back and forth in a horizontal direction in front of the face, whose features are distorted with a pronounced frown. Also HOMELY 2, UGLY 2.

UGLINESS 3, *n.* The "X" hands, crossed in front of the face, alternately move apart and recross. The facial features are distorted with a pronounced frown. Also UGLY 3.

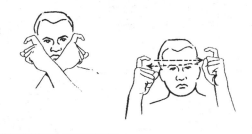

UGLY 1 (ŭg′ lĭ), *adj.* See UGLINESS 1.

UGLY 2, *adj.* See UGLINESS 2.

UGLY 3, *adj.* See UGLINESS 3.

ULTIMATE (ŭl′ tə mĭt), *adj.* (The little, *i.e.,* LAST, fingers are indicated.) With the hands in the "I" position, the tip of the right little finger strikes the tip of its left counterpart. The right index finger may be used instead of the right little finger. Also END 1, EVENTUALLY, FINAL 1, FINALLY 1, LAST 1, ULTIMATELY.

ULTIMATELY, *adv.* See ULTIMATE.

UMBRELLA (ŭm brĕl′ ə), *n.* (The natural sign.) The signer goes through the motions of opening an umbrella.

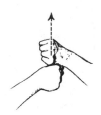

UMPIRE (ŭm′ pīr), *n.* (Judge, individual.) The sign for JUDGE is formed: the two "F" hands, palms facing each other, move alternately up and down. This is followed by the sign for INDIVIDUAL 1: both open hands, palms facing each other, move down the sides of the body, tracing its outline to the hips. Also JUDGE 2, REFEREE.

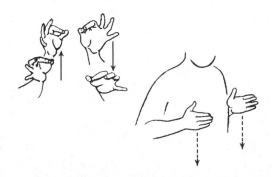

UN-, *prefix*. (Crossing the hands—a negative gesture.) The downturned open hands are crossed at the wrists. They are drawn apart rather quickly. Also NEGATIVE 1, NOT 1.

UNABLE (ŭn a′ bəl), *adj*. (One finger encounters an unyielding quality in striking another.) The right index finger strikes the left and continues moving down. The left index finger remains in place. Also CANNOT, CAN'T, IMPOSSIBLE 1.

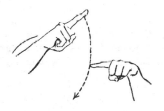

UNCLE (ŭng′ kəl), *n*. (The letter "U"; the "male" or upper portion of the head.) The right "U" hand is held near the right temple and is shaken slightly.

UNCLEAR, *adj*. (One hand obscures the other.) The "5" hands are held up palm against palm in front of the body. The right hand moves in a slow, continuous, clockwise circle over the left palm as the signer tries to see between the fingers. Also BLURRY, VAGUE.

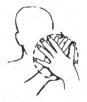

UNCONSCIOUS (un kon′ shəs), *adj*. (The "U" and "C" letters; under the conscious level.) The signer

makes a "U" and then a "C" with the right hand, which is held under the downturned left and moving in a small counterclockwise circle.

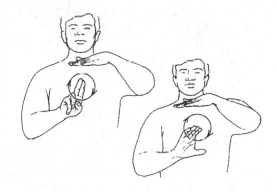

UNDER 1 (ŭn′ dər), *prep*. (Underneath something.) The right hand, in the "A" position, thumb pointing straight up, moves down under the left hand, held outstretched, fingers together, palm down. Also BELOW 2, BENEATH 1, UNDERNEATH.

UNDER 2, *prep*. (The area below.) The right "A" hand, thumb pointing up, moves in a counterclockwise fashion under the downturned left hand. Also BELOW 3, BENEATH 2.

UNDERNEATH (ŭn′ dər nēth′, -nē th), *prep*. See UNDER 1

UNDERSTAND 1 (ŭn′ dər stănd′), *v.,* -STOOD, -STANDING. (An awakening of the mind.) The right "S" hand is placed on the forehead, palm facing the body.

The index finger suddenly flicks up into the "D" position.

UNDERSTAND 2, *v.* (See rationale for UNDERSTAND 1.) The curved index finger of the right hand, palm facing the body, is placed with the fingernail resting on the middle of the forehead. It suddenly flicks up into the "D" position. Also COMPREHEND, UNDERSTANDING, UNDERSTOOD.

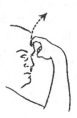

UNDERSTANDING (ŭn′ dər stăn′ dĭng), *n.* See UNDERSTAND 2.

UNDERSTOOD (ŭn′ dər sto͝od′), *v., adj.* See UNDERSTAND 2.

UNDERSTUDY (un′ dər stud′ ē), *n.* (One who is behind another, *i.e.,* backup.) The upturned right thumb is held behind the upturned left thumb. The sign for INDIVIDUAL 1 then follows.

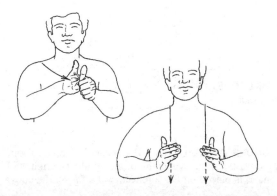

UNDERWEAR 1 (ŭn′ dər wâr′), *n.* (Indicating an undergarment.) Both open hands are held in front of the chest, palms facing the body and fingers pointing to either side, with the right hand nearer the chest and the left held just in front of the right. While the left hand remains stationary in this position, the extended thumb of the right hand rubs downward on the chest a short distance several times.

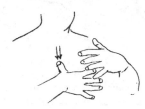

UNDERWEAR 2, *n.* (Pointing to the underclothes.) The right index finger, pointing down, is held on the upper chest near the opening of the collar. It moves down repeatedly an inch or two, returning each time to its original place.

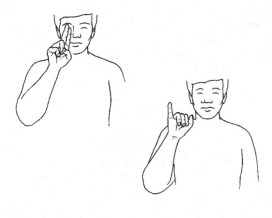

UNEMPLOYMENT INSURANCE (un em ploi′ ment in sho͝or′ əns), *n.* (A fingerspelled loan sign.) The letters "U-I" are fingerspelled.

UNFAIR 1 (ŭn fâr′), *adj.* (NOT, EQUAL.) The sign for the prefix UN- is made: the downturned open hands are crossed at the wrists; they are drawn apart rather quickly. This is followed by the sign for EQUAL: the downturned "B" hands, held at chest height, are brought together repeatedly so that the index finger edges come into contact.

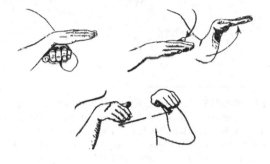

UNFAIR 2, *adj.* (Nicking into one.) The "AND" hands are held one above the other, palms toward the body, the right fingers pointing left, the left fingers pointing right. The upper hand then moves forcefully downward, striking its fingertips across those of the lower hand as it passes by. The "F" hands may also be used. Also UNJUST, UNJUSTIFIED.

UNFAITHFUL (un fāth' fəl), *adj. sl.* (Activity carried on out of view.) The downturned left hand, fingers pointed forward, is held at chest level. The slightly curved right hand, palm facing left, travels across the left fingertips, continuing on to the little finger side of the left hand. The sign is usually made twice. Typical expressions accompanying this sign would be one of guilt, eyes narrowed, or pursed lips.

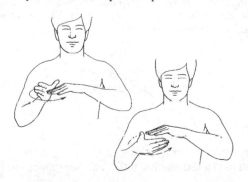

UNFORGIVABLE, *adj.* (NOT, FORGIVE.) The sign for the prefix UN-, as in UNFAIR 1, is made. This is followed by the sign for FORGIVE: the right hand, palm flat, facing down, is brushed over the left hand, held palm flat and facing up. This action may be repeated twice.

UNIFORM (ū' nə fôrm'), *adj.* (Parallel movement.) Both downturned "Y" hands, held a few inches apart, move simultaneously from left to right or toward and away from each other. Also SAME 3, UNIFORMLY.

UNIFORMLY, *adv.* See UNIFORM.

UNION 1 (yōōn' yən), *n.* (Joining together.) Both hands, held in the modified "5" position, palms out, move toward each other. The thumbs and index fingers of both hands then connect. Also AFFILIATE 1, ANNEX, ASSOCIATE 2, ATTACH, BELONG, COMMUNION OF SAINTS, CONCERN 2, CONNECT, ENLIST, ENROLL, JOIN 1, PARTICIPATE, RELATIVE 2, UNITE.

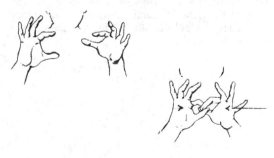

UNION 2, *n.* (The "U" fingers, making a circle to indicate unity.) Both "U" hands, touching, with palms out, move in a circle until they touch again, with palms now facing in.

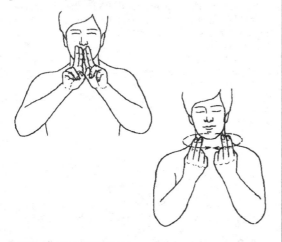

UNITE (ū nīt'), v., UNITED, UNITING. See UNION

UNIVERSAL (ū' nə vûr' səl), adj. (Encompassing; a gathering together.) Both hands are held in the right-angle position, palms facing the body and the right hand in front of the left. The right hand makes a sweeping outward movement around the left and comes to rest with the back of the right hand resting in the left palm. Also ALL, ENTIRE, WHOLE.

UNIVERSE (yōō' nə vûrs), n. (The letter "U"; the planet.) The right "U" hand, palm out, makes a clockwise circle around the left "S" hand, representing a planet.

UNIVERSITY 1 (ū' nə vûr' sə tĭ), n. (The letter "U.") The right "U" hand, palm facing out, rotates in a small clockwise circle.

UNIVERSITY 2, n. (The letter "U"; set up on a solid base; the concept of establishment of an institution.) The right "U" hand, palm facing out, rotates in a clockwise circle, and its base then comes down firmly on the back of the downturned left "S" hand.

UNIVERSITY 3, n. (The letter "U"; a higher school.) The base of the right "U" hand rests in the upturned left palm. It swings to the left a bit and up a few inches, describing an arc. Also COLLEGE, SCHOOL.

UNJUST (ŭn jŭst'), adj. (Nicking into one.) The "AND" hands are held one above the other, palms toward the body, the right fingers pointing left, the left fingers pointing right. The upper hand then moves forcefully downward, striking its fingertips across those of the lower hand as it passes by. The "F" hands may also be used. Also UNFAIR 2, UNJUSTIFIED.

UNJUSTIFIED (ŭn jŭs' tĭ fīd), adj. See UNJUST.

UNLIKE (ŭn līk′), *adj.* (Separated; different.) The "D" hands, palms down, are crossed at the index fingers or are held side by side. They separate once or a number of times. Also ASSORTED, DIFFERENCE, DIFFERENT, DIVERSE 1, DIVERSITY 1, VARIED.

UNSKILLED (ŭn skĭld′) (*colloq.*), adj. (The thickness of the skull is indicated to stress intellectual density.) With the thumb of the right "C" hand grasped by the closed left hand, the right hand is swung in toward the body, describing a small arc as it moves. The space between the curved right fingers and the closed left hand indicates the thickness of the skull. Also CLUMSY 2, DUMB 2, MORON, STUPID 2, THICK-SKULLED.

UNSURE (ŭn shŏŏr′), *adj.* (On a fence; uncertain.) The downturned right "V" hand straddles the index finger edge of the left "B" hand, whose palm faces right. The right hand sways slightly from left to right. Also INDECISION, UNCERTAIN, WAVER 1.

UNTHINKING (un thing′ king), *adj.* (The heart is empty, and therefore devoid of feeling.) The right hand slaps the heart, turns over to palm-up position, and moves sharply down, its fingertips grazing the left palm.

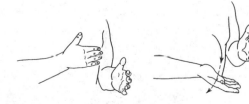

UNTIL (ŭn tĭl′), *prep.* (From one point to the next.) The extended right index finger moves forward slowly and comes to rest on the tip of the extended, upturned left index finger. Also TILL, TO 1, TOWARD 1, UNTO, UP TO, UP TO NOW.

UNTO (ŭn′ tōō), *prep.* See UNTIL.

UPHOLD (ŭp hōld′), *v.,* -HELD, -HOLDING. (Holding up.) The right "S" hand pushes up the left "S" hand. Also ENDORSE 1, FAVOR, INDORSE 1, MAINTENANCE, SUPPORT 1, SUSTAIN, SUSTENANCE, UPLIFT.

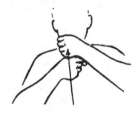

UPSET (up set′), *adj., v.,* UPSET, -SETTING. (The stomach is turned upside down.) The downturned open right hand is positioned horizontally across the stomach. It flips over so that it is now palm up.

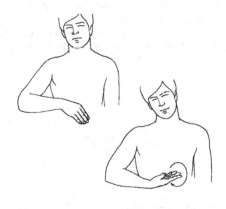

UP TO, *prep. phrase.* (From one point to the next.) The extended right index finger moves forward slowly and comes to rest on the tip of the extended, upturned left index finger. Also TILL, TO 1, TOWARD 1, UNTIL, UNTO, UP TO NOW.

UP TO NOW, *adv. phrase.* See UP TO.

UP TO YOU, *phrase.* (The thought is your own.) The right index finger touches the forehead in the modified THINK sign. Then the right "A" hand, with thumb pointing straight up, moves forward toward the person spoken to. See SELF. Also SUIT YOURSELF.

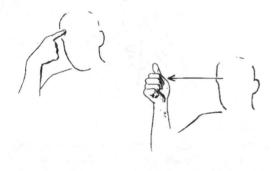

URGE 1 (ûrj), *v.,* URGED, URGING, *n.* (Pushing forward.) Both "5" hands are held, palms out, the right fingers facing right and the left fingers left. The hands move straight forward in a series of short movements. Also ENCOURAGE, MOTIVATE, MOTIVATION.

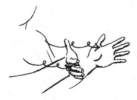

URGE 2, *v.* (Shaking someone to implant one's will into another.) Both "A" hands, palms facing, are held before the chest, the left slightly in front of the right. In this position the hands move back and forth a short

distance. Also COAX, CONVINCE, INDUCE, PERSUADE, PERSUASION, PROD.

URINATE 1 (yŏŏr′ ə nāt), *v.,* -NATED, -NATING. The right index finger, held pointing forward at the groin area, shakes up and down. Used for the male only.

URINATE 2, *v.* (The letter "P," for "pee.") The middle finger of the right "P" hand brushes off the tip of the nose. Also PENIS 2, URINATION.

URINATION (yŏŏr′ ə nā shən), *n.* See URINATE 2.

US (ŭs), *pron.* (The letter "U"; an encompassing gesture.) The right "U" hand, palm facing the body, swings from right shoulder to left shoulder.

USE (ūs), *n.* (ūz), *v.,* USED, USING. (The letter "U.") The right "U" hand describes a small clockwise circle. Also CONSUME 2, USED, USEFUL, UTILIZE, WEAR 2.

USED (ūzd), *v.* See USE.

USEFUL (ūs′ fəl), *adj.* See USE.

USE UP (yōōz up), *v. phrase.* (Pull something off the hand.) The right "C" hand, palm facing left, is placed on the upturned left hand. The right hand, moving right, quickly leaves the left while closing into a fist.

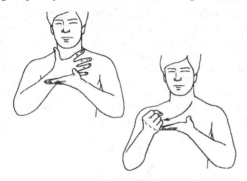

USHER (ŭsh′ ər), *v.,* -ERED, -ERING. (Opening or leading the way toward something.) The open right hand, held up before the body, sweeps down in an arc and over toward the left side of the chest, ending in the palm-up position. Reversing the movement gives the passive form of the verb, except that the hand does not arc upward but rather simply moves outward in a

small arc from the body. Also ADMIT 2, INVITATION, INVITE, INVITED, WELCOME.

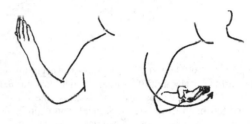

US TWO, *phrase.* (Two people interacting.) The right "V" hand, palm up and fingers pointing left, is swung in and out to and from the chest. Also BOTH OF US, WE TWO.

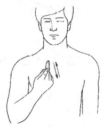

UTILIZE (ū′ tə līz′), *v.,* -LIZED, -LIZING. See USE.

UZI (ew zē), *n.* (A machine gun held in one hand.) The signer, holding an imaginary small machine gun in one hand, takes aim, and the arm and body shake repeatedly from the weapon's recoil.

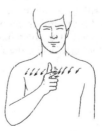

V

VACANCY (vā′ kən sĭ), *n.* (Devoid of everything on the surface.) The middle finger of the downturned right "5" hand sweeps over the back of the downturned left hand from wrist to knuckles and continues beyond a bit. Also BARE 2, EMPTY 2, NAKED, NUDE, OMISSION 2, VACANT, VOID.

VACANT (vā′ kənt), *adj.* See VACANCY.

VACATION (vā kā′ shən), *n.* (A position of idleness.) With thumbs tucked in the armpits, the remaining fingers of both hands wiggle. Also HOLIDAY, IDLE, LEISURE, RETIRE 3.

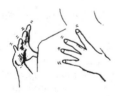

VACUUM CLEANER (vak′ yо̄о̄m), *n.* (Sucking up the dirt.) The extended right fingers are positioned above the upturned left palm. The right fingers move back and forth across the palm while the fingers open and close very rapidly.

VAGUE (vāg), *adj.* (One hand obscures the other.) The "5" hands are held up, palm against palm in front of the body. The right hand moves in a slow, continuous clockwise circle over the left palm as the signer tries to see between the fingers. Also BLURRY, UNCLEAR.

VALID (văl′ ĭd), *adj.* (Coming forth directly from the lips; true.) The index finger of the right "D" hand, palm facing left, is placed against the lips. It moves up an inch or two and then describes a small arc forward and away from the lips. Also ABSOLUTE, ABSOLUTELY, ACTUAL, ACTUALLY, AUTHENTIC, CERTAIN, CERTAINLY, FAITHFUL 3, FIDELITY, FRANKLY, GENUINE, INDEED, POSITIVE 1, POSITIVELY, REAL, REALLY, SINCERE 2, SURE, SURELY, TRUE, TRULY, TRUTH, VERILY.

VALISE (və lēs′), *n.* (The natural sign.) The downturned right "S" hand grasps an imaginary piece of luggage and shakes it up and down slightly, as if testing its weight. Also BAGGAGE, LUGGAGE, SUITCASE.

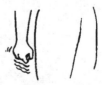

VALUABLE (văl′ yōō ə bəl, văl′ yə bəl), *adj.* Both "I" hands, palms facing each other, move apart, up, and together in a smooth, elliptical fashion, coming together at the tips of the thumbs and index fingers of both hands. Also DESERVE, ESSENTIAL, IMPORTANT 1, MAIN, MERIT, PRECIOUS, PROMINENT 2, SIGNIFICANCE 1, SIGNIFICANT, VALUE, VITAL 1, WORTH, WORTHWHILE, WORTHY.

VALUE (văl′ ū), *n.* See VALUABLE.

VAMPIRE (vam′ pīr), *n.* (Biting the neck.) The right curved thumb plus index and middle fingers make a bite at the right side of the neck.

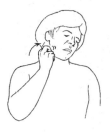

VANILLA (və nil′ ə), *adj.* (The letter "V.") The outstretched right "V" is shaken slightly.

VANISH (văn′ ĭsh), *v.,* -ISHED, -ISHING. (A disappearance.) The right open hand, palm facing the body, is held by the left hand and is drawn down and out, ending in a position with fingers drawn together. The left hand, meanwhile, may close into a position with fingers also drawn together. Also ABSENCE 1, ABSENT 1,

DEPLETE, DISAPPEAR, EMPTY 1, EXTINCT, FADE AWAY, GONE 1, MISSING 1, OMISSION 1, OUT 3, OUT OF.

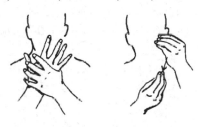

VANITY (văn′ ə tĭ), *n.* (All eyes on oneself.) The "V" hands, held on either side of the face with palms facing the body, swing back and forth simultaneously, pivoting at the wrists. Also VAIN, VAINLY.

VARIED (vâr′ ēd), *adj.* (Separated many times; different.) The "D" hands, palms down, are crossed at the index fingers or are held side by side. They separate and return to their initial position a number of times. Also ASSORTED, DIFFERENCE, DIFFERENT, DIVERSE 1, DIVERSITY 1, UNLIKE.

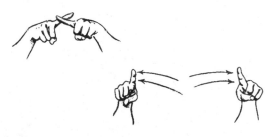

VARIOUS (vâr′ ĭ əs), *adj.* (The fingertips indicate many things.) Both hands, in the "D" position, palms out and index fingertips touching, are drawn apart. As they move apart, the index fingers wiggle up and down. Also DIFFERENT OBJECTS, DIVERSE 2, DIVERSITY 2, VARY.

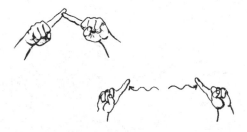

VARY (vâr′ ĭ), *v.*, VARIED, VARYING. See VARIOUS.

VCR, *n.* (A fingerspelled loan sign.) The signer fingerspells "V-C-R."

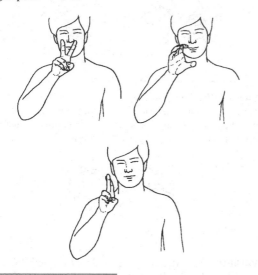

VEGETABLE (vej′ tə bəl, vej′ i tə-), *n.* (The "V"; chewing.) The index finger of the right hand, facing out, is placed against the right cheek and is twisted slightly.

VEND (vĕnd), *v.*, VENDED, VENDING. (Transferring ownership of an object.) Both "AND" hands, fingers touching their respective thumbs, are held palms down before the body. The hands are pivoted simultaneously outward and away from the body once or several times. Also SALE, SELL.

VENDER (vĕn′ dər), *n.* (Transferring ownership.) The sign for VEND is formed. The sign for INDIVIDUAL 1 is then made: both open hands, palms facing each other, move down the sides of the body, tracing its outline to the hips. Also MERCHANT, SALESMAN, SELLER.

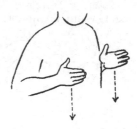

VENETIAN BLINDS, *n.* (The slats.) Both hands, palms down at chest level, are positioned with the right above the left, left fingers pointing right and right fingers pointing left. They both move down while each wrist swivels back and forth, imitating the opening and closing of the blinds.

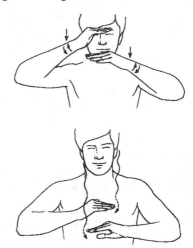

VERB (vûrb), *n.* (The letter "V.") The right "V" hand, palm facing the body and fingers pointing left, moves across the mouth from left to right.

VERBAL 1 (vûr′ bəl), *adj.* (Words tumbling from the mouth.) The right index finger, pointing left, describes a continuous small circle in front of the mouth. Also BID 3, DISCOURSE, HEARING, MAINTAIN 2, MENTION, REMARK, SAID, SAY, SPEAK, SPEECH 1, STATE, STATEMENT, TALK 1, TELL.

VERBAL 2, *adj.* (A small part of a sentence, *i.e.*, a word.) The tips of the right index finger and thumb, about an inch apart, are placed on the side of the outstretched left index finger, which represents the length of a sentence. Also INCH 1, WORD.

VERDICT (vûr′ dĭkt), *n.* (The mind stops wavering, and the pros and cons are resolved.) The right index finger touches the forehead, the sign for THINK, *q.v.* Both "F" hands, palms facing each other and fingers pointing straight out, then drop down simultaneously. The sign for JUDGE, *q.v.*, explains the rationale behind the movement of the two hands here. Also DECIDE, DECISION, DECREE 1, DETERMINE, MAKE UP ONE'S MIND, MIND 5, RENDER JUDGMENT, RESOLVE.

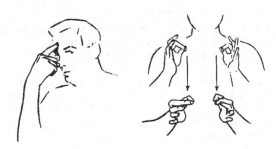

VERILY (vĕr′ ə lĭ), *adv.* (Coming forth directly from the lips; true.) The index finger of the right "D" hand, palm facing left, is placed against the lips. It moves up an inch or two and then describes a small arc forward and away from the lips. Also ABSOLUTE, ABSOLUTELY, ACTUAL, ACTUALLY, AUTHENTIC, CERTAIN, CERTAINLY, FAITHFUL 3, FIDELITY, FRANKLY, GENUINE, INDEED, POSI-

TIVE 1, POSITIVELY, REAL, REALLY, SINCERE 2, SURE, SURELY, TRUE, TRULY, TRUTH, VALID.

VERSUS (vûr′ səs), *prep.* (Two individuals pitted against each other.) The hands are held in the "A" position, thumbs pointing straight up, palms facing the body. They come together forcefully, moving down a bit as they do, and the knuckles of one hand strike those of the other. Also CHALLENGE, GAME 1, OPPORTUNITY 2.

VERTICAL (vûr′ ti kəl), *adj.* (The upright or vertical position.) The outstretched right hand, palm facing left, moves straight up and down. Alternately, the "V" hand moves straight up, either independently or from an initial position on the upturned left palm.

VERY (vĕr′ ĭ), *adv.* (The "V" hands, with the sign for MUCH.) The fingertips of the "V" hands are placed together and then moved apart.

VETERINARIAN (vet′ ər ə när′ ē ən), *n.* (A finger-spelled loan sign.) The signer spells out "V-E-T" with the fingers.

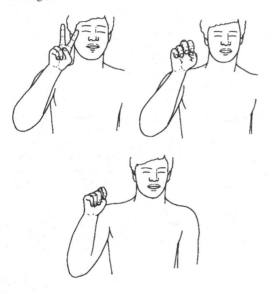

VICINITY (vĭ sin′ ə tē), *n.* (One hand is near the other.) The left hand, cupped, fingers together, is held before the chest, palm facing the body. The right hand, also cupped, fingers together, moves a very short distance back and forth as it is held in front of the left. Also ADJACENT, BESIDE, BY 1, CLOSE (TO) 2, NEAR 1, NEIGHBOR, NEIGHBORHOOD.

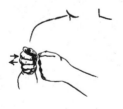

VICTORY 1 (vĭk′ tə rē), *n.* (Waving of flags.) Both upright hands, grasping imaginary flags, wave them in small circles. Also CELEBRATE, CELEBRATION, CHEER, REJOICE, WIN 1.

VICTORY 2, *n.* (Waving a flag.) The right "A" hand goes through the natural movement of waving a flag in circular fashion. Preceding this, the right hand may go through the motion of grabbing the flagstaff out of the left hand. Also EXULTATION, TRIUMPH 1, WIN 2.

VIDEOTAPE (vid′ ē ō tāp), *n., v.,* -TAPED, -TAPING. (The turning of the tape.) The left hand is held open, palm facing right. The right "V" hand makes a circle around the left palm, ending in the letter "T" and resting on the palm.

VIE 1 (vī), *v.,* VIED, VYING. (Two opponents come together.) Both hands are closed, with thumbs pointing straight up and palms facing the body. From their initial position about a foot apart, the hands are brought together sharply so that the knuckles strike. The hands, as they are drawn together, also move down a bit so that they describe a "V." Also COMPETE 1, COMPETITION 1, CONTEND 1, CONTEST 1, RACE 1, RIVAL 2, RIVALRY 1.

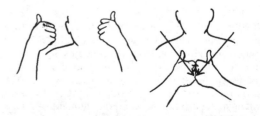

VIE 2, *v.* (Opposing objects.) The "A" hands are held side by side before the chest, palms facing each other and thumbs pointing forward. In this position the hands move alternately back and forth, toward and away from the body. Also COMPETE 2, COMPETITION 2, CONTEND 2, CONTEST 2, RACE 2, RIVAL 3, RIVALRY 2.

VIE 3, *v.* (The changing fortunes of competitors.) The "A" hands are held facing each other, thumbs pointing up in front of the body. Both hands are moved alternately backward and forward past each other several times. Also COMPETE 3, COMPETITION 3, CONTEND 3, CONTEST 3, RACE 3, RIVAL 4, RIVALRY 3.

VIEW (vū), *n., v.,* VIEWED, VIEWING. (Look around.) The sign for LOOK is made: the right "V" hand, palm facing the body, is placed so that the fingertips are just under the eyes. Then both "V" hands are held with palms down and fingers pointing forward in front of the body. In this position the hands move simultaneously from side to side several times. Also VISION 1.

VIOLATE (vī′ ə lāt′), *v.,* -LATED, -LATING. (An encroachment; parrying a knife thrust.) The left "A" hand is held palm toward the body, knuckles facing

right. The extended thumb of the right "A" hand is brought sharply over the back of the left. Also DANGER 2, DANGEROUS 2, INJURE 2, PERIL, TRESPASS.

VIRGIN 1 (vûr′ jin), *n.* The fingers of the right "V" hand are placed at the right corner of the mouth.

VIRGIN 2, *n., adj.* (One who has never had intercourse.) The sign for NEVER: the outstretched hand moves down in an "S" curve. This is followed by INTERCOURSE: both "V" hands are held palms facing, with the right above the left. The right hand comes down on the left repeatedly.

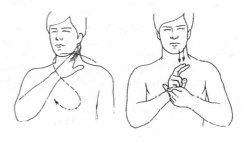

VIRGIN 3, *sl., n., adj.* (CHERRY, an extended slang term for hymen.) The sign for CHERRY is made: the fingertips of the right hand grasp the end of the left little finger and twist back and forth as if loosening a cherry from a branch. Also BERRY, CHERRY.

VIRTUAL (vûr′ chŏŏ əl), *adj. Computer term.* The index finger of the right "V" hand rests on the right temple. The hand moves forward and slightly up in a small spiral.

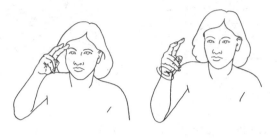

VISION 1 (vĭzh′ ən), *n.* (Look around.) The sign for LOOK is made: the right "V" hand, palm facing the body, is placed so that the fingertips are just under the eyes. Then both "V" hands are held with palms down and fingers pointing forward in front of the body. In this position the hands move simultaneously from side to side several times. Also VIEW.

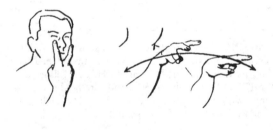

VISION 2, *n.* (The vision is directed forward into the distance.) The right "V" fingertips are placed under the eyes, with palm facing the body. The hand is then swung around and forward, moving under the down-turned prone left hand and continuing forward and upward. Also FORECAST, FORESEE, FORETELL, PERCEIVE 2, PREDICT, PROPHECY, PROPHESY, PROPHET.

VISION 3, *n.* (A sudden opening of the mind.) The sign for DREAM is made: the tip of the right index is

placed on the forehead. Then both "S" hands are held in front of the forehead, the left in front of the right. They open into the "C" position as the hands separate. The sign for DREAM may be omitted.

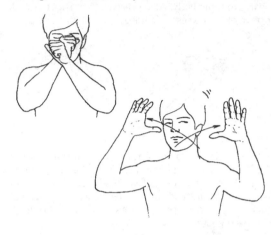

VISIT (vĭz′ ĭt), *n., v.,* -ITED, -ITING. (The letter "V"; random movement, *i.e.,* moving around as in visiting.) The "V" hands, palms facing, move alternately in clockwise circles out from the chest.

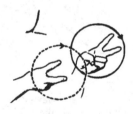

VISUAL AID (vizh′ ŏŏ əl ād′), *n.* (To see and to help.) The index and middle fingers of the right hand, palm facing the body, move away from the eyes. The left upturned open hand then pushes up the right fist.

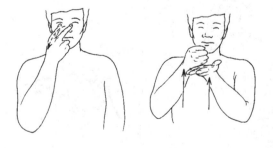

VITAL 1 (vī′ təl), *adj.* Both "F" hands, palms facing each other, move apart, up, and together in a smooth elliptical fashion, coming together at the tips of the thumbs and index fingers of both hands. Also DESERVE, ESSENTIAL, IMPORTANT 1, MAIN, MERIT, PRECIOUS, PROMINENT 2, SIGNIFICANCE 1, SIGNIFICANT, VALUABLE, VALUE, WORTH, WORTHWHILE, WORTHY.

VITAL 2, *adj.* (Being pinned down.) The right hand, in the "X" position, palm down, moves forcefully up and down once or twice. An expression of determination is frequently assumed. Also HAVE TO, IMPERATIVE, MUST, NECESSARY 1, NECESSITY, NEED 1, OUGHT TO, SHOULD.

VOCATION (vō kā′ shən), *n.* (Striking an anvil.) Both "S" hands are held palms down. The right hand strikes against the back of the left a number of times. Also JOB, LABOR, OCCUPATION, TASK, TOIL, TRAVAIL, WORK.

VOID (void), *adj., n.* (Devoid of everything on the surface.) The middle finger of the downturned right "5" hand sweeps over the back of the downturned left "A" or "S" hand from wrist to knuckles and continues beyond a bit. Also BARE 2, EMPTY 2, NAKED, NUDE, OMISSION 2, VACANCY, VACANT.

VOLCANO *n.* (The shape and the eruption.) Both "V" hands move up, coming together to form a peak. The hands are then closed and opened explosively, describing the eruption.

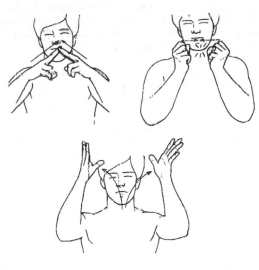

VOLUME 1 (vŏl′ ūm, -yəm), *n.* (Opening a book.) The open hands are held together, fingers pointing away from the body. They open with little fingers remaining in contact, as in the opening of a book. Also BOOK, TEXTBOOK.

VOLUME 2, *n.* (The "V" letters; an area is indicated.) Both upturned "V" hands, palms facing out, move forward, executing a circle, so that they now face the signer.

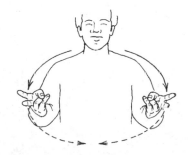

VOLUNTEER (vŏl′ ən tĭr′), *n., v.,* -TEERED, -TEERING. (Bringing oneself forward.) The right index finger and thumb grasp the clothing near the right shoulder (often the lapel of a suit or the collar of a dress) and tug it up and down gently several times. Sometimes one tug only is used. Also APPLY 1, CANDIDATE, OFFER 2, RUN FOR OFFICE.

VOW (vou), *v.,* VOWED, VOWING. (The arm is raised.) The right index finger is placed at the lips. The right arm is then raised, palm out and elbow resting on the back of the left hand. Also GUARANTEE 1, LOYAL, OATH, PLEDGE, PROMISE 1, SWEAR 1, SWORN, TAKE OATH.

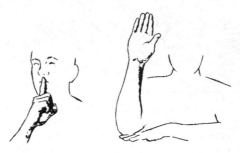

W

WAFFLE (wof′ əl), *n.* (The grid pattern.) Both hands face each other, fingertips forward and interlocked, right above left. The right hand moves down and back up a number of times, representing the cover of the waffle grill.

WAGE(S) (wāj), *n.* (Gathering in.) The right "5" hand, its little finger edge touching the upturned left palm, is drawn in an arc toward the body, closing into the "S" position as it sweeps over the base of the left hand. Also ACCUMULATE 1, COLLECT, EARN, SALARY.

WAGON 1 (wăg′ ən), *n.* (The wheels.) With index fingers facing each other and arms held quite close to the chest, the hands describe small continuous clockwise circles. The arms then extend forward a few inches, and the hands repeat their earlier movement.

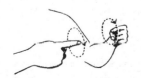 

WAGON 2, *n.* (Miming.) The signer pulls an imaginary wagon with both hands.

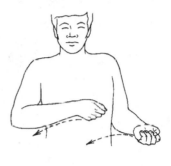

WAIT (wāt), *n., v.,* WAITED, WAITING. (The fingers wiggle with impatience.) The upturned "5" hands are positioned with the right behind the left. The fingers of both hands wiggle. Also PENDING.

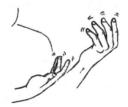

WAITER 1 (wā′ tər), *n.* (An individual who waits on someone.) The sign for WAITER 2 is made. This is followed by the sign for INDIVIDUAL 1: both open hands, palms facing each other, move down the sides of the body, tracing its outline to the hips. Also WAITRESS 1.

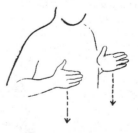

WAITER 2, *n.* (Passing the dishes one by one.) The upturned "5" hands move alternately toward and away from the chest. Also MAID, SERVANT, SERVE 2, SERVICE, WAIT ON 2, WAITRESS 2.

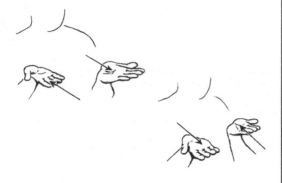

WAITRESS 1 (wā′ trĭs), *n.* See WAITER 1.

WAITRESS 2, *n.* See WAITER 2.

WAIVE (wāv), *v.*, WAIVED, WAIVING. (A wiped-off and clean slate.) The right hand wipes off the left palm several times.

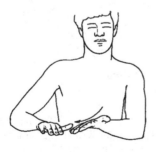

WAKE UP (wāk), *v. phrase.* (Opening the eyes.) Both hands are closed, with thumb and index finger of each hand held together, extended, and placed at the corners of the closed eyes. Slowly, they separate, and the eyes open. Also AROUSE, AWAKE, AWAKEN.

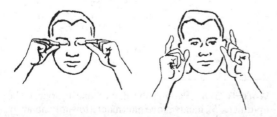

WALK (wôk), *n., v.,* WALKED, WALKING. (The movement of the feet.) The downturned "5" hands move alternately toward and away from the chest. Also PACE, STEP 1.

WALKIE-TALKIE (wô′ kē tô′ kē), *n.* (The shape at the ear.) The "Y" hand is held thumb against mouth, and then it moves up so that the thumb is against the ear. The movement is repeated.

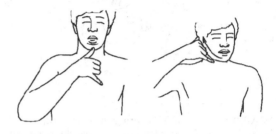

WALK TO, *v. phrase.* (The fingers do the walking.) The downturned index and middle fingers of either hand execute forward walking movement.

WALLET 1 (wol′ it), *n.* (Folding the wallet.) The two hands held with fingertips touching are brought together palm to palm and move flat against each other as if closing a wallet. This is a generic sign.

WALLET 2, *n.* (Placing the bills in.) The little finger edge of the open right hand, palm facing the body, is slipped into the space created by the thumb and other fingers of the left hand. The signer then mimes placing the wallet into a pocket. Also BILLFOLD 1.

WANDER 1 (wŏn′ dər), *v.*, -DERED, -DERING. (The natural motion.) The "G" hands are held side by side and touching, palms down, index fingers pointing forward. Then the right hand moves forward, curving toward the right side as it does. Also DEFLECT, DEVIATE 2, GO OFF THE TRACK, STRAY.

WANDER 2, *v.* (Random movement.) The right "D" hand, palm facing left, moves to and fro from right to left. Also ROAM.

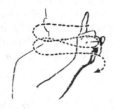

WANT (wŏnt, wônt), *v.*, WANTED, WANTING. (Grasping something and pulling it in.) The upturned "5" hands,

held side by side before the chest, close slightly into a grasping position as they move in toward the body. Also COVET 1, DESIRE 1, LONG 2, NEED 2, WILL 2, WISH 1.

WAR (wôr), *n.*, *v.*, WARRED, WARRING. (The contending armies.) The "4," "W," or "5" hands face each other and move simultaneously from side to side, representing the successive advance and retreat of contending armed forces. Also WAGE WAR.

WARM 1 (wôrm), *adj.*, *v.*, WARMED, WARMING. (The warmth of the breath is indicated.) The upturned cupped right hand is placed at the slightly open mouth. It moves up and away from the mouth, opening into the upturned "5" position, with fingers somewhat curved. Also HEAT 1.

WARM 2, *adj.* (Wiping off perspiration.) The extended, bent, right index finger is drawn across the forehead from left to right.

WARN (wôrn), *v.,* WARNED, WARNING. (Tapping one to draw attention to danger.) The right hand taps the back of the left several times. Also ADMONISH 1, CAUTION, FOREWARN.

WAS (wŏz, wŭz; *unstressed* wəz), *v.* (Something past, behind.) The upraised right hand, in the "5" position with palm facing the body, is held just above the right shoulder and is thrown back over it. Also AGO, FORMERLY, ONCE UPON A TIME, PAST, PREVIOUS, PREVIOUSLY, WERE.

WASH 1 (wŏsh, wôsh), *n., v.,* WASHED, WASHING. (Rubbing the clothes.) The knuckles of the "A" hands rub against one another in circles. Also CLEAN 2.

WASH 2, *v.* (The natural sign.) The signer goes through the motions of wiping his face with a towel. Also TOWEL.

WASH 3, *v.* (The natural sign.) The closed hands move up and down against the chest as if scrubbing it. Also BATH, BATHE.

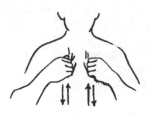

WASH DISHES, *v. phrase.* (The natural sign.) The downturned right "5" hand describes a clockwise circle as it moves over the upturned left "5" hand. Also DISHWASHING.

WASHING MACHINE, *n.* (The clothes are tumbled around.) The cupped, open hands, palms facing and one above the other, execute opposing circular movements.

WASTE 1 (wāst), *n., v.,* WASTED, WASTING. (Repeated giving forth.) The back of the upturned right hand, thumb touching fingertips, is placed in the upturned left palm. The right hand moves off and away from the left once or several times, each time opening into the "5" position, palm up. Also EXTRAVAGANT, SPEND, SQUANDER.

WASTE 2, *n., v.* (The "W" is indicated.) The same movement as in WASTE 1 is used, except that the right hand assumes the "W" position and keeps it.

WATCH 1 (wŏch), *v.,* WATCHED, WATCHING. (Careful, constant vision.) The downturned, left "V" hand sweeps back and forth from side to side beneath the downturned, right "V" hand, which remains stationary and pointing forward.

WATCH 2, *n., v.* (The eyesight is directed forward.) The right "V" hand, palm facing the body, is placed so that the fingertips are just under the eyes. The hand swings around and out so that the fingertips are now pointing forward. Also LOOK 1, PERCEIVE 1, PERCEPTION, SEE, SIGHT.

WATCH 3, *n.* (Time by the clock, indicated by the ticking of the clock or watch.) The curved right index finger taps the back of the left wrist several times. Also CLOCK, TIME 1.

WATCH 4, *n.* (The shape of the wristwatch.) The thumb and index finger of the right hand, forming a circle, are placed on the back of the left wrist. Also WRISTWATCH.

WATER 1 (wô′ tər, wŏt′ ər), *n.* (The letter "W" at the mouth, as in drinking water.) The right "W" hand, palm facing left, touches the lips a number of times.

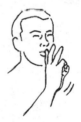

WATER 2, *n.* (The letter "W.") The right "W" hand, palm facing out, is shaken slightly, as in the rippling of water. This sign is used as a prefix for different bodies of water. Also LIQUID.

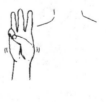

WAVER 1 (wā′ vər), *v.,* -VERED, -VERING. (On a fence; uncertain.) The downturned right "V" hand straddles the index finger edge of the left "B" hand, whose palm faces right. The right hand sways slightly back and forth, from left to right.

WAVER 2, *v.* (The wavering.) The downturned "S" hands swing alternately up and down. Also DISBELIEF 2, DOUBT 2, DOUBTFUL.

WAY 1 (wā), *n.* (The winding movement.) Both hands, palms facing and fingers together and extended straight out, move in unison away from the body in a winding manner. Also CORRIDOR, HALL, HALLWAY, MANNER 2, METHOD, OPPORTUNITY 3, PATH, ROAD, STREET, TRAIL.

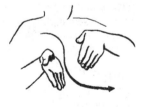

WAY 2, *n.* (The letter "W.") The sign for WAY 1 is made, but with the "W" hands.

WE 1 (wē; *unstressed* wĭ), *pron.* (An encompassing movement.) The right index finger points down as it swings over from the right shoulder to the left shoulder.

WE 2, *pron.* (The letter "W.") The right "W" hand, fingers pointing up, goes through the same motion as in WE 1.

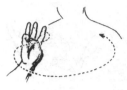

WEAK (wēk), *adj.* (The knees buckle.) The right "V" hand is placed with fingertips resting in the upturned left palm. The knuckles of the "V" fingers buckle a bit. This motion may be repeated. Also FAINT 1, FEEBLE, FRAIL, WEAKNESS.

WEAKNESS (wēk′ nĭs), *n.* See WEAK.

WEALTH (wĕlth), *n.* (A pile of money.) The sign for MONEY is made: the back of the upturned right hand, whose thumb and fingertips are all touching, is placed in the upturned left palm. The right hand then moves straight up as it opens into the "5" position, palm facing down and fingers somewhat curved. Also RICH, WEALTHY.

WEALTHY (wĕl′ thĭ), *adj.* See WEALTH.

WEAR 1 (wâr), *n., v.,* WORE, WORN, WEARING. (Draping the clothes on the body.) With fingertips resting on the chest, both hands move down simulta-

neously. The action is repeated. Also CLOTHES, CLOTH-
ING, DRESS, FROCK, GARMENT, GOWN, SHIRT, SUIT.

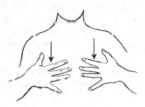

WEAR 2, *v.* (To use; the letter "U.") The right "U"
hand describes a small clockwise circle. Also CON-
SUME 2, USE, USED, USEFUL, UTILIZE.

WEATHER (weth′ ər), *n.* (The letter "W.") The right
"W" hand, palm out, moves straight down before the
body, trembling slightly as it does.

WEDDING (wĕd′ ĭng), *n.* (A joining of hands.) The
downturned "B" hands are joined together with a
flourish.

WEEK 1 (wēk), *n.* (Seven fingers, *i.e.,* days, are
brought together.) The downturned right "L" hand is
placed on the upturned left "5" hand, near the base. The

right hand moves forward toward the left fingertips, and
the left hand begins to close so that, in the final position, the fingertips of the left hand are closed and touching the tips of the right thumb and index finger.

WEEK 2 (*vern.*), *n.* (A modification of WEEK 1.) The
upright, right "D" hand is placed palm to palm against
the left "5" hand, whose palm faces right. The right
"D" hand moves along the left palm from base to fingertips. Also NEXT WEEK 2.

WEEP 1 (wēp), *v.,* WEPT, WEEPING. (Tears streaming
down the cheeks.) Both index fingers, in the "D" position, move down the cheeks, either once or several
times. Sometimes one finger only is used. Also BAWL
1, CRY 1, TEAR 2, TEARDROP.

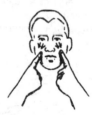

WEEP 2, *v.* (Tears gushing from the eyes.) Both "B"
hands are held before the face, palms facing forward,
with the backs of the index fingertips touching the
face just below the eyes. From this position both
hands move forward and over in an arc to indicate a
flow of tears. Also BAWL 2, CRY 2.

WEIGH 1 (wā), *v.*, WEIGHED, WEIGHING. (The balancing of the scale is described.) The fingers of the right "H" hand are centered on the left index finger or "H" hand and rocked back and forth. Also POUND 1, SCALE 2, WEIGHT.

WEIGH 2, *v.* (Turning thoughts over in the mind.) Both index fingers, pointing to the forehead, describe continuous alternating circles. Also CONSIDER 2, CONTEMPLATE, PONDER, SPECULATE 2, SPECULATION 2, WONDER 1.

WEIGHT (wāt), *n.* See WEIGH 1.

WEIGHTY (wā′ tǐ), *adj.* (The hands drop under a weight.) The upturned "5" hands, held before the chest, suddenly drop a short distance. Also CRUSHING, HEAVY.

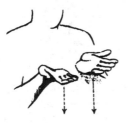

WEIRD (wǐrd), *adj.* (Something that distorts the vision.) The "C" hand describes a small arc in front of the face. Also CURIOUS 2, GROTESQUE, ODD, PECULIAR, QUEER 1, STRANGE 1.

WELCOME (wěl′ kəm), *n.*, *v.*, -COMED, -COMING. (Opening or leading the way toward something.) The open right hand, held up before the body, sweeps down in an arc and over toward the left side of the chest, ending in the palm-up position. Reversing the movement gives the passive form of the verb, except that the hand does not arc upward but rather simply moves outward in a small arc from the body. Also ADMIT 2, INVITATION, INVITE, INVITED, USHER.

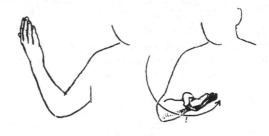

WELL 1 (wěl), *adv.* (Tasting something, approving it, and offering it forward.) The fingertips of the right "5" hand are placed at the lips. The right hand then moves out and into a palm-up position on the upturned left palm. Also GOOD 1.

WELL 2, *adj.* (Strength emanating from the body.) Both "5" hands are placed palms against the chest. They move out and away forcefully, closing and assuming the "S" position. Also BRAVE, BRAVERY, COURAGE, COURAGEOUS, FORTITUDE, HALE, HEALTH, HEALTHY, MIGHTY 2, STRENGTH, STRONG 2.

WELL 3, *n.* (Water in a hole.) The sign for WATER 1 or WATER 2, *q.v.*, is made. Then the right index finger, pointing down, traces a clockwise circle in the air, after which it drops straight down a few inches into the left "C" hand, whose palm faces right.

WELL 4, *interj.* (The natural sign, accompanied by a sigh.) With palms facing up, the signer heaves a distinct sigh, causing the shoulders to rise slightly. Also SO.

WE'LL SEE, *phrase.* (Modified from the sign for SEE.) The index finger of the right "V" hand, palm facing left, is placed at the corner of the right eye. The hand makes several very small back-and-forth movements. This is often accompanied by a very slight nodding.

WERE (wûr, *unstressed* wər), *v.* (Something past, behind.) The upraised right hand, in the "5" position with palm facing the body, is held just above the right shoulder and is thrown back over it. Also AGO, FOR-

MERLY, ONCE UPON A TIME, PAST, PREVIOUS, PREVIOUSLY, WAS.

WET (wĕt), *adj., n., v.,* WET or WETTED, WETTING. (The wetness.) The right fingertips touch the lips, and then the fingers of both hands open and close against the thumbs a number of times. Also CERAMICS, CLAY, DAMP, MOIST.

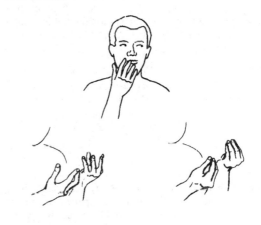

WE TWO, *phrase.* (Two people interacting.) The right "V" hand, palm up and fingers pointing left, is swung in and out to and from the chest. Also BOTH OF US, US TWO.

WHALE 1 (hwāl), *n.* (The blowhole.) The right hand, in the AND position, fingers pointing up, is placed on top of the head. It moves up off the head and opens into the "5" position, representing the whale blowing out through the blowhole.

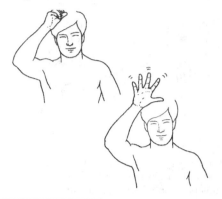

WHALE 2, *n.* (The letter "W"; the movement.) The right "W" hand makes a series of undulating dive movements in front of the downturned left arm, which represents the surface of the water.

W-H-A-T? (*colloq.*), *interj.* (A fingerspelled loan sign.) The letters "W-H-A-T" are spelled out rather slowly, but with force and deliberation, while the signer assumes a look of incredulity. This is the equivalent of a shouted interjection.

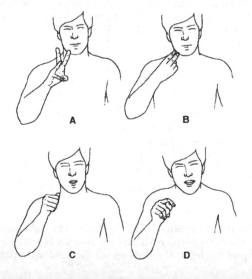

A   B

C   D

WHAT 1 (hwŏt, hwŭt; *unstressed* hwət), *pron., adj., adv., interj., conj.* (The finger passes over several specifics to bring out the concept of "which one?") The right index finger passes over the fingers of the upturned left "5" hand, from index to little finger.

WHAT 2, *pron., adj., adv., interj., conj.* (Throwing out the hands as a gesture of inquiry.) Both upturned open hands move slightly back and forth in front of the chest. The signer assumes a look of wonderment, emphasized by slightly upturned shoulders, raised eyebrows, or furrowed brow.

WHAT FOR? (*colloq.*), *phrase.* (For—For—For?) The sign for FOR is made repeatedly: the right index finger, resting on the right temple, leaves its position and moves straight out in front of the face. The sign is usually accompanied by an expression of inquiry, or annoyance.

WHAT IS THE PRICE? (Amount of money is indicated.) The sign for MONEY is made: the upturned right hand, grasping some imaginary bills, is brought down into the upturned left palm a number of times. The right hand then moves straight up, opening into the "5" position, palm up. Also HOW MUCH MONEY?, PRICE 1.

WHAT'S NEW? (The feelings well up and come out.) The open hands are placed near the chest, with middle fingers resting on the chest. Both hands move up and out simultaneously. A happy expression is assumed. Also THRILL 2, WHAT'S UP? HOW ARE YOU?

WHAT'S UP? See WHAT'S NEW?

WHAT TO DO? (*colloq.*), *phrase.* (Do—Do—Do?) This is a modified fingerspelled loan sign. The signer makes palm-up "D"s with both hands. These quickly assume the "O" position, with the palms remaining up. This is repeated several times, quickly, with an expression of despair or inquiry.

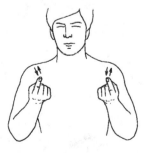

WHEELBARROW (hwēl′ bar′ ō), *n.* (Holding the handles and moving forward.) Grasping an imaginary pair

of handles and lifting with effort, the signer moves slightly forward. Also PUSHCART.

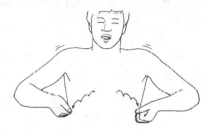

WHEELCHAIR (hwēl′ châr), *n.* (The wheels.) The signer makes simultaneous large forward circles at the sides of the body.

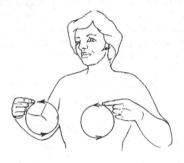

WHEN (hwĕn), *adv., conj., n.* (Fixing a point in time.) The left "D" hand is held upright, palm facing the body. The right index finger describes a clockwise circle around the left, coming to rest on the left index fingertip.

WHERE 1 (hwâr), *adv.* (Alternate directions are indicated.) The right "D" hand, with palm out and index finger straight or slightly curved, moves a short distance back and forth, from left to right. Also DIRECTION 1.

WHERE 2, *adv.* The open "5" hands, palms up and fingers slightly curved, move back and forth in front of the body, the right hand to the right and the left hand to the left. Also DIRECTION 2, HERE.

WHEREVER (hwâr ĕv′ ər), *conj.* Both hands, in the "5" position, are held before the chest, fingertips facing each other. With an alternate back-forth movement, the fingertips are made to strike each other. Also ANYHOW, ANYWAY, DESPITE, DOESN'T MATTER, HOWEVER 2, INDIFFERENCE, INDIFFERENT, IN SPITE OF, MAKE NO DIFFERENCE, NEVERTHELESS, NO MATTER.

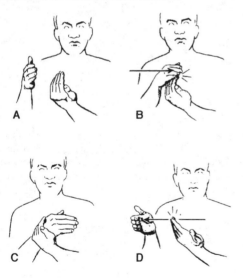

A   B

C   D

WHETHER (hwĕth′ ər), *conj.* (Considering one thing against another.) The "A" hands, palms facing and thumbs pointing straight up, move alternately up and down before the chest. Also EITHER 3, OR 2, WHICH 1.

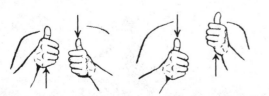

WHICH 1 (hwĭch), *pron. (esp. interrog. pron.)*, *adj.* See WHETHER.

WHICH 2, *pron.* (Something specific.) The down-turned right "Y" hand is placed on the upturned left palm. Also IT 2, THAT 1, THESE, THIS, THOSE.

WHILE (hwīl), *conj. only.* (Parallel time.) Both "D" hands, palms down, move forward in unison, away from the body. They may move straight forward or may follow a slight upward arc. Also DURING, IN THE MEANTIME, IN THE PROCESS OF, MEANTIME.

WHILE AGO, A 1, *phrase.* (A slight amount of time in the past.) The thumbtip of the closed right hand flicks off the tip of the curved right index finger. The hand then opens into the "5" position, palm facing the body, and swings back over the right shoulder. Also JUST NOW 1.

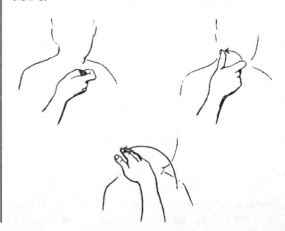

WHILE AGO, A 2, *phrase.* (The slight movement represents a slight amount of time.) With the closed right hand held with knuckles against the right cheek, the thumbtip flicks off the tip of the curved index finger a number of times. The eyes squint a bit and the lips are drawn out in a slight smile. The hand remains against the cheek during the flicking movement. Sometimes, instead of the flicking movement, the tip of the curved index finger scratches slightly up and down against the cheek. In this case, the palm faces back toward the shoulder. The same expression is used as in the flicking movement. Also JUST NOW 2, RECENT, RECENTLY.

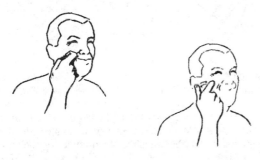

WHILE AGO, A 3, *phrase.* (Time moved backward a bit.) The right "D" hand, palm facing the body, is placed in the palm of the left hand, which is facing right. The right hand swings back a bit toward the body, with the index finger describing an arc. Also FEW SECONDS AGO, JUST A MOMENT AGO.

WHIP (hwĭp), *n., v.,* WHIPPED, WHIPPING. (The natural sign.) The left hand is held in a fist before the face, as if grasping something or someone. The right hand, at the same time, is held as if grasping a stick or whip; it strikes repeatedly at the imaginary object or person dangling from the left hand. Also BEAT 1, PUNISH 2.

WHISKEY 1 (hwĭs′ kĭ), *n.* (The size of the jigger is indicated.) The right hand, with index and little fingers extended and the remaining fingers held against the palm by the thumb, strikes the back of the downturned "S" hand several times. Also LIQUOR 1.

WHISKEY 2 (*arch.*), *n.* (Literally, strong wine, indicated by "W" making the color rise in the face.) The right "W" hand is placed, palm facing, against the face. It moves straight up the cheek. Both hands then close into the "S" position, palms facing, and drop down forcefully a short distance in front of the chest.

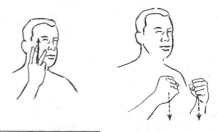

WHISPER 1 (hwĭs′ pər), *n., v.,* -PERED, -PERING. (Two people talk back and forth.) The right index and middle fingers rest on the lips. They individually go back and forth repeatedly striking the lips.

WHISPER 2, *n., v.* (Covering the mouth.) Cupping the hand over the mouth, the signer leans to one side, as if imparting private information to someone.

WHISTLE 1 (hwĭs′ əl, wĭs′ əl), *n., v.,* -TLED, -TLING. (The natural sign.) The index and middle fingers hold an imaginary whistle at the lips, and the signer purses his lips as if blowing the whistle.

WHISTLE 2, *v.* (The sound.) The extended right index fingertip moves in a wavy line out from the right ear. The lips are pursed.

WHISTLE 3, *n., v.* (Using the fingers to whistle.) The index and middle fingers, or the index and little fingers, are placed in the mouth and the signer mimes whistling.

WHO (hōō), *pron.* (The pursed lips are indicated.) The right index finger traces a small counterclockwise circle in front of the lips, which are pursed in the enunciation of the word. Also WHOM.

WHOLE (hōl), *adj., n.* (Encompassing; a gathering together.) Both hands are held in the right-angle position, palms facing the body and the right hand in front of the left. The right hand makes a sweeping outward movement around the left and comes to rest with the back of the right hand resting in the left palm. Also ALL, ENTIRE, UNIVERSAL.

WHOLE (THE), *n.* (An inclusion in the sense of a total number.) The left hand is held in the "C" position, fingers pointing right. The right hand, in the "5" position, fingers facing out from the body, palm down, is held above the left. With a horizontal swing to the right, the right hand describes an arc as the fingers close and are thrust into the left "C" hand, which closes over it. Also ALL 2, ALTOGETHER, INCLUDE, INCLUSIVE.

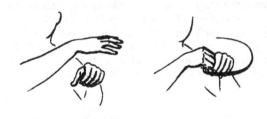

WHOM (hōōm), *pron.* See WHO.

WHOOPEE! (hwōō′ pē), *interj.* (Jumping up and down.) The downturned right index and middle fingers jump up and down repeatedly from the upturned left palm. The signer assumes an expression of unbridled glee.

WHORE (hōr), *n.* (The blood rushes up the cheek in shame—several times for emphasis.) The curved back of the right hand, placed against the right cheek, moves up and off the cheek several times. Also HAR-LOT, PROSTITUTE, STRUMPET.

WHOSE (hōōz), *pron.* (Who; outstretched open hand signifies possession, as if pressing an item against the chest of the person spoken to.) The sign for WHO is made: the right index finger traces a small counter-clockwise circle in front of the lips, which are pursed in the enunciation of the word. Then the right "5" hand, palm facing out, moves straight out toward the person spoken to or about.

WHY (hwī), *adv., n., interj.* (Reason—coming from the mind—modified by the letter "Y," the phonetic equivalent of WHY.) The fingertips of the right hand, palm facing the body, are placed against the forehead. The right hand then moves down and away from the forehead, assuming the "Y" position, palm still facing the body. Expression is an important indicator of the context in which this sign is used. Thus, as an interjection, a severe expression is assumed, while as an adverb or a noun, the expression is blank or inquisitive.

WIDE (wĭd), *adj.* (The width is indicated.) The open hands, fingers pointing out and palms facing each

other, separate from their initial position an inch or two apart. Also BROAD, WIDTH.

WIDTH (wĭdth), *n.* See WIDE.

WIFE (wīf), *n.* (A female whose hand is clasped in marriage.) The FEMALE root sign is made: the thumb of the right "A" hand moves down along the right jaw-bone, almost to the chin. The hands are then clasped together, right above left.

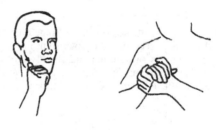

WIGWAM (wĭg′ wŏm), *n.* (The letter "W"; the sloping top.) Both "W" hands form the top. They move down in the shape of a pyramid.

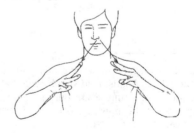

WILD 1 (wīld), *adj.* (Wild movements of the hands.) The "5" hands, held on either side of the head, twist in opposing circles as they move up from the head.

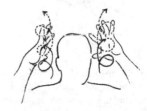

WILD 2, *adj.* (The "W" hands, with the same movements as in WILD 1.) Both "W" hands, palms facing out, are placed so that the index fingertips of each hand touch the respective temples. The same movement as in WILD 1 is then used, except that the hands remain in the "W" position.

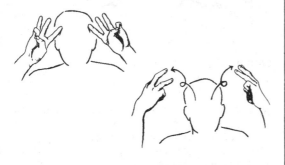

WILL 1 (wĭl), *v.*, WILLED, WILLING. (Something ahead or in the future.) The upright, open right hand, palm facing left, moves straight out and slightly up from a position beside the right temple. Also BY AND BY, FUTURE, IN THE FUTURE, LATER 2, LATER ON, SHALL, WOULD.

WILL 2, *n.* (Grasping something and pulling it in.) The upturned "5" hands, held side by side before the chest, close slightly into a grasping position as they move in toward the body. Also COVET 1, DESIRE 1, LONG 2, NEED 2, WANT, WISH 1.

WILLING 1 (wĭl′ ĭng), *adj.* (A taking of something unto oneself.) Both open hands, palms down, are held in front of the chest. They move in unison toward the

chest, where they come to rest, all fingers closed. Also ACCEPT.

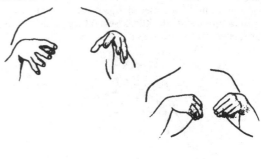

WILLING 2, *adj.* (A pleasurable feeling on the heart.) The open right hand is circled on the chest, over the heart. Also APPRECIATE, ENJOY, ENJOYMENT, GRATIFY 1, LIKE 3, PLEASE, PLEASURE.

WILLING 3, *adj.* (The heart is opened.) The right hand is placed over the heart. It swings quickly away to a position in front of the body with palm facing left. Also MAGNANIMOUS.

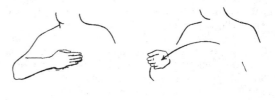

WIN 1 (wĭn), *v.*, WON, WINNING, *n.* (Waving of flags.) Both upright hands, grasping imaginary flags, wave them in small circles. Also CELEBRATE, CELEBRATION, CHEER, REJOICE, VICTORY 1.

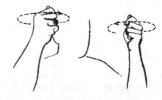

WIN 2, *v.*, *n.* (Waving a flag.) The right "A" hand goes through the natural movement of waving a flag in circular fashion. Preceding this, the right hand may go through the motion of grabbing the flagstaff out of the left hand. Also EXULTATION, TRIUMPH 1, VICTORY 2.

WIND (wĭnd), *n.* (The blowing back and forth of the wind.) The "5" hands, palms facing and held up before the body, sway gracefully back and forth in unison. The cheeks, meanwhile, are puffed up and the breath is being expelled. The nature of the swaying movement—graceful and slow, fast and violent, etc.—determines the type of wind. The strength of exhalation is also a classifier. Also BLOW 1, BREEZE, GALE, STORM.

WIND (wīnd), *v.*, WOUND, WINDING. (Turning the windup key.) The signer mimes turning a windup key on the left palm.

WINDOW (wĭn' dō), *n.* (The opening of the window.) With both palms facing the body, the little finger edge of the right hand rests atop the index finger edge of the

left hand. The right hand then moves straight up and down. Also OPEN THE WINDOW.

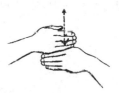

WINDSURFING (wind' sûrf' ing), *n.* (The natural movement.) The signer, standing on an imaginary windsurfer and grasping the boom, executes a series of swaying maneuvers, as if guiding a surfboard.

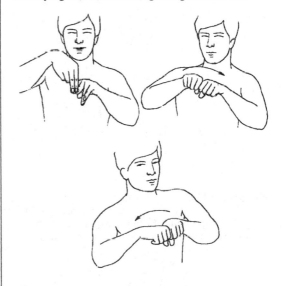

WINE 1 (wīn), *n.* (The "W" hand indicates a flushed cheek.) The right "W" hand, palm facing the face, rotates at the right cheek, in either a clockwise or a counterclockwise direction.

WINE 2 (*eccles.*), *n.* (Act of cutting a loaf of bread.) The left arm is held against the chest, representing a loaf of bread. The little finger edge of the right hand is drawn down over the back of the left hand several times to indicate the cutting of slices. Also BREAD, COMMUNION (HOLY) 2, HOLY COMMUNION 2.

WING (wing), *n.* (The flapping.) The right elbow moves in repeatedly against the right ribs.

WINTER 1 (wĭn′ tər), *n.* (The trembling from cold.) Both "S" or "W" hands, palms facing, are placed at the sides of the body. In this position the arms and hands shiver. Also CHILLY, COLD 1, FRIGID, SHIVER 1.

WINTER 2, *n.* (The letter "W.") The upright "W" hands, palms facing or forward, are brought together forcefully before the body one or two times.

WIPE (wīp), *v.,* WIPED, WIPING. (Wiping with a cloth or towel.) The flattened right hand makes a series of clockwise wiping movements against the open left palm.

WISDOM (wĭz′ dəm), *n.* (Measuring the depth of the mind.) The downturned "X" finger moves up and down a short distance as it rests on midforehead. Also INTELLECTUAL, WISE.

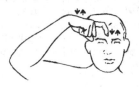

WISE (wīz), *adj.* See WISDOM.

WISH 1 (wĭsh), *v.,* WISHED, WISHING. (Grasping something and pulling it in.) The upturned "5" hands, held side by side before the chest, close slightly into a grasping position as they move in toward the body. Also COVET 1, DESIRE 1, LONG 2, NEED 2, WANT, WILL 2.

WISH 2, *n., v.* (The upper alimentary tract is outlined.) The right "C" hand, palm facing the body, is placed with fingertips touching midchest. In this position it moves down a bit. Also APPETITE, CRAVE, DESIRE 2, FAMINE, HUNGARIAN, HUNGARY, HUNGER, HUNGRY, STARVATION, STARVE, STARVED.

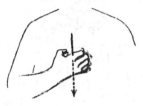

WITH (wĭth), *prep.* (The two hands are together, *i.e.,* WITH each other.) Both "A" hands, knuckles together and thumbs up, are moved forward in unison, away from the chest. They may also remain stationary. Also ACCOMPANY, TOGETHER, WANDER AROUND WITH.

WITHDRAW 1 (wĭth drô′, wĭth-), *v.,* -DREW, -DRAWN, -DRAWING. (Pulling away.) The downturned open hands are held in a line, with fingers pointing to the left, the right hand behind the left. Both hands move in unison toward the right. As they do so, they assume the "A" position. Also DEPART, EVACUATE, FORSAKE 1, GRADUATE 2, LEAVE 1, RETIRE 1.

WITHDRAW 2, *v.* (Removing.) The right "A" hand, resting in the palm of the left "5" hand, moves slightly up and away, describing a small arc. It is then cast downward, opening into the "5" position, palm down, as if removing something from the left hand and casting it down. Also ABOLISH 2, ABSENCE 2, ABSENT 2,

ABSTAIN, CHEAT 2, DEDUCT, DEFICIENCY, DELETE 1, LESS 2, MINUS 3, OUT 2, REMOVE 1, SUBTRACT, SUBTRACTION, TAKE AWAY FROM.

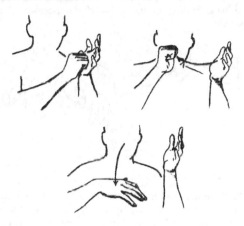

WITHDRAW 3, *v.* (Pulling out.) The index and middle fingers of the right "H" hand are grasped by the left hand. The right hand pulls out of the left. Also QUIT, RESIGN.

WITHDRAW 4, *v.* (Withdraw a resolution by pulling it off the agenda.) Both hands, facing forward, close and are pulled down.

WITHIN (wĭth ĭn′, wĭth-), *adv., prep.* (The natural sign.) The fingers of the right hand are thrust into the left. Also IN, INSIDE, INTO.

WITHOUT (wĭth out', wĭth-), *prep., adv.* (The hands fall away from the WITH position.) The sign for WITH is formed. The hands then drop down, open, and part, ending in the palms-down position. Also MINUS 2.

WITNESS (wĭt' nĭs), *v.,* -NESSED, -NESSING. (The vision is directed forward.) The tips of the right "V" fingers point to the eyes. The right hand is then swung around and forward a bit. Also GAZE, LOOK AT, OBSERVE 1.

WOMAN (wŏŏm' ən), *n.* (A big female.) The FE-MALE prefix sign is made: the thumb of the right "A" hand moves down along the line of the right jaw, from ear almost to chin. This outlines the string used to tie ladies' bonnets in olden days. This is a root sign to modify many others. The downturned right hand then moves up to a point above the head to indicate the relative height.

WONDER 1 (wŭn' dər), *v.,* -DERED, -DERING. (Turning thoughts over in the mind.) Both index fingers, pointing to the forehead, describe continuous alternating

circles. Also CONSIDER 2, CONTEMPLATE, PONDER, SPEC-ULATE 2, SPECULATION 2, WEIGH 2.

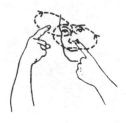

WONDER 2, *n.* (The hands gesture toward the heavens.) The "5" hands, palms out and arms raised rather high, are positioned somewhat above the line of vision. The arms move abruptly forward and up once or twice. An expression of pleasure or surprise is usually assumed. Also EXCELLENT, GRAND 1, GREAT 3, MARVEL, MARVELOUS, MIRACLE, O!, SPLENDID 1, SWELL 1, WONDERFUL 1.

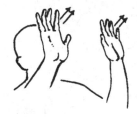

WONDER 3, *v.* (The letter "W.") The sign for WON-DER 1 is made, using the right "W" hand.

WONDERFUL 1 (wŭn' dər fəl), *adj.* See WONDER 2.

WONDERFUL 2, *adj., interj.* (The feelings are titillated.) With the thumb resting on the upper part of the chest, the fingers are wiggled back and forth. Also ELE-GANT, FINE 1, GRAND 2, GREAT 4, SPLENDID 2, SWELL 2.

WON'T (wōnt, wŭnt), *v.* Contraction of *will not.* (Holding back.) The right "A" hand, palm facing left, moves up sharply to a position above the right shoulder. Also REFUSE.

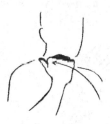

WOOD (wŏŏd), *n.* (The sawing of wood.) The little finger edge of the open right hand moves back and forth in a sawing motion over the back of the downturned left hand. Also LUMBER 1, SAW 1.

WOODCUTTER (wŏŏd' kŭt' ər), *n.* (Chopping down a tree.) The left upraised fist or open hand represents the tree. The upturned right hand (the axe) strikes the left elbow repeatedly. The sign for INDIVIDUAL 1 then follows.

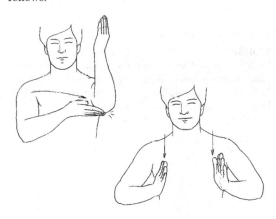

WORD (wûrd), *n.* (A small part of a sentence, *i.e.,* a word.) The tips of the right index finger and thumb, about an inch apart, are placed on the side of the out-

stretched left index finger, which represents the length of a sentence. Also INCH 1, VERBAL 2.

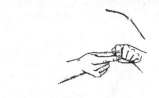

WORD PROCESSING *n.* (A fingerspelled loan sign.) The signer fingerspells "W-P."

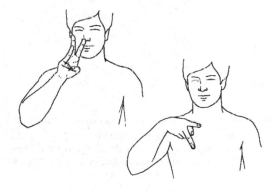

WORK (wûrk), *n., v.,* WORKED, WORKING. (Striking an anvil.) Both "S" hands are held palms down. The right hand strikes against the back of the left a number of times. Also JOB, LABOR, OCCUPATION, TASK, TOIL, TRAVAIL, VOCATION.

WORLD (wûrld), *n.* (The letter "W" in orbit.) The right "W" hand makes a complete circle around the left "W" hand and comes to rest on the thumb edge of the left "W" hand. The left hand frequently assumes the "S" position, instead of the "W," to represent the stationary sun. Also GLOBE 2.

WORRIED, *v.* (A clouding over; a troubling.) Both "B" hands, palms facing each other, are rotated alternately before the forehead. Also ANNOY 2, ANNOYANCE 2, ANXIOUS 2, BOTHER 2, CONCERN 1, FRET, PROBLEM 1, TROUBLE, WORRY 1.

WORRY 1 (wûr′ ĭ), *v.,* -RIED, -RYING. See WORRIED.

WORRY 2, *n., v.* (Drumming at the forehead to represent many worries making inroads on the thinking process.) The right fingertips drum against the forehead. The signer frowns somewhat or looks very concerned.

WORRY 3, *n., v.* (The "W" hands.) The sign for WORRY 1 is made, but with the "W" hands.

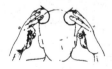

WORRY 4, *n., v.* (Making inroads on one's emotional equilibrium.) The middle fingers are thrust alternately and rhythmically against the chest. The signer frowns somewhat or looks concerned.

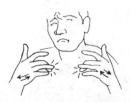

WORSE 1 (wûrs), *adj.* The "V" hands, palms facing the body, cross quickly. The comparative degree suffix sign -ER is often used after this sign: the upright thumb of the right "A" hand is brought sharply up to a level opposite the right ear. Also WORST 1.

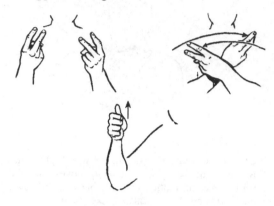

WORSE 2, *adj.* The same movements as in WORSE 1 are used, except that the "W" hands are employed. The comparative degree suffix sign may likewise follow. Also WORST 2.

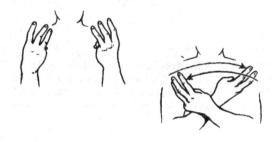

WORSE 3 (*rare*), *adj.* The "A" hands face each other, the right poised somewhat above the left. The right hand swings down in an arc, passing the stationary left hand. As it does so, the bases of both hands, or their knuckles, come into brief contact. Also WORST 3.

WORSHIP 1 (wûr′ shĭp), *n., v.,* -SHIPED, -SHIPPING (Worshiping.) The hands are clasped together, with the left cupped over the right. Both are brought in toward the body while the eyes are shut and the head is bowed slightly. Also ADORE, AMEN, DEVOUT, PIOUS.

WORSHIP 2, *v.* (Bowing to show respect or deference.) The right "W" hand comes down on its left counterpart as the signer's head remains bowed.

WORST 1 (wûrst), *adj.* The sign for WORSE 1 is made. This is followed by the superlative degree suffix -EST: the upright thumb of the right "A" hand is brought sharply up to a level a bit above the right side of the head. Also WORSE 1.

WORST 2, *adj.* The sign for WORSE 2 is repeated, followed by the superlative degree suffix sign, as in WORST 1. Also WORSE 2.

WORST 3 (*rare*), *adj.* The sign for WORSE 3 is repeated, followed by the superlative degree suffix sign, as in WORST 1. Also WORSE 3.

WORTH (wûrth), *adj., n.* Both "F" hands, palms facing each other, move apart, up, and together in a

smooth, elliptical fashion, coming together at the tips of the thumbs and index fingers of both hands. Also DESERVE, ESSENTIAL, IMPORTANT 1, MAIN, MERIT, PRECIOUS, PROMINENT 2, SIGNIFICANCE 1, SIGNIFICANT, VALUABLE, VALUE, VITAL 1, WORTHWHILE, WORTHY.

WORTHLESS 1 (wûrth' lĭs), *adj.* (The hands are thrown out from the sign for WORTH.) The "F" hands, palms down and held side by side or touching, close into the "S" or "E" position, palms still down. They are then thrown out and apart, opening into the "5" position, palms still down.

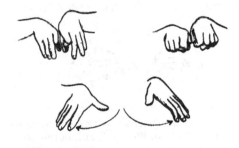

WORTHLESS 2 (*vern.*), *adj.* (A modification of WORTHLESS 1.) The "F" hands face each other, the right above the left. The right hand swings down in an arc, passing the left. As it does so, the thumb and index finger of the right hand strike the corresponding fingers of the left rather sharply. An expression of disdain is assumed. Also NO GOOD 2.

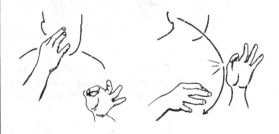

WORTHWHILE (wûrth' hwīl'), *adj.* See WORTH.

WORTHY (wûr' thĭ), *adj.* See WORTH.

WOULD (wŏŏd, *unstressed* wəd), *v.* (Something ahead or in the future.) The upright, open right hand, palm facing left, moves straight out and slightly up from a position beside the right temple. Also BY AND BY, FUTURE, IN THE FUTURE, LATER 2, LATER ON, SHALL, WILL 1.

WOUND (wŏŏnd), *n.* (A stabbing pain.) The "D" hands, index fingers pointing to each other, are rotated in elliptical fashion before the chest—simultaneously but in opposite directions. Also ACHE, HARM 1, HURT 1, INJURE 1, INJURY, MAR 1, OFFEND, OFFENSE, PAIN, SIN.

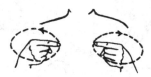

WRAP (rap), *n., v.,* WRAPPED, WRAPPING. (Wrapping up a package.) Both downturned hands, fingers pointing to each other, make a series of alternate clockwise circles, as if spreading wrapping paper around an object.

WRISTWATCH, *n.* (The shape of the wristwatch.) The thumb and index finger of the right hand, forming a circle, are placed on the back of the left wrist. Also WATCH 4.

WRITE (rīt), *v.,* WROTE, WRITTEN, WRITING. (The natural movement.) The right index finger and thumb, grasping an imaginary pen, write across the open left palm. Also PEN, SIGN, SIGNATURE.

WRONG 1 (rông, rŏng), *adj., n.* (Rationale obscure; the thumb and little finger are said to represent, respectively, right and wrong, with the head poised between the two.) The right "Y" hand, palm facing the body, is brought up to the chin. Also ERROR, FAULT 2, MISTAKE, SACRILEGIOUS.

WRONG 2, *adj., n.* (Going astray.) The open right hand, palm facing left, is placed with its little finger edge resting on the upturned left palm. The right hand curves rather sharply to the left as it moves across the palm. Also DEVIATE 1.

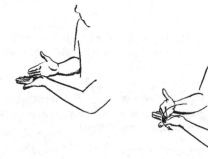

X

XEROX (zĭr′ ŏks), *n*. (The letter "X"; the movement of the light as it moves under the item to be copied.) The "X" finger moves back and forth rather rapidly under the downturned hand.

XMAS, *n*. See CHRISTMAS.

Y

YARD 1 (yärd), *n.* (A measuring off.) Both modified "O" hands are held before the face, palms facing each other. Then the right hand moves straight away to the right side, while the left hand keeps its original position.

YARD 2, *n.* (A fenced-in enclosure.) The "5" hands are held with palms facing the body and fingers interlocked but not curved. The hands separate, swinging first to either side of the body and then moving in toward the body, tracing a circle and coming together palms out and bases touching. Also FIELD 2, GARDEN.

YARD 3, *n.* (The letter "Y"; arm's length.) The downturned right "Y" hand is placed on the shoulder of the downturned left arm. The right hand moves down the arm to the left fingertips.

YARN (yärn), *n.* (The letter "Y"; unraveling.) The right "Y" hand is placed against the left little finger. The right hand moves away from the left in a series of small, circular, clockwise movements.

YEAR (yĭr), *n.* (A circumference around the sun.) The right "S" hand, palm facing left, represents the earth. It is positioned atop the left "S" hand, whose palm faces right, and represents the sun. The right "S" hand describes a clockwise circle around the left, coming to rest in its original position.

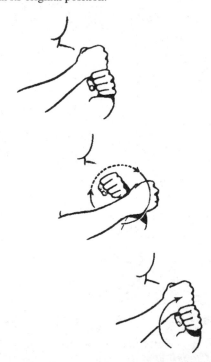

YEARLY (yĭr′ lĭ, yûr′-), *adj., adv., n.* (Several years brought forward.) This sign is actually a modification of the sign for YEAR, *q.v.* The ball of the right "S" hand, moving straight out from the body, palm facing left, glances over the thumb side of the left "S" hand, which is held palm facing right. As this contact is made, the right index finger is flung straight out, and the right hand, in this new position, continues forward. This is repeated several times to indicate several years. Also ANNUAL, EVERY YEAR.

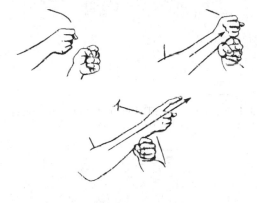

YEAR-ROUND (yĭr′ round′), *adj.* (Making a revolution around the sun.) The right index finger, resting on the left index, goes forward around the left once, coming back to where it began.

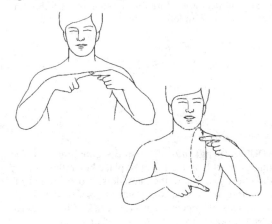

YEARS (yĭrs), *n. pl.* The sign for YEAR is made twice.

YEARS OLD, *phrase* (*regional*). (Showing relative height of a person.) The downturned "B" hand is placed against the stomach and moves off and up, coming to rest at chest level. This sign indicates the growth marks some parents make on the wall to chronicle the growth of children.

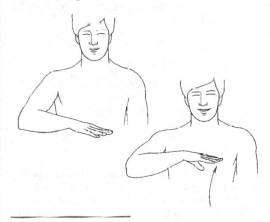

YES (yĕs) (*colloq.*), *adv., n.* (The nodding.) The right "S" hand, imitating the head, nods up and down.

YESTERDAY (yĕs′ tər dĭ, -dā′), *adv., n.* (A short distance into the past.) The thumbtip of the right "A" or "Y" hand, palm facing left, rests on the right cheek. It then moves back a short distance.

YET 1 (yĕt), *adv., conj.* (Duration of movement from past to present.) The right "Y" hand is held palm down in front of the right shoulder and is then moved slowly down and forward in a smooth curve. Also CONTINUE 2, STAY 2, STILL 1.

YET 2 (*arch.*), *adv.* The fingertips of the downturned right "5" hand execute a series of small jumps as they move forward along the upturned left palm from its base to the left fingertips.

YIELD (yēld), *v.,* YIELDED, YIELDING. (Throwing up the hands in a gesture of surrender.) Both "A" hands are held palms down before the chest and then thrown up in unison, ending in the "5" position. Also ABDICATE, CEDE, DISCOURAGE 1, FORFEIT, GIVE UP, LOSE HOPE, RELINQUISH, RENOUNCE, RENUNCIATION, SURRENDER 1.

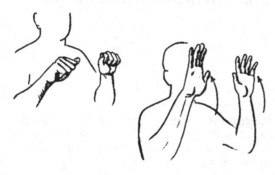

YOM KIPPUR 1 (yŏm kĭp′ ər; *Heb.* yōm kĭp′ ōor), (*eccles.*), *n.* (Day of Atonement, *i.e.,* Sorrow.) The sign for DAY is made: the right "D" hand, palm facing left, is held high, with the right elbow resting in the palm or on the back of the left hand. The right arm describes a 45° arc as it moves from right to left. The sign for SORRY or SORROW is then made: the right "S" hand, palm facing the body, is rotated several times over the area of the heart. The "S" hand may instead strike the heart. Also DAY OF ATONEMENT.

YOM KIPPUR 2, *n.* (The letter "Y"; beating the breast in penitence.) The right "Y" hand strikes the left breast several times.

YOU 1 (ŭ), *pron. sing.* (The natural sign.) The signer points to the person he is addressing.

YOU 2, *pron. pl.* (The natural sign.) The signer points to several persons before him or swings his index finger in an arc from left to right.

YOUNG (yŭng), *adj.* (The spirits bubbling up.) The fingertips of both open hands, placed on either side of the chest just below the shoulders, move up and off the chest, in unison, to a point just above the shoulders. This is repeated several times. Also ADOLESCENCE, ADOLESCENT, YOUTH, YOUTHFUL.

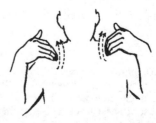

YOUR (yŏor), *pron., adj.* (The outstretched open hand indicates possession, as if pressing an item against the chest of the person spoken to.) The right "5" hand, palm facing out, moves straight out toward the person spoken to. This sign is also used for YOURS.

YOU'RE WELCOME 1, *phrase.* (Words extended politely from the mouth.) The fingertips of the right "5" hand are placed at the mouth. The hand moves away from the mouth to a palm-up position before the body. The signer, meanwhile, usually nods smilingly. Also FAREWELL 1, GOODBYE 1, HELLO 1, THANKS, THANK YOU.

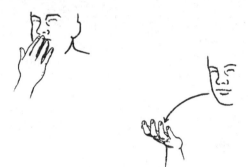

YOU'RE WELCOME 2, *phrase.* (A straightening out.) The right hand, fingers together and palm facing left, is placed in the upturned left palm, whose fingers point away from the body. The right hand slides straight out along the left palm, over the left fingers, and stops with its heel resting on the left fingertips. Also ALL RIGHT, O.K. 1, PRIVILEGE, RIGHT 1, RIGHTEOUS 1.

YOURS (yŏorz, yôrz), *pron.* See YOUR.

YOURSELF (yŏor sĕlf′), *pron.* The signer moves his upright thumb in the direction of the person spoken to. Also SELF.

YOURSELVES (yŏor sĕlvz′), *pron. pl.* The signer moves his upright thumb toward several people before him in a series of small forward movements from left to right.

YOUTH (ūth), *n.* See YOUNG.

YOUTHFUL (ūth′ fəl), *adj.* See YOUTH.

YO-YO (yō′ yō′), *n.* (Manipulating the toy.) The downturned "Y" hand moves up and down repeatedly in rhythmic progression.

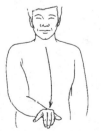

Z

ZEAL (zēl), *n*. (Rubbing the hands together in zeal or ambition.) The open hands are rubbed vigorously back and forth against each other. Also AMBITIOUS 1, ANXIOUS 1, ARDENT, DILIGENCE 1, DILIGENT, EAGER, EAGERNESS, EARNEST, ENTHUSIASM, ENTHUSIASTIC, INDUSTRIOUS, METHODIST, ZEALOUS.

ZIPPER (zip′ ər), *n*. (The movement of the zipper.) The signer mimes opening and closing a zipper on the chest or the side of the body.

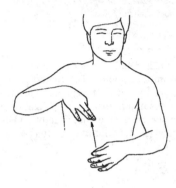

_____

ZEALOUS (zĕl′ əs), *adj*. See ZEAL.